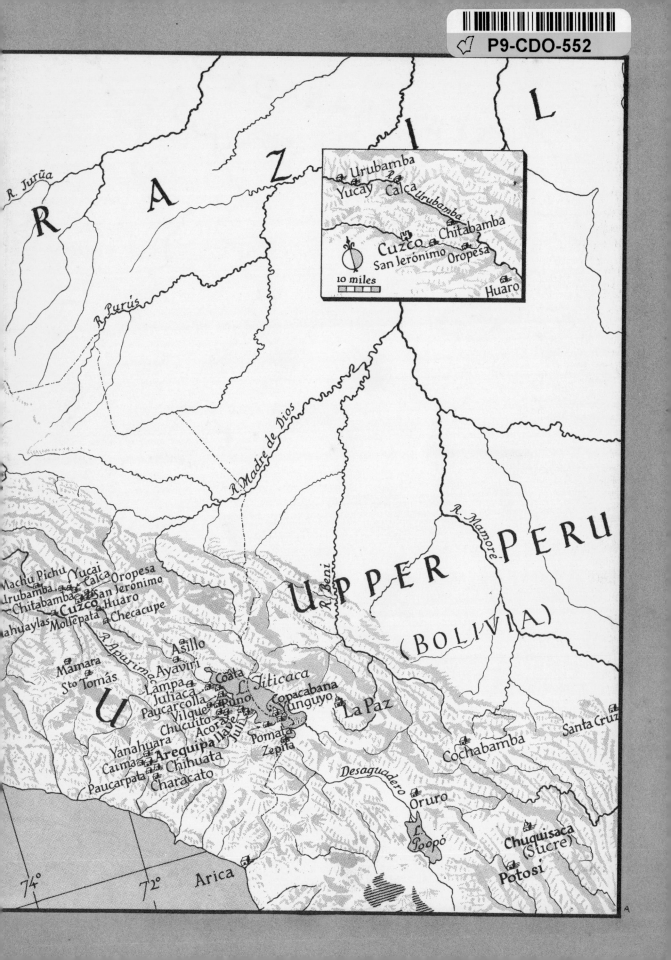

B R A Z I L

R. Jurūa

R. Purús

R. Madre de Dios

Inset map

Urubamba
Yucay   Calca
Urubamba
Chitabamba
Cuzco
San Jerónimo   Oropesa
Huaro

10 miles

U P P E R   P E R U

(B O L I V I A)

R. Beni

R. Manoré

Machu Pichu   Yucai
Urubamba   Calca   Oropesa
Chitabamba   San Jerónimo
Cuzco   Huaro
ahuaylas   Mollepata   Checacupe

R. Apurimo

Asillo

Mamara   Ayaviri
Sto Tomás   Lampa   Coata   Titicaca
Juliaca   L.   Titicaca   Copacabana
Paucarcolla   Puno   Yunguyo
Vilque   La Paz
Chucuito   Acora   Llave
Yanahuara   Caima   Juli   Pomata
Arequipa   Zepita   Cochabamba   Santa Cruz
Paucarpata   Chihuata
Charato   Desaguadero

Oruro

Poopó

Chuquisaca
(Sucre)

Potosi

74°   72°   Arica

COLONIAL ARCHITECTURE AND SCULPTURE IN PERU

COLONIAL ARCHITECTURE AND SCULPTURE IN PERU

Harold E. Wethey

CAMBRIDGE·MASSACHUSETTS
HARVARD UNIVERSITY PRESS · 1949

This book is published with the assistance of
the Horace H. Rackham School of Graduate
Studies of the University of Michigan, and
the American Council of Learned Societies.

LONDON · GEOFFREY CUMBERLEGE · OXFORD UNIVERSITY PRESS

TO A. S. W.

PREFACE

The present study is devoted to colonial architecture and sculpture within the boundaries of modern Peru, the leading cultural center of Hispanic South America during the colonial period. My initial plan to include all of the original viceroyalty of Peru, notably Bolivia, was abandoned because of the magnitude of the scope, and hence I have published elsewhere a series of articles on that region.

My research in Peru and Bolivia was carried out during 1944 and 1945 with the assistance of a grant from the Rockefeller Foundation. Subsidies from the American Council of Learned Societies and the Horace H. Rackham School of Graduate Studies of the University of Michigan made the publication of the book possible.

A number of Peruvian and American scholars helped me greatly throughout the course of travel and research. I am especially indebted to Padre Víctor Barriga of Arequipa, Dr. José Uriel García of Cuzco, and Padre Rubén Vargas Ugarte of Lima for their generosity in giving me unpublished documentary material. I have profited much by the advice and knowledge of Peru of Dr. Albert Giesecke, Dr. Alberto Santibáñez Salcedo, Dr. Jorge Basadre, Dr. Pío Max Medina, Dr. Horacio Villaneuva Urteaga, Dr. Franco Hinojosa, Señora Mercedes Gallagher de Parks, Emilio Harth-terré, Monseñor Juan Antonio Casanova, Monseñor Aurelio Guerrero, Padre Graciano Montes, and Padre Rosario Zárate.

I wish to acknowledge my sincere appreciation for permission to reproduce floor plans drawn by Mario Buschiazzo (Figs. 4, 7, 12–16), Alva Manfredi (Figs. 1–3, 9, 11), Emilio Harth-terré (Figs. 6, 17–19), Morales Macchiaveli

PREFACE

(Figs. 10, 20); those of the last two architects have previously been published in *Arquitecto peruano,* 1941–1942. I am grateful to Mrs. Elizabeth Kelemen for the use of three photographs (Figs. 233, 250, 320). The map for the end papers was prepared by Dr. Edwin Raisz of Cambridge, Massachusetts.

The criticism of my text by Dr. Robert C. Smith, the first American scholar to devote himself to the study of Latin American art, was of inestimable value. I am greatly indebted to Mrs. Delphine Fitz Darby for her advice in connection with the proofs and to my wife for expert assistance in the preparation of the manuscript and proofreading.

HAROLD E. WETHEY

Ann Arbor, Michigan
November 1, 1948

CONTENTS

IX

CONTENTS

ILLUSTRATIONS

Trujillo, Cathedral, High Altar, Detail

ILLUSTRATIONS

ILLUSTRATIONS

ILLUSTRATIONS

ILLUSTRATIONS

ILLUSTRATIONS

Introduction

I

THE EVOLUTION OF COLONIAL ART
IN PERU

TIME AND PLACE

PERU holds first rank among the Spanish colonies for high quality and for extraordinary quantity of artistic achievement, being rivaled only by Mexico. Lima was the capital of Hispanic South America from the start. Always in direct contact with the mother country, she clung to her position as the leading cultural center of the Spanish section of the continent until the nineteenth century. The early colonists, if not the conquistadors, numbered among them educated men, some of them university graduates. These men were no illiterate provincials, for many of them read the most recent literary works of Spain.[1] Even higher education was available in the New World at a remarkably early date. It began at Lima in 1574 with the opening of the University of San Marcos, just a little more than four decades after Pizarro's initial conquest of Peru.[2]

The best accomplishments of the Spanish colonial period in the arts lie in the field of ecclesiastical architecture and sculpture. The reasons are not difficult to discover. The Church held a position of unparalleled political, social, and economic power. Church and State were united as never before, as a result of the establishment of the Royal Patronage. By a series of agreements with the Spanish pope, Alexander VI, and with his successor, Julius II, the Spanish Crown secured the delegation unto itself of supreme authority in ecclesiastical matters throughout the Spanish territories of the New World.[3] The king of Spain was responsible for the physical well-being of the Church. The bishops and the religious orders were subject to him and to the Council of the Indies, and not to the pontiff at Rome. Without their authorization no church could be established, no religious order founded, and no member of the clergy could travel to the colonies.

The Spanish Empire reached its apogee in the sixteenth century. It held vast new territories, the extent and importance of which no one even suspected. Great wealth soon came pouring into Spanish coffers. The source was not merely the loot in precious metals which the conquerors gathered, but mines of silver in Mexico and Peru. The discovery of fabulous silver deposits at Potosí in 1545 and of mercury at

Huancavelica in 1563 brought economic prosperity to the viceroyalty of Peru which staggers the imagination. Large portions of that wealth went into the building and embellishment of churches and monasteries. By the seventeenth and the eighteenth centuries ecclesiastical vessels of gold, silver, and precious stones, like the monstrance of La Merced at Cuzco, were of surpassing beauty and priceless value. Silver altar frontals and tabernacles were commonplace. Great altarpieces of gilded wood filled the churches everywhere, even in the poorest Indian villages.

The society of Latin America was aristocratic, with privileges and wealth belonging to the few. The social inequality of the Hispanic colonies, where the wealth of the upper classes contrasted with the extreme poverty and the virtual serfdom of the masses, constituted an extension of medieval Spain. The Spanish concept of the gentleman and the exaggerated importance given to high birth were brought into even stronger relief in the colonies where the few of Spanish blood ruled over thousands of subject Indians.

The Spanish Church was an integral part of the aristocratic society and the feudalism of medieval Spain, inevitably and inescapably so. The position of the Church in Hispanic America was consonant with and a magnification of the increased power which it had begun to assume in Spain during the reign of Ferdinand and Isabella. With the Royal Patronage the State was united to the Church, one and inseparable. The spirit of the Reconquest of Spain from the Moors, which was com-

pleted in 1492 just before Columbus' discovery, was projected into the newly found lands. More worlds to conquer for the Crown and the Cross! The Counter Reformation of the Catholic church (its two greatest leaders the Spaniards, St. Ignatius Loyola and St. Theresa of Avila) gained momentum by the second half of the sixteenth century. Its full force carried into America with all of the vigor of youth.

The significance of the patronage of the Crown and of the upper classes can hardly be exaggerated in any consideration of the wealth and beauty of Hispanic ecclesiastical art. The nobles of Spain had always made vast donations to churches and monasteries and for the perpetuation of their favorite cults. In the New World they had still greater opportunities to found new religious establishments and to endow others. A rich landowner, Diego de Vargas, and his wife, Usenda de Loayza, were the original patrons of the monastery of La Merced in Cuzco. A miner of Potosí, Andrés Cintero, left money in 1643 for the foundation of the Dominican Colegio de Santo Tomás in Lima. Every man, rich or moderately successful financially, bequeathed legacies large and small to the Church, and ordered that masses be said for his soul. Anyone who searches through the testaments in notarial archives will be struck by this fact.

The Crown assumed the guardianship of the Church. Vast contributions were made for the construction of cathedrals, churches, and monasteries. These sums stood well in excess of the ecclesiastical tithes due to the king, at least in the first century and a half of colonization. Petitions to the Council of the Indies for money, and plans of buildings sent with them, have been preserved in the Archives of the Indies in Seville. Their publication by Diego Angulo Iñiguez has supplied a fund of invaluable data.[4]

In the reports of the viceroys the status of the clergy and of the churches and their furnishings are given full attention. Nothing escaped their zealous eyes. Francisco de Toledo berated the clergy and laymen of Cuzco for their delay in the construction of the cathedral on his visit there in 1571. The Conde de Lemos a century later is said to have been the driving force for the building of a new shrine to the Virgin at Copacabana.[5] The viceroy Amat, whose popular fame rests upon his love affair with the actress, La Perricholi, contributed substantially to the rebuilding of the nunnery of Las Nazarenas and their church in Lima after the earthquake of 1746.

Great churchmen like the bishops, Santo Toribio, Morcillo Rubió de Auñón, Martínez Compañón, Alonso Ocón, and Manuel de Mollinedo, were fired with religious zeal in their desire to increase the prestige and splendor of the Church. Manuel de Mollinedo, bishop of Cuzco, was the greatest single patron ever known in colonial Peru. The rebuilding of his city after the disastrous earthquake of 1650 is in great part his creation. He endowed churches, and gave altars, pulpits, silver altar frontals, and ecclesiastical vessels with princely munificence. Mollinedo was to Cuzco what the Medici were to Florence in the Renaissance. More is said of him in Chapter III.

To the first monks who evangelized Hispanic America is due much of the credit for the rapid success of the Spanish conquest. Some militant men like Fray Vicente Valverde had more of the spirit of the conqueror than of the evangelist. The celebrated Franciscan accompanied Pizarro on the first invasion of Peru, went on to Cajamarca in 1532, and two years later to Cuzco for its founding as a Spanish city. There he received his reward as first holder of the episcopal see of the region. Other churchmen were as brave as he, but possessed of far greater humanity. One of these was the Dominican, Fray Tomás de San Martín, likewise a member of Pizarro's expedition. From Cuzco he struck south in the rigorous altitude and cold of the Andes, penetrating to the shores of Lake Titicaca. There missions for the conversion of Indians were set up at Chucuito, Juli, Pomata, and other villages where the native population was heavily concentrated. The work of the Dominicans in the very first years of the conquest was the boldest and most courageous of all the monastic orders. Their numbers were few, but their spirit was mighty. They cannot be accused of self-advancement, for they faced terrible and incalculable hardship on every hand.

No one should be surprised to learn that the district of Lake Titicaca is one of the most important centers of sixteenth-century architecture. The churches built by the first Dominicans, however, have vanished with the probable exception of the east end of San Pedro Mártir at Juli. They were humble structures of adobe and thatch, which gave way to more enduring works later in the same century.

The Dominicans, Franciscans, and Mercedarians entered Cuzco at the time of its foundation in 1534, and Lima on January eighteenth of the succeeding year. The Augustinians arrived later, disembarking at Lima in 1551. Last in appearance among the great orders was the newly established Company of Jesus, which was to become the most powerful of all. Six Jesuits landed at the capital in 1568 and twelve more a year later. Beginning in 1576 the viceroy Francisco de Toledo took from the Dominicans their hard-won territory along the edge of Lake Titicaca and assigned it to the Jesuits.[6] The Jesuit expansion was bold and rapid, and they soon dominated most of the universities and educational centers throughout the continent of South America.

For all their missionary zeal the religious orders were relatively modest in their architectural and decorative ambitions during the sixteenth century. The viceroyalty of Peru and South America in general never saw anything comparable with the great monasteries and churches erected in Mexico by the Franciscans, Dominicans, and Augustinians.[7] The difficulty of travel and of transportation in Andean territory made any such rapid artistic development as that of Mexico impossible. Colonial Peru lay mainly in the heights of the Andes, except for the important cities of Lima and Trujillo which were situated at sea level on the narrow strip of coastal desert which borders the Pacific Ocean. Moreover, the Indian population of Peru was smaller and the natives did not need to be gathered by the thousands for religious instruction, as they were in Mexico.[8]

THE ARTISTS

OUR knowledge of the builders, architects, and sculptors of the colonial period is due largely to the investigations of Padre Vargas Ugarte and Emilio Harth-terré in Lima, Padre Víctor Barriga in Arequipa, and Dr. José Uriel García in Cuzco.[9] In the first years of the conquest the builders were carpenters and masons, for the most part modest artisans. Such was Juan de Escalante, carpenter, recorded at Lima as early as 1536. Diego de Torres, mason, who prepared the designs for the Town Hall in the capital, had something to do with the laying out of the streets, and also secured a license to sell soap (1549). Another mason, Jerónimo Delgado, received the commission to build the transept of the church of Santo Domingo (1547).[10]

A carpenter named Diego Martín was among the original settlers of Arequipa in 1540. In the same city a mason, Toribio de Alcaraz, erected the portal of the Iglesia Mayor (1544) before moving on to Potosí and Chuquisaca in the van of the great silver rush.[11] The most famous architects and sculptors of Spain could not have been expected to leave a prosperous and comfortable life at home to brave the hardships and uncertainties of the frontier. Francisco Becerra was the first outstanding master to establish himself in the viceroyalty of Peru. He was called there (1582) by the viceroy, Martín Enríquez de Almansa, after a laudable career in Mexico whither he had gone from Spain nine years earlier. The importance of his projects for the cathedrals of Cuzco and Lima is discussed in Chapters III and IV.

By the last years of the sixteenth century and the beginning of the seventeenth many competent artists migrated to Peru. Among them were Juan Martínez de Arrona and pedro de Noguera, architects and sculptors active in Lima. Those trained in the artistic capitals of Spain were still the leaders in their respective professions in the New World. They arrived by ship at Lima. Some were called from there to other centers, as Andrés de Espinoza and later Juan de Aldana (1643) were engaged to build the cathedral of Arequipa. A Portuguese, Constantino Vasconcellos, was exceptional in being an important architect of non-Spanish birth. He designed the new church and extensive monastery of the Franciscans at Lima in the mid-seventeenth century.

Some monks and churchmen also followed artistic professions, but their number and high position have been much exaggerated. The small adobe churches built by the priests and missionaries in remote Andean settlements were undoubtedly planned by the clergy. At the outset they were utilitarian structures and not highly sophisticated architectural schemes. San Cristóbal at Ayacucho (1540) is probably one of these (Fig. 35). Only the stone arch of the doorway would demand any knowledge of even the mason's craft. The actual laborers were, of course, the native Indians, then and always. They were highly skilled as workmen and builders, a fact which explains the rapid expansion of the constructional programs of the Spanish, especially in Mexico.

Some professional artisans were members of the religious orders. Early among these were Padre Juan Ruiz, carpenter, and the Italian, Padre Bernardo Bitti, a painter. Both Jesuits, they practiced their professions in the last quarter of the sixteenth century. Martín de Aizpitarte, another member of the Society of Jesus, was the architect of the Compañía in Lima (1624–1638).[12] The Mercedarians numbered among them the professional architects: Fray Pedro Galeano, designer of their new church in 1628, and Fray Cristóbal Caballero, who lived in the second half of the same century.[13] Contemporaries of Fray Pedro Galeano included the Augustinian, Fray Jerónimo de Villegas, and the Franciscan, Fray Miguel de la Huerta.

Some writers have assumed that Diego Arias de la Cerda, at first a priest at Urubamba and later canon of Cuzco Cathedral, was chief architect of that cathedral and a sculptor as well. The fact is that Padre Diego Arias held the office of administrator (*obrero mayor*) of the cathedral. His energy and devotion contributed much to the construction and embellishment of his church. No evidence at all supports the belief that he was an artist. This question is further elaborated in Chapter III. Other instances of the mistaken attribution of artistic achievement to the clergy will be encountered.

By the seventeenth century a number of artists were creoles, that is, born of Spanish parents in Peru. Miguel Gutiérrez Sencio, who passed the larger part of his life as chief architect of Cuzco Cathedral, was presumably native born. As time went on, more and more important figures were creoles, as those of Iberian birth decreased in number. In the eighteenth century Santiago Rosales, mulatto, the illegitimate son of a white man, reached the high office of chief architect (*maestro mayor*) of Lima Cathedral and held the same title for the monastery of the Augustinians.[14] This fact sheds an interesting light upon the comparative liberalism of Hispanic American countries in the matter of race mixture. Indeed, the earliest families to settle Peru soon had a generous admixture of Indian blood. Since the Spanish population in the sixteenth century was predominantly male, the creation of the new *mestizo* race was not long delayed.

The crossbreeding of cultures, like the mixture of races, was inevitable. From the first days of the conquest that phenomenon produced very beautiful hybrids in textiles. Predominantly native in materials and technique, they soon manifested the infiltration of Christian and other European themes.[15] The same conditions brought into existence the creole or *mestizo* style of sculptural and architectural decoration. It flourished in southern Peru from Arequipa through the *altiplano* along Lake Titicaca and down into La Paz and Potosí, the last two now within the borders of Bolivia. The native population far surpassed that of the whites or the mixed race (*mestizo*) in these regions, and it still does today except in the city of Arequipa.

Unfortunately few contracts relating to these monuments have been discovered and published. Whatever is known of the artists shows them to have been Indians. An Indian, Sebastián de la Cruz, was author of the fine *mestizo* tower of La Compañía at Potosí (1700–1707). He also began the church of San Francisco there (1707–1714) and was succeeded after his death by two other Indians, Joseph Agustín and Felipe Chavarría.[16] The Argentine writer, Angel Guido, states that the celebrated façade of San Lorenzo is the work of a *quechua* named José Kondori.[17] He gives, however, no indication of any source for the discovery of the name. There exists a notice of two Indian sculptors, natives of Juli, a town which is one of the chief centers of *mestizo* art. These men, Juan Huaicán and Marcos Rengifo received the contract (1705) for the high altar of a church at Moquequa at some distance from their home.[18] Simón de Asto, the man who signed the façade of Puno Cathedral, was surely a native with an Hispanicized name. As more documentary discoveries are made, evidence will surely accumulate to prove the predominance of the Indian artist in works of the *mestizo* style. One exceptional case is that of an artist of pure Indian blood whose architecture and sculpture are so completely Spanish that his race would never be suspected. He was Juan Tomás Tuyru Tupac, active at the end of the seventeenth century, architect of San Pedro at Cuzco, and sculptor of the Madonna of the Almudena.

STYLES AND TERMS

THE chronology of artistic styles in Europe varies considerably in different countries. In the Spanish colonies still greater deviation from the normal occurs. Gothic features such as decorative ribbed vaults survive in the New World well beyond the Gothic period. In Spain itself they persisted during the sixteenth century in the last of the Gothic cathedrals, for example, those of Salamanca and Segovia, and occasionally even during the Baroque age in the northern part of the peninsula. They are commonplace in the seventeenth and eighteenth centuries in the New World.

The Gothic pointed arch was used in Becerra's cathedral of Lima as late as 1598–1604. Very few examples of it still exist, however. They include the bay within the lateral portal (*circa* 1540–1552) of Santo Domingo in Lima, the crossing of San Pedro Mártir at Juli (*circa* 1560, Fig. 44), the chapel on the left and on the right on entering Cuzco Cathedral, and the former Franciscan cloister at Chiclayo.

Renaissance and Baroque are considered in the present volume as stylistic periods in the history of art. Hispanic Renaissance art both in Spain and the colonies corresponds to the sixteenth century, although continuing in its last phase into the early seventeenth in many cases. The word "plateresque" (*plateresco*), used by Spanish historians to distinguish the early decorated phase of Renaissance architecture in Spain (*circa* 1500–1560), is avoided as far as possible. English and American writers have extended the usage of the word to include late-Gothic works like the façade of San Gregorio at Valladolid. The intention is to define a surface-covering decorative scheme on the theory that it resembles the work of silversmiths (*plateros*). In reality the basis of this style is Islamic in its tendency to carpetlike patterns. Latin American critics expand the expression, plateresque, still further to include all lavishly decorated surfaces; they abandon the period limitations which are strictly observed by other historians. The reader will understand why it is preferable to avoid such unnecessary confusion.

The last period of the Renaissance in Spain (*circa* 1565–1610) is marked by the strictest classicism of the Italian High Renaissance. Juan de Herrera, architect of the Escorial, is the most famous Spanish exponent of the style, and, as a consequence, it is often known as "Herreresque." Francisco Becerra was its leading protagonist in Peru, but it continued well into the seventeenth century years after his death in 1605.

The Baroque extends over a long period from about 1600 to 1750. The first fifty years in Spanish architecture are distinguished by a relatively restrained treatment. The late Baroque (*circa* 1650–1750), on the other hand, is given to sumptuousness in decoration and a highly pictorial concept. Following the accession of the French dynasty to the Spanish throne in the person of Philip V, French culture and more specifically French rococo art gained the ascendancy. By 1750 its triumph was almost complete.

The name of José Churriguera is frequently applied to the last phase of the Hispanic Baroque. The spiral or salomonic column is the most prominent element of this style which is characterized by a lavish decorative scheme. As a matter of fact José Churriguera (1665–1725) did not create the "Churrigueresque," for it began in Spain about 1650 and reached Peru by 1665. The style gained its full momentum in the years *circa* 1690–1740.

The *mudéjar* is mentioned often in this volume because of its great popularity in the Spanish colonies. *Mudéjar* is distinguished by Islamic (Moorish in Spain) ornamental themes and techniques. Moslems living in Christian territory in Spain were originally called *mudéjares,* and thus the meaning of the word was extended to describe Christian art in Moorish style. The most typical are the geometric patterns of interlaces and star forms such as those used in Andalusian glazed tiles and in wooden ceilings composed of laths.

In the use of technical terms this book attempts to follow established usage. Many words, well known to historians of architecture and of the fine arts in general, will seem obscure to the layman. In dealing with Hispanic culture some terms are encountered for which no English equivalent exists. Thus the Spanish word *trascoro* refers to the wall behind the choir when the latter is placed in the nave of a church. The word "retable" is employed as an equivalent for *retablo,* meaning a large altarpiece. The English definition of a retable as a raised shelf behind an altar is never intended in the present book. Also

adopted from the Spanish is the term "salomonic column" (*salomónica*) signifying a spiral or twisted column. That feature is the very signature of the high Baroque style in Hispanic countries. Another expression which may need clarification is "triangular penetration." This refers to the slightly concave section of triangular shape which makes the transition from the barrel vault to the vertical wall containing the clerestory window, according to the usual practice in European architecture of the Renaissance and Baroque periods.

The remainder of this chapter will be devoted to a summary of the development of the architecture of colonial Peru, i.e., within the present boundaries of the country (see end papers). Upper Peru, which corresponds to the modern republic of Bolivia, belonged to the Viceroyalty of Peru until 1776. That region is not included within the scope of this book, but has been studied elsewhere.[19] In the succeeding chapters the monuments are studied by geographic divisions. Inasmuch as the chronology of colonial art follows geographic patterns, this procedure seemed the most workable. The material is so abundant that a purely chronological cross section would be confusing. In dealing with Lima, a catalogue of principal monuments and secondary monuments has been prepared (see Appendix) which may serve for reference. The major portion of the text is devoted to the development of the architecture. The sculpture is discussed by categories: choir stalls, pulpits, and retables. A general book like the present, which is the first of its kind, cannot hope to treat the material exhaustively. A whole volume might easily be given to the works included in each chapter.

THE EVOLUTION OF COLONIAL ARCHITECTURE

THE standard church of the sixteenth century was a long narrow edifice of adobe covered by a pitched roof of tiles or of cane and thatch. The earliest still extant appears to be San Cristóbal (1540) at Ayacucho (Fig. 35). Stone or adobe benches were placed along the walls of the nave, thus eliminating the need of chairs or pews. La Merced in the same city (Figs. 36–38), to be dated in the fifth decade of the century, is larger. Moreover, four lateral chapels and an elevated choir were included in the plan. Santa Clara in Ayacucho holds the distinction of being the earliest nunnery (1568) preserved. This church of single nave without chapels has upper and lower choirs on the short end opposite the sanctuary. It is exactly like the nunneries of Seville (Santa Clara, Santa Paula, San Clemente) and of many other Andalusian cities. The plan became almost universal in nuns' churches of Peru except that the lower choir was often placed at the right of the sanctuary. A triumphal arch precedes the apse, a characteristic of the sixteenth century to be noted also in San Jerónimo (1572) near Cuzco and in the Titicacan churches (Figs. 50, 54, 89). In Santa Clara a fine *mudéjar* ceiling still roofs the sanctuary.

Even the first cathedrals of Lima and Cuzco were humble structures of single nave. The Andalusian type of church with vaulted apse and a wooden covering of *mudéjar* interlaces over the nave was preferred in Lima throughout the sixteenth century. The mixture of the Gothic and later of the Renaissance styles with the virile Islamic tradition of southern Spain produced a distinctly regional school of architecture there. In Peru the cultural relations with Andalusia always remained strong throughout the colonial period. Lima, the capital, was constantly in communication with Spain and with Seville in particular. Hence there is no cause for surprise on discovering that the ecclesiastical architecture of Lima was derived to such a great extent from that important source.

The basilican church of Sevillian *mudéjar* origin was introduced to Lima by the three leading monastic orders in the mid-century: the Dominicans (*circa* 1540–1552), the Franciscans (1555), and the Augustinians (1574). Wooden ceilings were used in each case, those of the Dominicans and Augustinians being made of *mudéjar* interlaces. If only this precedent had been followed throughout the history of Lima's architecture, the perfect solution both structurally and artistically would have been reached. Instead, imitation barrel vaults of cane and plaster were adopted as the standard practice in the seventeenth and eighteenth centuries.

The church of single nave continued, however, to be the accepted type through the land in the sixteenth century. The Augustinians of Trujillo adhered to it in the second half of the century. The heavy walls of that building are incorporated into the nave of the present edifice. The original stucco ceiling of Renaissance arabesques and pine cones yielded to a barrel vault in the rebuilding after the earthquake of 1619.[20] A group of sixteen churches was begun in the villages on the shores of Lake Titicaca in 1590, and luckily half of them still exist. The plans of all are very similar, long and narrow with chapels in the position of the transept. Most of them have lost their original thatched or tiled roofs, which have been replaced by ugly coverings of galvanized iron.

The portals of La Merced (*circa* 1540–1550) and San Francisco (*circa* 1552) at Ayacucho afford the best examples of the earlier Renaissance phase in Peru (Figs. 38, 40). Here the classical orders and the frieze of cherubs' heads and rosettes in alternation are provincial versions of European work. Yet Peru can offer nothing to compare with the numerous fine Renaissance portals of Mexico. Nor does any surviving sculpture equal the beautifully carved arabesques on the doorways of Quito Cathedral in Ecuador.

The only Peruvian work which could conceivably be called plateresque is the portal of the Jesuit Chapel (*circa* 1570) in Ayacucho (Fig. 41), decorated with the arms of the Orue family. We are speaking, of course, of extant monuments. Doubtless, more splendid examples existed in the sixteenth-century churches of Lima, Arequipa, Trujillo, and Cuzco. The first church of the Jesuits, built in Cuzco in the last quarter of the century, is described

in some detail by an anonymous chronicler.[21] He praises the main portal as the best in Peru, but one must make allowances for that sort of hyperbole. Nevertheless, his description does contain the information that the portal was constructed of stone and that columns were grouped about the niches containing statues of saints. It was obviously a typical Renaissance composition of triumphal-arch division and without much question superior to anything still in existence today.

The best Renaissance carving is to be found on the capitals in the large cloister of San Francisco at Cuzco (Figs. 33, 34). The curious combination of a band of acanthus below an echinus embellished with volutes is paralleled by the Jeronymite cloister at Lupiana, in Santa Cruz at Toledo, and elsewhere in Spain. The pseudo-Corinthian capitals at Ayacucho are in reality very rustic (Figs. 38, 40).

The façade of the parish church (1572) at San Jerónimo near Cuzco is a Renaissance work (Fig. 88). It has a triumphal-arch entrance with niches and frieze of cherub heads which was imitated in the region well along in the following century. A more severe classical phase of the Renaissance appears in the Titicacan district (Figs. 45, 50, 52) at Paucarcolla (1563) and in the interior portals of La Asunción at Chucuito and San Miguel at Ilave (1590). The most interesting features of the latter building, however, are the entrances to the sacristy with the pointed arch in a rectangle, a *mudéjar* composition, known as the *alfiz* (Fig. 51). Thus the exotic Orientalism of Spain puts in an appearance at the most unexpected times and places.

Writers have often held that the Open Chapel or *Capilla de Indios* was an exclusive product of Mexican society of the sixteenth century. The practice of celebrating mass in a small chapel in the open air and the custom of preaching and instructing Indians in this manner were, to be sure, essentially Mexican developments. The reason lies in the large native population which could not be gathered conveniently within a church. Open Chapels did exist, however, in Peru. The Jesuits at Lima preached in the open air in the early years before their building program had reached fruition.[22] The Franciscans at Cajamarca said mass in an Open Chapel on Sundays and festivals, as explained in Chapter VII. The apertures in the apses of Santo Domingo at Cuzco (Fig. 79), Santiago at Pomata, and Santa Catalina at Juliaca, on the other hand, certainly cannot be interpreted as Open Chapels. Professor Kenneth J. Conant's suggestion that they were used for the display of relics is the most acceptable. Mass was said on feast days from a balcony in the façade of Lima Cathedral. This custom, described by Padre Cobo, is not peculiar to the Spanish colonies, however, and is not comparable with the special purpose of the Open Chapel.[23]

The first completely vaulted structure in Peru was the cathedral of Lima (1598–1604), the work of the famous architect, Francisco Becerra. Its rectangular ground plan (Fig. 8), probably derived from the cathedral of Jaén, had become a favorite in sixteenth-century Spain. The equal height of nave and aisles used in Lima Cathedral places it in the category of a hall church. That type was also of Andalusian parentage, and the piers at Lima, surmounted by a classical entablature block, unquestionably are descendants of those in Diego Silóee's cathedral of Granada. Becerra's groin vaults of brick were short-lived, for they suffered irreparable damage in the earthquakes of 1606 and 1609. The consequence was that a council of architects, held previous to the rebuilding of the church (1613–1622), decided upon ribbed Gothic vaults as the most resistant to earthquakes.

We have, therefore, the strange spectacle of the Gothic vault, apparently unused on a large scale in sixteenth-century Peru, widely adopted in the succeeding century at a time when it had passed out of favor in Europe. Gothic ribbed vaults covered the nave of the new church of La Compañía (1624–1638) in Lima, although small cupolas were placed over the aisles. La Merced, rebuilt in 1628, had Gothic vaults of brick over both the nave and aisles.

The type of single-naved structure known as Isabellan Gothic, which developed in Spain in the late fifteenth century, was the basic ancestor of the vaulted non-basilican churches of Santo Domingo, Mexico, Peru, and all other Hispanic countries excluding, of course, the Portuguese possessions in Brazil. In Mexico these Gothic monuments, mostly monastic, were erected in great quantity and high quality in the mid-sixteenth century. In Peru, as we have seen, the vaulted church delayed until the beginning of the seventeenth. One of the finest is the superb structure of single nave at Guadalupe, reërected after 1619. The monastic church of San Agustín at Saña (Fig. 168) and others in the same village, now ruined, belonged to the same category. As late as 1668 the architect, Francisco Jiménez de Sigüenza, designed the famous shrine of Copacabana (Bolivia) on the Isabellan model.[24] The dome over the crossing and the plain classical cornice of the nave alone suggest the lateness of its date.

The example of Lima extended to Cuzco. Gothic vaults were selected for the cathedral (1598–1654), the original project for which also came from the hand of Francisco Becerra (Figs. 65, 66). The success of these vaults in withstanding the earthquake of 1650 undoubtedly induced the Jesuits to adopt them for their own church, built shortly after the catastrophe. Elsewhere in Cuzco, the Gothic construction was limited to the sanctuary and the arms of the transept. Thus in San Francisco (1652) the decorative late-Gothic vaults (Fig. 77) are combined with domical vaults in the nave.[25] Their example was followed in the parish church at Ayaviri, combined there with barrel vaults in the nave.

The typical Renaissance-Baroque barrel vault is almost universal in Peru from 1650 onward with exceptions to be noted. Transverse arches or ribs separate it into bays. A concave section, generally triangular, makes the transition from the barrel vault to the vertical lunette of the clerestory. At Cuzco, by contrast, the lunette at the sides of the vault is arched and the window placed directly in the wall (Figs. 73, 77), wherever

the vaults are domical in section. This constitutes in reality a continuation of the same type of medieval construction as that used in Cuzco Cathedral and the Compañía, simply omitting the decorative Gothic ribs.

At times barrel vaults are also essentially medieval in the way the masonry curves up continuously from the horizontal springing. An example of this system occurs in Santiago at Pomata where the windows are splayed into the vault (Fig. 220). Fenestration is generally small in Peru, because of the tropical light and its increased intensity in the high regions of the Andes. In some of the churches of Arequipa, such as those at Caima and Paucarpata, a few small circular openings and an occasional window alone break the continuous surfaces of the vaults (Fig. 211).

The materials used in vaulting differ according to the geographic location. Finely cut ashlar characterizes most of the Andean region from Cajamarca to Arequipa and Lake Titicaca, extending also into Bolivia. On the other hand, the builders of Cuzco and Ayacucho preferred red brick, even though the stone of the Andes was available to them. The churches of Lima, erected in the first half of the seventeenth century, also received vaults of brick. Their repeated destruction by earthquake led the architects to resign themselves to the imitation of barrel vaults by means of cane coated with plaster. The first important work in which these methods were employed throughout was San Francisco at Lima (1657–1673, Fig. 92). That set a fashion never to be abandoned in the capital. At times wood alone sufficed and with sad results, as in the wooden Gothic vaults of the present cathedral. Other coastal cities, subject to conditions similar to those of the capital, followed in her wake. Only in Trujillo on the coast do many of the seventeenth-century brick vaults survive down to the present day.

The late Renaissance style known as the Herreresque triumphed in the cathedrals of Lima and Cuzco, designed first in 1582 but begun in their final form in 1598. The interior of Cuzco Cathedral, not finished until 1654, is the most complete representative, inasmuch as Lima Cathedral today is only a replica in wood and plaster, reconstructed in the mid-eighteenth century. The barrenness and austerity of the gigantic piers and the large molded entablatures of Cuzco are majestic and awesome (Figs. 65, 66). The example of the cathedral was so impressive that it established the norm for the school. The churches of the second half of the century, San Francisco, La Merced, San Pedro, and El Belén, clung to Doric pilasters and molded entablatures, maintaining a sober classical design (Figs. 75, 76, 82). Only the Jesuits showed independence in choosing Corinthian pilasters and a bracketed cornice (Fig. 72).

The interior of Trujillo Cathedral (Fig. 160), designed by Diego Maroto in 1643, is equally as sober as the churches of Cuzco. Indeed, any nonclassical work is the exception in this period. Very little in Lima itself save the chapel of La Vera Cruz and Nuestra Señora de Montserrat maintain vestiges of the early years. The cathedral

of Ayacucho (1632–1672) shows a slight divergence in the introduction of a dentelated cornice (Fig. 143). That detail set the standard for the local school during the next century and a half. Churches of the first half of the seventeenth century like Santa Clara in Cuzco, La Compañía in Ayacucho, and Santo Domingo in Trujillo (Figs. 59, 135, 161) have the direct earnest appeal of the utilitarian handiwork of the pioneer.

Portals in the first half of the seventeenth century remained sober, although less so than interiors. The portal of the chapel of La Vera Cruz in Lima, after the design of Diego Guillén in 1613, and the lateral entrance of Santo Domingo (Fig. 102) are late Renaissance works, comparable with monuments of the same date in Spain, such as Nuestra Señora de las Angustias at Valladolid (1597–1606).[26] Equally classical is the Doric entrance to the monastery at Guadalupe, north of Trujillo (*circa* 1619). Although exactly contemporary, the doorways of San Agustín at Saña (Fig. 167) retain more of an earlier Renaissance flavor in the frieze decorated with rosettes and the fluted pilasters in truncated form.

One work in Cuzco, the portal of Santa Clara (Fig. 61), affords a fixed date at this time (1603–1622). Its design is that of a simple Renaissance triumphal arch. The upper part was never completed. The peculiar capital, a Doric cushion topped by volutes, is so common throughout the city in the seventeenth century and perhaps earlier that it may be regarded as characteristic of the school. The side entrance of

San Juan de Dios (Fig. 58), now blocked up, is a fine sturdy composition of rusticated stone which appears to have originated in this period. Equally powerful, though not as well designed, is the portal of the seminary adjoining La Compañía at Ayacucho (Fig. 137).

The date, if not the quality, of the three portals of Santo Domingo in Cuzco (Fig. 55) may always be controversial. They belong precisely to the transition from the Renaissance to the more broken composition of the Baroque. They may have survived the earthquake of 1650, but I believe that they were part of the subsequent reconstruction. The same conservatism is manifested in the front entrance of La Merced (Fig. 56) dated in the sixteen-fifties.

Martínez de Arrona's design (1626) for the main entrance of Lima Cathedral (Fig. 105) reveals the Baroque in the abrupt transitions of contour and plane in the niches even more than in the broken pediment. The dimensions were large and the tendency to verticality might be regarded as a survival of Mannerism.

The full Baroque arrives in Peru with the portal (1654) of Cuzco Cathedral (Figs. 62, 63). Columns and wall surfaces are stepped out from the body of the façade moving toward the center. Planes and directions are constantly shifted. The breaking of cornices and moldings and the curve of scrolls both contribute to an expression of agitated movement and to a pictorial flow of light and shade. This is the dynamic pictorial style of the Baroque, so successfully analyzed by Wölfflin and contrasted to the sculptural stability of the Renaissance.[27]

Against the bare stone walls of the façade the cathedral portal stands out, concentrated and in sharp opposition. The effect is of a jewel shining in a sober setting. That scheme of contrasts is typically Spanish, being characteristic of Spanish architecture from the late Gothic thenceforth. To mention San Gregorio at Valladolid, Santa Cruz at Toledo, and Pedro Ribera's Provincial Hospital at Madrid will serve as a reminder. A still more persistently Spanish tradition should be noted in Cuzco Cathedral, and that is the use of flat terraced roofs. Even the Gothic style with its highly pitched roofs did not change the Spanish preference for the horizontal and rectangular silhouette. Both the southern Mediterranean customs of the Moors and the relatively warm climate lie at the root of that usage. In the New World, however, the pitched roof is much more common because of its practicality in a country subject to a rainy season. This type is characteristic of the unpretentious structures of the sixteenth century.

The façade of the cathedral established the Baroque style at Cuzco (Fig. 63). The portal of La Compañía (1668) is a close follower of it, distinguished by more sculptured ornament (Fig. 64). La Merced, San Pedro, El Belén, are all variants (Figs. 68, 69, 80). San Pedro manifests greater sobriety in its plain columns and undecorated wall surfaces. In many respects this church, designed by an Indian, Juan Tomás, is the most Spanish of all in its barrenness and dignity. The richly carved surfaces of San Sebastián (Figs. 70, 71) display greater Baroque exuberance.

The low proportions of the cathedral towers in relation to the broad façade (Fig. 62) are to be explained by the fear of earthquakes. The memory of the devastations of 1650 was still vivid when these belfries were erected (1654–1657). Far superior is the composition of La Compañía on the exterior (Fig. 67), extraordinarily fine in its scale and in the interrelation of all of its elements. The influence of this monument was second only to that of the cathedral in establishing the most notable school of architecture of Hispanic type in colonial Peru. The artistic authority of Cuzco was by no means limited to the city. Its artists worked throughout the entire region. The churches at Lampa and Ayaviri (Figs. 239–242, 245, 246) are dependent upon those of the Andean capital. In painting, the geographic range of influence was even greater, extending into Bolivia.

The mid-seventeenth-century façade of Ayacucho Cathedral (Fig. 139) has broad low dimensions and two towers which indicate its dependence upon the cathedrals of Lima and Cuzco. The composition is, however, very clumsy and faulty. It looks as though several architects had worked upon it, each with contempt for his predecessor. The exterior of Trujillo Cathedral, on the contrary, is unified and consistent in design (Fig. 158). The portals are good and decidedly conservative for the period (1643–1666). Here the school of Lima prevails and that is no wonder since the

architect, Diego Maroto, lived in the capital. The huge size of the towers was apparently an idea of José de la Sida, first introduced by him in San Agustín (1637) at Lima.

The important new direction taken by seventeenth-century architecture in Lima came with the rebuilding of the church and monastery of San Francisco (1657–1673). As previously explained, the decision to adopt imitation barrel vaults constructed of cane and plaster was decisive (Fig. 92). This expediency solved the problem of the earthquake-ridden city, and thenceforth no attempt was made to employ heavier materials. The *mudéjar* ornament in plaster, spread over the vaults and pilasters, marked the most wholehearted adoption of that style in a city where Andalusian *mudéjar* elements had always been conspicuous. La Merced, rebuilt in 1687–1706, was the most faithful follower of the Franciscan church in plan and type of construction (Fig. 93). In both cases chapels are domed and walls rusticated in plaster. A chain pattern of rectangles and ellipses in alternation on the walls of the nave replaces the Islamic patterns of San Francisco. The concept remains unmodified.

The basilican floor plan with single sanctuary, dome over the crossing, and the aisles covered by cupolas was introduced by the Jesuits in San Pedro (1624). Here the builders still clung to Gothic vaults in the nave. The Franciscans followed the precedent established in San Pedro, but substituted barrel vaults in the nave (Fig. 92), and the Mercedarians followed suit in 1687. The plan of San Pedro in Lima (Fig.

9) was partly derived, in my opinion, from the Jesuit church at Quito, begun in 1605, because the disposition of the two monuments is almost identical. Moreover, Martín de Aizpitarte, architect of San Pedro, had served his novitiate in the Jesuit house at Quito. To be sure Padre Nicolás Durán Mastrilli stated that he brought to Lima a model of the Casa Profesa in Rome. The church built in the time of Padre Durán shows marked differences from the Gesù at Rome, however. Writers have also claimed that La Compañía at Cuzco (Fig. 4) is based in its disposition upon the Gesù. It is built, nevertheless, in the form of a Latin cross with shallow lateral chapels. Hence it is the successor of a type common everywhere in the Gothic and Renaissance periods, and not in any way dependent upon the Jesuit prototype in Rome. A similar plan was used by the Jesuits in their church at Pisco and in San Pedro Mártir at Juli (Figs. 2, 6). Yet, elsewhere, they preferred a larger basilican edifice. The truth is that the Jesuit order never officially adopted a specific type of floor plan or church as its own in Peru or anywhere else.[28]

The plan of the Gesù in Rome was the source, though modified, of La Compañía at Quito. The Jesuits in Lima followed certain innovations of their order in Ecuador, even though they possessed the plans of the Casa Profesa of Rome. Thenceforth the plan of La Compañía in Lima was to become a basic type in Peru, employed by several religious orders, especially in Lima, Arequipa, and Trujillo. The Jesuits at Arequipa chose it for their new structure

(Fig. 16), begun about 1650, and the Mercedarians in 1657, the latter shifting the dome from the crossing to the sanctuary. The plan influenced the enlargements and rebuildings of the monastic churches of Trujillo: Santo Domingo, San Francisco, La Merced, and San Agustín. In these instances, domical vaults lighted from above take the place of cupolas, as they also do in Santo Domingo at Arequipa. San Antonio at Cajamarca (Fig. 11) falls into the same category. All openings from above are omitted in the aisles, however, a change explained by the intense light in this high altitude.

The façade of San Francisco (1669–1674) marks the rise of the full Baroque in Lima (Figs. 108, 109) just a few years later than its appearance in Cuzco. This frontispiece is, indeed, a retable transferred to the exterior of a church. Long ago the retable façade had started upon its course in Spain, as, for example, in a work of the late fifteenth century like San Gregorio in Valladolid. During the Renaissance it continued to flourish in such well-known monuments as San Esteban and the cathedral at Salamanca.

The treatment of the columns and the ornament on the Franciscan façade at Lima (Figs. 107–109) so closely resemble the retable of the Immaculate Conception in the cathedral as to suggest that both were designed by the same artist. In spite of the extraordinarily high quality of the portal, it is dwarfed by the gigantic towers and the heavy rustication of the walls. These unpleasing dimensions were introduced by José de la Sida in San Agustín

(1637, Fig. 111). As previously noted, they were successfully improved by Diego Maroto in his project for the cathedral of Trujillo (Fig. 158).

One of the best portals of this period is that of Santa Lucía at Ferreñafe (1690) near Chiclayo (Figs. 175, 176). The composition is refreshingly original and ingeniously put together. Female heads accompanied by cloth swags filled with fruit decorate the columns here, as they do those of San Francisco at Lima.

The ultimate in retable façades is reached in the large compositions of two or three stories in which spiral columns (*salomónicas*) enframe niches containing statues, and a prodigal wealth of ornament invests the entire monument. Vines and grapes usually entwine the columns, and the planes of the surface and the complexity of the moldings combine to create an expression of dynamically agitated exuberance. The first of these works in Lima was the frontispiece of La Merced (1697–1704), known today in a modern replica (Fig. 110). Virtuosity soared even higher in the filmy spun sculpture of San Agustín (Fig. 111), now unluckily recut and endowed with a gratuitous attic story and round window, both added in 1908. The true masterpieces of this type are three churches of the first half of the eighteenth century in the highlands of Cajamarca: the cathedral, San Antonio, and El Belén (Figs. 177–187). They are, indeed, Hispanic retables of gilded wood transformed into stone. The application of the term "Churrigueresque" to this type of Baroque art has become common, as previously explained.

It adds little or nothing to an understanding of the style.

A tendency to small churches characterizes the school of Lima in the eighteenth century and also districts subject to influence from the capital. In contrast to the type of monuments just discussed, sculpture and carved ornament are absent. The style is competent but undistinguished. The composition is one of relatively simple architectural elements. Two small belfries decorated with pilasters having volute capitals are the rule. An early specimen, Santa Rosa de las Monjas (1704–1708), was succeeded by numerous others in Lima. The two-towered churches of Ayacucho partake of the same general characteristics (Figs. 145, 146). The type traveled up and down the coast, and is found in structures such as Santa Teresa in Lima, El Belén at Trujillo, San José at Nazca, and La Compañía at Pisco (Figs. 115–117, 128).

About 1740 the French rococo began to filter into the art of viceregal Peru. It is responsible for the gay lilting spirit of the façade of Santa Teresa, now demolished. The sparkle and crisp rhythms of eighteenth-century music find their counterpart in such architecture. Some of these monuments of Lima cannot be dated exactly. The rebuilding of the city after the earthquake of 1746 saw the rococo style triumph over all others. This movement produced not only churches like San Carlos (1758–1766) and El Cristo de los Milagros (1766–1771), but also the tower of Santo Domingo, retables, and church furnishings (Figs. 114, 119, 329–336).

The most interesting innovation in the

floor plans of the eighteenth century is the elliptical shape (Fig. 18) of El Corazón de Jesús (1758–1766). Elsewhere in the Spanish colonies it also put in occasional appearances at this time. One of these was Santa Brígida in Mexico City and another, the Hospicio, at San Vicente in Salvador. The plan belongs to the rococo movement as do the centralized church of El Cristo de los Milagros at Lima and the Capilla del Pocito in Guadalupe, Mexico, even though the latter is based upon a Renaissance drawing of Serlio.[29]

For the most part, Lima's eighteenth-century churches are of the conventual type, small with a single nave. Barrel vaults of cane and plaster are universal. Doric pilasters and molded cornices persist, but the dentelated cornice is also widespread. The signature of the school is the use of a decorative bracket upon the cornice in the center of each bay. A bracket or volute capital was also very popular, occurring rather frequently in the preceding century too, but attaining an unparalleled vogue in the eighteenth century.

The death of colonial art in Peru came with the Neoclassic invasion of the first years of the nineteenth century. The chief apostle was a Spanish-born artist, Matías Maestro.[30] His own dull efforts are not too distasteful to cause particular resentment. The fact that he and his fellow enthusiasts ruthlessly destroyed and burned a vast portion of the priceless works of colonial art cannot be forgiven. He transformed the Baroque splendor of the interiors of San Francisco and Santo Domingo into the drab dismal spectacle which they present today.

Mestizo or creole art is the most original contribution of the Hispanic colonial period. Its distinguishing and flavorsome qualities were those of the Indian's heritage. *Mestizo* is the more accurate term, because this art like the new race was procreated by the crossbreeding of two races. Creole is the term generally employed, although its meaning fails in adequacy, since creole in Latin America refers to a person of European blood, born in the New World.

The *mestizo* style is limited almost exclusively to remote Andean regions where the population was largely Indian. It is concentrated in the south, extending from Arequipa through the regions of Puno, Lake Titicaca, and on down into La Paz and Potosí, now within the borders of Bolivia. As explained earlier in this chapter, all evidence points to the probability that the architects and sculptors were pure Indians or else *mestizos* who had had only a superficial contact with European civilization.

The chronology of the development is still obscure for lack of documentary information and because some of the earliest examples have surely been destroyed. At present Santo Domingo in Arequipa (1677–1680) occupies a key position, since it appears to be the first dated work (Fig. 201). The sculpture upon the face of the choir and the side portal already manifest a fully developed tradition. Thenceforth many splendid façades follow in its wake: La Compañía (1698), San Agustín, and those of the churches of Yanahuara (1750) and Caima (Figs. 193, 204–208). The luxuriantly carved cloister of La Compañía

(Figs. 196, 197) is dated 1738. To the same year belongs a fine example of domestic architecture, known as the Casa Ricketts.

In the architectural decoration masked heads, sometimes with long objects sprouting from their mouths, are the most striking of the pre-Columbian themes (Fig. 206). Local flora and fauna, particularly the lily of the Incas, called the *ccantu,* and the puma, are ever recurrent. The natural primitivism of the design and technique, however, is the most significant and determinative factor. The naïve primitive artist, at whatever epoch in history or at whatever part of the globe, creates simplified geometric patterns which he repeats over and over again. His technique is often rude, yet at times he shows great genius in his basic sense of form. Thus the Coptic or Merovingian carver may arrive at results very similar to those in the Andes of Peru.

By 1750 *mestizo* art had reached its peak. The façades of Puno Cathedral (1757) and San Francisco at La Paz (1753–1772) already suggest the overripeness of autumn (Figs. 250–252). Outside of Arequipa, the shores of Lake Titicaca showed its finest flowering in Santiago at Pomata, and in San Juan and Santa Cruz at Juli (Figs. 215–229). Tropical plants, fruit, birds, and monkeys contribute much to the exoticism of these rich products of the decorator's art. Furniture of inlaid wood whose highly stylized patterns display the same fantastic array of themes is a product of the same culture (Fig. 230). Manufactured in the same regions and also in the tropics of Bolivia, it probably contributed to the diffusion of these designs. Drawings

and textiles were also transportable media for the dissemination of such ideas.

Mestizo façades are the exception in northern Peru. The church of Santiago at Huamán (Fig. 165) near Trujillo is the work of a primitive master, although not by a *mestizo* artist of southern Peru. The presence of the mermaids playing the *charango* may possibly suggest some knowledge of Titicacan traditions. These mythical creatures are mainly concentrated in southern Peru and Bolivia. Although the theory cannot be proved, it is quite probable that they were associated by legend with Lake Titicaca, and that, just as in European lore, they lay in wait of the unwary. They appear on façades of the churches at Puno, Lampa, La Compañía at Arequipa, Nuestra Señora de Montserrat near Andahuaylas, San Lorenzo at Potosí, below the choir of San Miguel at Pomata (Fig. 235) and on houses at Oropesa, as well as on retables in Santa Clara of Cuzco and La Asunción at Juli.

No attempt is made in the present book to give an exhaustive account of civil and domestic architecture. The town hall with two stories of open galleries upon the main plaza was a standard type in the Spanish colonies.[31] It represented a continuation of the *cabildo* found commonly in small Spanish villages. Unfortunately nearly all of them in Hispanic America have disappeared in recent years during the rapid growth and expansion of cities. The Andean villages of Peru, like Huancavelica and Ayacucho, and tiny pueblos which have escaped modernization, still possess them (Fig. 154).

Virtually all Spanish cities in America were laid out upon the gridiron plan with a Plaza Mayor in the center. Charles V originally issued regulations for the urbanization of the colonies, and they were later elaborated by Philip II. Thus the urbanization of Lima and Trujillo was established at the very outset upon their foundation in 1535, whereas Cuzco maintained a great part of the plan of the Incaic city.[32] Cuzco alone, among the larger cities, however, has preserved its colonial domestic architecture almost unscathed. That of Lima has been destroyed in the present century. Arequipa lost the center of her public life in a conflagration in 1844.

The arcaded walks of Cuzco's plaza were reconstructed immediately after the earthquake of 1650, when the city endured the worst disaster in its history. A large painting in the church of the Triunfo presents a precise description of the city as it looked in 1650 (Fig. 21). The plaza has changed little from the time of the original foundation in 1534. Even the arcades of today go back in part at least to these early years.

Houses at Cuzco are of two stories in the center of the town, contrary to the general practice of limiting them to a single story. Every house had and still has its patio and is covered by a slightly pitched roof of red tiles. The force of tradition was so great that the Spanish took the patio with them even to the coldest climates. It originated in the warm Mediterranean world and is eminently suitable to the tropical coastal regions of Peru. Nothing could be less practical, however, in the rigorous cold of the Andean highlands, yet the Spanish built every house around a court. Social customs played their part in this matter. The seclusion of family life and the Oriental attitude toward women, who were shut up as though in a harem, are equally, if not more, important factors than architectural tradition.

Brick covered with stucco was employed in the small houses at Cuzco. Stone was plentiful, however, and for that reason even modest edifices enjoyed the added beauty of fine materials. The rich landowners and nobles of Cuzco built themselves large palaces of stone, often using Incaic structures as quarries. Most famous of them is the so-called Casa del Almirante (Figs. 22, 23). It has a large patio of two arcaded galleries supported by stone columns. The capital, a rather provincial type of Doric with the addition of volutes, became more or less the standard for the city. The vertical strip over each capital in the lower gallery establishes a rectangular *alfiz* arrangement of *mudéjar* origin, also present in the Renaissance cloister of San Francisco at Cuzco. The superstructure is made of brick. In one corner of the court a broad stairway leads to the second story. Here the main formal hall occupies the street side, following ancient custom in European palaces. The service quarters are consigned to an inner court.

The exterior of the Casa del Almirante is a rectangular mass, built of stone. The few windows, placed high in the second story, give an almost fortified aspect. One corner window with angle caryatid recalls many familiar prototypes in Renaissance Spain. The stone trefoil window like the *alfiz* of the patio introduces the Oriental *mudéjar* note. A fine stone portal, surmounted by escutcheons and a knight's helmet in good Spanish style, has the character of Renaissance design. It is difficult to say whether this palace is really a sixteenth-century structure or an archaistic work of a hundred years later. Related portals exist in Cuzco. The house known as the Casa de los Cuatro Bustos has four busts of men in mid-sixteenth-century costume upon the lintel of its doorway.[33] These busts, as well as the architectural elements, are very convincing pieces of evidence for dating the building in the sixteenth century. Investigation of the archives and identification of family shields must be achieved before a definitive solution of many of these problems is accomplished.

Throughout the seventeenth century Cuzco's arcaded patios of stone changed little. The second story sometimes has wooden posts and the flat Moorish type of capital known as the *zapata* (shoe). Projecting roofs like those which line the streets of Cuzco are universal in Spanish colonial towns. Their purpose is frankly utilitarian, for they afford protection to the house and to the pedestrian from sun and rain. Equally ubiquitous is the balcony, also ever present in small villages in the mother country.

A more peculiarly Oriental type of closed balcony provided a protected lookout for the women in the cities of Lima and Trujillo. The importance of social customs in their influence upon architecture is obvious here. The large carved balconies (called *miradores* by the Spanish) are especially beautiful in the Torre Tagle Palace at Lima (Fig. 24), now occupied by the Ministry of Foreign Affairs. A row of shutters upon horizontal bars could be tipped outward to allow the ladies to peer down upon passersby. The origin of these is to be sought in the Near East where they are very common in the streets of Cairo. The Moslems brought them to Spain, whence they traveled to the New World along with the Spaniard's definitely Oriental concept of women.

The Orientalism of the Torre Tagle Palace is not limited to the balconies. The main patio (Fig. 26) of trefoil arches, large and small in the upper gallery, is one of the finest pieces of *mudéjar* art in Peru. The Sevillian tiles upon the dado of the second story have the date 1735, sufficient as a guide to the period of the building. The tile pavement and fountain in the court are, on the other hand, modern. A splendid Baroque portal marks the street entrance, and another sets off the stairway within the court. A short corridor leading to the patio (Fig. 25) is richly carved in stone with flat lacelike designs of frankly *mudéjar* character. The second court is restricted to a carriage entrance and service quarters. As usual the principal salon runs across nearly the full breadth of the façade in the second story.

Lima was once a city of balconies. Those in the old section in the vicinity of the Plaza Mayor are now almost entirely of the nineteenth century, and only a few of them still remain in the Calle de la Vera Cruz. Virtually all of the single-storied houses with an occasional balcony on the street have disappeared. One stands picturesquely aslant of the large arches on the Paseo de Aguas, a broad promenade with pools of water in French style built by the Francophile viceroy, Amat.

Throughout the length and breadth of Latin America the houses of the common people were single-storied structures of adobe or brick. Roofs were generally tiled; frequently in primitive districts they were thatched. A small patio always stood in the center, and in larger establishments one or more patios were added, the last one for the service quarters.

At Trujillo a considerable amount of good domestic architecture of the colonial period gives distinction to the town. Portals are usually rectangular with a full entablature as cornice and truncated pilasters at the sides. The Casa Obregoso on the Plaza de San Agustín has a well preserved entrance of this type. A very handsome eighteenth-century façade is that of the Casa Ganoza Chopitea (Fig. 27) whose Baroque pediment provides a climactic element. The sheltered balcony, here at the right, was just as popular at Trujillo as at Lima. The large fine iron grilles, the very essence of Spanish architecture, are numerous and particularly good in quality at Trujillo. A short corridor leads into the main patio which is small in this region. Columns of wood topped by *zapata* capitals are the rule whether the court is single storied, or the more rarely used two-storied type.

No great variation in domestic architecture is noted up and down the coast whether it be at Lima, Trujillo, or Lambayeque (Fig. 28). Some extraordinarily long balconies run a full block on each side of a large house. A picturesque landmark of this sort is the Casa de los Herrera (Fig. 29) on the corner of the Plaza Mayor in Trujillo. Another stands near the center of Lambayeque.

The portals of the houses of Cajamarca (Fig. 30) deserve special mention in any discussion of domestic architecture. Related in type to those of Trujillo, they are more lavishly decorated with splendidly carved ornament. Although sometimes in stone, they are more frequently in stucco. At Trujillo itself the highly decorated frontispiece exists in only one example today, the Casa de los Arana.

Arequipa surpasses all other cities of Peru for the beauty of its ashlar construction, made of the gray volcanic stone of the region. Houses, like churches, are built in solid rectangular masses, making fine cubic volumes. The main salon is usually vaulted, a phenomenon for which there is no parallel elsewhere in the country. Windows are rectangular with a flat hood at the top and good iron grilles. The single-storied patios, generally small, have neither arcades nor the post-and-lintel system.[34] As explained in Chapter VIII, the stone portals carved with *mestizo* ornament achieve very beautiful decorative effects (Figs. 203, 205).

An attempt has been made in the present chapter to set forth the chief features of colonial architecture in Peru. In the succeeding chapters the material will be treated in some detail, including not only stylistic problems but also questions of historical and archaeological nature.

COLONIAL SCULPTURE

IN the last three chapters, which are devoted to sculpture, the material is arranged by categories of monuments: choir stalls, pulpits, and retables. The development is treated chronologically in each case. Since the material is studied in its broad general aspects, a synthesis of the sculpture has not been included in the present chapter, as in the case of the architecture. The choir stalls of the seventeenth and eighteenth centuries, principally in Lima and Cuzco, comprise an important corpus of works never before studied. Pulpits are still more prolific in numbers, and qualitatively unsurpassed anywhere in the world. The high point of achievement in this branch of artistic endeavor was reached in Cuzco in the second half of the seventeenth century.

To speak of Spanish sculpture is to think of retables. The gigantic altar filling the breadth and height of a chapel is an uniquely Spanish creation. This development which began in the fifteenth century is one more indication of the Spanish love of the grandiose and the luxurious. By no accident is the word *impresionante* one of the most often used in the Spanish language. The architectural style of retables closely follows the flux of movements in monumental buildings. In fact, the Baroque style of architecture is more complete and better fulfilled in retables than elsewhere. These structures are pieces of decorative architecture, resplendent in the beauty of their gilded wood. The figure sculpture itself never attained a position of great significance in the Spanish colonies, for it is conceived as subordinate to the decorative whole. The same is often true in Spain, yet the mother country did produce many sculptors whose fame rests upon their handling and interpretation of the human figure. No such master of outstanding distinction ever appeared in Peru.

The scope of the present volume does not extend to the inclusion of the minor arts, such as the countless magnificent works in silver. The altar frontals, tabernacles, and ecclesiastical vessels in precious metals deserve a special study in themselves, so great is their artistic worth. The entire field of colonial painting in Peru, likewise, has yet to be investigated. Although far less rewarding than the architecture and sculpture, a history of painting will add another interesting chapter to our knowledge of Hispanic culture.

Hispanic-colonial and Portuguese-colonial art in America constitute a new phase in the history of civilization. The New World must always be studied with reference to the Old, otherwise any comprehension of it is faulty. Yet, the colonial culture of America was far more than a provincial extension of that of the motherland. The different social, political, economic, and artistic factors in Spanish America produced new situations which find no exact parallel in Europe. The native Indian culture in Hispanic lands was joined to Old World traditions with an impact which was unprecedented in the history of man. Only in very recent years has a realization of their significance in respect to the fine arts come to the attention of historians at large.

Architecture

THE SIXTEENTH CENTURY

THE sixteenth century in Peru was the age of conquest, colonization, and conversion. Distances were great and travel over the Andean region demanded indomitable courage and physical stamina. Fired with the spirit of the crusades, Spanish friars accompanied Pizarro and his followers on their first adventures, setting up the Cross wherever they went. Their first churches were humble structures of adobe and thatch without architectural pretensions. At times they transformed an Incaic temple into a Christian church. Thus it happened at Cajamarca in 1532 that Fray Vicente Valverde set up a shrine to St. Francis in the Temple of the Sun.[1]

Early churches were long and narrow in the form of a single nave (Fig. 1). To this category belonged the first cathedrals of Lima and Cuzco, built in the second quarter of the century. In Lima throughout the sixteenth century the parish, monastic, and conventual churches were all of this plan with three exceptions. A vault over the sanctuary and a wooden *mudéjar* ceiling over the nave constituted the usual arrangement, a fact which points unmistakably to Andalusia as the architectural source of these monuments. When the three leading monastic orders built large structures of basilican type, they still turned to Andalu-

sian, or more precisely to Sevillian models. The Dominicans were the first to introduce the basilican plan in a large edifice *circa* 1540–1552, and shortly thereafter the Franciscans (1555) and the Augustinians (1574) followed suit. The Mercedarians (*circa* 1541–1542) seem to have combined the Andalusian wooden ceiling with some features of the Isabellan type of church: the single nave flanked by lateral chapels and the elevated choir.[2]

Churches of the simplest early type were replaced in the major centers by finer edifices as the colonies prospered. Earthquakes also took their toll. Consequently very few of the sixteenth century still exist today, and they are situated in remote regions. Those of Ayacucho and others upon the shores of Lake Titicaca are studied later in this chapter.

The colonists of Lima and Cuzco had illusions of architectural grandeur a quarter century after these capitals were founded. They proposed huge cathedrals in both cities to rival the best of Spain. Although the foundation stone was laid in Cuzco in 1560, and in Lima plans were under way in 1565, these projects came to naught. Not until the very end of the century were the two edifices begun in earnest upon plans by Francisco Becerra. They incorporate the style of the late classical Renaissance of Spain which carries over well into the seventeenth century.

Extant monuments of the sixteenth century are very few in Peru. Aside from the churches of Ayacucho and the Titicaca region, the cloisters of San Francisco and Santo Domingo in Cuzco (Figs. 31–34) are the only important structures. Both were erected in the mid-century. The upper gallery of the Dominican cloister appears, however, to have been reconstructed after the earthquake of 1650, as will be shown in Chapter III where the entire school of Cuzco is treated in some detail. Both cloisters consist of two stories, following the custom of important monasteries in Spain throughout the Middle Ages and later. The stone capitals are slightly provincial renderings of their contemporaries of the Renaissance in Spain. The particularly Spanish note is struck, however, by the vertical strip above each capital, thus establishing the *mudéjar* arch in a rectangle which is known as an *alfiz*. These cloisters of Cuzco are large and splendid and all the more precious because they are unique in Peru. They remind us that the Renaissance monuments of Lima were equally fine before earthquakes and necessary reconstruction swept them away.

The cloister (Fig. 173) of the former Franciscan monastery at Chiclayo in the northern coastal region apparently is a survival of the first building campaign (1572–1594). Its pointed arches spring from small piers and the material throughout is brick covered with stucco.

SAN CRISTÓBAL of Ayacucho is probably the oldest surviving colonial building in Peru, having suffered no transformation to the present day. It was erected in the fifth decade of the sixteenth century at the time of the first settlement of the town.[3] San Cristóbal has historical and sentimental importance, for it provides an extant example of the type of humble church of rubble and adobe which the first colonists built wherever they settled. Here are no pretensions, merely a long rectangular room, low and dark, crudely built, and covered by a pitched roof of basket-woven cane. A narrow bench is built into the left wall, a substitute for pews in the early days. Another such bench, in this case of stone, lines the wall of the façade within the tiny atrium. The portal (Fig. 35), unlike the rest of the building, is made of large blocks of stone. Its broad round arch and the simple channeled molding which takes the place of a capital are dignified and humble, like hundreds of others in rural districts of Spain. The single bell tower and the picturesque roof of red tiles add a note of charm to this relic of the early days of the conquest of Peru.

The convent of the Merced, founded according to Chávez de Guevara in 1540, San Francisco, established in 1552, and Santa Clara, inaugurated in 1568, all in Ayacucho, provide the only related group of mid-sixteenth-century structures in Peru.[4] Other works of the sixteenth century are the church of Paucarcolla (1563), and those of Chucuito, Ilave, Juli, and Zepita, contracted in 1590. As explained elsewhere, the great monastic structures of Saña and Guadalupe in northern Peru cannot be placed earlier than the sixteen-twenties.

The Merced represents a step beyond the primitive chapel of San Cristóbal, being considerably larger and having more architectural style, although the main walls are still rubble and adobe (Fig. 37). It is covered by a pitched roof of cane, supported by small wooden tie beams. Here, as in San Cristóbal, benches are built along the walls of the nave. To the single-naved plan are added chapels, two in the position of a transept, and a second chapel adjoining them on both sides. The entrances of the chapels with one exception take the form of a round arch with the channeled molding which acts as substitute for a capital. This same stylistic feature is characteristic of the school, recurring in the side portal of La Merced and also in the portals of San Francisco and San Cristóbal. The remaining chapel has an entrance decorated with one column at each side. The capitals are the same provincial Corinthian type as those of the exterior. By exception in a church of this sort the raised choir is supported on stone barrel vaults, which are reinforced by three transverse arches.

The façade, also partly of stone, was completely ruined in 1940, when a well-intentioned restorer covered it with a coat of cement. The photograph reproduced here (Fig. 36) has documentary value, since it was taken prior to the restoration. The channeled columns and rather crude Corinthian capitals closely resembled those of the portal of San Francisco (Fig. 40). Very strangely the upper part of the façade

received no architectural decoration, and it has only two small rectangular openings which give light into the choir. The single belfry to the left is simply handled with Doric pilasters and unornamented moldings, in general contemporary with, but more sophisticated than, the tower of San Cristóbal.

The side portal of the Merced (Fig. 38) escaped restoration, due to the fact that it is now blocked up and enclosed within a shed which houses the impoverished Indian sacristan and a chicken yard. For that happy accident we may be thankful, even though it is consequently impossible to photograph the monument satisfactorily. The broad round arch is constructed of large pieces of masonry, and the capitals consist of channeled moldings exactly like those of the chapels within the church. The same type of column which is used elsewhere in the edifice reappears here. The frieze of the entablature is decorated by alternate rosettes and cherubs' heads, a very common treatment in the sixteenth century. Considerable charm is added to the portal by the Annunciation carved in the spandrels; at the left Gabriel with his banderole bearing the phrase *Ave Maria gratia plena,* and at the right the Virgin Mary seated at her prayer desk. The sculpture is the equal of that found on many provincial churches in Spain itself, effective in its place, but not aesthetically important. The technique is distinctive in the repetition of flowing incised lines, recalling in a very general way the sculpture of the school of Avila, as represented by the *trascoro* of Avila Cathedral. The presence of the Mercedarian shield on the keystone of the arch and on the bases would be proof, if it were needed, that the monastic order brought this church into existence. Whether the top of the portal was crowned by a pediment, like that of San Francisco, cannot be determined because of the wooden shed which has been raised over it.

This side portal of the Merced has the distinction of being the only work of its kind dating from the mid-sixteenth century which has escaped the hand of the restorer. The façade of the church (Fig. 45) of Paucarcolla (1563) belongs to a more classical stylistic phase, as do the other churches of the Puno region, built at the end of the century.

The portal of San Francisco (Figs. 39, 40) is so nearly identical in style to that of the Merced that no doubt can be harbored that they are the work of one and the same architect. Columns, capitals, and frieze as well as the archway with its channeled molding repeat the Mercedarian side portal. The Franciscan shield of the five stigmata stands upon the keystone of the arch and the pedestals of the columns, in the same manner as the Mercedarian. The pediment contains the kneeling figure of St. Francis as he receives the stigmata while Brother Leo sleeps beside him. These reliefs, as well as the statues of St. Anthony of Padua and St. Clare atop the columns, the angels of the spandrels, and the frieze, were recut and refaced in the past ten years. Hence they have lost all of their sixteenth-century character. That fact can readily be understood by a comparison with the unscathed portal of the Merced. The lower

section of the tower, judging by the stone, is the only other part of the church which was left standing when the interior underwent a complete rebuilding in the early eighteenth century. The Franciscans came to Ayacucho in 1552, and they must have called upon the architect of the Merced to build their church, almost immediately after their arrival. The doorway of the small cloister, carved with the Franciscan cord, may also belong to the original structure, as Harth-terré and Marco Dorta have suggested.[5] It too has suffered from unintelligent restoration, in this case by an application of cement.

Santa Clara, the latest of the Renaissance foundations of Ayacucho, is accurately dated. Its inauguration took place in 1568, thanks to the generosity of the founder, Don Antonio de Orue.[6] In a small conventual church of single nave, a triumphal arch precedes the sanctuary opposite which are both upper and lower choirs. Covering the sanctuary is a magnificent *mudéjar* ceiling of interlaces, recessed octagons, and bosses, the earliest still extant in Peru, whereas the pitched ceiling of the nave was renewed and plastered in 1941. The stone body of the church is equally simple on the exterior. Its real distinction is due to the majestically beautiful bell tower (Fig. 149), added subsequently about 1712.[7] The principal side portal (Fig. 43), opening on the plaza, lacks the architectural significance of those of the Merced and San Francisco. The escutcheons, carved with elephant and griffin, beside the semicircular tympanum, are those of Antonio de Orue and his wife, Luisa Díaz de Rojas. The same channeled molding which is used in all six-teenth-century buildings of Ayacucho ap-pears at the springing of the arch of the doorway, and also upon the triumphal arch within the church. The capitals of the channeled shafts do not, however, follow the precedent previously established at Ayacucho. On the contrary, they have vo-lutes which resemble those in the cloisters of San Francisco and Santo Domingo in Cuzco.

The last of the Renaissance monuments of Ayacucho is the portal of a small chapel (Fig. 41) which stands at the right of the church of the Compañía. The patrons must have been the Orue family in this case once again, because their escutcheon provides the decorative motives of the stone tym-panum. Except for the replacing of the quartered shield of Antonio de Orue with AMR, monogram of the Madonna, we have a repetition here of the coat of arms on the choir wall within the church of Santa Clara (Fig. 42). The leaves are broader and longer, but otherwise there is little modification. The seated griffins of the Orue are used like guardian spirits, watch-ing at the sides. The elephant is a heraldic device of the same family, and cannot jus-tifiably be cited as an example of Far East-ern influence.[8]

This chapel is probably an early founda-tion of the Orues (*circa* 1570) about con-temporary with the church of Santa Clara. They must have ceded it to the Jesuits some time after the arrival of the first preacher of that order in 1583.[9] In the decoration of the portal there are no insignia of the Jesuits which would indicate that it was built by them. The designer of the portal displayed his independence in not follow-ing precisely the style of the other Renais-sance buildings of Ayacucho, just discussed above. The treatment of the columns, capi-tals, and frieze and the general decorative arrangement exhibit his originality. The lions' heads on the frieze over the columns and over the center of the doorway are new to the city, even though familiar motives in the period. This portal is indeed a rare example of Spanish plateresque architecture in Peru. In fact, it is the only work which may properly be called by that term, be-cause of the flourish and floridity in the handling of the foliate ornament. For that reason it is precious, as well as for its own innate provincial charm. Very recently, it has been damaged by clumsy pedestals added as reinforcement beneath the col-umns.

LAKE TITICACA

THE Dominican, Fray Tomás de San Martín, who accompanied Pizarro in his conquest of Peru, left Cuzco after its foundation in 1534 and set forth across the region of Lake Titicaca. Thence he pene-trated into distant Charcas, now Bolivia. In 1540, at the time of the erection of the province of the Dominican order in Peru, a monastery was about to be established at Chucuito. This house is mentioned as ex-isting in 1553, dedicated to St. Vincent, and there were other Dominican missions in Juli, Ilave, Zepita, Acora, and Yunguyo, these latter presided over by only one or two monks. The great importance of the lake district, known as the province of Chucuito, may be deduced by the fact that San Pedro Mártir of Juli held a full complement of twelve monks in 1565. It ranked third in size, next to Lima and Cuzco, among all of the Spanish Dominican establishments in South America.[10]

The rectangular apse and transept of San Pedro Mártir (Fig. 2) at Juli were probably constructed at that period, prior to the expulsion of the Dominicans from the whole region. On the initiative of the viceroy, Francisco de Toledo, they were replaced by the Jesuits (1576).[11] Hence this must be the earliest extant work (*circa* 1565) in the ancient province of Chucuito. The Gothic survival in the use of three pointed arches under the crossing (Fig. 44) provides the most interesting architectural feature, and one of the very rare instances of the pointed arch in the viceroyalty of Peru. It also occurs in the cloister (Fig. 173) of the former Franciscan monastery at Chiclayo (*circa* 1572–1594). Sixteenth-century examples of the pointed arch are to be found, however, in Santa Clara at Tunja, Colombia, in the cathedral of Quito, Ecuador, and in the crossing of San Francisco in the same city. Rubble and adobe were used in this early structure at Juli, now in a lamentable state of disrepair, the sanctuary covered with corrugated iron, and the transept roofed in wood. The low dome of cane over the crossing must, for structural reasons, have been rebuilt, when the new nave with its barrel vault of stone masonry was added at the close of the seventeenth century.

The earliest complete church still extant in the region of Lake Titicaca is that of the Inmaculada in a small village called Paucarcolla, just north of Puno. According to Meléndez, the bishop of Charcas, Fray Domingo de Santo Tomás, paid a visit here about 1563. Finding no church he ordered one built at his own expense "with walls of adobe, portals of brick, and a wooden roof."[12] The description may be based upon Meléndez's own familiarity with the building or upon a report of the bishop's pastoral visit which Meléndez undoubtedly had seen in documentary form. The present church follows the description, and the architectural style clearly indicates a date in the third quarter of the sixteenth century.

An excellent piece of design is the façade (Fig. 45), based in its disposition upon the triumphal-arch motive, and essentially of the late classical Renaissance in its application of pediments and in its undecorated surfaces. The stepping back of the pilasters at each end is a usage familiar in Michelangelo's work, such as the top story of the court of the Farnese Palace in Rome and the exterior of St. Peter's. The balustered colonnettes in the niches and on the frieze are effective, but simplified and provincial compared with Italian or Spanish usage. The treatment of moldings with dentils shows good taste, also in evidence in the general scale and proportions of the work. The familiar Renaissance medallion here is inscribed with a disk which turns up again in La Asunción at Chucuito (Fig. 46). The channeled capitals have precedent as far away as Ayacucho, in the churches of La Merced and San Francisco (Figs. 38,

40). Rather strange is the placing of the arched niche in the center of the main pediment. Within the church, the chapel to the right is preceded by a brick portal in which the same balustered colonnettes of the façade reappear. Other fine portals lead into the arms of the transept, in this case distinguished by recessed squares in the frieze and by Doric pilasters enframing the round arch.

The floor plan at Paucarcolla is long and narrow with chapels in the arms of the transept and with a polygonal apse, now in ruins. The same type recurs in the churches of La Asunción at Chucuito, San Juan at Acora, San Miguel at Pomata, and La Asunción at Juli.

The great similarity of the sixteenth-century churches in this region is explained by a contract of October 13, 1590, according to which Gabriel Montalvo y Peralta ordered the construction of sixteen churches by Juan Gómez and Juan López, carpenters, and Juan Jiménez, mason. Three churches were to be erected in Chucuito, three in Juli, and two each in Acora, Ilave, Pomata, Yunguyo, and Zepita. Another document of 1595 shows that ten of them had not yet been begun. By 1601 seven were in process but, on the other hand, eight still existed only as projects. The facts about the eight churches still extant today can be summarized thus: San Juan at Juli, San Miguel at Ilave, and San Miguel at Pomata were begun in 1590 and still incomplete in 1601; the churches of La Asunción at Chucuito, San Sebastián at Zepita, and San Juan and San Pedro at Acora were ready for inception in 1601; to

La Asunción at Juli there is no definite reference save that it was finished in 1620.[13]

All of the churches are of single-naved type (Figs. 1, 54). Some of them must have had a raised choir, as the remains of the wooden beams in San Juan at Juli demonstrate. No choir contemporary with the original building is preserved today. In two cases they were rebuilt in stone at the end of the seventeenth or at the beginning of the eighteenth century. The construction of the choir of La Asunción at Chucuito is especially interesting, because it is carried on square piers which support domical vaults in the lower story. The way the arches cut across the original doorway to the baptistry is clear evidence that they are of later date than the church. The type of construction and the curious ornament on the surface toward the nave also place them about the year 1700. Another choir, magnificent in its sculptured reliefs of the early eighteenth century, is that of San Miguel at Pomata (Fig. 235). Both of the above works will be discussed in more detail later.

From the architectural point of view the most interesting features are the portals. The churches are generally oriented laterally to the plaza with a side portal which enters the nave and another portal on the short side. Exceptions in which the normal façade on the short side overlooks the plaza are San Juan at Acora, La Asunción at Paucarcolla, and San Pedro Mártir at Juli, the latter still in its original disposition, even though the nave was rebuilt at the end of the seventeenth century.

The earliest and the most sophisticated of the portals is that of Paucarcolla (Fig.

45), already discussed. It had a follower in the side portal of San Pedro at Acora, where the shell niches with bulbous colonnettes and the stepping back of the pilasters give clear indication of the prototype. Imitation was not servile, however, for the general proportions at Acora are narrower and higher, while the use of disks in the frieze and the large medallion of the pediment have no precedent at Paucarcolla. The frieze of disks belongs, nonetheless, to the regional school, for it appears with good effect in the interior portals of La Asunción (Fig. 50) at Chucuito. A similar type of frieze distinguishes the portals of houses in Tunja, Colombia, at the end of the sixteenth century, indicating that it is a late Hispanic Renaissance feature, not limited to the highlands of Peru.[14]

The front portal of San Pedro at Acora has a sober design in excellent scale with the stepped pilasters again, disks in the spandrels, and a frieze of rectangular coffers. The latter type of frieze was the favorite of the builders of the region, for they used it in the front portal of San Juan at Juli (Fig. 47), the side portal of La Asunción at Juli (Fig. 48), the side portal of San Sebastián at Zepita, the side portal of San Miguel at Pomata, the interior portals of the chapels of San Miguel at Ilave (Fig. 52), and the façade of the same church. The earliest appearance of all, if we are correct in our dating, is upon the portals which give access to the chapels of the transept at Paucarcolla.

The use of large portals, as splendid as those of the exterior, to mark the entrances of the chapels of the transept is one of the most noteworthy features of the series of churches under discussion. They appear in La Inmaculada at Paucarcolla, La Asunción at Chucuito (Fig. 50), and San Miguel at Ilave.

The long nave of San Juan at Juli (Fig. 1) and the front portal (Fig. 47) still survive from the period of 1590, whereas its side portal, transept, and apse were rebuilt about 1700. The façade has been diminished in height by the raising of the ground level in recent years. Its sober design is one of the best of this group. Doric pilasters flank the round arch of the doorway and the pediment is loaded at the sides by urns. The globe of the world surmounted by a cross stands at the summit of the pediment. Unity of design, not always notable in these monuments, is achieved by the cross-inscribed disks of the spandrels and the larger medallion enclosing the IHS in the pediment.

The side portal of La Asunción at Juli (Fig. 48) constitutes an enlargement of that of San Juan by the addition of a pilaster and a medallion with the IHS at each side. That modification is sufficient to disrupt the fine dimensions of the other monument. The main façade, now in ruins as is nearly half of the long nave, followed the same style. Recently a covering of galvanized iron has been placed over the transept, apse, and part of the nave, and thus the church is being protected from further decay. The walls of the apse were reinforced with buttresses in 1944. The church may have been projected in 1590, but it underwent considerable delay and did not see completion until 1620.[15] La

Asunción's magnificent tower of stone (Fig. 233), since partly ruined by lightning, came into being about one hundred years later.

A provincial architect's attempt to achieve splendor is the impression given by the side portal of La Asunción at Chucuito (Fig. 46). Here the ornamentation of disks and niches and the channeled columns provide a more lavish composition than elsewhere in the region, but one which is poor in design, lacking any sense of the proper relation of the various motives. Certain details recall the church façades of Ayacucho and others in the province of Cuzco, such as those of San Jerónimo (Fig. 88) and Oropesa. There too the cherubs' heads occur in the frieze, so characteristic of the Renaissance; moreover, shafts and friezes are fluted.

Among all of the portals in the lake region, only those of La Asunción at Chucuito are built of stone. That fact alone does not make them superior to others of this group. The modest front portal of La Asunción with its simple Doric pilasters and channeled frieze is better than the more elaborate side entrance. Really excellent in scale and chaste in design are the large frontispieces of the lateral chapels within the church (Fig. 50). Here ornament is sparingly employed, being limited to disks on the frieze and in the spandrels.

The most interesting series of portals in any one church of the Titicaca district are those of San Miguel at Ilave (Figs. 51–54). Very rare in Peru is the use of the pointed arch. It appears here in the sacristy entrance and in the two portals of the lateral chapels, all on the interior of the church. The pointed arch enframed within a *mudéjar alfiz* makes the sacristy doorway a signal case of Hispanic archaism, one which astonishes the student on his first discovery of it. The large frontispieces of the chapels, on the contrary, have a sober late-Renaissance enframement of Doric pilasters and the familiar coffered frieze of the region. A curious note here is registered by the small colonnettes of the spandrels.

The front entrance of San Miguel is very nearly an exact replica of the corresponding section of the church of San Pedro at Acora, the closest neighboring village. At Ilave the pediment has disappeared and the stucco covering the brick has in large part disintegrated. The side portal at Ilave, which opens upon the plaza, has, in spite of its classical sobriety, a *mudéjar* frieze of interlacing quatrefoils. Here one sees variations upon local themes, the basic design of its companion on the other side of the building being modified by the use of channeled half columns and tiny voluted Ionic capitals, similar to those at Chucuito. Brick covered with stucco, following general practice in the lake region, is the material employed in all of these charming portals at Ilave.

The churches on the shores of Lake Titicaca usually have a single tower, large and devoid of architectural features, the belfry with two openings on each face. It is frequently located on the gospel side (Acora, Ilave, Chucuito [Fig. 49], Pomata), and occasionally on the epistle side (San Juan at Juli, Paucarcolla). The belfries of San Pedro Mártir and La Asunción at Juli, of San Pedro at Acora, and of San Miguel at Ilave were reconstructed in the late seventeenth or eighteenth century.

Materials employed in these late sixteenth-century churches are brick, rubble, and a generous admixture of adobe. The portals, as previously indicated, are constructed of brick and stucco, with the exception of the stone portals of La Asunción at Chucuito. The roofs were trussed on poles and covered with heavy thatch or tiles. Nearly all of the colonial roofs have disappeared and have given way to a practical but extremely ugly covering of galvanized iron. The roofing of the nave of San Juan at Juli is a trussed construction of branches, undoubtedly a replacement of

the eighteenth century. Some tattered fragments of painted silk cloth, which originally concealed the branches, supply evidence of an unusual method of enhancing the beauty of a church. On the outside, tiles combined with thatch still survive. Thus the picturesque charm of the exterior is preserved, as likewise in the thatched exterior of San Miguel at Pomata.

The atria within which the early churches stood have also disappeared with the centuries in great part. Some of the round-arched enclosure still stands at Paucarcolla. La Asunción at Chucuito (Fig. 49) is the most fortunate of all in that respect, its long open arcade rising in romantic abandon above the quiet spacious plaza.

III

THE SEVENTEENTH CENTURY: CUZCO

Cuzco, capital of the Incas, is unrivaled in all of the Americas, a city of two civilizations superimposed, the Incaic and the Hispanic. Situated in a valley at an altitude of eleven thousand feet with mountains rising high above on every hand, Cuzco is a land of breath-taking beauty. Legendary associations are said to have been the determining factors in the establishment of the Incan capital here. Yet it is difficult to avoid the belief that the natives were sensitive to the allure of the mountains and valleys, notwithstanding the rigors of the altitude and cold climate.

Although the Spanish conquerors attempted to destroy the society and the city of the conquered, they never succeeded, and still today the walls of Incaic palaces and temples serve as foundations of Hispanic convents, churches, and mansions. The magnificent stonework of the Incas, perfectly cut and fitted without use of mortar, can be seen on every hand, standing in sharp contrast to the European technique of ashlar and mortar which the Spanish employed in the churches of Cuzco. Availability of stone, both in the quarries and in the great Incaic palaces which the Spanish used as quarries, and the added advantage of skilled Indian ma-

sons made colonial Cuzco a city of stone. The fine brown Andean stone, called andesite, with its slight reddish cast gives to Cuzco a uniformity like that of Florence with its stone palaces of the Renaissance. Stone abounds in all of Cuzco's churches, its cloisters, its arcaded plazas, and in the portals and patios of its houses. Lima is a city of adobe and wood; Cuzco, a city of sturdy brown stone.

Spanish Cuzco, which Pizarro founded in 1534 on the ruins of the Inca empire, was later demolished, not by man but by nature, in the great earthquake of 1650. Diego de Mendoza, a Franciscan contemporary, asserts that among the churches only Santa Clara, San Juan de Dios, and the new cathedral escaped destruction in that fateful year.[1] Hence we have in Cuzco a city of the second half of the seventeenth century, a period of unbelievable activity, when a new and still more magnificent Cuzco arose. Unfortunately scarcely a building of the sixteenth century survived except the main cloister of San Francisco and the lower gallery of Santo Domingo.

The great architectural glory among many in Cuzco is its cathedral. Authorized by papal bull of 1553, it is the finest church of the western hemisphere, in my own opinion. The first stone on the present site was laid March 11, 1560. The architect in charge, Juan Miguel de Veramendi, who hailed from Viscaya, Spain, then resided in Chuquisaca, Bolivia. He had received the contract on the basis of plans submitted on October 10, 1559.[2] When in Bolivia I searched the archives of Chuquisaca with the hope of finding a record of Juan Miguel de Veramendi there, but succeeded only in discovering the name of an architect, Francisco de Veramendi, who was paid for work on foundations of a chapel of the cathedral in 1583. Since the Spanish population of the town was very small at that date, the two men named Veramendi must have been related, perhaps father and son.[3] Another architect, Juan Correa, appears as *maestro mayor* of Cuzco Cathedral in 1562.[4] These documents are of purely academic interest, however, since little was accomplished in the early years, and there is no reason to believe that Veramendi's plans were in any way related to the church as eventually built.

Nothing more is heard until the famous viceroy, Francisco de Toledo, with a show of anger ordered on October 9, 1571, that the church be finished within six years, stating that the plans, supplies, and everything necessary were available. One year later he became still more drastic. He lashed out and reduced the priests' salaries by seventy-five pesos monthly, ordered a tax on all inhabitants to contribute to the edifice, the Indians to fulfill their share by manual labor. Once again he reiterated that the church must be finished in six years, and little did he realize that it would

take eighty-two.[5] The structure was to have had three naves covered with vaults or a wooden roof as seemed best, with the reservation that the *capilla mayor* be vaulted. Moreover, of interest is a curious provision that there should be a choir but no *trascoro*, all of which proves that the plans of 1571–1572 were not those of the present church. After Francisco de Toledo left Cuzco, work on the cathedral was paralyzed, because the bishop refused to contribute the church's share of the cost, insisting that the king, citizens, and Indians pay for everything! The town council made feeble efforts to combat the bishop in 1574, but as usual nothing happened.[6]

The next and really important event in the complex history of Cuzco Cathedral is the appearance of the famous Spanish architect, Francisco Becerra, whose career is discussed as a whole in the section devoted to the cathedral of Lima. According to the testimony presented in court at Lima in 1585, Becerra had drawn plans for both the cathedrals of Cuzco and Lima at the command of the viceroy Martín Enríquez (died 1583), who had called him from Cuzco to Lima in 1582. Becerra's transfer to Lima at that time may partly explain why the construction at Cuzco seems to have been abandoned for a matter of sixteen years. Padre Reginaldo Lizárraga who visited Cuzco, probably in the period 1594–1597, remarked that the old cathedral of mud was very poor, and that considering the great wealth of the diocese he did not understand why the new one had not been built.[7]

In 1598 the viceroy, Luis de Velasco,

demanded less grandiose plans for Lima Cathedral which could be completed within a short time, and in the same letter stated, "I have ordered that the same be done in that of Cuzco which has also been begun in these days."[8] Although the letter does not say specifically that Becerra drew the new plans for Cuzco Cathedral, the evidence for such a belief is overwhelming. Most compelling of all is the similarity of the floor plans and pier construction of the two churches, and Becerra's authorship of the first cathedral of Lima (1598–1604) has been proven beyond a doubt by several documents. In 1603 the viceroy appointed a new *maestro mayor* of Cuzco Cathedral, an architect, Bartolomé Carrión, who had previously constructed the main portal of Tunja Cathedral in Colombia. He was ordered to proceed with the construction according to the plans he had recently drawn. Carrión remained in charge from 1603 until 1607 at least. Only in the latter year were this provision and a petition of the architect entered in the "Actas Capitulares."[9] Very little could have been accomplished in these years, considering subsequent history. Harth-terré's theory that Bartolomé Carrión should be given entire credit for the cathedral as it now stands is unconvincing, for many reasons.[10]

On December 2, 1616, the town council of Cuzco evinced enough interest to send the models of the church and a report of architects to the viceroy.[11] In November 1617 Fray Miguel de la Guerra, *obrero mayor* of San Francisco, Lima, turned in a report to the viceroy stating that in Cuzco

they had no plans for the cathedral, for they were in the viceroy's possession! He said the cathedral had been well begun by its first master "Francisco de Carrión," but that subsequent architects had made a thousand errors. The confusion of the names of Francisco Becerra and Bartolomé Carrión is indicative of the chaos which appears to have prevailed. The architect then in charge, Miguel Gutiérrez Sencio, submitted a statement, averring that he had had to make new drawings and plans since there were none, and explaining in some detail the system of proportions he had used, a scheme which does not correspond to the edifice as built.[12] In March 1619 the archdean petitioned the king that the bishop have the right to name the *maestro mayor* without the interference of the viceroy.[13] And so, matters dragged on interminably. Nineteen years later a royal *cedula* was forthcoming with the command that work on the cathedral proceed,[14] but the need was for an energetic bishop, at long last realized in the person of Alonso Ocón. When Bishop Ocón entered Cuzco in 1644, he found the walls of the church not more than half built,[15] and yet seven years later he was able to send a detailed account to the king and to state that only ten arches and seventeen vaults remained to be concluded. Fifty masons, significantly "all Indians," were at work upon the façade.[16] In the great earthquake of 1650 the damage to the new cathedral was slight, and by July 1654 the work was complete except for the towers which were delayed about three years more.[17]

Thus the actual construction of the cathedral for which the first stone was laid in 1560 may be summarized as follows: a plan by Francisco Becerra prepared in 1582; a final plan in 1598, most probably reworked by Becerra; subsequent modifications by Bartolomé Carrión and Miguel Gutiérrez Sencio and others; very slow progress until 1644, when due to the insistence of Bishop Ocón the structure was vaulted and brought to conclusion in ten years.

The question as to the author of the plans of Cuzco Cathedral may always remain a controversial issue. As previously stated, it seems to me impossible to avoid the conclusion that the original project of Becerra has survived in the main. This belief is based upon the virtual identity of Cuzco with Becerra's undeniably documented work, Lima Cathedral. Ample precedent for the use of the same plans long after the death of the original architect can be cited throughout architectural history: Diego Silóee's cathedral of Granada, completed a hundred years after the master's death, Alberti's Sant' Andrea at Mantua, and innumerable Gothic churches throughout Europe.

An attempt to give Bartolomé Carrión credit for the creation of Cuzco Cathedral is based on Miguel de la Guerra's report of 1617 that the cathedral had been begun by its first master "Francisco de Carrión." The confusion of the names of Francisco Becerra and Bartolomé Carrión is a symbolic coincidence. Whatever Carrión did is speculative, but the structure of the cathedral itself testifies to its blood relationship to Becerra's cathedral of Lima.

A man to whom much credit should be given was the canon, Diego Arias de la Cerda, who was the executive administrator of the work (*obrero mayor*) in these years. Writing to the king in 1657, the Bishop Pedro Ortega y Sotomayor praised him highly, stating "to his continuous presence, industry, and skill all of the work of this temple is due . . ."[18] People have erroneously concluded that Diego Arias was an architect and have accredited to his own hand the architecture of the façade, which is obviously a mid-seventeenth-century design, the sculpture of the choir stalls and the pulpit, and even the casting of the cathedral bells.[19] Undoubtedly it is due in great part to the zeal of Diego Arias de la Cerda that all of these projects were realized. His position was, however, that of administrator (*obrero mayor*) to which he was appointed in 1648, and not of chief architect (*maestro mayor*).[20]

The man who has been largely overlooked, but who, by several documents, is shown to have worked on the cathedral for at least thirty-two years, is Miguel Gutiérrez Sencio. He is mentioned as *maestro mayor* in 1617, in 1625, and again in 1628.[21] The latest document with his name, discovered by Monseñor Casanova, is a payment of salary in 1649.[22] In matter of length of service Gutiérrez Sencio easily outstrips all other contenders for honors as architect of Cuzco Cathedral. It was he who carried out Francisco Becerra's plans and, no doubt, modified them greatly. Gutiérrez Sencio's activity was not limited to the cathedral, however, for he was architect of a cloister of the Merced in 1634, a work to be discussed later on in this same chapter.

The name of one other man, Antonio de la Coba, is mentioned as architect (*alarife*) of Cuzco Cathedral in 1651,[23] but since that is the full extent of our information about him, little speculation can be hazarded. Just possibly, Gutiérrez Sencio, who was a man at least of middle age by that time, might have died. If the documents of Cuzco are ever systematically read and published, a fund of new data on the cathedral will surely come to light.

The ground plans of Lima and Cuzco (Figs. 7, 8), as previously stated, are alike in all essentials, differing in that Lima is one bay longer and that it originally had a chapel dedicated to St. Bartholomew behind the *capilla mayor,* whereas at Cuzco there is no chapel in that position. Both churches are of the hall type, consisting of three naves of equal height, and both have nonprojecting transepts without lantern. Perhaps most convincing of all is the identity in the shape of the piers of Lima and Cuzco Cathedrals, and the large Doric entablature block above the capital. The exact counterpart of these piers is not to be found anywhere in the world; hence the similarities are most noteworthy.

It may be argued that the stylistic relation between the two buildings is invalid because the cathedral of Lima was rebuilt after the earthquake of 1746. Nonetheless, the ground plan was retained throughout the numerous restorations and reconstructions as can be seen in the plan of 1696,[24] and there is no reason to believe that the shape of the piers at Lima was ever modi-

fied. Their Ionic capitals are noted by Vázquez de Espinosa about 1619.[25]

The differences between Becerra's original cathedral of Lima (1598–1604) and the present cathedral of Cuzco are the following: the former had pointed arches and groined vaults (for details see Chapter IV), whereas Cuzco has round arches and decorated Gothic vaults. Unquestionably Becerra's original plan for Cuzco was modified in detail by Bartolomé Carrión and Miguel Gutiérrez Sencio and others. Most certainly Becerra intended to use pointed arches, as is proven by the fact that the arches of the first chapel to the right and the first chapel to the left, on entering the church, are pointed. All other arches in the building are round, clear evidence of a change in plan. Becerra may also have intended groined vaults at Cuzco as at Lima, but that possibility lies in the realm of pure speculation.

The rectangular plan of Lima and Cuzco Cathedrals adheres to the type established in Spain in Seville Cathedral (1402) where it came into existence as a result of the use of the site of the Moorish mosque, which like all mosques was rectangular. Due to the great prestige of Seville Cathedral, this plan became very popular in Spain in the sixteenth century, particularly in Andalusia, whence it passed to the New World. Jaén Cathedral (1540) is the direct prototype of the cathedrals of Cuzco and Lima. In Mexico City, Puebla, Guadalajara, Mérida, Habana, and Panamá City, the rectangular plan was adopted, yet so different in proportion and detail from the Peruvian churches, as to further emphasize the close relationship between Cuzco and Lima.[26] The same is true of the like design of the cruciform piers with large entablature blocks in Cuzco and Lima (Figs. 65, 91). Their derivation as well as that of the ground plan and hall type are to be sought in Andalusia. Diego Silóee introduced the entablature block from Renaissance Italy, employing it first in Spain in Granada Cathedral (begun 1528), and thence it became characteristic of Andalusia, appearing in the cathedrals of Málaga, Jaén, Guadix, etc.[27] With the rectangular plan it spread to the new world: to Guadalajara (1561–1618), which like Cuzco has Gothic vaults and is a hall church, to Puebla and Mexico City where its design was very different from that of the massive cruciform piers of Cuzco and Lima.

The style of the interior of the cathedral of Cuzco (Figs. 65, 66) with its colossal proportions and austere simplicity is in marked contrast to the style of Mexico City (begun 1563) and Puebla (designed *circa* 1555–1575). Cuzco, replanned in 1598, represents the very last phase of the Spanish Renaissance, the rigorous classicism introduced to Spain by Juan Bautista de Toledo, when in 1559 he was called to Madrid from Spanish Naples to design the Escorial. This classicism was made famous by the great architect, Juan de Herrera, who succeeded as director of the building of the Escorial in 1567. The solemn bareness of the walls and the austere majesty of Cuzco are incomparable in the New World. Its majestic space is awesome, a space which might have appeared slightly

more vertical had pointed arches been used as first intended.[28] The late-Gothic vaults with decorative ribs do not disturb the Herreresque classicism of the piers, the walls, and the space. Gothic vaulting at so late a date is a reflection of the same conservatism seen on the Spanish peninsula in the sixteenth-century cathedrals of Granada, Salamanca, Segovia, and elsewhere. In the New World, too, Gothic vaults persisted in the Renaissance cathedrals of Guadalajara and Santo Domingo (1521–1541).[29] The return to Gothic vaults in Peru, after Becerra had used groined vaults in Lima Cathedral, is further explained, however, by the fact that architects believed that the Gothic construction would show greater resistance to earthquakes.

No small part of the grandeur of Cuzco Cathedral is explained by the beauty of the hard reddish-brown Andean stone of the Incas. Unfortunately the beauty of material has been damaged by painting the interior light gray. The vaults of brick, as usual in Cuzco, are now painted blue with the ribs white. The slightly domical shape of the vaults as well as the material became characteristic of Cuzco in the second half of the seventeenth century, although only in La Compañía are the Gothic ribs imitated. The Doric entablature block, on the other hand, was borrowed in other churches, notably for San Francisco, La Merced, El Belén, and San Pedro (Figs. 72, 73, 76, 82).

To the late Renaissance Herreresque interior of Cuzco Cathedral was added a façade (Figs. 62, 63), obviously designed in the mid-seventeenth century, and completely Baroque in its style. The portal in the center is composed of several planes which move toward the middle. The entire concept is pictorial, with the constant shifting of outlines and breaking of cornices, moldings, and entablatures.[30] The design is, nonetheless, architectural, for the elements employed are columns, pilasters, entablatures, and empty niches with a minimum of surface ornament, a contrast to the later, so-called Churrigueresque style of the eighteenth century, as represented by the façade of San Agustín, Lima, and the churches of Cajamarca (Figs. 111, 177–187). In these cases the façade is a tapestry of delicately cut ornament. On the contrary, the flat rather geometric patterns on the lower columns and bases of the Cuzco portal and the cloth swag containing apples upon the columns in the second story are entirely subordinated to the architectural whole. This portal set the standard for the entire school of Cuzco in the second half of the seventeenth century, serving as a model for the portals of La Compañía, El Belén, San Pedro, and San Sebastián (Figs. 67–70) with important modifications in each case. Retables, too, follow a similar style in the middle of the seventeenth century. Among them the high altar of Santa Catalina (Fig. 313) is the best example. Very characteristic is the contrast in the planes and the abrupt breaking of the pediments, with the wide gap over the main arch in the center. The curious webbed volute at the upper sides of the crowning of the cathedral portal recurs in the lunettes of the choir stalls within the church, as well as in the up-

per façade of La Compañía. The soberest classicism prevails in the two smaller rusticated doorways and in the simple rusticated pilasters of the towers. The balls and pyramids which crown the towers and roof tops likewise are survivals of the late Renaissance. Two features of the exterior of the cathedral are markedly Hispanic: the flat terraced roofs, which characterize Spanish architecture even in the Gothic period, and the disposition of the façade. By the latter is meant the emphasis on the central portal which is contrasted with the broad expanse of bare walls at the sides. This contrast of surface is an outstanding characteristic of Spanish architecture in the Renaissance and later, as for instance, the façades of the hospital of Santa Cruz in Toledo (1504–1514) and the cathedral of Gerona.[31] The latter portal furnishes an interesting parallel to the portal of Cuzco Cathedral, although the Spanish example is more restrained in design.

The proportions of the Cuzco façade (Fig. 62) are very broad in relation to the height of the towers. The reason for low towers is obviously a practical one, since they were completed only seven years after the disastrous earthquake of 1650 had ruined the city. This defect is less evident in the presence of the church than it appears to be in photographs. The whole mass of the church is rectangular and powerful, and the virile ruggedness of the brown Andean stone adds in no small measure to the solemnity and grandeur of the exterior. The particular disposition of the façade undoubtedly is derived from that of Lima Cathedral, as it appeared in the early seventeenth century, although the two façades vary greatly in detail and in proportions.

The architect who designed the façade of Cuzco Cathedral is unknown. Of the architects who were engaged here in the mid-seventeenth century only the names of Antonio de la Coba and Miguel Gutiérrez Sencio have been preserved.[32] Whoever he may have been, the author of the Cuzco façade was no provincial, but a man thoroughly familiar with the latest developments of the Baroque style in Spain. He must have been a Spaniard, and he was a highly original and gifted artist, one who set into motion Baroque architecture in Cuzco. He was a professional architect and surely not the zealous and able administrator, Diego Arias de la Cerda, canon of Cuzco and priest of Urubamba.

Architecture in Cuzco is accurately dated by the great earthquake of 1650 (Fig. 21), or rather series of earthquakes, which almost completely destroyed the city. The Franciscan chronicler, Diego de Mendoza, who was an eyewitness, gives relatively exact information as to the fate of the churches. The new cathedral escaped with slight damage, a fact confirmed by Bishop Ocón's letter; the churches of San Juan de Dios and Santa Clara were the only others which stood unharmed.[33] Having already discussed the cathedral (1598–1654), whose interior is late Renaissance and whose façade is Baroque, we now turn to these two churches as examples of pre-earthquake architecture.

The hospital of San Juan de Dios (Figs. 57, 58) has had a checkered career, having served as Casa de Moneda in the early nineteenth century and now as the Colegio de Educandas.[34] The church, modest in size and unpretentious in architecture, appears to belong to the early seventeenth century, probably rebuilt after 1617 when the monks came to take charge of the old hospital of St. Bartholomew.[35] Its long single nave has a pitched wooden ceiling with crossbeams which are decorated with the familiar *mudéjar* eight-pointed star, thus constituting the most interesting feature of the church. As for the equally unpretentious exterior with tiled roof, the stone portals are nondescript today, particularly the side portal of fine rusticated stone which has been blocked up and reconstructed.

Santa Clara (Fig. 59) is a far more important example of early Cuzco architecture. Although small and consisting of a single nave, as is customary in convents of nuns, it has interesting features, especially the domed vault with rectangular recesses over the sanctuary.[36] This simplification of a coffered Renaissance vault appears in no other extant building in Cuzco, but there may have been others prior to the earthquake. The coffered effect is found, on the contrary, in Bolivia, notably in La Merced and San Francisco in Sucre. The nave proper of Santa Clara consists of only three bays separated by stone arches and covered by groined vaults of brick. The groined vault, likewise, seems to represent an early phase of construction in Cuzco, since only one other case is found and that in the aisles of Santo Domingo, to be discussed later. The upper and lower choirs are very large and completely screened off from the nave, occupying the end of the church opposite the sanctuary. The two deeply splayed portals open in the long side of the church (Fig. 61). These portals on the outside are made of ashlar in the usual local brown stone, whereas the body of the church is built of irregular stone set in mortar. Both portals are late-Renaissance classical designs, one in simple rusticated pattern, the other in the familiar triumphal-arch arrangement with free-standing columns and entablature. The capitals, which are a curious combination of a Doric echinus topped with Corinthian volutes, are also found in the service patio of Santa Clara, and in numerous other *cuzqueño* buildings of the seventeenth century, both ecclesiastic and domestic.[37] This portal of Santa Clara was originally planned with a second story, but left unfinished as can be seen by the central plaque and the niches at the sides. The tower of Santa Clara stands in sober majesty, free from the body of the church. It must have been added in the second half of the seventeenth century, for it is identical in style with those of San Pedro (Fig. 68) and San Cristóbal built in that period.

The fabric of the church was complete for inauguration in 1622 on a new site for which the viceroy had given authorization in 1603.[38] Hence Santa Clara is the oldest extant church in Cuzco. According to Dr. José Uriel García, he once located contracts in the archives of the notaries of Cuzco which revealed the name of the patroness of the monastery of this period, Beatriz de Villegas, who engaged an architect called Juan Gutiérrez to begin the work. By agreements of May 24, 1599, a contract for the façade was let to Lucas Quispe and for the main arch (*arco toral*) to Pedro Zúñiga.[39] As Marco Dorta has already suggested, the present church is of later date, for the first church to be erected on the new site collapsed before it reached completion. Diego Mendoza is the authority for this information, which explains the fact that the nuns did not move into the new convent until 1622. Marco Dorta's attribution of the church to a Greek friar, Manuel Pablo, follows a tradition fostered by a recent prior of San Francisco who had the attribution painted upon the walls of the Franciscan cloister. Diego Mendoza again is the authority. In the biography of Fray Manuel Pablo, who was the head workman (*obrero*) in the Franciscan monastery at Cuzco, he states that Fray Manuel took charge of the rebuilding of the church and monastery of Santa Clara (*se encargasse de aquella obra*), a fact which does not imply that he was the designer and architect. Fray Manuel died in 1615, seven years before the inauguration of the new convent.[40]

It seems advisable to abandon the chronological plan of this chapter for a moment to mention two convents, Santa Catalina and Santa Teresa, which were built in the third quarter of the century, following the earthquake of 1650. Both consist of a single nave without transept and are modest in size, as is the rule with the churches of nuns. Santa Catalina, which had been founded in 1605, was completely ruined in the great earthquake.[41] Reconstruction of the church began immediately in 1651, and the nuns were able to return to the convent by 1653.[42] Judging from the style of the architecture of the church and its retables, it was finished in short order. Moreover, a series of pictures of the life of St. Catherine is dated 1669, a fact which may serve as indication of the approximate termination of the church. Santa Teresa (Fig. 60), a new foundation of Carmelite nuns of the year 1673, was ready for inauguration in 1676, according to the testimony of Bishop Mollinedo.[43] Both churches are covered with barrel vaults of brick separated into bays by stone arches, and in each case the bay corresponding to the sanctuary is larger with a small lantern raised over the center of a slightly domical vault. In both churches a broad molded cornice runs below the vault at each side. On the other hand the dado of colored Spanish tiles in the nave of Santa Teresa is unique in Cuzco churches. The entrance to Santa Teresa occupies the short side opposite to the sanctuary, and hence the lower choir is at the right of the high altar and the upper choir above the entrance. On the contrary, the two portals of Santa Catalina are on the long side of the church, and the upper and lower choirs are in the west end, separated from the body of the church, exactly as in Santa Clara. Neither church is of great architectural significance but both are substantial structures, Santa Catalina being the superior in scale and proportions. The simple rusticated portals of the latter are conservative Renaissance designs, and may be reconstructions of those built a half century earlier. In neither

Santa Teresa nor Santa Catalina is there evidence of the new Baroque architecture inaugurated in the façade of the cathedral. Their retables, on the contrary, fall into the full stream of the new style.

In Cuzco the most important architectural monuments after the cathedral are the monasteries of the leading religious orders, the Jesuits, Franciscans, Dominicans, and Mercedarians. The Augustinian monastery is in ruins. The oldest of these churches is the Franciscan, for which fortunately ample documentation was provided by the Franciscan historian, Diego de Mendoza, who lived in the monastery at Cuzco in the mid-seventeenth century. The site of the present church is the third, having been selected in 1549.[44] By the year 1645 the sixteenth-century church was in bad condition, and the monks decided to rebuild. Work had progressed well along when the fateful year of 1650 arrived. The tower fell and much damage was done to the church, but the vault of the nave withstood the shock of the repeated earthquakes. Hence the new church reached its conclusion in 1652, a solid edifice of brown Andean stone, covered with strong domical vaults of brick, separated into bays by stone arches. The nave (Fig. 76) is considerably broader and higher than the two lateral aisles.[45] The sanctuary, elevated 1.10 meters above the nave and approached by steps, comprises a single apse flanked by sacristies, the plan also followed in Santo Domingo. The influence of the cathedral (Fig. 65), then being brought to completion, is clearly in evidence here, in the use of a large entablature block on the piers of the crossing and in the nave. The same source may also explain the decorative late-Gothic ribs in the vaults of the sanctuary and the arms of the transept (Fig. 77). The use of Gothic vaults here, combined with domical vaults in the rest of the church, is unparalleled in the city of Cuzco. Similar disposition, however, has ample precedent elsewhere in South America and Mexico.[46] Like Santo Domingo and the Merced, the church (Fig. 13) has no side chapels, and the choir is raised over the main entrance according to Hispanic tradition. The choir is carried on simple groined vaults, and over the crossing is a domical vault with small lantern. Unfortunately the interior of San Francisco has been disfigured by ugly blue paint. Still worse, the great gilded retables of the colonial period were destroyed about the year 1900 and replaced by feeble imitations of Italian Gothic altars, made by a local carpenter.

The exterior of San Francisco (Fig. 78) is not impressive, in part because of the uninteresting use of irregularly cut stone set in mortar. The composition appears truncated, and yet judging by Mendoza's description there never was more than one tower. The main façade is obviously incomplete, otherwise it would be impossible to explain the curious disposition of blind arches in the upper section. Ashlar is used in the mediocre tower and in the imposing side portal, which occupies an intermediate stage stylistically between the Renaissance design of Santa Clara (Fig. 61) and the full Baroque of the cathedral, La Compañía, and San Pedro (Figs. 63, 64, 68).

It is less articulate, less emphatic than the other early Baroque portals of Santo Domingo and La Merced (Figs. 55, 56, 80), and is distinguished from them by the rectangular enframement of the first story. Here is the age-old Hispanic *mudéjar alfiz*, whose antecedent can be seen in the portal of the *mirab* in the mosque of Spanish Córdoba. It reappears in the small façades of the chapels of Loreto and San Ignacio which adjoin the church of the Compañía at Cuzco (Fig. 67). Another feature of San Francisco, and one unique in Cuzco, is the broad medieval type of narthex which occupies half of the space beneath the choir. Three arches flush with the wall serve as entrances to the narthex (Fig. 13) whence one continues into the church through a single door straight ahead, whereas a short passage to the left leads to the monastery. San Francisco is oriented curiously, as indeed are all of the churches of Cuzco, in this case with the sanctuary directed to the northwest.

The large cloister of San Francisco (Figs. 31, 33, 34) may well be the oldest structure in Cuzco, since its capitals of pure Renaissance type suggest a date in the second half of the sixteenth century. The capitals of the first gallery consist of a broad neckband topped by a projecting echinus which is decorated with the egg-and-dart motive. Long slender volutes rise from the lower part of the neckband to the four corners of the capitals. The capitals of the upper gallery have the same cushion shape, but are very differently ornamented. The neck has a single row of acanthus leaves, and on top of the echinus are two small volutes at each of the four corners. The bases of all of the columns are decorated with a stylized leaf, and of no small consequence in the beauty of effect is the reddish brown stone in which the columns and capitals are carved. The *mudéjar* again makes an appearance in the vertical strip upon the wall above each column, thus establishing the *alfiz* arrangement.

For Spanish parallels to these Renaissance capitals, Marco Dorta has already mentioned the Jeronymite cloister at Lupiana.[47] Others in the patio of the hospital of Santa Cruz at Toledo may be cited, and in each case the definite provincialism of the Cuzco sculpture is evident. Nor is apology necessary when one considers the remoteness geographically from Spain and the mid-sixteenth-century date of the cloister.

Not only the style but also Diego de Mendoza's detailed description of the monastery helps to confirm an early date. Throughout his very accurate account of the cloisters, their stairways, the fountains, etc., Mendoza fails to mention any damage caused by the earthquake of 1650, whereas he states specifically that the cloisters of Santo Domingo fell, and one side of the cloister of La Compañía. Hence there can be no doubt that the main cloister of San Francisco still stands as built in the second half of the sixteenth century. A marked contrast is afforded by the Baroque style of the retable of the Immaculate Conception, and above it the small wooden dome decorated with reliefs, which were added in the northwest corner of the upper gallery. Their date suggests the period *circa* 1650–1660.

The second cloister of San Francisco is pure Tuscan Doric. It covers an area about equal to that of the main cloister, both having ten arches to a side in the lower gallery. The upper galleries differ, however, in that the main cloister has an equal number of arches in both galleries, whereas in the second cloister the two-over-one scheme is used. This arrangement also appears in the neighboring cloister of the Franciscan Colegio de San Buenaventura (now Colegio Nacional de Ciencias), founded in 1690, but with piers instead of columns in the first gallery.[48] The first half of the seventeenth century seems to have been the period for the building of Doric cloisters, a great many of them with two arches in the upper gallery to one in the lower. For this reason, the second cloister of San Francisco may have been erected in that period, prior to the establishment of the Colegio.[49] The protracted survival of the late classical Renaissance in Spain doubtless accounts for the preference for Doric sobriety in the colonies. The change to the Baroque cloister arrived in Cuzco in the third quarter of the century with the famous cloister of the Merced.

The main cloister of Santo Domingo (Fig. 32), like that of San Francisco, quite surely dates back to the sixteenth century, but it met a fate less fortunate in the great earthquake. Mendoza states that it fell,[50] and its reconstruction after 1650 would account for the use of double the number of arches in the second gallery to that in the lower gallery. In this respect it differs from the principal cloister of San Francisco which has an equal number of ten arches in both galleries. The plan of Santo Domingo is slightly rectangular with ten and nine arches to a side. The capitals in the lower gallery are cushion-shaped, consisting of a broad neckband and large echinus, strangely topped with double volutes at the four corners. A small horizontal band of stylized leaves decorates the echinus and a half rosette appears just above in the center of each face. These capitals are almost identical with those in the upper gallery of San Francisco (Fig. 34), with the exception that the latter has a single row of acanthus leaves on the neckband which is absent in Santo Domingo. The workmanship of the Franciscan capitals is, however, much superior. The bases of the columns in both monasteries are decorated with four stylized leaves, and in both monuments the vertical strips forming the *alfiz* appear.

The capitals in the upper gallery of Santo Domingo are very different from those below: in size on account of the smaller scale resulting from the two-over-one scheme, and also in design and workmanship. On the northwest wing adjoining the church, the capitals are poor imitations of those in the lower gallery with a variation in the ornament on the echinus which in this case consists of two stylized oak (?) leaves placed diagonally. On the southwest side of the cloister there are three of the same type, but with an acanthus between the volutes, and also three copies of the capitals in the lower gallery. All other capitals on the same side and in the two remaining wings have a

different design. The latter might be called typically *cuzqueño* for they abound throughout the city and apparently were carved in something like mass production in the seventeenth century. It is the plain Doric cushion capital topped by volutes, similar to those in the portal and service patio of Santa Clara, the main cloister of the Recoleta, the house of the Condes de Peralta, the Casa Garmendía, and innumerable other patios throughout the city. Two capitals at the head of the stairway in the principal cloister of San Francisco belong to the same group and hence must be restorations after 1650.

Considering the evidence of the seventeenth-century capitals and the two-over-one system, the conclusion must be reached that the upper gallery of the Dominican cloister was rebuilt in its entirety after 1650. The lower gallery, on the contrary, with its sixteenth-century capitals seems to have needed only slight repairs and hence remains intact. Very famous is this cloister, not as a colonial monument, but for its Incaic walls which once formed part of the Temple of the Sun, Moon and Stars.[51] Substantial sections of the pre-Columbian structure were incorporated into the colonial monastery, and still survive despite Christian fanaticism and earthquakes.

The church of Santo Domingo is basilican in plan with nave and two lateral aisles, nonprojecting transept, a single apse with sacristy at each side, and a raised choir over the entrance. As in San Francisco and the Merced, the sections of the choir over the aisles serve only as passageways. The general disposition is similar to San Francisco, although the sanctuary is less elevated and the aisles are exceptionally narrow.[52] The restricted size and the low single-arched openings between the bays give the aisles the appearance of chapels. The nave is covered with a semicircular barrel vault of brick, separated into bays by stone arches. Consequently, the effect is entirely unlike the vaults of other Cuzco churches, because this vault is nondomical and makes much the same impression as a continuous barrel. One window is let directly into the vault at each side in each bay, an expedient which looks amateurish in the period of triangular penetrations. Only less surprising are the simple groined vaults over the aisles, in the arms of the transept, beneath the choir, and in the chapels below the choir. The only other church in Cuzco which has groined vaults is Santa Clara. As in San Francisco and the Merced a domical vault is raised over the crossing. The general nonconformity to the Cuzco school in the archaic structure of Santo Domingo leads to the belief that in the rebuilding subsequent to the earthquake of 1650, the plan of the older church of about 1610 was repeated in its main features. The fact that it was destroyed in the catastrophe of 1650 and rebuilt thereafter cannot be questioned. The statement of Meléndez in 1681 that the Dominican church at Cuzco was new confirms that fact.[53] Various other details find no parallels in Cuzco, for example: the very narrow aisles, the frieze with dentils in the nave, the capitals with rosettes, and the plain rectangular piers. The interior of Santo Domingo is the least interesting in Cuzco, even when one disregards the havoc

wrought by the restorers of 1895. They, like the renovators of San Francisco, destroyed the magnificent gilded retables and put in their places miserable imitations of Italian Gothic. They painted the fine brown stone, and still worse they changed the shape of the windows in the nave to suit their Gothic mania. The total result is disastrous.

The exterior of Santo Domingo (Fig. 79), although better, is not distinguished, and the irregularity of the stone clearly bespeaks a ruined structure rebuilt. The most famous and interesting part is the apse with its magnificent curving wall which once formed part of the great Temple of the Sun of the Incas. Above is a three-arched opening located behind the high altar, an unusual arrangement which led Buschiazzo to suspect an Open Chapel.[54] To place an Open Chapel here would be altogether peculiar, and moreover the ground falls off sharply in an unsuitable way. Professor Kenneth J. Conant's suggestion that this balcony was used for the display of relics seems more plausible.

The portals and the tower of Santo Domingo have considerable architectural merit. The latter represents the final step in the development of *cuzqueño* towers, having been built in the years 1729–1731.[55] The spiral columns on the belfry resemble those on the façade of Jesús y María (1733–1735) so closely as to suggest that the same architect designed both. The main portal, well proportioned and late Renaissance in its sober and symmetrical design, might have been built as early as 1625. Equally effective are the convent door to the left and the two windows in the same wall. The side portal (Fig. 55), too, a most satisfactory work by a first-rate professional architect, shows the same conservatism when compared with the Baroque concepts of the cathedral façade. This portal retains the traditional triumphal-arch motive very skillfully integrated with the niche above by the excellent spacing of the scrolls and pyramid pinnacles. The hand of the architect is sure and reveals greater knowledge of his profession than does the similar portal of Santa Clara. Judging by style alone the portals of Santo Domingo would be dated prior to 1650, but the probability is that they were redesigned and rebuilt entirely following the earthquake, since destruction of the church was complete. Harth-terré's attribution of the side portal to Bartolomé Carrión is unconvincing, since that architect's documented portal of Tunja Cathedral in Colombia (1598–1600) is stylistically unrelated.[56]

The two great monasteries of Cuzco which belong in their totality to the seventeenth century are the Merced and that of the Jesuits, commonly known as La Compañía. Both maintain uniformity in style and a high quality which place them on a much higher level architecturally than the Franciscan and Dominican establishments. Of the two, the church of the Jesuits is the finer monument. As for the cloisters, the Mercedarian is not only the better, but one of the most beautiful to be found in all Latin America.

The history of the rebuilding of the Merced after its destruction in 1650 can be reconstructed more fully than in the case of the other monasteries of Cuzco, because of the existence of a chronicle covering the second half of the seventeenth century. I had the opportunity to read the chronicle, which is an unpublished manuscript in the library of this monastery. Francisco Miranda Valcárcel y Peralta, the author of the work, called *Crónica de esta provincia del Cuzco 1650–1707*, states in the preface that his intention was to write only of the period of slightly more than fifty years, during which he had worn the habit of a Mercedarian. Miranda Valcárcel confirms the statement of Mendoza that scarcely a stone was left standing in 1650, and he praises Padre Juan Riquelme (commander, 1651–1657) for his great zeal in pushing forward the building of the new church.[57] By the year 1670 the church and cloister must have been completed, for the style suggests that fact as well as Miranda Valcárcel's statement that the viceroy Conde de Lemos who visited Cuzco in 1669 greatly admired the sumptuous beauty of the convent "which would serve as the palace of the king, our lord." [58]

The architectural fame of the Merced rests upon the main cloister (Figs. 84, 85), a work of great originality and surpassing beauty, built of the warm brown stone of the Incas, cut in blocks which are pronouncedly rusticated. The unknown architect showed genius in the use of materials and textures,[59] contrasting the virile strength of the rusticated walls with the opulent decoration of the free-standing columns. In the first gallery the columns have Corinthian capitals, and the shafts are carved with vertical rows of ornament which might be called a tongue motive. The lower section of the column is separated by two crowns of acanthus leaves, between which are horizontal rows of a scale motive, similar in type to that used in antiquity, and notably in the Florentine Renaissance by such sculptors as Donatello and Desiderio da Settignano.[60] The same treatment of columns is found on the retables within the church of the Merced (Figs. 311, 312), three side retables in Santa Catalina, the retable of the Trinity (dated by inscription 1655) in the cathedral (Fig. 310), and in other contemporary altars of the school of Cuzco. In the spandrels of the arches appear the familiar long stylized leaves, so common in architectural decoration in southern Peru and Bolivia. The columns of the upper gallery are different, the lower section being carved with a guilloche pattern running in spirals and contrasted to the vertical flutings above. The half columns at the sides play another variation on the same theme in which vertical bands of the tongue motive combine with conventional fluting. Both galleries carry an entablature with Roman brackets and a peculiarly large bracket over the capitals. The cloister has six broad arches to the side with equal division in both upper and lower galleries. The walk adjoining the church is covered with decorative late-Gothic ribbed vaults of stucco. The other three walks, except for the Gothic bay in each angle, have magnificently carved wooden ceilings of the second half of the seventeenth century in a good state of preservation. In the upper gallery only two sides, the northwest and southwest, retain their original wooden

ceilings of rectangular coffers, partly gilded.

Hispanic colonial architecture knows nothing more beautiful than the cloister of the Merced. Magnificent handling of open space, lightness and grace combined with sturdy virility of mass, the deep beauty of the color, extraordinary richness and originality in treatment of textures, unerring taste in scale and proportions, all this and more make the Mercedarian cloister unique.

As impressive as the cloister itself are the two monumental stairways which connect the upper and lower galleries. The same superb handling of rusticated stone distinguishes the construction which is carried on three broad arches in each story. On the side facing the Plazuela de la Merced a wide central ramp rises part way to a broad platform, and then breaks into double ramps which return and rise to the second story (Fig. 83). The stairway facing the Calle San Bernardo is planned in reverse fashion. Two ramps rise from the first gallery to a platform where they join into a single axial ramp. This second stairway was not constructed until 1692–1696.[61]

To these same years belongs the rebuilding of the second cloister (Fig. 86) of the Merced,[62] a large structure in serene Doric style consisting of piers carrying six arches to a side in the first gallery and double that number in the second gallery. The scale is excellent and far superior to that of the small third cloister which housed the *colegio* and was added in 1707.[63] For the second cloister, which had been erected prior to the earthquake of 1650, the original contract is preserved, dated October 30,

1634. The architect, Miguel Gutiérrez Sencio, was engaged to build *one* side, which was to consist of eleven arches of stone carried on ten square Doric columns.[64] Dr. García has stated that the second cloister was reconstructed after the earthquake of 1650, that is in 1692–1696, on the original plan of 1634. The disparity between the ten square Doric columns of the contract and the six rectangular piers of the existing structure does not justify that supposition.[65]

The church of the Merced follows in its plan (Fig. 12) the same tradition as that of the Franciscan (Fig. 13) and Dominican churches of Cuzco: nave and two aisles without lateral chapels, nonprojecting transept, raised choir, and single sanctuary; and, curiously enough, the floor plans of the three churches have almost the same measurements.[66] The Merced differs from the others in that the sanctuary is only slightly raised by three steps, and instead of closed sacristies at the sides, a small chapel without walls of separation occupies the space at either side of the sanctuary. Like San Francisco the interior of the Merced (Fig. 82) clearly reveals the influence of the cathedral of Cuzco in the use of the large entablature block over the pilasters of the nave. The body of the church is stone and, as usual in Cuzco, the vaults are brick. The vaults of both nave and aisles have a noticeably domical section, and they, like those of the other churches of Cuzco, are separated into bays by stone arches. Over the crossing is a domical vault with small lantern, just as in the case of San Francisco and Santo Domingo. Under the choir the vaults are of simple early Gothic type. The interior of the Mercedarian church is architecturally far more satisfactory in every respect than the Dominican and Franciscan. Moreover, unlike its companions, it escaped the extremes of the renovating frenzy of fifty years ago.[67]

The exterior of the Merced (Fig. 80) is placed laterally to the street and oriented to the southwest. The northeast door (Fig. 56) which would normally be the main portal adjoins the entrance to the convent. It is a single arched doorway flanked by Ionic columns and adorned with a blind niche above, which is brought into relation with the lower section by lateral scrolls and pyramids. The design is sober and dignified and like in spirit to the side portal of Santo Domingo (Fig. 55). The side portal of the Merced (Fig. 80), on the other hand, is the principal portal which, with the single tower at the left, presents a handsome grouping. A most interesting feature is the chapel provided with altar in the second story directly over the door. The presence of the altar leaves little doubt that mass was said here, while the populace assembled in the square below. Over the side portals of Santo Domingo and San Francisco is a niche in the corresponding position, but large enough only for the statue of the saint, and hence in neither case an open chapel. An excellent and conservative piece of Baroque architecture is this portal, planned in two stories of equal breadth. The influence of the cathedral façade (Fig. 63) will escape no one, a fact betrayed by the general concept, as well as by such details as the design of the lateral niches and the flat ornament on the lower section of the columns in the first story. This ornament is a skillful bit of *mudéjar* patterning and very different from the lozenge design on the columns above. The Merced façade has few planes and only four columns in each story, and hence is restrained compared with the more exuberant Baroque of the cathedral. According to Dr. García, Padre Riquelme let a contract for the construction of the church to two architects, Alonso Casas and Francisco Monya in 1654.[68]

The single tower (Fig. 81) at the left of the main portal ranks among the best in a splendid series of towers for which Cuzco is famous. Although the exact year of construction is not established, the Merced chronicle makes it entirely clear that convent, church, and tower were completed by 1696–1699.[69]

The earliest of the *cuzqueño* towers is that (Fig. 78) of San Francisco (1652) which lacks architectural style or distinction.[70] The series really begins with the cathedral belfries (1657) which have two arched openings on each side (Fig. 62), separated by rusticated Doric pilasters. A low cupola tops the structure, and the transition is made by round pinnacles at the corners and a square pinnacle between. The design is chaste and effective. The towers (Fig. 69) of El Belén (*circa* 1696) and the belfries of Santa Clara (Fig. 61) and San Cristóbal, both of the second half of the seventeenth century, are derived from the cathedral towers with an important change in the smooth, nonrusticated pilasters.[71] Other modifications of the cathe-

dral prototype appear in San Sebastián (Fig. 70; right tower 1664, and left tower 1799), where to the pilasters are added Corinthian half columns the lower part of which is decorated with the scale motive. The bracketed cornice too shows a rejection of the Doric simplicity of the cathedral, and is similar to the cornice of the Mercedarian tower.

The towers (Fig. 67) of the Compañía (*circa* 1651–1668) inaugurate a new design with the cupola raised upon a drum which has an arched opening in each face. The transitions at the corners are made by arched turrets. These two features had a great influence on other towers in Cuzco, yet strangely enough the other striking innovation was never copied in the city: the single elliptical opening on each side of the belfry. The humble village church at Tiquillaque, south of Cuzco, does have one tower containing this feature.

An interesting result comes about with the union of the two prototypes in the church of San Pedro (1688–1699). The belfries (Fig. 68) have two-arched openings and pilasters like those of Santa Clara (Fig. 61), San Cristóbal, and El Belén (Fig. 69), but they are topped by cupola on drum and angle turrets derived from the Compañía (Fig. 67). In the tower (Fig. 81) of the Merced (*circa* 1675–1680) the cupola with drum, even to its elliptical windows and angle turrets, is a descendant of La Compañía. The belfry, however, shows great originality, although the two-arched openings like those of the cathedral persist. The originality lies in the groups of half columns lavishly decorated with the scale motive in the lower part and a delicately incised lozenge design covering the rest of the shaft. The broad cornice with brackets closely resembles the cornices in the Merced cloister.[72] The tower of the Merced is one of the most original and surely one of the most monumental in the city. It is large and powerful rather than chaste and graceful like the belfry of Santa Clara. The tower (Fig. 79) of Santo Domingo (1729–1731), like the churches of Jesús María and the Triunfo, represents the aftermath, the twilight of the school of Cuzco. The Dominican tower is a copy of the Mercedarian with important modifications in the cupola and turrets. Here only among the *cuzqueño* towers spiral columns appear, and also carved moldings which reflect the same indigenous taste displayed in the two late churches just mentioned. These towers of Cuzco are among its most brilliant creations and they endow the city with some of its most characteristic and ingratiating aspects.

The Jesuits first arrived in Cuzco in 1571 under the leadership of the great pioneer, Padre Gerónimo Ruiz de Portillo. The history of their early years in Cuzco is related in a recently published manuscript in the Library of Congress at Washington.[73] The anonymous Jesuit who wrote in the year 1600 states specifically that Padre Portillo himself designed the first church and that the structure was completed under his successor Padre Joseph Tiruel. Although the chronicler undoubtedly exaggerates when he calls the principal portal the finest in all Peru, his description is valuable. The stone portal had many columns and niches enclosing statues of saints, probably a typical Renaissance triumphal-arch type. In the famous painting of Cuzco during the earthquake of 1650 (Fig. 21), which hangs in the church of the Triunfo at Cuzco, details of La Compañía are not explicit. It can be seen, however, that the church was small and unpretentious.

Of great interest is the fact that the canons of the cathedral instituted legal proceedings in the sixteenth century to prevent the Jesuits from locating their monastery on the Plaza Mayor, so near the cathedral. According to the *Anales del Cuzco* a like controversy arose over the rebuilding of the Jesuit church after the earthquake of 1650, but the Jesuits calmly ignored the injunction issued to restrain them.[74]

The additions to the Washington manuscript, which continue to the year 1653, include the history of the building of the chapel of Nuestra Señora de Loreto which stands at the left of the present church of La Compañía. This chapel was begun on the day of St. Augustine in 1651 and completed on the same day in 1653, constructed "with the aid and industry of Padre Juan Bautista Egidiano, with his constant assistance and his excessive work." Whether this means that Padre Egidiano was the architect or just the overseer is not entirely clarified.[75]

The chapel of Loreto (Fig. 67) has a small two-storied façade with a rectangular center which is derived from the side portal of San Francisco. The design is mediocre and might conceivably have been planned by an amateur like Padre Egidiano. The interior consists of three bays of barrel vaults with triangular penetrations, and a domical vault with tiny lantern over the sanctuary. The walls carry a simple molded cornice, and the whole chapel, whose portal on the outside has an inscription dated 1654, shows no relation in style to the principal church. The chapel of St. Ignatius (now the Artisans' Exhibition Rooms), which acts as a pendant to the chapel of Loreto at the right of the main church, has a single nave of three bays with triangular penetrations, each bay topped by a small lantern. The large bracketed cornice is like the cornice in the main church, and hence probably by the same architect. The façade, on the contrary, is a replica of that of the chapel of Loreto.

The problem as to who was the architect of the principal church of La Compañía in Cuzco is still unsolved, in my opinion. Recently Padre Vargas Ugarte has published the biography of Padre Egidiano, a Fleming who lived in the monastery at Cuzco from 1642 until his death in 1675. To him Padre Vargas attributes the church and also the design of the high altar.[76] The documentary basis lies in the Washington manuscript which connects him only with the chapel of Nuestra Señora de Loreto, also known as the *capilla de los indios;* and, in addition, in the *Carta de Edificación* written as a memorial one year after Padre Egidiano's death in Cuzco. Until further evidence is forthcoming, the architect of La Compañía must remain a problem.

The church of the Compañía is one of the best-known examples of colonial architecture in Latin America. After the destruction of the original monastery in the earthquake of 1650, rebuilding began the following year and it was ready for consecration in 1668.[77]

The church has the plan (Fig. 4) of a Latin cross with large dome over the crossing and shallow chapels on both sides of the nave, all of which are features new to the ecclesiastical architecture of Cuzco. This arrangement is commonly called the Jesuit plan. However, there is in reality no such thing as a Jesuit plan, for many Jesuit churches were built on the basilican plan, others without chapels, and conversely many non-Jesuit churches have the form of a Latin cross with chapels at the sides of the nave and dome over the crossing.[78] The only safe and scientific expedient is to refer to the Gesù plan, the problem of which is discussed in this book in the section devoted to San Pedro of Lima. Only one other church in Cuzco, San Pedro (Fig. 75), not a Jesuit foundation, was later to adopt the floor plan of the Compañía.[79]

The choir of the Compañía is raised over the main entrance as usual, and the five bays of the nave, the sanctuary, and transept are covered with late-Gothic ribbed vaults of brick which are copied from those of the cathedral (Fig. 72). Almost inexplicable is this reactionary use of Gothic vaults when the rest of the church is a Baroque monument representing a revolutionary departure from other works of the school of Cuzco. The walls of the nave are treated with double Corinthian pilasters between the arches raised on large bases 2.10 meters high. The chapels have double Doric pilasters which are much shorter and thus provide scale. This composition of wall surface originated in the Italian Renaissance, and soon passed to all European countries. A heavy cornice runs throughout, deeply projecting and with peculiarly awkward brackets, composed of an acanthus leaf supported by a volute. Bracketed cornices appear in Spain during the Renaissance on the exterior of the apse of the cathedral and of San Jerónimo in Granada. In the third quarter of the seventeenth century they became a characteristic of the interiors of churches in the school of Madrid.[80] Their appearance here at Cuzco in the nave of La Compañía clearly demonstrates the architect's knowledge of contemporary buildings in the capital of Spain. Atop this cornice at Cuzco a corridor with balustrade provides communication throughout the upper regions.

The large stone dome rises on a drum over pendentives which are intricately carved with the IHS as the central feature. At the crossing the pilasters give way to columns which are original in the placing of a band of basket weave just below the center of the shaft and a crown of acanthus leaves above it. The crown of acanthus leaves becomes universal as a decorative motive on the retables and the pulpits of Cuzco in the second half of the seventeenth century, and thence spreads throughout Peru.

The interior of the Compañía is serene, imposing, and harmonious in spite of the ugly cornice. It enjoys, too, the advantage of not having suffered from the hand of the restorer. The natural reddish brown stone has been painted an inoffensive light gray, and not even the blue vaults with white ribs can tarnish the dignity of the architecture.

In the proportions of the whole composition lies the secret of the beauty of the Compañía's exterior (Fig. 67). The mass of the church with its flat roof, prominent dome, and two graceful towers is superbly balanced and magnificently scaled. Here is the product of a first-rate architect who thought not simply of isolated details but of the entire monument.

The façade naturally demands principal attention. The central portal was inspired in its general disposition by the portal of the cathedral (Figs. 63, 64), but it differs greatly in detail. The proportions of the entire façade are in fact much superior to those of the cathedral. The portal itself shows a taste for profusion in ornament in contrast to the purely architectural quality of its prototype. Striking are the Corinthian columns with the crowns of acanthus leaves on the shafts, three in the first story and two in the second. The flat carved ornament over the niches, the design of the central section with additional recesses, the three windows of the second story, all add to the complexity of the composition but certainly constitute no improvement over the cathedral portal. The characteristic webbed volutes reappear here and much more prominently, and another detail of no great significance, the clusters of apples in a cloth swag on the columns of the third story. One of the most interesting elements of the Jesuit portal is the large trefoil shape of the top, another example of this uniquely Hispano-Moresque device. On the other hand, the most peculiar part of the façade is the large cornice which runs across the front and curves above the trefoil portal, the same strange cornice used within the church.

The singular beauty and originality of the towers (Fig. 67) have already been discussed. The idea of a single elliptical opening on each face is most successful, and yet curiously enough, never imitated in Cuzco. Neither was another innovation, the two-storied triumphal-arch niches on the lower part of the towers, for elsewhere in Cuzco the towers are undecorated below the belfry. The raising of the cupola on a drum and the use of angle turrets, which add much to the height and grace of the towers, were imitated thereafter, in the Merced, San Pedro, and Santo Domingo.

The full-sized dome of the Compañía (Fig. 74) was the first of its kind in Cuzco, and found only one successor in that of San Pedro. A low domical vault with small lantern at the top covers the crossing in San Francisco, Santo Domingo, and La Merced, and in the cathedral the crossing is treated exactly like any other bay of the vaulting. On the exterior of these three monastic churches the small lantern plays no part in the architectural composition, serving as a purely utilitarian source of light. The drum of the Jesuit dome, in contrast, is high and monumental with large double volute-shaped buttresses and four windows. The glazed tiles of green, yellow, and blue which cover the cupola add a colorful and most attractive note.

The former Jesuit convent now houses the University of Cuzco within its cloister (Fig. 87), a suitable adaptation of the once great monastery which the brothers left forever in 1767 when the Jesuits were expelled from all Spanish lands. The fine Doric cloister was entirely rebuilt after 1650, if one is to place any faith in the accuracy of the famous view of Cuzco of that date. It has eight and nine columns to the side in the lower gallery and, as so frequently in this period, double the number in the upper gallery. The columns are strictly Tuscan Doric without ornament except for a few in the northwest gallery which have four stylized leaves on the base and a small tongue ornament on the echinus. From the cloister one of the finest views of the church in profile is obtained, massive, austere, and imposing.

The former convent façade (Fig. 67) is very low compared with the church at whose side it stands, so much so that the effect is almost ludicrous. Built of the familiar red-brown stone, it is rather heavy and somber despite or perhaps because of its profuse ornamentation. Most prominent at first view is the projecting square device like a recessed coffer in reverse which decorates the pilasters throughout. The two-storied division carries columns ringed with an acanthus crown in the lower section, and the remaining wall surfaces are covered with stylized leaves, mask heads, a peculiar ball-and-tongue device, and long volutes beside the niches in the upper center. In the top center again appears the trefoil motive, and just below it another *mudéjar* variant of the same in the niche. The indigenous flavor prevails here but in a heavy-handed way, and without the exquisite fantasy of the true *mestizo* style.

San Pedro is the only church in Cuzco which follows in its ground plan (Fig. 75), and solely in its ground plan, the new type introduced to Cuzco by the Compañía. Known as San Pedro, its correct name is Nuestra Señora de los Remedios, so dedicated at its foundation in 1572 by Francisco de Toledo, but popularly called the Hospital de los Naturales in the colonial period.[81] The institution was rebuilt under the patronage of Bishop Mollinedo and his nephew, Andrés de Mollinedo, whose escutcheons appear over the first chapels to the left and right respectively on entering the church. The first stone was laid in 1688,[82] and in 1699 the local authorities sent a report to the Council of the Indies in Seville with a request for fifty thousand pesos needed to complete the building. Luckily the plans submitted with this report are preserved in the Archivo de Indias, this being the only building in Cuzco of which records are still extant there. Included is a description of the church, and the statement that they were then working on the windows and cornices, the vaults having been constructed.[83] Still more interesting is the information that the architect was an Indian, Juan Tomás Tuyru Tupac, none other than the sculptor of the pulpit in the same church and of the statue of the Virgin of the Almudena in the church of that name.[84]

The interior of San Pedro (Fig. 73), one of the finest in Cuzco, is built of stone, now painted gray, and covered with sturdy domical vaults of brick. Stone arches divide the nave into five bays and a sizeable stone dome rises on pendentives over the crossing. The choir, as usual elevated over the main entrance, is supported by a handsomely designed four-pointed arch. Although the ground plan and dome are derived from the Compañía the treatment of the walls (Fig. 72) shows no relation to that church.[85] The source of the style, characterized by colossal Doric pilasters stepped back at the sides and topped by a high entablature, is the cathedral of Cuzco (Fig. 65). An interesting evidence of change in taste is the use of domical vaults similar to those of the Merced and San Francisco, rather than ribbed vaults which prevail in the two churches from which San Pedro is otherwise derived. Smaller than the Compañía and less imposing, San Pedro nevertheless is in no way inferior in its handling of space and scale. No church in the city embodies greater purity of design or more serenity in mood, qualities which many will prefer to the more luxuriant Baroque of the Compañía.

The façade of San Pedro (Fig. 68) is less graceful and elegant than that of the Compañía, and it suggests rather power and simplicity in its lower proportions and barren walls. With its Doric belfries and unadorned towers it is more sober than the Jesuit church. Once again its two ancestors are the Compañía in the use of the cupola on a drum, and the cathedral, the portal being a simplified copy of the latter (Figs. 62, 67). The result is colder than either prototype, lacking in Baroque exuberance particularly in the details of the niches and in the ornament. The tone of classical serenity which was established by the interior of the cathedral set the dominant key for

Cuzco architecture of which San Pedro is one of the most satisfying and most majestic examples.

El Belén, originally founded by Francisco de Toledo in 1572,[86] was rebuilt contemporaneously with San Pedro and must have been well along toward completion in 1696, when Bishop Mollinedo mentioned it in his letter of that year.[87] The two Mollinedos, whose zeal for church building knew no bounds, were the chief patrons here as well as of San Pedro. The Bishop's shield appears over the doors at the left and right as one enters, and again on the silver altar frontal which bears the date 1696. Portraits of both men are included in devotional pictures flanking the altar, the bishop on the gospel side (left) and the priest on the epistle side.

The style of El Belén forces the conclusion that the Mollinedos employed the same architect here as they did for San Pedro, that is to say, Juan Tomás Tuyru Tupac. The interiors of the two churches are identical in the design of the colossal pilasters and huge entablature block and in their majestic austerity. The barrenness of the walls serve as an excellent background to the lavishly carved and gilded retables and the picture frames in the upper reaches. The brick vaulting is even more domical than in San Pedro, and the space differs due to the plan which in this case consists of one long single nave of seven bays with elevated choir.[88] El Belén was formerly the church of a convent of nuns, a fact which explains the omission of transept and dome. Here the size of the church far exceeds those of the other female orders in Cuzco,

such as Santa Clara, Santa Catalina, and Santa Teresa, and in every respect it is more luxurious, thanks no doubt to the Mollinedos. Without exact precedent in Cuzco are the three arched niches to a side in which small retables are set, and the small chapel on either hand just upon entering. El Belén is one of the outstanding works of Cuzco, ranking with San Pedro and the Merced, a fact which is all too generally overlooked, undoubtedly because of the superabundance of architectural riches which Cuzco possesses.

The façade of El Belén, obviously very similar to San Pedro (Figs. 68, 69), has one striking feature which sets it apart and that is the rectangular hood over the main door. This Hispanic shape, which has been noted previously in the lateral portal of San Francisco and in the façades of the chapels adjoining La Compañía, strikes a peculiar note here, for it cuts in half the two columns above at the sides of the window. The rest of the portal is almost identical with that of San Pedro except in details such as the omission of the webbed volutes. Juan Tomás reveals his provincialism, notwithstanding the fact that he was a great architect, in attempting to unite two incompatible types of design without resolving their differences. In the towers he returned to the two-arched opening and simple cupola, the tradition which starts with the cathedral and continues also in Santa Clara and San Cristóbal. Over the doorway in primitive relief sculpture the Holy Family kneel at the manger, guarded by the three kings on horseback. Despite its faults, the general proportions of the Belén façade are excellent, and it has an impressive exterior even though this is not equal to the harmonious and spacious interior.

San Sebastián, which stands in the village of that name in the suburbs of Cuzco, is the last in the series of two-towered churches to be mentioned, although not the last to be built. Also founded by Francisco de Toledo in 1572, it had a single nave with adobe walls nearly two meters thick.[89] In 1696 four arched openings were cut through each wall of the nave and an aisle was added at each side.[90] The unvaulted interior today presents the most forlorn and dilapidated appearance imaginable, its sloping cane roof covered in part with corrugated iron, its once lavish decoration of large paintings with gilded frames and its retables of the late seventeenth century ruined by neglect and drenched by years of exposure to tropical rains. Even now with national laws for the protection of works of art, execution of good intentions is woefully wanting.

If the façade of San Sebastián (Figs. 70, 71) is lacking in the excellent scale which characterizes related works in Cuzco, it should cause no wonder, for it was built in three stages. The right tower at its base has a long inscription with date 1664 and the names of bishop, priests, and noble Indians, but without mention of the architect. Located farther above, another legend gives the name of an architect, *Siendo Manuel de Sahuaraura, maestro mayor*. Much stress has been laid upon the fact that he was an Indian,[91] and this, indeed, is added proof of the important place in society held by Juan Tomás' compatriots. Interpreted strictly, it

must be confessed, nonetheless, that Sahuaraura is thus identified as architect of the tower, but not necessarily of the rest of the façade. The left tower, an exact replica of its mate, has a verbose inscription, dated 1799, in the lower section.[92]

The portal belongs to the second half of the seventeenth century on the evidence of style alone, since it is derived in its general disposition from the cathedral (finished 1654), and the rich ornament on the columns is almost identical with that of the choir stalls (Figs. 262, 263) of the cathedral (*circa* 1657–1678). In addition, documentary evidence is preserved in Bishop Mollinedo's letter of 1678 in which he said that the portal had been finished, "of such beauty that it might have been worked in wax." [93] It is probable that the façade was begun after Mollinedo's arrival in Cuzco in 1673, since he had his escutcheon placed in the upper center. His generosity did not end there, as is proved by the presence of his shield within on the magnificent silver altar frontal and on the left side of the high altar. Indeed, the splendor and luxury displayed in the retables and paintings of this church in a poor Indian village can only be explained by the munificence of Manuel de Mollinedo.

The towers of San Sebastián, as previously stated, follow the precedent created by the cathedral, with modifications in the use of Corinthian half columns, decorated with the scale motive in the lower section and carrying a cornice with brackets above. The really unique feature of the church, however, is the portal. The general scheme of the cathedral (Figs. 62, 63) has been altered only by the elliptical window in the center and the substitution of a single niche for the third story. A genuine devotion to surface pattern, such as is seen normally in retables, brought into being this lacily carved monument of stone, so exquisitely cut that Mollinedo aptly compared it with wax. The columns are covered with patterns of arabesques, of stylized volutes, leaves, and vines, and in the center of each is a big Spanish jar, wreathed in large leaves and containing pomegranates and peaches. For some reason, this obviously European classical variety of jar has been incorrectly described as an Indian *maceta*. Various ornamental motives, such as the female heads, and also the style of carving, suggest that the same sculptors who worked upon the choir stalls of the cathedral were also engaged here. The columns are ringed with crowns of acanthus, like the façade of La Compañía (Fig. 64), and in the upper set a cartouche is added. The decorative repertory of Cuzco is brought into full play everywhere, with the scale motive on the brackets below the niches, and the tongue motive on the pilasters at the sides. The façade of San Sebastián is more fascinating in detail than in its entirety. It is a decorator's triumph like the façades of Juli, Pomata, Cajamarca, and Arequipa, although stylistically of another sort.

The golden age of Cuzco architecture came to an end with the dawn of the eighteenth century. The great earthquake of 1650 had wrought havoc, but it produced a renaissance of fabulous extent. Only the epilogue remained to be performed, chiefly the continued building of retables, and the construction of the two churches adjoining the cathedral (Fig. 7). At the left the Sagrada Familia, begun in 1723, then abandoned, and later completed in 1733–1735,[94] is a small church of five bays with lateral chapels, and domical vaults. Its Doric pilasters recall the cathedral but it is an uninteresting building at best, rendered grotesque today by the ugliest paint in imitation of marble anyone could conceive. The exterior lacks distinction and is interesting chiefly because spiral columns are used on the portal, the only example in Cuzco and good testimony to the predominantly architectonic character of the Baroque in Cuzco. These spiral columns are identical with those of the tower of Santo Domingo and probably the work of the same architect.

At the opposite flank of the cathedral is the Triunfo, on the site of which once stood a mud structure which for more than a century served as cathedral. After the present basilica was inaugurated, the Triunfo received its much-needed reconstruction, under the aegis of the energetic Diego Arias de la Cerda, as recorded by the inscription of 1664 on the front of the building.[95] Not many years later the structure was demolished and the present church, designed in the form of a Greek cross by the Carmelite, Fray Miguel Menacha (1729–1732), replaced it.[96] The Triunfo has the distinction of being the only church of central plan in Cuzco, and it carries a fine stone dome on pendentives over the center. Indicative of the infusion of the *mestizo* taste are the carved bands of stylized leaves and cartouches on the arches beneath the dome. The rest of the church has domical brick vaults. It will be noted that the sober Doric piers persist, further testimony to the preponderant authority of the architecture of the cathedral throughout Cuzco's cultural life. The exterior does not measure up to the fine interior. Yet it maintains the reserve and good taste of *cuzqueño* tradition, and its three portals with familiar Cuzco ornament and lunetted skyline form a suitable pendant to the Sagrada Familia.

A few other ecclesiastical structures of Cuzco remain undiscussed, but they have not sufficient importance to receive more than brief mention in a general book of the present type.[97]

The Indian villages in the neighborhood of Cuzco, as throughout Peru, have churches filled with fabulous riches in retables, silver altar frontals, and religious paintings. Stone edifices like the large church at Urubamba (*circa* 1678–1696) are the exception.[98] Here the Latin-cross plan and nave with lateral chapels resemble the plan of the Compañía and San Pedro in Cuzco, although the vaults are made of cane rather than brick. The façade with three stories of Corinthian columns has only one tower completed. The parish church of Andahuaylas (department of Apurímac) resembles that of Urubamba slightly in its stone construction. Nevertheless the differences are great, although the period is contemporary, for the church at Andahuaylas followed the usual *pueblo* plan of long single nave without chapels, with raised choir and pitched roof. Its façade in two stories of Doric columns shows excellent taste in scale and in handling of ornament.

Virtually all village churches near Cuzco, as elsewhere, are adobe in construction with pitched roofs of cane and occasionally portals of brick. Most surprising of all is the enormous size of the parish churches, and the tiny scale of other village chapels. The plan almost universally is that of a long single nave without chapels or transept, and a raised choir, sometimes carried on arches as at San Jerónimo (Fig. 89) and at Huaro. The former, a foundation of Francisco de Toledo in 1572 may,[99] in spite of the earthquake of 1650, still preserve its original construction, for the capitals under the choir are identical with those in the large cloister of San Francisco at Cuzco, which belongs to the second half of the sixteenth century. San Jerónimo has other sixteenth-century features, such as the prominent triumphal arch preceding the sanctuary, and a façade composed of a three-arched narthex with balcony above (Fig. 88). The latter arrangement recurs at Urcos.[100] The balcony itself without narthex but with single tower (Calca, Oropesa, Andahuaylillas) or double towers (chapel at Checacupe, Fig. 90) is, on the contrary, a very common feature. The single attached tower is more prevalent than twin towers, and in addition the single isolated tower with atrium occurs (parish church, Checacupe). The portal of San Jerónimo consists of a triumphal-arch motive, a round-arched doorway with empty niches between the pilasters at each side, a type of design encountered repeatedly in this region. Some, like San Jerónimo, have a frieze of cherubs' heads over the portal (Oropesa, Calca) and in the other cases the frieze is plain (parish churches at Yucai, Checacupe, Andahuaylillas). A variant occurs at Chuquibambilla and Antabamba (Apurímac) where a row or rows of large blind niches cut across above the portal and the frieze of cherubs is lacking. The dates of these churches are problematic. San Jerónimo seems to preserve its original structure (1572). The triumphal-arched design of the portal and the frieze of cherubs' heads prove their adherence to sixteenth century models. On the other hand, nearly all of the other churches must have been rebuilt after 1650, as in the case of Yucai which dates about 1685.[101] That conclusion is forced upon us not only by the earthquake, but by the fact that retables, pictures, and altar frontals belong almost entirely to the late seventeenth and early eighteenth centuries, with rare exceptions like the pulpit at San Jerónimo (*circa* 1625) and two side retables in the parish church at Checacupe. Although the majority of the churches are oriented with the short side facing the plaza, the reverse situation with the long side upon the plaza is not infrequent (Checacupe, Yucai, Andahuaylas).

Small Andean chapels of adobe usually with one tower, occasionally with two (Checacupe, Fig. 90), characterized by a small porch formed by the projection of the pitched roof, are innumerable, visible on every hand in villages and in private haciendas as one drives through the countryside (Yucai, Chitabamba). Unpretentious from without, every chapel holds within unbelievable riches in retables and altar frontals. Unity of style, both inside and out, prevails with surprising consistency.

Occasionally novelties are forthcoming, as in the delightful little chapel of San José at Urubamba, formerly a Franciscan Recoleta (founded 1613),[102] where a high broad tower of reddish-brown stone with two open arches at the top replaces the usual mud structure. Or again, a greater novelty comes to pass in the large stone church, standing in complete isolation in the fields called Tiobamba, where two broad open towers flank the usual narthex. Here the portal, also in stone, and richly carved in primitive *mestizo* style in the eighteenth century, would be not surprising in Puno, but is rare in the district of Cuzco. The Ermita at Oropesa (1685) likewise has a stone doorway,[103] charming in its naïveté and indigenous stylization, which would seem more at home in the region of Lake Titicaca, although not specifically a product of that school.

Cuzco is without question the greatest center of Hispanic architecture in South America. Qualitatively, as well as quantitatively, it might have been challenged by Lima had not repeated earthquakes reduced the latter city to rubble, especially in 1746. The great earthquake of 1650 in Cuzco, on the other hand, came early, when colonial Peru was still at its apex, and so the city arose anew, more magnificent than ever it had been before. Remote as it was, and still is, Cuzco had the force of tradition behind it, as the capital of the Incas, and so under the Spanish it became a still greater city. At the start, even Upper Peru (Bolivia) was subject to ecclesiastical rule from Cuzco, the bishopric extending to the shores of Lake Titicaca, and the monasteries, too, ruled by the mother houses in Cuzco.

Great patrons played a decisive role in the building of religious Cuzco and noble families in the erection of many vast palaces. The early bishops were no patrons of the arts, and it will be remembered that Bishop Sebastián Lartaún sabotaged the viceroy's intentions of bringing to completion the cathedral within six years by refusing to contribute the financial share of the church. Not until Bishop Ocón (1644–1652) assumed his charge, were energetic measures taken to give to Cuzco at long last the magnificent cathedral which still stands today. Immediately upon the heels of the earthquake, the churches and monasteries were rebuilt with incredible rapidity, a virtual renaissance, explained by the men of great zeal with whom the city was endowed at this time. First among these was Manuel de Mollinedo, the greatest bishop Cuzco ever knew, and the most munificent patron of the arts in the history of Spanish colonies, a virtual Medici of the seventeenth century (1673–1699). At the time of his death it was said that he had donated fourteen churches of brick, thirty-six of adobe, fourteen pulpits, eighty-two *custodias,* and twenty frontals of silver.[104] His letters, as well as the prodigal quantity of works extant bearing his shield, add further testimony. Many silver objects have been melted down for money in years past, but in Cuzco itself magnificent frontals bearing his escutcheon are still in place in El Belén (1696), San Cristóbal, San Sebastián, and in the village of San Jerónimo (dated after his death in 1702). It would be tedious to list all of his donations: the majority of the pulpits in Cuzco, many retables such as that of the *trascoro* of the cathedral, the high altars of San Sebastián and San Blas. Entirely rebuilt at the expense of Bishop Mollinedo and his nephew Andrés were El Belén and San Pedro, probably the finest church after the cathedral, la Almudena, and San Sebastián in great part. He built the tower of San Cristóbal; he contributed to San Antonio, Santa Catalina, and Santa Teresa. Not even Julius II or Lorenzo de' Medici has a better record, and yet present-day cynics, unable to understand such a phenomenon, scoff and say the bishop placed his shield everywhere at will. The contemporary history, the bishop's letters, and the style of the monuments belie such an attitude. Mollinedo was not the only patron of the day, but his example was inspirational. There is no other explanation for the prodigality of retables and silver altar frontals (such as Yucai, Urubamba, San Juan de Dios in Urquillos, Oropesa) throughout the region in the late seventeenth and early eighteenth centuries. And still nothing has been said of the vast quantity of pictures which Mollinedo donated,[105] nor of the astounding productivity of Cuzco in painting and sculpture in this period.

The style of *cuzqueño* architecture was set to a considerable degree by the cathedral which, so far as its interior is concerned, is a product of the late classical Renaissance of Spain, usually known as the Herreresque. San Francisco in the mid-century, and even at the end of the seventeenth century San Pedro and El Belén, still preserve the style of the cathedral, designed a hundred years before. In general, exuberance in ornamentation is reserved for retables and choir stalls against a sober architectural background. Nowhere in Cuzco itself does one encounter the lavishly ornamented architecture which characterizes the *mestizo* style of Arequipa and Lake Titicaca. In the great capitals like Cuzco and Lima the Spanish tradition predominated in all matters cultural and the indigenous element was suppressed. Only in the Indian villages of the province and to a reserved degree in the cloister of the Merced does that factor make an impression.

The exteriors of the churches of Cuzco give a general impression of mass and sobriety. The strength and character of the reddish-brown stone, so distinctive of the region, contributes in no small measure to the majesty of *cuzqueño* architecture. Color, texture, and mass are inherent in the material, the legacy of the magnificent edifices of the Incas. The flat rectangular silhouette of Cuzco architecture is, however, strictly Hispanic, characteristic of churches and domestic architecture of that peninsula far back into the Middle Ages. The façades of Cuzco, too, are marked by architectonic sobriety in the main. The portal of the cathedral, advanced architectural Baroque, was decisive in founding a school and in breaking with the more conservative classicism which had preceded it, and which continued even after 1650 in the portals of Santo Domingo and in the front portal of La Merced. The school was established in La Merced, San Pedro, El Belén, and San Sebastián. The façade of the Compañía, too, followed the precedent established by the cathedral, but added ornament to produce a more lavishly Baroque edifice. In the matter of vaulting, the cathedral and the Compañía with their Gothic vaults are surprisingly enough the most conservative structures. Elsewhere they found no imitators, for even Santa Clara in the early seventeenth century had groined vaults. Otherwise, domical and barrel vaults prevailed after 1650. An interesting case is San Francisco with domical vaults, save in the arms of the transept and sanctuary, where late-Gothic ribbed vaults are used for purely decorative reasons. This solution, however, is not of local origin, but one, as previously explained, widespread in Mexico and Bolivia.

As one thinks of Cuzco, one sees towers of red-brown stone, massive stone churches, sober solemn interiors, and above all the unforgettable majesty of the cathedral. The school of Cuzco is not provincial. It is Hispanic, and it is colonial because it was of the Spanish colonies. Here the great traditions of the past did much to spur the haughty Spaniard to make his Cuzco still more magnificent than ever it had been under the fabulous rulers who preceded him, the mighty Incas.

IV

LIMA

LIMA, the capital of South America in colonial days, held unbroken sway until the nineteenth century, when she fell behind the modern metropolises, Buenos Aires and Rio de Janeiro. Lima too has grown and expanded in the past half century, her present population of a half million spreading out into modern suburbs far beyond the limits of the original city. Little remains of the colonial setting except the churches.

In the realm of domestic architecture, the Torre Tagle Palace (Figs. 24–26), the portal of the Casa de Pilatos, an eighteenth-century balcony on the Paseo de Aguas, other balconies on Calle Santa Cruz opposite Santo Domingo, these and other scattered bits give hints of the former charm which men have done their utmost to destroy. The end has not yet come, for the present plan of urbanization in Lima sweeps all before it. The Plaza Mayor has already been ruined forever, and largely within the past ten years. Antonio Rivas' superb bronze fountain of 1650 still presides serenely over the thronged streets, where the vast square was once tranquil and expansive. On the east side, the arcade built under the Conde de Moncloa in 1699 is the only vestige of colonial domestic architecture left. Opposite stands the new and unattractive Government Palace (1937) which so recently replaced the colonial Casa del Virrey.

Nature as well as man has conspired to harm the Spanish colonial city. Repeated earthquakes have devastated Lima, the worst of them in 1687 and 1746, and the most recent serious catastrophe in 1940. Not a single edifice has survived without damage at one time or another. Little did Francisco Pizarro foresee the tragedies to come when he founded his capital on the banks of the Rimac in 1535, a site located just three miles from the sea on the flat plain which borders the Peruvian coast. The conquerors chose to build the city here, because they found a river at hand and ready communication with the sea through the port of Callao. That the warm climate was a factor in their choice is doubtful, for those intrepid men cared little about the amenities of life. Climate as well as the geographic situation, however, is an important factor in architectural development. For example, the lack of rain in Lima made possible the roofs of cane and mud, which were universally adopted after brick vaults of colonial churches proved cumbersome and dangerous in a land of many earthquakes.

The history of *limeño* architecture in

the sixteenth and seventeenth centuries must be reconstructed almost entirely from literary sources. Not a building survives from the first century of Lima's existence, and even the seventeenth century can be evoked in completeness in just one important monument, the church and monastery of San Francisco. The eighteenth century, on the other hand, is well represented by churches entirely of that period and by numerous reconstructions on earlier foundations. To the nineteenth century belongs the tragedy of wanton destruction by the hand of man in a frenzy of Neoclassic modernization. The churches of Lima and other cities were stripped of their magnificent Baroque altars which were consigned to the fire. Thus priceless and irreplaceable works of art were burned, not even sold. The cathedral, San Francisco, La Merced, nearly all of them save San Pedro suffered this ravage. Only a relatively poor and modest church like Jesús María was overlooked, and hence today it possesses the finest colonial interior in Lima.

For all of man's stupidity and the earthquakes again and again, Lima is still rich in ecclesiastical monuments. The recently formed Consejo Nacional de Restauración y Conservación de Monumentos Históricos y Artísticos has made a valiant effort, and has arrested much destruction. They have been unable to save Santa Teresa, however, and overthoroughness of restorations has sometimes resulted in loss.

A catalogue of the churches of Lima, dividing them into principal monuments and secondary monuments, has been prepared (see Appendix). The material is vast

and at the same time cumbersome because of the numerous rebuildings subsequent to earthquakes. Hence a catalogue supplied with facts, description, and bibliography seemed the best method of handling the innumerable problems involved in this study. Fuller references will, therefore, be found in the Appendix. The present chapter is regarded as an introduction to the catalogue in which the stylistic evolution of the architecture is traced from the sixteenth century up to the early nineteenth century.

Documents relating to Lima's churches have been studied and published to a greater extent than in any other part of Peru with the possible exception of Arequipa, which has recently been so thoroughly investigated by Padre Víctor Barriga. Unfortunately very few of the monuments of which the documents speak are still extant, whereas in Cuzco the reverse is true. There the archives have scarcely been touched, but the works of art still exist in abundance. For Lima much excellent work in the archives has been done by the late Fray Domingo Angulo and Horacio Urteaga who published their finding in the *Revista Histórica*. Padre Rubén Vargas Ugarte in many books and articles and Lohmann Villena have brought to light important information.[1] Harth-terré has contributed extensively to the study of *limeño* documents in various articles, the most important of which have been collected in his recent book.[2]

Much of our knowledge of lost monuments is based upon the descriptions left by chroniclers, nearly all of them priests and monks. Among these works which will be cited in due course, the *Historia de la Fundación de Lima,* written by Padre Bernabé Cobo, is the most important source for a study of the churches of Lima which were built in the sixteenth and early seventeenth centuries. Padre Cobo, a Jesuit, lived many years in the monastery at Lima, where he wrote his invaluable history about 1629, although he did not sign the preface until 1639 after a sojourn of ten years in Mexico.[3] His work is extraordinarily accurate, particularly for his day, and is replete with dates of foundations and with brief but explicit statements about types and construction of churches.

INTERIORS

IN the year 1535 at the very beginning of Lima's existence, a humble church was begun on the Plaza Mayor. Six years later it was elevated to the rank of cathedral, and hence the first Spanish founders felt the urgent need of a better edifice to suit its high station. The need was met in 1551 by a structure with vaulted apse, a single nave covered with a wooden ceiling, and an elevated choir. A simple type of single-naved church without lateral chapels and covered by a pitched wooden roof was the rule throughout Peru in the sixteenth century, as already explained in the second chapter. Few examples of that early period survive today except in the region of Lake Titicaca and in Ayacucho. The humble cathedral of Lima of 1551, with only its sanctuary covered by a vault of brick, established, however, a precedent

which was widely followed in the city. Santa Ana (about 1553) had the same features, and likewise the Espíritu Santo built some twenty years later. The nave in these later churches, however, had paneled wooden ceilings, whereas the rudimentary pitched roof appears to have been used in the cathedral. The same type of church without lateral chapels continued well along into the seventeenth century, as, for example, in the church of Santa Catalina (1624). A slight modification, in that the crossing as well as the sanctuary was vaulted, took place in the Encarnación (1562), the Concepción (1573), and El Belén (1606). Other single-naved churches of the sixteenth century apparently had the wooden roof throughout: San Pedro, Santos Cosmé y Damián, and later in 1604, Santa Clara.

The Spanish prototypes for these churches are to be found in Andalusia, where the single nave covered by a wooden ceiling is characteristic of the fourteenth, fifteenth, and sixteenth centuries. Frequently the apse alone was vaulted, just as in the parish and conventual churches of Lima. Late examples in Seville, like Santa Paula, Santa Clara, and San Clemente, which were reconstructed in the fifteenth and sixteenth centuries, approximate these first religious edifices in the Peruvian capital. The sixteenth-century churches of Granada also belong to the same tradition.

The basilican type, composed of nave and two side aisles, and covered by wooden ceilings of *mudéjar* interlaces, was introduced to Lima from Andalusia by the Dominicans, Franciscans, and Augustinians. The Andalusian models are so numerous that only a few, such as Omnium Sanctorum, San Lorenzo, and San Andrés in Seville, need be cited.[4] The Dominicans apparently anticipated the other orders when they began their large new church in Lima *circa* 1540–1552. It was followed by those of the Franciscans in 1555 and the Augustinians in 1574.

The Mercedarians' church, begun in 1542, had a floor plan derived from late-Gothic Isabellan models of Castile and a paneled wooden ceiling of the Andalusian school. This particular combination, judging by Padre Cobo's description, seems to have been followed in San Sebastián, a church for which Francisco Becerra drew plans in 1585.

Meanwhile, an ambitious scheme for a great vaulted cathedral of basilican type, to equal the best of Spain, was proposed in 1565. The matter dragged on ineffectually for more than a quarter century. Francisco Becerra's plans of 1582–1584 came to naught until the viceroy, Luis de Velasco, instructed Becerra to reduce the size of the project. Shortly the church begun in 1598 was half finished, and ready for dedication six years later.

This church was the first completely vaulted structure known to us in Lima. It had groined vaults and pointed arches, an unusual type of construction which was not repeated. The rectangular floor plan (Figs. 7, 8), the hall type of church with nave and aisles of equal height, and the pier construction were, however, repeated in Cuzco Cathedral (Figs. 65, 91). This fact seems sufficient proof that the plans of both churches are based upon Becerra's original projects of 1582. Both structures underwent numerous modifications, but they maintained in common the features mentioned, and they have no exact duplicates anywhere in the world. The rectangular plan, as explained elsewhere, is derived from sixteenth-century Spanish architecture, probably from the cathedral of Jaén. The pier construction with large entablature block is an offshoot of the Andalusian school, originating in Diego Silóee's cathedral of Granada.

With the severe damage done the brick groined vaults of Lima Cathedral in the earthquakes of 1606 and 1609, a council of architects was called to consider what course should be followed in the reconstruction. The decision was reached to reduce the height of the piers and to replace the groined vaults with ribbed Gothic vaults of brick. Vázquez de Espinosa, who lived in Lima in 1619–1620, describes this new church of 1613–1622, mentioning the Gothic vaults and Ionic piers. Hence it is certain that in the rebuilding of the edifice in wood and plaster (1751–1755), because of the devastation caused by the earthquake of 1746, they faithfully reproduced the ruined church. In this state the cathedral exists today.

The adoption of the Gothic vault in 1613 was a matter of constructive expediency and not a question of stylistic preference, for the Gothic had long since become outmoded in favor of the Renaissance barrel vault. Unfortunately, nobody thought of suggesting a paneled wooden ceiling of Renaissance type or a *mudéjar* ceiling, both of which were employed extensively in Lima in the sixteenth and early seventeenth centuries. Aesthetically such a solution would have been highly satisfactory for the cathedral, and for Lima in general. It would also have been the best adaptation to a region subject to repeated earthquakes. Instead, imitation barrel vaults of wood or of cane and plaster became the rule throughout *limeño* churches from the mid-seventeenth century thereafter. Today every church in Lima has imitation vaulting and the effect is in most cases highly unsatisfactory.

The turn to completely vaulted churches at the start of the seventeenth century was short-lived by necessity. It included the cathedral, the Dominican Recoleta (1611), San Ildefonso (1612), La Trinidad (1614), San Pedro (1624), and La Merced (1628). The nave vault of Santo Domingo is only a copy in wood and plaster of those of the cathedral, having been reconstructed in 1660–1666 (see Appendix). The new basilican church of the Merced (1628) had ribbed Gothic vaults throughout. San Pedro, however, represented a strange combination of Gothic vaults in the nave and cupolas in the aisles. The cupolas were to have a profound effect all over Peru, being adopted in the new church of San Francisco (1657), in the rebuilding of La Merced after the earthquake of 1687, and passing far afield to Arequipa and Trujillo.

Gothic vaults in Lima ran their course in the first three decades of the century, and a definite and distinct change appeared in the new church of San Francisco (1657–1673). The vaults (Fig. 92) were then constructed of cane and plaster, and thenceforth appeared no serious attempt to use heavier construction on a large scale. These vaults of San Francisco are the oldest in Lima, having withstood numerous earthquakes. The nave has a barrel vault, but the aisles, following the innovation of San Pedro, are covered with cupolas. No less important than the construction is the *mudéjar* plaster work of extraordinary richness and invention which decorates vaults and pilasters. The *mudéjar* ornamentation has precedent in the Compañía at Quito (1605–1616). There, however, the star designs, interlaces, and chain patterns are cut in stone upon the piers with plaster only on the upper walls and vaults. At Quito an indescribably sensuous beauty is produced by the gilded patterns in relief against a red background; here the oriental sumptuousness of the Alhambra lives again in the New World. At Lima the color is lacking. The walls are whitewashed, and the geometric patterns do not invest the entire surface. Indeed, the chapels and piers are finished like rusticated stone, done in plaster over a brick core. It appears highly doubtful that the interior of San Francisco at Lima followed the fashion set by that great masterpiece of Hispanic American architecture, the Jesuit church at Quito. The case could be argued in the affirmative, due to the similarity of floor plans, the use of cupolas in the aisles, as well as the *mudéjar* designs on the wall surfaces. The plan, however, already existed in San Pedro at Lima. The ornamental motives in Lima are not identical with those employed in Quito. More probably the style came independently from Spain, where similar decoration is encountered on the interiors of Andalusian churches, for example, San Lucas at Jerez de la Frontera, and Nuestra Señora de la Angustias at Granada. Comparable effects also occur in the contemporary façade of San Miguel at Jerez (1672).[5] Here is more evidence of the constant influence of Andalusian art upon that of colonial Lima.

The basilican floor plan with single sanctuary, dome over the crossing, and the aisles covered by cupolas (Fig. 9), was introduced by the Jesuits in San Pedro (1624). They derived it from the Compañía of Quito, begun in 1605, even though they possessed a model of the Casa Profesa at Rome, as explained on pages 17, 18. The Mercedarians adopted the same ground plan for their new church in 1628 and the Franciscans in 1657 (Fig. 10).

The new church of San Francisco provided the model for the rebuilding of the Merced, after it fell in ruins during the earthquake of 1687. The basilican plan of the brick church of 1628 was retained, but the ribbed Gothic vaults were replaced by a construction of cane and plaster (Fig. 93) in imitation of the Franciscan edifice. The aisles follow the prototype closely in the use of domes, in the pronounced rustication of the walls in a plaster imitation of stone masonry, and even in the lunettes over the arches. The nave too has a barrel vault and rusticated piers with the *mudéjar* ornament limited in this case to the pilasters and transverse arches. The Mercedari-

ans used the ornament much more sparingly than the Franciscans. They employed as the chief decorative device a chain consisting of rectangle and ellipse in alternation, a motive which is found in identical form on the portal of the Compañía in Granada, and in the chapel of the Archiepiscopal Palace at La Zubia, a suburb of the same city.[6]

The nave vaults, many times rebuilt, at present have no decoration, whereas, on the contrary, the aisles and the elliptical dome of the choir contain geometricized leaves in relief. This large elliptical dome over the first bay of the raised choir provides an unusual and impressive architectural feature as well as allowing for an interesting play of light. The ellipse also indicates the turn of the new century in which the church was reconstructed (1688–1706). Trefoil arches cut across the angle of each arm of the transept. This is an extraordinary arrangement not found in San Francisco, although the *mudéjar* trefoil in itself is so widespread as to be almost commonplace in colonial art.

San Francisco and the Merced have a relation to each other similar to that between the Compañía and the Merced at Quito, that of innovator and follower. It may be, as previously stated, that the *mudéjar* interior traveled from Quito to Lima, but I believe, because of stylistic differences, that both were imported independently from Andalusia.

The normal type of seventeenth-century interior with plain vaults, Doric pilasters, and molded cornice, like San Francisco and San Pedro at Cuzco, certainly existed in many churches of Lima. The restored interiors of the chapel of the Vera Cruz (about 1613), attached to Santo Domingo, and Nuestra Señora de Montserrat belong to this group, although nearly all others have been destroyed.

As the eighteenth century advanced in Lima, new styles appeared, leaving San Francisco and La Merced without followers. It may be, however, the result of the *mudéjar* spirit which led to the decoration of the aisles of San Pedro (Fig. 94) with gilded wooden panels, carved in flowing arabesques. The patterns themselves are not *mudéjar*, but the taste for allover ornament is, as well as the revetment of glazed Sevillian tiles. The date of this lovely decoration is subsequent to the earthquake of 1687. Similar arabesques, although in stucco, appear beside the transept windows of the Compañía at Pisco (1678–1728), and on the walls of the stairway in the cloister of the Seminario de Santo Toribio in Lima. The precedent of the Merced, nevertheless, explains the use of a geometric pattern in the clerestory of the church of the Carmen.

The new churches of the eighteenth century in Lima were for the most part of the nunnery type, small and of single nave. The exception is the basilican San Francisco de Paula Nuevo, a mediocre and unfinished structure (1748–1814), which presented no innovations. Jesús María (1698–1721), too, might have been built in the preceding century, so far as the design of the interior is concerned, for it has traditional Doric pilasters with molded cornice and barrel vault. The shell tympanum within the main portal and the retables, however, manifest its later period.

At the very start of the new century (1704–1708) the nuns' church, Santa Rosa de las Monjas, introduced a new feature in the dentelated cornice, which has a large bracket in the center of each bay. An unusual arrangement occurs in the termination of the wall pilasters halfway to the floor. The placing of a decorative bracket midway between the pilasters in a molded cornice became a characteristic feature of *limeño* architecture in the eighteenth century (Fig. 95), appearing in San Carlos and the Corazón de Jesús (both dated 1758–1766) and in the churches of the Carmen and the Virgin of Copacabana. The latter were rebuilt subsequent to the earthquake of 1746. The bracketed cornice without pilasters found favor in the sacristy of San Agustín and in the small chapel which adjoins the sacristy of San Francisco. The bracket seems to have reached the height of its popularity in the mid-century. It traveled up the coast to Trujillo, which always followed in Lima's footsteps, and there put in an appearance in Santa Rosa (1758–1777) and in Santa Teresa (about 1759). A somewhat monumental variant of the *limeño* bracket was developed in San Antonio at Cajamarca (Fig. 183) where the cornice projects deeply above it. Arequipa, occasionally an artistic disciple of Lima in the colonial period, adopted the dentelated cornice with bracket in the rebuilding of Santo Domingo after the earthquake of 1784.

Another interesting use of the bracket

occurs in Las Trinitarias (1722), where it replaces the usual pilasters below each of the transverse ribs of the nave and also terminates the ribs of the dome. Las Trinitarias is one of the most complete representatives of the eighteenth century in Lima and a more important architectural monument than is generally realized. This substitution of the bracket for the pilaster had a follower in the church of Magdalena la Vieja, and also far off in the northern sierra in the cathedral (Fig. 181) of Cajamarca (1686–1762).

A fine small interior of different sort is that of the chapel of the Virgen del Patrocinio (1734). It has a large dome over the sanctuary instead of the crossing. This scheme was a favorite in nunneries. Good examples of it in the seventeenth century are the churches of Santa Clara (Fig. 59), Santa Catalina, and Santa Teresa (Fig. 60), all of them in Cuzco. Later the type was followed in Bolivia in Santa Teresa (1753–1790) at Cochabamba and in the Oratorian church of San Felipe Neri at Sucre (1795). The interior of the Patrocinio at Lima is sober and good in scale, with a large dentelated cornice adding to its dignity.

An elliptical floor plan set within a rectangle, something entirely new to Lima, was introduced in the Corazón de Jesús (Fig. 18), also known as the Huérfanos. The main portal and sanctuary occupy the short ends of a rather elongated ellipse. To the right are chapels and sacristy. The rococo spirit of the period (1758–1766) prevails in the ornament throughout the church and in the reversed curves which constitute the outline of the choir. The shell tympana in the doorways and in the baptistry (Fig. 96) add a charmingly gay decorative note. Mention has been previously made of the corbeled cornice, so characteristic of *limeño* architecture of the time.

As for the elliptical plan, it is common enough in Italy during the seventeenth century, whereas in Spain its use is less widespread. Among the few examples there which can be cited are the Bernardas at Alcalá de Henares and the Desemparados at Valencia. In the mid-eighteenth century a general trend toward circular and elliptical plans is apparent: San Marcos, Madrid; the chapel of Nuestra Señora del Pilar, Saragossa Cathedral; Agustinos, Valladolid; San Francisco, Madrid, and others.[7] To this phase of Hispanic architecture the Corazón de Jesús of Lima adheres. Elsewhere in the New World too the elliptical building was occasionally adopted. Fairly close parallels to the plan used in Lima are those of Santa Brígida (1740–1745) in Mexico City, recently demolished, and the Hospicio at San Vicente (1765) in Salvador.[8] At Cochabamba in Bolivia the Carmelites started out to build a structure of the same type, but changed it into a conventional single nave (1753–1790).

The one complete rococo monument of Lima is Santo Cristo de los Milagros (Las Nazarenas) erected in 1766–1771, and, if we are to believe the inscription upon the viceroy Amat's portrait within the convent, he was the architect. Recent investigations have revealed Amat's extensive activity as a military engineer.[9] To what extent he practiced architecture has yet to be established. That he donated funds for the new church, and took a direct interest in the project cannot be doubted. French taste, introduced to Spain by Philip V and his court, spread throughout the Spanish colonies in the second quarter of the eighteenth century. The popular legend that Amat himself introduced the rococo to Peru is utterly without foundation, since he did not arrive in Lima until 1761, well after the style had been adopted there.

The main feature of the church of the Milagros (Fig. 97) is the large dome over the crossing preceded by a short nave of two bays. An interior narthex lies beneath the elevated choir, attached to a centralized plan. The walls of brick and plaster are divided inside into bays by Corinthian half columns and the effect of marble is simulated throughout in grayish paint. Here for once the marbleized treatment has been handled tastefully and is not offensive. The same fashion prevails in the high altar which is related in design to the interior as a whole. We meet for the first time a complete break with the ancient Hispanic tradition of gilded wood sculpture, a glorious tradition which was never to rise again. Throughout the church the rococo details are charming: the hoods over the four small doors in the crossing, the ornament of the niches, and the altars of the nave. Moldings in all cases are gilded, as usual in rococo works. Very effective is the handling of the numerous reversed curves in the façade of the raised choir. The interior of Santo Cristo de los Milagros has unity, every detail being planned as part of the whole composition, even the altars,

and the fine bulging pulpit (Fig. 304). Contrary to all else the wooden grilles (Fig. 98) of the sanctuary and choir betray their Hispanicism in retaining *mudéjar* patterns but with a rococo sauce in the *rocaille* motives of the tympana. Santo Cristo de los Milagros is the epilogue of colonial architecture in Lima. It was followed by the Neoclassicism of Matías Maestro. He destroyed and restored to make way for his own academic works, which are at times more redolent of the French Empire than of true Neoclassicism. Because of his activity and the taste of his day the leading churches of Lima were stripped of their Baroque retables. Thanks to Matías Maestro, much of the colonial grandeur of Lima has been lost forever.

SACRISTIES

THE sacristy of Lima Cathedral is the oldest of the city, having originated surely in the early seventeenth century. The rectangular room, much smaller than the sacristies of the chief monastic orders, has a barrel vault, Doric pilasters, and a cornice the frieze of which is decorated with rosettes. Whether Becerra's design of 1598 still remains here is a moot question, but the Renaissance character is evident. The most notable feature of the sacristy, however, is the fine series of apostles (Fig. 309) carved in wood by Martínez de Arrona in 1608.

Among the best monuments of colonial Lima are the ante-sacristy and sacristy of San Agustín. The original contract for the work, dated 1643, has recently been published in full by Alberto Santibáñez Salcedo. The ante-sacristy preserves its magnificent coffered ceiling of wood, superbly worked, as was usual in the period. The sculptor, named Diego de Medina, also made the ceiling of the sacristy, now lost, and the statuettes (1643–1651), which are still extant (Fig. 333). The ante-sacristy with its lovely dado of glazed tiles is in the main a splendid work of the mid-seventeenth century. Modifications were introduced a hundred years later in the form of the shell tympana over the doors and windows. The sacristy itself fell into ruins in the earthquake of 1746, and it was rebuilt with a barrel-vaulted ceiling of cane and plaster which rises from a cornice decorated with corbels in typical *limeño* style of the period. The vault collapsed again in 1940, and underwent reconstruction with conscientious exactitude immediately thereafter.

The sacristy of San Pedro (Fig. 99), like all of the others under discussion, is a rectangular room of good size. The wooden ceiling by exception is flat, and is covered by three long rows of octagonal paintings. A large array of pictures lines the walls, set in tabernacle-like frames of gilded wood. These frames take on architectural significance by virtue of their size and permanence. In the wood carving of filigree and arabesque lies the glory of the sacristy of San Pedro, lavish and luxurious, one of the high lights of Lima. If anyone doubts the splendor of colonial Peru, its fabulous wealth, and its unlimited cultural aspirations, he need but tarry a moment here, and reflect. The style suggests a date

in the turn of the century, contemporary with the carved and gilded decorations in the aisles of the church. Prominent are the long stylized leaves like those which decorate the façade of the Merced (1697–1704).

A bronze plaque near the entrance of the sacristy of San Francisco bears a legend which divulges the year of its erection in 1729. The portal has the name of the architect, Lucas Meléndez, carved in the upper regions. A ponderous example of late architectural Baroque with heavy projections, it also includes foliate and scroll ornamentation related to the interior of the sacristy. The sacristy proper, broad, high, and barrel vaulted (21 × 10 meters), consciously maintains the style of the church, built more than fifty years previously. Florid plaster work characterizes the vault, in which scrolls and arabesques play a prominent part. Few of the strictly *mudéjar* motives, so strikingly significant in the church, recur here. Thus the span of time is betrayed. The magnificent large shell tympana of doors and niches clearly indicate the eighteenth century, as likewise do the small gilded retables. The tiny domed chapel which adjoins the sacristy has unadorned walls and a corbeled cornice which belong completely to the style of the eighteenth century. Here the relative anachronisms of the main hall are missing.

The sacristy of San Francisco, spacious and imposing, fittingly climaxes the *limeño* series. La Merced provides the epilogue, a joyous bit of rococo, dating from 1773–1776, and notable especially for its delightful set of chests and cupboards with their panels of Frenchified paintings on glass. The tiny Islamic domes which provide the roofing to this small room are the most interesting feature from the strictly architectural angle. They are another case of the unexpected in colonial art, appearing to date originally from 1765–1768. They were reconstructed in 1912 without the original *mudéjar* ornament.

CHAPTER HOUSES

CHAPTER houses of the leading monastic orders have in most cases little architectural interest, being significant instead for their furnishings. The room is normally long and narrow with a tribune at one end and an altar at the opposite end, occasionally enlarged as at San Francisco into a chapel. The chapter house of San Agustín has simple Gothic vaults which, along with the simplicity of the room, support the belief that it is the room mentioned by Calancha.[10] Hence it is to be dated in the late sixteenth or early seventeenth century. The ledge of seats and the continuous uprights against the wall, with good but unpretentious wood carving, must have originated at that period. Paintings set in the end wall bear the date 1657, and the superb tribune beneath them is mentioned in the *Libro de Gastos* about 1670.

The chapter house of San Francisco (Fig. 101) has lost its original vaults, but is otherwise well preserved and contemporary with the new church and monastery, erected in the third quarter of the seventeenth century. Two rows of seats, like upper and lower choir stalls, which run the full length of the hall are crisply carved with scale and tongue motives, and the upper row carries Doric colonnettes. A narrow chapel with tile dado and tile altar frontal contains a small salomonic retable of the early eighteenth century. The masterpiece, however, is the superb tribune. The ornament is gilded against a red background, and a splendid relief in the lunette represents St. Anthony of Padua's Vision of the Madonna. The arabesque upon the Corinthian columns are beautifully designed and cut, while the pilasters in the upper section have the peculiar bracket capitals which are also found on Manuel de Escobar's side portal of the church. The decoration of the hall is completed by a row of paintings of Franciscan saints set in gilded frames against the upper wall. The original vaulting has been replaced by a plain modern ceiling of wood.

The chapter house of Santo Domingo (Fig. 100) marks the high point of the *limeño* group in a broad and lofty hall roofed with a large barrel vault of cane and plaster. Huge long brackets replace the usual pilasters, and produce a striking and rather bizarre effect. Paintings on the walls, the massive tribune, the prior's throne and the friars' seats are worked into one unified scheme, magnificently integrated. Rusticated plaster enframement is provided for doorways and niches which are topped by crisp and decorative shell tympana. Unity is attained with superb balance and good taste on a definitely luxurious scale. No better wood carving is to be found in Lima than on the grandiose tribune or in the strictly *mudéjar* balcony of the viceroy which hangs aloft above the main portal. Here the colonial City of the Kings put forth its best about the year 1730.

PORTALS

THE earliest portal in Lima appears to be that of the chapel of La Vera Cruz, attached to Santo Domingo. The work of Diego Guillén in 1613, its original composition as shown in Meléndez's print (Fig. 102) has escaped modification in several rehabilitations.[11] The sober classicism with one broken pediment is exactly what would be expected in the Spanish colonies. In the mother country itself the late Renaissance of Herrera was still the prevailing style. The side entrance of Santo Domingo cannot be far removed in date. About a decade later is the façade of San Agustín at Saña (Fig. 167). To the same period belongs the first story in the central section of the cathedral façade (Figs. 103–105), begun in 1626 after the design of Juan Martínez de Arrona. It still retains the main features of the original, despite repeated restorations, as can be seen by a comparison with the architect's drawing which was discovered and published by Harth-terré. The Renaissance is dominant in the giant Corinthian columns and the triumphal-arch motive, but the niches with their broken pediments and moldings herald the Baroque style. In the drawing, however, the entablature does not break forth over the columns, as it does in the present structure. Details of ornament and the carved frieze are also missing in the sketch.

The second story, dated 1722 by inscription, harmonizes extremely well with the older section. That is achieved to a great extent by the repetition of a similar entablature in both stories, replacing the more severe classical design of 1626. The rustication of wall and pilasters fits satisfactorily into the whole composition, as does the conservative Baroque handling of the central section. This main portal of the façade is the best architectural feature of Lima Cathedral in its present-day status.

In the field of domestic architecture the portal of the house, known as the Casa de Pilatos, is the one important survivor of the first half of the seventeenth century. Its dignified early Baroque composition is indeed admirable. The balcony and window are modern, and the interior of the house throughout has been considerably reconstructed.

San Francisco provides the best architecture of seventeenth-century Lima. The entrance of the monastery and the façades of the church and the chapel of the Soledad, all belong to the time of Luis de Cervela (1669–1674) and are visible in an engraving of 1673, published by Suárez de Figueroa. The first of these is broad with trefoil portal flanked by large windows which are covered by a flat arch and filled with iron grilles. The rusticated wall surfaces and the *mudéjar* latticework of the frieze correspond exactly to the style of the church interior. Oval windows which were to become very popular in Lima make their first securely dated appearance here in the second story and in the cloister. They were probably antedated, however, by the oval openings in the main cloister of Santo Domingo. The problem is discussed in the section devoted to cloisters in this chapter. Another interesting detail is the large volute capital used on the pilasters of the central section of the monastery entrance of San Francisco. It turns up again in the lateral portal of the church, dedicated to St. Louis of Toulouse, which has the date 1674 and the name of Manuel de Escobar cut in the spandrels. This type of capital was adopted by architects of the following century to the extent that it became a signature of *limeño* buildings.

The monastery entrance of San Francisco constitutes a felicitous union of *mudéjar* and Baroque elements resulting in an original composition which is almost symbolic of colonial Lima. The pronounced pyramids which space the windows and load the pilasters seem like a throwback to the days of Herrera, a hundred years before. The same pinnacles, in larger scale, load the buttresses of the church and rise starkly against the skyline.

The side portal of San Francisco (Fig. 106), as already stated, bears the date 1674 and the name of the well-known architect, Manuel de Escobar. Despite the volute capitals and the half-disk ornament on the pilasters, like those of the upper center of the monastery entrance, the two works are very unlike in style. The latter, due to its homogeneity with the church, may be from the design of the first architect, Constantino de Vasconcelos. Escobar's portal introduces ponderous but effective Baroque masses which are constructed in four deep planes as the entablatures break

from the center sidewise and in depth toward the wall. Although the Tuscan order and comparatively undecorated surfaces are sober in themselves, the composition as a whole carries a sonorous Baroque forcefulness. Here is the germ from which developed the later and more lavish portals, such as that of the sacristy of San Francisco and the chapel of the Carmen in the Descalzos. A detail which Escobar started upon a notable new career is the crisp shell of the central niche and of the side lunettes. It turns up again and again in *limeño* architecture of the eighteenth century, especially in doorways.

The façade of the chapel of the Soledad, a member of the Franciscan group, catches the eye because of the unusual handling of the rustication in large oval shapes, combined with more conventional horizontal bands. Oval windows as well bring the composition into relation with the monastery entrance nearby. The modification of the central part of the façade and the towers took place under the hands of the Neoclassicists of 1815. Both the difference in style and the documentary evidence of the engraving published by Suárez de Figueroa prove the fact.

One other portal in Lima, related in style to San Francisco, is that of Nuestra Señora del Prado. It is doubtful that it corresponds to any of the three portals designed by Juan de Aldana in 1638, since the description of them does not seem to apply. Stylistically, the use of brick and plaster with rusticated pilasters and frieze, and the prominent ovals of the spandrels and sides connect it with the Soledad. At present disfigured by the modern wooden frame and balustrade at the niche, the Prado portal is, nevertheless, discreet and excellent in scale, the work of a first-rate architect, apparently of the third quarter of the seventeenth century. It might, on the other hand, have been completed by the time the church was inaugurated in 1640. That possibility seems unlikely, for in that case the Prado portal would be a forerunner rather than a follower of the style which triumphed in San Francisco.

The main façade of San Francisco (Figs. 107–109) is by far the most important of seventeenth-century Lima (1669–1674). Materials are brick and plaster treated to imitate rusticated courses of stone, and at present painted gray with moldings, architraves, and cornices in white to afford contrast. Proportions are broad and massive, but instead of creating an impression of power and monumentality the effect is overweighted and clumsy. The composition lacks scale, and suffers very distinctly in comparison with a contemporary façade, such as that of the Compañía in Cuzco. In the latter case, relations of the whole composition are beautifully integrated, whereas in San Francisco at Lima the portal is dwarfed by the excessive breadth of the structure and the ponderously large towers. These faults must have originated in the façade of San Agustín, as first projected by José de la Sida whose name with the date 1637 is inscribed in the base of the left tower. Although the present portal is dated 1720, the bases of the colossal two-storied towers establish the proportions of the structure, leaving no doubt that San Agustín was the prototype of San Francisco.

The portal itself, on the contrary, is one of the most interesting works of colonial Peru. Of stone, unlike the rest of the structure, it has a yellowish color as the result of numerous coats of paint, a fact which does not interfere with its effectiveness. Suárez de Figueroa's description of the main portal in 1674 and the engraving in his book establish without any doubt the date of the present work. Mugaburu states that portals and towers were still incomplete in 1672.[12] Its exact contemporary, the side portal, which bears an inscription with the year 1674 and the name of the architect, Manuel de Escobar, differs so strikingly in style as to suggest that another man, probably a sculptor, was the author of the principal entrance. To be sure, the two portals have a few details in common: the extremely calligraphic shell niches, the pilasters with volute capitals, and the half-disk ornament on the pilasters.

The concept of the main portal is not architectural, however, but sculptural in its extensive application of surface ornament. The pictorial handling of the masses, with pronounced projections of moldings, broken cornices, and the constant movement throughout which makes the eye dance fitfully hither and yon, give it an advanced Baroque character which anticipates the developments of the eighteenth century. It has been suggested that the very top constitutes a modification of the latter period because of the almost rococo rhythms of cornices and lunettes. This suggestion cannot be accepted. The webbed volutes are also present in retables and on the façade of the Compañía at Cuzco (Fig. 64) in the third quarter of the seventeenth century. The main portal of San Francisco is in reality a retable like those of gilded wood, translated into stone, and viewed in that light its style is homogeneous and consistent with its date (1672–1674). Lima has lost nearly all of her retables of that period, but other cities have many, for instance, the altars of the Compañía of Cuzco and that of Santa Teresa (1675) in the same city. The retable of the Immaculate Conception (Fig. 324) in Lima Cathedral itself has the same decorative details as the portal to such a degree that it must be either by the same sculptor or derived from the portal. This retable was reconstructed by the famous *retablero,* Diego de Aguirre, in 1692–1696, according to a document mentioned by Harth-terré.[13] Unfortunately none of the other retables of the artist is preserved so that it is difficult to determine on stylistic grounds to what extent he remodeled the retable of the Immaculate Conception or whether it is almost entirely his own creation. Both the Franciscan portal and the retable have the same columns: a spiral base, the fluted shaft decorated with draped female heads and swags of cloth containing flowers and fruit, and at the top Corinthian capitals. The frieze also includes the draped female head. These combined with swags may justly be termed choir-stall themes, since they are found among the ornament of all of the principal stalls of Peru in the seventeenth century. They first occur in the choir of Lima Cathedral which was de-

signed by Pedro de Noguera in 1623. One other instance of their use in a monumental way on the façade of a church is that of Santa Lucía (Fig. 175) in Ferreñafe (1690).

Figure sculpture is restricted to the statue of the Virgin of the Immaculate Conception in the upper center accompanied by kneeling figures of St. Francis and St. Dominic. The Hispanic taste for surface patterns reveals itself in the panels of arabesque on the base, the jambs, and intrados of the arches, as well as the spiral and zigzag bases of the columns.

The portal of San Francisco is the first important retable façade of Lima, and one which possesses great originality in its design as a whole, as well as in the ingenious manipulation of its multiple ornamental devices. Baroque unity is manifest in the swelling crescendo which rises to the statue of the Madonna through the upward curve of the broken pediment to the central niche. It finishes off at the top with a flourish of volutes and lunettes, and is brought to a quiet conclusion by the oval window and the final curve of the gable overhead. The presence of figure sculpture, as well as relief ornament, helps to produce an effect of richness which makes San Francisco the forerunner of the salomonic façades of the eighteenth century.

Lima's churches in this latter period which brought the colonial era to a close are small in scale, and the façades constitute a homogeneous school of late architectural Baroque. The exceptions were provided by the two great monastic orders, the Augustinians and Mercedarians, whose large and magnificent churches suffered almost complete destruction in the earthquake of 1687, and were rebuilt with lavish "Churrigueresque" façades. The latter term is generally used in Hispanic lands to describe retables and decoration of late Baroque style in which spiral (salomonic) columns play a predominant role. This style began about 1650, and reached its climax *circa* 1690–1740. The Spanish usage of the word "salomonic," which is employed to signify the twisted or spiral column, has been adopted in this book, because it is specific and useful in writing. The word is explained by the legend that a spiral column in St. Peter's came from Solomon's temple.

The façade of the Merced (Fig. 110) was the first of its type in Lima, dating from 1697–1704. Demolished at the beginning of the present century, it was reproduced in replica in 1940, under the direction of Harth-terré.[14] This modern copy follows the original, as known in old photographs, with painstaking accuracy. Slight modifications were made in the cornices of the top story and in the central niche. The carving itself is hard and mechanical, lacking the beauty of touch and exquisite quality of original works like the façades of Cajamarca. Saints in niches and paired spiral columns entwined with vines and bunches of grapes, make of the Merced façade a true retable translated into stone. The arrangement of the rectangular Hispanic frames over the doorway and central niche introduces a discordant note in the otherwise flowing melodious style, an observation which can better be understood by comparison with the façade of San Agustín where the gables do not exist. Both monuments strike one as strangers who have penetrated within the walls of Lima. The façade is carved in gray stone with cornices and moldings painted rose.

San Agustín, like the Merced, was laid waste in the great earthquake of 1687. The new portal (Fig. 111), dated 1720 by inscription, is the only original work of its type in central Peru. In the restorations of 1903–1908 the statues were drastically modified and the decorative sculpture recut, so that much of the quality of the carving has been lost. A heavy coat of gray paint and some use of plaster also mask the richness and freshness which the surface of the stone itself would convey. The oval window and broken Baroque cornices at the top were replaced by the present round window, and by a new small story surmounted by a continuous molding. Thus the builders of the neo-Romanesque interior sacrificed stylistic consistency. The façade remains, nonetheless, a very effective work.

The central niche above the doorway in which stands a large statue of St. Augustine is the iconographic and compositional focus of the façade. The broken cornices above the entrance carry the eye upward, and the progressive diminution of the height of the stories combines to bring the work into Baroque unity. The sculpture is a filigree of exquisite lace which envelops the entire wall. Spiral columns, draped with vines and bunches of grapes, and ringed in the lower section, flank the niches, both major and minor. The niches themselves have shell tympana, crowned by fantastic architectural fragments. In the third story, originally the last, are pilasters with bust-length caryatids which turn at the waist into long plumelike frills. The frieze in the entablatures is cut with heads and arabesques. One strong touch of local idiom is the *mudéjar* chain pattern on the jambs and archivolt of the doorway, an unmistakable reminiscence of San Francisco's decorative repertory.

The original portal of San Agustín was a noteworthy work of colonial Peru, and it still is, in spite of the added top story and the recutting of the sculpture. Its design is immeasurably superior to that of the Merced which we know in photographs and in the modern replica. The only similar works in Peru which surpass it are the three churches of Cajamarca (Figs. 177–187) whose remoteness has spared them the hand of the modern restorer. It is not fitting to classify San Agustín with the façades of Arequipa and the Titicaca region, since they represent the indigenous interpretation of the Hispanic retable façade, and constitute a separate and a distinctive style in themselves.

San Agustín is now towerless, but the huge bases remain, the left of which has an inscription with the name of the architect, José de la Sida, and the date 1637. The huge belfry above fell victim to the restorers of 1903 and is known only in photographs which, however, give an excellent idea of its style.[15] The volute capitals of the pilasters as well as the cane and plaster materials suggest that it was rebuilt after the earthquake of 1687. The interesting fact about this façade is that its proportions with two colossal towers overshadowing the portal are exactly like those of San Francisco (Fig. 108). Moreover, the date 1637 proves that José de la Sida first introduced this heavy ungainly composition to Lima, and that of San Francisco (1657–1674) is the follower, not the originator.

Lamentable as the restorations of the early twentieth century were, matters would have been even worse, had the façade of San Agustín been crowned with a central tempietto flanked by domes, as the architect then proposed. His design, published in 1908, never saw fulfillment, thanks to the good fortune that funds were lacking.[16]

The great and devastating earthquakes of 1687 and 1746 brought such widespread destruction to Lima that little save San Francisco, prior to the eighteenth century, has survived. Hence ecclesiastical architecture of Lima is predominantly of this later period. Notable are the numerous façades of small churches which constitute a uniform and original school. Persistent features are the two small towers which flank the façade. Santa Rosa de las Monjas (1704–1708) and Nuestra Señora de Copacabana (1700) are early in the development. In both the small belfries are decorated with pilasters which have volute capitals. The tall slender bases upon which the belfries stand are faced with colossal pilasters. The same arrangement prevailed in the destroyed church of the Caridad and in the recently cement-surfaced Nuestra Señora de Cocharcas (1777). The belfries are simplified and rather ugly in the cases of Las

Trinitarias (1722) and the Patrocinio (1734).

Very charming and beautifully designed were those of the destroyed façade of San Marcelo and of Santa Teresa (Figs. 115, 116), a precious work which, likewise, has been demolished (1946). In these two cases the belfries rested upon a plain undecorated wall beneath. The general style falls into the first half of the eighteenth century.

Occasionally a wooden balustrade surrounds the belfries as in Nuestra Señora de Cocharcas, La Compañía at Pisco (Fig. 117), San José at Nazca (Fig. 118), and the destroyed façades of San Marcelo and La Caridad at Lima. These towers are not limited to coastal Peru alone, but are found as far south as Concepción in Chile. A drawing for the cathedral of Concepción is interesting not only in its stylistic relationship to the school of Lima, but likewise in its corroborative date of 1744.[17]

A simplification in design, which includes an abandonment of volute capitals and domed turrets in favor of molded pilasters and flattened roofing, sets in with the second half of the century in San Carlos (1758–1766) (Fig. 114) and Santo Cristo de los Milagros (1766–1771). The results are dull and uninteresting, lacking in the charm of their predecessors. Another innovation, unsuccessful and without progeny, was introduced in the Corazón de Jesús in the form of broad heavy octagonal towers. Possibly this might be regarded as a reincarnation on a small scale of the ponderous massiveness which characterizes the façades of San Francisco and of San Agustín.

At the very beginning of the eighteenth-century development is the portal of La Concepción (Fig. 112), dated 1699 and the work of the architect, Diego Pérez de Guzmán.[18] The style of the seventeenth century is still present in the flat *mudéjar*-like ornament of the pilasters and frieze. The new period prevails in the fine shell tympanum in the upper center and in the upward sweep of the broken cornices over the door. These details have a long line of descendants of various types in the eighteenth century, but not often so interestingly manipulated. The curious oblique wall with single tower attached to the side of the church was conditioned by the location of the building on the corner of two narrow streets. The graceful tower, distinguished by volute capitals and cupola, is identical with the belfries of Nuestra Señora de Cocharcas (1777), and hence must be dated in the same period and attributed to the same architect.

Specific variants of the Concepción portal are the two rear entrances of the cathedral (Fig. 113), dated 1732, which display greater simplicity in the elimination of all surface ornament, save rustication. They are also more emphatically architectural in the depth of planes between wall, column, and entablature. Good taste and excellent scale, although with less fantasy than in some of their contemporaries, make them pleasing. A reduction of the cathedral portals and far inferior is that of the Patrocinio (1734) which betrays its model in spite of numerous changes from the prototype, such as the elliptical windows.

Santa Rosa de los Padres, begun in 1676, did not reach completion until 1728, and it was in the later years that the façade must have been built. It represents an intermediate stage between the portals of the Concepción and the cathedral, with the oval window of the choir the most striking variation. This oval window started its career in the monastery entrance of San Francisco (1669–1674). It became virtually a characteristic of *limeño* portals, as well as of her cloisters of which more will be said later. In the eighteenth century the best known examples are the façades of the Trinitarias, Patrocinio, Santa Rosa de los Padres, San Marcelo, Cocharcas, and the parish churches of Surco and Huaura.

The Trinitarias (1722) belongs in the same category as Santa Rosa de los Padres, its many variations notwithstanding. The narrower and more compact composition of the latter is difficult to judge from the point of view of quality because of the destruction of the gable. The second story lacks articulation, however, because of the short heavy pilasters and the shallowness of contrasting planes. Very broad, on the contrary, is the exterior of Nuestra Señora de Cocharcas, the latest edition (1777) in this series of related works.

The entrance to the chapel (1703) of the viceroy's palace, to judge by an old photograph, ranked as one of the most advanced architectural designs of its day. It was destroyed in 1937. Of the same period (1704–1708), but without exact counterpart, is the small portal of Santa Rosa de las Monjas, flanked by Corinthian columns, and notable especially for the lovely shell tympanum over the doorway. The placing of the calligraphic shell in that position is an extension to the exterior of a device very common in eighteenth-century interiors; the one other case of exterior usage being the side entrance, Portada de los Guitarreros, of the Merced, which Padre Barriga dates very late, in 1765–1768.[19] The style, on the contrary, locates it in the first half of the century. The contours of moldings and cornices strike a gay note, abetted by the deep projections of the second story. As usual a narrow vertical border of scrolls enframes the portal at the sides. The original monument, alas, no longer exists. It was dismantled after slight damage in the earthquake of 1940, and replaced by a cement copy which has none of the charm of the colonial work.

The façade of San Marcelo (Fig. 116), recently demolished (1925–1933), reached a climax of eighteenth-century brilliance. Its wide rhythmic portal embodied new variations on familiar themes, as in the four oval cameos on either side of the central niche which in turn was topped by a *limeño* oval window. The proportions of the exterior were perfectly adjusted, characteristic towers giving the final touch of completion.

The masterpiece of the century in Lima was the façade of Santa Teresa (Fig. 115). It was destroyed in 1946, along with its lovely cloister, in order to widen a street. Needless to say, such disregard of the priceless heritage of the past is lamentable; especially in the case of a work which was the very personification of the charm of its epoch. Familiar and typical were the graceful towers, the pilasters with volute capitals, and the lilting melodious flow of the moldings. Unique was the particular composition of them and impeccable the scale and the creative fantasy. The stories diminished in height and breadth from the broad arch and pilasters of the doorway, through the niche above and to the rococo curves of the large window at the top. The volutes and curves were woven by repetition into a rhythmic calligraphic unity. Not the least effective in the picturesque beauty of Santa Teresa was the play of shadows over the walls and niches, like stillness broken by soft music.

A marked change of style appears in the churches of the third quarter of the eighteenth century. It takes the direction of greater sobriety, indicative of more influence of contemporary French art. Two of them, San Carlos (Fig. 114) and El Corazón de Jesús, are exactly contemporary (1758–1766), and the portals similar in disposition. In both cases the first story with simple Doric pilasters and entablature is contrasted with the second story where the curious volute capitals reappear. The broken rococo pediments and the urns on the two churches are nearly identical, but the general composition and detail of San Carlos make it infinitely the superior of the two. The finishing off with small towers makes a very pleasing façade, whereas El Corazón de Jesús's large polygonal towers result in a heavy and ungainly grouping.

The façade of Santo Cristo de los Milagros (1766–1771) breaks with the traditions of Lima in the modified simplicity and rectangularity of the design of the towers and in the entire composition of the portal between them. The breadth of the portal, and the use of two windows in both first and second stories, have no exact analogue. The rococo is less in evidence than within the church, although some of the moldings have that flavor. The use of Corinthian capitals and the curiously close grouping of the half columns and pilasters indicate an unmistakable stylistic relation to the famous tower of Santo Domingo. That fact raises anew the question of the supposed activity of the viceroy Amat as an architect. His portrait which belongs to the nuns of Las Nazarenas states that Amat designed and directed the construction of their church, Santo Cristo de los Milagros. Tradition holds that he also designed the tower of Santo Domingo which was built by the engineer, Juan de la Roca. Although his activity as a military engineer in the fortification of the coast of Peru and Chile has been established, nothing is known of the exact extent to which he engaged in the profession of architect. It may be that he was an interested amateur who made suggestions with a regal sweep of the hand. Flattery to the powerful would easily motivate giving him more credit than was due.

The tower of Santo Domingo (Fig. 119) is grandiose in size, and it virtually dwarfs the church beside it. Except for its three stories and polygonal shape, it bears no relation to the earlier tower as seen in the engraving published by Meléndez.[20] The undecorated first story is succeeded by Ionic columns in the second and Corinthian in the third. The rococo spirit is projected in the small broken curves of the pediments and in the close spacing of the columns. The tower of Santo Domingo is successful as a monument which looms large and imposing over the roof tops of Lima, a memorial to the splendor of her colonial past.

The epilogue of viceregal architecture of Lima included the now demolished portal of the Augustinian Capilla de la Guía (about 1760) which was purely rococo. It was overlaid by cartouches in stucco, much in the manner of retables of the same time. San Francisco de Paula Nuevo (1748–1814) is an academic throwback to the large towered façade of San Francisco. The uninteresting portal is dependent upon the earlier group represented by the rear entrances of the cathedral. The crash came, however, with Matías Maestro and the dull Neoclassic Portada de las Maravillas, a Doric triumphal arch of stucco and imitation marble. It marked the passing of Hispanic colonial architecture.

CLOISTERS

Lima's cloisters are her loveliest ecclesiastical structures of the colonial period, and by good fortune they exist in considerable numbers. The most picturesque and striking are those which have arches of trefoil shape. That these arches were introduced as early as the seventeenth century is unmistakably proven by the print of Santo Domingo (Fig. 102) which Meléndez published in 1681. Trefoil arches in the second cloister can clearly be distinguished. Lizárraga in his description of Santo Domingo (*circa* 1602) says that Salvador de Ribera (1582–1586) finished the cloister and *portería*, indicating that no more than one had yet been erected. Hence the original construction of the second cloister must be placed later in the first half of the seventeenth century, and given a presumed first place in the long line of *mudéjar* patios for which Lima is famous. It has been much restored, and hence lacks the beauty of later structures of the same type. The cloister of the Dominican novitiate, in wretched condition and largely dismantled, also preserves a few trefoil arches. It is impossible to say whether the original work of 1586–1590 had the same design. My belief is that this section and the extremely beautiful second story (Fig. 120) with its handsome domed staircase were reconstructed in the eighteenth century. The corbels and other decorative details point emphatically to that conclusion. The ribbed dome is closely analogous to the one over the crossing of the Trinitarias (1722). Moreover, the materials of wood and plaster were adopted universally in Lima in the eighteenth century, with brick frequently used in the first story. The stone cloisters of the earlier years had to be abandoned because of their unsuitability in this land of earthquakes.

A most enchanting corner of Lima was the cloister of Santa Teresa (Figs. 121, 122), built in 1683–1686 and destroyed in 1946 to widen a street. The trefoil arches had very shallow lobes in this case, and were used only in the first story. The rustication in stucco over a brick core was adroitly designed to make an interesting wall surface and cornice. There were many charming details, such as the oval openings in the corner piers, the lovely shell ornaments, and the slim pilasters pendant on a leaf which filled the spandrels of the arches. The second story of Santa Teresa was of cedar, stained dark brown, with fine *zapata* capitals carrying a horizontal roof. The contrasts between arches below and lintel construction above, between the white stucco and the dark brown wood were highly effective. A balustrade in the upper gallery added to the horizontality and helped to give scale to the composition.

Another patio with trefoil arches in the first story only was that of Espíritu Santo, the second story of which was remodeled in the nineteenth century. The whole structure was destroyed in 1946 to make way for the new basilica of Santa Rosa.

Very common is the contrary arrangement in which trefoil arches occupy the second story and round arches the lower gallery. Santa Rosa de las Monjas (1704–1708) provides a dated example where Doric columns of wood in both stories support this arrangement of the arches. The two inner cloisters of San Agustín, now part of the Augustinian school, also have trefoil arches only in the upper gallery which is manifestly of eighteenth-century design because of the typical corbel in the spandrels of the arches. Both have been miserably restored and covered with cement. That of the Augustinian seminary is unusual because of the projecting points of the lobes.

The very beautiful cloister of San Francisco Solano (1732–1734), now part of the seminary of Santo Toribio, is in ruinous condition, subsequent to the earthquake of 1940.[21] The round arches, the pilasters, and the rustication of the first story are made of stucco over brick, whereas cane and stucco are employed in the upper gallery. Here the graceful trefoil arches separated by corbels suspended on tiny lobed arches rise from small rectangular piers.

The large cloister of the Merced (Fig. 123) with its beautiful garden and picturesque *mudéjar* second story is the most memorable colonial site in Lima, and all the more so since the patio of Santa Teresa has vanished. Luckily the second story is dated by the rebuilding of 1777–1780. Thus it is established as the last of its kind before the Neoclassic invasion. The large trefoil arches alternate with small trefoil arches in a graceful and rhythmic progression, the same arrangement which is so effective in the patio (Fig. 26) of the Torre Tagle Palace (about 1735). Doric columns of cedar marked by an exaggerated entasis, a very common peculiarity of Hispanic colonial architecture, provide the usual contrast of materials in the second story of the Merced. José Gabriel Navarro has stated that both features originated in Quito and thence spread throughout Hispanic America. This claim that the exaggerated entasis first came into existence in the sixteenth century in the cloister of San Francisco (*circa* 1573–1581) at Quito has yet to be proven. Navarro's other assertion which gives priority in the use of alternately large and small arches to San Agustín at Quito, under construction in 1650, must definitely be rejected. The Augustinian cloister of Lima begun in the last quarter of the sixteenth century and described by Calancha (publication of 1638) is at least one monument in which that usage definitely preceded its adoption in Quito.[22]

Judging by Calancha's accurate description, the present main cloister of San Agustín is a copy of the structure which collapsed in 1687. Instead of the original stone piers, brick covered with stucco was substituted in the rebuilding, and the vaults of the first story gave way to wooden ceilings. The main cloister of the seminary of Santo Toribio, originally dedicated to San Buenaventura, follows the same scheme with rectangular piers in the first story and the alternation of small and large arches in the upper gallery. The simple rusticated panels in stucco and the oval of the spandrels recall the large cloister of San Francisco, to the great monastic complex of which the seminary belongs. The later date (1734) is revealed by decorative details like the great masks in the upper corners of the court and still more by the lovely stairway between the cloisters of San Francisco Solano and San Buenaventura, where arabesques and large masks are spread over the wall at the turn of the steps, recalling the decorative fantasy of the transepts in the Compañía at Pisco. These two eighteenth-century cloisters of San Francisco are outstanding works of colonial Peru. Just one more instance of the alternation of large and small arches in the second story should be mentioned, the patio of Jesús María (1698–1721).

The main cloister of San Francisco (Fig. 124) retains the ground plan of the original structure which, according to Padre Cobo, was erected in the time of the Marqués de Cañete (1556-1561). Córdoba Salinas in his description (1651) of the sixteenth-century monument speaks of eighty-eight columns of stone, presumably in the upper gallery. The present work belongs to the rebuilding of 1669–1674. Unquestionable proof of that fact is afforded by the engraving of the cloister published by Suárez de Figueroa in 1675.[23] The only discrepancies between the print and the preserved work are the mudéjar interlaces of the frieze and the corbel ornaments as contrasted with the rectangular pattern in the frieze and the pyramidal hoods in the spandrels which appear in the engraving. These minor variations can logically be attributed to the engraver's lack of interest in subordinate details, other instances of which are found in the print of the exterior of the church and monastery.

The materials of the second story are wood and plaster, the design being notable for the large oval openings. These as well as the mudéjar frieze and the rustication in stucco carry through the same stylistic features as the church itself. The alternating large and small arches link the cloister with those of San Agustín and San Buenaventura, both of which, on the other hand, are much smaller in area.

It would be logical to conclude that San Francisco was the innovator in the use of oval openings because of their appearance throughout the church and monastery. Yet Meléndez's print of 1681 shows a portion of the upper gallery of the main cloister of Santo Domingo (Fig. 102) which has the same design as the corresponding part of San Francisco. For stylistic reasons it is difficult to believe that the Dominican cloister could date from the time of Salvador de Ribera (1582–1586), or to be sure that it was contemporary with the tiles which have the years 1604, 1606, and 1620 inscribed upon them. The question is a purely academic matter, but one which is interesting to the historian. The conclusion must be reached, however, that the elliptical openings probably made their first appearance in Lima in the Dominican cloisters on the occasion of a reconstruction during the early seventeenth century. Perhaps a later revelation of the archives will further clarify this interesting chronological problem. The present upper gallery of wood with plaster ornaments seems to identify a remodeling subsequent to the earthquake of 1746.

Unmistakably an offshoot of the school of San Francisco is the Claustro de los Doctores of the Merced, a work of strikingly *mudéjar* character, which like the church of the same order, must have been built anew after the earthquake of 1687. It follows the usual type of construction in the use of brick in the first story and wood in the second covered by rustication and patterns in stucco. The disposition of the arches and the oval openings, as well as the *mudéjar* motives, indicate its relationship to the Franciscan cloister, without, however, equaling the high quality of design and workmanship of the latter. Today the Mercedarian cloister suffers from the extraordinarily ugly paint, vivid blue and white in the upper gallery and, unbelievable as it sounds, red in the lower.

The cloisters of nunneries and the lesser male orders are usually single storied and modest in size, but often very pleasing. The Descalzos Franciscanos and the former Augustinian College of San Ildefonso which now houses the Academia de Bellas Artes have small courts in which piers support round arches, the materials being brick covered with a plain coat of white stucco. The inner precincts of the Mercedarias and the Monasterio del Prado follow the same scheme. Rusticated stucco work of seventeenth-century type was the variation on the same theme in the Encarnación, now destroyed. In Arequipa and Trujillo even the great monastic orders, the Dominican, the Jesuits, and the Mercedarian, preferred the single-storied structure on piers (Figs. 163, 196–198).

In eighteenth-century Lima, Doric columns of cedar carrying slender round arches became very popular. Good examples are the cloisters (Fig. 125), in the Casa de Ejercicios (1777) of the Franciscans, the cloisters of the Nazarenas (1766–1771), Santa Clara, and the Casa de Ejercicios of the Descalzos Franciscanos. Inner patios in which *zapata* capitals with the post-and-lintel system make a picturesque and eminently Hispanic composition still survive in Santa Clara and the Mercedarias. Once very numerous both in conventual and domestic architecture, they have now dwindled to very few.

Unique in Peru is the large circular cloister of the Colegio de Santo Tomás (Fig. 126), a work which appears to have been rebuilt after the earthquake of 1746. The most likely Spanish prototype for the plan is the unfinished palace of Charles V at Granada. There the circular court reflects the enthusiasm for round buildings which flourished during the Renaissance. The groined vaults of Santo Tomás are cane and plaster resting on brick walls and piers. Very curious is the entablature block arrangement of the piers and the pilasters attached to the wall, a late instance of the influence of the pier construction of Lima Cathedral.

Any discussion of Lima's beautiful cloisters should include a mention at least of the lovely tile revetments in the lower walks of certain of them. Among the most magnificent in the world are the Sevillian tiles upon the walls and piers of the large court of San Francisco. In a number of places the dates 1620 and 1639 occur in the tiles themselves. The late patio of the Franciscans (Fig. 125) also contains a fine set (1777) into which rococo elements have found their way. The earliest of all line the walls of the main Dominican cloister (Fig. 127), the dates 1604 and 1606 appearing repeatedly and the year 1620, just once. A legend in the ceramics of the north wall reads *Me fecit Garrido 1606*. The name is surely that of a Moor.

The glazed tiles of Seville, heritage of the Moslem civilization in Spain, are eloquent evidence of the prominent position *mudéjar* art held in colonial Peru. In the capital, Lima, the closeness to Andalusian Spain is even more striking than elsewhere. Tile revetments also decorate the walls of the churches of San Pedro at Lima, Santa Teresa at Cuzco, and the sacristy of San Agustín at Lima. Although the majority of the tiles were imported from Spain, some were fabricated in Lima itself. Dated examples at Seville in Santa Clara (1578), San Clemente (1588), and the Museo Provincial, are nearly identical with those in Peru.[24]

CITIES TO THE SOUTH OF LIMA: PISCO, NAZCA, ICA

THE most important churches in the coastal region of southern Peru between Lima and Arequipa are three Jesuit foundations: the Compañía at Pisco, and the churches on the haciendas of San José and San Xavier in the valley of Nazca. Here the country is completely arid, and for many miles a pure desert of sand and dunes stretches in picturesque desolation. Thus it begins just south of Lima, and so continues for three hundred miles until the mountains rise to the north of Nazca. Thereafter they grow increasingly large as the traveler goes to the south. The first two churches mentioned represent an extension of the school of Lima. San Xavier at Nazca, on the other hand, although it shows some evidences of *limeño* influence, must be placed within the orbit of Arequipa. Thus the two churches at Nazca divide their allegiance between the two great cities of the coast, a fact which is symbolic of their geographic position, just midway between Lima and Arequipa.

Pisco, one hundred and fifty miles south of Lima, is nearer to the capital both in its location and in the style of its one fine colonial church, originally erected by the Jesuits. The earthquake of 1687 left the earlier building in ruins, promptly to be replaced by the present delightful work which stood ready in 1723.[25] A commemorative portrait in the sacristy records the name of the patron and founder of the new Jesuit *colegio,* Andrés Ximénez de Vilches y Vallés.[26] Its Latin-cross plan (Fig. 6) with single nave flanked by lateral chapels, its dome over the crossing, and the single apse resemble in a general way the Jesuit churches of the Compañía at Cuzco and San Pedro at Juli. The *limeño* coastal tradition, on the other hand, is in evidence not only in the stylistic features but also in methods of construction, that is, in the use of brick and plaster walls topped by a barrel vault with triangular penetrations and a dome, both made of cane and stucco.

The interior is small in scale and the chapels rather shallow. The white walls, the chaste molded piers and entablature establish a restrained mood which is modulated, like eighteenth-century music, by occasional florid embellishment. Here it involves volutes and arabesques of extraordinarily beautiful quality beside the windows of the transept and in the pendentives of the dome. The style recalls the arabesques in panels of gilded wood which decorate the aisles of San Pedro in Lima and the fine stucco work over the stairway in the Franciscan Colegio de Santo Toribio. Bits of ornament accent the frieze in the center of each bay of the nave at Pisco, and the clerestory windows also carry volutes beside them. An unusual arrangement here is the isolation of each window by a balustrade instead of the usual continuous balustrade atop the cornice, so commonly used in Jesuit churches. One other architectural detail of the interior deserves mention, and that is the fine shell tympanum, so typi-

cally *limeño,* over the transept door. Before quitting the interior of the Compañía, mention must be made of the very beautiful pulpit and salomonic retables which shine like gold reliquaries against the white walls. In period and quality they resemble the fine collection of sculpture in Jesús María at Lima (Figs. 292, 294, 327, 328).

Moving out to examine the façade (Fig. 117) of the Compañía at Pisco, we find that it has the small towers characteristic of Lima in the eighteenth century. Analogous were the towers (Fig. 116) of the façade of San Marcelo, even to the plain base and the wooden balustrade about the belfry itself. In the same category were the towers of Santa Teresa (Fig. 115) and the Caridad, also demolished in recent years. The façade is marked by an oval window of *limeño* parentage, but the design is provincial in detail. The first and second stories lack coördination both in scale and in unifying decorative elements. The silhouette of the central section forms a trefoil and the same *mudéjar* motive recurs in the monastery portal to the right. Despite its provincialism the façade of the church at Pisco is pleasing with its yellow walls against which the columns and ornament stand out in white. The rusticated transept portal and entrance to the former monastery are offshoots of the style introduced in the monastery entrance of San Francisco at Lima, and hence belong to an earlier stylistic phase than the rest of the Compañía at Pisco. The ruins of the cloister show an altogether unconventional type of pier with great bulbous curving base, which has a Spanish parallel of the eighteenth century, however, in the cloister of San Hipólito at Córdoba. The moldings at the springing of the arch cut curiously into the swelling side. At the roof level, beams are carried on *zapata* bracket capitals. Only an amateur could have invented such a bizarre and fantastic piece of architecture.

One hundred and thirty-five miles south of Pisco lies the valley of Nazca, site of a great pre-Columbian civilization in the early centuries of the Christian era. Here stand, half ruined, two Jesuit churches of extraordinarily high quality, far surpassing anything of that period in Lima itself. The façade of San José (Fig. 118), damaged as it is, is unrivaled of its kind throughout all Peru. The two fine *limeño* belfries closely resemble those of the Compañía at Pisco. The composition as a whole has excellent dimensions, and it identifies the hand of a far more gifted architect than that of the latter church. The *mudéjar* patterns of interlocking squares which cover the pilasters of the towers (Fig. 129) undeniably betray an admiration on the part of the designer for the patterned interior of San Francisco at Lima.

Most striking is the portal (Fig. 128), in truth a salomonic retable of two stories with niches occupied by Jesuit saints. The columns are divided into three horizontal bands, the center smooth and the others channeled, by crowns of gaily flamboyant acanthus leaves. The arabesques in the middle section of the portal and around the oval window represent the art of the colonial decorator at its best. The material is stucco over a wooden framework in the upper part, with brick and adobe forming the body of the structure. This salomonic retable on the exterior of a church has no exact parallel in Peru, those of Huancavelica being constructed of dark red stone and decorated with columns entwined in the usual grapevine. The spiral shaft at Nazca with three-part division also occurs in the portal of the Compañía at Quito, a fact which does not, however, presuppose any artistic relation between the two works. The façade of San José at Nazca was probably the creation of a *retablero* who traveled down the coast from Lima. A partly defaced inscription on the façade contains the date 1744. Another in the sacristy states that the first stone of the church was laid in 1740 and that it was finished on March 19, 1744.

The side portal (Fig. 130) of San José at Nazca is embellished with lovely scroll-and-leaf ornament, a *mudéjar* frieze with the oval chain pattern similar to that of La Merced at Lima, and curious half columns suspended on tiny corbels. The entrance to the sacristy is exceptionally interesting, less for its arabesques in stucco than for the grimacing masks, some of them with projecting tongues. Here the student encounters an undeniable case of the reappearance or survival of an ancient pre-Columbian theme, so thoroughly characteristic of Nazca pottery and textiles, which were produced in this same valley many centuries before the arrival of the Spaniards.[27] Similar heads can also be discerned on the upper part of the towers.

The single-naved interior of San José lies in a grievous state of ruin, its vaults having been shaken to the ground in the earthquake of 1940. The sanctuary is elevated by four steps, and behind the high altar a rectangular chamber constitutes an unorthodox practice in Peruvian churches, although it does occur in the Jesuit church of San Pedro at Lima and in Puno Cathedral. The stucco patterns here, unlike those of the more lavish church of San Xavier at Nazca, are limited to the transverse bands of the barrel vault and the moldings about the clerestory windows. The patterns of rosettes and heart-shaped scrolls, Islamic in character, resemble metal chains in their sharp crisp outlines. A really extraordinary piece of stucco work adorns the face of the choir loft: masks with plumed headdresses and serpents in great calligraphic coils. Once again a pre-Columbian theme is reborn, for the serpents are very common in the pottery and textiles of Nazca and Paracas. No better proof of native Indian influence could be forthcoming, yet the motive is usually passed off as Asiatic. The truth is that both indigenous and *mudéjar* factors explain this exoticism, without recourse to hypothetical missionaries bearing to the New World the arts of the Far East. Witness the fine *mudéjar* tiles of green and yellow upon the floor of the nave and sanctuary.

A broad molded cornice runs the length of the church, and a cedar balustrade isolates the windows, the same disposition previously noted in the Compañía at Pisco. Corbels rather than pilasters indicate the division into bays between the wall recesses within which the retables were set. A fine *limeño* shell tympanum tops the side door within the church, while another decorates the deeply splayed doorway in the sacristy.

The church of San Xavier del Ingenio in the valley of Nazca is undated, but its style very clearly places it in the first half of the eighteenth century. The nearest clue to documentation is the fact that the Jesuits of Lima purchased some land in the district called Arpicho in the Valle de Ingenio in the year 1713.[28] I have not been able to ascertain whether that is the exact spot upon which the church now stands. San Xavier surpasses even its companion just a few miles away in decorative fantasy. Here, too, grimacing masks with open mouths and projecting tongues peer from the friezes of the towers and façade (Figs. 132, 133). Their grotesque headdress defy description and evoke admiration for the unrivaled decorative skill and imagination of their anonymous masters. The flourish and rhythm of the foliate ornament throughout the church is achieved with consummate artistry, both in the bands upon the façade and inside of the church, in the frieze, pilasters, and ribs of the vault. Bust-length female figures with plumed headdresses accent the friezes at regular intervals above the pilasters. The pilasters (Fig. 134) next to the sanctuary carry in addition to the foliage a tall seated figure about which encircle two dragons in heraldic opposition. A great lily plant rises below from a classical vase, and the human body itself interpenetrates the highly stylized design. Once again Asiatic elements have been declared present, but indigenous tradition and fantasy seem to be the only logical and reasonable explanations. The *mudéjar*, too, puts in its appearance in the geometric molding under the frieze and in bands of the vault.

The stucco work throughout the interior is of surpassing beauty. Even the font for holy water is part of the unified scheme which was originally complemented by a series of large paintings upon the walls, now, alas, in ruinous condition. The plan of San Xavier is that of a single nave like San José with the usual elevated choir. To the left of the sanctuary stands the large sacristy covered by a dome.

The interesting fact about the façade of San Xavier (Figs. 131–133) is that it appears to be the product of crossed influences from Lima and Arequipa. From the latter, nearer city come the large polygonal towers adorned with grotesque masks. The prototype is the tower of Santo Domingo in Arequipa, originally designed by Juan de Aldaña in 1649 and twice rebuilt subsequently. The two-storied central section with its curving broken pediments and elliptical window is derived from the school of Lima, as seen in the rear entrances of the cathedral (1732) and the church of Santa Rosa de las Monjas (1702–1704) (Fig. 113).

The two churches at Nazca, now in a pitiful state, half ruined and virtually abandoned, belong to large haciendas whose owners, it is to be hoped, will protect them from still greater decay. Each is unique, without any exact counterpart either in style or in quality throughout South America.

Ica, the largest and most important modern city on the coast of Peru between Arequipa and Lima, has lost nearly every vestige of its colonial heritage. The present parish church is the only one which retains its colonial plan, a nave with barrel vault and the aisles covered by domes. This follows the type of the Merced and San Francisco in Lima. The materials are brick and adobe in the walls, whereas cane coated with plaster provides the vaults. The façade suffered rebuilding in Neoclassic style in the nineteenth century, and at the same time the interior was much altered. Two small retables of *limeño* origin in the transept and a beautifully carved shrine with ivory crucifix are the best colonial remains in the city. The church, originally established as part of the new Jesuit foundation in 1746, passed into the hands of the Mercedarians in 1780 after the expulsion of the Company of Jesus.[29]

Much-rebuilt churches of other monastic orders in Ica have recently been demolished: San Francisco in 1945 and San Agustín in 1943. Neither the convent of Augustinian nuns, designed by Cristóbal de Vargas in 1769, nor the church of San Jerónimo (1692–1700) exists today.[30]

Ica is equally impoverished in the field of domestic architecture. The present post office functions in an eighteenth-century building in the patio of which are two wooden columns with *zapata* capitals and a large pair of eighteenth-century doors. Across the way on the main plaza are the ruins of a house with an interesting portal which opens into the patio, the former residence of the Marqueses de Torre Hermosa.

V

CENTRAL PERU

AYACUCHO

AYACUCHO's primary importance in architecture lies in the exceptional number of her monuments of the sixteenth century. These works of the earliest days of the conquest, San Cristóbal, La Merced, San Francisco, Santa Clara, and the plateresque portal of the Jesuit chapel, have already been examined in Chapter II. Only the region of Lake Titicaca with its numerous churches of the fifteen-nineties can vie with Ayacucho. Churches of the seventeenth and eighteenth century also abound here, but they do not occupy the same high rank within their periods.

The history of the churches of Ayacucho has been well established, thanks to the splendid recent monograph by Dr. Medina and the earlier studies of the diocese by Bishop Olivas Escudero. Dr. Medina gives the dimensions of each building and various historical data of value.[1]

Most important in the seventeenth century are the Compañía, the cathedral, and Santo Domingo. The earliest is the church (Fig. 135) of the Jesuits, begun about 1614, nine years after the founding of the colegio here on August 15, 1605.[2] The construction is low, its massive walls of stone and brick barrel vaults very solid and utilitarian in their purpose and without archi-

tectural pretensions. Its rather heavy rude simplicity has a serious and humble appeal. Light is dim, for there are just two round openings in the nave vault, a window in the raised choir, and no dome. The transverse ribs of the barrel vault hang suspended on corbels, and a simple rounded molding runs along the springing of the vault. This is a church of pioneers and missionaries in a newly conquered land. The single-naved plan without lateral chapels has the same humble forthrightness. It belongs to no school and to no type, and is entirely innocent of any connections with a so-called Jesuit plan.

Chapels occupy the position of a transept, as in the late sixteenth-century churches of the Titicaca region and the Merced in Ayacucho. Both are domed. The one on the left has pendentives covered with designs in stucco consisting of octagons and other *mudéjar* motives, and the cross within interlaces decorates the dome. The stucco work, like the fragment of a fine retable in the same chapel, must be dated in the second half of the seventeenth century. Contemporary is the sacristy, large and more sophisticated than the original church, its barrel vaults surfaced with stucco panels.

On the epistle side of the church is the chapel of Loreto. It is lower than the church proper, but otherwise identical in its massive construction and humble simplicity. Light enters only from the main door and a single window above. Narrow stone benches line the walls, showing still further how closely the chapel adheres to the customs practiced in the early days of the conquest. The nearest thing to decoration are the small rosettes and shells upon the cornice. Simple recesses in the wall permit the setting of a statue here and there. The walls, newly painted, glare in their barren whiteness, yet they are refreshing compared with the ugly marbleized paint in the church proper.

At the left of the Compañía façade is the entrance to the former *colegio* of the Jesuits (Fig. 137), now occupied by the Colegio Seminario de San Cristóbal. Although plans were drawn as early as 1645, the main body of the *colegio* was under construction in 1674, and work upon both it and the church continued as late as 1687–1693.[3] Nevertheless the massive portal is of sober classical design with pronounced rustication in deep red stone. The diamond points on the wall, so common in Spanish and Italian palaces of the Renaissance, make for added vigor. The same style and the same red stone prevail in the original portals of the church and the chapel of Loreto. The Doric order and the plain uncarved stone manifest the austerity of the late Spanish Renaissance. These are more sober than the portals of San Agustín at Saña but of less significance architecturally. Cuzco possesses works of similar style, such as the main entrance of the chapel of the Educandas, formerly San Juan de Dios.

The two large towers of the Compañía (Fig. 136) are clearly additions to the original façade in the first half of the eighteenth century. Nine horizontal rows of four-leaved ornament, highly stylized, give a unique appearance to the entire structure. Nothing comparable with it can be found in Peru, although precedent for similar rows of ornament exists on the atrium gate and great tower of La Asunción at Juli. The latter works display a far more highly developed sense of decorative design. It may have been, nonetheless, some wandering builder from the Juli region who created this original piece of *mestizo* art in the towers of the Compañía at Ayacucho. The vertical bands of ornament which he added at the sides of the main doorway are in typical *mestizo* idiom of which the churches of Santa Ana and La Magdalena provide other instances. The belfries differ from numerous others of the type in the same city in the bulbous onion dome at the top. The façade of the Compañía at Ayacucho has unique and attractive features compensating to some degree for its lack of unity, which is the almost inevitable result of modifications and alterations. Some of these are frankly clumsy, for instance, the middle section between the towers, constructed of brick, with an acceptable window but a weak and ineffectual gable at the top.

The cathedral of Ayacucho merits attention by virtue of its size and the influence which its architecture had upon subsequent buildings, rather than for anything notable about its quality. The façade (Fig. 139), its poorest feature, is frankly bad in scale and in the complete failure to solve the problem of bringing some sort of coördination among the upper story, the first story, and the towers. The general idea of a broad façade having three portals and flanked by towers is borrowed from the cathedrals of Cuzco and Lima, but there the connection stops. The central section with the awkward niche over the portal and its free-standing columns is mediocre in itself, but even more the complete lack of harmony with the smaller portals produces a shock. The latter constitute an interesting phenomenon in the cutting of the rusticated stone, now painted red, which resembles pre-Columbian technique. Doubtless the native Indian workman was responsible for this survival from an earlier epoch. The towers, built in the time of Bishop Castilla y Zamora (1669–1672), established a prototype which was repeated again and again in the following century. Characteristic are the single-arched openings in the front, the cupola, the pyramidal pinnacles, and the dentils in the cornice. The band of rosettes upon the cupolas and the four-leaved ornament at the corners also recur later. These towers of Ayacucho Cathedral are effective in themselves, but too small in relation to the breadth of the façade. The generally poor aspect of the frontispiece has been further damaged by layers of cement in modern times. The general mass of the cathedral is pleasing, however, when viewed laterally (Fig. 138) across the varying roof levels of

nave, aisles, and transept topped by the fine low dome. A lateral portal on the gospel side with channeled Doric pilasters and triangular pediments carries over the severe classicism of the late sixteenth century.

This portal must be identified with the first campaign in the building of the cathedral which lasted four years, 1632–1636, only to be paralyzed until 1662. In the second campaign the work was carried as far as the vaults (Fig. 143) which were erected along with the towers and dome (1669–1672) under the great benefactor of the diocese, Bishop Castilla y Zamora.[4] His power, wealth, and munificent ways are explained by the fact that he was a natural son of King Philip IV of Spain. An inscription in the aisle on the epistle side records the consecration of the church on May 19, 1672, in honor of the Madonna of the Immaculate Conception.

The plan of the cathedral of Ayacucho is rectangular, thus following the tradition established in Peru by the cathedrals of Lima and Cuzco, whose influence has also been noted in the broad proportions of the two-towered façade. Further than that the dependence does not extend. At Ayacucho the nave is slightly higher than the aisles and the sanctuary stands against the extreme wall without aisle behind it, contrary to the arrangement at Cuzco and Trujillo. The most pronounced stylistic feature of the building is the large cornice with dentils which was later to be imitated in several churches within the city. The barrel vault of common seventeenth-century type collapsed in 1881 and was restored thereafter. Slightly domical vaults are used in the aisles which leave them rather dark. A magnificent burst of light illuminates the church, however, through the fine dome on pendentives over the crossing. The choir occupied its traditional place in the nave until the early twentieth century, when it was transferred to the sanctuary.

The earliest section of the church is clearly the sacristy and the small chapel at each side of the sanctuary. These parts are lower and heavier in construction and covered with a longitudinal barrel vault. Rather curiously each of the chapels receives light from a round window in the center of the vault. After this initial campaign in 1632, plans were radically changed in the direction of a larger church, as the small scale of this part of the building unmistakably indicates.

The cathedral of Ayacucho is spacious and dignified, but lacking in architectural refinements. A contemporary work with which it might logically be compared, such as the cathedral of Trujillo, although not one of the masterpieces of Peruvian art, outstrips it on every point, from scale relations to details of moldings.

The convent of the Dominicans, established in Ayacucho in 1548, was one of the earliest foundations of the order in Peru. Of the original convent nothing is left today, and the rather nondescript church has been twice rebuilt. A royal provision of 1606 refers to the fabrication of a new church, a piece of evidence which Meléndez corroborates in his statement that Fray Bartolomé Martínez, prior in the early seventeenth century, completed the church

and choir, and that Padre Gaspar de la Fuente made the stone cloister. Another document refers to building a new church a century later in 1715.[5] Survivals of the early seventeenth century are the monastery portal and the baptistry (Figs. 141, 142). The first has an extraordinary tympanum decorated with the sun and moon, taken over from native Indian rather than Christian worship. They are combined with the Sacred Heart, vegetable patterns, and a knight's escutcheon, the identification of which would still further clarify the date. The general shape of the tympanum suggests a trefoil. The same fusion of pagan and Christian themes takes a still more naïve and primitive form in the portal of the baptistry. Here the stars, sun, and moon from the native Indian altar combine with the cross, the diadem of Mary, the Dominican shield, and the pomegranate. The iconography recalls a still more famous work, the portal of San Lorenzo, Potosí (1728–1744), which from the point of view of sculpture and decoration is a masterpiece which does not brook comparison with this humble chapel of Ayacucho.

The exterior of the church of Santo Domingo (Fig. 140) produces an unusual impression because of the large narthex and the open porch above it. Although Santo Domingo in Lima also has a deep narthex, the best comparison to be singled out is the church at San Jerónimo near Cuzco, a work of the late sixteenth century. The explanation of the upper porch both in these instances and commonly in the Andean region seems to be that they were designed for preaching to large crowds and for the display of relics. It is probable that the rebuilding of 1715 did not constitute a complete abandonment of the old church and that the façade still antedates the rest of the church by a hundred years. From the standpoint of style that seems to be a reasonable explanation. The belfries, on the other hand, clearly fall into the Ayacuchan series of eighteenth-century date, and are related to those of San Juan de Dios and San Francisco de Paula (1783) (Fig. 146).

The body of the church is built of gray stone throughout, including the barrel vaults and dome. The building has suffered by miserably inept painting, some of it white and some of it black, not to speak of the white stripes on the exterior. The interior has the most garish overlay of blue marbleized paint in all Peru which, although most distressing to see, is not irremediable.

The Latin-cross plan without lateral chapels and the raised choir place it in the usual category of monastic churches. The cornice with dentils is a signature of the local school, subsequent to the building of the cathedral, whereas the corbel in the center of each bay is unique in Ayacucho. That peculiarity was borrowed from the school of Lima, where it found great favor in the eighteenth century.

The dome takes first place in this church, for it is large and refulgent within, and built up in four levels on the exterior into an impressive mass, roofed in fine red tiles. Other matters to be recorded on the exterior are the side portal, difficult to analyze

because of its unfinished state, and the open *espadaña,* the whole upper section rebuilt in brick not more than fifty years ago.

The mid-sixteenth-century portal of San Francisco (Figs. 39, 40), the only important survivor of the original church, has previously been discussed. By virtue of its style the belfry falls into the group of eighteenth-century monuments, and may be dated with a fair degree of accuracy at the time of the rebuilding of the church. A large painting in the sacristy bears an inscription which states that the high altar, the sacristy, and the picture were concluded in 1712. The consecration of the church delayed until May 30th, 1723.[6] The style and plan (Figs. 19, 147) fall completely outside of the traditions of the local school, an indication that an architect from without was responsible. Its basilican plan, the only church except the cathedral which has nave and two aisles, is most unusual. A deep entrance corridor of two bays passes beneath the raised choir into a broad rectangular area of three bays which terminates in a single apse. Four large cruciform piers carry the vaults, those of the nave being domical in section without clerestory, and slightly higher than the aisles. Over the first two bays of the side aisles are half domes constructed on ribs, an altogether peculiar scheme which would suggest a central type of church. The piers at the crossing receive dramatic emphasis by the use of the large entablature block which descends from the cathedrals of Lima and Cuzco. A chain motive decorates the lower molding. The setting is prepared as for a dome, but the vault of the crossing differs from its neighbor only in the placing of a circular window in the top. The ends of the transept are barrel vaulted, like the choir, apse, and sacristy. The interior of San Francisco reveals the mind of a definitely unorthodox architect. That qualification is not synonymous with provincial, because the building must be characterized as a distinct success, the work of a man who knew his professional technique, as has been demonstrated in Harth-terré's analysis of the geometry of the plans.[7] Broad, spacious, and harmonious, San Francisco of Ayacucho deserves a place in the upper reaches of Peruvian colonial architecture.

From an architectural viewpoint the eighteenth century in Ayacucho was most productive. It saw the completion and consecration of Santa Teresa in 1703, the foundation of the order of San Francisco de Paula in 1713, the establishment of the monastery of the Buena Muerte (1720–1726), and the rebuilding in part of San Francisco, La Compañía, San Agustín, San Juan de Dios, Santa Ana, La Magdalena, and the addition of the tower to Santa Clara.

The house of Carmelite nuns owes its establishment to Padre Francisco de la Maza in 1683. To his brother, Diego, some writers have credited the architecture of the church and convent.[8] The historical facts provide little basis for the belief that he was anything more than the spiritual and financial benefactor. The style of this church of single-nave type, general in nunneries, suggests a limeño architect. The dentelated cornice suspended on corbels instead of pilasters recalls Las Trinitarias (1722) in Lima. The shell tympana over both doorways within the church are frankly limeño, the only other appearance of this motive in Ayacucho being in the main portal of the cathedral, a phenomenon which must be regarded as an eighteenth-century modification. The interior impresses one by its unusual height and resultant spaciousness, crowned by a fine barrel vault with a gilded rosette in the center of each bay. Like other churches of the interior of Peru, Santa Teresa has the good fortune to have retained her splendid collection of colonial retables and a fine pulpit. Especially magnificent and, in fact, unique is the beautiful wooden grille of the upper choir, which is gilded and inlaid with mother-of-pearl.

Passing to the exterior, the small two-towered façade (Fig. 145) is also related to the Lima tradition of the late seventeenth and eighteenth centuries, although it differs in detail from works of the vice-regal capital. The Ayacuchan tradition is seen in the belfries, the first being those of the cathedral (1669–1672), the second those of Santa Teresa (1683–1703), to be followed by every one of the churches listed at the beginning of this discussion as built or remodeled in the eighteenth century. Just one exception is to be noted here, the fine bell tower of Santa Clara (Fig. 149), added, about 1712, to the sixteenth-century church.[9] This beautiful tower soars serene and lofty in excellently cut masonry. It is unmistakably modeled upon the towers of Cuzco of the previous century, and no doubt upon that of Santa

Clara in Cuzco (Fig. 61) which it resembles more closely than any other. Moreover, the tower in the two Franciscan nunneries occupies the same position relative to the church. The most notable difference is that the belfry at Ayacucho has two stories, whereas the Cuzco towers have one.

The exterior of Santa Teresa manifests a sobriety which becomes a characteristic of the entire school of the city. The general verticality and slimness of proportions are an eighteenth-century Peruvian trait. The rusticated portal, made of brick and stucco, is exceptional in the omission of a window to light the choir. The general effect, however, is one of greater dignity than that of contemporary works of the city, notwithstanding the fact that the entire frontispiece has suffered from an overlay of cement surfacing in recent years.

Three of the churches of Ayacucho, San Francisco de Paula (founded 1713), the Buena Muerte (1720–1726), and San Juan de Dios, have façades (Fig. 146) similar enough to be the works of the same architect. All are distinguished by the usual towers and dentelated cornices, varying chiefly in the details of the belfries. Those of San Francisco de Paula more closely resemble the towers (Figs. 39, 145) of San Francisco (*circa* 1712–1723) and Santa Teresa (1703), but have cherubs' heads at the angles and the four-leaved ornament which also appears upon the cathedral towers. The belfries of the Buena Muerte, San Juan de Dios, and San Agustín are virtually identical, differing from the others in the smaller diameter of the high cupola at the crowning.

A round-arched doorway topped by an entablature, a single window also with round arch, and two oculus openings above constitute the simple elements in the portals of San Francisco de Paula and the Buena Muerte. A negro monk of the Benedictine order is said to have been the architect of the latter, and it does not seem hazardous to attribute the former to him. Final consecration of San Francisco de Paula did not take place until 1783, an event which often delayed many years, whereas the foundation belongs to the early part of the century.

The façade of San Juan de Dios, somewhat inferior to the others, must either be ascribed to the same architect or be regarded as an imitation. The foundation of the hospital goes back to the year 1555, and it was later taken over by the brothers of San Juan de Dios (1630). At that period the church was first erected, but it underwent much modification or amplification in the eighteenth century, and was inaugurated in this new guise in 1783.

A similar history holds for San Agustín, whose friars settled in Ayacucho in 1637. Their church was reconstructed in 1767 and again modified in 1871.[10] The latter cannot be regarded as a major operation, and was limited to the portal whose row of niches and Renaissance frieze speak for the revivalist eclecticism of the past century.

The interiors of these churches are also very similar. San Francisco de Paula (Fig. 144) has a very shallow transept surmounted by a fine dome on pendentives. The cornice is of the simple molded type, and the retables stand within wall niches. Stone prevails throughout, as elsewhere in the city, both in the barrel vaults and the cupola.

San Juan de Dios, the Buena Muerte, and San Agustín are all small churches such as are frequently associated with religious orders. They have single naves and raised choirs with barrel vaults throughout, and in no case do more splendid features such as dome, transept, and lateral chapels exist. The same school or even the same architect produced them all, in each case using the dentelated cornice and simple pilasters, ubiquitous in Ayacucho.

Santa Ana (Fig. 148) and La Magdalena, both parish churches of sixteenth-century origin, were enlarged and rebuilt in the second half of the eighteenth century. How persistent and consistent was local tradition strikes one forcibly in the repetition of the same towers, these almost a duplicate of the Franciscan belfry. The earliest of the series were those of the cathedral (Fig. 139) in 1669–1672, now brought to a close by La Magdalena whose right tower has the date 1797, a span of one hundred and twenty-five years. The portal of this church is decorated by volute pilasters, scroll ornament at the sides, and an elliptical niche in the tympanum. The masonry of the broad façade reveals how it was lengthened and increased in height, by adding on to the original walls. The small interior in the form of a Latin cross has a pitched roof of cane, the only unvaulted church of any importance in the city, a

fact which in itself symbolizes the poverty and insignificance of this humble structure.

The façade of Santa Ana (Fig. 148), unlike that of La Magdalena, is well designed as a unit and well built. The *ayacucheño* towers enframe a portal which has no exact counterpart in the city, but which does fall into the same style and period as the portal (Fig. 150) of San Francisco (1772) in Huancavelica. The same master or school must have been responsible for both, and that is only one of the instances of interrelations between the two cities. The free-standing column on each side of the doorway may have been suggested by a Renaissance portal, such as that of San Francisco at Ayacucho (Fig. 40). Contact with the *mestizo* taste which appears in the exterior of the Compañía (Fig. 136) is evident here in the stylized vine and leaves at the sides, an exact replica of the ornament beside the doorway of the Compañía in Ayacucho. The interior, despite its dome and stone barrel vault, is small and unprepossessing. It does, however, contain an array of colonial painting in a state of complete abandon, open to the elements and the birds, as well as a splendid high altar of the seventeenth century, and a sumptuous silver altar frontal and altar back with candelabra, dated 1796. In the silver work French rococo influence predominates. As so frequently, the visitor is both amazed by the great luxury of the colonial past and depressed by the fact that it is now moldering away, neglected and forgotten.

In summary, the seventeenth- and eighteenth-century architecture of Ayacucho is characterized by good solid construction in which the gray stone of the region is employed throughout, in vaults as well as in walls. Arches of windows are frequently made of brick, a material also present in the façade of Santa Teresa. The style is generally sober and very restrained in decoration. The chief exception in the period is the appearance of the *mestizo* style in the rows of stylized leaves upon the façade of La Compañía. Towers are the most distinguished feature of the region, small, good in scale, and well placed. Those of the Jesuit church again prove the exception to the tradition with their curving Baroque moldings and onion-shaped cupolas. One other exception remains to be recorded, the unimportant chapel called Pampa San Agustín, a mid-eighteenth-century building with salomonic portal and single *ayacucheño* tower. A builder from Huancavelica or perhaps just a simple *retablero* was its architect.

Interiors throughout are sober, with barrel vaults, usually a dentelated cornice, and flat pilasters. The exceptions in Santa Teresa and San Francisco have already been discussed. Strangely enough not a single cloister of the many monastic houses has survived from colonial times, a phenomenon which is largely explained by the exclaustration of the monks in the nineteenth century. The cloisters of the nuns of Santa Clara have met a better fate, but they are invisible to the male student of architecture. The true fame of Ayacucho rests, in the last analysis, upon her Renaissance monuments, La Merced, San Francisco, San

Cristóbal, Santa Clara, and the Jesuit portal, not solely because of their quality, but still more because they are unique in all Peru.

HUANCAVELICA

HUANCAVELICA lies in the remote heights of the Andes at an altitude of 12,500 feet, where cold and bitter winds sweep the year around. Its fame spread far and wide in colonial days, due to the prodigious wealth of its mercury mines, the discovery of which allegedly took place in 1563. Francisco de Toledo issued the official charter for the foundation of the city in 1571, and a year later he expropriated the mines as property of the Spanish crown.

This discussion cannot be anything more than a superficial account of the religious architecture of Huancavelica, since my visit there was limited. It was impossible to study the monuments satisfactorily or to secure sufficient photographic documentation. The state of neglect and disrepair of the churches is worse than in any other city of Peru, the roofs being inadequate to keep out the rain and the state of dilapidation inside beyond belief. No monasteries or nunneries function today, and the former churches and houses of the Jesuits and Augustinians have totally disappeared.

The churches of Huancavelica are built of the gray stone of the region and covered by wooden vaults or roofs in every case. This method deviates from the usual custom of vaulting the churches with stone in mountainous regions. The latter practice was followed in Ayacucho, Arequipa, and the Titicaca district, whereas in Cuzco brick was preferred. The two largest structures of Huancavelica are the *matriz* and Santo Domingo, both basilican in plan with nave and two aisles, the former covered by a clumsy wooden barrel vault and the second by a sloping wooden roof. Both are constructed with piers and Doric cornices decorated with dentils as though vaulting had been originally planned. The general style is related to the cathedral of Ayacucho, and the local school must be in part an offshoot of it.

It seems likely that the same architect directed the construction of both the *matriz* and Santo Domingo in the second half of the seventeenth century. Meléndez, who affords the only documentation, states that the Dominican house became a priory in 1590, and that in the time of Fray Domingo de Montenegro the first adequate church was built. Judging by the context and the fact that Meléndez speaks of Montenegro as alive in one passage and in another states that he died the day after the church was finished, we may conclude that the friar died about 1675.[11] The period is corroborated by payment for unspecified work on the *matriz* in 1668.[12]

The exteriors of the *matriz* and Santo Domingo (Figs. 152, 153) are also similar but not identical. Both have very large flanking towers with two-storied belfries topped by cupolas. The towers of Santo Domingo carry the usual complement of pilasters and entablatures, whereas the towers of the *matriz*, because of their extraor-dinary bareness, may possibly be incomplete. Although the bulk and mass of the latter church are impressive, the appearance is more provincial and less refined than that of its companion. The great size of these towers makes one think of San Francisco and San Agustín of Lima, but otherwise they have no points of contact.

The salomonic portals in soft red stone make the two churches still more like nonidentical twins. Both must be dated in the first half of the eighteenth century when they appear to have been added to the original façade. The unfortunately poor quality of the stone, which has crumbled and deteriorated, interferes with the otherwise good decorative effect of the work. The two portals, unmistakably by the same hand, have an elliptical window in the upper center of each, like the eighteenth-century churches of Lima. They differ from each other in detail and in the fact that the *matriz* consists of two stories and Santo Domingo of one. As previously suggested, the portal of the chapel in Ayacucho, called Pampa San Agustín, may be an offshoot of the school of Huancavelica. Spanish prototypes, especially in Andalusia, such as Santa María in Alicante, are easily cited.

The interiors of the two churches present a lamentable disarray of paintings and retables in a ruinous and neglected condition. In large part the works of art date from the eighteenth century, the high point of the prosperity of the town. Especially beautiful is a lavish chapel in Santo Domingo, the walls of which are invested with carved and gilded wooden panels. The donor was Jerónimo de Solá y Fuente, governor and superintendent of the mines in 1744. A fine primitive portrait with long inscription preserves the memory of him.

The most sophisticated in plan of the churches of Huancavelica is San Francisco, laid out in the form of a Latin cross without lateral chapels. As usual in a building of single nave, the choir is raised above the main entrance. A molded cornice, Doric pilasters, and a dome on pendentives over the crossing fulfill the usual requirement of a Baroque church. Cane coated with plaster, as in Lima, imitates stone vaults, in this case designed to give the impression of groined vaults between transverse arches.

The style of San Francisco is consistent with the date 1772, inscribed in the upper center of the façade (Fig. 150). The left tower was never completed, and the stucco work upon the façade itself is fragmentary. The portal with its free-standing Corinthian columns resembles that of Santa Ana in Ayacucho (Fig. 148) more closely than any other. It is beautifully designed, like a Renaissance work, but the lack of conventionality in the handling of detail and the ornamental motives themselves betray the later *mestizo* spirit. Sharply cut arabesques in alternate progression occupy their customary place at the sides, and the familiar four-leaf stylization decorates the curious double frieze and also the elliptical window which opens into the choir.

The classical spirit prevails even more strongly in the portal of San Sebastián (Fig. 151) which stands upon the same plaza near San Francisco. Double Doric columns flank the doorway with a very strange provincial interpretation of a Doric frieze. The rectangular window of the choir is set between pilasters in the form of atlantes, old men swathed in togas. This theme is of rare occurrence in Peru, being present in the tiles of San Francisco at Lima, dated 1620, and in the former portal of San Andrés of Cuzco, a work of the second half of the eighteenth century. The abundance of retables of caryatid type, dated in the latter period, as well as the late classicism of the portal of San Sebastián, suggest that general time for its origin. No other architectural monument in Peru is exactly comparable with it in style. The quality is pleasing, sober, and in good taste, although unconventional in usage. A two-storied open *espadaña* rises to the left of the façade. The interior is small, one nave and two short aisles, and an interesting wooden ceiling still survives over the sanctuary and part of the right aisle. The ruinous and dejected state of the churches of the town finds no exception here, an example being the really fine pulpit from which the moldings have been partly ripped away.

The other churches of Huancavelica were visited in a downpour of rain which made study or photography well-nigh impossible. The small single-naved church of Santa Ana, roofed in wood, has a few modest retables of the eighteenth century. The façade is simple, with a single tower to the right and a doorway topped by a molded entablature including dentils. The humble church of the Indians, dedicated to the Ascension, calls for no particular comment, its portal being in red stone and the interior of single nave. The larger church of San Cristóbal stands on the outskirts of the city. The broad two-towered façade enfolds a portal whose first story has plain spiral columns and the second story curious voluted capitals of provincial invention.

The picturesque church and hospital of San Juan de Dios lack noteworthy architectural features. Square piers and red-tiled roofs make for a charming and simple patio, while the little church has a plain façade and single open bell tower. The buildings of this institution, originally founded in 1608,[13] are dated 1771–1776, by virtue of a long inscription upon the portrait of the benefactor, Domingo Antonio Jáurequi y Aguirre, governor of the city, which hangs within the former hospital.

The domestic architecture follows the usual pattern of the Hispanic colonial tradition in remote centers: one- and two-storied houses, tiled roofs, balconies, and arcaded sidewalks. It is picturesque, although it lacks the distinction of beautiful portals, like those of Cajamarca and Trujillo. Dilapidation prevails everywhere. But that in itself possesses at least one virtue in that the town has escaped bad restoration which is limited here to the Prefectura. The town hall (Fig. 154), except for modern balconies, is well preserved and typical with an arcade over the sidewalk and an open loggia in the upper center where the wooden posts have *zapata* capitals. The date 1673 upon the city's coat of arms may record the year the hall was built. Huancavelica, although not one of the most important centers either in ecclesiastical or domestic architecture, deserves more study.

OTHER ANDEAN CHURCHES

MY original hope to compile a complete catalogue of the colonial monuments of Peru had to be foregone because of the vastness of the project. The whole region of the Callejón de Huaylas was omitted because of the lack of time to visit that region. The fact that the architecture there is very provincial, consisting in large part of Andean chapels of the usual type, means that our understanding of Peruvian architecture does not suffer by its exclusion. From Colombia and Ecuador through Peru and Bolivia down into Argentina, the Andean chapel is essentially an expression of the same humble provincial architecture.[14] Usually of adobe, sometimes of brick, it generally has a pitched roof of wood covered with thatch or with tiles. The use of the slightly recessed porch formed by the salient roof is widespread through all of the countries, and undoubtedly was intended as shelter from sun or rain. When the interior is vaulted, the round-arched recess reveals the fact. Towers are of varying sorts: the open arched belfry (*espadaña*), the single-staged tower, or double towers flanking the façade. The latter type with balcony between is one of the most common, having been discussed in the chapter devoted to Cuzco. A good example can be cited at Santa Rosa de Ocopa and it extends even into North America in the well-known mission churches of the state of New Mexico. Wherever well preserved, these chapels have picturesque charm, as for instance the thatched-roofed churches at Rosapata near Juliaca and at Coata near Puno.[15] The region of Huancavelica abounds in them. Too often the incursion of galvanized-iron roofs as a substitute for the original thatch or tiles has broken the spell of the past, and replaced it with the tawdriness of ugly cheap materials.

In the region of Huancayo no architecture of significance has come down to us, save numerous Andean chapels in the valley of the Río Mántaro, photographs of which have been published by Harthterré.[16] The famous monastery of the Franciscans at Ocopa is, alas, entirely devoid of interest, having been completely rebuilt after a disastrous fire in 1900.

Notice must be given of four interesting churches in the remote fastnesses of the Andes: Cocharcas, Mamara, Santo Tomás, and Andahuaylas. The first two lie far in the mountains without roads and can only be reached by mule or on foot. The latter two stand upon a road, passable by automobile. Of the four, I have visited only Andahuaylas.

San Pedro at Andahuaylas is a large structure of fine stone masonry, consisting of a long high single nave. Salient pilasters separating the interior into bays indicate an intention to use vaults, an intention which was abandoned in favor of a pitched cane roof. The large choir at the entrance is raised upon a barrel vault. The splendid quality of the stone and the tile roof make for a good sober exterior. The façade with

single tower to the right has a fine portal composed of Doric columns in triumphal-arch disposition, the second story narrower than the first. The stylized rosettes and the leaf ornament upon the portal belong in the category of primitive *mestizo* design, so familiar in rural districts. The church, on the whole, is not provincial, but must have been planned in the seventeenth century by some architect who had been reared in the school of Cuzco.

The most splendid of all the remote Andean churches is the sanctuary of Nuestra Señora de Cocharcas (Fig. 155) in the province of Andahuaylas, whose cult long ago spread into other regions of Peru, and into Bolivia and Chile. The substantial stone structure has the plan of a Latin cross with dome over the crossing and an elevated choir at the façade end. Glazed tiles decorate the pavement and the interior of the dome.

The exterior, known to me only by photographs, appears large and impressive with two towers flanking a simple portal of Doric pilasters and moldings. The portal of the atrium is an interesting case of provincial craftsmanship in which simple geometric interlaces and linear patterns cover the surface. It appears to be a case of natural primitivism rather than of *mudéjar* influence. Nor would there seem to be any stylistic relation to the *mestizo* churches of Arequipa and Lake Titicaca.

According to documents in the archives at Cocharcas, the present church was begun in 1672. An inscription upon the high altar states that it was complete by 1675, an astoundingly short time.[17] Hence this structure is the third upon the site, the first having been begun in 1598, only to be replaced shortly thereafter by the second in 1623.[18]

Scarcely less important than Cocharcas as an architectural monument is the parish church (Figs. 156, 157) of an Andean village called Mamara (province of Andahuaylas). No historian either of architecture or of the Church has ever braved the rigors of mountain passes by muleback to visit it. Luckily it is known as the result of an expedition of a photographer of Cuzco.

The style of both the church and the retables within attests to its derivation from Cuzco, probably at a date sometime in the first half of the eighteenth century. Whether documentation exists either in the form of archives or inscriptions only investigation on the spot will reveal. The general type of stone church with façade in two stories, flanked by towers, is derivative from Cuzco. Details supply further evidence, for instance, the elliptical openings of the towers (La Compañía, Cuzco), and the elliptical window in the second story which opens into the choir (San Sebastián, Cuzco). In the side portal at Mamara the architect imitated the columns of the Mercedarian cloister at Cuzco, copying the scale and guilloche patterns, as well as the crowns of acanthus leaves and the capitals. The columns of the main portal, on the other hand, are more eclectic in their decorative themes, although the origin remains the same. Throughout, the carving in low flat planes and the high degree of stylization place the church in the category of *mestizo* work. To the familiar rectangular leaf pattern is added the shell in great abundance. Most extraordinary of all are the cherubs' heads in the spandrels of the main portal, with their fantastic calligraphic lines, made to fill the architectural space. A low wall surrounds the atrium into which entrance is given by a fine portal of the same character. The church at Mamara, virtually buried and forgotten, is a notable testimony to the vigorous spirit of viceregal Peru.

Mention should be made of an important and unpublished church in the village of Santo Tomás in the southern part of the province of Cuzco, near the province of Arequipa. Although now reachable by road, it is virtually unknown. Judging from a poor photograph, I suspect that the richly carved portal should be regarded as derivative from the school of Arequipa, to be dated in the first half of the eighteenth century. No one can doubt the splendor of this church of finely cut masonry, crowned by an unusually prominent dome.

VI

NORTHERN PERU—I

TRUJILLO

TRUJILLO is situated on the coastal desert of northern Peru, and today is the most important center to the north of Lima, although numbering only about forty thousand inhabitants. The Andes rise deceptively close at hand, seemingly within the plain of sand and desert grass along the sea. Slightly inland the valley of Chicama harbors great sugar plantations and farms, and in Trujillo's own valley of Chimú lies the great pre-Columbian capital, Chan-Chan, not to speak of lesser archaeological sites. Farther north are Chiclayo, which has flourished as a commercial center in recent years, and still beyond toward the equator, Piura, the first town Pizarro founded. Cajamarca, an Incaic capital and the site of one of the most famous episodes of the conquest, nestles high in the Andes, still a colonial city, but one which has suffered utter degeneration, forgotten and forlorn in this present world.

Architecturally the city of Trujillo has less to offer than Cajamarca, that is, in quality not in quantity, and churches in Guadalupe and Saña far surpass anything the present regional capital has to offer. Trujillo, nevertheless, maintains much of its colonial aspect, particularly in the portals of houses which, after Cuzco, Arequipa, and Cajamarca, are the finest in all Peru. Its ecclesiastical architecture lacks the great vitality and originality of that of southern Peru and of Cajamarca, and might be described as agreeable and moderately interesting. Retables, on the contrary, are both abundant and of exceptionally high quality.

The cathedral of Trujillo, like that of other coastal cities, has suffered from repeated earthquakes and constant restorations, but unlike many others, it retains its colonial design. Thanks to the scholarly monograph on the diocese by García Irigoyen, with its thorough documentation from the cathedral archives, the complex history of the edifice is known.[1] When the diocese of Trujillo, embracing all northern Peru, was actively separated from that of Lima in 1616, the parish church on the plaza served as cathedral. After the earthquake three years later, they began a new building under the architect, Bartolomé de Cueva. One of the most severe earthquakes came later in 1635, after which the Dominican architect of Lima, Diego Maroto, presented plans for a new and larger cathedral (1643). That structure, finally begun four years later, and consecrated in

1666, seems to be in all essentials the fabric of today. Diego Maroto supplied the plans, but probably never directed the work personally in Trujillo; at any event a man named Francisco Balboa was in charge in 1664.[2] Another earthquake in 1687 caused much damage which was thoroughly repaired in the time of Bishop Mimbela (1721–1740). He gave the church many jewels, constructed the Sala del Cabildo (1732), and apparently donated a pulpit and the present high altar, as well as the silver tabernacle and *sagrario,* now lost.[3] In 1755 the church council sent the king the report of an architect, Toribio Ramírez, requesting eight thousand pesos for repairs,[4] but presumably no action was taken before the next and last great catastrophe of 1759. Cristóbal de Vargas, of wide reputation from Lima to Potosí, is said to have had charge of the subsequent restorations in 1768–1771,[5] and reconsecration took place in 1781. New towers (1782–1784), badly constructed and involved in litigation, had to be reërected by the contracting architect, Tomás Rodríguez. Since that time no radical alteration in the edifice has been made except the transfer of the choir stalls to the sanctuary and the destruction of the *trascoro* (1911) which had occupied its traditional Hispanic place in the nave.[6]

The ground plan as reproduced from the work of Martínez Compañón shows a rectangular church with the choir in the nave and an elevated sanctuary approached by a flight of steps.[7] The arrangement is like that of the cathedral of Cuzco (Fig. 7) with the difference that Trujillo has no lateral chapels. The sanctuary of Lima Cathedral was originally in like position, but there were two bays to the rear and a chapel dedicated to St. Bartholomew. Other than in the floor plan the cathedral of Trujillo bears no relation to either of the other famous rectangular churches of Peru: Cuzco and Lima. At Trujillo a fine dome over the sanctuary produces a climactic effect in a simple and dignified interior (Fig. 160) which is marked by cruciform piers with molded capitals and the customary molded cornice beneath the vaults. Exceptional is the use of groined vaults throughout with the bays separated by the usual transverse arches. Niches for altars, four to the side in the aisles, are decorated with large canvases of the seventeenth century, one of them being dedicated to Santo Toribio and bearing the date 1681. There can be little doubt that Trujillo Cathedral should be regarded as Diego Maroto's creation and as his masterpiece. The floor plan he obviously based upon that of Cuzco Cathedral, and the austere interior just as unmistakably carries the stamp of the surviving classicism so typical of Peru in the seventeenth century. The exterior (Fig. 158) embodies a like spirit of conservatism, Doric portals with broken pediments but without any suggestion of Baroque movement and devoid of surface decoration. The elliptical window over the main portal affords some light in an extremely dark interior. The design of the portal and window later served as model for the façades of El Belén and Santa Rosa, both of Trujillo. The cathedral throughout is constructed of brick covered with stucco.

The school of Trujillo never adopted a genuinely Baroque style like that of the façades of the cathedral and La Compañía in Cuzco. In this region Santiago de Huamán and Santa Lucía at Ferreñafe (Lambayeque) (Figs. 165, 176) are the exceptions to the rule. It was solely in Cajamarca that the late Baroque of the eighteenth century flourished in northern Peru, and that must be regarded as an independent school. Otherwise, the cathedral of Trujillo did much to establish the seventeenth- and eighteenth-century style for the entire diocese which included all that lies to the north.

The chief religious orders were represented in Trujillo and at an early period. The Franciscans are said to have come shortly after the foundation of the city which took place in 1535, the Mercedarians presumably in the same period, the Augustinians in 1558, the Jesuits in 1627, and the Bethlehemites in 1680.[8] The first Dominican house, now destroyed, was located nearby in Chicama, a foundation of Fray Domingo de Santo Tomás, mentioned by Cieza de León in 1553.[9] The same friar established a convent in Trujillo itself some time between that date and his transfer to Chuquisaca as bishop in the year 1563. These facts and his many virtues are recorded in the legend on his portrait which hangs in the Dominican church at Trujillo, probably a contemporary picture but many times repainted and now in a dilapidated condition.

Except for San Agustín, none of the churches of Trujillo antedates the earthquake of 1619 in anything save the ground plan. Calancha avers that the walls of the Augustinian structure withstood the great catastrophe.[10] The plan of the long nave (Fig. 159), so characteristic of Peruvian churches of the sixteenth century, corroborates the written word. Part of the heavy walls and surely the low barrel vaults belong to the reconstruction of the sixteen-twenties. Presumably at this time the aisles, or more properly chapels, were added, two chapels to the right and three to the left. The irregular shapes of the latter and the clumsy construction of the piers which were cut through the original walls can be noted both within the church and from the roofs. They leave no doubt that the church was never planned thus at the outset.

In 1931 the present neocolonial façade was erected, replacing the original of which a photograph hangs in the reception room of the monastery. The unpretentiousness of the Trujillo school prevailed here too in the simple doorway flanked by pilasters and the one tower to the left. To the left of the church, the early seventeenth-century façade of the convent (Fig. 162) furnishes a striking contrast to the contemporary imitation of the colonial. The wall of brick covered with white stucco is topped by crenelations. A very fine portal, flanked by Doric half columns, supports a curiously shaped tympanum at each side of which are pyramidal pinnacles. Most striking of all is the repeated pattern of octagonal coffers within the tympanum. The convent doorway of San Agustín, authentically colonial, surpasses all else of its type, either religious or domestic, which has survived from the mid-seventeenth century in Trujillo.

The church of San Francisco, likewise rebuilt after 1619, has much the same character as San Agustín in its heavy walls, clumsy proportions, and low barrel vaults. Very curious is the heavy cornice, which projects too much in an amateurish way. Fear of further upheavals of nature and hasty reconstruction explain the appearance of both buildings. In San Francisco, too, arches cut through continuous walls communicate with the side aisles in such a way as to suggest that it was previously a cruciform structure of single nave. The windows, one in the center of each bay of the nave vault, were added in recent years, so great was the desire for more light. The ugly pink and imitation-marble paint further damages a makeshift interior, and the elevated choir is modern.

The exterior of the church was subjected to the fate of cement surfacing, a common phenomenon in the twentieth century. Its principal feature is the large octagonal tower to the left of the façade which was erected subsequent to the earthquake of 1759. These towers are characteristic of northern Peru in the eighteenth century, as witness the single octagonal towers of San Lorenzo in Trujillo, Mansiche, and San Pedro at Lambayeque. Santa Lucía at Ferreñafe (1690) has twin towers (Fig. 176) of the same shape and very large.

The Dominican is the best of the early churches, dating in part at least, from 1641, to judge by an inscription in the left aisle. This reads: *Esta capilla se hizo de la limosna de los esclavos y esclavas de la Madre de Dios. Año de 1641.* The word "slaves" is not to be interpreted literally, for thus devotees of the Madonna of the Rosary called themselves. According to Meléndez, the pre-earthquake structure was made of stone and topped by a cedar roof of interlaces. The church of his own day, apparently the edifice which has come down to us, was of brick and mortar, perfected in the time of the prior, Padre Esteban Bara.[11]

The interior of Santo Domingo (Fig. 161) is the most satisfactory among the monastic churches of Trujillo, dignified and broad in its feeling of space, even if somewhat low in proportions. Its molded cruciform piers and general austerity recall the cathedral, from which it differs strikingly in the lack of clerestory. The general style of Santo Domingo may have influenced the later design of the cathedral itself, so far as its barrenness and Doric piers are concerned. The plan of basilican type with projecting sanctuary belongs to the Lima-Arequipa group, formerly discussed, especially in respect to vaulting, characterized by barrel vaults in the nave and domical vaults topped by lanterns in the aisles. In Arequipa, La Compañía and La Merced, and in Lima, La Merced and San Francisco, all have this arrangement. Trujillo adheres to the same coastal tradition in Santo Domingo, San Francisco, La Merced, and San Agustín, although the vaults are domical rather than cupolas as in Lima and Arequipa. All of these churches suffered in the earthquake of 1759 according to Feyjóo's celebrated report, but chiefly in the vaults; none was completely demolished.[12]

The only unusual features of the interior of Santo Domingo are the peculiar long U-shaped choir and the double pilasters for each transverse arch in that section. The façade with single tower to left has a conservative Doric portal with niche above. The portal recalls in style the portals of Santo Domingo and the front doorway of La Merced in Cuzco (Figs. 55, 56), although the Trujillian work does not have volutes in the second story and also differs in other details. It is, of course, a matter of the classical style of the period rather than of any direct relationship. The side entrance of Santo Domingo in Trujillo with its shell niche within the door must be an eighteenth-century reconstruction, I should judge by its style.

The Dominican cloister which now serves as the local prison has no architectural distinction, being of single story with round arches carried on plain square piers. In Trujillo none of the colonial cloisters of monks continues in monastic service today, for all were transferred to secular use in the exclaustration of the early republic. The cloister of San Francisco, originally similar to that of Santo Domingo, now serves in a much altered state, as the Colegio Nacional de San Juan. The Jesuit cloister and that of the Mercedarians (Fig. 163), also of single story and both rusticated in surface, have been altered and transformed into the University of Trujillo and the Court of Justice respectively. San Agustín, the only cloister of two stories in Trujillo, existed until demolished in 1931 to make way for a street and a market. Four forlorn arches of brick covered with plaster can still be seen within the monastery. Two half columns of the Doric order are attached to the piers, an arrangement exactly like that of the Augustinian cloister of Saña, discussed later in this chapter. They are certain evidence of stylistic connection between the two houses of the same monastic rule.

Small and unpretentious in size, La Merced today holds the sad distinction of being the dirtiest and most neglected church in Trujillo. The basilican plan, with barrel-vaulted nave and the aisles covered with domical vaults lighted from above, has already been mentioned in the discussion of Santo Domingo. Like San Francisco the dimensions are heavy and clumsy, the Merced differing from the other seventeenth-century monastic churches of Trujillo in the shortness of its nave. One feature should be noted: the lack of cornice in the nave even in the presence of a clerestory, an omission common in Bolivia, as in the Merced at La Paz, Santo Domingo and La Merced of Sucre, and Santo Domingo at Cochabamba.[13] Only the stone reliefs (Fig. 164) of the life of San Pedro Nolasco in the pendentives of the dome, now wooden, merit consideration. The façade of the Merced is by far superior to the interior, due in large part to the open-arched belfries which are graceful and recall those of La Recoleta in Cajamarca. They were built after the earthquake of 1759, in which La Merced suffered severely, according to Feyjóo. The portal with three orders superimposed, Doric, Ionic, and the top indescribable, is simple and pleasing.

One of the best of the monastic churches

of Trujillo was the Compañía, at present half ruined, its vaults partly destroyed, and used as a storehouse by the university which functions in the cloister. In contrast to others it has excellent scale and space relationships, unmistakably indicative of the hand of a professional architect. The rustication of the pilasters and transverse arches contrasts in texture with the wall, the material throughout being brick coated with stucco, except for the cane-and-plaster barrel vaults. The Latin-cross plan with niche chapels in the nave conforms in a general way to the erroneously so-called Jesuit type and is the only example of it in Trujillo. The skillful placing of the elevated choir over a flattened arch, and the successful design of the dome over the crossing contribute to an effective interior. The towerless façade comprises two stories with Ionic half columns below at the portal and Corinthian above, where a single large window gives light into the choir. An interesting Palladian detail is noted in the use of brackets beneath the cornice of the portal. As for the date of the church, it may be presumed to have been erected in the mid-seventeenth century, sometime after the first fathers came in 1627.

Considerable damage befell the church and hospital of El Belén, founded in 1680, in the earthquake of 1759. It must be considered as largely rebuilt immediately thereafter. In the hospital only one small cloister of single story, like the others of Trujillo, remains. The simple cruciform plan of the church, the dome on dentelated cornice, and the barrel vaults constitute a good unpretentious interior, and one which enjoys

good care and cleanliness. The façade, clearly of eighteenth-century facture, resembles its contemporary, Santa Rosa, in its two small towers and the elliptical window with its rusticated wall surface above the portal. The small twin towers characterize most of the mid-eighteenth-century churches in Trujillo: El Belén, Santa Rosa, Santa Ana, and Santa Teresa.

El Belén has undergone unfortunate disfigurement in recent times on the exterior, particularly in the ugly pseudo-Russian top placed on the dome, and a side buttress, clumsily set against the nave to support recent fractures.

Santa Teresa met the common fate of severe damage in 1759 at the moment it was to have been inaugurated, just thirty-five years after the foundation of the Carmelite nuns in Trujillo. Restoration followed and the consecration at last took place in 1773.[14] The church is small with single nave of nunnery tradition (Fig. 20), having, as so commonly, a lower choir to the right of the sanctuary and the elevated choir above the main entrance. The cornice with a corbel in the center of each bay betrays its connection with the contemporary school of Lima, where that detail is a signature of the mid-eighteenth century. The ever-present dome rises in its customary position in the bay corresponding to the crossing, and as usual there are barrel vaults in the rest of the church. The retables have brought to the church exaggerated local fame, for in no way does Santa Teresa equal Jesús María in Lima, nor Santa Teresa in Ayacucho, nor many others in the sierra. Architecturally the interior is satisfactory but undistinguished. Frankly bad is the only description which can be given to the façade, with its small twin towers, its two-storied division with heavy Corinthian columns below and curious bulging pilasters above, all of which lack scale and result in a heavy ugly composition. The building does little credit to its architect, General Mateo Vitores de Velasco.

The other nunnery in Trujillo, Santa Clara, established in 1743, has been transformed into neo-Romanesque within recent years, and hence can no longer be classified as colonial. The ground plan belongs to the same type as that of Santa Teresa, although considerably larger. Here, as in La Merced, the one interesting survival is the series of stone reliefs carved on the pendentives of the dome, in this case, naturally enough, dedicated to the life of Santa Clara.

Among the parish churches Santa Rosa claims the distinction of being the best. Rebuilt by Bishop Luna Victoria (1758–1777),[15] it resembles El Belén in the elliptical window and rusticated treatment of the center and its other contemporaries of Trujillo in two small towers. Newly restored with simplicity and good taste, it has become a small chapel with the apse abandoned. The corbeled cornice recalls Santa Teresa, but in the modern rebuilding of the vault the customary transverse bands have been omitted.

Santa Ana and San Lorenzo, Bishop Luna Victoria likewise restored, the former much in the style of Santa Teresa so far as the façade is concerned with the difference that

the portal has a large triumphal-arch motive. The single-naved interior of Santa Ana [16] now can be characterized only as a complete ruin, and the cruciform San Lorenzo is a very poor structure of wood. The unpretentious façade has a single polygonal tower of Bishop Luna Victoria's day, similar to the tower of Mansiche. The fame of this church, however, must rest upon its magnificent high altar (Figs. 350, 351), a fine monument to the bishop's memory, and one which is discussed in the chapter on retables.

For the sake of completeness, there remains the mention of the chapel of the Seminario de San Carlos y San Marcelo, first built by Bishop Juan de la Calle y Heredia, but now Gothicized beyond repair,[17] and the church variously known as the Portada de la Sierra or the Capilla de la Unión. The latter, a long narrow edifice of one nave crudely built, retains no vestige of the church reërected in 1786, and soon after restored by the architect Evaristo Noriega (1798–1801), for which documents are preserved in the Archivo de Indias in Seville.[18]

In pueblos near Trujillo interesting churches are found at Huamán, Mansiche, and Huanchaco. The single-naved plan, brick walls, and wooden roofing prevail in all, the first two having simple pitched roofs and the last a barrel vault of cane and plaster. A single large tower suffices at Mansiche and Huanchaco, both undoubtedly posterior to the earthquake of 1759, and belonging to the series of towers characteristic of northern Peru in this period, which have already been mentioned in connection with San Francisco of Trujillo. The façade of Mansiche is two-storied with the Doric order below and peculiar flat pilasters ending in pyramids above. The elliptical window which let into the choir, now destroyed, occurs repeatedly in the Trujillian school, following the model first established in the cathedral. The portal of Huanchaco also has the oval window, but the design consists of the broad single story of classical orders like the Jesuit church in Trujillo. Huanchaco's true glory is its dramatic situation, rising upon a desolate sandy height, surrounded by an atrium wall, and overlooking the open sea of the Pacific Ocean. The sites of both Mansiche and Huanchaco were established early, but the present buildings belong in large part to the time of Bishop Vitores de Velasco (1705–1713),[19] their towers to the post-earthquake (1759) period, plus various modern restorations.

The church of Santiago at Huamán deserves recognition as possessing the most interesting façade (Fig. 165) in the region of Trujillo. Two towers, now very much aslant, flank a portal of triumphal-arch design with statues of saints in the niches. Santiago, the patron, appears as *matamoros* on horseback, and the rest represent Mercedarian saints, to which order the church pertained, as the Mercedarian shield also indicates. Over the doorway are two recumbent mermaids complete with fish tails, playing the *charango*, a surprising appearance of the mermaid motive in northern Peru, the only case known to me. It occurs, on the contrary, with frequency in the sierra of southern Peru and Bolivia: Lampa, Puno Cathedral (Figs. 251, 252), Santa María de Montserrat (near Andahuaylas), in a retable of Santa Clara in Cuzco, houses in Oropesa (Cuzco), San Lorenzo, Potosí, and elsewhere. Other interesting details at Huamán are the draped heads on the frieze, a motive which also embellishes the choir stalls of Trujillo Cathedral, and retables in San Francisco, San Agustín, and La Merced. The draped head in much more elaborate fashion decorates the columns on the façade of the church at Ferreñafe (Fig. 176). Its derivation from the school of Lima is discussed in the chapter on Lima, and in the section on retables.

The façade of Santiago de Huamán is another instance of native Indian taste in the allover decoration of wall surface, and it contrasts sharply with the sober restraint of the façades of Trujillo itself, from which such exuberance is conspicuously lacking. The cherubs' heads on the arch of the doorway strike an anachronistic note, a revival of Renaissance usage in the eighteenth century. Strips of ornament like side pieces of a retable recall such devices of southern Peru. Charming and amusingly primitive is the large scroll-like stylization of flowers in the corners beside the mermaids. The yellow paint of the background against the white reliefs and columns plays no small part in the gaiety and naïve charm of this surprisingly original composition.

The religious architecture of Trujillo is unpretentious and definitely conservative. Santo Domingo and the cathedral in the middle of the seventeenth century established the norm which prevailed throughout. These two churches deserve praise for their dignity, sobriety, and good taste. Santo Domingo tends to low, heavy proportions which in the case of San Francisco and San Agustín descend to clumsiness and rusticity. The Compañía, now in an abandoned state, must have been elegant in its prime, and the eighteenth-century church of El Belén, inside at least, is well planned. The destruction in the earthquake of 1759 was limited, according to Feyjóo's account, to vaults and towers, and in the restorations the seventeenth-century character of the churches was not lost. The numerous retables of Trujillo antedate 1759 with a few exceptions, another proof that damage was not as extensive as might have been expected. Brick and mortar prevail because of lack in this region of stone, a material which nowhere occurs in any edifice. Brick vaults were replaced by cane in some instances in the eighteenth century, for experience proved it the more serviceable material along the whole coast of Peru, so frequently visited by upheavals of nature.

The best of Trujillo, however, lies in its retables and in its domestic architecture. Trujillo boasts a good collection of retables of the eighteenth century, having suffered less than Lima in the renovations of the nineteenth. After Cuzco, which possesses by far the largest number and the best in quality, and Ayacucho, which falls well below Cuzco, Trujillo ranks as the third city of Peru in the variety and quantity of its wood sculpture.

GUADALUPE

THE former Augustinian monastery of Nuestra Señora de Guadalupe stands in the village which inherited its name on the Pan-American highway, one hundred and thirty kilometers north of Trujillo. The church and cloister are accurately dated by Calancha who states that the house established in 1564 fell to the ground in the great earthquake of 1619.[20] Three days later on May 17, 1619, the site of the new establishment was chosen at a distance of one quarter of a league from the original location. The present church and cloister were erected, therefore, in the sixteen-twenties. Since Calancha was prior of the Augustinians at Trujillo at the time of the earthquake, there is no reason to doubt the accuracy of his statement. He speaks of "the most sumptuous church of vaults and *lacerías*," the usual terminology for describing, in the seventeenth century, Gothic vaults (Fig. 171) with decorative ribs. Calancha aptly stresses too the "sumptuous cloister" and its fine vaulting.

The Augustinian churches at Guadalupe and Saña are located near each other geographically, and they are so similar in style that they must be the work of the same architect. The man was undoubtedly Blas de Orellana, who was engaged upon the church and cloister of San Francisco at Saña and upon San Agustín in the same city in 1617–1619.[21] The vaults of the latter (Figs. 168, 169) are especially like those at Guadalupe, where the late-Gothic decorative ribs rest upon corbels. The designs of the ribs are not, however, identical, those of Guadalupe being more sophisticated and purer Gothic than the nave vaults of Saña. Particularly lovely are the circles and ogive ellipses which the ribs describe. The plan at Guadalupe follows the usual single-naved type with an elevated choir. The exterior of the church, much restored, has lost its original aspect.

The large cloister of single story is severely classic and sober in its use of a Doric half column attached to each molded pier on the court side. Simple groined vaults of brick rest upon corbels placed against the wall and against the piers. The cloister portal, the very essence of late Renaissance dignity, far surpasses in that respect the portals of San Agustín at Saña. Its Doric columns and molded pediment are austerely barren of all ornament. To the right the bell tower of two open arches has an interesting rusticated treatment, as likewise do the three windows which open into the second story of the monastic quarters. The material throughout is brick covered with stucco.

The church at San Pedro de Lloc, a short distance south of Guadalupe, has suffered considerably from restoration. At best a provincial building, it has an interesting main portal.

SAÑA

O N the northern coastal desert of Peru lie the ruins of Saña, once the capital of a province and after Trujillo the most important city of the region. The crumbling walls of its seven churches, overgrown with brush, rise in romantic desolation (Fig. 166). Saña recalls other dead cities of Hispanic America: Antigua in Guatemala, overwhelmed by earthquake, and Old Panama City, abandoned after the ravage it suffered from the English pirate, Henry Morgan, in 1671. None of these is more picturesque, and none so remote from the world of today as Saña, where dim echoes of the past grandeur are hidden amid a flat expanse of desert sands, dotted here and there by low brush. Founded in 1563, the city grew to prosperity in the production of sugar and leather, until catastrophe overtook her when the English pirate sacked the region for seven days in 1686. The deathblow fell later on March 18, 1720, in the form of a torrential flood which swept away the entire city within a few hours. Only the churches, because of their solider construction, remained to some degree intact.[22] They gradually disintegrated into still greater ruin, and Saña never lifted her head again, for her citizens moved off to Trujillo and Lambayeque. Her unfavorable geographic position was too great a drawback and could not withstand the onslaughts of both man and nature. Today a poor village of humble peasants lies on the rim of the old city, the plan of whose very streets is lost. Only the ruined walls of her churches, overgrown with vine and brush, rise up ghostlike in quiet pastures.

The convents of the Augustinians, the Franciscans, and the Mercedarians, as well as the *matriz*, were large and important structures. Less so were Santa Lucía, San Joaquín, and San Juan de Dios, the latter small and modest according to the chronicler of the order.[23] This church still exists, though much rebuilt and rededicated to Santo Toribio, for the sainted archbishop of Lima died in Saña on March 23, 1606, while making his third pastoral visit to his see, which at that time stretched from Lima far to the north.[24]

The monastery of Nuestra Señora de las Mercedes was the latest of the religious orders to be established in the city, the monks resettling here in 1637, after having previously abandoned their monastery because of the unhealthy climate.[25] Today only the brick skeleton of the church façade (Fig. 174) and a side portal mark the site of the Mercedarian house. There is sufficient to reveal, however, a restrained classical style similar to that of the school of Trujillo in the seventeenth century. The two-towered façade has a dignified doorway flanked by Doric pilasters and surmounted by a simple broken pediment. The window above, which repeats the same design, gave light into the choir loft.

The portal of the *matriz* (Fig. 166) is almost an exact repetition of the Mercedarian and for that reason would seem to belong to the sixteen-thirties. The vaulting of late-Gothic style, on the other hand, is characterized by ribbed construction on corbels, very closely related to that of the church of San Agustín at Saña. The *matriz* surpasses all other monuments of this dead city of Peru in its picturesque desolation. It is so buried in sands and thicket that only an excavation could fully reveal the extent of its large basilican floor plan.

The exact disposition of the single-naved church of San Francisco is even more conjectural and its crumbling walls still more fragmentary. The triumphal arch looms awesomely alone and intact, and at some distance stands the main wall of the façade. The church and cloister were ordered by an agreement of October 30, 1617, from a mulatto architect, named Blas de Orellana. He was under contract to the Franciscans and Augustinians at the same time, a situation which caused him considerable difficulty. In 1618 the local magistrate served notice upon the architect that he must fulfill his obligations to both religious communities without further salary. In order to obtain first rights to his services, the prior of San Agustín took Orellana into his religious community as a monk. The Franciscans appealed on the grounds that Orellana was married and hence disqualified for a monastic career! Later they reached a compromise, whereby he was allowed to complete his work in San Francisco before continuing with the construction of San Agustín.[26] These events took place previous to the great earthquake of May 14, 1619, which destroyed the monastery at Guadalupe, south of Trujillo. As we have seen, the Augustinian monastery there was rebuilt immediately afterwards at one quarter of a league from the site of the sixteenth-century establishment. The close similarity between San Agustín at Saña and at Guadalupe leads to the conclusion that Blas de Orellana, the mulatto friar, was the architect of both.

The church and cloister at Saña (Figs. 167–170) are well enough preserved to give an excellent idea of their original magnificence. Calancha, writing about the year 1635, described "the excellent vaulted church with beautiful chapels." [27] The plan of the church is most extraordinary, giving the impression in its ruinous condition of three small churches in parallel alignment. In reality the church proper has a nave with rectangular sanctuary and the usual raised choir above the portal. At the right hand is a short aisle consisting of only three bays. The opposite aisle runs the full length of the church, and terminates in a large sacristy which projects well beyond the apse. The material throughout is brick, originally covered with plaster. The three bays of vaulting in the nave, which have survived in relatively good condition, provide adequate testimony to the splendor of the edifice in its heyday. They are late-Gothic ribbed vaults with liernes and tiercerons, but not highly decorated. The ribs spring from corbels, and the bays are separated by broad transverse arches of seventeenth-century type. The elevated choir is reached by a stairway from a chamber which is connected with the cloister, according to established practice in monastic houses, so that the friars could enter it directly from the monastery. The vaulting of the truncated aisle to the right, only one bay of which survives, was like that of the nave. The four vaults of the opposite aisle, all in existence, have an exceptionally lovely design with a large rosette in the center upon which converge eight ribs. In one of the drawings in his manuscript of 1681 the Spanish architect, Simón García, introduced a similar vault. It reflects the school of Rodrigo Gil de Ontañón who lived in the preceding century. [28] These vaults at Saña are rivaled in beauty throughout all Peru only by those of the contemporary church of Guadalupe.

The main entrance to the church of San Agustín (Fig. 167) consists of a fine classical portal flanked by Doric pilasters and loaded at the sides by pinnacles. The metopes of the Doric frieze are decorated with disks in Renaissance style, while the approach of the Baroque period is suggested by the broken pediment. The window just above, which gives light into the choir, has a semicircular hood suspended on truncated pilasters, likewise in late Renaissance style. The convent door at the left hand, topped by the same Doric frieze, conforms to the same late-classical spirit, which in Peru continues well into the seventeenth century, and crossbreeds with the Gothic in such an interesting fashion here at Saña, at Guadalupe, and in the cathedral of Cuzco.

The huge cloister (Fig. 170) numbers nine round arches to the side, each pier carrying two Doric half columns upon the inner face. Like the cloister at Guadalupe it is limited to one story, but in the latter the compound piers have single Doric half columns. Very little can be said of the monastic quarters, since only the hall and chamber on the west wing of the first floor have endured to the present day.

San Agustín was without a doubt one of the most splendid of all monastic establishments in South America. Of the three monuments, related in type, which have survived the ravages of earthquakes, floods, and reconstruction, all are Augustinian houses: those of Saña, Guadalupe, and Copacabana.

Some day, perhaps, excavations will throw more light upon the lost architectural history of Saña. Little new documentary information can be expected, since the archives were of a certainty destroyed in the great flood of 1720.

CHICLAYO

CHICLAYO, a modern city, has only one colonial monument of importance, the former Franciscan convent, and that is about to be demolished to widen a street. The main cloister (Fig. 173), which for many years housed the Colegio Nacional de San José, possesses a feature apparently unique in Peru: pointed arches carried on rectangular molded piers. Whereas the Gothic arch occurs with some frequency in Mexico, it is found rarely in Peru: in the crossing of San Pedro at Juli (Fig. 44), in the first chapel to the left and to the right in Cuzco Cathedral, just within the lateral portal of Santo Domingo in Lima,[29] in the Sala Capitular of La Merced at Arequipa, and in the church at Azángaro.

The foundation of the Franciscan monastery at Chiclayo took place in 1561. Work on the construction of the church and monastery was in progress during the years 1572–1594, and I am inclined to believe that the main cloister belongs to this period.[30] The structure of brick and stucco, now picturesquely overgrown with trees and shrubbery, is unique in Peru, and deserves a better fate than the guillotine to which local authorities have condemned it. It consists of a single story of five pointed arches to each of the four sides. The second cloister, already in ruinous condition and employed until recently as a basketball court, possesses but moderate interest. Its round arches and molded piers suggest the seventeenth century, a date contemporary with the church. Two gables with scroll ornament rise strangely lost amid the ruins, in sections which once housed portals.

The original church, covered with a wooden roof, collapsed in the great earthquake of 1618, and the rebuilding began in the following year. Progress must have been rapid for that age, since Vázquez de Espinosa spoke of the monastery (*circa* 1630) as "elaborate and architecturally very interesting."[31] The church (Fig. 172) is unpretentious although sizeable, far more satisfactory outside than within. It can be classified in a general way as an offshoot of the school of Trujillo of the seventeenth century. The side portal with molded pilasters and plain semicircular hood, broken in the center, is dignified and conservative like the Trujillian prototypes. The two-storied façade, likewise, embodies classical restraint and good dimensions. The gable above and the towers are neo-Romanesque additions of modern facture, fortunately not unduly incongruous. The one feature which gives the church a definitely colonial stamp, and imparts a certain picturesqueness, is the use of crenelations, an anachronism very common in Hispanic America as late as the mid-eighteenth century.

The plan of the church includes nave and two aisles without lateral chapels, a projecting sanctuary, dome over the crossing, raised choir, and molded rectangular piers. The eight bays of the nave are separated by transverse arches, and covered by heavy barrel vaults of cane and adobe. The materials used in the vaults indicate that they were reconstructed in the eighteenth century. Walls throughout are brick, covered with plaster. The exceptional use of transverse barrel vaults in the aisles strikes an unusual note, in a frankly provincial and mediocre interior.

For the sake of completeness, mention should be made of the one other colonial church in Chiclayo, formerly a private chapel and now a parish church dedicated to Santa Verónica. A small modest edifice with roofing of wooden beams and adobe, its walls are constructed of a series of piers. The two-towered façade, low and humble, has a simple doorway, flanked by Doric half columns which suggest an eighteenth-century date.

Much the finest church façade (Figs. 175, 176) on the coast of northern Peru is that of Santa Lucía in Ferreñafe, a village nineteen kilometers northeast of Chiclayo. It has the added virtue of being dated by a large inscription at the base of the left tower within the present parochial office, *Año de 1690.* The composition is excellent with a two-storied Baroque portal between large polygonal towers. The latter belong to the series of octagonal towers located in northern Peru, and previously discussed in connection with San Francisco at Trujillo. Those of Ferreñafe are perhaps the earliest, because of the destruction of the others in Trujillo in the earthquake of 1759. The octagonal tower of San Pedro of Lambayeque, much nearer Ferreñafe, is also an eighteenth-century structure.

The style at Ferreñafe is severe, with Doric pilasters and a frieze of triglyphs and disk metopes. Here is unmistakable evidence of local tradition, in view of the similarity to the frieze on the portals of San Agustín at Saña. The two-storied center of the church at Ferreñafe establishes the unknown architect as a man with an excellent sense of relative dimensions. The traditional scrolls unify the design, rather than act as pure decoration. The ball-and-tongue ornament, common in Trujillian domestic architecture, and in churches in Lima, Cuzco, and elsewhere, puts in an appearance in the upper center. Most intesting of all is the recurrence of the draped female heads on the columns, a motive found not only in Lima in the main portal of San Francisco, and the retable of the Conception in the cathedral, but also in the choir stalls of Trujillo Cathedral and a few small retables in the same city. Even the typical choir-stall motive, a draped cloth filled with fruits, is used: tropical fruits produced locally, such as cherimoyer and papaya, along with the traditional and allegorical grape and apple. Unfortunately the excellence of the Ferreñafe façade is partly masked by ugly red paint in imitation of bricks, a condition, however, which another coat of paint could easily rectify. The handling of the window in the upper center is effective and original with the rather prominent balcony, the repetition of scrolls laterally, and the shell with pediment above. Just below the balcony two nude sculptured youths hold the escutcheon of the town of Ferreñafe, a plate upon which are displayed the eyes of the patroness, St. Lucy.

The side portal is a curious two-storied affair composed of giant rusticated columns, made of brick and stucco as is the whole church. The architect could scarcely have been the same man who designed the main façade. Here a coat of paint consisting of alternate bands of red and white produces an altogether bizarre effect. The interior, originally a long single nave, has lost all of its colonial appearance, and is described here merely as an example of degeneration of taste. Tall thin columns of wood, painted like marble, were added in 1911 to give the illusion of a basilican church, and the retables were destroyed or modernized. Only the fine shell tympanum within the main portal remains unharmed. The roof, now wood and tin, must have been vaulted in times past. Otherwise there would be no explanation for the enormous buttresses added at the sides, at a period subsequent to the original construction. For all its miserable interior, Santa Lucía at Ferreñafe deserves front rank among churches of northern Peru, by virtue of its highly original and exceptionally beautiful façade.

In the village of Lambayeque, the churches have been reduced from four to two, the larger being the parish church of San Pedro (1691) which resembles in plan and style Santa María in Chiclayo and adheres to the school of Trujillo.[32] A large basilican structure with molded piers, barrel vaults in the nave, domical vaults in the aisles, and a modern dome of tin, it has been completely ruined by restoration, consisting of cement on the exterior, a modern façade, and grotesque painting of the interior in imitation red marble (1942). Only the lateral door of simple rusticated design has escaped the destructive hand of remodelers.

At the side of San Pedro stand the ruins of three other churches, joined together in parallel alignment. The one now under the jurisdiction of the Third Order of the Franciscans is intact: a long single nave and a simple façade with two bell towers of open arches. Another façade, two-storied in brick and stucco, with imitation rustication, is the best architecturally of these churches in Lambayeque. The interior has been destroyed, as well as that of the fourth church, which has a single door in a nondescript exterior.

A few colonial houses in Lambayeque deserve mention. The most complete is the house at 91 Calle 8 de Octubre which has a strangely original portal with ruined balcony above. Two half columns topped by turrets flank the door against a background of half columns, all of which consists of stucco veneer over brick. An arched passage leads directly into a charming patio (Fig. 28) of single story, on two sides of which run porches carried on wooden columns with *zapata* capitals. On the street side an open stairway leads to the single room and balcony in the second story of the façade. Very striking for its length is the wooden balcony of another house which extends continuously for a block on one side of the house and a half block on the other. Lambayeque today is for the most part dull and colorless, with just a flash here and there, as a reminder of greater prosperity in days gone by.

VII

NORTHERN PERU — II

CAJAMARCA

CAJAMARCA, once a capital of the Incas, lies in the mountains of northern Peru. Situated in a valley, at an elevation of ten thousand feet, it is rich in eucalyptus and mountain vegetation, and overhung with radiant blue sky and the great billowing white clouds of the sierra.[1] Much like Cuzco in its landscape, Cajamarca is further testimony to the Incas' appreciation of nature. Here Pizarro came in November 1532 with his small band of adventurers which included the celebrated Franciscan friar, Padre Valverde. It was here that Atahualpa, the emperor, fell prisoner, languished incarcerated for a year, and then was put to death notwithstanding his willingness to submit to baptism into Christianity at the hands of Fray Valverde.

On the arrival of the Spanish an Inca Temple of the Sun was promptly transformed into a Christian church dedicated to St. Francis. About 1562 the Franciscans built a new church of rubble and brick covered by a wooden roof. It was long and narrow, the familiar type of the mid-sixteenth century in Peru, like La Merced and San Cristóbal in Ayacucho, San Juan at Juli, and San Jerónimo near Cuzco. This church was dismantled in 1687, previous to the inauguration of new construction.

Some walls remained behind the present Capilla de la Dolorosa until they were cleared away for no apparent reason in 1928–1931.[2]

Unmistakable evidence of the existence of an Open Chapel in the early days of Cajamarca is divulged in Santo Toribio's report of his pastoral visit, apparently made in 1593. He says, "Although large, the church does not hold all of the people of the village in it . . . and thus they say mass on Sundays and festivals in a chapel (adjoined to the same church) which is in the cemetery. In the latter all of the people of the village gather all the morning, etc." [3] That the Open Chapel was an expedient of the frontier throughout the Spanish colonies, and not limited to Mexico, becomes more and more apparent as Hispanic studies progress.

Cajamarca belonged to the diocese of Trujillo until 1908. Nonetheless, the style of ecclesiastical architecture in the two cities is strikingly different, due to the remoteness of Cajamarca and to geographic and climatic conditions completely unlike those of Trujillo. The latter stands in the desert near the sea, and in its architecture relied upon brick and stucco. Lofty Cajamarca, like Puno and Arequipa, used stone throughout, even in the vaults, and developed façades luxuriantly sculptured. Notwithstanding these features in common, the school of Cajamarca is independent of southern Peru. Its façades are identical in technique and decorative motives with the gilded retables of eighteenth-century Peru. The indigenous elements which characterize Puno and Arequipa are of minor significance here. Very few decorative themes of indigenous type appealed to the Cajamarcan sculptors. The flat primitivism of *mestizo* design is notably absent except in some details of the façade of San Antonio and the interior of the Capilla de la Dolorosa. Both Cajamarca and Puno belong to the late Baroque period of effervescent floridity, but the former is essentially Hispanic and the south of Peru, *mestizo*.

Cajamarca possesses six churches. San José, a humble Andean chapel of adobe, with single bell tower and salient roof to form a porch, has no particular interest save its inscription which gives the date of its construction in 1683.[4] In addition, there are the Franciscan Recoleta and La Inmaculada Concepción, but the glory of Cajamarca are the three eighteenth-century churches with retable façades: San Antonio de Padua, the cathedral, and El Belén.

The present cathedral of Cajamarca, originally a parish church, was raised to the category of *matriz* in 1682,[5] at which time a new structure was begun. Eighty years elapsed before the consecration of the church took place in 1762, and even then the façade was unfinished, and thus it remains today.[6] The floor plan and side portal, however, fall within the later years of the seventeenth century. This side portal (Fig. 178) bears the royal escutcheon of Spain and the inscription, *Año de 1686.* It and the contemporary portal of the Sagrario beside it present a restrained architectural design characterized by the pilasters pendant on corbels, and by the stylized leaf in rectangle, both upon the frieze and on the surface of the arch. The dated portal has a clearly seventeenth-century character in the rectangular emphasis of the design and in the use of the familiar scale motive on the central corbel. The Sagrario portal must have been delayed in the finishing, judging by the scrolls in the second story which so closely resemble those of the eighteenth century on the main façade. The magnificent escutcheon with flourishing plumed helmet is that of the city of Cajamarca.

Some relationships between Cajamarca and the coastal region of Peru are found in the plans of the churches. The basilican type with single apse, dome over the crossing, and barrel vaults in the nave, transept, and sanctuary is common to Lima, Arequipa, Trujillo, and Cajamarca. They differ, however, in the vaulting of the aisles. In the churches of San Francisco (Fig. 10) and La Merced of Lima, and in La Merced and La Compañía (Fig. 16) of Arequipa, each bay of the aisles is covered with a small dome lighted from above. Instead of a dome, a domical vault, lighted from above, is used in the aisles of Santo Domingo of Arequipa, and likewise in the churches of the monastic orders in Trujillo: Santo Domingo (Fig. 161), La Merced, San Agustín (Fig. 159), and San Francisco. In all of these churches the large dome over the crossing is lacking only in La Merced of Arequipa, where it has been transferred to the sanctuary.

Among the churches of Cajamarca, San Antonio (Fig. 11) follows the coastal tradition the most closely. It varies only in the omission of light from above in the domical vaults of the aisles, and surely less light is needed in this region than in Lima and Trujillo. The cathedral of Cajamarca (Fig. 181) omits the large dome over the crossing, as well as the lighting of the aisles from above. The aisle vaults of the cathedral have the peculiarity of an elliptical shape, an indication of their eighteenth-century date.

The piers in the cathedral of Cajamarca are extremely large, so much so that the nave in reality has continuous walls with arched openings which connect with each bay of the aisles. The same heavy ungainly construction follows the precedent set in San Francisco and San Agustín (Fig. 159) in Trujillo. In the latter church the arrangement results from the alteration of a Latin-cross plan by the addition of aisles. The appearance is unfortunate, but San Agustín of Trujillo seems to have provided the model for San Francisco in Trujillo and the cathedral of Cajamarca. One striking and important difference is to be noted, that the heavy pilasters in each bay of the nave are omitted in Cajamarca. A corbel at the height of the cornice replaces each pilaster, a device repeatedly encountered in the eighteenth century. The interior of Cajamarca Cathedral is severe, bar-

ren, and lofty in proportions, far superior to its Trujillian prototypes. Cajamarca too has the advantage in beauty of materials, for dressed stone masonry is employed throughout the entire church in vaults as well as in walls. Solid stone construction is always limited to the sierra regions, such as Cajamarca, Puno, and Arequipa. In Cuzco and Ayacucho, on the contrary, stone walls are combined with vaults of brick.

The present Franciscan church, dedicated to San Antonio, was begun about 1699 following the plans drawn by the architect Matías Pérez Palomino. An earlier effort (1690) to replace the inadequate old structure had come to naught. The confused problem of the origin of San Antonio has been solved by Padre Vargas Ugarte's recent publication of several important documents. An inventory of 1737, discovered by the Jesuit scholar, shows that the vaults of the choir and a few others in the main body of the church were still incomplete in that year. The architects in charge at that time were José Manuel and Francisco de Tapia, successors of Pérez Palomino, who was undoubtedly dead. Just how far along the sculpture of the portals had progressed by 1737, we do not know for lack of documentary information.[7]

Two years later the Bethlemite brothers of Cajamarca secured a temporary injunction to prevent the Franciscans from quarrying more stone in the hill of Santa Apolonia. The quarrel with the Bethlemites had begun long before in 1677 when the Franciscans tried to prevent them from taking charge of the local hospital.[8]

Fray Vicente Valverde had played an historic role in the first conquest of Cajamarca by Pizarro, and the Franciscans thenceforth had always been entrusted with the teaching of the Indians there, a privilege which they guarded zealously. For more than a half century the monks defied orders from the king and viceroy to abandon their church and turn it over to the Indians, a quarrel which is recorded in documents of 1811 preserved in the Archivo de Indias.[9] These papers say that the Indians had built the church in 1717, a statement not to be taken literally, for the work endured for more than one year (1699–1737), but it does corroborate the period.

San Antonio is a magnificent large structure 73 meters in length and 26.70 meters in breadth within the walls. Its floor plan (Fig. 11), as already noted, derives from the coastal tradition of Peru, the chief variation being the omission of lighting from above in the aisle vaults.[10] Niche chapels, large enough only to contain altars, flank the aisles within the thickness of the walls. The interior of San Antonio (Fig. 183) differs radically from the cathedral, due not only to its greater size and to the large dome over the crossing, which the cathedral lacks, but also to the design of the interior. Large cruciform piers with Doric pilasters and plain cornice provide the framework of a grandiose composition. The large bracket in the center of each bay of the cornice is a familiar eighteenth-century feature, here boldly placed like a ledge beneath the clerestory. The window frames inside are carved in stone with a curious tongue in a rectangle, repeated at the top and down the sides. No other part of the interior is carved, the vaults being in fine smooth stone masonry, unlike the elaborately worked vaults of El Belén and the Capilla de la Dolorosa. The interior of San Antonio is one of the best in all Peru, awesome in its majestic space composition and technically expert in detail. The present elevated choir with its rococo shape is not the original but a refabrication of 1880, the time during which most of the restorations in the church were made.[11]

The great distinction of the religious architecture of Cajamarca lies in the remarkable sculptured façades of San Antonio, the cathedral, and El Belén. They are contemporary works of the first half of the eighteenth century, constituting one school. Curiously the façades of all three were left unfinished in the upper parts and the towers only begun. The explanation might easily be financial, when a city the size of Cajamarca attempted three such ambitious structures contemporaneously. That will be realized readily by considering their known dates. The cathedral was begun about 1682 and consecrated in 1762; San Antonio, started in 1699, was still under construction in 1737. The monks of El Belén in 1677 took charge of the old hospital of Cajamarca which they found very miserable. They began a new church about 1699, but the major share of the construction was carried out between 1727 and 1744. An inscription upon the pedestals of the statues in the second story states that the façade was finished by José Morales on May 18, 1744.[12]

The façade of the cathedral (Figs. 177–180) is the largest and the most lavishly decorated, yet lacking completion at the top. It is easy to see that work stopped abruptly one day, and was never resumed. El Belén (Figs. 186, 187) has a complete façade and one tower half finished, whereas San Antonio (Fig. 182) is the farthest from termination and technically drier than the others. The cathedral looks rather forlorn because of its truncated condition, but that should not obscure the luxuriant magnificence of its stone reliefs. The central section rises two and one half stories, divided into the triumphal-arch division by spiral columns with niches between them in the traditional manner. The two side portals have single columns and a broad attic section. Above in the second story three open arches are hung with bells. The entire arrangement is puzzling, for this second story does not correspond to the center of the façade. If bell towers were to have risen still another story, what was to have been done with the clock tower to the left? It is possible that the use of bells here is a subsequent modification and that simple niches were in the original plan. Observe the irregular filling in of the niches from below, a clear indication of nonprofessional modification. San Antonio suffered a similar fate as late as 1941, when the ugly octagonal tower was added, and the wall to the right was quite inexplicably finished off with a sloping top.

The great beauty of the sculpture in the first story of the cathedral façade and in the entire central section would be difficult to exaggerate. The crispness of the carving and the exquisite decorative qualities of the design have no equal except in the finest gilded retables. When first completed, the façades of San Agustín and La Merced in Lima (Figs. 110, 111) might have approached the Cajamarcan school in quality. Today the former is but a shadow of itself, the carving having lost its vigor in restoration and recutting, while the Merced is a replica of the original and completely mechanical, so far as the sculpture is concerned. Grapes and vines entwine the spiral columns of Cajamarca Cathedral, the large luxuriant bunches overshadowing the vines and leaves. Customarily, the latter predominate, and the grapes are relatively inconspicuous. This reversal in the decorative emphasis is especially notable in the cathedral portals. Flamboyant birds with crisp broad feathers peck at the eucharistic grapes in one of the oldest themes of Christian symbolism. An occasional pomegranate emerges. The columns of the side portal rise from a lower drum cut with the zigzag motive, also very common in retable design.

In the central portal, on the contrary, the drum is cut with arabesques, as a contrast to the spiral part above, except in the top story. The most flamboyant and calligraphic in their sweeping rhythm are the great volutes, also of retable origin, along the sides of the two smaller portals. A tapestry of crisp full leaves spreads over the upper center of the façade. Strangely out of key are the lateral sections with their rectangular stones slightly concave and the obviously unfinished pedestals and volutes. The frieze in the first story is composed of rectangular blocks carved with stylized leaves in the side portals; the main portal has alternately flower pots and cherubs' heads accompanied by pomegranates. Human figures are limited to the graceful recumbent angels in the main spandrels who carry the keys of Paradise and censers, pairs of angels with the Sacred Heart over the niches, and grotesque busts.

The peculiar attic section of the side portals contains a European motive which became very popular with *mestizo* artists. They used it frequently in colonial textiles and in portals of the regions of Arequipa, Puno, La Paz, and Sucre, as well as in retables and pulpits of Bolivia. That motive is the human bust, here male, which turns into stylized leaves at the waist. It would be wearisome to describe every bit of ornament on this lavishly exuberant façade, ornament which comprises classical motives like the egg and dart, dentils, as well as the guilloche pattern, stock-in-trade cusps in unconventional usage, along with the fantastic inventions of an artist who was without doubt a decorative genius. The diamond points in the upper left wall, on what presumably was to have been a tower, play a much greater role in the church of El Belén. The façade of Cajamarca Cathedral is one of the remarkable achievements of Latin American art, and one likely to be underestimated in photographs, because of the sadly truncated state of the upper story.

The façade of San Antonio (Fig. 182) is the farthest from completion of the three contemporary churches of Cajamarca. As previously stated the ugly conical tower,

the upper wall over the right portal with its very poor stonework and diagonal top, and also the gable of the upper center were added in the year 1941. The appearance was more satisfactory before these recent changes, as can be seen in an old photograph, which shows three open arches hung with bells in place of the tower.[13] The entire wall surface was to have been carved with stylized leaves and rosettes, as can be deduced from the walls of the right portal. In the second story of the central section the carving was started from the lower rows but stopped when scarcely under way. On the left side the carvers began at the top and completed two rows before the work was paralyzed forever. Clearly the original scheme embraced two large towers, as was also the case for the Belén.

The cathedral façade (Fig. 177), particularly the central section which is copied in all essentials, served as model for San Antonio, which stands opposite it across the broad Plaza Mayor. Evidence that the cathedral inaugurated the Cajamarcan school lies in its greater fantasy and invention, and the fact that San Antonio is a simplification of its prototype. Moreover, the craftsmanship of the carving of the Franciscan church is far inferior. That is not to say that the façade of San Antonio is poor, but rather that it does not achieve the same decorative brilliance, and the carving is a drier repetition of its model. A comparison of the angels of the spandrels of the two main portals brings out the mature handling of form in a graceful and accomplished *contrapposto* in the cathedral, whereas the angels of San Antonio although derivative are rustic, technically inexpert, and devoid of decorative design. Amusing in this case are the stylized clouds in the form of balls inscribed with volutes, recalling medieval conventions, such as the stylized ground in the reliefs of Santo Domingo de Silos in Spain. Similar conventions do not necessarily indicate interrelations, but rather independent arrival at a similar conclusion at Cajamarca by a naïve mind, for surely this is native Indian invention.

The spiral columns of San Antonio were copied from those of the cathedral, but rather dryly and superficially, without producing the richness in contrasts of light and shade which are so notable in the cathedral sculpture. The nude babies in the vines of San Antonio are an exceptional and playful touch, the most pleasing among the variations from the prototype. The statues of saints in the niches do not rise above the commonplace and the provincial. Considerably more originality is displayed in the flanking portals, although they too betray derivation from the cathedral, in this case from the lateral portal (1686) and the Sagrario entrance (Fig. 178) beside it. These doorways of San Antonio might be said to carry on the same tradition in a later and more florid stage of stylistic development. The corbels in place of pilasters rest upon an object which resembles a melon and two stylized lilies. An interesting treatment is the handling of the window over the door with diagonal moldings which rise like a truncated pyramid. The long stylized leaves against the wall

beside the windows recall the same motive so widely disseminated in southern Peru and Bolivia.

The portal of the Capilla de la Dolorosa (Fig. 184), the chapel which adjoins San Antonio, is contemporary with and very similar to the works just discussed, although variations in ornamental details are numerous. The wall of the chapel is composed of smooth masonry rather than rusticated. The window rises higher, larger, and unadorned in a façade which is of greater scale. The enveloping semicircular lunette, which represents the barrel vault within, provides a rather bold and dramatic frame against the swinging rococo curves of the gable above it. Small and sparkling bell towers with the same eighteenth-century gaiety top the buttresses. The composition as a unit is peculiar, perhaps not thus planned at the outset, but nevertheless arresting in its contrasting masses. The chapel was begun in 1722, and if it followed the usual pattern of the day, the work was in progress for ten to twenty years. A report of 1760 demonstrates that it had been finished well before that year.[14]

The façade of El Belén (Figs. 186, 187) holds the distinction of being the most complete of the three contemporary churches of Cajamarca, and, moreover, an original creation both in design and in detail. Although obviously of the same school and possibly by the same artist, El Belén does not copy the cathedral, which seems to be the first in the series, and upon which San Antonio so closely depends. El Belén lacks only its towers, one of them half finished and its mate never begun, so that aesthetically the aspect of the whole composition is by far the most pleasing of the three monuments. We note here the age-old Hispanic scheme of contrasting a profusely decorated portal with a bare expanse of wall, in this case the bases of the towers. The extraordinary bulk of these towers takes on the appearance of a fortification. The bases combined with the façade proper would have formed a better composition without the proposed hexagonal belfries. Rows of projecting lozenges or diamonds decorate the frieze of the towers, the entire surface of the belfry, and the pilasters and base of the lower portal. They also invest the walls and vaults within the church. This motive became a signature of Cajamarcan art of the eighteenth century, appearing in the cathedral façade, on the windows in San Antonio's smaller portals, on the façade of the Women's Hospital of El Belén, on the convent portal of the nuns of the Concebidas Descalzas, in domestic architecture, and on the high altars of La Recoleta (nineteenth century) and San Antonio (1863). The covering of an entire wall surface with an ornamental motive, as employed on the tower and within the church of El Belén, has ample precedent in Spain in such famous buildings as the Casa de los Picos at Segovia, the palace of the Duque del Infantado in Guadalajara, the Casa de las Conchas in Salamanca, and the Palacio de Javalquinto at Baeza.[15] It occurs even in Italy, for example the Casa dei Diamanti at Ferrara. The Moorish basis of this aesthetic is obvious, since surface decoration in repeated patterns is the very foundation of Islamic art and of all of its Spanish derivatives, such as the *mudéjar* and the original manifestations of Spanish plateresque art.

Returning to the façade of El Belén, we discover the same two-and-one-half-story division as that of the cathedral but very different in detail. Striking is the window of the second story which opens into the choir, quatrefoil in shape and excellently placed within the well-proportioned design of the whole façade. The quatrefoil, which has an origin in both Gothic and Islamic art, is not uncommon in the Spanish colonies. The sixteenth-century façade of the chapel at Santa Mónica in Mexico has this type of window in the same position.[16] It is the natural companion of the trefoil doorway, as in Santo Domingo at Cochabamba. Considerable imagination is shown in the placing of the shell beneath the window, an illogical procedure, but nonetheless an inspired thought from the decorative point of view.

If any criticism of the design of the Belén is made, it would be that the niches of the second story are small in relation to the wall above and that the omission of columns or pilasters in the top story constitutes a rather abrupt change of key. The cornice finishes with fine sweeping reversed curves of the eighteenth century which, combined with other factors, and the dated inscription of 1744, lead to the conclusion that El Belén is the latest of the three monuments. The sculptured ornament rises to the same high standard as that of the cathedral, both in design and technique. The spiral columns are cut with a vine-and-leaf pattern, completely unlike the spiral of the cathedral and San Antonio. The friezes and archivolt of the doorway have continuous ornament instead of the carved blocks of the other two monuments. Very lovely is the handling of the rinceaux, that is, the vines in rhythmic curves which enclose stylized flowers and leaves. They comprise the principal ornament over the entire surface and are handled with great clarity, emphasis, and contrast, which result in decorative articulation superior to that of the upper reaches of the cathedral, where many of the same patterns are to be identified. Angels recline in the spandrels of the doorway, in the same position as in the cathedral, here supporting the three crowns of the Bethlemite shield in one hand and a ring of clouds in the other. Not to be overlooked, in passing, are the exquisite shields in iron upon the wooden doors just below. The stone statues in the niches of the façade do not rise above the commonplace, one more proof that the sculptors of colonial Peru were great decorators but inferior figure sculptors, a fact amply illustrated by the abundant retables throughout the land.

For sculptural magnificence the three church façades of Cajamarca are unique in Peru. Truly retables in stone adapted to an architectural purpose, they display inventive imagination in design and nothing short of genius in the decorative fantasy of the relief sculpture which both technically and creatively will stand the test beside the best which Spain itself or any other land has to offer. A few years later than these monuments is the small façade of the former Hospital of Women, now used as a *colegio*, whose portal is dated by inscription above it in 1763–1767.[17] The work is a rustic interpretation of the same motives, so magnificently manipulated on the façade of El Belén. The poor provincial artisan lacked any sense of decorative design, handling the patterns clumsily without understanding of formal relations, and the carving itself is only slightly less inept.

The church of El Belén (Fig. 188) consists of a single nave without lateral chapels, except for the baptismal chapel to the left beneath the choir upon entering by the front portal. An extremely bizarre impression greets the visitor, and, although it somewhat diminishes after the initial surprise, it never fades. The first impression, that the stone walls are entirely covered with large projecting diamond points, proves on examination to be inexact, for in reality the rows of geometric ornament are limited to the window frames, to the pilasters, the frieze, the broad transverse arches, and a wide band which runs longitudinally in the center of the vault for the full length of the church. This latter feature is most unconventional, and only increases the general feeling of heavy-handedness which the interior admittedly possesses. The sacristy portal in the right wall of the sanctuary is, on the contrary, very pleasing and in good scale, with its single row of diamond points on frieze and pilasters, the large calligraphic shell over the doors, and the rococo busts at the top. The sacristy within has a well-constructed stone barrel vault.

Strangest of all is the large stone dome (Fig. 189) with reliefs of the four Evangelists in the pendentives and eight half-length angels who appear to sustain the dome of heaven above them. These angels have naked human torsos which turn into long stylized leaves at the waist. As previously stated, their origin is European, but the compositional arrangement of them as well as the magnification of their size and the erect frontality of their posture are highly original and distinctly the creation of a native *mestizo* craftsman. Other, less spectacular appearances of the same theme are on the façades of the cathedral and the Women's Hospital. I know of no dome similar to this work, for that (Fig. 214) at Chihuata (Arequipa) has full-length angels which fit into a tapestrylike pattern. A garish coat of modern paint with the reliefs in red and green against a blue background produces a crude impression at Cajamarca which was surely no part of the original intention. In the upper reaches of the dome rows of peculiar volutes and leaves alternate with bands of flowers interspersed with cherubs' heads. Rather quaint are the large flowers, recalling pond lilies, which decorate the frieze below the dome.

The interior of El Belén is an interesting experiment but one not often repeated. An allover pattern can produce a sumptuously rich effect, and one of the highest quality aesthetically, as is proven by the interior of the Compañía in Quito, one of the world's great churches. Like success was not achieved here at Cajamarca.

The two patios of El Belén were never of importance architecturally, and today, with their poor state of repair, they are without interest. A small belfry rises at one corner adjacent to the church, and the dome cuts a compact, sturdy silhouette against the sky. The men's hospital, of eighteenth-century date, and still the only hospital in the city, stands upon the first patio. It is a stone structure in the form of a cruciform church with barrel vaults. Bays are separated by transverse arches, and a large stone dome tops the crossing. Light comes in from a clerestory, and in every respect the hospital looks like a church, even with altar for mass, and as unfitted for the sick as can be imagined, according to modern ideas of hospitalization. Unlike the church proper, the walls are plain and undecorated. The hospital continues, of course, the Spanish medieval tradition, as seen in the Hospital de Santa Cruz at Toledo.

Another interior with abundant stone sculpture in relief, but different from El Belén, is that of the Capilla de la Dolorosa (Fig. 185) which adjoins the church of San Antonio. The façade of the chapel has previously been discussed. The interior consists of five bays and nearly equals the church of El Belén in size. There are no lateral chapels. The elevated choir occupies its usual place above the main entrance, and in the spandrels on the front wall are Gabriel and Mary in the mystery of the Annunciation. The barrel vault, like that of El Belén, has a broad longitudinal band in the center, in this case carved with stylized leaves. The vault over the sanctuary is entirely worked in stone relief giving an effect similar to embroidery. The window frames are decorated with the same stylized leaves as well as various unconventional moldings, one of which looks strangely like an Islamic blind arcade. Quite without parallel is the broad frieze containing heads of Franciscan saints, both male and female, while in the sanctuary seven busts of kings at each side replace the saints, the busts separated, amusingly enough, by large flower pots. All of the figured reliefs have been crudely painted in recent years, and the poor quality of the sculpture has not been improved thereby.

At the sides of the sanctuary are two large scenes in stone relief, the Last Supper at the left and the Washing of the Feet of Christ at the right. The sculpture is crudely provincial both in design and in technique. Most peculiar of all is the placing of figured reliefs above the clerestory windows in the following manner: on the right wall, the Circumcision, Christ among the Doctors, Ecce Homo, Christ with Angels Holding Instruments of the Passion; on the left wall, the Nativity, the Flight into Egypt, Ecce Homo, Christ with Angels Holding Instruments of the Passion. The poor quality of the figure sculpture does not interfere with the effectiveness of the chapel as a whole.

The structure is well planned and proportioned, and has additional interest for those interested in curiosities of religious iconography. This chapel is delightfully naïve and entertaining, yet it cannot take rank with the stone-carved interiors of Santiago of Pomata and San Pedro of Juli,

where decorative genius of the highest order is revealed. Nor can it compare technically with the façades of the cathedral and El Belén of Cajamarca itself, where artists of extraordinary endowment were engaged.

Two other monuments, La Recoleta and the Church of the Immaculate Conception, belong to a later period and to a stylistic phase unrelated to the works just discussed. The former Franciscan monastery of the Recoleta, which now houses the Colegio Nacional, was founded in 1650,[18] and the first cloister is dated 1668–1678 by an inscription over the principal entrance: *Empeçóse este convento en 14 de julio de 1668 y se acabó el año de 1678.* It is a small cloister (Fig. 191) of single story with Doric half columns attached to the piers on the court side. The vaults of the galleries rest on corbels against the wall. The second and larger cloister, likewise of single story and groin vaulted, is presumably of eighteenth-century facture, because of the rectangles and diamond points which decorate the walls and piers of the court. The style of this cloister is so unlike that of the small cloister of 1668–1678 that it leads to the conclusion that the later work was added in the mid-eighteenth century, a period in which the use of surface decoration was characteristic of Cajamarca. The materials of both structures are brick and stucco. Cajamarca has no other cloisters of importance, those of the large monastery of San Antonio being humble single-storied buildings of brick and stucco with wooden posts for columns, originating during the rehabilitation of 1868–1870.[19]

The church of the Recoleta is a single-naved structure of no great size, as usual in the houses of the Franciscan novitiates. Most impressive of all is the great stone dome at the crossing, which appears especially monumental above the mass of the church, as seen from the large cloister. The interior of the church, its barrel vaults, molded cornice, and raised choir look mechanical and dull as a result of the resurfacing with cement in 1937. The façade (Fig. 190), however, entirely of gray stone, and topped by two open bell towers, is a spirited composition. The eighteenth-century verticality of the towers and the gaiety suggested by the whirling volutes are delightful. The small tabernacle over the portal has been added in recent times. In spite of the dedication of the church by Bishop Mimbela in 1736, recorded in a picture which hangs in the choir, I believe that the façade was erected thirty to forty years later, contemporary with the towers of the Merced in Trujillo which were rebuilt after the earthquake of 1759.

The nuns of the Concebidas Descalzas del Velo Negro came to Cajamarca in 1747, and their church was consecrated in 1806.[20] The single-naved edifice has thin Doric pilasters which rise to the full height of the walls both within and without. It is a cold academic design of early Neoclassic taste. The large polygonal tower, unfinished, seems to be a late member of the series of such towers in northern Peru, like that of San Pedro at Lambayeque and the towers of Santa Lucía at Ferreñafe (Fig. 176). The roof is now covered with galvanized iron, and the ceiling within is made of plaster over reeds. The convent portal is a picturesque and somewhat rustic revision of Cajamarcan domestic architecture with large diamond points covering the pilasters and frieze.

In this review of the ecclesiastical architecture of Cajamarca I have attempted to point out some of the relations of the churches of Cajamarca to those of other regions of Peru and to emphasize the great originality and extraordinarily high quality of the cathedral, El Belén, and San Antonio. So far as anything is ever original, the façades of the three churches are that. They are offshoots, to be sure, of the Hispanic family tree, and their distant antecedents are to be found in the great retable façades of San Gregorio and San Pablo of Valladolid in the epoch of the Catholic Kings; or later in the sixteenth century in the façade of San Esteban in Salamanca and the transept portals of the cathedral in the same city.

Many of the Spanish colonies developed the retable façade in the seventeenth and eighteenth centuries to an extent far exceeding that of the mother country. Particularly notable are churches of this type in Mexico, at Guanajuato, Taxco, Zacatecas, Mexico City, San Luis Potosí, etc.[21] Many similarities are to be explained by their common Iberian sources and the working of indigenous influences in similar fashion both in North and South America. The latter might well account for a decorative motive such as the long stylized leaf, somewhat resembling a fern, which is extremely common in southern Peru and Bolivia, turns up occasionally in northern Peru as on the lateral portals of San Antonio in Cajamarca, and is also known elsewhere, as, for example, in Mexico on the façade of the cathedral of Aguascalientes.[22]

In the viceroyalty of Peru itself the *mestizo* façades of Arequipa, Puno, La Paz, and Potosí form a separate school, notable for their markedly indigenous character both in design and technique. As already indicated, the triad of Cajamarca has no close parallel save the façades of San Agus-tín and La Merced in Lima in their prime. There would be no justification for presuming, however, that *limeño* sculptors worked at Cajamarca, since the composition and the decorative motives used in Lima have *limeño* ramifications and are unlike those of Cajamarca. Conversely, some *mestizo* traits do give an individual character to the local school, most notably in the interior of the Capilla de la Dolorosa and the dome of El Belén.

VIII

SOUTHERN PERU: THE MESTIZO STYLE — I

AREQUIPA

AREQUIPA, the second largest city of Peru, ranks first as a land of blue skies and radiant sun. Situated at an elevation of eight thousand feet, it lies at the foot of snowcapped mountain ranges among which the great conical peak of Mount Misti rises sheer and majestic. Edifices of white stone built in solid rectangular mass, houses of single story, ecclesiastic and domestic portals lavishly carved in exotic *mestizo* style give to Arequipa's architecture its own distinctive character. The city of Arequipa, founded in 1540, has preserved only a faint shadow of its heritage. Here even more than in Lima tragedy has stalked in the form of earthquake after earthquake which have reduced the city to ashes time and again. The worst of these were in 1582, 1600, 1687, 1715, 1784, and 1868. On the last occasion the local newspaper, *La Bolsa*, under date of August 19, 1868, mourned the fact that "ten minutes were sufficient to bring to the ground the work of three centuries, churches and buildings which resisted the terrible earthquake of May 13, 1784, which was, without doubt, in no way comparable with that which occurred on the afternoon of August 13, 1868 . . . beautiful Arequipa exists no more!"

An earlier catastrophe, the great fire of 1844, had totally destroyed the magnificent seventeenth-century cathedral, and hence the city is in large part a product of the second half of the nineteenth century. The plaza belongs to that period,[1] the altars and furnishings of the churches, and the majority of the houses. Yet domestic architecture has preserved the white stone construction of single story, the patio and the grilled windows of colonial days, with the result that Arequipa still maintains its individuality. There is no disguising the fact, however, that the story of *arequipeño* architecture is the story of what once existed more than of monuments extant today.

Not a vestige of the sixteenth century remains. Toribio de Alcaraz built the portal of the principal church on the plaza (1544) before migrating to Potosí in the wake of the discovery of silver mines there. I have shown elsewhere that this man who is traceable in Sucre and Potosí from 1549 until 1573 could not have been the same person who also practiced architecture in Mexico.[2] Gaspar Baez, resident of Lima, made plans for the Franciscan church (1569) and for the church and *colegio* of the Jesuits (1573).[3] These and other meager notices tell us little about the buildings themselves.

The chief ecclesiastical monument of the seventeenth century was the huge cathedral, a basilican structure of stone covered with Gothic vaults of brick. A well-known architect of Lima, Andrés de Espinoza, prepared the project and began the work in 1621, but death overtook him seven years later. It was carried on by the architect Moscoso in 1634. After further interruptions, the church came to completion under Juan de Aldana (1643–1656), a Spanish architect, who moved from Lima to a long career in Arequipa.[4] The present cathedral (1844–1847), a neo-Renaissance edifice, replaces its colonial predecessor, destroyed in the fire of 1844.

The one church which has survived intact from the repeated disasters to which Arequipa has been subjected is La Compañía. Higher tribute to its builders could not be imagined. Only its tower, shaken to the ground on various occasions, is modern (1919). The first church, the project for which Gaspar Baez prepared in 1573, collapsed in the earthquake of 1584. The Jesuit fathers did not actually become established in Arequipa until 1578, after five years of negotiation.

Another church was begun in 1595 under the direction of a Jesuit, Padre Diego Felipe. The inception of the present structure, however, seems to date from approximately 1650. By contract of 1654, a builder named Simón de Barrientos agreed to construct the lateral portal of stone, two vaults in the nave, two chapels, the enclosure around the church, and a stairway leading from the ante-sacristy to the roof. The vaults were not entirely finished until 1690,

and the work presumably came to an end with the façade which has the date 1698 inscribed upon it.[5]

This façade (Figs. 192, 193) is the city's finest work in the *mestizo* style of architectural decoration. The whole problem of this style will be discussed later along with the façade of San Agustín, the portals of Santo Domingo and Santa Rosa, and the churches of nearby pueblos, Caima, Yanahuara, and Paucarpata. The façade of the Compañía is basically the type of two-storied structure so common in European churches of the sixteenth and seventeenth centuries. From Rome, the place of origin, it spread throughout the Christian world. In Arequipa, however, the native element is so strong that it all but submerges the European frame in a carpet of exotic *mestizo* ornamentation. The trefoil pediment is Hispanic but strikingly original in its application here. The columns have great collars of zigzags in the lower story and a more modest spiral in the second story, in both cases ringed above and below by a crown of leaves. Between the columns at the lower left a shield bears the words *El Año* and on the right side of the door, *De 1698*. In these flat spaces and in the strips of ornament at the sides of the portal, fantasy is given free rein in a flat tapestry of stylized ornament: vines and bunches of grapes, pomegranate, *ccantu* flower, heraldically disposed birds, a cherub whose body consists of swirling leaves, and long volutes. The frieze carries a meandering vine with geometric rosettes, flowered angels, and the letters *SD—SF—SI—MN* (*Sanctus Deus, Sanctus Fortis, Sanctus Im-*

mortalis, Miserere Nobis). These words, taken from the Good Friday mass, appear in full on the façade of the church at Asillo (Fig. 244) and upon two houses in Arequipa, formerly owned by the Jesuits.[6] I have been unable to discover any explanation for their peculiar association with Jesuit buildings.

In the upper center the large flowers, square and rectangular, stand forth prominently, along with the crowned double-headed eagle of the Hapsburgs. Upon the frieze are carved the monograms of Christ, Mary, and Joseph. The puppet-like St. Michael in the niche of the pediment is flanked by angels and filling ornament as abstract in their natural primitivism as any of their Merovingian, Coptic, or Mozarabic predecessors. At the extreme sides the classical shell and volute are mingled with grotesque Indian masks, profile heads like gigantic caricatures, and an Indian head with high feathered crown. The grotesque faces out of whose mouths flow long serpentine objects are throwbacks to Nazca pottery and textiles. If any art or race was ever crossbred, if ever there was a mixture of European and native Indian, the monuments of Arequipa and Puno are the proof thereof.

The side portal (Fig. 194) is much earlier and less fantastic, having been commissioned in 1654 of the same Barrientos who worked upon the vaults. In the tympanum a relief of Santiago Matamoros, to whom the church is dedicated, shows the saint brandishing his sword to slay the turbaned Moors lying crushed beneath his charger's hoofs. The stylization with good archaic flavor turns the horse's mane into long serpentine coils and the mandorla into a shell-like niche. The horse's body stands in profile and the head in full face, thus approximating the Egyptian convention. The primitive mind of the sculptor conceived objects in a simple two-dimensional aspect. Hence he placed St. James in a frontal position, sidesaddle upon his mount.

Below the relief, two mermaids with angels' wings (!) naïvely recline like heraldically opposed guards. Thus the mermaids of Lake Titicaca who lured the unwary, like their Greek predecessors, are Christianized and transformed into angels. The lion of St. Mark and the ox of St. Luke with iconographical peculiarity occupy the frieze between clusters of grapes and papaya. The half-disk pattern, also met in Cuzco and Lima, turns up here on the pilasters set between the columns.

In floor plan (Fig. 16) the Compañía has one nave, two side aisles, single projecting sanctuary, and raised choir. Stone masonry is maintained throughout including the dome, the barrel vaults, and the three small domes in each aisle (Fig. 195). Ionic half columns carry the high entablature which serves as a large cornice in the nave, large enough to afford a balustraded corridor at the springing of the vaults. The interior is painted white with red balustrade atop the cornice, red pendentives, and gilded dentils. It has a refreshing well-kept appearance. In La Compañía three retables, a number of colonial pictures in their gilded frames, and a fine pulpit of the late seventeenth century help to recall what Arequipa once was.

One of the finest parts of the building is the sacristy, square in shape and covered by a huge stone dome which comes down very low on pendentives. Interesting early mural paintings of purely decorative nature representing flowers, apples, bananas, watermelons, and nude *putti* decorate the surface of the dome.

Another fine sacristy, though smaller, is that of San Agustín (Fig. 213), the only part of the interior not destroyed in 1868. It is an octagonal chamber, 7.60 meters in diameter, likewise domed. Ionic pilasters upon the walls end abruptly on corbels halfway to the floor. The decoration of the dome is carved in the stone with great skill. Highly stylized leaves, rosettes, *ccantus*, stars, and volutes spread over the surface which is subdivided by ribs, themselves covered with the scale motive. This dome is a masterpiece of *mestizo* art, characterized by the highly geometric quality of design which is the very essence of the style.

The basilican plan with single sanctuary like that of the Compañía was adopted by the Mercedarians, Dominicans, and Franciscans (Fig. 15), all of whose churches maintain their ground plans of the second half of the seventeenth century, but have been repeatedly restored. Their similarity to San Pedro, San Francisco (Figs. 9, 10), and La Merced in Lima is surely no accident. Architects from Lima like Andrés de Espinoza and Juan de Aldana transferred their activity to Arequipa, and there is no reason to doubt that European ideas emanated from the capital. As already pointed out in Chapter IV, I believe the basilican plan in which the aisles are covered by cupolas was first introduced to Peru in the Jesuit church (1624) at Lima. The Franciscans and Mercedarians borrowed it from them, using barrel vaults in the nave instead of the Gothic vaults, originally in San Pedro. Thence the plan passed to Arequipa and Trujillo. The Compañía of Arequipa was built largely in the second half of the seventeenth century (*circa* 1650–1698), whereas the church at Lima was consecrated in 1638.

The Merced in Arequipa was rebuilt in 1657 on the same scheme as the Compañía, under the direction of Juan de Aldana.[7] Here again an architect, originally from Lima, took over the prevailing architectural ideas of the capital. Stone is used throughout, however, as usual in Arequipa, both in the barrel vault of the nave and the cupolas over the aisles. The heavy, rather ungainly dimensions were doubtless chosen with the hope that thick walls would resist earthquakes. Padre Barriga is the authority for the information that the sanctuary was reërected after the earthquake of 1687. The construction of the apse is peculiar, the first bay being barrel vaulted and the second topped by a large dome. The only near parallel is found in the nunneries of Cuzco, where a dome is placed over the sanctuary instead of the crossing.

In 1868 some of the Merced vaults collapsed,[8] apparently those in the center rather than the domes over the aisles. With the rebuilding the sober Doric piers and simple cornice were touched up with incongruous frills: a Gothic corbel table under the cornice and Renaissance leaves with cherubs' heads on the frieze!

The exterior of the Merced is disappointing, the façade having been modernized.[9] The former convent door, decorated with rosettes and vines, is now blocked up. The best view of the flat roofs and terraced mass, so peculiar to Arequipa, can be seen from the garden side. Here too stands the fine lateral portal, a simple round-arched entrance crowned by a tall sculptured group of the Madonna of Mercy. The Madonna is placed within a large shell niche supported on spiral columns, details indicative of a date in the late seventeenth or early eighteenth century.

The single-storied cloister of square piers, above which is a modern second story, lacks distinction, but the old Sala Capitular, now used as a storehouse, is a superb relic of the past. It is composed of two large bays, the first carrying a simple quadripartite Gothic vault and the second a fine late-Gothic vault with clover design in its ribs. Here stands the only survivor in Arequipa of the Gothic style of the seventeenth century. Its quality is excellent, and the whole room seems strangely like a page torn loose from medieval Spain.

Two original stone inscriptions establish the date of the ground plan and walls of Santo Domingo. In the vault under the choir an inscription says *Año 1677*, and a plaque on one of the piers records the consecration of the church in 1680. The plan falls into the same category as those of La Compañía and La Merced, also originating in the third quarter of the century. The piers (2.32 meters thick) are gigantic with the intent of resisting earthquakes. They as well as the choir remain intact. The church was badly damaged, however, in the earthquakes of 1784 and 1868.[10]

The design of the nave betrays the remodeling after 1784 in the treatment of the dentelated cornice. Here a projecting corbel is used as a decorative accent in the center of each bay. This device, so common in Lima in the eighteenth century, does not occur elsewhere in Arequipa. The vaulting throughout appears to date from the reconstruction of 1873, recorded by an inscription upon the triumphal arch.[11] The barrel vaults in the nave and transept, the domical vaults in the aisles and lantern, which are lighted by an oculus in the center of each, are heavy and uninteresting. The extent of the degeneration of architecture in the nineteenth century is much in evidence. Then they rebuilt the sanctuary with an ugly ribbed semidome and wall pilasters. To cap the climax, pointed neo-Gothic windows were added in the clerestory and leaf patterns in the spandrels of the nave.

Juan de Aldana originally designed the large free-standing polygonal tower in 1649. Born in Spain, he had built three portals in the church of Nuestra Señora del Prado at Lima in 1638. Moving to Arequipa, he became the leading architect of the city in the mid-century. He brought the new cathedral to its conclusion (1643–1656), and had charge of the rebuilding of La Merced (1657).[12] Later in the first half of the eighteenth century, Aldana's tower of Santo Domingo influenced those of San Xavier at Nazca. The Dominican tower, badly ruined in 1784 and 1868, is now a mediocre reconstruction of 1891.[13]

The main façade of Santo Domingo is a

chaste and majestic composition of the seventeenth century, built in two stories with Doric columns and deeply projecting entablatures. Its style would normally suggest a period thirty years earlier than 1677–1680. Yet chronological consistency is never to be relied upon in colonial art. This façade has no analogue in Arequipa today. The only hint of the local *mestizo* style is to be found in the semi-abstract ornament in the spandrels of the archway and upon the window above.

The earliest dated example of *mestizo* carving in its full development is the decoration on the face of the choir (1677) within the church.[14] It consists of long leaves and rosettes, partly gilded, and the escutcheons of the Dominicans and Franciscans. The lateral exterior portal (Fig. 201) of Santo Domingo has similar ornament, and it would normally be assigned the same date. On the other hand, the style is so similar to that of Paucarpata (Fig. 202), and the portals (Figs. 204, 206–208) of Caima (1719–1730) and Yanahuara (1750), that the student must pause to reflect. The model established at Santo Domingo in 1677–1680 was apparently followed for seventy-five years. Otherwise, it would be necessary to assume that the Dominican portal also is later. More documents will help to solve these problems, which will be studied in greater detail later in the present chapter.

Also very much refashioned is San Francisco, although it suffered less in the earthquakes than Santo Domingo. The foundation of the monastic order in Arequipa took place in 1552, and the church is mentioned by Diego de Mendoza in 1664 as having a single vaulted nave and a domed sanctuary.[15] Harth-terré believes that the church preserved today still retains the plan prepared by Gaspar Baez in 1569.[16] It seems clear, however, that Mendoza in 1664 was describing Baez's structure of 1569. Hence the rebuilding and enlargement of the edifice by the addition of aisles must be placed later in the seventeenth century, possibly after the earthquake of 1687. The walls of the sixteenth-century edifice may be incorporated in the huge supports and piers of the nave.[17] Heavy banded barrel vaults of stone follow the local tradition throughout. In the aisles the vaults are exceptional in that they are placed transversely. The purpose may have been to provide buttressing for the nave. That the scheme was structurally successful is demonstrated by the fact that they apparently have survived the earthquakes since their construction at the end of the seventeenth century. The crossing and the chapels in the transept are domed. The one at the right (Fig. 199) is a most surprising and interesting gored or melon dome. Here again the art of Islamic and medieval Spain is projected into the New World.

The best part of San Francisco is the fine stone choir raised over the entrance. The face is skillfully carved with reliefs in *mestizo* style: vines and rosettes, and figures of the Madonna of the Immaculate Conception, St. Francis, and St. Dominic. They are superior to the similar decorations on the choirs of Santo Domingo and Santa Teresa. In date they apparently lie just between the two, the former dated 1677 and the latter about 1710. Extremely interesting too is the frieze of fruit and flowers beneath the choir. The treatment of the walls in this section is almost unique in the way the surfaces are corrugated vertically and divided into panels by the Franciscan cord.

The most drastic changes in San Francisco were introduced in the nineteenth century. Then colossal Corinthian columns, exactly like those of the high altar, were set against the piers of the nave. The effect is grotesquely incongruous. New pieces of ornament touch up the section beneath the small dentelated cornice of an earlier day. The date, 1871, on the exterior of the tower gives the clue to the period of this refurbishing.

The façade and tower are surprisingly nonacademic for that time. The first story is paneled and embellished with rococo-like arabesques. In the upper part, there hang suspended from mask heads great sprays of roses which are delicately naturalistic like wax flowers in a Victorian glass case. Strangely enough the façade is pleasing and highly original. The old entrance to the monastery, now blocked up at the right of the church, has one noteworthy feature: a window in the shape of an Islamic poly-lobed arch.

Attached to the left transept of San Francisco stands the smaller church of the Tercera Orden, built in 1775–1777. It fell in 1784, and was promptly reërected.[18] The church, a perfect Latin cross with a fine dome over the crossing, incorporates the academic correctness of the approaching Neoclassicism. The grayish stone, the flat mass, and the prominent buttresses still maintain the local methods of building, however. The portal brings to an end the Arequipa series of *mestizo* sculptures. The strips of vines and rosettes upon the buttresses at the sides and the tympanum have a quaintly archaic tinge. In the latter, a medallion encloses the kneeling figures of St. Francis and St. Clare who adore the Host in a large monstrance placed between them. The plain twisted columns which border the doorway are unorthodox in this last lingering note of a great period.

All of the cloisters of Arequipa are single storied with arches on square piers. Only one is exceptionally distinguished and that is the lavish Jesuit cloister (Figs. 196, 197), for many years left to ruin and recently restored as an office building. A small patio with the date 1738 inscribed over the archway precedes the main court which is abnormally small for a monastery, four and five arches to a side. Each pier (.80 m. x .80 m.) is carved in identical style on each of the four faces: cherub's head, grapes, papaya, shell, rosettes, *ccantus*, and enfolding vines. On the keystone of each arch is a rosette topped by three large Indian feathers like those of the Puno region. The spandrels have the monograms of Christ, Joseph, and Mary, so commonly displayed on Jesuit buildings. Figure sculpture is limited to small figures of St. Ignatius and St. Francis Xavier in the spandrels on the entrance side.

The surface-covering richness of the Jesuit cloister has the spirit of Oriental luxuriance, but to suggest the influence of the Far East, as has so frequently been done, seems to me preposterous. Not a single motive is Oriental, nor is there any technical aspect which might be so interpreted. The exotic decorative repertory and the technique are autochthonous in every respect. An Italian painter, Sartorio, set the fashion for this hypothesis of Orientalism in the New World. Antúnez de Mayolo spoke very sensibly and convincingly in refutation of these theories, and recently Martha de Castro and others have added their voices with the same rational judgment.[19]

The second cloister of La Compañía, now completely ruined, was built in one story of plain rectangular piers supporting round arches. All of the others in the city are alike in type: La Recoleta,[20] Santa Teresa, San Agustín (now the University), La Merced, Santo Domingo, and San Francisco. Three patios in the latter monastery have modern upper stories, to their great architectural loss. They and the cloister of Santo Domingo (Fig. 198) are groin vaulted in fine ashlar. Indeed, the excellent dressing of the stone is one of the best qualities of the school of Arequipa. Next to the main cloister of the Compañía, the Dominican (*circa* 1677–1680) is the most important in the city. Its massive square piers are austere and imposing, and the decoration is limited to a band of stylized leaves and volutes on the frieze. A low modern wall between the piers and the modern balustrade at the roof level are unfortunate. Yet the patio is spacious and beautifully overgrown with palm trees, and it affords a splendid side view of the church.

The colonial nunneries of Arequipa are three, Santa Catalina, Santa Teresa, and Santa Rosa, all of which maintain the tradition of such churches in their single naves without chapels. Santa Teresa alone has an ample lower choir to the right of the sanctuary. In the others both upper and lower choir stand at the end opposite the sanctuary. All are barrel vaulted in stone and all have lost their gilded retables, replaced by neo-Renaissance altars in the second half of the nineteenth century. Santa Catalina, the first convent of nuns in the city, was founded by authorization of Francisco de Toledo in 1576. Rebuilt by Archbishop Almoguera after its ruin in 1662, it underwent restoration, by another archbishop, Juan Bravo del Rivero (1743–1752), to which the date 1758 in the choir grille must refer. It appears to have been refurbished in its present condition when consecrated in 1874, an event recorded by a picture on the wall.[21] Disappointing as the interiors of these churches are with their modern appointments, the exterior of Santa Catalina (Fig. 200) has, in its fortress-like massiveness, its flat roofs, powerful rectangular buttresses, and sturdy dome over the sanctuary, no equal in the whole school of Arequipa. Moreover, the yellow walls with white buttresses and white dome are enchantingly picturesque against the cloudless blue skies of Arequipa. The modest and dignified tower has the distinction of being the only colonial tower in the city, for it alone withstood the earthquake of 1868.[22]

The convent of Santa Teresa of rather late foundation (1700) opened in 1710,[23] and although it has never suffered much damage from the forces of nature, it has lost virtually all of its colonial aspect. That is because the neo-Renaissance façade, the tower, and retables are "modernizations" of the later nineteenth century. Judging from photographs, generously supplied by the mother superior, the interior of the convent in *clausura* has been less renovated, since numerous colonial paintings adorn the lower choir, refectory, library, and inner chapels. Within the church, the fine stone barrel vault and the face of the upper choir are intact. The latter, carved with leaves, four-petaled flowers, the *ccantu*, and the Carmelite shield, is reminiscent of the Dominican and Franciscan choirs. The frieze upon the wall of the nave was much redone in the past century, neo-Renaissance cherubs' heads and leaves having been added.

Santa Rosa held the distinction of being the newest of the nunneries (1744–1747) when the catastrophe of 1868 came.[24] It must have been the poorest in construction, for it collapsed to the ground, and had to be rebuilt. A very fine side portal withstood the shock. Inscriptions say that it was erected in 1745 and reërected in 1871, but surely the sculpture was unharmed. The reliefs are replete with the full *mestizo* repertory of flower vases, grapes, papaya, nude *putti*, and puma heads. Appropriately, a large geometric rose plays a prominent part in the decoration here and not in other buildings.

Within the church the rows of Corinthian columns in the sanctuary imitate the neo-Renaissance cathedral, and the retables belong to the same style. The Doric half columns of the nave and the barrel vault of stone seem to have been rebuilt on the original scheme, however. The church today consists of only four bays instead of the seven mentioned by Travada y Córdoba in 1752, unless his method of calculation was different. Of especial interest is the treatment of windows, some let in at the sides by lunettes, and others as oculi set in the top of the vault. On the whole, windows are very small in the churches of Arequipa and this region because of the sun, brilliant for ten months of the year. Oculus windows in the center of the vaults are especially characteristic of the school, occurring in the aisles of La Merced, Santo Domingo, and San Francisco, and in the naves of Santa Rosa, Yanahuara, Caima (Fig. 211), Paucarpata, and Characato.

Sculptured portals in *mestizo* style are the most distinctive contribution of Arequipa to colonial art. The beginnings are found in the lateral portal of La Compañía (Fig. 194), the work of Barrientos in the year 1654. Stylization of a natural primitive sort already marks the design of the tympanum and the grotesque heads upon the pedestals beside it. The lower section, however, is essentially European and devoid of specifically local themes or technique.

The side entrance of Santo Domingo (Fig. 201) occupies the first position chronologically among the numerous *mestizo* monuments of the region. It seems to belong to the church of 1677–1680, in view of the appearance of the same style of carving upon the face of the choir. The composition manifests great originality, not only in ornament but also in the way the pilasters are raised in a series of three entablature blocks. Thus is established a powerful frame surmounted by a curving tympanum at the top of which are two volutes. St. Paul stands in the upper center in an elliptical mandorla wreathed with vines and bunches of grapes. Heavy vines meander down the broad border at the sides of the portal. Here the grotesque masks in profile with stems growing from their mouths are the most striking instances of the survival of pre-Columbian themes. Highly stylized versions of Indian corn and the native lily or *ccantu* flower sacred to the Indians are included within an European concept. Nude *putti*, as in European Renaissance ornament, clamber among the foliage. Other clothed *putti* blowing horns recline cross-legged in the spandrels. The square flowers and rosettes upon the archivolts and supporting pilasters are less exceptional. They find a place in the ornamental schemes of provincial artists almost everywhere in Latin America.

The lateral portal of the church at Paucarpata (Fig. 202), just a short distance from Arequipa, is so similar to that of Santo Domingo that they seem to be the work of the same master. The chief difference between the two is that the architect used half columns at Paucarpata instead of the pilasters in tiers. The tympana with their broken contours, central volutes, and sculptured medallions leave no doubt of their close relationship. Christ bearing the Cross occupies the place of honor at Paucarpata. The broad bands of ornament are nearly identical in the two

churches except that the toy pumas at the bottom occur only in the village church. In both instances *putti* recline cross-legged in the spandrels, each blowing a horn and holding a long-stemmed flower.

These artists were naïve and unselfconsciously primitive. At the same time they had a natural sense of humor which no one who studies their work can miss. Their sense of design was most acute, and they were above all great masters of decoration.

The main façade of La Compañía (1698), already discussed (Figs. 192, 193), is the most important monument of the *mestizo* style in Arequipa. By that time the school had reached its apex. It was to continue to flourish without any major variation for another sixty years.

Next to that of La Compañía, the façade of San Agustín is the most lavish in the city. The columns and sculpture are painted white against a green-gray background. The general impression is very colorful and rich in the way the carving stands out like lace over the surface. The compositional basis is European with its two-storied division and the symmetrical balance of doorway and niches. In these niches the shell tympanum adds a touch of decorative elegance. The columns of the first story have no exact parallel. The spiral band of the ornament dotted with balls is set on the lower section between two crowns of leaves. In the second story, half-length angels occupy the corresponding space in a fashion similar to those on the church at Caima (Fig. 208). As usual the sides of the portal display broad bands of curving vines and leaves. The repertory of ornament which spreads out over the façade is familiar: flower vases on the pilasters, the double-headed eagle of the Hapsburgs in the upper story as in the Compañía, long-stemmed vines, heavy leaves, rosettes, and cartouches. The date of the Augustinian façade has not been established by documents. Judging by the school as a whole, I should place it in the first half of the eighteenth century.[25] The shell niches and half-length angels are prominent on the façades (Figs. 204, 207) of Caima and Yanahuara (1750). The style of San Agustín is nearer to these monuments than to the Compañía.

Mestizo monuments of the eighteenth century abound in Arequipa. They include portals of private homes, the most important of which are the Casa Ricketts and the Casa del Moral (Fig. 203). The large tympanum filled with a thick carpetlike mass of flat ornament is typical of domestic as well as ecclesiastical architecture. The themes carved in the portal of the latter house are especially significant, for they include puma heads out of whose mouths coil long serpentine objects. They are, as previously stated, related to Nazca pottery and textiles. Other native themes include Indian dancers in flounced skirts and the *ccantu*, sacred lily of the Incas. This house and the Casa Ricketts have lost much of their authenticity so far as the quality of the carving is concerned, because of recent and overconscientious restoration. Five large *ccantu* flowers in strict profile and rigid symmetry fill the center of the tympanum of the Casa Rick-

etts. Its date of 1738 is carved in stone within the patio. The cloister of the Jesuits originated in exactly the same year, as the inscription over the entrance shows.

Hence sufficient inscribed works survive to indicate that the *mestizo* style flourished in Arequipa from at least 1677, the date of the Dominican choir, to 1750, the year of the Yanahuara façade. The side entrance of Santa Rosa (1745), although pleasing, does not measure up to the best standards. The last lingerings of an age, already slightly anachronistic, best describe the fine lateral portal of the Third Order of the Franciscans (1775). Even as late as 1794, the traditional local composition steadfastly persisted in the doorway of the Casa de Moneda. The ornament had been transformed, however, from *mestizo* into rococo. Meanwhile, the lateral entrance of Santa Marta was carved some time in the mid-eighteenth century. The design includes local characteristics but is less consistent than usual. The placing of the monstrance as the predominating theme in the tympanum is explained by the fact that the church was famous for its celebration of the festival of the Host.[26] The female heads upon the half columns have surely been recut in modern times.

In Caima and Yanahuara, pueblos in the suburbs of Arequipa, are the two finest churches of the eighteenth century in the region. Especially beautiful are their façades (Figs. 204, 206–208), that of Yanahuara with date *Enero 29 Año 1750* being almost an identical twin of Caima (*circa* 1719–1730).[27] The lacelike effect of the white reliefs against a background painted yellow is rich and sparkling in the bright sun. Both façades are two storied with double columns at the sides of the doorway over which is a large niche of shell form. The elements of design in the second story are better organized at Yanahuara in the relation of the central niche to the smaller one at each side and in the setting off of the three-part cornice at the summit. A relief of the Madonna of the Rosary upon a crescent moon occupies the upper center, and just below in the large niche is St. John the Baptist, to whom the church is dedicated. Beside him stand St. Francis and St. Dominic with the shields of their respective orders above them. Statues of St. Anthony of Padua and St. Vincent Ferrer load the buttresses at the very top of the façade.

Each column of the first story is decorated with a cherub's head crowned with long-feathered headdress, so frequently encountered in *mestizo* churches but not often in this particular location. In the lower section are two crowns and a cartouche. The same stock of motives occurs in the border ornament at the sides of the portal, as on the side entrances of Paucarpata and Santo Domingo (Figs. 201, 202), but the spacing here is wider and hence the pattern stands out more clearly. There is also a greater tendency to verticality in the position of the stems which rise from the cornucopia and mask heads. At the sides of the door contemporary fashion is curiously introduced in the hat worn by the half-length figures, just as the angels of San Juan (Fig. 219) at Juli are dressed in full-skirted coats.

The façade of San Miguel at Caima is similar to that of Yanahuara (1750), although the church was consecrated as early as 1730. The consecration does not imply that the structure was entirely complete at that time.[28] The white reliefs against a yellow ground are lovely in their decorative organization. As already noted, the composition of the second story is somewhat less expert than Yanahuara's. St. Francis and St. Dominic kneel here adoring the Madonna of Candlemas of whom there is a famous miracle-working statue within the church.

Curious details are the half-length angels (Fig. 208), with baskets upon their heads, who decorate the lower band of the columns. The same iconographic peculiarity is repeated upon the convent door of San Agustín in Arequipa. Details of ornament differ considerably from those at Yanahuara, particularly in the broad strips at the sides of the portal. The twin towers are inscribed with the year 1876, showing that they were reërected after the earthquake eight years earlier. In the left tower appears still another date, 1783, indicative of its first construction, and the words *Beato Michali Arcangel*. To St. Michael the church is dedicated.

The church was first designed in 1719 by the architect, Pérez del Cuadro, in the form of a single nave. The consecration took place on February 10, 1730. The celebrated priest of Caima, Juan Domingo Zamácola y Jáuregui, enlarged the structure by the addition of lateral aisles in 1783–1802. This fact is learned by inscriptions in the left aisle and his initials, *JZJ*, carved in the vault. In 1782 Zamácola engaged the architect, Carlos Aranchi, to design the dome.[29] The inscriptions and the construction, as well as the former side entrance (Fig. 212) which now opens into the right aisle, show that aisles were built in two bays alongside of the original nave. Arches were opened in each wall to allow for two passageways into the aisles. Probably there was only one tower, on the right, at the outset, just as at Yanahuara, and so the date 1783 on the left tower would indicate that it was added at the time of the enlargement of the church. The devotion of nineteen years to this building campaign is explained to some degree at least by the severe damage the church endured in the earthquake of 1784.

The tympanum over the side portal (Fig. 210) in the wall of the original church of single nave still exists. It contains a relief of St. Michael, now half concealed by the roof of the right aisle. The sculpture can be studied upon the roof, and though badly weathered, enough is preserved to give evidence of a work of good quality.

The church (Fig. 211) is barrel vaulted in stone, including the original sacristies which flank the apse and have transverse vaults. The sanctuary by contrast carries a ribbed groin vault in the center of which is a small oculus window. The other oculus and four lateral windows are let into the crossing. The arches between the bays of the nave, contrary to general practice, are suspended on corbels richly decorated. The vaults have reliefs: St. Rose of Lima under the choir, and in the succeeding bays, St. Dominic, the shield of Castile (?) erad-

icated, and the papal insignia. The *camarín* of the miraculous Virgin of Caima, an elevated chamber behind the high altar, which is reached by stairway from the sacristy, has been redecorated in recent years.[30]

The views of San Miguel at Caima taken at the side and upon the roof (Figs. 209, 210) give an excellent idea of the superb ashlar construction in gray volcanic stone. This fine material and workmanship are among the best features of the school of Arequipa and very typical. Walls are built straight upward and then stepped into terraces at the haunch of the vault. Roofs are uniformly flat. The barren geometric mass is particularly attractive to the modern eye. This is virtually abstract art.

The church at Caima is a unique gem. It is significant not only for its excellent stonework and its lavish *mestizo* façade, but also for the romantic beauty of its location. It stands in an enchanting setting upon the plaza of a small village which still maintains its architecture, and is evocative of the secluded tranquillity of the colonial past.

The church at Yanahuara has been truncated rather than enlarged like its neighbor at Caima. It has lost the apse and the right transept of its Latin-cross plan, both of which now lie in ruins. The high altar stands beneath the dome of the crossing and the sacristy occupies the left transept. The interior is low and heavy with oculus windows in the vaults. The indifferent proportions along with the modern furnishings make for dullness. The massive dome and the cubic terraced construction, as seen from the side or rear on the exterior, are very impressive here, as in all of these churches.

The Espíritu Santo in a tiny and desolate pueblo called Chihuata (Fig. 214) deserves consideration for its very remarkable sculptured dome of the eighteenth century. It ranks second only to Pomata as a creation of *mestizo* art in which, likewise, the Spanish *mudéjar* in the ribbed design is curiously crossbred with the indigenous. Twelve angels in flounced feathered skirts stand with arms upraised vertically, separated by twelve strips of rectangular flowers which rise from vases. Over the head of each angel is the monogram of Mary and at a distance below the feet a molded pedestal. Cherubs' heads with feathered headgear decorate the circular cornice and upon it stand nude *putti*. Full-length reliefs of St. Francis, St. Dominic, St. Anthony of Padua, and St. Vincent Ferrer occupy the four pendentives. Scattered rosettes and other *mestizo* ornament fill the space surrounding the saints. Technically the carving is not the equal of that at Pomata, and the design lacks the rhythm which is almost terpsichorean in the more famous sanctuary on Lake Titicaca. The stone at Chihuata is white, and the background of the dome, painted blue, makes for a two-color effect like a fine tapestry. This dome, virtually unknown, ranks as one of the most original works of the colonial period.

The fabric of the structure at Chihuata, a small Latin cross in solid masonry, is no more notable than hundreds of other village churches. It has suffered much from restoration, as its altars dated 1878 and 1880 would suggest. A decorated side portal of the eighteenth century is a rustic product of the *arequipeño* school, not comparable in quality with any of the works previously discussed. All of the usual exotic motives appear but manipulated by an artisan lacking in skill and sense of design.

The churches at Caima, Yanahuara, Chihuata, and Paucarpata, all were Dominican foundations in regions first evangelized by Fray Pedro Ulloa.[31] The *mestizo* portal of the latter has already been studied in this chapter. The church is a single-naved structure with stone barrel vault, a type very common in small villages of the district. Window openings are few, in this case limited to a small oculus in the center of each vault of the nave and to four lunettes at the sides. The sacristy had to be reërected after the earthquake of 1784, and the neo-Renaissance façade, which is almost the rule hereabouts, has the date 1875 upon it. Very similar is the façade (1876) of the parish church at Sanbandia nearby.

The interior of the Mercedarian foundation at Characato is single naved with barrel vaulting and a method of lighting following the same system mentioned at Paucarpata. The church was rebuilt from the foundations after the earthquake of 1687.[32] The front portal with a few bits of ornament is a modest product of this time. The Doric lateral entrance, inscribed 1787, points ahead to the Neoclassic and away from the local *mestizo* style. At this same period the vaults had to be replaced following the catastrophe of 1784.[33] The chief attraction of the church lies in the characteristically massive construction of the Arequipa school. Against the rectangular silhouette of the structure are set gigantic curving buttresses, 2.78 meters deep. They recall somewhat the exterior of Santa Marta in Arequipa, and were undoubtedly added in the light of the experience with the late eighteenth-century earthquake.

The remote parish church at Yanaquigua, at some distance from Arequipa, is known to me only in photographs. For the sake of record, it is mentioned as a handsome ashlar monument of the Arequipa school. The *putti* blowing trumpets of the Dominican lateral entrance have found their way to the same position here. Otherwise, the sculptured doorway at Yanaquigua has no counterpart in the regional capital. Its columns are decorated with rosettes borrowed from Arequipa's wood-carved retables of the eighteenth century rather than from her architectural sculpture. Other churches of importance in isolated villages surely exist, awaiting discovery by investigators of colonial art.

It is hoped that the present chapter will supply the basis for an understanding of *arequipeño* architecture of the colonial period. When Padre Barriga's investigations of the archives are completed, many chronological problems will be solved and the lacunae left by destruction partially filled. If one stops to consider the fact that two thirds of Arequipa's artistic past has been lost in upheavals of the earth, the imagination is left aghast at the thought of her vanished colonial splendor.

IX

SOUTHERN PERU: THE MESTIZO STYLE—II

THE geographic range of the creole or *mestizo* style extends from Arequipa in southwestern Peru through Puno and the district of Lake Titicaca down to Potosí in Bolivia. During the colonial period Upper Peru (Bolivia) fell within the jurisdiction of the viceroyalty of Peru until the establishment of the viceroyalty of La Plata in 1776. Thereafter Bolivia was ruled from Buenos Aires. Hence it causes no wonder that the art of central South America displays stylistic unity. Moreover, the archbishopric of La Plata at Sucre, founded in 1552, included Bolivia and the region of Lake Titicaca. A later reorganization in 1605 placed the district of Chucuito in the diocese of La Paz. Not until 1866 was the present bishopric of Puno created.

An exact chronology of the development of the *mestizo* style cannot be established until more documentary evidence is forthcoming. With our present knowledge, the church of Santo Domingo in Arequipa, rebuilt in 1677–1680, seems to be one of the earliest monuments. The carving upon the choir and the side portal are thus important in the inception of the style. The façade of La Compañía (1698) marks the apex of the movement which was to continue with full force for another sixty years in Arequipa.

Some writers have characterized *mestizo* art as the "Arequipa style," thus making that city the center in which it was created and from which it disseminated.[1] It exists all over Latin America, however, and cannot be regarded solely as Peruvian, although the highest expression was attained there.[2] Even in the viceroyalty of Peru, the question arises as to whether the *mestizo* façades of Potosí were created independently or whether workmen from Arequipa transplanted the style there. Here is where our need for more documentation is imperative before the problem can be resolved. On the other hand, most of the Potosí monuments are later than those at Arequipa: Santa Teresa (1685–1692), the façade of La Compañía (1700–1707), San Francisco (1707–1714), and San Lorenzo (1728–1744). The other *mestizo* façades in the region all belong to the eighteenth century: El Belén, La Merced, San Bernardo, and the Casa de Moneda (1753–1773) in Potosí and the recently discovered façades in the neighboring villages of Santa Lucía and Salinas de Yocalla.[3] The same period holds for the splendid church of San Francisco at La Paz (1753–1772).

The region of Lake Titicaca and Puno which lies geographically between the extreme points of Arequipa and Potosí was the recipient of influences from both directions. There seems to be no possibility that the first origins are to be sought here, since none of the churches can antedate 1690–1700. The lack of dated works is particularly to be regretted. The quality, on the other hand, is unsurpassed along the lake shores. Santiago at Pomata, the transept of San Juan at Juli, Santa Cruz at Juli, and San Pedro at Zepita represent the finest flower of *mestizo* art (Figs. 215–238).

Mestizo art, like the *mestizo* race, is the product of the crossbreeding of the European with the indigenous. The most superficial study of the problem makes that apparent, and all historians agree upon the subject. The natural primitivism of simplified geometric design is the expression of the naïveté of the Indian. That same preference for two-dimensional pattern characterizes the art of all prehistoric and primitive peoples; it is indicative of a certain state of intellectual development. Dr. Neumeyer in his recent stylistic analysis of the whole phenomenon of *mestizo* art in North and South America rightly calls attention to parallel developments in Europe which were produced by similar fusions of different cultures.[4]

The very fact that *mestizo* art is concentrated in remote Andean regions, largely populated by the native alone, proves that he is the determining factor. The names of the workmen and architects in the region are Indian. The builder of the tower of La Compañía at Potosí was an Indian, Sebastián de la Cruz. He also began the church of San Francisco in the same city, and was succeeded after his death by two others of indigenous stock, Joseph Agustín and Phelipe Chavarría.[5]

Far more surprising than the natural primitivism of native artists is the survival of pre-Columbian decorative themes. The masks of Nazca and Tiahuanacu culture occur in the ornament upon the portals of Arequipa and Zepita. Their appearance has also been pointed out in San Xavier at Nazca. The grotesque heads with serpentine objects issuing from their mouths have been noted in Arequipa as survivals of the distant past. The inclusion of local flora, such as the sacred lily or *ccantu,* and local fauna, like the puma, is undeniably indicative of the contributions that native folklore made to this artistic phenomenon.

The popularity of the papaya and the banana, monkeys, and tropical birds in the repertory of *mestizo* decorators has led some scholars to propose that these elements were brought to the highlands by missionaries from Paraguay and the lower Amazon.[6] The sources of the style itself cannot be placed in those regions, however, since no prototypes of Andean decoration exist there. Media for the diffusion of tropical themes throughout the highlands were undoubtedly textiles, drawings, and even furniture, and their carriers must have been the clergy, since they were the principal European overlords. *Mestizo* marquetry (Fig. 230), a virtually unstudied ramification of the development, involves the same aesthetics and the same problems as the architectural decoration and textiles.

One other factor must be mentioned in connection with the formation of the *mestizo* style. That is the Spanish *mudéjar* (Hispano-Moresque). Other writers have recognized that the characteristics of *mudéjar* art, i.e., the abstraction of ornament into stylized patterns and the covering of large areas of surface with flat designs cut into the plane, reënforced the same tendencies in the mind of the indigenous artist.[7] Moreover, specific *mudéjar* types of architectural construction are encountered, as for example, the ribbed domes of Pomata and Chihuata (Figs. 214, 221).

REGION OF LAKE TITICACA

THE masterpiece of the *mestizo* style in South America is the church of Santiago at Pomata (Figs. 215–224), a small village on the southern shore of Lake Titicaca. Built of rose-colored stone throughout, it is incomparable in its beauty of design and fine workmanship. The Dominicans, who evangelized this region in the fifth decade of the sixteenth century, had established a house in Pomata before 1553. Probably no more than two or three monks lived there. In 1569, with the expulsion of the Dominicans from this region, which the viceroy handed over to the Jesuits, the Dominicans left Pomata but were permanently reinstated in 1600. From that time forward the importance of their mission grew, and by 1606 the house at Pomata was elevated to the rank of a monastery.

The exact dates of the present magnificent church are problematic. Meléndez in his chronicle, published in 1681, which is the source of our knowledge of the Dominicans' activity in the lake district, says, speaking of the monastery, "They are building sufficiently [sic], it has a most beautiful church and in it a miraculous image of Nuestra Señora del Rosario, the church adorned with rich retables, carved images and fine paintings." [8] The very fact that Meléndez does not make any reference to the church as being entirely of stone, as he usually does in such cases, suggests that the present edifice had not yet been begun. The statement, *está edificando*, refers to the monastery of which nothing whatsoever remains today.

The archives of Santiago at Pomata have not yet been thoroughly searched. Harthterré did find, however, three valuable references in the inventories of the sacristy: the completion of the high altar in 1722, and repairs done to the vaulting in 1729 and 1732.[9] From this evidence it is safe to conclude that the church was erected in the first quarter of the eighteenth century.

Various dates appear in inscriptions in the church, but they are subsequent to the main fabric. The atrium arch with its legend and year 1763 is a provincial structure, unconnected stylistically with the masterpiece to which it gives access.[10] On the base of the left tower is the inscription: *Quiroga acabó 1794*. The curious fact that the belfry of this tower does not exist, whereas its mate to the right does, leads to the conclusion that the upper part collapsed at some subsequent period. The surviving tower with its two-arched openings is in a general way derivative from the school of Cuzco. It resembles the tower of the church at Lampa (Fig. 239), notably in the division of the base into sections by horizontal moldings.

The ground plan of Santiago at Pomata is almost identical with that of San Pedro Mártir (Fig. 2) at Juli: a Latin cross with single nave and six lateral chapels at each side. Richly carved doorways beneath the elevated choir give access to the baptistry at the right and to the tower at the left. The two churches clearly belong to the same school and may even be the work of the same architect, although Santiago (Fig. 220) is by far the superior in space and dimensions and infinitely richer in sculptural detail. In both cases the chapels are shallow, and the bays are marked by a broad transverse arch. Stepped-back pilasters and a large cornice come out strongly *en ressaut*. In the apse a small subordinate rib occurs between the broad transverse arches, a scheme similar to the vaulting of the church at Lampa. The clerestory windows are deeply splayed into the vaults without the triangular penetration of European and of most colonial Baroque. The curve of the barrel vault at Santiago is semicircular, while that of San Pedro at Juli flattens out at the summit. The dome at Pomata (Fig. 221) soars, lofty and imposing, over the crossing in excellently cut masonry, whereas at Juli a low dome of cane and plaster was accommodated to the sixteenth-century east end. A curious architectural feature is the window, opened in the apse behind the high altar at Pomata, possibly for the display of relics. Analogues were noted previously in Santo Domingo at Cuzco and Santa Catalina at Juliaca.

Santiago at Pomata lingers in one's memory primarily because of the hauntingly lovely rose hue of its stone and the indescribable richness of the carving which abounds in every part. Moldings on the bases and cornice are rather numerous but satisfactory in scale. The sculptured ornament, on the other hand, surpasses the imagination. Crisply cut and highly stylized patterns form continuous bands on the arches of the chapels. Most interesting and original is the placing of a cone-shaped candelabrum of leaves in the spandrels of the arches. Wooden candelabra upon picture frames are common in Cuzco and Checacupe but obviously less practical than these of stone. The splays of the windows (Fig. 224) are superbly decorated with large classical jars, from which palmettes and star flowers rise stiffly. The arch is covered by broad palmettes or fronds accompanied occasionally by monkeys or *putti*. The word "fabulous" only suggests the luxuriant beauty of the windows in the apse with long palmettes, rosettes, baskets overflowing with grapes and papayas, and at the top the monogram of Christ held by two *putti*. A rectangular shield of ornament occurs repeatedly on the pilasters, on the frieze, on the transverse arches, and throughout the vaults. The pilasters under the crossing come in for still greater emphasis with pots of flowers, leaves, and shells, similar to the decoration of the façade. The mermaid playing the *charango*, so beloved of *mestizo* artists, turns up at Pomato too, in the vault of the apse.

The dome is one of the most celebrated in colonial art. It rises loftily on pendentives upon which are stone reliefs like woven tapestries. Stems and leaves placed in great pseudoclassical urns are interspersed with flat-petaled flowers, grapes, and occasional birds.[11] The bust-length figure, so common in *mestizo* art, acts as caryatid to the vase in each pendentive.

In the dome itself (Fig. 221) eight flat bands radiate from the center in what is an undeniably *mudéjar* scheme, common in Spanish medieval architecture. A large medallion of great beauty is woven between the ribs in an exquisitely rhythmical pattern. A convincing prototype for the whole composition is the dome in the chapel of La Mejorada at Olmedo (Fig. 222) near Valladolid in Spain. This appearance, in the eighteenth century, of a dome basically *mudéjar* in design is not unique. Another example has been cited in the church at Chihuata (Fig. 214), but it is in Spain that we find them most commonly in the Baroque period, especially in Andalusia. The dome in the church of Santo Domingo at Archidona (Fig. 223), in the province of Málaga, is a splendid Baroque monument, the contemporary of that at Pomata. In actual design, however, the latter adheres more closely to their common medieval forerunners.

The Pomata design has been interpreted as a native dance, but it must be assumed that any suggestion of dance rhythms was unpremeditated. Dr. Neumeyer believes that angels are represented according to long established European custom, but here carried to an unusual degree of symbolic abstraction.[12] This latter seems the more likely explanation. Few will question the undeniable beauty of the work both in composition and decorative detail. The predominant motives are many-petaled flowers in flat frontality, long stems and leaves, and, within the rings of the center of the vault, stylized lilies which may represent the *ccantu*.

Decorated interior portals are two, one on the gospel side of the apse (Fig. 224) and another in the transept, both of them entrances to the sacristy. Rather top-heavy in proportions because of the shortness of the pilasters in relation to the broad entablature, they are nonetheless showpieces of decorative splendor. The urns of cut flowers which flank the tympanum stand in inflexible symmetry, completely stone in texture and quality. This primitivism of design and technique suits the standards of taste set by twentieth-century conventions of criticism.

The small portal on the exterior which gives access to the right transept is good in its dimensions and hence much superior to the sacristy entrances. The design is beautifully calculated throughout. The main thematic devices are stems, leaves, and flowers, sometimes rectangular in pattern, at other times with petals which curve as in a whirling disk. The abstract volutes at the sides which recall an Oriental fire motive are also noteworthy on the façade of San Francisco at La Paz and on the high altar of San Francisco in Cochabamba, both in Bolivia.

The main façade of Santiago (Fig. 215) at Pomata stands within a round-arched recess. This arrangement is frequently encountered in southern Peru (Ayaviri,

Asillo, Lampa, Juliaca, Zepita, Figs. 236, 241, 249) and in Bolivia (Santo Domingo at La Paz; San Lorenzo, La Merced, El Belén at Potosí). At Pomata the carved reliefs are limited to the columns and cornices, the walls themselves being left bare. This extraordinary simplicity suggests that the façade is earlier in date than the side portals. Its three and one-half stories diminish in height as they rise, leaving the large square window which lights the choir unrelated to the arched doorway and to the three rows of niches. The ornament on the columns (Fig. 216) has the quality of good Byzantine relief, especially in the first story, where a crisp shell alternates with an eight-petaled flower within interwoven medallions. At the base of the column is the familiar half-length caryatid figure.

The side portal (Figs. 217, 218), somewhat later and far more lavish, is like an embroidery of long palmettes which spread over the semicircular tympanum and spiral columns and flare out above the niches. A hard solid stem winds about the shafts to effect the spiral curve, and amid the leaves appear parrots, monkeys, catlike pumas, and tropical fruits such as bananas and papayas. More primitive-looking puma heads decorate the corbels below. The two sun-faced disks on the columns of the second story are to be explained by indigenous sun worship rather than as the attributes of the Dominican, St. Thomas Aquinas. The same theme recurs in the Jesuit church of San Juan at Juli and on the façade of San Lorenzo at Potosí. It formerly existed over an arch in the left aisle

of La Merced at Sucre, until the restorations of 1944 cleared it away.

The church at Pomata in its entirety is incomparable, a complete and perfect jewel. It is rivaled in details by San Juan and Santa Cruz at Juli but neither of the latter possesses the same unity and completeness, nor the same beauty of material, the rose-colored stone. This monument at Pomata alone would suffice to prove the original genius of colonial builders, and the peculiar qualities of imagination which the crossbreeding of European and native cultures produced.

San Juan at Juli, originally built about 1590, of rubble, brick, adobe, and wood, received a new transept and apse as well as a new portal, all in dark brown stone, about the year 1700. In quality of carving it equals Pomata and even surpasses it in lavishness, but San Juan lacks the unity of the neighboring church. The floor plan (Fig. 1) is a Latin cross with single rectangular apse. A destroyed sacristy on the gospel side of the apse and the portals which communicated with it from the apse and left transept do not appear in the plan reproduced here. An octagonal baptistry (Fig. 225), connected with the right arm of the transept and the apse, is covered by a fine stone dome on pendentives constructed with eight ribs. The doorway inside has a round arch within a Moorish label or *alfiz*, the center of which rises in extraordinary fashion in two volutes. The flanking spiral columns are twins of those within the transept and on the side portal. The sacristy is a large room, like a chapel, built in four bays of banded barrel vaults, all in well-cut masonry. It is lighted by four windows, deeply splayed in heavy stone walls.

The crossing and transept (Fig. 226) are the highlights of San Juan at Juli, the only church in Peru where four large spiral columns stand free under each of the four corners of the dome. Above rises a large square drum of masonry which is topped by a low dome of wood, lined with a painted silk covering. The monumental scale of the columns, resting upon a high base and crowned by a deep massive entablature, produces a truly grandiose effect, the high point of the Baroque splendor of Jesuit art in Peru. At each end of the transept stands a colossal stone arch, semicircular within a rectangular label. The flat decorative ornament which is spun across the entire surface defies description. Clearly of the same school as Pomata, the ornament, nevertheless, varies considerably in detail, further proof of the creative fancy of these *mestizo* sculptors. On the pilasters double rows of flat-petaled flowers, subtly varied in shape, rise from a classical urn at the base. The flat crisp textile-like treatment of the stone is exactly comparable with the technique used in the wood carving of the gilded picture frames and altars nearby. Both gilded wood and stone fuse into a sensuously sumptuous unity.

A richly carved doorway stands in each of the lateral walls of the apse and above them is a deeply splayed window, magnificently carved with the familiar vase of flowers, grapes, and birds. Exactly the same arrangement recurs in the apse of Santa Cruz at Juli (Fig. 232). Another portal in the right transept opens into the baptistry, and in the same position in the left transept a portal, now blocked up, gave access to a sacristy which has fallen into ruin. These stone-carved doorways are related to the others in the same location in Santiago at Pomata, but are better in scale, lacking the ponderous entablature and tympanum of the latter. The door in the gospel side of the apse of San Juan is particularly fine with the large triple rosettes and the pomegranates in the spandrels. Round and square rosettes alternate on the surface of the arch, and at the sides the interlacing vine enclosing a flower recalls a similar theme in the Casa Ricketts of Arequipa. Specific relations to Pomata are indicated by the cone of leaves which seems to be a candelabrum. It flanks the arches throughout both these churches of Santiago at Pomata and San Juan at Juli. The baptistry door in the right transept has a flatter, crisper allover pattern of many-petaled flowers and, at the sides, volutes which spin around dynamically.

The exterior side portal of San Juan (Fig. 219) completes the stone sculpture of the church. It inevitably invites comparison with the side portal of Pomata (Fig. 218). The free-standing columns are shorter and heavier with rather large, clumsy capitals, and the scale of the composition is ponderous and more provincial throughout. In detail the sculpture of San Juan very nearly equals that of its rival. Peculiar in the decorative repertory is a long pod which looks like a red pepper. Clusters of grapes are more predominant here than at Pomata, and the cutting is perhaps flatter and less varied. Otherwise, the two monuments must be considered works of the same school, although not of the same master. Very charming are the trumpeting angels in the spandrels at San Juan, wearing wig and full-skirted coat, fashionable in high society in the early eighteenth century. Similar figures are found in colonial painting of the same period.

No less magnificent than the stone sculpture are the carved and gilded picture frames which line the interior of the nave enclosing a series of scenes of the life of St. John the Baptist. Whereas the frames cannot strictly be regarded as architectural decoration, the carved wood adornment of the splayed windows might logically be so classified. It would be difficult to surpass them as decoration, their patterns so beautifully stylized in rigid symmetry. The Middle Ages in Europe never knew anything finer. Technically and stylistically they differ from the Byzantine only in their more rhythmic exuberance and hence less geometric severity. The thematic material is common to the stone carving of the period, flower pots from which grow branches interspersed with star-shaped flowers. Among the foliage are birds usually in heraldic opposition, *putti*, and monkeys, favorite of this region. At the base recur the tropical fruits, papaya and bananas, also popular in the lake district, while rather exceptionally a pair of opposed peacocks act as corbels with elegant flourish.

The nave of San Pedro Mártir at Juli was entirely rebuilt by the Jesuits at the end of the seventeenth or beginning of the eighteenth century. The plan (Fig. 2) and construction are almost exactly like that of Santiago at Pomata with a number of variations in detail. For example, the piers of San Pedro have high molded bases, somewhat awkward in treatment, which occur in Santa Cruz at Juli (Fig. 228) but not at Pomata. The barrel vaults in San Pedro Mártir are lower and flatter in section, and a small intermediate rib reinforces the vault between the transverse arches. This arrangement is also found in the apse at Pomata. At Juli sculptured ornament is sparingly limited to stylized leaves in the frieze and a large rectangular piece in the center of each bay of the vault. Later in the eighteenth century, ornament was painted upon the walls of various chapels in *mestizo* style. In the second chapel to the left, behind the altar, stands a blind arch the jambs of which are beautifully carved with the vertical stem and leaf, punctuated by an occasional flower. A comparable pattern decorates the exterior doorway of the transept at Pomata.

Pier buttresses support the transverse arches on the outside of San Pedro Mártir, and the roof level of the chapels falls well below that of the nave. The walls consist of irregular stone instead of the dressed masonry of the interior. At Pomata (Figs. 215–224), on the contrary, ashlar is used throughout, and the nave walls rise straight without buttresses or contrast in roof levels. San Pedro Mártir at Juli is modest and provincial in every respect in comparison with the finished masterpiece at Pomata. The two monuments are obviously related in period and style, that of Juli possibly the earlier of the two, although it would be dangerous to be categorical about the chronology without some specific documentary evidence.

The main façade of San Pedro Mártir at Juli (Fig. 227), the wall of which is a nondescript mixture of rubble, brick, and adobe, is a stylistic and chronological problem. In spite of the classicism of the freestanding Doric columns in two stories, nothing of the type is known in Peru before the seventeenth century. The façade, of very retarded style, is probably contemporary with the nave, for reasons of construction including the use of brown ashlar. The shells in the spandrels of the first story are like those in the pendentives of the sixteenth-century crossing, but the latter ornaments must have been added at the time of the rebuilding when a new dome of cane replaced the old. The long *mestizo* leaves in stucco on the second story of the façade seem strangely out of relation to the rest of the design.

The eighteenth-century tower to the right is considerably later than the nave and portal. Spiral columns carved with vine and grapes enframe the elliptical openings, and below, a cornice with corbels effects the division between the belfry and the main body of the tower.

The same architect was undoubtedly the master of the great square tower, now half ruined by a thunderbolt, which looms majestically beside the late-Renaissance church of the Asunción at Juli (Fig. 233). Its exceptional bulk, the excellent brown ashlar, and the effective scale which the decoration affords make it one of the most imposing monuments of colonial Peru. The belfry, almost totally destroyed, had two round openings to a side, and single spiral columns. Most unusual is the spacing of the story just below the belfry, where pyramidal entablature blocks stand just above and just below the spiral columns. The tapering corbel is a signature of the local school, appearing in the vaults of San Pedro at Zepita, Santa Bárbara at Ilave, and San Pedro at Acora. The multiplication of moldings in the cornices strikes a peculiar note which, though provincial, is justified by the problem of scale. Notable here, as well as upon the contemporary archway of the atrium (Fig. 234), is the characteristic *mestizo* ornament, the square and rectangular multipetaled flowers.

A complete monument of the eighteenth century in *mestizo* style and one of surpassing decorative beauty was Santa Cruz at Juli, now abandoned and disintegrating. Four bays of the nave vault of brown ashlar survive intact, while the rest of the church is open to the sky. Rubble walls fill the intervening sections between the ashlar of the piers, transverse arches, and vaults. The portals and windows are also in stone, and beautifully decorated.

The Latin-cross plan falls into the same group as those of San Pedro Mártir at Juli and Santiago at Pomata except that arched recesses for the retables rather than shallow chapels line the nave. As usual the masonry barrel vault is separated into bays by transverse arches supported by pilasters and a half column. The entablature block is limited to each bay and to the four angles of the crossing (Fig. 228), leaving the walls of the interior without continuous cornice. The most extraordinary originality is displayed in the use of a band of basket weave, topped by a double row of flowers, which cuts across the piers. This peculiar flower motive may be a version of the *ccantu* It is also placed upon the base of the pilasters. The capital too is unusual in the crisply cut leaves and the thin volutes above. The latter indicate that it is a long-distant descendant of the Roman composite capital.

The sculptured decoration is the true glory of Santa Cruz at Juli. As in Pomata the deeply splayed windows of the clerestory are superbly carved with the same motives, large vases filled with stylized plants and flowers, scattered through with birds in heraldic opposition. Occasionally the sun face puts in an appearance. In the center of some windows appears the IHS and in others AM, the favorite though not exclusive monograms of the Jesuits.

The lateral windows and doorways of the apse (Fig. 232) are especially luxuriant in their handling. Winged harpies with Indian profiles and bust-length angels with volutes at the waist are carved in crisp archaic technique. The instruments of the Passion are worked into an abstract design with the crown of thorns encircling the IHS surmounted by a cross. The composition is enclosed by a long stem which ends in the familiar *ccantu* flower. The doorways below, about equal in size to the windows, originally gave access to the sacristies.

The high point of decorative invention throughout the entire region is reached in the triumphal-arch portals (Figs. 229, 231) placed laterally below the choir at the main entrance of the church. The thematic material is common to the regional school, but it bursts forth with exceptional exuberance here. The cutting is deeper with a richer play of light and shade than in the side portals of Pomata and of San Juan at Juli. The capitals with their sharply cut rows of leaves are similar to those of the latter monument but better in scale. Not usual in the school is the horizontal band of leaves which subdivides the shafts. Monkeys play an exceptionally prominent role here, clutching papayas or large bunches of grapes. Although they belong to the *mestizo* repertory of the lake region, nowhere else are they so amusing and so prominent. They must be regarded as the inheritance of pre-Columbian art. They are ubiquitous in textiles and pottery of the late indigenous cultures.

Also very much in evidence in Santa Cruz are bunches of grapes, large pomegranates cut through laterally revealing a sizable core of seeds, papayas, bananas, and birds. The arch of the doorway is cut with the long leaves and starlike flowers common to the Juli-Pomata school, here treated with particular flourish and luxuriance in their calligraphic curving rhythms. A curious double shell occupies the keystone. Fantasy and playful imagination combine in a work which is the ultimate achievement in this exotic art, the result of the crossbreeding of the native with European culture.

The façade of Santa Cruz is a badly planned provincial work, by no means the creation of the same architect who designed the interior. A poor bell tower of three open arches is constructed of brick and adobe. The portal itself lacks distinction of any sort, being badly jumbled in composition and poorly carved. The spiral columns of the first story lack the fine quality of the portals within the church. The upper sections attract the attention solely because of their naïveté. Two tall angels, Indians in dress and features, hold instruments of the Passion of Christ as they stand guard beside the large shell niche. The monogram of Christ within a large crown of thorns occupies the tympanum.

Reflections of the Juli school of *mestizo* art leave their traces in domestic architecture of the town, the most interesting examples of which are the stone carved portals of the Casa Zavala on the main plaza.

San Pedro at Zepita (Fig. 236) is a highly original monument, a product of the Titicaca region, but one which shows great individuality in detail. It must be the work of an independent disciple of the Juli-Pomata school. The church of Latin-cross plan has no lateral chapels, and the transverse arches of the barrel vault are suspended on corbels. The latter with their three rows of stylized leaves resemble the ornaments in the spandrels of Santiago at Pomata and San Juan at Juli. The interior is barren and sober without further decoration except for some carving upon the sacristy portal. The usual raised choir is placed over the doorway opposite the sanctuary. Unexpectedly a narrow bench is built along the wall on each side of the nave, preserving the custom of sixteenth-century rural churches which was generally

abandoned long before the advent of San Pedro at Zepita.

On the exterior the church stands laterally within a large atrium. The fine bell tower, very similar to that of Santiago at Pomata (Fig. 215), the low dome, salient transept, and recessed portal make an extremely effective composition. A functional note is struck by the way the tile roofs reveal the curves of the barrel vault. The dark red stone adds immeasurably to the picturesque beauty of this building which also has the advantage of being located near the shores of Lake Titicaca.

The fame of the church rests, however, on the large sculptured lateral portal (Figs. 237, 238) which is recessed within an arch. To the left the titular St. Peter stands within a niche and to the right his companion, St. Paul. The two-storied division into a broad triumphal arch with free-standing columns is European in descent, but the detail is the most exotic of all churches of the *mestizo* school in southern Peru. The short columns bulge out in extraordinary fashion, and the lower half is divided off by a ring of stylized leaves. The interwoven chain devices have no parallels in other *mestizo* monuments. They are probably analogous to rather than specifically *mudéjar*, just as the application of flat ornament like tapestry to the wall is natural primitivism which occurs independently throughout the world at many different epochs. The grotesque masks, at times feline, and the frontally seated figures at the extreme sides can permit of no doubt that they are a combination of pre-Columbian survival and natural primitivism. The theory that they reflect Asiatic influence brought by missionaries seems utterly romantic.[13] These female figures with pendant breasts in geometric symmetry put in their appearance again and again at Asillo throughout its decoration and in pulpits as far south as the Merced at Sucre (Bolivia). Most startling and fantastic of all is the enormous vertical volute which rises out of the headdress, springing into crisp knobs at the sides, and cut down through the center in slightly projecting scales.

The filigree relief of the doorway and friezes is more lacelike than elsewhere in the Titicaca region. The thematic material, however, has been encountered often before, especially in San Juan at Juli: triple rosettes, spiral rosettes, long ferns, vases with flowers and leaves, and heraldically opposed birds. More numerous than elsewhere are the *putti* who take part in the large abstract compositions occupying the niches of the second story. Loading the verticals are large urns with stiff metallic-looking plants and flowers, triumphs of the decorator's art, and prime favorites of *mestizo* sculptors, not only here but also at Pomata (Fig. 224) and elsewhere.

The small front doorway at Zepita does not startle, yet its stone embroidery is impeccable, as exquisitely drawn and cut as the finest colonial textiles. The light-colored stone of both portals has been painted a dark red.

The master of Zepita produced a still finer achievement in the magnificently carved wall piers (Fig. 235) which support the choir added in the eighteenth century to the church of San Miguel in Pomata.

The style of carving and motives match those of Zepita, and even surpass them in quality. The ingenious interlacing chain pattern covers the entire columns in San Miguel. Great vertical headdresses grow like huge plants over the heads of the mermaids who play the *charango*. This is indeed a sumptuous example of the archaic formalism and majestic symmetry of *mestizo* design. Its beauty is hard to match.

Another eighteenth-century choir in a sixteenth-century church must be mentioned, that of La Asunción in Chucuito. In this case the sculptured decoration is limited and unimpressive, consisting of acanthus leaves over the arch and between the arches large bowls of papayas, apples, and pomegranates. The construction here provides more interest than the ornament, the choir being sustained on four small square piers which carry six small domical vaults.

The church of Santa Bárbara at Ilave, dating from the late seventeenth or early eighteenth century, is a building entirely of masonry and without notable architectural features on the exterior. The atrium archway of stepped form resembles the still finer one of La Asunción at Juli (Fig. 234). The decorations in *mestizo* style consist of disks, flat reliefs of saints, and spiral colonnettes, the latter the only indication of the date of the church. The type of monument, the long single nave covered with barrel vaults suspended on corbels, belongs to the regional group, more similar to San Pedro at Zepita than to any other. Certain peculiarities are observed in the way the barrel vault of the apse is raised higher than that of the nave. The very limited fenestration in the nave consists of only one window near the crossing and another which illuminates the raised choir. Carved decoration, so characteristic of the *mestizo* school, is altogether lacking here.

PROVINCE OF PUNO

INTERMEDIATE geographically between Cuzco and Puno and intermediate stylistically as well is a group of churches which includes those of Lampa, Ayaviri, Asillo, Juliaca, Pupuja, Pucará, and Vilque. The finest of these is at Lampa, reached by automobile from Juliaca. This church was formerly in the diocese of Cuzco, and none other than the great Bishop Mollinedo reported in 1678 its inception and in 1685 its completion.[14] Lampa (Fig. 245), like the other churches of this group, has the plan of a Latin cross with extremely long nave, single rectangular apse raised by four steps, elevated choir, and a broad molded cornice which runs the full length of the church. One rather large chapel is placed at each side below the choir, but otherwise the nave has no chapels, an arrangement which occurs also at Juliaca and Ayaviri. The churches in the region are barrel vaulted in stone, and carry a large dome over the crossing. Asillo, the exception, had a thatched roof originally.

The vaults of Lampa have an unusual and original character, for between the transverse arches of stone in each bay, two intermediate arches are added. The ribbed effect which results is very satisfactory because of the considerable length of each bay. Equally unusual is the handling of the U-shaped choir. It is not merely suspended on a vault, but also has two large supporting columns at each side (Fig. 243). The columns are ungainly with their huge capitals and short thick shafts upon which appear two crowns of stylized leaves. The doors of the two chapels beneath the choir are flanked by half columns of similar design. A rather fantastic note is obtained by the gigantic decorative shell at each side below the choir. Otherwise ornament is sparingly used, in contrast to the Puno region. It is limited to three rectangular shields of stylized leaves in three of the four bays of the nave and the three large leaves in each pendentive of the dome.

The Latin-cross plan without side chapels is clearly related to that of the churches of the Puno region. The influence of Cuzco, on the other hand, is equally clear in the Doric cornice and in the entablature block at the crossing and over the pilasters, which first entered the school of Cuzco in the cathedral there. Other features, nonarchitectural, such as the picture frames with spiral columns in natural cedar, are *cuzqueño* in origin, as is the pulpit which in a general sense is related to the type of pulpit found in Cuzco Cathedral. Even more pronounced influence of the school of Cuzco appears in the main portal (Figs. 239, 241) which is based directly on that of La Compañía (Fig. 64). Most striking are the columns ringed with two crowns of acanthus leaves, the use of flat carved ornament in the central section, and even the general composition of the façade with its three stories, the window giving into the choir, and the placing of the niches. The reddish-stone portal of Lampa is in no sense a copy of the Jesuit church at Cuzco, but the prototype is unmistakable. The familiar arched recess, within which the Lampa portal is set, is typical, on the contrary, of the Puno-Bolivian region. Also popular in the south are the mermaids who guard the shield of the Virgin just above the door. Mermaids reappear in the same position on the façade of the church at Asillo (Fig. 244). The side portal at Lampa is a reduction of the principal portal, but consisting only of two stories.

The general composition of the church (Fig. 239) from the exterior, set within a large atrium, is excellent. The fine bell tower of masonry is separated into three stages by plain broad cornices. Its isolated position is definitely a rural feature, unknown in Cuzco, but common in small pueblos like Checacupe. Simple ball pinnacles load the buttresses of the nave and the dome. The unusual size of the two chapels at the front gives something like the impression of a second transept as seen from the distance. Their sloping red-tiled roof and the brown stones of the structure blend well with the reddish stone of the portals. The parish church at Lampa is outstanding among those of the small villages of Peru, notable for the high quality of its workmanship and the originality of its composition. It is interesting too in the way it shows its descent from the architecture of both the Cuzco and Puno regions.

The church at Ayaviri (Fig. 246) is very similar to that at Lampa, consisting of a Latin cross with single sanctuary elevated by four steps. It has only one chapel at each side beneath the choir, a prominent dome on pendentives over the crossing, a large cornice with entablature blocks at the crossing and over the pilasters. The portal is based directly upon that of Lampa (Figs. 241, 242). On the word of Bishop Mollinedo the church at Lampa is dated 1678–1685, and Ayaviri had been finished by 1696.[15] These data, plus the higher quality of Lampa throughout, leave no doubt as to which is the earlier. The portal at Ayaviri shows a greater taste for ornamentation than its model, adding the frieze of stylized leaves in the first story and the rosette and interlace in the second story. Both are redolent of the Puno region. Although the general proportions at Ayaviri are excellent, the detail is coarser with a show of more provincial taste, and the light brown stone has far less flavor than the reddish. The composition of the exterior at Ayaviri, when seen as a whole standing within its spacious atrium, in some respects surpasses its rival. The twin towers of Cuzco derivation present a well-balanced unity and the two chapels toward the front are small and inconspicuous without the medieval silhouette of those at Lampa. The flat roof and strong rectangular buttresses are well fitted into the composition (Fig. 240), but the appearance of the church today is sadly marred by the recent restorations using galvanized-iron roofs for the transept and dome.

Within as well as without, the two churches (Figs. 245, 246) differ in detail, although less so within. The fine stone barrel vault at Ayaviri is divided into five bays with a single transverse arch at each bay in traditional style, in contrast to the four bays and two intermediate arches at Lampa. The choir too follows the traditional method of construction, being suspended on a flatly arched vault. The less usual features in Ayaviri are the use of early Gothic ribbed vaults in the arms of the transept and the large blind arch supported by columns in the ends of the transepts. The same taste for ornament displayed in the portal comes to light in the shield, floral and scroll, in the center of each bay of the vault and the flat scroll designs in the pendentives. The influence of the school of Cuzco here again is not limited to the architecture alone, but appears still more eloquently in the high altar, the pulpit, and the large pictures of the nave. The latter are signed by Isidoro Francisco Moncada of Cuzco in 1768. It is difficult to do full justice to the church of Ayaviri, because of the very dilapidated condition of both interior and exterior today, whereas the church at Lampa is in an excellent state of preservation.

The church at Asillo, under construction 1678–1696, has a façade (Fig. 244) which is modeled directly on its contemporary at Ayaviri some twenty miles away.[16] The two-towered façade with three-storied portal of red stone differs, however, in the thoroughly primitive Indian character of the dimensions and the ornament. Everything is done with a strong *quechua* accent. The columns swell more than usual; the acanthus crowns of Cuzco, via Lampa-Ayaviri, are heavy and coarse. The Sacred Heart is carved above each of the side niches, which have Indian guardians with feathered headdresses. In the second story the three hearts bear the inscription: *Sanctus Deus, Sanctus Fortis, Sanctus Immortalis*, also present in abbreviated form on the façade of La Compañía at Arequipa. The irregular stone of the lateral walls and the bright red portal of Asillo are imposing in this tiny Indian village of eight hundred souls. But this art is rustic and provincial without the exquisite qualities of the best primitive work. Today the church is roofed with galvanized iron, which has replaced the thatched original, a mournful loss for its picturesqueness.

The Latin cross persists at Asillo as do the single apse, now raised only two steps, and the broad cornice. Lacking are the stone vaults and the stone dome of the region. The fenestration strikes an entirely new note here with two large windows in each wall of the nave instead of the small openings placed high in each bay at Lampa and Ayaviri.

The interior of Asillo is rustic, and even though the specialist is delighted by iconographic and ornamental curiosities in the altars and pictures, he must not forget that aesthetically they possess no great merit. Far better is the really awesome interior of the cruciform church at Pucará with its enormously long and narrow nave, its high stone barrel vault, its large dome, and the tiny raised choir. This church is barren and austere like a Mexican monastic church of the sixteenth century, although judging by local style, it belongs to the late seventeenth or early eighteenth century. The clumsiness of the exterior, consisting of portal and flanking towers with the left tower unfinished, is partially offset by the bright red stone of the portal and the starkness of the landscape setting.

Vilque, once an important commercial center, to which Argentines went from Salta to sell their mules, is now an abandoned village of one hundred inhabitants. Facing the plaza is a splendid church entirely of stone, light tan in color, with single tower of *cuzqueño* lineage to the left. This church, finished in 1696, on the word of Bishop Mollinedo, obviously is a close relative of Ayaviri and Lampa.[17] The handling of the rectangular buttresses is identical, but the quality of the cut masonry is superior to any others of the group. In plan there are striking differences, for here at Vilque the church has a single nave and no dome. The barrel vault of masonry counts only six bays throughout, and in general the scale is smaller than in the others. A plain molded cornice runs below the vault, and the bays are indicated by stone arches carried on pilasters. The windows as at Lampa are small and the middle bays unlighted. A baptistry is located to the right under the choir, and a stairway in the lower part of the tower to the left leads to the choir. These projections and the sacristies flanking the sanctuary give contrasts in roof levels on the exterior. The roofs, originally of red tiles, have recently been covered with the prevailing curse, galvanized iron.

The portal is an addition of the late eighteenth century and the retables and pulpit were all replaced in the mid-nineteenth century, only the silver candelabra having survived from about the year 1700. The high altar was donated by Doña María del Ribero in 1847 according to an inscription above it. In stone letters beneath the choir appear the following words: *Hiso el Dr. Don Manuel de la Peña Montenegro esta iglesia. Se empesó en el año de 1790 y se acabó 1793.* This statement that the church was built in 1790–1793 by Manuel de la Peña Montenegro is an exaggeration, for it can refer only to the portal. The church and tower clearly are contemporary with the churches at Ayaviri and Lampa, as the style and the word of Mollinedo prove. The portal, on the contrary, was obviously remade in the eighteenth century and fitted rather awkwardly into the recessed niche which is too small for the huge capitals and projecting entablatures. This portal is a late adaptation of the side entrance of Lampa. The capitals consist of two rows of large incised leaves topped by volutes, and the shafts are encircled below by two crowns of leaves, as at Lampa. An allover decoration of grapes, leaves, and pomegranates betrays the later date and the influence of the *mestizo* façades of Puno, Juli, and Pomata. This is a tame reflection of the sumptuousness of the latter, however, the postscript to a greater past. Technically the façade is inferior to the body of the church, whose best feature is its beautifully cut masonry. The side portal, which unmistakably belongs to the original construction of the late seventeenth century, is a dignified composition of two stories with unchanneled and undecorated shafts topped by a Corinthian type of capital possessing large volutes.

The parish church at Santiago de Pupuja in the vicinity of Pucará is a fine structure in reddish stone. It has a two-towered façade and a Latin-cross plan with dome. I believe it is modeled on the church at Ayaviri, although it is known to me only in photographs. An inscription beneath the choir is said to state that the construction was finished in 1767, a date which is clearly betrayed in its façade of *mestizo* style.[18] Although the general disposition of the architectural design descends from Ayaviri, the flat ornament covering the entire surface has an unmistakable Puno-esque flavor. This crossbreeding of the two regions produces a highly exotic offspring. Most notable are the columns which taper sharply toward the top and consist of a succession of crowns carved with leaves. Here are the acanthus-leafed crowns of Cuzco, multiplied and presented in a completely native and *mestizo* guise, as reinterpreted by artists steeped in Puno traditions.

Juliaca lies farthest to the south, nearest to Puno, a fact which might be surmised from the architecture of its church, Santa Catalina (Fig. 249). Like Santiago de Pupuja, it incorporates, but in a different way, the Indianism of the south. The date too is of the eighteenth century, for an inscription on the portal which I could decipher only in part reads: . . . *se acabó esta portal año 1774* ("this portal was finished in 1774"). The late period is attested by the spiral columns and the lack of ornament, indicative of the change to a more classical taste. The fact that the composition is based upon that of the façade (Figs. 250, 251) of Puno Cathedral (1757) also shows

that the inscription is correctly read as 1774 and not 1711.[19]

The portal stands within a semicircular recess like so many others of the region. The curiosities, such as the cherub heads on the stilt block above the capitals, the frieze of cherubs over the upper niche, the half-length figure with pendant breasts as in Puno Cathedral and the retables of Asillo, interest the spectator but the design and workmanship are second rate.

Definitely not so is the body of the church, again set in a broad atrium and facing upon a large plaza. The front, with its single bell tower at the left and a side glimpse of the dome and buttresses, is picturesque. Magnificent is the view from the opposite extreme with the apse and transept rising to equal heights and the dome soaring above (Fig. 247). The buttresses are loaded with pinnacles, enchanting in their fantasy, with rows of crisply stylized leaves. To complete the circuit of the exterior, mention must be made of the side door of trefoil shape whose moldings are carved with pomegranates, vines, and grapes. In the rear wall of the apse is an arched recess enclosing a broad window. Here is a rare feature and an exact parallel to the balcony (Fig. 79) in the apse of Santo Domingo, Cuzco, which Buschiazzo interpreted as an Open Chapel.[20] As previously explained, greater probability favors the theory that the opening in the apse was intended for the display of relics.

The interior of Santa Catalina (Fig. 248) strikes one immediately by its enormous length, and then by its fine dome and stone barrel vaults. All of these features occur at

Lampa and Ayaviri as do the chapels on either hand beneath the elevated choir. Quite new to the churches in the present group are the shallow arched niches, in each bay of the nave, which from the outside give the mistaken appearance of chapels. The sacristy at the right also looks more prominent than it should, as it does at Lampa. The Puno-esque character comes forth in the ornament of the frieze with its alternation of rosette and rectangular stylized flower, a signature of Puno-Arequipa-Bolivia. The vaults too have large stylized shields similar to those of Puno Cathedral (Fig. 254). The six bays of the nave are thus decorated: with female head (St. Catherine?); with stars, sword, crown, and half wheel (the attributes of St. Catherine of Alexandria); with the giant face of the sun; with stars; with AM (Ave Maria); and with the monogram, IHS. The dome too carries the monograms of Christ and Mary and a row of stylized flowers. The right transept has the Franciscan crossed-arms in its vault, perhaps a later addition, and the left transept the Bethlemite shield of three stars and crown. Hence the church, at present in charge of the Franciscans, seems to have belonged to three religious orders, for the IHS and the pierced heart upon the façade suggest the Jesuits. This description gives no adequate picture of the peculiar and primitive charm of the interior of Santa Catalina at Juliaca, charm which persists, although a fire stripped it of all its original retables and furnishings.

The new cathedral of Puno, dating from the first half of the eighteenth century, was begun at the expense of a rich miner, Don Miguel Jacinto San Román, at the time of whose death of unrecorded date the structure had been completed except for the vaults.[21] The Latin-cross floor plan (Fig. 3), the only type used in important churches of the Andean region of southern Peru during the eighteenth century, has no lateral chapels at Puno. It follows the same plan as the churches at Lampa and Ayaviri. Everything about the construction of Puno Cathedral (Fig. 254) places it stylistically with the churches in the region just to the north of the city: the stone barrel vault with penetrations, the severe molded cornice, the raised choir, and the fine stone dome on pendentives over the crossing. The same holds for the exterior with its excellent ashlar, the flat roof, the stone dome loaded by turrets, and the pronounced rectangular buttresses, like those of Ayaviri and Vilque. Novelties are the low buttresses of the transept and apse, rising little more than half the height of the church, like a deep wall with curving top. They recall the large curving buttresses massed against the wall of the church at Characato near Arequipa. Unfortunately the appearance of the exterior at Puno is badly marred by the galvanized iron which has recently been placed over the stone vaults.

Ample sacristies of rectangular shape flank the apse of Puno Cathedral, each with doors opening both into the transept and the sanctuary. The square chamber which projects beyond the apse might be interpreted as a *camarín*, not very commonly placed in that position, although a good example of it can be cited in the church at

Copacabana. The analogue is less certain in the churches of San Pedro at Lima (Fig. 9) and San José at Nazca. The *camarín* is a special chamber or shrine placed behind an altar containing a cult statue of the Virgin or other saint. It appears to be particularly characteristic of Latin America.

The sculptured decoration of the interior is limited to the center of each bay of the vault, and to the long figures (now destroyed) with great feathered headdresses in the pendentives of the dome. The placing of a saint in relief enframed in stylized leaves in the vault follows the precedent of Arequipa, as seen in the churches of Caima and Paucarpata. At Puno the Immaculate Conception appears over the sanctuary, the Madonna and Child in the transepts, followed in the bays of the nave by St. Rose of Lima, a praying figure, St. Michael, St. Dominic, and St. Francis. Today the interior of Puno is disappointing because the altars and furnishings are entirely modern, as the result of a fire in 1930. The original high altar was transferred to the church at Taraco in 1877, and there it still exists.

The façade (Figs. 250, 251) and side portals of the cathedral constitute an amalgamation of the style of Arequipa and that of Juli and Pomata. The main fabric of the church, on the other hand, belongs to the regional school of Ayaviri and Lampa. These sculptured portals, in contrast to others of the lake region, are exactly dated. That on the epistle side (Fig. 253) has an inscription, *Año de 1754.* In the spandrels of the front doorway (Fig. 252) are two inscriptions giving the date of completion,

May 25, 1757, and the name of the sculptor, Simón de Asto. They read as follows: *Se acabó es(ta) portada oi 25 de maio de 1757 años* and *El maestro que hiso esta portada fué Simón de Asto.* On the columns of the second story the date is repeated, *Acabó año de 1757.*

The general composition of the façade of Puno Cathedral with its high portal between two square towers is derived from the school of Cuzco where it originated in La Compañía (Fig. 67), followed by San Pedro and El Belén at Cuzco and by the church at Ayaviri. Otherwise, the style is related to the *mestizo* works of southern Peru. The bases of the towers are divided into stories by moldings as at Zepita. The belfries seem to have been added by an architect who changed the original designs, for they are small and slightly out of proportion to the mass of the towers. The stone used in the belfries has a light yellow color, unlike the gray stone throughout the rest of the church, another indication of a lapse of a few years, probably at the time of San Román's death. The plain colonnettes, ringed by crowns of leaves and pinched in the center by a band, and the large capitals with rigid leaves point in the direction of the Ayaviri-Lampa circle rather than toward Juli-Pomata in the south. Puno Cathedral throughout stands at the crossroads where the two schools meet.

The highly decorated portal by Simón de Asto is the work of a man who had practiced his trade at Juli, judging by his repertory of ornament. A heavy vine twists about the columns, dividing them into spiral bands as on the portals of Pomata and of San Juan and Santa Cruz in Juli (Figs. 218, 219, 231). The familiar *mestizo* motives (grapes, papayas, flat crisp-petaled flowers, and broad leaves) stand out prominently. The carving here is hard and dry, lacking in the luxuriance and decorative exuberance of the best work at Juli and Pomata. The mermaids, popular in southern Peru and Bolivia (Arequipa, Juli, Pomata, Potosí), play their *charangos* as they float over the niches within which stand solemn evangelists.[22] Interesting as the façade of Puno Cathedral is, its extremely static rigidity produces the effect of coldness which makes it fall aesthetically into a category well below the churches of Juli, Pomata, and Zepita.

From the archaeological standpoint the Puno façade (Figs. 250–252) is intriguing because it gathers up and combines crosscurrents from the Titicaca region and from Arequipa. The composition of the portal in two stories and the general disposition indicate that Simón de Asto had visited Arequipa, and had admired the façade of the Compañía there (Fig. 193). The fragment of an entablature at the sides which makes a transition between the two stories is borrowed directly from the Compañía. Likewise derivative from Arequipa is the use of a broad flat fringe of vine-and-leaf ornament (Figs. 201, 202, 206) at the outer edges of the portal. To be sure, the artist modified the prototype radically in proportions, in detail, and especially in the introduction of figures of saints, as though in a great retable. The large empty niche, which must have contained a statue of the

titular saint of the church, Charles Borromeo, is accompanied at the sides by Saints Peter and Paul. Just below, the Madonna of the Immaculate Conception is sustained in an elliptical mandorla by tiny angels, and adoring her are Saints Dominic and Francis. Over the doorway, a *quechua* St. Michael, wearing a feathered headdress and flounced skirt, slays the dragon. The short primitive statues in the main niches, negligible in merit, represent St. Mark at the right and possibly St. Matthew at the left.

A number of interesting details of the façade deserve mention. The spiral column to the left of the doorway, now reënforced by iron bands, is the only one which, like Santa Cruz at Juli (Fig. 229), has monkeys in the decoration. An acanthus crown of leaves, of Cuzco tradition, also appears here and on the columns of the second story. The frieze over the columns is carved with a rosette topped by three feathers, the latter like an Indian headdress. The feathers turn up now and again in *mestizo* art and with especial frequency among the ornament within the church at Asillo and in the cloister of the Compañía at Arequipa.

The two side portals (Fig. 253) of Puno Cathedral, like the façade, are adaptations of the Arequipa school, but so modified as to become original works. The general arrangement: round-arched doorway with pilasters, a horizontal frieze or entablature above, a rounded tympanum with voluted hood, a niche or sculptured relief in the center, are found, though differently proportioned, at Paucarpata and in the side portal of Santo Domingo at Arequipa (Figs. 201, 202). The corbel beneath the niche, supported by a nude *putto,* is also *arequipeño,* as for example in the portal of Caima (Fig. 208). Only the spiral colonnettes belong to the lake region, the rest of the ornament being definitely of *arequipeño* flavor. Especially notable in that respect are the grotesque heads in profile and even the designs of the vines, the leaves, the rosettes, and rectangular flowers. The side portals have excellent scale and most effective composition, combined with decorative invention. The ornament, both in technique and motives, is sufficiently unlike that of the façade to suggest that some other master, rather than Simón de Asto, conceived it.

Sculpture

X

CHOIR STALLS

THE extraordinary importance of the choir stalls of colonial Peru has passed hitherto almost unnoticed. Only the series in Lima Cathedral has received much attention, in spite of the fact that the churches of Lima alone contain five superb sets of the seventeenth and eighteenth centuries. Furthermore, Cuzco has three fine series and Trujillo one. No other country in South America possesses anything comparable either in quantity or quality.

The earliest choir stalls in South America, so far as I know, are those in the cathedral of Sucre in Bolivia, a city known in the colonial age as La Plata and as Chuquisaca. Among the books and loose papers in the cathedral archives which record the expenditures of the late sixteenth century are numerous payments to Christóval Hidalgo, sculptor of the stalls (1592–1599). Funds were collected from all over the diocese, as far away as Chucuito, at that time within the episcopal jurisdiction of Chuquisaca.[1]

These interesting stalls of the late sixteenth century have been considerably damaged by later alterations (Fig. 255). Not the least is the white paint with touches of gilt on details of ornament, thus masking the natural color of the cedar and giving an artificial look to the sculpture.

The paintings of apostles and saints in half length which occupy the main panels have been retouched on numerous occasions. The most drastic changes took place, however, in 1825 when the choir stalls were moved from their traditional Hispanic location in the nave to their present position in the apse. The elliptical backs of red plush with gilded frames were added then, as well as the late rococo gables at the top. Perhaps it would clarify the situation to state the case positively and say what has survived of Christóval Hidalgo's work: the large panels which serve as backs to the upper stalls, the bishop's throne, and the caryatid figures between the seats. The seats of the upper stalls and the lower stalls in their entirety are later.

Hidalgo's style reveals clearly that he was Spanish born. The large decorative cartouches of the late Renaissance serve as frames for elliptical paintings of apostles, and balustered colonnettes separate the panels. The freedom of Renaissance artists from adherence to strict classical usage is manifest in the free interpretation of the Ionic capitals and in the association with them of a Doric frieze. The bishop's throne with its fine canopy supported by the same balustered colonnettes is an outstanding example of Renaissance craftsmanship.

The choir stalls of Sucre Cathedral are unique in South America. Only one other series stands near them in date, that of Tunja Cathedral in Colombia (1598–1603), the work of a certain Francisco Velázquez. The style of the latter is unrelated to the church furniture of Peru and Bolivia. Most extraordinary is the arrangement of these stalls as separate chairs, each of which has a prayer desk before it.[2]

The earliest set of choir stalls in Peru is located in Santo Domingo at Lima (Fig. 256). They are assignable by style and literary allusion to the first quarter of the seventeenth century. Padre Lizárraga, who departed from Lima for Chile in 1603, makes no mention of them throughout his detailed description of the church. On the other hand, Padre Cobo in his history of the city (circa 1629) speaks of the fine stalls with many carved figures of saints.[3]

By some miracle these stalls have escaped destruction in numerous earthquakes, although the church has suffered repeatedly. Damage has been limited to the pinnacles and moldings at the top which are modern in large part. The backs of the seats in both the upper and lower ranges have a mudéjar pattern which is repeated almost without modification throughout. A vertical channeled motive constitutes the rectangular frame, and within are elliptical interlaces. Similar mudéjar designs decorate the lower sections of the seats in the four other series of choir stalls in Lima, the only feature which those of Santo Domingo have in common with them.

Forty-seven panels, each carved with the figure of a saint, are arranged in the usual manner above the seats of the upper stalls. Their architectural enframement clings to an early Renaissance design, even at this late date. Columns, fluted in the upper two thirds of the shaft and topped by a Corinthian capital, separate the panels. The frieze displays the freedom of Renaissance interpretation of classical themes in the use of the triglyph over the column and in the molding of dentils, while the main section over each saint is filled by an arabesque.

The saints represented include an imposing array of Dominicans, the apostles, the Fathers of the Latin Church, and the major personalities of sacred history, such as St. Catherine of Siena, St. Catherine of Alexandria, St. Agnes, St. Ursula, St. Lucy, St. Sebastian, St. Martin of Tours, etc. The patroness of Spanish America, St. Rose of Lima, was added in the late seventeenth century. The usual custom in Dominican and Franciscan churches of placing over the prior's throne the meeting of St. Francis and St. Dominic at Rome is observed here.

Each of the panels has a round arch at the top, and the saint in most cases is crowded in the space. This crowding of the figure and the animation attempted in many of the postures are in general characteristic of the sixteenth-century stalls of Spain.[4] The swaying of the body, in the reliefs representing St. Michael, St. Agnes, and others, suggests the Gothic hip-swing. Close examination, however, leads to the suspicion that Renaissance contrapposto was the real intention of the sculptor. The attempt to rotate the body at the hips and to throw forward one leg and one shoulder is not successfully accomplished. For the most part the handling of the human figure ranges from competence to failure. St. Sebastian and St. Agnes fall into the latter category. In general, the artist paid little attention to the problem of composition either of the figure or of its relation to the space about it. The technical equipment of the artist was not equal to the task in such panels as St. Martin and the Beggar, or Santiago Matamoros. These reliefs do have a naïve charm which appeals to the specialist, but our critical sense would be inadequate, if we did not recognize the provincial quality of the work.

Certain figures like that of the Magdalen are touched by the classical style in the disposition of the pallium. On the whole, however, the drapery displays an attitude which is naturalistic rather than concerned with decorative qualities or effects of style.

The choir stalls of Santo Domingo are definitely retarded works of art. In Spain they would be dated about 1530, that is approximately one hundred years earlier. The most surprising archaism of all is the relief devoted to St. Anne, Mary, and the Infant Christ (Fig. 261), which retains the iconography of the *Annaselbsdritt*, so common in northern Europe in the fifteenth century whence it penetrated to Spain.[5] The group in Lima is dignified and expressive, one of the most successful pieces of sculpture on the stalls.

The sculptor of the Dominican stalls was surely Spanish born and just possibly a monk. He was acquainted with the church furniture of the mother land, but he was an amateur without the technical equipment which was known to first-rate artists in Spain. Because of the belated nature of the sculpture and the personal naïveté it embodies, direct stylistic relations with any specific school of Spanish sculpture would be difficult to establish. The non-professional artist, very frequently the member of a religious order, is by no means a rarity in the cultural history of Hispanic America.

The choir stalls of Lima Cathedral (Figs. 257, 258) may be justifiably called the most important in Peru, not only because of their high quality, but also because of the precedent which they established for subsequent works. After a period of competitive bidding among the chief sculptors of the day, the contract for them was awarded to Pedro de Noguera, one of the outstanding colonial artists of the seventeenth century. Noguera won this highly prized competition in April 1623. The following year he engaged to work with him under his direction two of the men who had been his rivals in the bidding: Luis Ortiz de Vargas and Martín Alonso de Mesa.[6] The latter died in 1626, and hence probably accomplished comparatively little upon the left side of the stalls which was assigned to him.[7] Luis Ortiz de Vargas' share consisted of the right side. How much he completed is difficult to surmise, for he was back in Seville in 1628. Highly significant is the fact, however, that ornamental details, such as the *putti* supporting the canopy and the draped female heads, are used both on the Lima stalls and on those of Málaga Cathedral in Spain. Ortiz de Vargas, himself, was entrusted with the decorative carving of the latter in the six- teen thirties. Notices of his activity in Lima are limited to the years between 1622 and 1627.[8]

It must be admitted that the style of the choir stalls is uniform throughout, giv- ing little evidence of the collaboration. Pedro de Noguera prepared the designs, and he must have had a number of sculp- tors and carpenters to carry out his plans under his close supervision. The workshop coöperated as a well-organized unit, as was customary from the Middle Ages to the nineteenth century.

The stalls originally occupied their tra- ditional Hispanic position in the nave. During the restorations and alterations of Lima Cathedral in 1895–1897 the *trascoro* was destroyed and the stalls transferred to their present place in the sanctuary. In the reinstallation the positions of the saints were so completely rearranged that it is impossible to say exactly what the pre- vious disposition was. An old photograph, published by Martín Noël, shows that the bishop's throne with the figure of the Sal- vator Mundi occupied its customary place in the center of the rear wall.[9] Seven apos- tles and the *Purísima* were placed in two groups on each side of Him. Today the bishop's throne stands at the left of the high altar as the spectator faces the altar. In this region at both the left and right of the throne appear empty panels without seats below. These sections are modern imi- tations of the original carving.

The lower stalls as usual have only deco- rative ornament. A saint in full length, carved in high relief, is placed within the niche above each of the upper stalls. To- day, as one approaches the choir, the four Fathers of the Latin Church, the Four Evangelists, and the apostles are equally divided between the left and right sides facing each other. With them are other saints, such as Joseph, Michael, and Sebas- tian. Their arrangement is confused, be- cause of errors made in their transfer from the original choir to the sanctuary. On both sides near the altar there follow female saints such as Barbara, Agnes, Clare, Theresa, Catherine of Siena, and the Mag- dalen. With them stand Franciscans and Jesuits. The rear wall, likewise, is mainly devoted to monastic saints, in large part of the Dominican and Franciscan orders. A second bishop's throne holds its normal position in the center of the rear wall. Padre Rubén Vargas Ugarte generously ex- plained to me the reasons for the peculiar occurrence in Lima of the two episcopal chairs and of still a third which is in reality the stall of the dean of the canons. The presence of this third and most extraordi- nary feature Padre Vargas solves on the basis that the dean of Lima often acted for the bishop and hence was especially hon- ored in that city. His stall stands on the right side and is given the same prominence as that of the primate. The existence of the first bishop's throne at the left is easily understood, because the position of the high altar in the middle of the sanc- tuary relegates the normal throne to a dis- tant and unsuitable location.

The style of the figure sculpture dis- plays considerable animation in the poses of the saints. The lower part of the body with one knee bent forward assumes virtually the same position in each relief. The torso is swung slightly to the left or right, and the movement of the head usually follows the same direction. In some cases the postures are badly motivated, the desire to introduce variety of action having prevailed to the disadvantage of composition. The poorest relief is that of the Visitation in which an ugly distortion of body results from the projection of the knees and the inability of the artist to cope with the problem of two figures embracing. The confused and disorganized handling of the draperies still further distresses the critical observer.

In general, the style of drapery is characterized by sharp-edged folds, numerous creases, and puckers. The intention is clearly to create a pictorial play of light and shade. Although a successful effect is achieved in some instances, the drapery usually appears metallic, and is lacking in good design and in motivation. The classical handling of rounded folds with channeled divisions, seen in Martínez de Arrona's Apostles (Fig. 309) in the sacristy of the cathedral, was the point of departure for Pedro de Noguera's drapery. He transformed it into a metallic pictorial concept. Among the most successful reliefs are the four Fathers of the Latin Church and St. Francis which display composure and hence suffer from no straining for effect. The Salvator Mundi on the bishop's throne would logically be regarded as the most important piece of sculpture. The body is posed with dignity and the drapery is pleasing. Yet it is overelaborated in the manner

of secondary artists who lack that instinct for selection native to really great masters.

Even though the figures of the saints must frankly be termed mediocre, that fact does not alter the splendor of the stalls as a whole. The reliefs of St. Rose of Lima and San Francisco Solano, canonized in 1671 and 1726 respectively, are excellent sculptures beautifully conceived with a fine sense of composition and motivation. Especially memorable is the graceful movement of the latter's arm which holds the bow of the violin. These figures are in contrast to the kneeling St. Jerome whose distraught and penitent mind is reflected in the nervous draperies. The figures of the two local saints of Lima must have been added subsequent to 1726, the date of San Francisco Solano's canonization, since they are both by the same hand. Possibly they were carved by Santiago Rosales when he restored the stalls after the earthquake of 1746. Still later, belonging to the Neoclassic period of the nineteenth century, are two colossal wooden statues in the round, which represent St. Rose and St. John the Evangelist. One stands in each corner of the choir behind the high altar.

The architectural scheme of the Lima stalls belongs to the early Baroque phase, even though the ornamental motives might be classified as Renaissance. The niches enclosing the figures of saints are topped by two volutes upon each of which reclines a female figure. A rectangle fills the space between the volutes, itself finished by a broken pediment and more volutes. The constant change of direction, the breaking of lines, and the contrast of planes constitute the first major appearance of the Baroque in Lima. Even the rectangle of the niche and the other small rectangle above it break out at the corners.

The canopy at the top likewise carries through the Baroque spirit in the agitated movement resulting from the interplay and contrast of numerous curving lines. The pinnacles in the shape of molded candlesticks cause the attention to fluctuate restlessly. The draped female heads and lion heads which alone interrupt the moldings and volutes are also employed prominently in the ornament upon the chairs and columns below. The frieze with its channeled design, similar to a triglyph, strikes a sober note. Nude *putti* act as caryatids as they bend forward with the curve of the canopy, an arrangement found in the Baroque choir stalls of the cathedrals of Málaga and Cádiz. Within the curve a large shell inscribed in an ellipse set in a rectangle makes a pleasing and restful transition between the upper and lower registers.

The columns carry fine Corinthian capitals upon a channeled shaft with pronounced entasis. On the broad band at the lower end are carved festoons of fruit grouped about a draped female head. Just below each column a lion's head acts as corbel. In the narrow panel between the heads is carved a decorative motive comprising two swags of cloth containing apples. A cartouche in the center of the panel provides the stabilizing feature. The swag with apples is repeated again and again on the backs and on the sides of the chairs. That particular motive is not common in

decorative ornament in European art. It does occur prominently upon the high altar of San Miguel at Huejotzingo (1580) in Mexico. The apple may or may not be symbolic in intention. If symbolism is implied, it would have reference to sin, brought upon mankind when Adam and Eve ate of the fruit of the Tree of Knowledge.

The chairs themselves are first rate in design and sculptural decoration. On the sides between the seats is a half-length female figure, a classical European theme, with pendant breasts and large abdomen in which the navel is prominently stylized. The profile of these panels separating the seats is composed of inward and outward sweeping curves, a triumph of Baroque composition. A grotesque mask, generally human but occasionally that of a lion, finishes the outward swell of the curves. Another type of mask head, like that of a satyr with grimacing open mouth, is carved upon each of the misericords. These heads are fanciful and imaginative in addition to being superb in their decorative organization.

The backs of the seats show considerable variety in handling, although most commonly the draped female head occupies the center of the panel with swags of cloth containing apples arranged about it in curvilinear patterns. Frequently two eagles in heraldic opposition confront a fountain and the female head flutters above it. This thematic repertory undergoes many variations, but unity prevails in the general scheme. The few restorations, probably those carried out by Santiago Rosales shortly after 1746, are easy to recognize, for the imitation of the original ornament is perfunctory.[10] Note, for instance, the columns with mask heads and the narrow panels accompanying the figures of St. Rose, St. Jerome, and San Francisco Solano. Still later modifications were made in 1895–1897 when the choir was transferred from the nave to the sanctuary, and the neo-Gothic canopy was placed over the bishop's throne on the left side. The restraint of the design is self-effacing, so that no unpleasant conflict is established with its Baroque environment.

The derivation of the ornament of the Lima choir stalls is classical, coming from Italy via Spain. Swags, masks, caryatids, and arabesques are, needless to say, the very essence of antique ornament, as reinterpreted in the Renaissance and Baroque periods. The geometric panels on the lower sides of the seats are the only details which may be specifically termed as Spanish because of their *mudéjar* character. They put in their first appearance in the stalls of Santo Domingo, and passed into Peruvian tradition, being used on the choir stalls of San Francisco, La Merced, and San Agustín in Lima as well as on those of San Francisco at Cuzco.

The most beautiful and the most Renaissance sections of the cathedral sculpture are the two columns which support the canopy over the Visitation. They recall works of a century earlier. Arabesques like those of the Ara Pacis of Augustus, masks, shells, and the draped female head are woven into a design, carved with a skill equal to the best European standards.

The draped female head, a favorite of Pedro de Noguera, is of Renaissance origin. See, among many Spanish examples: the retable in the sacristy of Avila Cathedral (1549–1553), the retables in the parish church at Palenzuela (1591), the pulpit at Villafranca del Cid; as well as choir stalls in southern Italy and in Switzerland, and Italian engravings of ornament.[11] It soon passed from the cathedral stalls into the main body of Peruvian art at Lima, Cuzco, and Trujillo.[12] In fact, the work of Pedro de Noguera is the foundation of the Peruvian school of the seventeenth century. Nearly all of the subsequent choir stalls owe something to him. Those of San Francisco in Cuzco are virtually a copy of the cathedral series. In addition to the introduction of the decorative motives already mentioned, his use of the nude female busts,[13] the swag of cloth containing apples,[14] and the mask upon the misericord [15] was widely emulated. All of these features he had come to know in Spain where they belong to the main body of European tradition.

The choir stalls of Lima Cathedral hold first rank among the several fine series of Peru. They are the work of Spanish artists in the New World, and they deserve recognition even on comparison with sculpture in European lands. To be sure, the figures do not measure up to those of a masterpiece like Alonso Berruguete's stalls in Toledo Cathedral. They are, however, not inferior to Guillén de Olanda's reliefs in Valladolid [16] and may be compared with many other similar works in Spain and Italy.

San Francisco at Cuzco possesses a series of choir stalls (Figs. 259, 260) which are discussed next because of their direct dependence upon those of Lima Cathedral. The sculptor was unmistakably instructed to use the latter as his model, a fact made obvious by the most cursory examination. The columns, the capitals, and the architecture enframing the saints at Cuzco are copied with only slight modification from the earlier set. The changes involve the elimination of the recumbent female figures which are stretched out on the volutes in Lima and minor variations in ornament. The canopy above the upper stalls at Lima is copied at Cuzco where the elliptical shell, the nude *putti,* and the channeled frieze are repeated. The greatest difference in the two works occurs in the crowning at Cuzco. Here saints in niches replace the earlier decorative cartouches. The seats follow their model with great fidelity. Some variation occurs in the handling of the details of the swags of cloth and fruit and in the geometric panels in the lower reaches. The grotesque masks upon the misericords, the female figures with pendant breasts, and the volutes ending in masks, all appear again.

The quality of the carving is somewhat drier in the stalls at Cuzco than at Lima. Yet the relationship is so close that it is difficult to avoid the supposition that some of the artists moved on to the Andean capital after finishing their first contracts. Such a large project, which included thirty-four lower and forty-six upper stalls, demanded the services of several woodcarvers and carpenters working under the direction of the chief master. Dr. José Uriel García discovered a contract in the notarial archives at Cuzco by virtue of which Sebastián Martínez agreed in 1631 to make the choir stalls of San Francisco within three years.[17] This document seems to be contradicted by Fray Diego de Mendoza's statement that the sculptor was a Franciscan friar, Luis Montes.[18] From the same author we learn that the stalls were damaged by the collapse of the church tower in the earthquake of 1650.[19] Dr. García suggested that Fray Luis Montes' share in the work was probably limited to their restoration after 1650. That indeed may have been the case, for it is difficult to believe that a single friar could have carried out the project alone. A modern inscription painted upon the walls of the choir states that Fray Luis Montes was assisted in 1652 by two brothers of the Third Franciscan order, Isidro Fernández Inca, carpenter, and Antonio de Paz, workman. Because of the loss of the archives verification of that information is impossible. The inexactness of a number of these modern inscriptions in San Francisco makes one hesitate to accept them without qualification. The style of the decorative sculpture, so closely modeled upon the choir stalls of Lima Cathedral (1623), is compatible with the document of 1631 identifying Sebastián Martínez as the master. Fray Luis Montes may have assisted in planning the iconographic scheme and in the carving too. The restorations after the earthquake of 1650 were carried out in such a way that no change of plan or style is discernible.

In contrast to the decorative part, the

figure sculpture of San Francisco shows no relation to that of Lima. The style is more sober and the garments fall in simple vertical folds for the most part. The conventional forward bend of one knee, so common in Peruvian sculpture of the period, was adopted. The repetitiousness of the great number of Franciscan saints tends to monotony, although certain of the friars have a Spanish intensity of feeling which is emotionally stirring (Fig. 260). The figures are far more spirited than those of the Franciscan choir stalls in Lima, to be discussed later.

The saints in the Cuzco series comprise a total of forty-six large panels and forty-five smaller reliefs at the top. Inscriptions originally identified each saint, all of whom are male Franciscans with the exception of a few Franciscan nuns and certain major church personalities such as St. Peter, St. John the Baptist, St. Anthony Abbot, St. Sebastian, etc.

The choir stalls of La Merced (Fig. 264) at Lima fall, like those of the cathedral and those of San Francisco at Cuzco, into the second quarter of the seventeenth century. A document of 1628 indicates that their donor was Bernardo de Villegas, the great benefactor of the monastery.[20] Solely on stylistic grounds they would be placed earlier than the contemporary stalls just mentioned, inasmuch as Baroque elements of the architecture are notable for their absence. The scale of these stalls is smaller, because of the lack of a canopy at the top and the reduced size of the figures. All of them are angels dressed in the Mercedarian habit. The idea of a choir exclusively of angels replacing the usual array of saints is indeed charming. The slender childlike angels, each carrying a book, stand within shallow round arches. The space above is strangely barren of adornment except for a small corbel or cartouche. Instead of a canopy, a shell lunette alternates with a head centered in Renaissance arabesques, spaced by pinnacles.

The pilasters place the design of the Mercedarian stalls in a category without counterpart in Peru. Nude *putti* act as caryatids supporting a capital from which an acanthus leaf springs forth like a great plume. Long sprays of acanthus ending in a cluster of apples complete the pilaster below.

Notwithstanding the originality of the main features of the Mercedarian stalls in relation to the other Peruvian works, the seats in both rows are based directly upon those of Lima Cathedral. The chief difference consists in the more extensive use of arabesques of pure Renaissance type in the Mercedarian choir. Otherwise, the design and the decorative repertory are uniformly alike, with the quality of the carving distinctly the superior in the earlier work in the cathedral. The differences are those usually distinguishable between original creation and school repetition. Cherub heads take the place of the lion heads below the pilasters, and the anatomy of the female busts between the seats is considerably under-emphasized. The two large panels which join the angles contain a Mercedarian shield, accompanied by floating *putti* set in a splendid sheaf of Renaissance arabesques.

A life-sized statue of Nuestra Señora de las Mercedes presides in the center of the choir stalls. The statue, now painted white, is a splendid eighteenth-century work in spite of its disfigurement by a large crown and modern jewels. The central niche and the smaller shrine above it with its statue of St. Michael have been restored in an unsatisfactory fashion. That the spiral columns did not belong to the original scheme of 1628 can be seen in the way they are set in the second story without logical relation to the niche. The first alteration clearly belongs to the period when the statue of the Madonna was added. The crude uncarved sections must be twentieth-century restorations.

Only a brief reference can be made to the choir stalls of Santa Clara in Cuzco, inasmuch as they are unphotographed and inaccessible. I was allowed to see them at a distance and in dim light, looking through the screen which separates the choir from the nave of the church. They number thirty-four upper stalls, and their decoration is entirely architectural without human figures. The design appears to be datable in the mid-seventeenth century, because the same style was current then in the retables of La Merced and in the high altar of Santa Catalina at Cuzco (Figs. 311–313). The pilasters are decorated with the tongue motive, so popular in the city at that time, and a scroll occupies the position of the capital in most instances. The webbed scrolls upon the triangular pediment at the top are the very signature of mid-seventeenth-century Baroque in Cuzco, as witness the façades of the cathedral and La Compañía (Figs. 63, 64), not to speak of numerous retables. The Franciscans informed me that the choir stalls of Santa Clara originally belonged to the dissolved monastery of the Augustinians.

Cuzco Cathedral has the distinction of possessing the most lavish set of choir stalls in Peru (Figs. 262, 263). They are datable between 1657 and 1678. A letter directed to the king in the former year gives a report upon the cathedral but makes no mention of the stalls. In 1678 Bishop Manuel Mollinedo spoke of them in high praise as part of the work completed after his arrival in 1673.[21]

Forty-three panels carved with full-length saints form the wall behind the upper seats. Above them is a row of three-quarter-length figures, all female saints and female martyrs. On the same level the Infant Christ stands within a niche in one corner faced by the infant St. John the Baptist who occupies the corresponding position opposite. San Francisco in Cuzco (Fig. 259) provides the only precedent in Peru for this smaller secondary row of saints in the upper register. The iconography is developed on traditional lines with the Madonna of the Immaculate Conception behind the bishop's throne. In a great niche above her is the royal escutcheon crowned by a large canopy and a profuse Baroque architectural setting. Eight apostles occupy the main panels of the rear wall with the two leaders of the church, Saints Peter and Paul on each side of the Madonna.[22] On the long sides the remainder of the apostles appear, together with the Evangelists and the Fathers of the Latin Church. Each saint is identifiable not only by his attributes but also by his name in gold letters on a Baroque shield above his head.[23] The selection and iconographic grouping of the saints may well have been evolved by the canon, Diego Arias de la Cerda, who is known to have been a most energetic and enthusiastic administrator (*obrero mayor*) of the cathedral at this time. The attribution of the sculpture itself to him or to Francisco Domínguez de Chávez y Arrellano, whose personality is entirely unknown, cannot be maintained.[24] No light has yet been shed upon the sculptors and carpenters who must have labored upon the project for many years.

The Cuzco stalls constitute a new trend in the Peruvian school, independent of the tradition established by the first important set in Lima Cathedral. The nude female figures which decorate the arms of the seats are the only important survival from the latter. The misericords and the *mudéjar* panels of the earlier works have been abandoned. The Renaissance survivals in the ornament have given way to the full Hispanic Baroque. A salient cornice like a canopy over each column provides abrupt contrasts in planes and deep shadows. The multiplication of subordinate moldings, the variety of contrasts, and the general lavishness of ornament are carried through with the dexterity of a first-rate master of the Baroque style. The arabesques upon the columns and in panels upon the seats are spun out with great imagination and virtuosity. Here the draped female head appears again, having passed into the repertory of Peru-

vian ornament after its initial introduction in the choir stalls of Lima Cathedral.

Nearly all of the elements of the architectural and decorative style of the school of Cuzco of the second half of the seventeenth century come to a focus in the stalls. The webbed volutes and the voluted cartouches so prominent on the choir stalls are equally so on the façade of the Jesuit church which stands nearby upon the Plaza Mayor. The façade (Fig. 71) of San Sebastián (*circa* 1673–1678) is related in design and ornament to such a degree that the same workshop must have produced both monuments. Other wood sculptures which show stylistic affinity are the pulpit and high altar of Santa Teresa (Figs. 302, 317) in Cuzco (1675), by the sculptor Diego Martínez de Oviedo.[25] It is to be hoped that a thorough search of the archives in Cuzco will eventually provide a basis for a more complete study of these relationships. The high altar, side altars, and pulpit of the Jesuit church (Figs. 280, 319, 359) also fall within the same orbit and may eventually prove to have come from related workshops. The extraordinarily beautiful spiral columns at the sides of the episcopal chair belong in a like classification. The angel's head against a shell is a somewhat novel device placed beneath the columns and in the hoods upon the cornice of the choir stalls.

The figure sculpture maintains a high level of excellence throughout, and although several sculptors must have been engaged upon it, no appreciable variation in style is detected. The poses are natural and reposeful with few exceptions. The convention of one knee projecting to give variety of surface continues here as in virtually all Peruvian stalls. Ancient classical custom is likewise repeated in the way the mantle is caught at the waist leaving the arms free. The modeling of surface is broad and naturalistic without any trace of the Renaissance channeled folds which were noted in the choir stalls of Lima Cathedral.

The choir of Cuzco Cathedral is perfect in its completeness down to the last detail of the wooden gates and of the balustrades in the organ loft. As a monument to the munificence of the colonial age and to the splendor of Baroque imagination, it would be difficult to surpass.

The choir stalls of Trujillo Cathedral were moved from the nave to the sanctuary in 1911, and undoubtedly that fact plus the numerous earthquakes explain why only eight upper stalls in addition to the bishop's throne have come down to us (Figs. 265, 266). There must have been at least thirty or forty when they were originally carved. Their date is unrecorded but the style suffices to make them contemporary with the construction of the new cathedral (1643–1666) or very nearly so. They are the most important stalls in Peru in which figure sculpture is absent.[26] Their creator probably came from Lima. The style prompts that assumption, and we know by the architectural history of Trujillo that most of the artists active there came from the capital.

Large elliptical panels, like escutcheons filled with interlocking volutes about a central cartouche, form the upper wall behind the seats. The Corinthian colonnettes have an exaggerated entasis in the channeled section and a cartouche is carved upon the band at the base. This general type of colonnette is essentially of Renaissance origin and in that respect analogous to those of Lima Cathedral. The panels on the seats also have points of contact with the school of Lima in the use of the draped female head centralized and balanced on each side by a draped cloth filled with apples. At first glance the Trujillo stalls may impress one as secondary in importance. Such is not the case, it seems to me, for they are first rate in technique and in expertness of design. The bishop's throne, a work of extraordinary beauty, has the draped female head as the major theme upon the colonnettes. In the center of the main panel are the attributes of St. John the Evangelist, the eagle and the chalice. At the top, as usual on the bishop's chair, appear the tiara and keys, insignia of the pope whose authority is invested in the bishop. A few widely spaced arabesques are interwoven in the setting and the panel is topped by a trefoil arch. Anything superior in decorative quality would be difficult to find at any time or place.

San Francisco at Lima is the largest monastery in Peru, and fittingly it possesses the biggest set of choir stalls (Figs. 267, 268). Seventy-one upper stalls and sixty-two lower fill the deep broad space of the choir, testimony to the great numbers of Franciscans who dedicated themselves to the church in the colonial age. When a new organ was installed some years ago, three upper and three lower stalls were removed and sold. In 1912 they were donated to the

Hispanic Society of America in New York where they are now on exhibition.[27]

Fray Luis de Cervela under whose administration the rebuilding of the monastery was completed (1669–1674) was also responsible for the furnishing of the choir. The stalls were nearing completion in 1674 according to the report of Fray Juan de Benavides, but unfortunately he makes no mention of the names of the sculptors and carpenters who were engaged upon them.[28] They continued some of the features introduced in Lima with the choir stalls of the cathedral, but in other respects, particularly in the design of the main wall behind the upper range, they broke into new paths.

The masks of the misericords with their open mouths and large tongues, grotesque in their humor, have become familiar to the reader by this time. It is significant to contrast the smooth curvilinear designs of the cathedral misericords with these of San Francisco, which are sharp, angular, and pictorially planned in a Baroque manner. The heavy-breasted females, half-length and changed into leaves below the waist, recur in a manner at once more sophisticated and less subordinated to the decorative scheme. Other ornamental devices which descend from the sculpture in Lima Cathedral are the *mudéjar* panels beneath the seats, the swags of cloth filled with apples, and the draped female head. The patterns of arabesques on the backs and sides of the seats display, however, an independence of previous models in Peru. Drawings were prepared by the chief master in charge and the same designs were repeated again and again. In several instances a classical urn forms the center of the composition. The theme is given several variations, at times with vines and grapes looped about the urn. In others there are vines and leaves very much like distant descendants of the ancient vines and rosettes on the Ara Pacis of Augustus in Rome. Peacocks in heraldic opposition are added in several cases in a manner analogous to early medieval sculpture. The Franciscan shield of the five wounds is also employed in the center of several panels, and in the space about it is spun a cartouche of volutes.

The sides of the chairs display great originality. In general, the irregularly shaped panel is filled with vine and leaves, but in a number of them are lions in a miniature landscape, or an eagle, and occasionally a fish. The puma appears twice and likewise the elephant, rendered with delightful humor, as can be seen in the illustration (Fig. 267). The elephant looks Chinese, suggesting that the wood carver used a textile or print for his model. Here is an indication of some familiarity with Oriental art, but there is no question whatsoever of Eastern influence upon the style of carving.[29]

Turning to the wall of saints in the upper range, one discovers elements entirely new to Peruvian tradition. For the first time a cherub's head within a shell forms the tympanum, the top of which is semicircular and crowned by two inverted volutes. Stepped rectangular moldings act as frames to the subdivisions such as the pilasters, tympana, and reliefs of saints.

The pilasters offer a number of surprises, most of all in the transposition of the female figures, half-length and ending in acanthus leaves, from their usual place between the chairs to their new positions as caryatids. They have become more youthful and angelic in their faces and more fully clothed in body. Possibly the original idea of caryatids upon the pilasters was borrowed from the Mercedarian choir stalls in Lima where nude *putti* perform the same function. The latter are closer to the Renaissance in every respect. The caryatids of the Franciscans support a long capital, concave in shape and divided into four compartments, each very curiously containing an apple. Below the caryatid is suspended a drumshaped object with a frill around it ending in a tassel. For all of their quaintness many of these devices are more unusual than effective.

A great array of sixty-two male saints, most of whom are Franciscans, six Franciscan nuns, and two Dominican nuns preside over the choir. Behind the bishop's throne stand St. Francis and St. Dominic, founders of their respective orders, as they embrace in commemoration of their meeting at Rome in 1216. The same event is also made the iconographic high point on the stalls of Santo Domingo in Lima. In an elliptical medallion in the upper region the Madonna of the Immaculate Conception stands with the crescent moon and cherubs' heads at her feet. The two smaller medallions, one at each side of the Madonna, must have been carved with reliefs which have since been destroyed. This whole central section is set back within a niche and raised to considerable height. It is topped by the usual projecting canopy, embellished by a flourish of volutes and interlocking moldings. The tortuous spirals of two large "salomonic" columns create a feeling of dramatic tension about the center of the composition that they enframe. The columns themselves are divided horizontally into four bands, alternately fluted spirally and carved with the eucharistic grape and vine. These are the first dated *salomónicas* of the type in Peru, so far as I know. The bishop's throne in Cuzco Cathedral is given similar dramatic emphasis, but the columns there are continuous spirals carved with arabesques and girded in the lower third by two crowns of acanthus leaves.

The quality of the figure sculpture of the Franciscan choir is frankly poor, well below the general standard of such work in Peru. Some monotony might be expected because of the repetition of so many monks in Franciscan habit. They lack, however, the fervor and intenseness of feeling which places the Franciscan saints in their monastery at Cuzco on a much higher artistic plane (Fig. 260). These saints in Lima are mechanical puppets with few exceptions. The sculptors were unable to manipulate the body with any significant motivation because of their poor technique and their intellectual shallowness. Several different wood sculptors were at work here, a fact which is evident from the variation in degree of effectiveness. The best results were obtained in the saints upon the episcopal throne, and in the panels adjoining it. To these the chief master clearly gave his attention. The poorest are the panels upon the long range at the sides.

The choir stalls of San Francisco at Lima are notable for their great number, and they are pleasing as church furniture from a decorative point of view. In detail they do not measure up to the design or craftsmanship of the other series of Peruvian stalls hitherto discussed.

Two works remain to be considered, both of them of the first quarter of the eighteenth century, one in the Mercedarian church at Cuzco, the other in the Augustinian church at Lima. The former can be dated about 1710, inasmuch as the style belongs to that period. Other pertinent facts are that the Mercedarian chronicler of 1650–1707 does not mention them and that the large paintings in the choir have an inscription with the year 1708.[30] The date of these paintings would indicate that the completion of the furnishing of the choir took place at that time. Moreover, a comparable period style, so far as the use of spiral columns and of elliptical medallions is concerned, can be observed in the choir stalls (1702) of the Carthusian church of Seville, part of which are now in Cádiz Cathedral.[31]

Here is the only instance in Peru where spiral columns enframe the niches, thus giving a highly Baroque feeling of richness and movement (Fig. 269). Leaves and branches of nondescript fruits serve as ornament on the columns. The sculpture is hard and dry in quality and not equal to the highly effective decorative design of the whole monument. The eighteenth-century character of the work is in evidence in the complex curvilinear involutions of the ornament upon the arms of the chairs and, likewise, in the hoods upon the cornice. A comparison with the choir stalls at Cuzco Cathedral (Figs. 262, 263) is significant, because it shows that the sculptor of the Mercedarian relied to some extent upon the earlier series in the two sections mentioned. Yet his own style constitutes a later stage of development. Elliptical medallions of half-length saints replace the rectangular panels used in the upper register of the cathedral choir.

The figure sculpture lacks distinction in the motivation of drapery and in emotional expressiveness. Most of the saints stand with their shoulders bent slightly forward and the head tilted to the side. The result is a weakly sentimental attempt at piety. Thirty-five saints and Venerable Fathers, most of them Mercedarians, occupy the niches behind the upper stalls, whereas in the medallions are male and female saints of various periods and religious orders.[32] A long rectangular relief with excellent carved frame fills the space over each doorway, the saints represented being the Magdalen and St. Mary of Egypt, both in penitence. If regarded as church furniture, the Mercedarian stalls fulfill their function as luxurious products of the decorator's art.

The choir of San Agustín in Lima (Figs. 270, 271) was described by Calancha, writing about 1637, as a magnificent work in cedar which cost thirty thousand *pesos*. A saint stood between each pair of columns with a relief illustrating some episode from his life placed above him. The same arrangement is found in the Spanish Renaissance stalls of Burgos and Jaén Cathedrals.[33] Disastrously damaged in the earthquake of 1678, enough fragments were salvaged in 1717 to supply chairs for the Augustinian choir. A new row of saints for the wall behind the upper stalls, added in the years 1721–1725, brought the sculpture to its present status.[34] The chairs themselves and also the columns are clearly of early seventeenth-century design, but the quality of the carving is so mediocre that it must be assumed that most of it was restored and recut in 1717. Much of the work can be regarded only as an early eighteenth-century reproduction after the original models.

Egiguren states that he has discovered a contract with the date August 17, 1620, in which Pedro de Noguera was awarded the commission for the Augustinian choir.[35] Even though the fabrication of the chairs as they exist today cannot be regarded as a product of Pedro de Noguera's shop, the details of ornament and the type of column are very similar to his masterpiece in Lima Cathedral. Hence it is entirely possible that he supplied the sketches for the works so enthusiastically described by Calancha. The only other choir stalls in Peru which have Renaissance columns of this sort are those of San Francisco at Cuzco. They, as we have seen, are replicas of Noguera's prototype. The art of Noguera would explain why the intertwining circular vines upon the columns in Cuzco (Figs. 259, 260) and those of the Augustinians in Lima are almost identical. The draped female head is replaced in the Augustinian series, however, by a grotesque head or mask. In all three cases masks are carved upon the corbels beneath the columns, and upon the misericords, only a few of the latter in San Agustín having withstood the repeated earthquakes of Lima.

The dilapidated condition of the Augustinian choir in 1945 made investigation difficult. The church, damaged in the earthquake of 1940, was still unrestored. It was necessary to climb through scaffolds, brush off layers of dust, lift heavy coverings of cloth, and peer through at the stalls. The swags of cloth and apples, the arabesques, and the geometric panels beneath the seats constitute the decorative repertory as they do in Lima Cathedral. The quality of the sculpture is in no way comparable, however, and the designs are imitatively mechanical. The eighteenth century is unmistakable in the heads with plumed helmets upon the backs of the seats and in the male heads, like hermae, upon the arms between them.

The full-length saints in high relief are documented in the period 1721–1725, as previously noted. Under the present arrangement thirty figures form the back wall of the upper stalls, set up in this way during the rebuilding of the church in 1903–1908. Nine panels of monks and seven of nuns are kept in storage.[36]

The sculptor of these figures was a skillful technician who shows great ability in the handling of the human body as an instrument of expression. The saints stand in high relief, modeled with vigor in massive sculptural volumes. They reflect the academic traditions of the Baroque period with their slow majesty, inherited in a general sense from antique sculpture. The word "academic" should not necessarily be regarded as a term of condemnation, but rather as constituting traditional style and high standards. So it was regarded in the eighteenth century and in this sense it is employed here. Qualitatively these sculptures surpass all other figures upon the several series of Peruvian choir stalls. They are superior even to Juan Martínez de Arrona's fine apostles (1608) in the sacristy of Lima Cathedral. The latter show their dependence upon the antique still more clearly, especially by the channeled folds and by the disposition of the drapery. In speaking of the reliefs of the Augustinian stalls with such high praise, I refer only to the best of them which represent the hand of the chief master. Several less able assistants in the workshop collaborated. With the exception of St. Mary of Egypt,

clothed only in her long flowing hair, the panels kept in storage belong in the category of apprentices' work. The row of saints at the left, a detail of which is reproduced (Fig. 271), contains the best. The right side of the stalls is unknown to me because of their inaccessibility following the earthquake of 1940. The sculptor of the Augustinians was a well-trained and competent artist, even if not one of the world's great geniuses.

The church furnishings of the colonial age, presented in this chapter, are products of European culture in their religious iconography, their style, and their technique. At times the Spaniard manifested a complete resistance to his New World environment. Yet in certain regions, his culture united with the native to create *mestizo* art, a phenomenon already investigated. The choir stalls, on the contrary, reveal scarcely a trace of the native, for they are Hispanic through and through.

XI

PULPITS

THE importance of preaching as an integral part of the program of evangelization in the New World is reflected in the great number of superb pulpits of the seventeenth and eighteenth centuries. Lavishness in ecclesiastical furniture prevails throughout Hispanic America in the colonial period. Nevertheless, no country, not even Mexico, can equal Peru in the number and quality of wood-carved pulpits nor in the variety of types and styles.

The earliest datable pulpit is in San Francisco at Cuzco (Fig. 273). The only one of its kind known to me, it is composed of inlaid woods and ivory. The date can easily be established because of the fact that in design, materials, and workmanship it is identical to the lectern (Fig. 272) in the choir of the same church. The latter has an inscription upon it with year 1628 saying it was made during the guardianship of Fray Pedro Gómez. I verified the reading of this date, previously interpreted as 1678, by a search of the archives of the Franciscans at Cuzco. Pedro Gómez is recorded as guardian in the years 1627–1630.[1] If further proof of the correctness of my reading of the date be needed, both the lectern and pulpit are described in Vasco de Contrera's report of 1650.[2]

The octagonal base of the lectern with its eight Tuscan colonnettes is made of cedar. In each panel a niche is flanked by scroll-capitaled pilasters and topped by a broken pediment. The arabesque inlays of lighter wood, presumably *carey*, decorate the base, the frieze, and main panels on the four principal sides. The pilasters of these four windowlike niches have delicate inlays of ivory. The same material is used for St. Francis' shield containing the stigmata, placed above the capitals, and for the Franciscan escutcheon. The latter consists of a crucifix standing upon the globe of the world within a medallion and the arm of St. Francis crossed by the arm of Christ. This shield appears upon each of the four sides of the bookrest and also in the frieze below. The inlaid arabesques are particularly beautiful in their arrangement upon the upper sloping sides of the lectern, the surface of which is studded with brass knobs to prevent the books from scratching the wood.

The technique and design of the Franciscan pulpit are so nearly identical with the lectern that they must be assigned to the same anonymous artist. Red cedar is the principal material. Ebony is used for the pediments of the niches, and numerous inlays of ivory decorate the pilasters and the friezes. The Tuscan colonnettes like those of the lectern and the flat inlaid arabesques place the Franciscan work in a stylistic category entirely unrelated to other pulpits of the school of Cuzco, produced a quarter of a century later. The chasteness of the design of the niches may be characterized as the earliest phase of the Baroque in Peru, more restrained, for example, than the contemporary choir stalls of Lima Cathedral. On the pulpit, the Franciscan shield and the stigmata in ivory medallions occur several times. The escutcheon also fills the large panel beneath the canopy. A death's head and cross bones below it are a reminder to the faithful of the need for repentance in this transitory life. The domed canopy over the speaker's tribune is the simplest in Cuzco, as would be expected at this early date. Four volutes upon the cupola notwithstanding, the outline is comparatively closed, with none of the lavish detail of later works. The four volutes upon the base of the pulpit give far more Baroque expression.

Restoration has marred the wall panel beneath the canopy, and ugly modern paint has made the statuettes in the niches garish. These images are constructed of wood and dressed in cloth stiffened by plaster, a technique very common in Hispanic colonial art. They represent St. Dominic, a pope who may be St. Gregory, and two bishops. The letters upon the base of one of the latter read *Cisneros*. A statuette of St. Francis in wood atop the canopy is bereft of an arm, a fact which accentuates the almost Gothic swing of the body.

The beautiful gilded pulpit in the parish church of the village of San Jerónimo near Cuzco can be dated by its style about 1630. The free-standing colonnettes are now Corinthian instead of Tuscan, but the simplicity of design and the supporting volutes beneath the pulpit place it near in date to that of San Francisco. Two of the paintings, the Crucifixion and the Assumption of the Virgin, are modern. The remaining two representing St. Dominic and St. Anthony Abbot are originals of the colonial period. The beauty of this pulpit, however, lies in the excellence of its architectural design and in the polychromy. The medallions of the red and gold frieze suggest the sun, attribute of St. Dominic, and the Dominican shield with its Maltese cross is painted in the upper corners of the niches.

In Santa Clara at Ayacucho the pulpit (Fig. 274) has the unusual distinction of an inscription with the year of its origin, 1637.[3] The art historian is ever grateful for such rare accidents, since they provide a secure ground upon which to establish chronology. Like the work in San Francisco at Cuzco the colonnettes are Tuscan, but in this instance channeled and with a noticeable entasis. The architectural niches are similar in design, except that the pilasters in Ayacucho have additional vertical bars of ornament and the pediments are loaded with spherical pinnacles. The diamond points and the oval ornaments in general recall the imitation of gems in similar fashion on medieval reliquaries and altar frontals. The cedar wood of the pulpit was given a dark brown stain and the statuettes repainted in ugly colors by a local carpenter in 1941. Only the figure of St. Francis atop the canopy retains the original black and gold polychromy. The other statuettes are: St. Clare beneath the canopy, and upon the pulpit, St. Elizabeth of Hungary, St. Louis of Toulouse, St. Catherine of Alexandria, and St. Anthony of Padua. The abbess, named Catherine according to the inscription, must have been a relative of the Orue who founded the nunnery. Her patron saint, as we have noted, occupies the middle niche upon the pulpit. The architectural designs and the use of inlays set these works of San Francisco at Cuzco and Santa Clara at Ayacucho entirely apart from other extant pulpits in Peru.

The next group is formed by the sculpture of Martín de Torres, who signed the contract for the two ambones (Fig. 275) of Cuzco Cathedral in 1656.[4] Torres was a leading sculptor of his day as can readily be deduced by the number of retables mentioned in various documents. The high altar of the Mercedarians (1631) was destroyed by fire in the nineteenth century, and two others among his works have also disappeared.[5] The design of the cathedral ambones fits perfectly in the architectural style of the mid-seventeenth century in Cuzco. The band of diamond points on the paired colonnettes and the handling of the niches with their stepped rectangular tops, as well as the pediments of webbed volutes with an elliptical cartouche in the center, are comparable with the retable of Martyrdoms (circa 1660) in the left transept of La Merced. The five apostles on

each of the ambones stand in erect quiet poses. That they belong to the same regional school as the figure sculpture of the cathedral choir stalls is immediately recognized.[6]

Another pulpit now in the chapel of the Colegio de Educandas, badly repainted and regilded, and second rate in quality, must be located chronologically in the mid-century. By exception in this type of monument, the pilasters are decorated with the tongue ornament which was so commonly used at the period. The statuettes of the four Evangelists manage to look pleasant and typical of the school, even though smeared with recent gilt. The pulpit is said to have been transferred here from the destroyed chapel of San Andrés and can therefore be dated circa 1650–1665.[7]

One of the finest colonial examples of ecclesiastical furniture stands unnoticed in the church of San Francisco at Arequipa (Fig. 276). On style alone it should be placed about 1660–1670. Perhaps some day a document will reveal the name of the sculptor who was without a doubt one of the leading Peruvian artists of his day. Most surprising is the expression of vigor and movement and the heroic proportions of the bodies. These saints represent Franciscans and St. Agnes. The niches, though similar to those of the ambones of Cuzco Cathedral, receive added complexity by the placing of volutes vertically along the sides. The spiral bands on the lower part of the colonnettes establish a contrast in tension to the vertical channels above, which are repeated in the vertical bars of the frieze. Another interesting feature is the rolled bracket upon the pedestal beneath the colonnettes. Grotesque masks, so popular on misericords, and in sculptured decoration of the seventeenth and eighteenth centuries in Peru, here occur upon the long scrolled brackets beneath the pulpit. Some modern restoration, conscientiously carried out, can be detected here.

Most unexpectedly I found a provincial copy of the Franciscan pulpit of Arequipa in the shrine of Nuestra Señora at Copacabana. The repetition of the architectural details with only slight variations can leave no doubt of this, even though the proportions and quality of the carving throughout are inferior. The ugly modern blue paint does much to disfigure this work of the second half of the seventeenth century.

A pulpit which must be placed very high on any list is in the chapel of the Colegio de los Sagrados Corazones in Lima, brought there from the destroyed church of El Belén (Fig. 277). Here again the design of the niches is similar to those just discussed and the spiral bands separate the lower part of the shaft from the upper. The most exceptional details for a pulpit are the draped heads and swags of fruit just below the capitals. They are similar enough to the main portal of San Francisco in Lima (1669–1674) to make one believe that the pulpit must be contemporary. Similar too are the interlocking arabesques upon the base. The volutes with masks and the contours are smoother and less complex than usual. It is easy to distinguish the school of Lima with its stronger Renaissance traditions, to be observed even in the delicate arabesques of the frieze. Smaller than usual

are the saints in the niches, St. Peter Nolascus, San Ramón Nonato, St. Andrew, and a Doctor. The circular ledge on the top seems to be the only important piece of restoration.

The tribune in the Sala Capitular of San Agustín is a superb piece of ecclesiastical furniture deserving mention here. A seated figure of St. Augustine presides in the niche within the recess of the wall. An intricate juxtaposition of rectangles, interrupted spiral volutes, flower pots, and involuted arabesques in the niches provide a dynamic Baroque design. The draped female head is cut upon the frieze above the colonnettes. Padre Graciano Montes, a zealous student of the Augustinian archives, informed me that a record of payment about the year 1670 mentions this masterpiece of the wood carver's art.

Returning to Cuzco, we approach the golden age of pulpits of colonial Peru. Groups can be established which surely correspond to individual workshops. In some cases, separate groups may represent a single workshop at different stages of development. Following upon Martín de Torres' ambones of Cuzco Cathedral (1656), next in the chronology come the pulpits of La Merced and Santa Catalina (Figs. 278, 279), both of them by a single artist. Suffice it to observe the identical design of the niches, the two masks upon the volutes beneath the colonnettes, the delicately cut patterns like goldsmith work, the swags with fruit upon the frieze, the exact repetition of the hemispherical base and its flat leaves, the pendant pine cones, and the horizontal chain of ellipses upon the molding. The gilding which is limited to details of ornament and costume has the same technical features throughout, although both pulpits have undergone the misfortune of recent retouching. Only one important difference exists in that the paired colonnettes are smooth spirals in the Merced and the shafts in Santa Catalina are cut in zigzags. Even the large panel beneath the canopy has the same elliptical mandorla cut with the scale motive and a similar treatment of the ornament on the rectangular frame. The architectural design of the nuns' pulpit stands very close to that of the retable (Figs. 311, 312) of the Soledad (1660) in the right transept of La Merced.[8] Hence both pulpits seem to belong to that period (1660–1670). The figures in the two works are handled in a broad sculptural way, their draperies disposed in full deep folds, and the movements suggestive of vigorous inner life.[9]

We may suspect that these two pulpits are early works of Diego Martínez de Oviedo who in 1675 signed the contract for the pulpit and high altar of Santa Teresa (Figs. 281, 317). The specification that the Carmelite pulpit should be identical with that of the Merced, or San Agustín, or La Compañía (Fig. 280) is no final proof of common authorship, but it is a link in a chain of evidence.[10] Diego Martínez reproduced the Jesuit model in Santa Teresa, and both are sufficiently akin to our first group to be regarded as a later phase in the career of the same sculptor.

The document, just mentioned, establishes the Jesuit pulpit about the year 1675

and that of Santa Teresa, *circa* 1675–1680.[11] The third, belonging to the destroyed church of San Agustín, has disappeared. The Jesuits with their tendency to the sumptuous in church decoration had their pulpit completely gilded. For that reason its luminous richness against the cold stone wall of the church makes an unforgettable impression, even though the wood carving itself is equaled and even surpassed elsewhere in Cuzco. The Carmelites, whose patron was the munificent Bishop Mollinedo, were content with the gilding of the edges of ornament and costume, leaving the natural cedar otherwise untouched. The Jesuit pulpit has suffered from vandalism in recent years, and is lacking several colonnettes.

The canopies with volutes and torches, the panels beneath them, and the speakers' boxes, are nearly identical in the pulpits of the Carmelites and the Jesuits (Fig. 72). A new style is inaugurated here with the use of the carved spiral colonnettes. Niches are surmounted by curving voluted pediments, elliptical cartouches, and angular stepped moldings. The same features distinguish the high altar of Santa Teresa. As already explained, Diego Martínez de Oviedo received the contract for both the pulpit and high altar of this church in 1675. Another innovation in the pulpits under discussion is the greater complexity of the hemispherical base to which have been added a concave molding of acanthus leaves, two projecting bands of ornament, and corbels of nude female figures turning into a long acanthus leaf below the waist. This latter motive has been men-

tioned before because of its repeated occurrence on Peruvian choir stalls. As a
matter of fact, the Jesuit pulpit terminates
like the top of a splendidly carved inverted
urn. The Carmelite pulpit combines the
new multiplication of moldings with the
hemispherical base of the earlier examples,
that is, of Santa Catalina and La Merced.
In the church of Santa Teresa, Martínez
also repeated the small chain pattern.

In every case the figure sculpture is less
interesting and significant than the decoration, and the style shows considerable
variation. The chief master, Diego Martínez, must have had numerous assistants
in his workshop. On the preacher's box of
La Compañía five priests, undoubtedly
Jesuits, dressed in red and white robes,
stand in the niches. A statue of St. Ignatius
holds forth upon the summit of the canopy. A second Jesuit is carved upon the
large panel which is always placed against
the wall behind the spot where the speaker
stands. The pulpit in Santa Teresa displays upon the canopy the statue of a
monk with a sword in his breast, possibly
St. Albert, patriarch of Jerusalem, and a
relief of a Carmelite monk in the usual
position beneath the canopy. In the niches
St. Theresa of Avila, the greatest of the
Carmelites, holds the scene by herself, appearing five times either kneeling or standing. On one occasion the presence of an
angel indicates the vision in which her
heart was transfixed by an arrow, symbolic
of divine love. In two reliefs the Infant
Christ stands upon her prayer desk as she
kneels before it.

The pulpits of La Merced and Santa

Catalina may be assigned to Diego Martínez de Oviedo in the sixteen-sixties and
those of La Compañía and Santa Teresa in
the following decade. Another example,
the one in the church of the seminary,
dedicated to St. Anthony Abbot, must be
his work or that of his shop in the latter
period. It is nearly a replica of the type he
established in Santa Teresa, even to the
technique of gilding only the edges of the
ornament and leaving the rest of the wood
in its natural color. The chief variation is
the omission of the nude female caryatids
in the seminary. Appropriately, the patron
of the church, St. Anthony Abbot, is
given the most prominent position atop
the canopy, and second place is awarded
St. Thomas Aquinas on the large panel.
The iconography of the saints in the four
niches is obscure, although they should
logically be the four Fathers of the Latin
church. Bishop Mollinedo reported the
building under construction in 1678, and
the wood sculptures fall within those
years.[12]

A much discussed artist of the late
seventeenth century in Cuzco was a man
of noble Indian lineage, named Juan Tomás
Tuyru Tupac. Even the king of Spain
heard his praises sung, when in 1699 funds
were requested of the crown for the completion of the church of San Pedro which
Juan Tomás had designed. On that occasion his sculpture as well as his architecture
was extolled.[13] Previously he had completed and gilded the retable (Fig. 307)
of Nuestra Señora del Buen Suceso (1678–
1679) in the church of San Blas, and he
had carved the *Virgen de la Almudena*

(1686) for the church dedicated to her (Fig. 364).[14] Bishop Manuel de Mollinedo, who had been the priest of the church in Madrid where her cult originated, brought with him to the New World a small piece of wood taken from the statue of the Virgin in Madrid. He had the token placed in the head of the new work which he ordered and consecrated to her cult.[15] The statue, now heavily dressed in real clothes, is hardly visible, and somewhat repainted in the face, yet nevertheless a work of considerable grace and charm. Her original garment is a gold and blue cope lined in red with a rose tunic, very lovely in the handling of the polychromy.

Dr. García's discovery of the testament of Andrés de Mollinedo, the bishop's nephew, provides further information about Juan Tomás. He is proved to be the author of the pulpit in San Pedro and of the doors of the sacristy.[16] His chief patrons were the two Mollinedos for whom he worked in both San Pedro and the Almudena. The historian is justified in assuming both on documentary and stylistic grounds that Juan Tomás was the general director of the sculpture and architecture of the two buildings.[17]

Inasmuch as the pulpit of San Pedro is a documented work of Juan Tomás, the similar work in the Almudena must be ascribed to him (Figs. 285, 286). The close relationship between the sculpture of the two churches is at once recognizable in the general proportions, the handling of the niches with their flat tops, the comparatively large area above them, and the rosettes upon the spiral colonnettes. As usual in Cuzco, crowns of acanthus separate the lower part of the shaft. The iconographic scheme in the Almudena involves the four Evangelists in the niches and an apostle under the canopy. The cedar wood, intended to be left unpainted, has a recent coat of ugly green house paint and in general the state of preservation is bad. The canopy eluded the hand of the dauber, thanks to its higher position and the probable lack of a ladder to reach it, a very common phenomenon.

The iconography in San Pedro is similar in that the Evangelists recur, St. Matthew and St. John remaining and the other two having been lost. The Madonna with the Child is given the central niche, while the titular saint, Peter, stands in the customary position behind the speaker's box and St. Paul, his companion, holds forth upon the canopy.

Of major significance is the pulpit of Cuzco Cathedral (Figs. 282, 283), carved in natural cedar, unpainted and ungilded. The whirling interplay of Baroque lines reach a high point of artistic expression in the balustrade of the steps which lead up to the speaker's box. Spiral colonnettes, dominant and subordinate, adorn the composition. The statuettes have liveliness and sparkle here, their iconography following the same scheme just mentioned above. With our present information it is impossible to attribute the sculpture either to Diego Martínez or Juan Tomás. Notwithstanding the close relationships of the school, stylistic details are different from the previous works. The pulpit has been ascribed to Diego Arias de la Cerda, general administrator (*obrero mayor*) of the cathedral at that time. The chronicler of Cuzco states that he made the pulpit, choir stalls, ambones, and numerous other works in the cathedral.[18] He was not an artist. The documents show that Martín de Torres carved the ambones. The attempt to make the canon an architect and sculptor of prodigious activity is not reasonable.

Surely by the same hand as the cathedral pulpit is that in Santo Domingo (Fig. 284). It has unfortunately suffered the loss of all of the figure sculpture except the St. Dominic upon the canopy who is well out of reach of common vandals.

The climax of the *cuzqueño* school is reached in the famous pulpit of San Blas (Figs. 287, 288), first mentioned by Bishop Mollinedo in 1696.[19] No documentary notice regarding the sculptor has been forthcoming. Its attribution to Juan Tomás[20] does not carry weight in view of the dissimilarity of the style of his authentic work. Now the spiral columns have dissolved into undulations, showing freedom and fantasy in the manipulation of ornament which would be difficult to rival. Numerous tiny cherubs' heads appear amid the swirl of palm leaves, long torches, and episcopal mitres. At the top of each shaft is carved a chalice with the Host, accompanied by eucharistic grapes. A domical canopy projects over the niches, another innovation of which there are legion in this masterpiece of San Blas. Tiny nude *putti* stand like caryatids beneath the colonnettes. Below, gay grinning masks spring forth at the end of each bracket, the beard terminating in a bunch of grapes. Decorative leaves turn back and forth with spirited abandon.

The niches are occupied by vivacious statuettes of the *Purísima* and the four Evangelists. The canopy, topped by a large figure of St. Paul, is equally remarkable in its virtuosity. An array of smaller statuettes includes the four Fathers of the Latin Church and angels bearing the instruments of the Passion. The eucharistic grapes put in another appearance suspended beneath the tiny bust-length angels on the edge of the canopy. St. Blas on the panel beneath is a surprisingly dull piece of sculpture which must be the handiwork of a helper of the chief master. The pulpit of San Blas deserves its wide renown not only in Peru, but as a major manifestation of the high Baroque at its fantastic best, anywhere in the world.

The Indian village called Checacupe a few miles south of Cuzco has a humble adobe church, yet it is sumptuously furnished with retables, paintings, and a pulpit (Fig. 289). The latter is a modified replica of that of San Blas. The master of San Blas certainly supplied the design and part of the sculpture of the Checacupe pulpit. The statues of St. Paul at the summit of the two works are identical. The canopy at Checacupe is simplified by the omission of the many smaller figures. The splendidly draped and energetic image of St. Peter is eminently characteristic of the San Blas Master. The main body of the pulpit, likewise, is much simpler, the more usual spiral colonnettes entwined with vines and grapes recurring here. The domed canopies over the niches and the spirited masks upon the brackets underneath clearly betray their relationship to their prototype. The *Purísima* and the four Fathers of the Latin Church in the niches were left in large part to assistants who followed the master's sketches. This sculpture is excellent and it suffers only on comparison with its exceptionally brilliant prototype and predecessor, that of San Blas.

Two other pulpits of Cuzco are related to those just discussed: that of El Belén (Fig. 290), reported by Bishop Mollinedo in 1696 and a ruinous specimen in San Sebastián. The canopy of the latter, as usual out of reach of unathletic vandals, falls within the present group. Saints Peter and Paul have both survived, but the niches are stripped bare. To El Belén befell a like fate, so far as the saints are concerned, for only the beaconing St. Paul persists aloft. The speaker's box, in natural cedar, is lovely with its twisted colonnettes spotted with cherub heads. Here the main niches are trefoil, the only case in Cuzco, and topped by a crownlike canopy lifted on a voluted pediment. Still more novel is the introduction of a smaller secondary group of niches below the major row.

With our present lack of documentary information it is impossible to attempt more than the general classification of the pulpits as proposed here. Undoubtedly a goodly number of these works come from a single sculptor's shop, if one allows for intentional diversity in style and design and the intervention of many assistants. The inventiveness and the first-rate quality of these works can hardly be exaggerated. To the patronage of the Bishop Mollinedo much credit is due. Only at a period of extraordinary productivity and economic prosperity could such a state of affairs exist.

With the pulpit of Santa Clara in Cuzco we move into the early years of the eighteenth century. The edges are gilded, its ornament an exquisitely delicate filigree, with new motives such as the shells over the niches. An inscription, twice stated, reads as follows: *De este monasterio la flor Doña María de Peralta.* The nunnery archives would doubtless reveal the time at which this lady lived there, were one of the sisters inspired to search out such data. The pulpit is in lamentable condition, all but two of the colonnettes torn away and two of the niches empty. St. Anthony of Padua holds the uppermost position with St. Francis beneath him and in the niches St. Clare and two Franciscans.

Cuzco sculptors went far and wide in southern Peru. To pursue their peregrinations in detail would require years of research and a large volume for the compilation of the results. The fine pulpit in the church at Lampa, for instance, is of Cuzco derivation, especially to be observed in the canopy, but it cannot be assigned to any particular group. The iconography used here is also the most common in Cuzco, although not exclusively limited to that region. The four Evangelists on the speaker's box have red and blue polychromy, and the *Purísima* in the large panel against the wall is untouched. The rest, alas, has been daubed with white paint, a crime of bad taste, all too widespread.

Farther afield geographically, in San Pedro at Juli, the exquisitely gilded pulpit is further removed in design and facture. Here is another tradition iconographically too, for the *Purísima* tops the canopy and the wall panel is blazoned with the Jesuit escutcheon. As so often, the statuettes have disappeared. Winged busts with exaggeratedly long pendant breasts, a theme recurrent in southern Peru, bend like brackets beneath the speaker's box.

The absence of niches and figure sculpture upon the tribune distinguishes a number of pulpits throughout Peru. This type is usually gilded. A lovely specimen is that of La Compañía in Arequipa (Fig. 291), the gilding of which renders it particularly unforgettable. Elliptical shields with the IHS and the monogram of Mary, AMR, are set in the flat panels of arabesques. A small cartouche at the base of the otherwise plain spiral colonnettes and various decorative motives suggest a date about 1675. Only one statue, the image of St. Ignatius, is used and that in the customary situation upon the canopy. Unspectacular as the pulpit may appear in a photograph, it is in reality very beautiful, far more effective in the original than many more virtuoso and more celebrated productions.

The pulpit in San Antonio, Cajamarca, now covered with a recent brown stain, is mentioned because it is an early example of a type prevalent in Ayacucho and the school of Lima in the early eighteenth century. This design can be dated about

1650, however, because the pilasters are still flat and they carry a vertical strip of the tongue motive. At the top and bottom they curve into volutes. The most interesting parts are the large elliptical panels of flat ornament covered by small voluted canopies. A painting of a Franciscan fills the wall panel in an exceptional usage. This canopy, with just a few volutes and crockets and encased in the scale pattern, is simple, pleasing, and also indicative of an early date.

About the beginning of the eighteenth century a sculptor active in Ayacucho provided several of the churches with new pulpits. Those of Santa Teresa (*circa* 1703), the cathedral, and La Magdalena, apparently came from his shop. The best of these, in the cathedral (Fig. 293), is large and in natural cedar, now given a brown stain. All of them resemble each other in the shape of the elliptical panel on each of the five sides, centered by a smiling angel's head in the midst of a spirited play of volutes and arabesques cut in low relief. A single spiral colonnette fills the vertical space at each angle in the usual way. The wall panel in the cathedral has a fine relief of the *Purísima* and on the canopy is the image of Christ.

The pulpit of Santa Teresa is gilded in its entirety and devoid of figure sculpture, although a crowning statue, now lost, may have existed. The base cuts off flatly without the long pointed silhouette seen in the cathedral. In La Magdalena the wood carving also shines in gleaming gold, and here St. Dominic stands in low relief against the wall as though he were the orator. An angel with trumpet finishes off the composition above.

The most enchanting of all is the pulpit of La Compañía (Fig. 295), round rather than the customary polygon and carved in a filigree of low relief, all of it exquisitely gilded. A winged cherub's head stands out at the top and at the bottom of each spatial division, as well as upon the frieze of each twisted colonnette. The naked heavy-breasted females in half length adorn the corbels below, as they do in some sculptures of Cuzco and so commonly the arms of choir stalls. Without a modicum of documentary guidance it is difficult to determine what relation the sculptor of La Compañía bore to the author of the group previously discussed. The ellipse is a basic shape in all cases, and this is still more emphatic in the sumptuous shield of the giant-sized wall panel, emblazoned with the Jesuit IHS. St. Ignatius fittingly receives the hierarchical distinction of the place of honor upon the canopy. These wood carvings, as well as the splendid array of retables, give Ayacucho an enviable distinction in the field of Peruvian colonial sculpture.[21]

Falling completely outside of the pattern of the Ayacuchan school is the beautiful pulpit, carved in natural cedar, in the church of San Francisco de Paula (Fig. 296). Instead of niches, four panels are carved in high relief with figures of the four Evangelists, accompanied by their symbols and clouds of cherubs' heads. Nothing in Peru exactly comparable with this sculpture is known to me. The compositions are spirited and the Evange-

lists ecstatic in their expressiveness. Spiral colonnettes enframe these scenes and also the *Purísima* upon the wall panel. Otherwise the decorative details are restrained. They are consistent with the traditions of the local school in which niches, canopies, and intricate complexity of planes are notably absent. The crowning statue of a bishop must be a Franciscan, possibly St. Louis of Toulouse.

Lima, the viceregal capital, was surely the center in which first developed the pulpit with elliptical panels separated by spiral colonnettes. Even though it is not possible, in view of the destruction of earthquakes, to establish chronological priority, the primacy of the cultural center of South America can hardly be challenged. The pulpit of Jesús María in Lima (Fig. 292), in general contemporary with the high altar of 1708,[22] is classifiable in the same category as the works in Ayacucho, although presumably not designed by the artist who was active there or shipped his wood carving from Lima to Ayacucho. The monograms of Christ and Mary stand out upon the elliptical shields, and at the top of each is an angel's head. The round arch above and the small bracket below suggest a lingering in the designer's mind of the traditional niche arrangement. St. Joseph upon the wall beneath the canopy, within an ellipse between spiral colonnettes, and St. Bonaventure at the summit are logical iconography in a Carmelite nunnery. The cut-out openwork of the domical portion of the canopy establishes a new and unusual note here. The quality of gilding of the entire surface maintains the high standards of colonial production. Much of the same sort is the pulpit in the small but precious church of Magdalena la Vieja.

A nonconformist to the contemporary school of Lima is the example in Santa Rosa de las Monjas. The canopy and wall niche with its relief of St. Dominic are far more florid. The main body, unlike the pulpits of the previous group, contains niches in which stand St. Rose of Lima and four Dominican nuns. Partly nude female busts are in this instance competently clothed in paint and gilt. The design and workmanship point to the hand of some mediocre practitioner of the wood carver's art, or perhaps two men, since the upper section is distinctly the better.

Two related works of the elliptical panel type are those of La Compañía at Pisco (Fig. 294) and San Xavier at Nazca. The latter is in natural cedar and the former gilded, but they are alike enough to have come from the same shop about the year 1720. The school of Lima projected itself into this coastal region, and can easily be recognized on a comparison with the wood sculpture in Jesús María and Magdalena la Vieja in the capital. Backed against the wall between deep hoods at Pisco is a billowing figure of the *Purísima*. St. Ignatius is perched aloft. The entrance here is made by a flight of steps, whereas at Nazca a passageway penetrated the thickness of the wall. The door opening into the pulpit has been destroyed, and further damage has been inflicted in replacing the lost spiral colonnettes with Tuscan pilasters.

Recognizable as very much akin to the Pisco pulpit is that of the Iglesia del Prado in Lima, now painted white. It has been remodeled, most noticeably in the volute pilasters which were originally spirals and in the ugly modern balustrade and canopy. Pulpits of the paneled category must have been legion in the eighteenth century. Only a few of them have withstood the vicissitudes of time. They are to be localized in Lima and her subsidiaries, which for some reason included Ayacucho.

Traveling north from Lima to Trujillo, we come to a city distinguished as an outstanding center of wood sculpture. The earliest pulpit is the one in which San Francisco Solano is said to have preached in 1603, foretelling the earthquake of 1619. It has greater importance as a relic than as a work of art, since it is only a fragment and not of high quality. Rectangular stylized leaves, so common in rustic carving, and channeled pilasters are the chief motives. The best one can do is conjecture its date as about 1600. This saint's relic is kept in the church of San Francisco, whose regular pulpit (Figs. 297, 298) in the nave is unusually fine. The panels of the tribune of the latter have an urn in the center, and out of it curve long stylized vines and leaves. At the foot of each panel a draped female head is centered, accompanied by two swags of cloth, filled with apples. The same female head substitutes for a capital, and suspended beneath it is a cluster of apples. The wall panel bears the Franciscan escutcheon and the stigmata of St. Francis. The composition finishes off with a fairly simple canopy, underneath which hovers a dove. A small archangel flutters at the top. A slightly later copy of this pulpit, now painted an ugly brown, belongs to the church of the neighboring village of Mansiche. The problem of dating these monuments is considerable, since they do not correspond to other types whose chronology can be established. The decoration of choir stalls, such as those of the cathedral and La Merced in Lima, furnish the most satisfactory analogies. Hence we may suggest that these pulpits belong to the second quarter of the seventeenth century.

The gilded pulpit of Santo Domingo (Fig. 299), modest but lovely, has just one statue, that of St. Dominic placed upon the canopy. The horizontal flat piece upon the tribune is modern, as likewise the door opening upon the staircase within the walls. The arabesques in two interweaving heartshaped patterns fill the vertical sides of the pulpit, separated by spiral colonnettes. They are undecorated except for the flat entwining vine. Here is a fine composition without exact counterpart, presumably produced about 1670.

Moving on to the second quarter of the eighteenth century, the pulpit in Santa Clara at Trujillo (Fig. 301) is a beautiful work, entirely gilded, which has an unusual combination of the shell tympanum in trefoil division over the panels of the four Evangelists. The iconography and also the placing of the figures on flat panels instead of within recessed niches indicate some common denominator in tradition between the monuments of Santa Clara in Trujillo and San Francisco de Paula in Ayacucho. The *Purísima* upon the wall

panel and the founder, here St. Francis, upon the canopy follow established iconographic practice.

Perhaps less distinguished in quality but fitting into the same category is the pulpit of Cajamarca Cathedral. The iconography differs only in the canopy statuette which probably portrays St. Catherine of Alexandria, titular saint of the church. The gilded ornament tends to flatness with some faint hint of the rococo in the frilled curves with cherubs' heads between. The Evangelists move with emphatic and imploring attitudes. Most charming in her tall primitive slimness is the Madonna, like a Zurbarán female saint, in rich and fashionable dress.

The climax is reached in Trujillo with the pulpit of San Agustín (Fig. 300) which has the distinction of possessing the most extraordinary canopy in all Peru. It sweeps upward like lashing flames in a swirl of golden leaves spotted through by large black flowers. Floating at the apex, St. Augustine stretches out his arms in the act of blessing. Upon the body of the pulpit the four Fathers of the Latin Church are placed full length in shallow trefoil arches. The carving tends to emphasize flat planes here again, as it does in most monuments of later date, in this instance, one would conjecture about 1760. The reversed curves of the molded top unmistakably introduce a French rococo note. The Madonna and Child within a roundel upon the wall panel are modern.

The rococo triumphs completely in the pulpit of Santa Teresa (Fig. 302) at Trujillo where spiral colonnettes give way to a series of ripples in lieu of pilasters. The trefoil arches are transformed into rhythmic curves edged by the typical scalloped molding of the rococo, and the rest of the ornament is consistently French. Only the general components of the composition carry over from the Spanish Baroque. A painting of St. Theresa decorates the door of the speaker's tribune, this usage representing a departure from established precedent. Polychromed figures of the titular saint and other Carmelites fill out the composition. Thus we have approached the end of a long tradition, whose direction changed at the moment of the restoration of the church (1759–1773) after the great earthquake of the mid-century.[23]

The three major rococo pulpits of Lima fall into the third quarter of the eighteenth century when the churches in which they are located were rebuilt: San Carlos and El Corazón de Jesús (both 1758–1766). The best is the first mentioned (Fig. 303), a fact not disguised by the ugly black paint of fifty years ago. The pilasters spring out in reversed volutes like the legs of a Louis XV table. The body of the tribune, entirely changed in its proportions, compared with earlier works, curves inward and then rounds out into plain classical moldings. Familiar rococo cartouches and scalloped moldings prevail with a few cherubs' heads at salient points. The highly expressive statue of a Jesuit at the summit, St. Ignatius no doubt, is a reminder that the church belonged to his order.

The pulpit in El Cristo de los Milagros (Fig. 304) is completely French with no Spanish antecedents. The tribune swells out in a full rococo silhouette without carved ornament of any description. The moldings are gilded, and the stylistic unity of the church is maintained throughout. A contrary situation obtains in El Corazón de Jesús where a local sculptor of retables produced a work altogether devoid of understanding of the new style. The tiny busts are familiar in retables and ecclesiastical furniture of the day. Provincial rococo designs characterize the shields in the center of the hexagonal panels, bearing the instruments of the Passion of Christ. These cartouches and bits of ornament are gilded against a background of tan paint.

The new style spread everywhere in Spanish America. By the end of the century it had passed into Bolivia to the churches of Santa Teresa at Cochabamba and Sucre, and to San Felipe and the chapel of Guadalupe at Sucre.[24]

The iconography of pulpits in the representation of saints is varied. Religious orders place their founder either upon the canopy or the wall panel behind the speaker. The niches on the tribune contain other saints of the same order. The women's branches of the Franciscans and Dominicans always include the male founder and other leading male saints.[25]

Occasionally that tradition is abandoned in favor of placing the four Fathers of the Latin Church in the niches. The Augustinians and the Bethlemites at Trujillo displayed that independence. In the case of Augustinians the iconography is logical, since their founder is one of the four. The seminary at Cuzco, because it is a school for priests, would also understandably prefer to honor the chief medieval authors of Christian doctrine.

By far the predominant favorites for representation upon the preacher's tribune are the four Evangelists. They, as preachers of the Christian gospel, are indisputably the consistent choice. In the present chapter eleven examples of that iconography have been mentioned. Among the religious orders the scheme is less common, yet it was adopted in the churches of La Merced at Cuzco, Santa Clara at Trujillo, and San Francisco de Paula in Ayacucho, respectively, Mercedarian, Franciscan, and Minorite.

All but three of the eleven pulpits containing the Evangelists are located in Cuzco or its vicinity. That phenomenon may be explained by local tradition and also by the fact that so many pulpits are preserved there. The Evangelists alone occupy the niches upon the speaker's tribune in seven of them.[26] In the remaining four, all of the Cuzco school, the Evangelists are accompanied by the *Purísima* in the central niche.[27] The Madonna very frequently holds a more prominent place upon the wall panel behind the speaker. Such is the case in four of the present group.[28] Even in pulpits whose tribunes are unadorned with statues she sometimes holds this same important position.[29]

The statue upon the canopy is often reserved for the founder of the religious order in whose church the pulpit stands[30]

or for the saint to whom the church is dedicated.[31] St. Michael, occupant of high places in medieval times, occasionally receives that distinction on pulpits.[32] At Cuzco the two leading apostles, Saints Paul and Peter, are given primacy in a number of pulpits, appearing upon the canopy and the wall panel respectively.[33] Frequently the dedicatory saint of the church appears on the wall panel instead of aloft upon the canopy.[34]

The absence of the figure of Christ in any of these iconographic groups is noticeable. The only instance known to me of His appearance on a pulpit is the figure of the Infant Jesus upon the canopy of the pulpit in Ayacucho Cathedral. The explanation of His presence here lies in the local cult of the "Weeping Christ Child" of whom there is an image in the same church.

Peruvian sculptors put forth their best efforts in the creation of pulpits. The same men were also active as architects and producers of retables, a fact specifically documented in the cases of Pedro de Noguera at Lima and of Diego Martínez de Oviedo at Cuzco. The architectural and decorative designs follow the same stylistic evolution whether they be façades of churches, choir stalls, retables, or pulpits. The two latter categories of monuments allow for the greater scope in decorative fancy. Colonial artists of Peru were equal to the opportunity presented. No one who studies their work can fail to admire their inventiveness and their technical skill.

XII

RETABLES

THE large Spanish retable, mounting upward in several stories and frequently spanning the breadth of a chapel, came into being in the fifteenth century at the time of the rising political and economic power of Spain. The sculptured altars of Vich and Tarragona in the early part of the century are only a prelude to numerous vast works a few years later, such as the high altars of Toledo Cathedral, Seville Cathedral, and the Carthusian church of Miraflores.[1] Painting and sculpture are frequently combined in these monuments of the late-Gothic period, and the same tradition is carried into the Renaissance and Baroque periods. Alonso Berruguete's high altar (1529) of the Colegio de los Irlandeses in Salamanca, a masterpiece of the Spanish Renaissance, is cited as one of many similar works of the period. The New World too saw Renaissance monuments of great splendor and high quality in the retables of Huejotzingo (*circa* 1580) and Xochimilco in Mexico.[2]

In South America, including Peru, the peak of sculptural magnificence was attained during the second half of the seventeenth and the early eighteenth centuries. The viceroyalty of Peru has lost its sixteenth-century treasures which once adorned the monastic churches at Lima.

Today no Renaissance sculpture of importance has escaped the slipping sands of time. The triumphal-arch retables in the four corners of the Dominican cloister at Cuzco (Fig. 305) are Renaissance in style, probably of the second half of the sixteenth century. They are, however, so rustic in nature, fabricated in stone and plaster by an unskilled workman, that their interest is solely archaeological. Similar are the two side altars in the parish church at Checacupe and another at Huaro, both near Cuzco and placeable at the end of the century.[3]

How retarded the colonies could be is proven by two small altars in the Andean village of San Jerónimo, near Huancayo. The paintings and the architectural setting of wooden balustered columns in the altar of the Crucifixion (Fig. 306) would be dated about 1530 in Spain, whereas the legend in gold letters at the lower right clearly includes the year 1609. The other, a fragment by the same master, belongs to 1614 according to the lengthy inscriptions on the predella. The columns are hung with clusters of fruit and centered by a lion's head. The design is surprisingly good, in spite of ineptitudes in the irregular fluting.[4]

The transept altars of La Asunción at

Juli apparently fall in the same decade, inasmuch as the church itself was probably not initiated until after 1590 and it was completed in 1620.[5] Of brick and stucco, they are set into the body of the wall. The capitals, composed of Ionic volutes joined to a channeled collar, can be sought as far back as the Hospital of the Holy Cross in Toledo (1504–1514),[6] yet the cartouches of the frieze point to a later day. Again the architectural arrangement is good, whereas the statues of Jesuits are primitive Indian pieces. Attention should be drawn to the clearly Spanish character of the crucifix and the Risen Christ in the altar of the left transept. The elongated mannerist proportions of the latter figure elicit more interest than usual, because of the rarity of this style in colonial Peru.

The dated work (1618) in a lateral chapel of the Augustinian church at Copacabana (Fig. 308) was originally the high altar and the shrine of the miracle-working Madonna.[7] It has more than usual importance, because it is the best example of the Renaissance style in the viceroyalty of Peru. For that reason it is included here, although Copacabana lies within the modern boundaries of Bolivia. Only the broken pediment in the top center and the cornices and volutes at the sides suggest the early seventeenth century. Possibly the volute pilasters with human-headed capitals might also be included among these auguries of a later style. Otherwise, the Renaissance prevails in the architecture and in the frieze, decorated with cherubs' heads and lighted lamps. Faith and Hope in stucco reliefs recline upon the sloping cornices at the sides. In the predella the four Fathers of the Latin Church stand guard beside reliefs of the Nativity and Birth of the Virgin, while the six elliptical medallions about the central niche enclose half-length figures of the sibyls. Clusters of fruit, winged *putti,* and nude female busts add to the decorative assembly. The paintings and statues are a miscellany, not belonging to the altar originally.

The high altar of Sucre Cathedral (1604–1607), long since destroyed, occupied a position far more advanced in style and was first rate in quality. Its author, Joseph Pastorelo, was without question European born, perhaps Italian, judging by his surname. The original drawing, attached to the contract of 1604, I had the good fortune to discover in the archives of the cathedral.[8] Here we meet the turn from Renaissance to Baroque, the classical features soberer, and the Baroque in evidence in broken pediments and in the irregular outlines of the voluted tabernacle. The same volutes, carved with the scale pattern, act as pilasters flanking the Crucifixion in the attic story. The pyramidal pinnacles descend from the school of Juan de Herrera, but the bracketed frieze is new. The figures, tall and slender with small heads, are in the full stream of Mannerism. Such a retable as this would be a priceless manifestation of colonial greatness, but alas, none exists. The sketch gives us some hint of the beauty which abounded in the churches of Lima, Cuzco, and other capitals, even within the first hundred years of settlement.

Numerous documents attest that Spanish sculptors and painters of first rank shipped their works to the Indies.[9] Few of them have come down to us; far fewer than reasonable, because of the extraordinary destruction caused by repeated earthquakes. The retable of St. John the Baptist (1607–1612), in the church of La Concepción at Lima, carved by the celebrated Sevillian, Juan Martínez Montañés, is the only work of its kind which the New World still possesses. The fact that it is one of the artist's earliest achievements adds to its importance, even though repaint and minor restorations have inflicted unnecessary damage upon it.

A fragment of a Spanish retable of the same period, possibly imported from the mother country, stands in a side chapel of San Francisco at Ayacucho. Placed above a later altar of the eighteenth century, it is dedicated to St. John the Baptist whose statue occupies the central niche. Panels in relief relate the chief episodes of his legend. Lack of detailed photographs and the high location of the altar make a more accurate analysis impossible. Up to the present it has escaped the attention of students of Hispanic art.

The nearly life-sized reliefs of Christ and fourteen apostles in the sacristy of Lima Cathedral cannot be classified literally as a retable, yet they seem to fit best in the present chapter (Fig. 309). They rise like a wall in cedar above the chests (*cajonería*) in which ecclesiastical vestments are stored. Their documentation to the hand of the well-known sculptor and architect, Juan Martínez de Arrona, in 1608 makes them doubly significant to the historian. Recorded in Lima as early as 1599, he became chief architect of the cathedral in 1614, a post which he held until his death in 1635. His most important contribution to colonial architecture was the design for seven portals of the cathedral (1626). The drawing of the main portal, discovered by Harth-terré (Figs. 104, 105) shows that the first story, however much remade, still incorporates some features of his composition.[10]

The Apostles in the sacristy embody the last stage of Renaissance classicism. The approach of a new age is betrayed only in the row of cartouches at the crowning. The Corinthian columns are handled correctly, and the frieze of rinceaux with precision. Martínez de Arrona was an academic master, highly competent and well grounded in his craft, yet uninspired. The prevailing classicism, drawn from the fount of ancient Roman sculpture, is unmistakable in the well-poised bodies and in the draperies, fluted in the antique manner. These sculptures would win respect anywhere. They are good enough to make one wish that the artist had been more than academic, that he had had just one spark of the temperament and emotional insight which might have made him a great master. His extant sculpture is the only representative of classicism in Peru bequeathed to us. His dominant position in the school of Lima figures in the discussion of Pedro de Noguera's choir stalls of Lima Cathedral.

Knowledge of the retables of Lima during the first half of the seventeenth century is limited to documents, the works themselves having been lost, for the inevitable reason: earthquakes.[11] The fine choir stalls of the cathedral and La Merced do much, however, to fill the sculptural lacuna.

CUZCO

Cuzco too has little to offer in the early years, thanks to the same caprices of nature. The retables by Martín de Torres in La Merced (1631), in San Agustín (1639), and in the cathedral (1646) have disappeared. Of all the work by this important sculptor, only the ambones of the cathedral (1656) survive.[12]

After the earthquake of 1650 the rate of productivity was extraordinarily high in all branches of artistic endeavor. The two lateral altars in Santa Catalina seem to be among the rare works which antedate the earthquake, in this case possibly by two decades. The shafts are carved with the scale motive except in the lower band which is fluted spirally. Conservatism too stamps the first lateral altar of La Compañía, dated 1651.[13] Its arrangement has been confused by subsequent alterations. The Doric order is exceptional, but other types of ornament of the period, such as voluted brackets and the tongue motive, are included.

An important milestone, the retable of the Trinity in Cuzco Cathedral (Fig. 310), provides the point of departure for a study of the school during the second half of the seventeenth century. An inscription with the year 1655 runs in several lines above the seated statues of the Trinity. The figure of St. Peter to the left has lost its companion, St. Paul, who on the right is replaced by a borrowed though colonial piece. The sculptures, like the paintings, are local products of Cuzco, and the iconography is confused and unconventional. The *alfiz* setting of the central niche reminds the student of the contemporary portals of San Francisco and the Capilla de Loreto in Cuzco. Most significant, however, is the decorator's skill in manipulation of ornament. Tiny pearled strips run vertically upon the shafts of the columns, the lower band of which has a lozenge pattern in the second story, and in the first story a variant of a basket weave. Columns of this type are the signature of the Cuzco school in the mid-century. The broken pediments centered by a niche begin here, and will develop greater complexity in later works. •

The Merced has a large array of altars of the period immediately following the earthquake, only the high altar and those of the two chapels at either side being of the nineteenth century. The retable in the right transept (Figs. 311, 312), dedicated to the miraculous image of Nuestra Señora de la Soledad, was completed and gilded in 1660 by Juan Calderón.[14] Greater Baroque involutions in broken cornices and contrasted planes distinguish the architectural design from that of the Trinity altar five years earlier. The gilded columns are beautifully handled with beaded zigzags and a band of volutes and arabesques in the lower section. Smaller columns look like palm trunks with the scale motive below. The close similarity of this wood carving to the pulpit in Santa Catalina (Fig. 278) is noted in Chapter XI. The well-preserved set of paintings relate the Passion of Christ. The modern restorer ruined the central section of the altar by stripping off the Baroque ornament, as he did the companion piece in the left transept. The latter work is contemporary, and probably by the same architect. The pictures which are devoted to Martyrdoms are outstanding for their unusually high quality. Charming statuettes of the four Evangelists and a relief of the Epiphany badly daubed with modern paint constitute the predella. The same men who worked upon the cloister of the Merced must also have designed these retables. The stone columns of the cloister (Figs. 84, 85) like the wood sculpture are cut with vertical strips of a knob ornament and the lower section with the scale motive or spirals. The only notable difference is the use of the crowns of acanthus leaves to separate the lower band, missing in these early retables. The later salomonic retables adopted them almost universally from about 1675 thenceforth.

Two retables of paintings, one in each of the arms of the transept in La Compañía are very closely related and perhaps from the same workshop as the transept altars of La Merced. The Jesuit works are more luxuriantly carved in the first story: notably the columns of arabesques and the female torsos used like brackets over the capitals. They stand out in sharp distinction from the salomonic retables nearby.

The high altar of Santa Catalina (Fig. 313) fits into this same group, although slightly later, perhaps about 1665. The niches have become deeper and the moldings more intricate. The now familiar carving of the columns, the heart-shaped cartouches, and webbed moldings recur. On the other hand, the spiral column, in this case plain above a spiral band, makes its appearance, quite possibly for the first time in Cuzco.[15] As previously observed, façades and retables pursue the same stylistic course, but the latter are always more exuberant in decoration. Allowing for difference of function the façades of the cathedral and La Compañía are unmistakably products of the same school as the Santa Catalina altar, although probably not of the same workshop.

To the south of Cuzco on the shores of Lake Titicaca, the high altar of La Asunción at Juli (Fig. 315) is a fine structure of gilded wood, datable about 1660, but in a state of ruin and collapse. The large shell niches in the center do not belong here, and the painting above replaces the original relief of the Assumption of Mary which is now stored in the transept. The Mannerist style lingers on in the elongated bodies of saints and angels, both in the sculpture and in the paintings. The lake region shows the force of tradition in the familiar mermaids woven into the frames at the sides.

Ayacucho, next to Cuzco, has preserved the best collection of mid-seventeenth century wood sculpture. The altar of the Capilla de Loreto, addorsed to La Compañía, surely is not later than 1650, its fluted columns and its general conservatism comparable with the altar of 1651 in the Jesuit church at Cuzco. In the same manner as the Mercedarian altars of 1660 is the high altar of Santa Ana at Ayacucho, excluding the eighteenth-century central section. The fine architectural setting for the paintings of the life of St. Francis Xavier in the Jesuit church fits also in this category, and perhaps is a product of the identical workshop. More strikingly original is the altar of Jesús Nazareno in the same church (Fig. 316). Here, by exception, the statues are first-rate Hispanic sculptures, both the Christ Bearing His Cross and St. Ignatius. The large framework of columns builds up splendidly, the columns very beautiful in their alternate bands of cartouches and spiral flutings.[16]

The high altar of Ayacucho Cathedral holds first rank among the masterpieces of the seventeenth century. It was probably in place at the time of the consecration of the new church in 1672 or shortly thereafter. The most suitable stylistic comparison is with the altar of Nuestra Señora del Buen Suceso in San Blas at Cuzco (Fig. 307), mentioned as existing in 1678. Here the spiral columns rise above a lower band decorated with cartouches. Although not identical with the first story in Ayacucho, it is at least comparable in period. The second row of columns also recalls the Cuzco school, but in this case the earlier phase, as represented by the cloister and altars of La Merced (Figs. 84, 311). It would be hazardous to propose, however, that the sculptor active in Ayacucho was specifically a *cuzqueño* artist. The ornamental vocabulary must have been widely diffused in the period, including Lima, although no visible evidence has survived in the capital.

The niches of the first story are devoted to sacred vessels containing relics of saints. The panels on the two upper stories have paintings of saints and in the top center the Crucifixion. The central niche which enshrines a statue of the Madonna was re-embellished in the mid-eighteenth century, and various mirrors were then inserted in this section. The silver tabernacle is specifically said to be the gift of Bishop Gutié-rrez Gadeano (1745–1749).[17]

Returning to Cuzco, we find that the last third of the seventeenth century, that is to say, the period of Bishop Manuel de Mollinedo, was one of unparalleled artistic production. Retables and pulpits poured forth from sculptors' shops, refurbishing all of the churches. No really accurate chronology of them can be established, however, until the notarial and episcopal archives are thoroughly searched for documentation.

The retable of Nuestra Señora del Buen Suceso (Fig. 307) in the church of San Blas was begun *circa* 1673–1675, presumably at the request of Bishop Mollinedo, since the latter mentions it in his letter to the king, dated 1678. Payments for the completion and the gilding of the altar were made to the famous Indian sculptor, Juan Tomás Tuyru Tupac in 1678–1679.[18] The spiral column makes one of its earliest appearances in Cuzco in this work. That fact is evident in the relatively chaste handling, with fluting but unadorned by foliate ornament and grapes like others appearing within a few years thereafter. The band with cartouche sets off the shafts in the first story. Probably from the same shop is a lateral altar of Santa Clara, the center of which was later modified by the superposition of a glass niche, dated 1779.

Just how the spiral column was introduced to Spanish America is uncertain. The most important single factor in its widespread popularity throughout Europe was Bernini's *baldacchino* (1627–1633) in St. Peter's at Rome. A replica designed by Diego de Aguirre was projected for Lima Cathedral in 1675 but never realized.

By the middle of the seventeenth century the spiral or salomonic column appeared in several retables in Spain.[19] The first certain example of it in America seems to have been the high altar of Puebla Cathedral in Mexico, a work carried out by the sculptor Lucas Méndez after a drawing sent from Spain by Martínez Montañés. The engraving of it, dated *circa* 1650 and indubitably prior to the death of the engraver, Juan de Noort, in 1652, places the altar in the fifth decade of the seventeenth century.[20] In Peru spiral columns decorate the episcopal throne of the choir stalls in Cuzco cathedral, a monument designed about 1660. The same feature is repeated in the choir of San Francisco at Lima (1674). Nearly all of the retables and pulpits at Cuzco adopted it after 1670. The altar of Nuestra Señora del Buen Suceso in San Blas, mentioned above (*circa* 1673–1678), the high altar and pulpit of Santa Teresa commissioned in 1675, and the project for the high

altar of Lima Cathedral (1675) were among those which launched the style. Shortly the salomonic retable controlled the field unchallenged, and it held sway until the advent of the rococo in the mid-eighteenth century.

A monument of considerable importance is the high altar of Santa Teresa (Figs. 60, 317), awarded by contract to Diego Martínez de Oviedo in 1675. It was to be identical with the high altar of La Merced, now destroyed.[21] The spiral column fills the dominant positions in all three stories. Only the smaller shafts which flank the niches cling to the older tradition, as exemplified by the Mercedarian transept altars. Two crowns of acanthus leaves encircle the lower section, establishing the one-to-two-part division. The vocabulary of ornament grows increasingly richer. Among the new themes are cherubs' heads and nude *putti* amid the grapevines on the columns. The bracketed frieze and the draped female head upon the cornice join company with the familiar scale motive, the half-disk or tongue moldings, the dentelated edges, and the broken hooded niches which are topped by the elliptical cartouches. Gilded throughout, the high altar of Santa Teresa is a masterpiece, although its beauty is partially concealed by the new glass cages placed around the statues, and the atrocious sunburst and Lamb of God in the center. The latter with its tin crown was placed there by the nuns of the present century. This damage could easily be repaired. Modern clothes, too, obscure the statues of the Madonna and three Carmelites. St. Theresa herself and Christ are modern religious images of the waxworks variety, no doubt bought in Paris or New York.

Diego Martínez de Oviedo was apparently the leading sculptor of the second half of the seventeenth century in Cuzco. The numerous pulpits which came from his shop were studied in Chapter XI. They include those splendid monuments in La Merced, Santa Catalina, Santa Teresa (1675), La Compañía and the seminary (Figs. 278–281). His documented retables are the high altars of Santa Teresa and San Sebastián (1679–1680).[22] The provision that the former was to be exactly like the main altar of La Merced would suggest that Martínez was the author of the chosen model. Surely it could not have been the work ordered from Martín de Torres in 1631, for the spiral columns like those of Santa Teresa were not used at that date.

The similarity in the designs of Martínez de Oviedo's two altarpieces is easily recognized in spite of the extensive modern additions to the Carmelite retable and the dilapidated condition of its companion in San Sebastián. The latter was on the verge of collapsing to the ground until partially reënforced in recent years. Many of its spiral columns have been lost and various mirrors have been added. In general the state of preservation is very poor in this monument whose donor's shield, that of the priest, Juan de Cárdenas, is placed upon the lower niches.

For decorative splendor and extraordinarily fine quality of figure sculpture, the high altar of La Compañía excels all others in Cuzco (Figs. 72, 318, 319). It is a glorious array of gilded Baroque wood carving, painted canvases, and polychromed statues. Three life-sized Jesuits in wood sculpture, painted black and gold, fill the dominant niches in the upper section. They are majestic, broadly draped with full rounded folds which are arranged in groups and gathered in at the waist. The style is reminiscent of the Sevillian school of the seventeenth century. The figure of the Madonna, in the central position, is entirely gilded. She is unmistakably a Baroque copy of a Gothic prototype which the artist had admired or one the Jesuits wished him to reproduce. The type is very close to the fourteenth-century statue in Toledo Cathedral, known as Nuestra Señora la Blanca. The Christ Child is omitted at Cuzco, and the subject is the Assumption.

A painting of the Transfiguration of Christ appears just above the Madonna, and on either side of her a painting of an archangel. The statues in the niches beside the tabernacle do not pertain to this altar, although they are colonial. The statuettes of the predella are lost, but one fine statue of a Jesuit, like the three others previously mentioned, still remains on the lower right, where the retable turns against the wall of the sanctuary (Fig. 319). It is possible here to comprehend the dignity of interpretation, combined with a consuming fervor, so eminently Hispanic. These lateral niches are trefoil in shape.

Most imposing of all is the beauty of the architectural setting, built up in two high columned stories and finished off with an attic of niches, gables, and cartouches.

The large spiral columns of the first story create an added sense of restlessness in which the Baroque delights. Acanthus crowns encircle the lower third of the shafts, and the usual arabesques and grapes spread over the surfaces. Nude *putti* occur here as in the high altar of Santa Teresa. Still more in evidence are the unmistakably female nudes, most of them turning into flowing leaves at the waist. This theme, so popular upon the arms of choir stalls, also decorates the brackets and the friezes here repeatedly.

The columns of the second story have beautiful long-stemmed foliate ornament ending in three stylized flowers. By contrast a zigzag is carved into the lower band. Secondary columns display considerable versatility in treatment, with arabesques and shields the most noteworthy. Spinning over the surfaces recur many familiar devices of the Cuzco school: the scale motive, channeled moldings, the ball and tongue, brackets, beaded edging, etc.

It would be impossible to exaggerate the beauty of the high altar of the Compañía in Cuzco, or to overestimate its historical significance. It is the greatest masterpiece among the altarpieces of colonial Peru. Without any documentary information as to the author, an attribution would be hazardous in view of our limited information about artists of the period. The style is close to the work of Diego Martínez de Oviedo, although the quality is somewhat superior. The altar of the Immaculate Conception in the right transept of La Compañía is a splendid work by the master of the high altar. At present the lower niches contain two excellent statues of St. Jerome and St. Francis (Fig. 359), brought here from the destroyed chapel of San Andrés.

The high altar of the famous shrine of Copacabana (Fig. 320) on Lake Titicaca lies beyond the present geographic borders of Peru. Nonetheless, it is a dated monument, and for that reason, it helps to establish the chronology of the period. The present church was begun in 1668 and an inscription upon the retable states that it was gilded in 1684.[23] Hence it is approximately contemporary with the high altars of Santa Teresa, La Compañía, and San Sebastián in Cuzco. More conservatism is suggested by the adoption of the spiral column only in the secondary positions flanking the niches. The major columns display a rich overlay of arabesques and elliptical shields comparable with the small shafts beside the Madonna of the Jesuits in Cuzco. It would be hazardous to suggest, however, that the Cuzco school projected itself to the shores of Lake Titicaca. In view of the lack of documentary information and of exact stylistic relationships, speculation as to the origin of the sculptor is unjustified. The architectural composition as well as details of ornament are better in the Jesuit retable at Cuzco, and the figure sculpture attains a much higher level of quality. For all of that, the Copacabana retable is a brilliant work. The mutilations of the tabernacle in the present century and the neo-Renaissance round-arched enframement of the miraculous image are unfortunate but not disastrous.

Precise information is available in regard to the date of the high altar of San Blas (Fig. 314) in Cuzco, since the bishop claimed it to be the best in the city in 1696, when it was being gilded.[24] At the end of the century the spiral shaft excluded all other types of columns which had been conspicuous by their variety hitherto. In San Blas the difference in period and workshops is also noted in the predominance of the rosette instead of the usual grapevine. Whirling movement and decorative richness mark the last phase of the Hispanic Baroque, so frequently yet incorrectly called "Churrigueresque." Very charming are the scrolled pediments with shell in the second story. The *mudéjar* trefoil establishes the shape of frame in four of the paintings. As usual the sculpture is superior to the oils. The statue of the *Purísima* is especially lovely. The others too, St. Blas, Saints Peter and Paul, and the two Saints John, are effective and somewhat similar to the figures on the pulpit in the same church. The mirrors and glass canopy do not belong to the original composition, but were added about 1750.

The *trascoro* of Cuzco Cathedral (Fig. 66) shines with great splendor, making the entry into this church dramatic beyond that of all others in Peru. The huge spiral columns, hung with clusters of grapes and vines, and brilliantly gilded, are extraordinarily beautiful. The smaller columns beside the cult picture of Nuestra Señora de la Antigua by contrast are carved in a series of rosettes. Bishop Mollinedo's escutcheon in the upper center combines with the style to place the *trascoro* in the last decade of the seventeenth century. The large academic paintings are uninteresting additions of the nineteenth century.

So many other altarpieces and decorative sculptures were produced in Cuzco at the turn of the century, that a whole volume would be needed for a thorough study of them. The interior of the seminary, works in the cathedral, and the high altar at Checacupe are representative. For a half century the traditions remained without essential variation. The principal altar in the church of San Pedro (Fig. 321), ordered of Lorenzo de Vega in 1720, is a gigantic three-storied structure that maintains the high standards of the school.[25] The division of the niches between paintings and statues is especially characteristic of Cuzco, although it does occur to a lesser extent in Lima. The tabernacle has recently been restored in colonial style. The statues of Mercedarian saints are also recent as a result of the transfer of the church to sisters of that order.

The high altar of Jesús María must be contemporary with the rebuilding of the church in 1733–1735. Possibly the same workshop produced the main altar in the parish church of the town of Oropesa, one of the masterpieces of the province. Because of its rural location, the sculpture has escaped later alterations such as those which mar the related monument in Cuzco. The flatness of pattern and the sharper distinctions between planes suggest that a native Indian artist created this slightly more static interpretation of the late Baroque.

The fine altar of natural cedar, ungilded, in the sacristy of San Francisco at Cuzco has flat lacy borders and broad openwork moldings which also indicate this late period. The main panels are devoted to paintings of the Passion of Christ. The zigzag columns of the second story are the only case in the city of an imitation of the pulpit of San Blas, somewhat exaggerated, to be sure (Figs. 322, 288).

One utterly charming altar of the eighteenth century in Santa Catalina (Fig. 323) remains to be mentioned. Dedicated to the Madonna, her small statue stands within a closable circular shrine in the center. The Dominican saints beside her are modern, but the niches and columns are exquisitely jewel-like. The elliptical reliefs in stucco above depict the Trinity, the Ascension of Christ, and the Descent into Limbo. Upon the summit sit spirited little figures of nude angels playing harps and guitars. For fantasy of invention and delicacy of expression, this altarpiece would be difficult to surpass.

LIMA

THE sculpture of Lima in the seventeenth century is well documented, thanks to the study of archives made by Lohmann Villena, Padre Rubén Vargas Ugarte, and Harth-terré.[26] Juan Martínez de Arrona, architect and sculptor, has already been discussed at the beginning of the present chapter in connection with his fine series of Apostles (Fig. 309) in the sacristy of Lima Cathedral (1608). The most important figure of the first half of the century, or so today he appears to have been, was Pedro de Noguera whose

masterpiece, the choir stalls of the cathedral, is studied in Chapter X. Noguera, a Catalan born in 1592 at Barcelona, is first mentioned in Lima in 1619. He married two years later, and enjoyed a long and distinguished career, succeeding Martínez de Arrona as *maestro mayor* of the cathedral in 1638. He carried on the building of the cathedral portals, carved retables and pulpits, and prepared the design for the fountain in the Plaza Mayor at Lima. Only the latter work and the choir stalls have survived. He is last mentioned in 1655.[27]

Martín Alonso de Mesa, active in Lima from 1595 until his death in 1626 and Luis Ortiz de Vargas, both of whom collaborated with Noguera on the choir stalls, were also creators of retables. None of them has come down to us. The same fate has befallen the prolific production of Asencio Salas. Not a single work from his hand has survived. Born at Logroño, Spain, in 1612, he practiced his art in Lima from 1637 until his death in 1669.[28]

The most important extant sculpture in Lima dating from the mid-seventeenth century is the series of saints over the wardrobes (*cajonería*) in the sacristy of San Francisco. Across one end of the room twelve monastic saints, in large part Franciscan, stand on either side of the main central niche which enshrines the image of Christ. The Immaculate Conception holds the central position in the left wall, accompanied by a row of ten saints. On the opposite wall her pendant is St. Catherine with twelve saints. Individual figures are competently managed, if uninspired. The general impression of the architectural setting with the figure sculpture is rich and splendid. On the basis of the style a date *circa* 1650, long before the rebuilding of the sacristy in 1729, is indicated.

The refurbishing of the sacristy of San Agustín in 1643 included the ceiling and a series of twenty-eight saints.[29] The luxurious chests and the wall of niches above them (Fig. 333) now belong to the period about 1760, subsequent to the great earthquake. The statues are generally believed to have escaped the disaster of 1746 as they did in 1940. Pleasing graceful figures in wood, subdued in their polychromy, they number thirty today. It is not at all certain that these sculptures are entirely the work of Diego de Medina. A soft flowing movement in many of them seems to suggest the eighteenth century.

The leading sculptor of Lima in the second half of the seventeenth century was Diego de Aguirre. He is called sculptor and *ensamblador* (joiner) signifying that he was a specialist in retables. Many commissions are recorded from the year 1667, when he made a large tabernacle for the nuns of Santa Catalina, until his death in 1718. The project for the high altar of Lima Cathedral (1675) which was to reproduce Bernini's *baldacchino* in St. Peter's at Rome makes an impression upon any art historian.[30] Thus we realize that Lima was not isolated from the ecclesiastical and artistic capitals of Europe. The death of the archbishop who proposed the new altar meant the abandonment of the undertaking. Aguirre was then engaged upon the high altar of San Agustín (1673) which must have done much to establish his repu-

tation. An important work came in 1681 when he agreed to provide an altar for the Capilla de Animas in San Marcelo. It was to comprise two stories and eighteen *salomónicas*. This notice is of significance for it signalizes the definitive triumph of the spiral column which Bernini had done so much to popularize.[31]

Just one of Diego de Aguirre's many works has daunted the hand of fate which has swept away the major portion of Lima's artistic past. That is the retable of the Immaculate Conception (Fig. 324) in the cathedral, originally the work of Carlos Pavia. Diego de Aguirre was engaged to dismount and reconstruct it (1692–1696) because of the damage it suffered in the severe earthquake of 1687. The exact date of Pavia's design is unknown, but it must be placed about 1675, contemporary with the main façade of San Francisco.[32] As explained in the analysis of this latter monument, the relationship to the retable is so close that the façade may also be attributed to Carlos Pavia. The alternative possibility is that Pavia was a pupil and close follower of Constantino Vasconcellos, architect of San Francisco.

It is difficult to be sure that Aguirre contributed more to the retable than the shell tympanum in the center and the elliptical panels. The rococo details of the lower sides postdate Aguirre, belonging to the second half of the eighteenth century. At this time the gray background and gilded details replaced the traditional Hispanic method of gilding the entire monument. The statue of the Madonna and the altar furnishings are modern Gothic. The original reliefs at the sides are episodes in the life of the Virgin: the Presentation in the Temple, the Marriage, the Annunciation, and the Nativity.

The church of San Pedro in Lima is a virtual museum with its nine retables of the late seventeenth and early eighteenth centuries. They have not been visible since the earthquake of 1940, on account of the restoration of the church. Hence an adequate discussion of them is impossible. Judging by a photograph, the retable of the *Purísima* has a second story of about 1650, a first story redone in 1700, and modern statues.

The retable of St. Francis Xavier (Fig. 325), it seems to me, should be dated about 1700. Padre Vargas Ugarte has generously furnished me with valuable information by letter to the effect that the retable of St. Francis Xavier was mentioned as recently completed in the Annual Letter, i.e., the report of the Jesuits of Peru, in the year 1648.[33] The same source states that they had placed a statue of the saint by the hand of Martínez Montañés in the altar. The large standing figure of the Jesuit in polychromed wood which occupies the main niche seems most probably to be that very work. It resembles somewhat the statues of St. Ignatius and St. Francis Xavier in the University Chapel at Seville.[34] Padre Vargas believes that the figure of St. Francis Borja in San Pedro at Lima should also be attributed to Martínez Montañés. The retable of St. Francis Xavier in Lima, however, cannot possibly be dated *circa* 1648, since the style of architecture and spiral columns are later.

The conclusion must be reached that it was damaged in the earthquake of 1687 and replaced by the existing structure not long afterwards. The entire church was redecorated at that period, and the wood carvings and paintings were added to embellish the aisles.

In the first story of the altar, horizontal rings divide the spiral columns into four zones, a usage which seems to characterize one particular workshop of Lima. In the second story only one ring separates the lower third of the shaft which is curiously decorated with melons in addition to bunches of grapes. Above the large statue of St. Francis Xavier the Madonna is enthroned beneath a canopy, delicately cut with a lacelike filigree of open work. Pulpits of Lima also have similar canopies. The shell tympanum behind the Madonna likewise testifies to the stylistic unity of the school in which doorways of the eighteenth century carry the same feature. This gilded altar of St. Francis Xavier is eloquent evidence of the high quality of *limeño* retables of the second half of the seventeenth century. Very few of them have survived.

The altar of the Trinity in San Pedro appears in the photograph to be a splendid monument (*circa* 1700). The treatment of the spiral columns, here using the rosette instead of grapevines, is more common than the style of the workshop just discussed.

No counterpart exists in Peru for the altar of St. Ignatius in the transept of San Pedro (Fig. 326) for the simple reason that it is a copy of the transept altars dedicated to St. Ignatius and to St. Francis Xavier in La Compañía at Quito, Ecuador. These altars in turn were derived in their composition from those by Andrea Pozzo in the church of Sant' Ignazio at Rome.[35] The giant spiral columns in single story enframing one large niche are Italian in origin. The altar in Lima had no imitators. It is a foreign importation which is less satisfactory today because the wood is painted black, one of the nineteenth century's worst aberrations. Thus in Spanish America the Italian marbles were replaced by wood. At Quito the Hispanic gold and polychromy united with the Italian composition to produce splendid results. These altars are subsequent to the year 1700, the approximate date of their Roman prototype.

The first half of the eighteenth century in Lima and the coastal region was one of the best and most prolific periods in retable production. Lima seems to have been, and logically, the fountainhead. As a point of departure for study, the rich array of wood sculpture in Jesús María serves admirably. The high altar (Fig. 327) was commissioned of Joseph de Castilla in 1708. He must have been one of the leading and one of the most influential masters of his day. Documents of his activity range from the year 1701 until his death in 1739, and yet only one other work mentioned in the records may still exist.[36] That is the retable for El Belén, a church which was destroyed in recent years and its altars rearranged and transferred to the modern edifice of the Sagrados Corazones.

The focal point in the high altar of Jesús María is the central niche over the tabernacle, occupied by life-sized statues of the Holy Family. As in colonial painting they are presented standing, with the Infant Christ between Mary and Joseph. A relief in the upper center depicts the Coronation of the Virgin by the Trinity. The niches contain Franciscan and Dominican saints: St. Francis, St. Clare, St. Dominic, and St. Rose of Lima.

The proportions of the altar in two stories are broad and low on account of the size of the sanctuary. The architectural ornament is spun out with greatest delicacy, weaving back and forth in spirited curving rhythms. Much of the verticality of preceding altars is lost in a complex rippling play of lines and masses, dissolved and diffused in a flow of golden light and shade. The deeper niches and broader undulating pediments all contribute to the enchantment of this rich glowing expression of spiritual warmth. The rococo had not yet reached Lima, and yet pure Hispanic art underwent a leavening which seems to be native to the new century.

For high quality and unity of a single period it would be difficult to surpass the interior of Jesús María. Nearly all of the lateral altars may have come from the shop of Joseph de Castilla, they are so similar. Particularly lovely is the altar of San Ildefonso, completed in 1734. Here the figures of the saint upon his knees and the Madonna and the angels are arranged and modeled with great charm. The altar of the Crucifix (1714–1718) in the transept (Fig. 328) likewise merits special consideration.[37] The unusual breadth of the design is again noteworthy, a characteristic of works of this period.

The altars in the church of Magdalena la Vieja in Lima are contemporary with those of Jesús María and much akin in style and quality. Several workshops must have functioned in close relationship, judging only by the few preserved monuments. The high altar has much the same disposition as that of Jesús María, here enshrining the Magdalen in the upper story and the Immaculate Conception in the principal niche, the latter badly repainted and adored by waxwork angels. The other major statues represent St. Peter, St. Francis, St. Dominic, and another Franciscan. Rosettes decorate the spiral columns to the exclusion of grapes. The clusters of apples which by exception were favored by the artists of Jesús María were not adopted here. The six side altars, all of like facture, make this interior a veritable jewel box of unforgettable luster.

Several retables from the first half of the eighteenth century, formerly in El Belén, now in the Sagrados Corazones, have lost their original gilding and are now stained in natural cedar. On the contrary, the pristine beauty of the small altar of the Crucifix and of the altar dedicated to the *Purísima* still remains intact in the sacristy of San Francisco. The rebuilding of the sacristy in 1729 in addition to their style provides adequate evidence of their period. The altar in the Sala Capitular fits into the same group, as will be recognized when the refabrication of the top story is taken into consideration.

South of Lima upon the coast, the town of Pisco boasts of the Compañía, a fine church of the first quarter of the eighteenth century whose high altar, transept altars, and pulpit alone suffice to establish an enviable claim to fame. Some *retablero* of Lima answered the call to practice his art there or else he shipped his creations from the capital. Anyone will recognize that he was a contemporary of Joseph de Castilla. His altar of the Crucifix is outstanding, worthy of the best Castilla ever achieved. The high altar and the altar of St. Joseph do not quite measure up to this standard, and indeed are probably by another hand. One is struck by the division of the spiral shafts into three registers by horizontal rings. Ornament, composition, proportions are clearly *limeño*. The Madonna and four Jesuits comprise the sculpture of the high altar which is set against a scalloped shell, another favorite arrangement of Lima.

The Jesuit church in Arequipa possesses three splendid retables all of the same style and period. As a result of earthquakes and still more of the Neoclassic mania in the nineteenth century they are the only colonial altars of any importance in the entire city. The one dedicated to St. Francis Xavier was gilded by a certain Felipe Morón de Carmona in 1717.[38] Lavish and luxuriant, this structure of three stories sparkles with the rosette type of *salomónica*. The statues of wood and cloth reinforced with plaster carry a convincing religious fervor. The stylistic features, such as the deep niches with shell tympana the ribs of which are carved in foliate ornament, indicate connections with Lima rather than with Cuzco. They do not correspond, however, in general composition to the school of Joseph de Castilla.

Documents of some nonextant sculpture of Arequipa have been published by Padre Barriga. The high altar of the cathedral (1733) by Antonio de Torres and Joseph Flores was lost in the fire which destroyed the whole church in 1844.[39] Padre Barriga has discovered contracts for several altars by Antonio de Torres who died in 1732. Perhaps the man named Flores, of Arequipa, was related to the family of sculptors known in Lima. One of the latter, Antonio Flores, left a signed inscription upon a side altar (1764) in San Francisco de Paula in the capital.

Ramifications of the workshops of Arequipa could be traced throughout the neighboring provinces. A side altar in the church at Yanaquiqua, known to me by photograph, is an indication of the existence of others unseen and unpublished. This particular example has been badly daubed with white paint, an all too frequent custom in southern Peru and Bolivia.

The mid-eighteenth century in Lima heralds the last phases of colonial art. The chastened design and the reversion to Renaissance clusters of fruit in the tomb of Bishop Morcillo Rubió de Auñón hold new portents. The treatment of the broken pediments recalls, however, the school of Joseph de Castilla. This monument of wood and plaster is very much like a retable, the work of a certain Felipe Santiago Palomino in 1743.[40]

The rebuilding of Lima after the earthquake of 1746 brought an outburst of new activity. The French rococo took the scene with a show of force which was soon to sound the death knell of the Hispanic Baroque.

The armless bust-length caryatid placed upon voluted pilasters is one of the most striking new rococo ornamental devices of the third quarter of the eighteenth century. The lateral altar of St. Anthony of Padua (Fig. 329) in the church of San Francisco de Paula Nuevo is a work of high quality which represents the new style at its best. An inscription (Fig. 330) on the predella gives the date, 1764, and the name of the sculptor, Antonio Flores. The altar is painted white with polychromy limited to the statues. This feature marks the abandonment of the Spanish tradition of gilded wood sculpture, which began to disappear in Spain itself after the succession of the French Bourbons to the throne in the early eighteenth century. The general composition of the altar in two stories, the niches and their pediments still retain a semblance of the style of the first half of the century. The details, however, are rococo, with numerous cartouches surrounded by crisp rippling leaves, sparkling shells, and the lattice motive. These sculptors of Lima must have owned books of engraved ornament published by French architects, such as François Cuvilliers' *Livre de Cartouches*.[41]

A whole series of small altars, in which bust caryatids without arms strike a new note, appears throughout Peru. A charming small work of this type in La Merced at Lima is dedicated to Nuestra Señora de la Antigua. The painting, a copy of the celebrated cult picture, as well as the carved ornament, displays an eighteenth-century grace and naïveté.[42] In Lima the churches of San Marcelo, Santa Rosa de las Monjas, Sagrados Corazones, and the Iglesia del Prado all have altars of the type dating from the third quarter of the century. The finest carving of the period is, however, the woodwork of niches enclosing Augustinian saints in the sacristy of San Agustín (Fig. 333). A mask in the center of the pilasters and an urn at the bottom create a gay and fantastic mood. Most original of all are the flame-like rococo tympana over the niches and the handsome rococo chests for ecclesiastical vestments.

The Carmen of Trujillo possesses a lateral altar (Fig. 331) of this category, dedicated to the Infant Christ (*circa* 1759–1773). The custom of gilding is still maintained here. The bust caryatid without arms was at the height of its popularity in the sixties and seventies, although the fashion did persist later with some retarded masters. The altar to the Marriage of the Virgin (1782) in La Merced at Trujillo and another devoted to Santo Toribio (1790) in the cathedral exemplify that fact. The latter's chief claim to fame lies in the fact that the donor was the famous bishop, Martínez Compañón. Although of no great importance, the names of the artisans were Diego Fernández Briseño, sculptor, and Inocencio de Heredia, architect.[43]

Just as common as the armless bust caryatid is another type in which the human torso with arms is displayed down to the waist. This category will be called the atlas group. These figures occupy the upper part of the columns in the large retable of San José in La Merced at Lima. Otherwise the composition is still Hispanic, although rococo ornamental themes intervene. A dark mahogany stain of nineteenth-century origin now gives a gloomy cast to the wood which once was gilded.

The atlantes on the high altar (Fig. 332) of San Carlos (*circa* 1758–1766) swing about in energetic *contrapposto* and their arms rise up, as if to support the capitals. The major shafts are giant spiral columns set diagonally. Influence of Italian Baroque altars and of José Churriguera's retable in San Esteban in Salamanca, Spain, may be suspected here. The altar with colossal columns rather than with the three-storied division was adopted, however, not only by José Churriguera but by numerous masters throughout Spain in the eighteenth century. Its appearance at Lima is retarded on comparison with the mother country. To all of these features are added rococo ornament. The altar of San Carlos, in truth, should be recognized as a highly original work of considerable merit. Its chief blemish is the ugly and lugubrious mahogany stain. The four caryatid maidens of the tabernacle are Neoclassic, falling entirely out of the style of the original structure, and the Madonna belongs to the twentieth century.

The simple type of atlas retable was found in the old church of El Belén at Lima, and still exists in La Merced at Ica and elsewhere.[44] Cuzco, surprisingly enough, possesses three fine retables of the atlas group, all of them unmistakably by the same workshop. They are strictly importations from Lima, planted on foreign soil. The best stands against the end wall of the cathedral behind the sanctuary. The others are side altars in La Compañía and Jesús María. The cathedral altar (Fig. 334) strikes one as strangely out of key, it is so alien to the Cuzco environment. High quality, however, meets with approval at any time or place. The architectural setting can be described as Hispanic, overlaid with the new French rococo fashion of the third quarter of the eighteenth century. For some reason, probably financial, the wood was left in natural cedar. The really superior statues of apostles and saints did reach the stage of polychromy which is beautifully preserved and unmolested.

More or less as an aside, while still in Cuzco, it is fitting to speak of the superb array of mirror altars in Santa Clara (Fig. 59). The most extraordinary of its kind anywhere is the high altar, composed entirely of mirrors, and arranged in two and one-half stories. The side altars and the central section of another, added to an altar of *circa* 1675, are all contemporary. This latter is the only one which has a dated inscription. It is recorded twice for good measure and reads thus: *Este retablo se dedicó haser la devota sor Isadora Baca el año 1779.* The pilasters of green enameled glass are rather curious. The two mermaids playing the *charango* on the lower ledge are unique in Cuzco altars, and a reminder that the lake region where they flourish is not far to the south.

The habit of decking out the principal niche of a retable with a frame of mirrors is widespread in Andean Peru and Bolivia in the second half of the eighteenth century. Large individual mirrors, as though taken from a boudoir, were often scattered about. Witness the high altar of Ayacucho Cathedral and the altar of San Blas in Cuzco (Fig. 314), both of the seventeenth century and given these later embellishments.

After this digression we return to Lima and to the third category of caryatid and atlas retables. In this case the full-length figure, sometimes female and other times male, is employed. The first of these, the retable of Nuestra Señora de la Luz in San Francisco at Lima, has a dated inscription of 1761. It combines full-length and half-length caryatids. The mediocrity of the sculpture is not improved by the garish pink, blue, white, and gold paint of recent times. The retable of San Diego in the same church has the twelve apostles as atlas figures. It is of slightly later date, but the quality shows no improvement. These works mark the lowest ebb of Peruvian colonial art.[45]

The last monument in Lima which must be recorded in this group is the high altar of San Marcelo, painted black in the nineteenth century but regilded in our times. The spiral columns and the composition of the early century were brought up to date (*circa* 1770) by four apostles in the first story and four angels in the second. Some other details, such as the urns beneath the columns, identify a conservative master who was forced to adopt some of the ideas of his contemporaries. How late the full-length caryatids and atlantes persisted in the provinces can be judged by the large retable of Nuestra Señora de las Mercedes in San Pedro at Lambayeque. An inscription tells of the completion of the gilding in 1796. The rococo is in evidence throughout, as it is likewise in other altars of related style in the same church. However provincial the workmanship, the general impression is sumptuous.

Caryatid or atlas figures are not restricted to eighteenth-century retables in Peru. They are also common in Mexico. It will suffice to mention those in San Agustín at Guanajuato and in the church of the same order at Salamanca, not far away.[46]

The last bloom of the Hispanic rococo in Lima arrives with the high altars of San Sebastián and of La Concepción (Figs. 335, 336). The sculptor, Llorente, completed the latter in 1783.[47] Both works are painted light gray with gilding limited to a few high spots. The curious bulging urn-shaped columns, the broad proportions of the two stories, and the deep recesses also characterize the two monuments. In detail, however, the former is more rococo in the fine rollicking play of the moldings and the crisp flowing cartouches. These cartouches recall the earlier retable of Antonio Flores in San Francisco de Paula, but such patterns are so popular in the period that an attribution to him on that basis alone would be unjustified. Strangest of all are the wheeled cartouches upon the lower columns and the unexplained symbols in the second story. Inasmuch as the church has been concealed by the restorer's scaffolds since the earthquake of 1940, the work could be studied only by way of a photograph.

The altar in the church of La Concepción is drier, plainer, and less spirited in design, scarcely more than mediocre. Numerous modern repaintings and various revisions, such as the heart-shaped moldings which hold electric light bulbs, have not improved matters. Here too, trees, fountains, and towers are peculiarly placed upon the columns.

The church of Santo Cristo de los Milagros, supposedly designed by the viceroy Amat, is the most complete surrender to French taste in Lima. Throughout, the walls are painted to suggest marble and the high altar too is given the same appearance. In the unity of the structure (1766–1771) lies its greatest charm.[48] The high altar (Fig. 97) still clings to one feature of local origin, the large fine shell tympanum which acts like a halo to the angels and flaming urns at the top. The latter in truth disappoint any careful observer by their ugly bulging shapes. Compared with the gilded salomonic retables of earlier days, this altar is cold and dull. The keynote is simplification by the use of plain shafts and walls of simulated marble. Nonetheless, the great broken pediments of the attic and the rococo moldings put the design in a category as yet far removed from the Neoclassic.

Altogether surprising results came into being in the altars of the church at Surco, a suburb of Lima. There a local yet daring provincial master bent columns and even turned niches aslant in his desire to create rococo movement. It is doubtful whether anyone except a modern fantastic architect like the Catalan, Gaudí, ever sought such unconventional effects.

Beyond the borders of colonial art lie all of the revivalisms of the nineteenth century. Not much enthusiasm can be aroused in the various transitions to the Neoclassic, as exemplified by the interior of the church of La Trinidad. The cathedral at Lima, alas, was subjected to much rehabilitation at that time. French academic Baroque, replete with musical instruments and tasseled curtains, is the style of an altar dedicated to the Madonna, and, according to the inscription, made in 1796 and painted in 1802. Soon Matías Maestro was to start bonfires of colonial art, and replace it with his own sterile Neoclassic efforts.

AYACUCHO

THE large number of magnificent retables of the eighteenth century in Ayacucho, a small village of eight thousand inhabitants, serves to remind us of the treasures which have been lost elsewhere. Because she fell into decline in the first century of independence, Ayacucho escaped the destructive forces of that period. Serious earthquakes, too, have been spared her. Preservation, then, is the reason why her riches in this field are much greater in quantity than those of Lima, the viceregal capital.

The huge high altar of Santa Teresa (Fig. 337), dated 1703, inaugurates the century with splendor.[49] It is constructed in three high stories in a combination of paintings and statues amid a lavish architectural setting. Its size and the arrangement of its components more closely resemble Lorenzo de Vega's altar in San Pedro at Cuzco (Fig. 321) than works of the school of Lima. In this respect the circular paintings in subordinate positions are unusual, a feature which was to become a characteristic of the school of Ayacucho. Points of contact with Lima (Fig. 327) will also be observed in the lacelike complexity of ornament, the shell niches, and their beaded moldings. Until some documentary information about the workshops is forthcoming, however, the school of Ayacucho must be regarded as a separate entity although it certainly drew from the fountainhead at Lima and possibly somewhat from Cuzco.

The three-part divisions in the upper center of the Carmelite retable are unusual and they established a precedent which was often followed within the city. Grapes and vines entwine the spiral columns which are also decorated with occasional rosettes and birds. The statues of the cloth and plaster variety have been garishly repainted. Otherwise the condition of the altar is excellent. The round mirrors are nineteenth-century intrusions, and the rectangular mirror at the top occupies the niche formerly given to a saint. The high altar of Santa Teresa is one of the most important works of art of colonial Peru, far superior to a better-known monument, such as the Carmelite altar in Trujillo.

The next step chronologically in Ayacucho leads to the high altar (1712) of San Francisco.[50] Unmistakable dependence upon the altar of Santa Teresa is betrayed in the tripartite composition of the center in all three stories. Another master must have been active here, however, for his architecture is blunter and harder, especially noticeable in the angular terraced arrangement of the crowning. Various other ineptitudes are noticeable in the rings placed almost in the center of the spiral shafts. The entablatures and columns are now somewhat askew, in spite of recent reconditioning and the fortunate removal of an ugly tabernacle of the nineteenth century. The statues, on the other hand, are exceptionally good, their contemporary dress notwithstanding.

Mention should be made of the principal retable of La Merced, if for no other reason than that it is dated by an inscription in the year 1718.[51] Simpler than the others and less expensive, it is still a fine gilded structure. The tripartite center and the medallions of the local school continue here. The ugly canopy in the center is a modern intrusion out of scale with the original composition.

The first approach to the study of Ayacucho's sculpture is easy, thanks to dated monuments. Thereafter the situation becomes very complex. Here we can do no more than record the existence of an unexplored mine of eighteenth-century sculpture. Indeed, the altars of the cathedral deserve a volume in themselves.

The church of Santo Domingo alone possesses an excellent high altar and five side altars of the eighteenth century.[52] The principal retables of La Compañía and San Francisco de Paula, the latter now painted white and blue, and many smaller works have passed unnoticed. The main altar of Santa Clara is a production of 1650 upon which an eighteenth-century center has been engrafted.

Most astounding of all is Ayacucho Cathedral with its eight retables of the eighteenth century including the two gigantic structures in the transepts. The latter (Fig. 338) were donated by Bishop Romaní y Carrillo in 1764, according to the inscriptions upon plaques near them. Both are so similar in style to the earlier retable in Santa Teresa (1703) that I was at first inclined to discredit the Carmelite document and to believe that this high altar should be placed nearer 1750. However, it seems more likely that a remote school like that of Ayacucho was less subject to changes of fashion than the capital at Lima. For that reason, the sculptors of Ayacucho trod the same path without marked deviation for a matter of seventy-five years.

The monument in the left transept is dedicated to the Immaculate Conception and its companion piece in the right transept to the Christ of Burgos.[53] They are almost identical except that the Madonna is placed within a closable tabernacle and the crucifix is not. Both combine painting and sculpture and have the same architectural composition. Essentially they continue the style first introduced in the church of Santa Teresa (Fig. 337).

The altar of the Assumption located beside the Christ of Burgos is also identified in the inscription as the gift of Romaní y Carrillo (1764). This right wall of the church holds an incredible array of superb sculpture. Among the best are the altars of St. Joseph with a fine relief of the San Ildefonso miracle in the upper center and that of the Madonna with the splendid statue of St. Peter Nolascus at the top.

TRUJILLO

TRUJILLO was one of the leading centers of retable production in the seventeenth and eighteenth centuries. Many withstood the earthquake of 1759, and the Neoclassic wrought little damage, probably because of lesser economic prosperity than in Lima. Small retables in the Merced, San Agustín, and Santo Domingo have been reconstructed out of fragments of different periods. The worst are those of the Merced, badly wrecked by neglect and by white paint over the gold. On the whole, however, the large altars are in excellent condition, and with the present renewed respect for colonial art, they have very good prospects for the future.

Among the earliest are several small altars whose style is distinguished by a certain type of column which flourished about 1650–1670. This column has a band carved with a cartouche in the lower section. The remainder of the shaft is channeled and is draped with swags of cloth filled with fruit. The draped woman's head, so familiar on choir stalls, is part of the ornamental repertory, and is often placed upon the shaft. At times a cherub's head supplants it. Variations of this column and the same motives embellish the splendid choir stalls of Trujillo Cathedral (Fig. 265) which, on stylistic grounds, seem contemporary with the building of the cathedral, hence about 1660. The best-known monument where the draped column is used is the main portal (Fig. 107) of San Francisco at Lima (1669–1674). Wood sculpture with these features slightly precedes the sudden adoption of the spiral column all over the Spanish possessions in Peru approximately in the years 1670–1675.

The retable of the Virgen del Carmen (Fig. 339) in San Francisco provides a good example of the swag-bedecked shaft, although much remade and now painted with a brown stain. The same fate of repeated modifications has befallen another, dedicated to the Sagrado Corazón in San Agustín. Somewhat related but without fluting on the shafts are the disastrously dilapidated altars of the Crucifix and the Virgen del Carmen in La Merced.

Early adoption of the spiral column marks two lateral altars in Trujillo Cathedral, one devoted to paintings of the four Evangelists and the other dedicated to St. John the Baptist. The latter is accompanied by paintings of the four Fathers of the Latin Church. The spiral shafts carry no carved ornament and they rise from a band with cartouche similar to the works just discussed. This early stage, really one of transition, probably occurred about 1665. The columns in the second story are identical with those of the choir stalls in the same cathedral and without swags. This combination of two sorts of columns in different stories is typical of retables of the period everywhere, and does not imply that the separate stories were pieced together from different structures.[54]

No one seems to have noticed that the life-sized statue of St. John the Baptist in the central niche of his altar is a good work of the Andalusian school of the mid-seventeenth century, by a follower of Martínez Montañés. The brutal daubing of the statue by a recent house painter has obscured the importance of this sculpture. The bust of the Dolorosa on the predella is lovely and undamaged. The rose of her robe and the blue and gold of her cope maintain the best technique of polychromed sculpture.

The relative flatness in the design of the eighteenth-century retables of Trujillo is a feature which distinguishes them from other works of the type in Peru. From the broad flat wall of the structure, columns are set forth, and niches are stepped back in recess. By contrast, in Lima, Cuzco, and elsewhere the planes shift constantly. The center may project, and numerous transitions are established by the moving back and forth of cornices and subordinate columns. This flatness of the basic design is then a local feature of Trujillo. The broad exposed surfaces are cut with repeated patterns which add again to the general effect of single plane.

Chronology is the most difficult problem in the Trujillian school of sculpture. Only two monuments are dated: the high altars of Santa Teresa (1759) and of San Lorenzo (1774). Hence a provisional chronology is established here on the basis of comparison with the schools of Lima and Cuzco. By the discovery of documents, later historians may prove it to be erroneous in part, since local conditions often vary radically. Witness the great gap in the dates of the retables at Ayacucho.

The high altar of San Francisco may be placed in the first quarter of the eighteenth century, although it could be slightly earlier. The division of the spiral shafts into four registers (Fig. 340) has precedent at Lima, for instance in the altar of San Francisco Xavier, in San Pedro (Fig. 325), and in several others. To repeat, the striking distinction from the school of Lima is the broad flat surface of the Trujillian composition. Just possibly, there were decorative shields upon the cornices in San Francisco at Trujillo which might have been destroyed in the earthquake of 1759. The very large deep central niche with the Madonna is without precedent in Peru. A similar arrangement exists in the high altar of the Compañía at Quito. The whole middle section has been subjected to modern alterations in neocolonial style, including the tabernacle which is new. Hence, to draw final conclusions is dangerous. The top region has been somewhat pieced together, but it certainly never had a third story, local speculations notwithstanding, for the vault of the sanctuary is too low. The two Franciscans in the upper niches are fine colonial statues; the rest are either modern or much redressed.

In far better condition is the high altar of Santo Domingo, a church which has been reopened to the cult after years of inactivity. Fluted spiral columns are separated in the lower third from the leaf-covered upper section by a crown. The composition builds up effectively to St. Dominic over the tabernacle and to the meeting of Saints Dominic and Francis at the top. Three identical figures of the Trinity complete the iconography. The two saints in the upper niches are excellent, whereas, as usual, the saints in the first row of niches have been badly repainted and decked out in real clothes.

Many details of the altar are excellent, as for instance, the charmingly naïve Madonna of the Rosary at the lower left (Fig. 341). Splendid as it is, and interesting in detail, the composition of the whole manifests provinciality, placing the altar well below the best of Lima, Cuzco, Ayacucho, and even small cities.

Two large retables in the transept of San Francisco are without parallel in other schools of Peru. Instead of statues or paintings, they contain series of carved reliefs. Precedent for this treatment exists commonly in Spain in the Gothic, Renaissance, and Baroque periods.[55] The closest analogues in Spanish art of the eighteenth century are the splendid retables with spiral columns and elliptical reliefs at Arenys de Mar, Palafugell, and Cadaquers in Catalonia.[56] Whatever other works of the type were produced in Peru have passed into the great beyond. Hence, if for no other reason, the Franciscan altars are worthy of note. The one in the right transept is dedicated to the Passion of Christ (Fig. 342). The crucifix hangs in the principal niche of trefoil shape. The Last Supper, Christ Before Pilate, the Flagellation, the Ecce Homo, and the Via Dolorosa are the subjects of the reliefs. Prints may have provided the compositions, some of which are archaic enough to have been late Gothic. The Last Supper is Mannerist, more or less in the period of Ribalta's painting in the Colegio del Patriarca, Valencia.[57]

The retable in the right transept, dedicated to the Madonna, presents her statue in the tabernacle. Her life is told by the conventional episodes: her Birth, her Presentation in the Temple, the Annunciation, the Visitation, her Assumption. With the exception of the Assumption, the compositions are unmistakably of late-Gothic origin. Again engravings were undoubtedly the source, indicated by iconography and composition.

These two retables are by the same master. His provincialism is still more apparent in the reliefs than in the architecture. In Spain they would be vaguely classified as Hispano-Flemish, *circa* 1510, although the iconography of some scenes is later. Flatness and lack of Baroque exuberance again impress the spectator. The grape and vine upon the surfaces as well as upon the spiral columns might have been copied from books or prints. They are neither pictorial nor sculptural, and rather halting and stilted. It may sound as though these monuments were being consigned to a contemptible category. They are not. They are impressive decorative structures when seen in their setting. They are not important works of art.

The same workshop produced the high altar of Santiago de Huamán, a suburb of Trujillo. Four reliefs of the Passion (Arrest of Christ, Christ Before Pilate, Ecce Homo, Gethsemane) have been placed in a modernized setting. The original salomonic tabernacle now embellishes a lateral altar.[58]

The masterpiece of the Trujillian school is the high altar of the cathedral (Fig. 160), very ingeniously composed to suit its elevated location in a sanctuary which has a transverse aisle behind it. The altar rises like a screen at the end of a vista, in two stories of open arches, the statues silhouetted against the light of day at the rear (Figs. 343, 344; frontispiece, plate section). Below on either side of the tabernacle are Saints Peter and John the Evangelist. Above them is the *Purísima*, accompanied by St. Rose and St. Stephen. The bodies of the first two saints in fine blue, gold, and red polychromy sway and swing in an ecstatic outburst of Baroque emotion. For this type of art, they have no equal in Peruvian colonial sculpture. They are indeed unforgettable, and are in good condition except for some repaint on the head of St. Peter. Among the other statues, the *Purísima* seems to be the only one which might be contemporary with the original altar. The architectural setting is beautifully conceived and with great originality. The slim spiral columns have the familiar grape-and-vine decoration. Here some of the gilding has been retouched but with discretion. The beholder must, of course, discount the electric-light bulbs, the plants, paper flowers, and other regalia. Through these he must penetrate to comprehend one of the finest expressions of Baroque genius in Hispanic colonial art.

The exact date for the high altar of the cathedral is difficult to establish. It might have originated at any time during the first half of the eighteenth century. Very possibly it was part of the extensive restoration and redecoration of the church in 1738.[59]

Although the victim of refurbishings and pseudoclassical additions, the high altar of Santa Clara could be returned to its original state without much difficulty. The altar of the Crucifixion (Fig. 346) at the side is in good condition, if one discounts the bad repaint of pink and blue on the statues. The lower part has been regilded and some pieces replaced, but they match the original. These two altars in Santa Clara are by the same master and of very high quality. The rosette type of spiral column was the one preferred by him, and he displays originality in the handling of the background, consisting of the stylized leaf in a rectangle, placed in repeated rows.

The fine crucifix is older than its setting, for it resembles the model established by Martínez Montañés in the early seventeenth century. It is not a creation of the famous Spanish sculptor, but one influenced by his work.

The master of Santa Clara is also the author of a large retable in the right transept of La Merced. Only the architectural setting and one colonial relief in the upper center still exist. An inscription, the last cipher of which is missing, places the altar in the seventeen forties. Hence this bit of evidence helps corroborate a dating of the Santa Clara retables and similar works in the fifth decade of the century. The convent of Franciscan nuns was founded in 1743.[60] That fact and the style of the sculpture leave no problems about the chronology unanswered. Another altar related to those under discussion is the one in La Merced, dedicated to the Madonna, and now painted black.

A very beautiful retable, with some suggestions of primitivism in the hard precise outlines of the ornament, is that of Nuestra Señora del Rosario (Fig. 345) in Santo Domingo. It has a lavish splendor about it, and is rather bizarre with its large voluted cupolas over the three niches of the first story. The reticulated background is more prominent here than in the case of the Crucifixion in Santa Clara. The sections alternate between grapes and leaves. The statues comprise the Baptist, Saints Joseph and Elizabeth in the upper register, with Joachim, Mary, and Anna below. St. John the Baptist represents an attempt to copy the fine prototype in the cathedral, formerly discussed. The altar of the Rosary is hard to place, although in certain technical features it most closely resembles the transept retables of San Francisco. For some reason, it makes a more vivid impression than any work of its type in Trujillo. Photographs do it little justice.

The high altar of Santa Teresa (Fig. 347) is signed and dated by an inscription cut in the predella. It was carved by a man with an Indian name, Fernando Collao, and completed in 1759.[61] Collao is the *quechua* designation for the region of Puno, and this may signify that he came from there, although his art gives no indication of that fact. The whole middle section has been ruined by the insertion of a neoclassic silver tabernacle and a gilt niche above, as recently as 1920.[62] The original tabernacle is said to be the one now located in the high altar of San Lorenzo and to judge by the style and the presence of the Carmelite shield, it must be so.

Fernando Collao's art is accomplished and mature, not unlike contemporary creations in Lima, Arequipa, and Ayacucho. His design is richly laden with an interplay of stepped moldings, and leaf-and-rosette *salomónicas*. Dominant and subordinate themes are well correlated. The candelabra upon the columns provide an unusual touch, and one wonders if they ever ran the risk of placing lighted tapers there, however lovely would have been the effect. The borders of open patterns which run above the entablatures are broad and florid, as they are in Lima and Ayacucho in the first half of the century. As for the statues, only those in the two upper niches have escaped replacement.

Collao's style can also be traced in some of the lateral altars in the church of Santa Teresa. Of far greater import is the probability that he was also the author of the high altar of San Agustín. The composition is the same as that of Santa Teresa, particularly in the arrangement of the main and subordinate niches. Details of ornament in the rosette type of spiral column and in the moldings are closely akin, although not identical (Figs. 348, 349). No comparison can be made between the central sections of the two works in view of its nonexistence in the Carmelite church. That portion surrounding St. Augustine in the other instance breaks with the commonplace. The statue of the founder of the order is set forth with dramatic emphasis as the curving pediments and the large central space act like a large frame about him. The *Purísima* in the tabernacle is the only modern intrusion, the Augustinians being, one and all, fine statues of polychromed wood. Among the large retables in the city, these of Santa Teresa and San Agustín are very significant.

The most original, next to the cathedral's high altar, is, however, the principal retable of San Lorenzo (Figs. 350, 351). Here, at a time when the rococo began to sweep away the Hispanic tradition, is a highly ingenious and original creation which proves the exception to the general rule. Instead of a dull and misunderstood adaptation of a foreign style, it is altogether charming. The columns are composed of rows of urns, and upon the face of each a shell or formalized plant. Similar effects in the high altars of San Sebastián and La Concepción at Lima (Figs. 335, 336) were uninteresting. The large closed tabernacle enshrining the dedicatory statue is the dominant note in the structure. Rococo motives are subordinated to a well-organized and comparatively quiet scheme. The Carmelite shield on the tabernacle indicates that it was transferred here from Santa Teresa. The spiral columns very clearly do not belong to this altar. The nondescript statues have been collected together without much regard for the size of the niches. St. Lawrence at the lower left is the exception, and he is the patron of the church. The statue is very expressive from the emotional point of view, notwithstanding the cloth vestments. The saint is well posed, and the head and the face have an intense expression of spiritual exaltation. Surprises such as the originality displayed in this altar are rare and appreciated. An inscription upon the lower section states that it was the gift of Bishop Francisco Xavier de Luna Victoria and that Manuel García gilded it in 1774.[63]

The bust-caryatid altar, a favorite medium of the rococo style, enjoyed considerable popularity in Trujillo. These works are for the most part mediocre, and they have already been mentioned in connection with the appearance of the type in Lima.[64]

CAJAMARCA AND THE REGION OF LAKE TITICACA

ONE other work which even surpasses the altar of San Lorenzo at Trujillo in originality and imagination at a period of creative decline is the high altar of Cajamarca Cathedral (Figs. 352, 354). It should be dated contemporary with the consecration of the church in 1762, and hence in the heyday of rococo influence. The French style blends into the Hispanic tradition with extraordinary success to produce a retable of great beauty. Most unusual and spirited ornaments are the pilasters resembling musical notes. The rococo curves are light and gay. The same mood carries throughout the swinging rippling movement of the attic story and in the flat patterns about the niches. The excellent gilding adds to the brilliance of this fine piece of decorative architecture. The only colonial statue still remaining in the altar is that of San Francisco Solano to the upper right. The original tabernacle has been replaced by a poor thing in imitation of marble.

Few retables have been preserved in the region of Lake Titicaca. Those of belated Renaissance style in La Asunción at Juli have already been studied. A monument for which no extant parallel exists is the high altar of San Juan at Juli (Fig. 356). Undoubtedly others of similar type have been lost in earthquakes at Lima, Arequipa, and Cuzco. Hence this Jesuit altar has more than usual interest because it is the unique representative of a body of lost works. The columns have plain gilded shafts, and they are surmounted by a provincial Corinthian capital having three rows of acanthus leaves instead of the orthodox two. The voluted hoods and beaded pilasters of the niches are handled in a restrained manner suggestive of the period about 1650. In addition to the dignified architectural setting, the polychromed reliefs of wood maintain a superior level of quality. The sculptor must have been one of the leading artists of his day and possibly Spanish by birth. The Apparition of Christ to St. Ignatius reveals a highly skilled technician in the modeling of the bodies of Christ and the cherubs. The figure of St. Ignatius is competent, but not inspired. On the opposite side of the retable, the relief portrays the Apparition of the Madonna to the Jesuit founder. Three figures, grouped in simple poses, tell the story with the direct naturalism of Spanish Baroque art.

The *mestizo* style has left its mark upon one important retable, that of the famous church dedicated to Santiago at Pomata (Figs. 353, 355). By good fortune a document exists showing that it was completed in 1722.[65] Most exotic of all are the capitals of serpent heads whose snouts turn into volutes. The scale motive decorates their necks. This predilection for the fantastic is native to the Indian mind, as the art of the pre-Columbian period so vividly displays. The same capitals recur upon the pulpit and the high altar of La Asunción at Yunguyo. One master was active in the creation of these wood sculptures in neighboring villages upon the shores of Lake Titicaca. The long coiling body of the serpent or whale is intertwined with grapes, papaya, and pomegranates at each side of the retable at Pomata. Only the monkeys and birds, which the sculptors of stone at Juli and Pomata introduced with such gay decorative abandon, are missing here. The other features of the retable are more conventional, although the twisted column rising from a beaded spiral base is of a type common fifty years earlier. The tabernacle of the Madonna is modern and some colonial alterations are detected in the attic story. Again the superiority of the architectural and decorative design to the pictures is consistent with general conditions of colonial art.

The retables of colonial Peru are set in luxuriant richness against the sober interiors of Baroque churches. In Cuzco particularly, the stern Andean stone and the severe Herreresque architectural traditions provide a restrained setting for the splendor of gilded altars and ecclesiastical furniture. This combination of power and sobriety in the architecture with sensuous richness in decoration is unforgettable in churches such as the cathedral, La Compañía, El Belén, and La Merced in Cuzco.

The decorative handling of an architectural interior is rare in Peru, far less frequent than in Spain or Mexico. The *mudéjar* ornament upon the walls of San Francisco and La Merced at Lima, the diamond points within El Belén at Cajamarca, and the lavish *mestizo* ornament of stone in the churches at Pomata and Juli are the exception rather than the rule. In all of these cases the gilded retables are correspondingly less significant than elsewhere.

The unity established between architectural decoration and the altars of gilded wood, so noteworthy in Mexican churches like Santa Prisca at Taxco and the Jesuit church at Tepoztlán, has no exact counterpart in Peru. The interior of Santo Cristo de los Milagros at Lima was designed as a complete and harmonious whole, but in the rococo style, and hence not comparable with the lavish decoration of the late Mexican development. The eighteenth-century altars in which the pilasters take the shape of an inverted pyramid (estípite) originated in Andalusian Spain, and they became the established type in Mexico during that century. Peru, on the contrary, shifted from the late Baroque altar with spiral columns to the rococo phase in the mid-eighteenth century, never partaking in the estípite development. There in the first half of the century the richly laden salomonic altars of Ayacucho, Lima, and Trujillo are the final stage of a style which began in Spain about 1650. The last seventy-five years of the colonial period brought a decline from the previous high standards. Rococo ornament and white paint marked a change in taste which ultimately led to the Neoclassic and the final abandonment of the Hispanic Baroque.

FIGURE SCULPTURE

FIGURE sculpture never attained an importance in Peru comparable with the decorative effect of retables, pulpits, and choir stalls. In these monuments themselves the statues of saints and the reliefs rarely equal the quality of their setting. The statues of the high altar of La Compañía at Cuzco (Figs. 318, 319) are exceptional in that respect.

The medium of colonial sculpture is usually polychromed wood, thus continuing the Spanish medieval and Baroque traditions. Upon the coat of plaster applied to the wood, gold leaf and flesh tints are laid.[66] Red, blue, and green constitute the basic colors of the costumes except those of the monastic saints. In these cases the habit of the order established the scheme to be followed. Even so, some latitude is allowed the artist. The Jesuit saints in Cuzco, for instance, are partly gilded, to add brilliance to their black frocks.

A second type of statue is that in which garments of cloth, reënforced with plaster (tela enyesada), are superimposed upon the wooden image. This technique was widely adopted in the Spanish colonies. It fulfilled the realistic mood and had the virtue of pliability. When well designed and well painted, works of this sort may be almost as effective as others in a more durable medium. The statue of St. Anne (Fig. 357) in San Francisco de Paula at Ayacucho is very lovely in color. She wears a rose dress and a gold mantle. If not carefully protected, however, the cloth may become torn and deteriorated in general. Polychromed statues of wood and heavy cloth are not new to the Spanish colonies, but are, on the contrary, a medieval survival. Some Romanesque and Gothic sculptures of the type have come down to the present day. A superb Spanish work of the fourteenth century, in the museum at Worcester, Massachusetts, still retains its fine gold polychromy upon the heavy cloth and wood. Even great Spanish masters of the seventeenth century like Martínez Montañés occasionally used this medium.

Most common of all in Hispanic America are dressed images (*imágenes de vestir*). The great vogue for them reached its height in the mother country and the colonies in the seventeenth century. The heads, hands, and feet of these works are carved in wood. The rest of the statue is a clothes model upon which real garments are placed. The custom developed from the great popularity of religious processions in which statues are driven through the streets upon floats or carried upon the backs of men. A favorite cult image had and has a large wardrobe which includes costumes for various occasions. Since the wardrobe is constantly refurbished throughout the centuries, the costumes worn by these images today rarely are more than one hundred and fifty years old.

The passion for reality in contemporary Hispanic Catholicism is so great that the tendency is to put real clothes on all statues. Good works of art are thus disguised. Crucifixes are generally dressed with long skirts, and wigs of false hair are placed upon the heads. No complete study of colonial sculpture can be made until some enterprising scholar is able to secure permission to divest images of their robes and photograph them. The statue of St. Francis (Fig. 358) in the sacristy of his church at Cuzco is a fine example of the ecstatic and contemplative mood of religious art of the seventeenth century. The saint meditates upon the crucifix and upon death, symbolized by the skull. The robe of costly embroidered velvet, made fifty years ago, and the later halo are superior to the usual. How much more effective, nevertheless, an original statue unadorned can be, is seen by a comparison with the kneeling St. Francis in La Compañía (Fig. 359). The fact is that the robes of dressed images fall outside of the realm of plastic art, however interesting they may be as costume.

Harder materials such as stone are almost unknown in Peru except in architectural sculpture. Sepulchral monuments, so important in Spain and other European countries in the Baroque period, were not developed in the colonies. The kneeling effigies in Lima Cathedral are exceptions and without particular artistic significance.[67]

A local school at Ayacucho produced quantities of small objects both secular and religious in the soft stone of the region.[68] Huamanga, the colonial name of the district, is still used to distinguish the school and the stone. These works are numerous in private collections and occasionally in churches. An interior chapel of the Franciscan monastery at Ocopa contains an interesting series of small reliefs. These Huamanga carvings belong in the realm of the minor arts and cannot be regarded in the same category as monumental sculpture.

A number of ivory crucifixes, averaging about two feet in length, demonstrate the conviction among colonial peoples as among Europeans that this medium was particularly suitable to the subject. Most of them are carved and designed with primitive rigidity.[69] The small group in the parish church at Ica includes the Madonna and St. John the Evangelist (Fig. 365). The curve in the body of Christ and the distortion of the arms make for a somewhat more brutalized version than usual. The polychromy heightens that impression still more. The decorative richness of the eighteenth-century niche demonstrates the lavishness of the age, although much has been lost in covering the gold with black paint. Other crucifixes follow more closely the Baroque sophistication of European traditions.[70] Because of their ready transportability, crucifixes have also found their way into foreign collections and hence have become familiar to peoples of other lands, whereas far more important products of colonial culture still remain among the unknown.

Cult images, venerated for centuries, exist in abundance throughout Peru. Most of them lack artistic significance and whatever they may possess is hidden under heavy robes and false hair. The Christ Bearing the Cross in Santa Clara at Ayacucho gives the impression of being a splendid work, because of the strength of the face and hands, the only parts of the sculpture which are visible. In remote regions very primitive objects, often dressed in the clothes of native Indians, exist in abundance.[71] They have attained a popularity today entirely out of relation to their true artistic worth, because of the world-wide interest in the expression of primitive peoples and because they appeal to the jaded palate. They are amusing in their ingenuousness, but often no more than that. The

Apparition of the Virgin at Sunturhuasi, a relief in Santa Clara at Cuzco is naïve, and yet the figure of the Virgin is pleasantly handled. The event concerns the miraculous intercession of the Virgin to save the Spanish at Cuzco during an Indian revolt in 1536.[72] The relief has lost some of its character by the modern repaint of recent years.

At the opposite pole from popular cult images are the works imported from Spain. The altar of St. John the Baptist (1607–1612) in La Concepción at Lima, as previously noted, was shipped to the New World by the famous Sevillian sculptor, Martínez Montañés. Many works in Lima and elsewhere have been attributed to him, solely because he is the best-known Spanish sculptor of the Baroque period.[73] In addition to the altar of St. John, he may also be the author of the statue of St. Francis Xavier in San Pedro in Lima. The discovery of the documentation of it by Padre Vargas Ugarte was discussed earlier in the present chapter.

The modern gray paint and various restorations on the retable of St. John the Baptist have diminished greatly but have not destroyed its effectiveness. The crucifix has suffered most, for the loin cloth, usually handled by the artist in a decorative arrangement, has been almost entirely cut away. Padre Vargas Ugarte succeeded in convincing the nuns of the present generation that the Christ should not be dressed in a skirt.

Another splendid crucifix in La Merced (Fig. 360) at Lima has passed almost unnoticed. Known as Nuestro Señor del Auxilio, it hangs in the center of a nineteenth-century altar in which are included five other figures of the Passion of Christ from a retable of the seventeenth century.[74] The crucifix is Sevillian, and I believe from the hand of Martínez Montañés. In the contract of 1603 for the crucifix of Vázquez de Leca, now in the sacristy of Seville Cathedral, the artist agreed to deliver a work better than the one which he had recently shipped to the Indies.[75] The Merced statue must be, it seems to me, that very work. It is characteristic of the master in the type of Christ, the disposition of the drapery, and even in the unusual crossed position of the feet. This latter iconographic detail he repeated in the image he carved for Vázquez de Leca. At first inclined to attribute the Lima sculpture to Juan de Mesa, I changed my opinion completely after doing research upon the problem in Seville. The observations of Antonio Sancho Corbacho were most helpful in reaching what appears a convincing solution. It is also probable that this same statue is the one which Padre Cobo said existed in La Merced at Lima in his day and was known to have come from the hand of the most famous sculptor in Spain.[76] Today it is finer than the Concepción crucifix, because it has suffered less maltreatment, in spite of the modern painting of the head and the daubing of the body with painted streams of blood. This sculpture of polychromed wood is life-sized. Dignity and tragic poignancy combine with fine decorative treatment in the modeling of the body and loin cloth.

The other sculptures of the altar of La Merced at Lima comprise the Christ at the Column, Ecce Homo, Carrying of the Cross, Christ on Gethsemane, and the Pietà. Except for the last, they are single figures. The sculptor's style is more pictorial and at the same time qualitatively far inferior to that of Martínez Montañés. He must have been a local Hispanic artist of the first half of the seventeenth century. On the contrary, the statues of St. John the Baptist and the Mater Dolorosa in Trujillo Cathedral, already mentioned above, must have been imported from Seville, since they betray the style of some follower of Martínez Montañés. The latter's St. John the Baptist in Santa Clara at Seville served as prototype.

Another fine Spanish crucifix of polychromed wood, in this case small in size (.86 cm.), stands in the sacristy of La Recoleta at Cuzco. Only the crown of thorns is modern. The style suggests that it may have been carved in Seville in the second half of the seventeenth century. The mood is one of intense suffering and agitation, unlike the calm resignation characteristic of Martínez Montañés and Juan de Mesa. The feet are transfixed by two nails instead of one, following the practice approved by Francisco Pacheco.[77] Even though it is much calmer, the crucifix at Mollepata near Cuzco (Fig. 361) strikes the observer as a work inspired by that in the Recoleta. The Mollepata artist was a colonial and not a native Spaniard. He stylized the anatomy, and handled the loin cloth with an almost Gothic linear grace. The state of preservation of this seventeenth-century sculpture is good, and only the modern wig and crown of thorns mar its effectiveness.

The famous cult image in Cuzco Cathedral, known as Christ of the Earthquakes, is reputed to be a Spanish crucifix presented to the city in the sixteenth century by Charles V of Spain. That legend is not substantiated by the sculpture itself, for it is a provincial colonial statue without any particular artistic significance.

The chapel of St. Joseph in Lima Cathedral contains a splendid life-sized group of the Holy Family in polychromed wood sculpture (Fig. 362). The Madonna's costume is painted in rose and gold. St. Joseph wears a red and gold cope over a blue and gold tunic. The Holy Family is composed with dignity and restraint, represented as though walking, with the Christ Child in the middle. The iconography, familiar in Hispanic art of the seventeenth and eighteenth centuries, became especially popular in the painting of the school of Cuzco.[78]

To identify this work with a retable ordered of the sculptor, Martín de Oviedo, in 1602, is tempting but untenable.[79] The terms of the contract demonstrate clearly that it was not the same retable which Echave y Assu mentioned in 1688.[80] The latter speaks of a life-sized group composed of Joseph, Mary, and the Christ Child in the central compartment. His description and the style of the sculpture identify the extant figures as the sole survivors of the large monument which existed in his time. The naturalism and the general technical expertness of the work suggest a Spanish-born master active in the second quarter of the seventeenth century. The Christ Child is surprisingly inferior to the other figures, and it should be remembered that the crowns and halos are later additions.

As previously explained, there is no claim to completeness in the present discussion of figure sculpture. I have intended only to call attention to a few interesting works which are not entirely hidden by heavy modern garments. The life-sized Christ at the Column in the Jesuit church at Ayacucho (Fig. 363) unites a feeling for beauty with a spirit of religious resignation, which is deeply moving. The position of the arms and the slight turn of body still carry a suggestion of Renaissance *contrapposto*, although the sculpture must date from the first half of the seventeenth century. The understanding of anatomy to such a degree as that displayed here indicates an artist of Spanish background. The beard of Christ has been badly painted in recent times. In photographing the work, it was impossible to remove the wig and the brocaded loin cloth.

The superiority of the Ayacucho Christ is evident on comparison with the sadistically bruised Christ at the Column which stands in a passageway to the choir of San Francisco at Cuzco. The latter work does possess, however, some formal organization in its composition, a quality altogether lacking in the grotesquely ugly statue of the same subject in San Agustín at Lima.[81] The nude figure is rarely represented in colonial art, and then without much success. The statue of St. Sebastian in the church of that name at Cuzco is mannered in body and in spirit, shallow and devoid of dignity. In spite of its technical flaws, the St. Jerome in Penitence in San Pedro Mártir at Juli achieves far greater distinction. The seriousness of his mood is unmistakable.

The persistence of the medieval liturgical play took on a national character in Spain, where sculptured scenes of the Passion of Christ were carried through the streets during Holy Week. The altar of the Descent from the Cross in San Juan at Juli is one of these colonial *pasos,* although it is stationary and hence apparently never transported in procession. The medium is polychromed wood and plastered cloth. Discounting the loss of parts of the costumes by the women in the center, the action constitutes a highly dramatic and vividly stirring presentation. No claim for the altar as a great work of art can be proposed. Living reality was the aim of the Church in order that the faithful might experience the suffering of Him who died for them.

The Jesuit saints in the high altar of La Compañía at Cuzco (Fig. 319) mark a high point in achievement in colonial sculpture, a fact already remarked. They are designed in broad, tall proportions and the draperies are arranged in heavy deep folds. The artist unhesitatingly exaggerated breadth and depth in the knowledge that the statues were to be located at a great height and distance from the spectator. To dignity of bearing is added an expression of intense spiritual life in the burning fervor of the faces. In the realm of religious ecstasy of the Counter Reformation, the kneeling St. Francis (Fig. 359) in the transept altar of the same church is the most memorable in Peruvian colonial art. The saint is transfixed in a state of rhapsodic exaltation which mounts to a climax as at the conclusion of a symphony. Very

few works more successfully fulfill the aims of religious Baroque art. Another St. Francis in El Belén at Cuzco achieves in a mood of contemplation something of the same dramatic emphasis.

In Chapter XI the famous Indian sculptor and architect, Juan Tomás Tuyru Tupac, was briefly discussed. His statue of the Madonna, dated 1686 and known as Nuestra Señora de la Almudena (Fig. 364), is surprising in its pure and undiluted Hispanicism without suggestion of the author's race or environment.[82] Despite its small size (1.25 m.), the statue is composed with the breadth and monumentality of a life-sized figure. The traditions of the Sevillian Baroque school are fostered here by a man reputedly of noble Indian lineage. The charming statuette of the Immaculate Conception (Fig. 366) in Santa Catalina at Lima with its flounced and billowing cope is gay beside Juan Tomás' grave Madonna. The change of mood from the seventeenth to the eighteenth century is responsible for the contrast in the two works, far more than any difference in the temperaments of the two masters.

The Hispanic colonial age was one of great luxury for the church and the landed gentry. Because of the almost inexhaustible mineral wealth of the New World and the cheapness of Indian labor, few were the limitations placed upon the embellishment of her churches. That was a society which sought splendor, and splendor it achieved.

Appendix

LIMA: CATALOGUE OF MONUMENTS

(Arranged alphabetically)

PRINCIPAL MONUMENTS

Cathedral of Lima
Colegio de Santo Tomás
Corazón de Jesús (Los Huérfanos)
Jesús María
La Merced
San Agustín

San Carlos
San Francisco
San Pedro (La Compañía)
Santa Teresa
Santo Cristo de los Milagros (Las Nazarenas)
Santo Domingo

SECONDARY MONUMENTS

Descalzas de San José
Descalzos Franciscanos
Desemparados
Espíritu Santo
Magdalena la Vieja
Mercedarias
Nuestra Señora del Belén
Nuestra Señora de la Buena Muerte
Nuestra Señora de la Cabeza
Nuestra Señora del Carmen
Nuestra Señora de Cocharcas
Nuestra Señora de la Concepción
Nuestra Señora de Copacabana
Nuestra Señora de la Encarnación
Nuestra Señora de Guadalupe
Nuestra Señora de Guía
Nuestra Señora de Montserrat
Nuestra Señora del Patrocinio
Nuestra Señora del Prado
Nuestra Señora del Rosario

Recoleta Domínica
San Andrés
San Francisco de Paula Nuevo
San Francisco de Paula Viejo
San Ildefonso
San Lázaro
San Lorenzo
San Marcelo
San Pedro Nolasco
San Sebastián
Santa Ana
Santa Catalina
Santa Clara
Santa Liberata
Santa Rosa de las Monjas
Santa Rosa de los Padres
Santiago del Cercado
Surco
La Trinidad
Las Trinitarias

LIMA: CATALOGUE OF PRINCIPAL MONUMENTS

Cathedral of Lima

Historically the cathedral of Lima holds first place among the churches of the city, but the present edifice has very slight architectural worth, much less than many humble village churches in the mountains which still retain their colonial beauty. It is necessary, however, to recount the long and tedious story of the first cathedral of Peru, to enumerate the repeated earthquakes which have so often destroyed it and the still more numerous rebuildings and restorations which have been scarcely less disastrous.[1]

The first small church which stood upon this site was inaugurated in 1540, only to be raised to the rank of cathedral three years later. A humble structure of wood and adobe, it gave way to the second building in 1551. Still small and of a single nave, it was provided with a *capilla mayor* of stone which was built with funds donated by Francisco Pizarro's daughter. The kingdom of Peru was growing apace, however, and soon a colossal church of three naves was projected to rival the most celebrated cathedrals of Spain. Alonso Beltrán, the *maestro mayor*, presented the plan in 1565, and on an unspecified date between 1569 and 1575 the first stone was laid by the first archbishop, Jerónimo de Loayza, in the presence of the famous viceroy, Francisco de Toledo.[2] Very little seems to have been accomplished, and soon Beltrán's plans were replaced by those of another architect, whose career is of such importance that it will be necessary to digress to discuss it.

Among all of the Spanish architects who came to the New World in the sixteenth century, Francisco Becerra had the most notable career. Only Claudio de Arciniega in Mexico might be considered a near rival. Documents relating to him were first mentioned by Ceán Bermúdez well over a hundred years ago,[3] and recently his biography has been much amplified by Marco Dorta, Padre Vargas Ugarte, and Harth-terré.[4] Knowledge of his life rests chiefly upon the documents presented in court at Lima when he sought the title of chief architect of the kingdom of Peru in 1585. The originals preserved in the Archivo de Indias at Seville were published in some detail by Marco Dorta. Becerra was born at Herguijuela near Trujillo in Spain of a family of architects, his father having practiced that profession as well as his grandfather, who had been *maestro mayor* of Toledo Cathedral. When still young he worked on the church of Santa María, the chapels of Santa Isabel in Trujillo and later built a chapel in the cloister of the famous monastery of Guadalupe. In 1573 he obtained permission to go to the New World, and set sail for Mexico accompanied by his wife. There he appears as *maestro mayor* of the cathedral of Puebla in 1575, and according to his own testimony given in Lima ten years later, he designed and began that church. Diego Angulo is probably right, however, that the plan is more likely by Claudio de Arciniega who worked in Puebla and made the plan of the cathedral of Mexico City.[5] The two churches are very nearly twins. Becerra also was employed in Puebla on the churches of San Francisco, Santo Domingo, San Agustín, and the Colegio de San Luis. He mentions activities on the church of Santo Domingo, Mexico City, and in the villages of Teotimehuacán, Cuautinchán, Tlalneplantla, in Cuernavaca, and in the "Marquesado de Tepoztlán." It is reasonable to suspect that many of these projects were of no great significance, but they make an imposing list. Dr. Kubler holds that none of the Mexican churches as they stand today, except Puebla Cathedral, shows any vestiges of Becerra's intervention.[6] About 1580 Becerra turned up in Quito, Ecuador, as architect of Santo Domingo and San Agustín, the ground plans of which are undoubtedly his. The latter has a Latin-cross plan with side chapels and the former a nave and two aisles with projecting transept. In both cases the elevated choir is used and Santo Domingo preserves its magnificent *mudéjar* ceiling of the sixteenth century. Becerra also built three bridges and lived a year in Pichincha.

The next and important step in Becerra's career came in the year 1582 when the viceroy Martín Enríquez, whom he had known in Mexico, called him to Lima from Cuzco where he had been residing. By his own testimony we know that Becerra made plans for two cathedrals, Cuzco and Lima, at the specific command of the viceroy. Whoever studies without bias the ground plans and type of pier of the two churches can arrive only at one conclusion: that they are the creation of the same architect and that despite numerous modifications and reconstructions, the original project of Becerra survives in both cases. On June 17, 1584, the title of *maestro mayor* of Lima Cathedral was officially confirmed, but the following year Becerra failed in his attempt to be called chief architect of Peru. He did, however, secure the office of architect of the city, and in that capacity he worked on the viceregal palace and the fort at Callao. Other official opportunities still on record include the plan for the church of San Sebastián, many times rebuilt since, and the portal of the house of a man named Ferrer de Ayala.[7]

To return to Lima Cathedral, although Becerra took charge in 1582, very little had been accomplished until the new viceroy, Luis de Velasco, finally ordered a reduction of its size to about half that originally intended. New plans (Fig. 8) were drawn for both Lima and Cuzco in 1598, and by 1604 half of the church at Lima was ready for dedication.[8]

This church of Becerra's had groined vaults without any decoration, on the word of Padre Cobo to whom is due the major part of our knowledge of the religious architecture of Lima in the early seventeenth century. The arches were pointed and all of equal height, a scheme sarcastically derided as bad construction by a rival architect Fray Jerónimo de Villegas.[9] A very old tradition holds that the plan of Lima Cathedral is modeled on that of Seville, a completely erroneous notion still frequently repeated.[10] As a matter of fact the court, called the Patio de los Naranjos, on the right side at Lima is the only imitation of Seville Cathedral. The hall type and the disposition of the floor plan are derived from the cathedral of Jaén, a problem discussed in greater detail in Chapter IV.

Hardly had the church been opened for worship when the earthquake of 1606 damaged the vaults severely, as Padre Cobo relates. It was followed by still another in 1609. Several architects were consulted for their opinions as to the best way to reconstruct and complete the edifice. Among them were Alonso de Arenas, Pedro Blasco, Juan del Cerro, Juan del Corral, Clemente de Mansilla, Antonio Mayordomo, and Jerónimo de Villegas.[11] Becerra is not among them, since he had died four years previously, on April 29, 1605.[12] Villegas submitted a denunciation of Francisco Becerra's church and haughtily rejected the suggestion of wooden vaults, the solution which finally had to be accepted for all *limeño* architecture. Juan Martínez de Arrona, the *maestro mayor*, favored Gothic ribbed vaults of brick in his report of 1613.

At length it was decided to reduce the height of the piers and employ Gothic vaults in the hope they would better withstand the earthquakes.[13] Construction then went forward rapidly and Padre Cobo was able to report in 1629 that the church had been finished in 1622, the towers in 1624, and that the portals and choir stalls were in progress. This building which in its plan exists today involved a complete modification of Becerra's vaults but retained his floor plan.

Vázquez de Espinosa, who lived in Lima in 1619–1620, describes the church, mentioning its Gothic vaults and Ionic piers, and Córdoba Salinas in an unpublished manuscript specifically refers to the same features.[14] Hence it can be assumed that the extant church is a faithful reproduction of this monument of 1613–1622, reërected in wood and plaster after the earthquake of 1746.

Seven portals of the cathedral were projected in 1626 by Juan Martínez de Arrona whose drawing for the main entrance on the plaza was discovered by Harth-terré in the notary's contract.[15] The interesting fact is that the first story except for the entablature still preserves the design of 1626 in spite of repeated rebuildings, the latest in 1942–1945. The style is early

Baroque but with a strong classic flavor in the handling of the Corinthian columns. The design of the niches and the peculiar tongued ornament, however, belong to Baroque vocabulary. The second story of the portal is clearly dated by inscription (*Reedificóse año 1722*). Although the style of its rusticated walls and lavishly ornamented center does not correspond to the lower section, the general effect is satisfactory. The entablature of the first as well as of the second story dates from this period. Little can be said for the dull neoclassic statues in the niches which were imported from Europe about 1870 (Figs. 104, 105).[16]

A major catastrophe was the great earthquake of 1687 when nearly all of the city fell in ruin. A plan with date 1696 which is preserved in the Archivo de Indias and a report of 1704 show that the vaults of the *capilla mayor* and neighboring bays collapsed, but damage was not as extensive as first accounts seemed to indicate. The vaults of the crossing and three adjoining bays even at this time were made of wood, possibly dating from 1630.[17] The second story of the main portal, as previously stated, was rebuilt in late Baroque style, corresponding to the date, 1722, inscribed in the center of it. To the same period belong the rear portals of San Cristóbal and Santa Apolonia on both of which are inscribed the name of the viceroy, the Marqués de Castellfuerte, and the year 1732 (Fig. 113).

The final *coup de grâce* was given to the seventeenth-century cathedral in the great earthquake of 1746. The towers fell, the vaults of the nave and of some of the chapels,[18] and so complete was the destruction that only the outside walls could be utilized. The main portal had to be dismantled and rebuilt with the same stones. This time they decided to use wood of Guayaquil for the piers, arches, and vaults,[19] but work was not begun until 1751 with a Jesuit from Bohemia, named Juan de Rher, in charge.[20] Four years later the building had sufficiently advanced to permit its return to religious services, an event celebrated with great festivity.[21] Fortunately a plan of the church and a report by Salvador de Villa are preserved in the Archivo de Indias with explicit information about the progress of the reconstruction and also drawings for the towers by Pedro Antonio de Molina, dated 1794.[22] The latter were added in 1794–1797.

Thus the present fabric of the cathedral of Lima (Figs. 91, 103, 104) belongs entirely to the second half of the eighteenth century, barring numerous subsequent restorations. In 1895–1897 the wood of the vaults was renewed and presumably painted in the manner which prevails at present, the ribs gilded and the surface of the vaults in blue and rose. The worst damage was done, however, in the destruction of the *trascoro* and transference of the choir stalls to the sanctuary. This change resulted in the disappearance of the chapel of St. Bartholomew by its inclusion in the *capilla mayor*. The retables today are in the main works of the nineteenth century with the only notable exception that of the *Inmaculada*. Several were destroyed in the earthquake of 1746, and many others were burned by the Neoclassicists.[23]

The interior of Lima Cathedral today is a dismal sight with its painted wooden vaults, its wood and plaster piers topped by gilded semi-Ionic volutes, its dreary neo-Gothic confessionals of oak, and its mediocre retables. There is scarcely a suggestion, save in ground plan, shape of piers and Ionic capitals, of that magnificent edifice described in great detail by Echave y Assu just prior to the earthquake of 1687.[24] Of the lavish array in retables and sculpture little has survived the fury of nature and the stupidity of man. Today there re-

main from the seventeenth century only the choir stalls, the *Apostolado* in the sacristy, and a sculptured group of the Holy Family.

The exterior of Lima Cathedral has suffered less than the interior, although it too has been frequently restored. In 1895–1897 the windows were pointed to suit the Gothic mania. Earlier the portal in the Calle de Judíos had been redressed in neo-Renaissance fashion. After the severe earthquake of 1940, the restoration completed in 1945 included resurfacing of the entire exterior and a replacement of all of the masonry and sculpture of the main portal with modern replicas.

The façade of the cathedral which stands on the plaza is frankly in very bad scale, due to the oversized towers and their extraordinarily ugly profile. The story of Lima Cathedral is a sad one, rich in history, but the building is now utterly impoverished of architectural merit.

The Sagrario, which stands at the left of the cathedral, is a church of single nave and slightly projecting transept, with dome over the crossing. It was begun in 1663 under the direction of a Dominican, Fray Diego Maroto, then *maestro mayor* of the cathedral, and completed in 1684. Although it withstood the earthquake of 1687, damage was severe in 1746.[25] The present barrel vaults and dome are wooden, like all others in Lima. In 1945 the façade of the Sagrario underwent reconstruction to return it to its pre-nineteenth-century design. The church has suffered too many alterations to hold a place of importance as a colonial monument.

[1] Angulo, Domingo, "La metropolitana de la ciudad de los Reyes," in *Monografías históricas sobre la ciudad de Lima* (Lima, 1935), II, 3–88, is the most complete history of the church; Cobo, Padre Bernabé, *Historia de la fundación de Lima,* written about 1629–1630, and published in *Monografías históricas,* I, is the most important early literary source; Mendiburu, *Diccionario,* VII (1933), 437–453.

[2] Angulo, Domingo, *op. cit.*, pp. 10–12. Vargas Ugarte, *Ensayo de un diccionario*, p. 61.

[3] Llaguno y Amírola, *Noticias de los arquitectos, con Adiciones de Ceán Bermúdez* (Madrid, 1829), III, 56–58.

[4] Marco Dorta, Enrique, "Arquitectura colonial, Francisco Becerra," *Archivo español de arte*, XVI (1943), 7–15; Vargas Ugarte, "Notas para un diccionario de artífices virreinales," *Cuaderno de Estudios*, Universidad Católica, Lima, II (1942), 152, 185; Harth-terré, "Francisco Becerra," *Comercio de la tarde* (Lima), April 26, 1944; *Comercio de la mañana*, Jan. 1, 1945; *Artífices*, pp. 69–87.

[5] Angulo, Diego, "Las catedrales mexicanas del siglo XVI," *Bol. Real Acad. de His.*, Madrid, CXIII (1943), 137–81; also *Historia del arte hispano-americano*, I, 429–438

[6] Kubler, George, *Mexican Architecture of the Sixteenth Century*, pp. 123–124.

[7] *Cabildos de Lima* (Lima, 1942), X, 82; Schofield, Sophy, *Indices, 1535–1601*, p. 451; Harth-terré, *Artífices*, pp. 73–74.

[8] Cobo, *op. cit.*, p. 145; Marco Dorta, *Archivo español de arte*, XVI (1943), 14.

[9] Vargas Ugarte, "Notas," p. 185; Martínez de Arrona also opposed the retention of the hall plan; Angulo, Domingo, "La metropolitana," p. 67.

[10] Echave y Assu, *Estrella de Lima* (Antwerp, 1688), pp. 47–48; Montalvo, Francisco Antonio, *El sol del Nuevo Mundo* (Rome, 1683), p. 44; Angulo, Domingo, *op. cit.*, pp. 9, 17.

[11] Vargas Ugarte, "Notas," pp. 161, 165, 169, 174, 177, 185; both Villegas and Juan del Corral in 1609 named Becerra as the author of the cathedral. The latter said, "A los demás reparos que se deben enmendar a la traza que hizo Francisco Becerra que está ya plantada en superficie," Harth-terré, *Comercio de la tarde* (Lima), April 26, 1944; Vargas Ugarte, *Ensayo de un diccionario*, pp. 281–282.

[12] Lohmann Villena, *Historia del arte dramático en Lima durante el virreinato* (Lima, 1941), p. 98.

[13] Vargas Ugarte, "Notas," p. 176; Cobo, *op. cit.*, p. 146. Vargas Ugarte, *Ensayo de un diccionario*, pp. 199–200.

[14] Vázquez de Espinosa, *op. cit.*, pp. 430–431; Córdoba Salinas, "Teatro de la Santa Iglesia metropolitana . . . Lima," folio 8 reverse (manuscript dated 1650 in New York Public Library).

[15] Harth-terré, "Imafronte de la catedral de Lima," *Arquitecto peruano*, June, 1941. Work on the portals was presumably continued by Pedro de Noguera after Martínez de Arrona's death in 1635. The stone was quarried at Cañete in 1625 and not imported from Panama as usually stated. Vargas Ugarte, "Notas," p. 287.

[16] García Irigoyen, Manuel, *Historia de la catedral de Lima* (Lima, 1898), p. 70.

[17] Angulo, Diego, *Planos de monumentos*, pl. 25, pp. 652–658; Angulo, Domingo, "El terremoto del año de 1687," *Revista del Archivo Nacional del Perú*, XII (1939), 10, 141. The architects in charge of the reconstruction when it began in 1693 were Fray Cristóbal Caballero, Juan Iñigo de Eraso, and Alonso Pérez. Harth-terré, "La catedral de Lima," *Arquitecto peruano*, May, 1941.

[18] Mendiburu, *Diccionario*, article on Manso de Velasco, ed. 1935, VII, 169; Odriozola, *Terremotos* (Lima, 1863).

[19] *Memorias de los Virreyes* (Lima, 1859), IV, 121–122. Letter of Manso de Velasco.

[20] Vargas Ugarte, "Notas," pp. 193–194.

[21] Angulo, Domingo, *op. cit.*, pp. 75–76.

[22] Angulo, Diego, *Planos*, pls. 202–204, pp. 738–747. The ground plan was first published by Torre Revello, "De arquitectura colonial," *Revista Azul*, II (1931), 55.

[23] Angulo, Domingo, *op. cit.*, pp. 83 ff., gives in considerable detail the numerous changes which have taken place in the cathedral; also García Irigoyen, *Historia*, pp. 68 ff.

[24] Echave y Assu, *op. cit.*, pp. 44–123.

[25] Vargas Ugarte, "Notas," p. 175; Angulo, Domingo, *op. cit.*, pp. 22, 41; Mugaburu, *op. cit.*, II, 157. Vargas Ugarte, *Ensayo de un diccionario*, pp. 195–197.

Colegio de Santo Tomás

The Dominican college of St. Thomas of Aquinas, since its establishment in the mid-seventeenth century, has undergone many transformations. In recent years it served as a prison for women, and at present it is under restoration after the earthquake of 1940 with the intention of converting it into a museum of colonial art. This extremely unusual and interesting structure certainly merits preservation.

The original manuscript of the constitution of the college, which is to be found in the archives of Santo Domingo, Lima, is dated 1650, and it states that the foundation of the institution was effected by Andrés Cintero, a miner of Potosí, in his testament dated February 8, 1643.[1] Among the interesting clauses of the constitution is the provision that professors of the University of San Marcos should be allowed the privilege of living in the college.

The present buildings are not those originally erected, for they suffered destruction in the catastrophe of 1687.[2] In the small circular room which connects church and cloister, there is a large inscription on the upper wall under the dome which reads, "This work was constructed in the year 1783" (*Se edificó esta obra el año 1783*). Whether this date refers to the entire establishment including church and cloisters, or just to the room in which it appears, is a moot question. The style of architecture shows no notable variation throughout, and the work as a whole must belong in large part to the mid-eighteenth century.

An enormous circular cloister (Fig. 17) gives the Colegio de Santo Tomás a unique position architecturally. Circular churches, so much in vogue in Renaissance Italy and still more so later in the Neoclassic period, are unknown in Peru. Spain itself took up the circular church with some degree of seriousness from the time of the Jesuit college of St. Ignatius (1689) in the founder's birthplace, Azpeita, and thereafter.[3] Cloisters in that form are rare indeed, Spain presenting only two analogues, the circular courts of the castle of Bellver and of Charles V's unfinished palace at Granada.[4]

The large circular cloister of single story dominates the buildings of Santo Tomás as can easily be seen in the plan, drawn and first published by Harth-terré.[5] The photograph (Fig. 126), taken during the restorations, shows a section of the circular walk with wall pilasters which have capitals surmounted by an entablature block. The arrangement, although awkward here, is more successfully used on the court side and within the church. It must be regarded as a strange case of adaptation from the entablature-block scheme of the sixteenth century which still survives in replica in Lima Cathedral. As usual, cane and plaster vaults, placed upon brick and plaster walls and piers, prevail throughout the edifice. The adjustment of the groined vaults of the cloister walk is achieved with obvious effort and distortion, not easily judged in the examination of the floor plan. The volutes, used decoratively on the court side of the cloister piers, are typical of the second half of the seventeenth and the eighteenth century.

Only part of the walls of the library and second cloister serve as skeletons upon which to rebuild these sections of the *colegio*. The *portería* or entrance of the monastery too will be entirely resurfaced and modern when completed.

The exterior of the church lacks interest due to its nineteenth-century façade and the virtual ruin of the side portal. Within, the elevated choir is reached by steps rising from the circular room between the church and the cloister. The disposition of the space of the single nave, with the crossing and sanctuary occupying nearly half the length, has no exact parallel. Unconventional too is the arrangement of just a few large side chapels. The arches of the chapels and the supporting arch of the choir have a very flat profile. That feature, the entablature-block scheme of the pilasters, and the other peculiarities already noted produce a novel interior for which I know no exact counterpart. The vaults and dome of cane and stucco were under reconstruction in 1945

[1] "Miscelanea, Papeles pertenecientes al antiguo Colegio de Santo Tomás": "Constituciones del colegio," 12 pp., archives of Santo Domingo, Lima.

[2] *Revista del Archivo Nacional del Perú,* XII (1939), 33.

[3] Schubert, Otto, *Historia,* p. 308.

[4] Lámperez y Romea, *Arquitectura civil española,* I, 336, 374.

[5] Harth-terré, "El colegio de teología de Santo Tomás," *Arquitecto peruano,* August, 1940.

Corazón de Jesús (Los Huérfanos)

Next to Santo Cristo de los Milagros, this church is the most interesting ecclesiastical building of rococo tendency in Lima. A contemporary report affords fairly complete documentation of the edifice.[1] The site was purchased in 1742 and work begun immediately under the direction of the "master architect Cristóbal de Vargas, Juan de Matamoros, and Manuel de Torquemada." Judging by the use of the term "master architect," it is probable that the originator of the design was the famous architect, Cristóbal de Vargas, but the passage lacks clarity.[2] It may also be interpreted so that the man last mentioned would be the architect.

Work on the church, interrupted by the great earthquake of 1746, was suspended for twelve years. The building as it now stands dates from 1758 to 1766, the consecration taking place in the latter year. Whether the plans underwent modification from those originally prepared in 1742 is an open question. The long elliptical shape of the church (Fig. 18) has no parallel in Peru, although it is common enough in European churches of the seventeenth and eighteenth centuries. Well-known Spanish examples are the Bernardas in Alcalá de Henares and the Desamparados in Valencia.

It must be regarded as belonging, however, to the later phase of the mid-eighteenth century in Spain, represented by a number of elliptical and circular churches.[3] Still closer in ground plan were the church of Santa Brígida (1740–1745) in Mexico City and the Hospicio at San Vicente (1765) in Salvador.[4] The relationship of the Peruvian plan to those in Central and North America is one more piece of evidence of the cultural unity of the Hispanic colonies.

The interior of El Corazón de Jesús (Fig. 95) is divided into equal units by molded pilasters placed vertically upon the walls. A molded cornice topped by a balustrade provides the eye with the usual feeling of support for the vaults. The corbel in the middle of each bay of the cornice, so typical of Lima in the eighteenth century, is effectively used here. Neither imagination nor architectural skill, however, was displayed in the treatment of the sanctuary which a Bernini would have handled with indirect theatrical lighting. The archway which opens into the apse is particularly weak and ineffectual. The high altar itself (1765) by Joseph Manuel Palomares,[5] even discounting restorations and modern statues, is badly designed, and in every respect an inferior work.

The vaulting of the church is handled in the form of semidomes at the ends of the ellipse and barrel vaults with triangular penetrations over the main body of the nave. Even though of cane and plaster, they collapsed entirely in 1940, and the whole church was restored and rededicated in 1943. Green and white paint on the walls replaces the former imitation marble, and the vaults now have a conservative cream color. The pulpit of 1765 remains intact, while the side altars have been much modified, and the confessionals are neo-Gothic.

A number of rococo motives supply the most interesting and successful aspects of the church. The raised choir, for example, takes the form of two reversed S-curves. Notably characteristic of Lima in the period are the large and highly decorative shell vaults which here add luster to the inner part of the front and side portals. Great charm results from the diminutive shell tympana over the two small doorways at each end of the ellipse. The best in the church is the chapel of the Baptistry (Fig. 96) to the right on entering. Here a small dome rests on pendentives which are gaily decorated with the flourishing *rocaille* ornament. An oculus window in the main wall is set in a large flamboyant rococo shell with scalloped edges, and in the corners of the chapel caryatids appear to support the vault. The caryatids consist of four bodies, two above two, instead of the usual single figure, and they are manipulated in a frankly decorative way. This chapel was by far the most original part of the building. The past tense is used advisedly. It was ruined in the recent restorations, when the walls and stucco ornaments were plastered over with cement and the quality of the work thus lost forever.

The façade of the church is provincial, chiefly because of the short, ugly, octagonal towers. The portal, although satisfactory, cannot redeem the composition as a whole. Above the first story in restrained Doric style rises the rococo second story whose pilasters with corbel capitals, shell niche, and curvilinear hood are signatures of the *limeño* school of the mid-eighteenth century. The portal of San Carlos, which is dated 1766 and stands a short distance away, is similar enough in style to be the work of the same architect, as Harth-terré has suggested. Nonetheless, there seems to be no reason to attribute them to Juan de Rher.[6]

[1] "Relación . . . la compra del sitio y fábrica de la nueva iglesia de los Huérfanos," in *Revista del Archivo Nacional del Perú*, X (1937), 53–76.

[2] *Ibid.*, p. 56, "Se hizo el deseño de la iglesia cuyos cordeles y demarcación se delignió por el maestro alarife Cristóbal de Vargas, por Juan de Matamoros, y por Manuel de Torquemada que hizo un mapa en que delignió todo el sitio, dando en él la forma y planta que ha de tener . . ."

[3] Schubert, Otto, *Historia del barroco en España*, pp. 140, 293, 400, 405–433.

[4] Fernández, Justino, "Santa Brígida de México," *Congreso internacional de historia de América* (Buenos Aires, 1938), III, 438–454; Angulo, Diego, *Planos de monumentos*, pl. 174.

[5] *Revista del Archivo Nacional del Perú*, X (1937), 71.

[6] Harth-terré, Emilio, "La iglesia del Corazón de Jesús," *Arquitecto peruano*, January, 1942; Eguiguren, L. A., *Calles de Lima*, pp. 210 ff.

Jesús María

Jesús María is included among the principal monuments of Lima, not because of architectural importance but because it preserves complete and unspoiled its Hispanic Baroque interior. This fortunate circumstance is due not solely to its escape from serious damage in earthquakes. It also escaped destruction at the hands of nineteenth-century renovators. The magnificent unity of the interior, with its salomonic retables of gilded wood, its side altars, pulpit (Figs. 292, 327, 328), and the walls hung with good colonial pictures, has no superior in central and northern Peru. In Lima the small contemporary church of Magdalena la Vieja is also splendid, but not the equal of Jesús María.

Architecturally the church of Jesús María is modest and small, a Latin-cross type without chapels, with an elevated choir over the entrance, and a lower choir at the left of the sanctuary. Double pilasters, double transverse bands, and molded cornice separate the space into bays with the usual barrel vault now made of wood. Scroll ornaments decorate the wall beside the windows of the sanctuary, as they do in other churches of the period. The walls are pleasantly painted in rose color with the vaults and pilasters gray.

The history of Jesús María is well known, thanks to the excellent documented study of Santiago Antúnez de Mayolo.[1] Subsequent to the foundation of the convent in 1698, work progressed rapidly and the church was inaugurated in 1721. In recent years the exterior of the church has suffered severely by drastic restoration. The picturesque atrium disappeared, and the walls of the church were covered with a coat of cement. This lamentable practice, more than anything else in recent years, has destroyed colonial monuments. Not even the ornamental details of the portal were respected, and the exterior of the church is now an inaccurate cement copy of a former colonial work.

[1] Antúnez de Mayolo, Santiago, "Iglesia de Jesús María," in *Lima precolombina y virreinal,* pp. 181–224.

La Merced

Next to San Francisco, the Merced is the best preserved monastic house in Lima. The complex history of its architecture has been completely revealed by the splendid publication of Padre Víctor Barriga in a thick volume of documents. I shall give only an outline of the main course of events.

The Mercedarians established their house with the very foundation of the city in 1535. Their first large church was begun in 1541–1542. According to Padre Cobo it had a vaulted sanctuary, a single nave roofed with wooden panels and chapels at the sides. The contract for the first tower of brick was let to Alonso de Morales in 1589 and, on Cobo's testimony, finished ten years later.

About 1614 the architect, Andrés de Espinoza, rebuilt the *capilla mayor* and *capilla de la Piedad,* and in 1621 he signed a contract to erect anew the rest of the church. In the same year, however, he went off to Arequipa as architect of the new cathedral. In consequence, a Mercedarian friar, Pedro Galeano, took his place with new plans in 1628. Work continued for at least a decade. The floor plan of nave and lateral aisles is still preserved today, but the original elevation differed considerably. In addition to the documents we have the word of Cobo who describes the building as made of brick and mortar. Most interesting of all, the vaults were Gothic, thus following the general trend in Lima from wooden ceilings of the sixteenth century to the Gothic vaults of the following century.

In 1687 the church fell in ruins, and when it arose again, the materials were brick, wood and stucco with barrel vaults of wood and plaster replacing the earlier Gothic vaults of brick. Although by 1706 the church was complete, the cells and cloisters were still in a ruinous condition. The present edifice, with its patterns of rectangles and ellipses which decorate the vaults and piers, is the third church of 1688–1706 (Fig. 93). Not only the chain ornament but the rusticated wall surfaces are stucco veneer, not masonry. Most interesting and unusual are the trefoil arches which cut across the corners in each arm of the transept. The main body of the church has been frequently repaired in subsequent years, but except for the destruction of many Baroque altars, it has suffered no drastic modification other than the imitation curtain suspended below the cornice.

The façade (Fig. 110) has had an exceptionally checkered career even for Lima. It was originally erected in so-called Churrigueresque style about 1697–1704, judging by the fact that they began to collect the stone for it in the former year and that in the latter the funeral eulogy of Fray Luis Galindo de San Ramón included words of praise for his activity in raising funds for the façade. Slightly damaged in a revolution in 1895, it was demolished a few years later and replaced by a pseudo-Renaissance affair. Very recently in 1941 a modern copy of the Baroque façade, correct but cold in execution, was reconstructed under the direction of Harth-terré.

The side portal, called the Puerta de los Guitarreros, is dubiously attributed by Padre Barriga to Ventura Coco on the ground that the architect constructed two vaults in the church near the portal in 1765–1768. This portal (*circa* 1740), a splendid example of Lima's rococo with prominent shell motive, built of cane and stucco, was damaged in the earthquake of 1940. It was thereupon demolished and replaced by a copy in cement, tragically the present method of "restoring" colonial monuments in Lima.

As for the cloisters, three remain of the five which existed in the seventeenth century. The contract for the main cloister under date of 1592 called for eight *danzas de arcos* in contrast to the nine arches to a side now present. The cloister is large and very lovely (Fig. 123), its brick piers and round arches faced with stucco in the lower gallery. In the upper gallery (1777–1780) the dark brown Doric columns of wood are distinguished by an exaggerated entasis in the shafts. The arches in trefoil shape with smaller trefoil arches alternating between the large are clearly derived from the charming *mudéjar* patio of the Torre Tagle palace, the only other edifice in Lima which has precisely this feature.

The grand stairway between the two cloisters, which was reconstructed in 1759–1762, is mainly brick and stucco, and it is spanned by a wooden vault and dome. Large pedimented niches alternate with scrolled and voluted niches in abundance to produce flourishing sumptuousness. A curious plaited motive decorates the soffit of the arches in the ground story, the same device which occurs in the wooden ceiling in the *portería* of San Agustín.

The second cloister is called that of the Doctors after busts of Doctors of the Church in the spandrels of the second story. The first gallery of brick and stucco in rusticated design has a coat of red paint, and the upper gallery of wood and stucco is bright blue and white. The effect is extraordinarily ugly. The elliptical openings between the arches recall, of course, the main cloisters of San Francisco and Santo Domingo. The present construction is surely post-1746, but it may repeat a seventeenth-century original, a fact suggested by the ellipses and the *mudéjar* stucco patterns which resemble those within the church of San Francisco. The small third patio, its second story rebuilt in the nineteenth century, lacks any interest.

The sacristy is a completely charming product of French rococo influence, dating in its woodwork chests, and fashionable episodic paintings on glass, from the period immediately following its destruction by fire in 1773. The small domes, mentioned in the *Libro de Gastos* in 1765–1768, have been replaced at least twice and as recently as 1912 when the *mudéjar* ornament was omitted! These suspended domes are indeed a curious rebirth of medieval Islamic beehive construction in America.

Barriga, Padre Víctor, *El templo de la Merced de Lima, Documentos para la historia del arte* (Arequipa, 1944); Fuentes, Manuel A., *Estadística de Lima* (Lima, 1858), p. 361.

San Agustín

The first church and convent of the Augustinians were erected shortly after their arrival in 1551 on the site of the church of San Marcelo. The community moved to the present location in 1573, and the following year the new church was begun. This fine structure, described by Calancha, consisted of nave and two aisles roofed with a *mudéjar* ceiling of wood. It was richly furnished with fourteen retables and a fine set of choir stalls. The main cloister, in stone and of two stories, had alternately large and small arches in the upper gallery. That feature persists today despite many rebuildings.

According to the chronicler, Padre Juan Vázquez, the first church was torn down in 1681 in order to build an entirely "modern" structure. Very shortly the great earthquake of 1687 laid the convent and church in ruins. Apparently the lower gallery of the main cloister, the ante-sacristy, the tower though badly ruined, and part of the church survived. The presbytery was restored with cedar covering in 1693–1697, whereas the remainder of the church progressed slowly in the succeeding years, coming to a conclusion with the big façade (Fig. 111) which is dated by inscription *Año 1720*. The earthquake of 1746 once again caused considerable damage which was slowly repaired in the second half of the century. Finally the church and tower were demolished in 1903 to build the present ugly structure of pseudo-Romanesque-Gothic style, completed in 1908.

In the year 1945 the walls of the transept and apse of the church built at the end of the seventeenth and at the beginning of the eighteenth century still stood. A project was under consideration to destroy the edifice of 1903–1908 and reconstruct the one demolished at that time. Such is the change of fashion even in architecture.

The main cloister of San Agustín is preserved as rebuilt in brick after 1687. The alternating large and small arches in the upper gallery suggest that the design of the late sixteenth century, described by Calancha, is still maintained. A small inner cloister of square piers has been modernized in cement beyond all interest. The other two cloisters now serve as the seminary and both consist of two galleries, the lower carrying round arches on square piers and the upper trefoil arches. In one case small square columns of cane and stucco are used in the upper story, and in the other Doric columns of wood.

The most important parts of the monastery of San Agustín are the sacristy and ante-sacristy for which the contract of 1643 with an architect, Luis Fernández Lozano, was recently published in full. Absolutely intact, the ante-sacristy has a fine carved wooden ceiling of coffers, the work of Diego de Medina in 1643–1651. The dado of Sevillian tiles was bought from the monks of San Francisco in 1661. The large shell tympana over the main door and the windows are, however, alterations of the eighteenth century.

The sacristy proper no longer preserves the *artesonado* of 1643, but is covered by a barrel vault of the second half of the eighteenth century which was restored after the earthquake of 1940. Here too the characteristic shell motive appears over the doorways, and the cornice repeats the familiar motive of the eighteenth century: the corbel used as a decorative device.

Thirty statuettes of Augustinian saints are arranged in niches of the second half of the eighteenth century around the hall. A contract for twenty-eight statuettes was made with Diego de Medina in 1643. The woodwork ordered of Asencio Salas ten years later must have been lost in the earthquake of 1746, since the style of the existing niches with their bust-length caryatids and flamboyant *rocaille* tympana clearly belongs to about 1760–1770 (Fig. 333). The Sala Capitular, although at least of the seventeenth century, has less architectural character, being notable chiefly for its ribbed Gothic vaults. The tiles, benches, and tribune of the first half of the seventeenth century are worthy of note.

The façade of San Agustín, the only original retable-façade in Lima, luckily has a dated inscription including the year 1720. It is discussed in Chapter IV. Domingo Angulo quoted Padre Vázquez' chronicle as authority in stating that the façade was the work of the sculptor, Diego de Aguirre. Padre Vázquez says that Aguirre carved the high altar in 1673, but he makes no further reference to him. The tower to the left, which was torn down in 1903, has an inscription in its base, with the name of the architect, José de la Sida, and the date 1637. The photograph published by Jacinto Monasterio shows the materials of cane and stucco and decorative details consisting of rolled brackets which indicate that the belfry was reconstructed after the earthquake of 1687. The general proportions of the façade with its enormous two-storied towers were very similar to those of San Francisco, which is later in date (1657–1674). Hence the inscription of 1637 in the base of the left tower of San Agustín proves that José de la Sida was the originator of this type of structure in Lima. According to Padre Vázquez (vol. II, p. 337), who wrote in the year 1721, the *portería* was made in that year. Unfortunately its lavish baroque portal fell victim to the restorers of

1903 who left only the trefoil door and the fine *artesonado* ceiling within it.

Calancha, Antonio de, *Crónica moralizada* (Barcelona, 1638), I, 247–250; Vázquez, Juan Teodoro, "Crónica continuada de esta provincia del Perú de N. P. S. Agustín," dated 1721 (unpublished manuscript preserved in the Museo Prado, Lima). The most important references to the church and convent are quoted in the following: Monasterio, Jacinto, *Recuerdo de la inauguración del templo de San Agustín* (Lima, 1908); Montes, Fray Graciano, "Los agustinos en el Perú," in the periodical, *Expresión*, I (1939), 55–60; Vargas Ugarte, "Notas," pp. 152, 156, 159, 173, 181–182, 188, 294; Angulo, Domingo, "La portada de la iglesia de San Agustín," *Arquitecto peruano*, January, 1938; Lohmann Villena, "Notícias inéditas," *Revista histórica*, XIII (1940), 16; Santibáñez Salcedo, Alberto, "La restauración de la sacristía del templo de San Agustín," *Cultura peruana*, vol. V (1945) no. 22; Montes, Padre Graciano, *La sacristía del templo de San Agustín* (Lima, 1944).

San Carlos

The church of the Jesuit novitiate dedicated to St. Anthony Abbot became part of the Real Colegio de San Carlos in 1770 after the expulsion of the Jesuits. The University of San Marcos now functions in the cloisters, and the church has been made the national pantheon for heroes of the war of independence. In 1924 it was remodeled for that purpose by sinking a well in the floor of the crossing in imitation of Napoleon's tomb in the Invalides, Paris. Large neocolonial windows were introduced in the transept, and the side altars were transferred to the church of San Marcelo.

The first stone of the present church of San Carlos was laid in 1758, and the year of completion is indicated by an inscription over the lower niches of the façade, *Año 1766*. This façade (Fig. 114) with its small twin towers and its two-storied portal is one of the best eighteenth-century works in Lima. Stylistically the portal closely resembles that of the Corazón de Jesús, although immeasurably superior. The upper story, broader by four pilasters and the side niches, expresses the gaiety of the rococo in a restrained and highly successful manner. Decorative shell niches, the curious *limeño* volute capitals, and the swinging curves of the cornice build up a pleasing composition which is loaded at the top by large vases stepped upward. The material of the second story is brick and plaster. The first story, on the contrary, in sober Doric style with plain frieze and dentils in the cornice, is stone, and the only part of the edifice in this more durable material. The Doric design of the lower façade is closely repeated in the side portal. The dome, very tastefully planned, suffers from the superposition of an ugly modern lantern, entirely out of harmony with the exterior of the church as a whole. A secondary dome covers an adjoining chapel.

The small interior, in the form of a Latin cross without lateral chapels, has good proportions and a simple, pleasing design. Barrel vaults and a dome over the crossing, molded pilasters and cornice with the *limeño* bracket in the center of each bay are familiar elements in contemporary churches of Lima. Equally characteristic shell vaults surmount the main portal and the side door within the church. Rebuilding of the nave vault was necessary subsequent to the earthquake of 1940, at which time general repairs took place.

Lima, precolombina y virreinal, pp. 309–318.

San Francisco

The splendidly documented monograph on San Francisco which was recently published by Fray Benjamín Gento Sanz provides an exhaustive history of the church and monastery. Consequently only a brief résumé of his findings will be given here. Although the first Franciscans came to Lima in 1535, the actual foundation of the monastery delayed until 1546, when they took possession of the site still occupied by their vast precincts. The first church was humble, equipped with adobe seats built along the wall, an arrangement still seen in sixteenth-century churches such as San Cristóbal at Ayacucho and La Asunción at Chucuito.

A large new church was begun in the time of the Marqués de Cañete (1556–1561), according to Padre Cobo, a statement confirmed by a royal decree (1555) in favor of the church.[1] This church was basilican in type with nave, two aisles, transept, and sanctuary. The paneled wooden ceilings of the body of the church, constructed by Juan de Grajales and Francisco de Xuara in 1560, were later replaced by new *artesonado* ceilings under the Marqués de Montesclaros (1607–1615). At the same time the domed transept and sanctuary were rebuilt. Valuable descriptions by Padre Cobo[2] and Padre Córdoba Salinas[3] give us an excellent idea of this church. The latter in 1651 mentions a dome over the sanctuary as well as over the crossing, the arms of which were covered with decorated Gothic vaults. The domes had been reconstructed in 1638–1645.[4]

In 1656 the *capilla mayor* collapsed and rebuilding began the following year upon plans prepared by a Portuguese, Constantino de Vasconcellos. The architect died some time before 1671 leaving the completion of the project to Manuel de Escobar whose name appears upon the side portal of the church.[5] Work was completed up to the transept by 1664, and the final impetus came from Padre Luis de Cervela who spent five years in Lima (1669–1674), as *comisario general* of the order. When

Padre Cervela returned to Spain, he left a new church (Fig. 10) with its magnificent portals, one tower already erected, and numerous gilded retables. Moreover, the *portería*, the *ante-portería* and the Capilla de la Soledad had been built anew. The solemn consecration of the church had taken place in 1673 with Manuel de Mollinedo, the famous bishop of Cuzco, who had just arrived from Spain, officiating.[6]

A very rare book which describes the collapse of the church, its rebuilding, and the progress achieved under the enthusiastic guidance of Fray Luis de Cervela provides the major part of the new documentation. This book, which was first brought to light by Sánchez Cantón,[7] was independently discovered in manuscript form by Padre Gento Sanz when he searched the Franciscan archives at Lima. The descriptions of the portals and above all the engraving of the exterior, dated 1673, which is included in the printed work are invaluable as irrefutable proof that the façade of the church, the monastery entrance, and the façade of the Soledad all belong to this period. The towers and upper center of the Soledad were restored in 1815, as both style and the print of 1673 confirm.

Of major interest is the portal of the church (Figs. 107–109) which both the print and the verbal description reveal in its present status. Thus any theory that it is a composite of sixteenth, seventeenth, and eighteenth-century rebuildings is disproven. The major variation between church and print is found in the towers, which in the latter have three stories, and are smaller in relation to the portal than the building as it exists today. There is no reason to believe in a subsequent reconstruction of the towers, and Sánchez Cantón may be correct in suggesting that the engraver followed an architect's drawing which was not put into effect. The towers of the engraving are far

superior, in design and in their scale relations to the portal, than the structure as completed. Some details of the print show carelessness and inaccuracies on the part of the engraver. The position of the side portal of the church, details of the buttresses and dome, and the drawing of the monastery entrance are inexact. The side portal (Fig. 106), which is very vague in the print, is dedicated to St. Louis of Toulouse. It has an inscription cut in its stone spandrels containing the architect's name and the year: *E. Manuel de Escobar Fabciebat ano 1674* [*sic*].

The interior of San Francisco (Fig. 92) presents a disappointing aspect today for it has lost its great array of Baroque retables, silver altars, and ecclesiastical furnishings, the very description of which dazzles the imagination. Rodríguez Guillén's account of the church in 1735 makes the wanton destruction of such beauty in 1803–1805 all the more painful.[8] Yet Matías Maestro, who directed the tearing out and burning of colonial treasures, has his followers today in those who destroy churches like Santa Teresa in order to widen a street. The Capilla de la Soledad met the same fate of "restoration" in 1815. The Capilla del Milagro was reërected after a fire in 1835.

The previously mentioned book of the seventeenth century by Suárez de Figueroa and Benavides contains an engraving of the new cloister of the time of Luis de Cervela (1669–1674). Some slight variations occur, the *mudéjar* frieze and the volute decorations of the corbels being replaced in the print by simple rectangles in the frieze and a pyramidal hood motive in the spandrels. Probability speaks for inaccuracy on the part of the engraver. The original ground plan of the cloister (1556–1561) was not disturbed in the rebuilding. Córdoba Salinas in 1651 speaks of eighty-eight stone columns apparently in the upper gallery.[9] That would suggest an arrangement contemporary with and similar to the Franciscan cloister in Cuzco. In the new structure the oval openings and the alternating large and small arches are noteworthy. Both features had previously been introduced in Lima. The oval shapes of the second story probably appeared first in the main cloister of the Dominicans. This problem is more fully discussed in the general section of Chapter IV.

The magnificent tile revetment in the lower walk of the principal cloister is one of the finest in the world. The date 1620 occurs repeatedly, and an inscription discloses that it was imported from Seville: *Fray J. Gómez y sus bienhechores de Lima enviaron por estos azulejos a Sevilla.* Another inscription reads: *Nuevo oficial trabaxa que todos gustan de veros, estar haciendo pucheros del barro de por acá.* It is repeated several times above or near the tiles which contain grotesque atlantes. The usual interpretation has been that these tiles were manufactured in Lima, a theory difficult to accept because of their high quality and thoroughly Sevillian techniques. Another set of lovely tiles revets the lower wall of the entrance hall (*portería*) of the monastery, these dated 1643 by inscription and the gift of a certain Menacho. The latest date, 1749, is located below the tile portrait of St. Francis on one of the piers of the main cloister. It apparently refers to restoration done on the figure after the earthquake of 1746.

The extraordinary array of tile dados was not the only *mudéjar* feature of the Franciscan cloister. Another was the magnificent cupola of wood with typical Moorish star-shaped interlaces. Unfortunately it collapsed in the earthquake of 1940.

The portal of the sacristy has an inscription including the name of the architect: *Alférez Lucas Meléndez me fecit.* On the opposite wall is a bronze plaque which dates the sac-

risty in the year 1729. Thus is provided a date for the sacristy portal which in general style resembles numerous contemporary works, such as the rear entrances of Lima Cathedral.

The cloister of the infirmary of San Francisco Solano is small, single storied with square piers, and is largely reconstructed. The chapel in this cloister has an interesting elliptical dome of the eighteenth century. The small patio (Fig. 125) of the Casa de Ejercicios (1777) is restricted, likewise, to a single story. Its Doric columns of wood and its tiles, already transformed into rococo patterns, contribute to the charm of one of the finest corners of colonial Lima.

The present seminary of Santo Toribio occupies the two latest sections of the Franciscan properties. The best is the former cloister of San Buenaventura (1734), distinguished by the alternation of large and small arches, the same arrangement used in the main cloister of San Agustín. The second cloister, formerly that of San Francisco Solano (1732–1734), is another good example of the type in which trefoil arches in the second story stand above round arches in the lower gallery. An attractive stairway has arabesque ornamentation recalling the transepts of La Compañía at Pisco. The chapel attached to this section is bizarre but interesting in the curious ribbed barrel vault of the nave, and a huge shell vault of *limeño* type expanded to support the elevated choir.

[1] Gento Sanz, Benjamín, *San Francisco de Lima* (Lima, 1945), pp. 73–74, 110–113, 174–177; introduction by Harth-terré, p. vi.

[2] Cobo, *op. cit.*, pp. 240–241.

[3] Córdoba Salinas, Diego, *Crónica franciscana* (Lima, 1651), *Libro* III, pp. 173–183.

[4] Gento Sanz, *op. cit.*, p. 120.

[5] *Ibid.*, pp. 128–129; Lorea, Antonio de, *Santa Rosa . . . su admirable vida* (Madrid, 1671), pp. 6–7; Vargas Ugarte, *Ensayo de un diccionario*, pp. 158–159, 275–277.

[c] Gento Sanz, *op. cit.*, p. 144; Mugaburu, *Diario*, I, 36–37, 104; II, 27, 36, 40, 143.

[7] Sánchez Cantón, "El Convento de San Francisco de Lima," *Revista de Indias*, IV (1943), 527–551.

[8] Gento Sanz, *op. cit.*, p. 163.

[9] Córdoba Salinas, *Crónica, Libro* III, p. 181.

San Pedro (*La Compañía*)

With the arrival of six Jesuits in Peru on March 28, 1568, the newest of the great monastic orders first set foot in the New World. They were led by a zealous missionary, Padre Jerónimo Ruiz del Portillo. The small chapel which they built almost immediately is described by Padre Anello Oliva, writing in 1598. That chapel was replaced by a fine church as early as 1575.[1] A large broad structure of single nave, according to Cobo,[2] probably covered with a wooden roof, it gave way fifty years later to the church, which with modifications still exists today. The first stone was laid in 1624 and the dedication took place in 1638.[3] Padre Nicolás Durán Mastrilli, arriving in Lima in 1623, brought with him the plans of the Casa Profesa of Rome, according to his own statement.[4] Similar dependence on the Gesù of Rome is claimed for the Jesuit church at Quito.[5] Navarro has asserted, however, that the latter was modeled upon Sant' Ignazio in Rome whose foundations were laid in 1626. Such a belief is chronologically impossible, since the Compañía in Quito antedates Sant' Ignazio by twenty-one years, having been begun in 1605 and the main body of the church completed by 1616.[6] The truth is that the churches at Quito and Lima were influenced by the Gesù of Rome, but are in no sense replicas of it.

Little attention has been given to a consideration of what true resemblances there were between San Pedro in Lima, as it looked in the seventeenth century, and the Gesù of Rome. The description of Padre Cobo, who lived in the Jesuit monastery, when he wrote his famous history of Lima in 1629, precisely mentions Gothic ribbed vaults (*crucería*) in the nave and cupolas in the aisles. The materials were brick, stone, and mortar.[7] The present barrel vault of cane and plaster in the nave must date from the early nineteenth century, judging by style and materials. It will be understood, therefore, that San Pedro in Lima, when first built, resembled the Gesù in Rome even less than it does today. The ground plans of the two churches differ considerably. The Gesù has a single nave with intercommunicating lateral chapels, a broad transept, and a single semicircular apse. The plan of San Pedro (Fig. 9) consists of nave and two aisles (not chapels) with niche chapels for retables flanking the aisles, a transept much narrower in proportion than in the Gesù, and a rectangular apse with sacristies at each side. The features which San Pedro and the Gesù have in common are the large dome over the crossing and cupolas over the side bays. This usage in the vaults of the aisles appears in Lima for the first time in San Pedro (1624) whence it passed to San Francisco (1657) and to La Merced (1687), as well as to Arequipa and in modified form to Trujillo.

It is my belief that the floor plan and elevation of San Pedro in Lima were influenced by the Jesuit church in Quito whose inception anticipates that of Lima by nineteen years. The former was begun in 1605, the body of the church completed in 1616, and the crossing in 1616–1634.[8] The two churches have exactly the same general disposition, a basilica with domes over the aisles, a large dome over the crossing, and a rectangular apse. The use of domes passed from the Gesù in Rome to the

Jesuit houses in America. The second great Jesuit church in Rome, Sant' Ignazio, reverted to the basilican plan, although built under the influence of the Gesù in respect to vaulting. Sant' Ignazio with its basilican disposition stands closer to the churches in Lima and Quito but could not have influenced them, since it was begun in 1626, subsequent to the South American structures.

It is possible, of course, that Lima and Quito arrived at the same plan independently under the influence of the Gesù vaults. The indisputable priority in date of the Compañía in Quito tends, nonetheless, to invalidate such a supposition. Moreover, Martín de Aizpitarte, architect and Jesuit brother in Lima, who directed the construction of San Pedro until his death in 1637, had passed his novitiate in the Jesuit college at Quito.[9] He was transferred from Quito to Lima in 1604, proof enough, if proof were needed, that relations between various houses of the same order in America were intimate.

Granting that Padre Nicolás Durán Mastrilli brought the plans of the Gesù to Lima in 1623, as documents show, the facts prove that they were not used. The basilican plan was too firmly entrenched in Lima to allow for the adoption of the Gesù's single nave. Only the sixteenth-century Merced was of that type, to be abandoned by the Mercedarians too in 1628. The Jesuits of Peru understandably wanted their church no less large and impressive than the basilican structures of their rivals, the Franciscans, Augustinians, and Dominicans.

Modifications of the Jesuit church at Lima have been frequent and drastic. The first of these was the redecoration of the aisles about 1700 (Fig. 94), perhaps in the wake of slight repairs after the earthquake of 1687. Gilded panels of arabesques carved in wood cover the wall surface along with insets of oil paintings on canvas. A large rectangular picture occupies the upper part of the wall, not visible in the photograph, while long narrow pictures flank the arches below, and the composition is completed by the symmetrical placing of three small paintings just beneath the cornice. The lovely tile dado completes the decoration which has no superior in all Peru for richness combined with good taste. Nor is there any exact parallel for this combination of gilded wood carving and pictures. The closest analogy is to be found in the crossing of La Merced in Sucre, Bolivia, where the pictures of the Life of San Pedro Nolasco and the Birth of the Virgin bear the signature of the famous Bolivian painter, Pérez Holguín. Another contemporary series of pictures signed by the same artist in the same church bears the date 1710.

A magnificent example of the investiture of walls with gilded wood carving, but without pictures, is the chapel of Jerónimo de Solá y Fuente in Santo Domingo at Huancavelica. The inscription on the donor's portrait there carries a date of 1744 in the legend, the approximate period of the chapel. Other stylistic comparisons can be made with the stucco ornament in the upper walls of the Jesuit church in Pisco (1687–1723). The combined evidence points to the early eighteenth century as the period of the exquisite wall decoration of the aisles of San Pedro in Lima.

Another and more radical transformation of the interior of the church was the substitution of the original Gothic ribbed vaults (1624–1638), no doubt of the ornate type, for a barrel vault of cane and wood which is covered by a cloth painted to imitate stone coffers. No record has been discovered to indicate when the brick vaults gave way to plaster. The official report of the damage caused by the earthquake of 1687 says that the main vault of San Pedro withstood the shock, although the dome of the crossing and the towers fell.[10] Immediate rebuilding of the towers and repairs in the church took place under the direction of Padre Blas Ferrando.[11]

The condition of San Pedro after the great catastrophe of 1746 is less explicitly told. As usual the towers collapsed.[12] The present barrel vaults of cane and plaster seem to be subsequent to 1746, since it is known that the brick vaults withstood the earthquake of 1687. Judging by the style, the nave must have been redecorated entirely at the turn of the nineteenth century and probably by Matías Maestro. In fact, Bermúdez, in his eulogy of the latter, states, without giving details, that Maestro restored San Pedro.[13]

Of pure Neoclassic taste are the Doric pilasters and Doric frieze of nave and transept, surely not part of the seventeenth-century design. The disposition of the crossing with the setbacks in the piers under the dome and the placing of two niches in each are an academic derivation from the crossing of St. Peter's in Rome. The barrel vault, covered with cloth and painted in imitation of stone coffers, is an unadulterated piece of Neoclassic stage scenery. The gallery over the aisles, often found in Jesuit churches, disappeared in the remodeling of 1894–1897.[14] The woodwork of the tribunes and the trefoil arches at the sides of the sanctuary are of modern facture, neocolonial in a Neoclassic setting.

The original façade of San Pedro fell before the executioner's axe in 1896–1897, and was replaced by the dull academic work which still existed in 1945. The inscription, prominently placed at the entrance, recorded the names of pious donors and dates. At the present time, the intention is to alter the façade again, upon the design of a contemporary architect, Héctor Velarde, and without reference to its colonial predecessor.[15] The new scheme is part of the campaign of repairs, necessitated by the damage caused by the earthquake of 1940. It must be confessed that the colonial façade, whose towers collapsed with every earthquake, is by far the most interesting of the three, to judge by the engraving published by Manuel Fuentes.[16] The main features of the first story, including the portals, still survived in 1896–1897, but the cement surfacing and the exclusion of niches and statues of the original destroyed its effectiveness. The rusticated upper story and the low colonial towers were infinitely superior to the 1896 edition, for they at least had the virtue of stylistic authenticity. What a pity that the atrium wall too was demolished. Thus was lost one more bit of the charm of old Lima, now almost vanished entirely and forever.

Adjoined to San Pedro is a small church, known as the Penitenciaria, and said to be located upon the site of the first chapel of the Jesuits in Lima. It gives the appearance of a hall church, although the elliptical domes of the nave are slightly higher than the cupolas of the aisles. The plan is a perfect rectangle with two rows of small square piers bearing molded capitals. The church suffers from ugly blue wall paint, and its chief interest lies in a fine series of mural paintings.

Padre Cobo makes no mention of the Penitenciaria in 1629, from which fact it must be concluded that it was built in the mid-seventeenth century. Reference is made to the collapse of its vaults in 1687 which, having been rebuilt, had the strength to survive the earthquake of 1746.[17]

The sacristy of San Pedro (Fig. 99) with its superb array of carved and gilded niches and frames is one of the most fabulous remains of colonial Lima. It appears to have been redecorated at the beginning of the eighteenth century at the same time as the aisles of the church. Certain details of ornament, such as the long crisp leaves, have close analogues on the façade of the Merced (1697–1704), a fact which is further indication of a date at the turn of the century.

[1] Anello Oliva, Juan, *Historia del Perú y varones insignes de la Compañía de Jesús* (Lima, 1895), pp. 164, 204–205. The editors, Pazos Varela and Varela y Orbegoso, date the manuscript 1598. Vargas Ugarte in *Historia del Perú, Fuentes* (Lima, 1939), p. 250, dates it 1628. Mateos, F., *Historia general de la Compañía de Jesús en la provincia del Perú, Crónica anónima de 1600* (Madrid, 1944), I, 26–27.

[2] Cobo, *op. cit.*, p. 246.

[3] Vargas Ugarte, *Los jesuitas del Perú* (Lima, 1941), pp. 169–170.

[4] Mendiburu, *op. cit.*, VII, "Mastrilli." Padre Vargas Ugarte gave me the following quotation from Padre Durán Mastrilli's *Carta Anua del año 1638*. Speaking of the newly inaugurated Jesuit house in Lima Padre Durán says: "es un modelo del de la Casa Profesa de Roma cuya planta traje yo." The original manuscript is in the Jesuit archives at Rome, and a copy exists in the Jesuit archives at Toledo, Spain.

[5] Navarro, José Gabriel, *La iglesia de la Compañía en Quito* (Madrid, 1930), p. 65.

[6] Navarro, *Religious Architecture in Quito* (New York, 1945), p. 16; Furlong and Buschiazzo, "Arquitectura religiosa colonial," *Revista Archivum* (Buenos Aires, 1942), I, 22.

[7] Cobo, *op. cit.*, p. 248.

[8] Furlong and Buschiazzo, *op. cit.*, p. 22.

[9] Vargas Ugarte, "Notas," pp. 159–160; —, *Ensayo de un diccionario*, pp. 120–122.

[10] Angulo, Domingo, "El terremoto del año de 1687," *Revista del Archivo Nacional del Perú*, XII (1939), 31, 154.

[11] Vargas Ugarte, *Notas*, p. 171.

[12] Angulo, Domingo, *op. cit.*, p. 31; Mendiburu, *op. cit.*, VII, "Manso de Velasco."

[13] Bermúdez, José Manuel, *Fama póstuma* (Lima, 1805), p. XCIII.

[14] Vargas Ugarte, *Los jesuitas del Perú*, p. 180.

[15] Velarde, Héctor, "Algo sobre la reconstrucción de San Pedro," *Arquitecto peruano*, March, 1944.

[16] Fuentes, Manuel A., *Estadística general de Lima* (Lima, 1858), p. 389.

[17] Odriozola, Manuel, *Terremotos*, p. 37; Mendiburu, *op. cit.*, VII, "Manso de Velasco."

Santa Teresa

The convent of Santa Teresa set something of a record for speed in construction and destruction. Its first stone laid in 1683, it was inaugurated December 21, 1686, only to be ruined within ten months by the earthquake of October 28, 1687. Of the original structure the large cloister must have been salvaged or immediately rebuilt, and it had the distinction of being the finest of the nunneries.

In the beauty of its cloister (Figs. 121, 122) it stood second only to San Francisco and La Merced. Its charm and picturesqueness was inferior to none of them. The large court had seven trefoil arches to a side carried on small square piers in the first story. Stucco over brick gave the impression of rustication which was skillfully designed on the wall surface and in the frieze. A peculiar feature was the pilaster suspended on a leaf corbel in the spandrels of the arches. The handling of the four corners of the cloister was manipulated in highly successful fashion, particularly the elliptical openings in the piers and the dexterous placing of two shells at the base of the arches.

The second story in brown wood had a post-and-lintel construction with fine *zapata* capitals, long and beautifully carved. The open balustrade added to the horizontality of the upper gallery which, with its contrasting color, acted as a foil to the white rusticated arches below. The basis of the style is, of course, *mudéjar*, altogether delightful in its interpretation here.

The vaults of Santa Teresa collapsed in the earthquake of 1940, and the church, left in ruinous condition, was demolished in 1946 to widen a street. So far as the interior was concerned, it was no great loss, and the mediocre eighteenth-century altars were moved to San Sebastián. It was a single-naved building with molded pilasters, molded cornice, barrel vaults, and domical vault over the crossing. The façade (Fig. 115), however, was the best rococo exterior in Lima and in all Peru for that matter. Its loss is greatly to be regretted, and it is one more proof of the disregard of the civic authorities for the preservation of their artistic heritage. The two small towers with volute capitals on the rusticated pilasters and their domical turrets were very similar to the towers of San Marcelo, before the façade of that church was destroyed to give way to the present monstrosity (Fig. 116).

The portal of Santa Teresa was completely charming, a masterpiece of Peruvian rococo. The curious volutes were used not only as capitals but also at the bottom of the pilasters in some cases. Lovely shell ornaments appeared beside the doorway as well as in the niche overhead. Three stories of diminishing height culminated with a window of rococo curves which were interrelated with the calligraphic flow of the volutes below and over the sides. A magnificent iron grille and gates enclosed the small atrium before the church. The façade of Santa Teresa must have been rebuilt in totality about 1750, after the devastation of 1746.

Mugaburu, *Diario*, II, 147, 191–192; *Revista del Archivo Nacional del Perú*, XII (1939), 32–33.

Santo Cristo de los Milagros (Las Nazarenas)

The Milagros is the finest rococo church in Peru and the most complete representative of this style which dominated Lima in the second half of the eighteenth century. The convent of the Nazarenas, inaugurated in 1730, met with destruction in the great earthquake only sixteen years later. Finally the viceroy Amat turned good angel to the nuns and ordered the church rebuilt in 1766. Its consecration in 1771 and other data are recorded in a volume published in commemoration thereof.[1] Amat is accredited as architect of the church, a tradition based upon the inscription contained in a famous portrait of him dated 1771, which the nuns, the Nazarenas, possess. The legend reads: to him "are due the fabric of their church which he designed and directed from the first stone which he placed in its foundations to its total completion with the beauty and strength which it possesses."[2] I am somewhat skeptical about the literal accuracy of the above statement. No doubt Amat supplied funds and used his all-powerful influence to expedite the project. No other evidence except this laudatory inscription is forthcoming, as yet, to shed light upon his excursions into the practice of architecture. As a military engineer, however, he took an important part in the fortification of the coast of Peru and Chile.[3]

The church (Fig. 97) is small with a large dome over the crossing which is given the principal emphasis in the spatial design. At the entrance, a narthex occupies the space below the upper choir and gives into the nave through three openings. The nave itself, very short in two bays with niche chapels, prepares the way to the large crossing and the rectangular sanctuary. The climactic feature is the great high altar which is topped by an enormous shell like a semidome. At each side of the sanctuary a magnificent wooden grille (Fig. 98) with typical *rocaille* ornament in the upper section screens the lower choir and an inner room of the convent. Definitely rococo is the treatment of the crossing which projects slightly beyond nave and apse. A diagonally placed wall across the corners provides the transition to the pendentives of the dome. Two half columns on high bases meet the transverse arches on the four corners of the crossing, and the same half columns of the Corinthian order separate the bays of the nave. A molded cornice finishes off the composition at the springing of the vaults. Niches in the angles of the crossing and small doors below provide scale, giving an impression of greater height than would otherwise be suggested. Over the narthex the upper choir is shielded from the body of the church by a fine wooden screen divided into a three-part scheme which corresponds to the arches below. Moldings throughout are rococo in profile with characteristic reversed curves. Charming rococo patterns, likewise, serve as over-door decorations on the four lateral doors of the crossing.

Barrel vaults of cane and plaster cover the nave and sanctuary and are painted in a restrained rectilinear pattern. Light-colored, slightly marbleized paint decorates the walls of brick and plaster. This case is the only one known to me in which imitation marble walls are done with restraint and good taste, and give no offense.

The Cristo de los Milagros represents the transplantation of a new style and a complete reaction against the Hispanic Baroque tradition. Salomonic retables of gilded wood which were universal in the eighteenth century give way here to white marble (in this case imitation) with gilding limited to capitals, moldings, and a few ornaments. Spiral and other Baroque columns are discarded for plain shafts and Corinthian capitals. To me the Hispanic colonial version of the French rococo in no way equals the beauty or originality of Hispanic Baroque. Nevertheless, it is interesting as a stylistic phenomenon, and an example of change of taste.

The beauty of the church of the Cristo de los Milagros is its unity of design throughout. The six lateral altars and the high altar, the rococo pulpit, the confessionals, and every detail of decoration are integral in the composition and plan of the whole church. Fortunately, the destructive fury of the nineteenth century spared its hand here, and so the church fostered by Amat remains as a perfect representative of his age in Lima.

The façade of the church in no way measures up to the interior. Its two towers, oft rebuilt following earthquakes, terminate in flat tops instead of the cupolas which can be seen in the church as it appears in the background of Amat's portrait. The portal shows the rococo tendency to multiply small motives in composition. On the whole, the façade is conservative and rather dull.

The cloisters, which have recently been amputated to widen a street, are known to me only in photographs published by Ismael Portal.[4] They are single-storied structures of wood, arcaded and without architectural significance.

[1] Colmenares Fernández de Córdoba, Felipe, *El día deseado* (Lima, 1771), pp. 29–56.

[2] *Exposición de cuadros y objetos de arte virreinal* (Lima, 1942), unpaged. Portrait and inscription reproduced.

[3] Rodríguez Casado and Pérez Embid, *Memoria del gobierno del virrey Amat* (Seville, 1947), pp. lxiii–lxxi; —, *Construcciones del virrey Amat* (Sevilla, 1949).

[4] Portal, Ismael, *Lima religiosa* (Lima, 1924), pp. 226–228.

Santo Domingo

The first Dominicans entered Lima in the year of the city's foundation, 1535, and five years later their monastery was made a priory. The chronicler, Lizárraga, writing *circa* 1602, provides valuable information about the first church, the plan of which still exists. He states that a church of three "naves" was begun in the time of the provincial, Fray Tomás de San Martín (1540–1552), and that the church, cloister, and *portería* were finished under Salvador de Ribera (1582–1586).[1] The magnificent coffered wooden ceiling of the *portería* follows a design reproduced in Villalpando's edition of Serlio. The contract for the crossing and two vaulted chapels was awarded to an architect named Gerónimo Delgado in 1547.[2] Meléndez's excellent description of the church in 1681 includes the information that the nave had a wooden ceiling of interlaces, that is, in *mudéjar* style. Still more important, he published an excellent floor plan (Fig. 5) of the entire monastery which leaves no doubt that the exact disposition of today already existed then.[3] Padre Cobo, writing still earlier in 1629, characterized the church as very large and mentioned the wooden roof of the nave, Gothic vaults in the "chapels," and the "vaulted" *capilla mayor*.[4] The terminology which Padre Cobo used has led people to believe that the plan in his day was that of a single nave with noncommunicating chapels, and Domingo Angulo has even stated that an alteration was made, opening them into the aisles *circa* 1683–1684.[5] Both Meléndez's plans of 1681 (Fig. 5) and the testimony of Lizárraga prove beyond question that the plan of Santo Domingo has always been the same since its inception in the fifth decade of the sixteenth century. Moreover, a careful observation of Padre Cobo's descriptions of churches will show that his architectural terms are frequently confusing. He also refers to the aisles of the Jesuit church of 1624 as "chapels."

An important change in the church of Santo Domingo took place in 1683, when a contract was let for the rebuilding of the transept.[6] The dome over the crossing is said to have been the work of the Dominican architect, Diego Maroto. It seems reasonable to suppose that the present vaults of cane and plaster in the nave, imitating the Gothic ribbed construction of the cathedral, were erected then or after the earthquake of 1687, replacing the *mudéjar artesonado* which was still in existence when Meléndez wrote in 1681. Domingo Angulo's attribution of this imitation Gothic vault to Martínez de Arrona in the early seventeenth century is contradicted by the testimony of Cobo and Meléndez, previously cited.[7] Harthterré's recent statement that the present vaults replaced the original *mudéjar* ceiling in 1660–1669 is also difficult to reconcile with Meléndez's words.[8] This problem remains unresolved until fuller documentation is available.

The next major alteration in the church came with the new tower of 1774–1775, which replaced the old structure seen in the prints published by Meléndez (Fig. 102). The latter tower had collapsed in the earthquake of 1746. There persists a romantic legend that the amorous viceroy Amat drew the plans and left their execution to an engineer Juan de la Roca. The truth of any of this has yet to be established.[9] The tower of 1774–1775 is characterized by rococo influence in the moldings, the style which appears all over Latin America in the second half of the eighteenth century, but the polygonal shape of the tower as shown in the engraving published by Meléndez is preserved. The tower, damaged in the earthquake of 1940, was repaired under the direction of Harth-terré in 1942–1944, and the cupola at the top, altered in the nineteenth century, was returned to its original design.

The worst damage befell the colonial church in the nineteenth century, first in the early years under the Neoclassicist Matías Maestro.[10] Then the large half columns with Ionic capitals must have been put in place. The famous *camarín* of the Virgin, all done in Neoclassic style, with its paintings in the second story by José del Pozo dated 1798, has a lower chamber in which are found exactly the same Ionic pilasters as those in the nave. Moreover, this modification of the orders is specifically mentioned in an epic poem which was published in 1807 to celebrate and to extol the complete renovation of the church.[11]

The renovation brought the wanton destruction of three centuries of colonial art, known to us now only by Meléndez's description. How many magnificent Baroque retables were dismantled and burned at that time, it is difficult to say. Not one exists today. Maestro covered the vaults with his own oil paintings which in their turn were consigned to the flames in the modernization of 1898–1901. Then the wooden ribbed vaults of the church were once more revealed to an astonished public. The vaults of the aisles were, however, replaced by wooden cupolas with imitation Gothic ribs, destroying the former groined vaults. Pointed windows were let into the nave, and the dome was rebuilt and redecorated.[12] All of the altars of the church were brought up to date by an Italian named Francesco Scicale whose reputation is proclaimed on the basis that he had worked in palaces of Egypt and Constantinople, as well as in the Opera House in Paris. Hence he was eminently qualified to construct altars *a la porcelana* in Lima, Peru!

The very latest modification in Santo Domingo took place in 1942–1944 when false ribs were added to the choir vaults to give them the same appearance as the rest of the nave. These vaults had been burned in 1834, and, when remade in wood, the ribs had been omitted.

In recapitulation, the sad tale of the church of Santo Domingo ends with the present state of the edifice as follows: floor plan of about 1540; the bay within the side portal including pointed arches and some ribs, probably of this period; the imitation Gothic vaults of the nave of the second half of the seventeenth century; the Ionic half columns of the nave added in 1807; the interior otherwise refurbished 1898–1901 and 1942–1944; the tower of 1773–1775 and the portals restored in 1942–1944.

The history of the monastery is somewhat less depressing. The Chapter House is a magnificent room with two deep windows. The niche of the tribune and two doors are covered by large shell vaults, superbly decorative, and a signature of their eighteenth-century date. The style of this period is also pronounced in the large volutes which are applied as decoration below the cornice. The banded barrel vault with smooth white surface furnishes a good contrast in textures to the rusticated walls. Materials, as usual, are brick and stucco for the wall, cane and stucco in the vaults.

The main cloister in the time of Meléndez (Fig. 102) boasted stone construction in both galleries, but today the upper story of wood with stucco ornaments must belong to the eighteenth century, after the earthquake of 1746. The general disposition and the elliptical openings, nevertheless, retain the original design shown in Meléndez's print of 1681, another proof that reconstructions were frequently made without change of style. The lovely Sevillian tile dado (Fig. 127) shines as resplendently as when first installed. The date 1606 occurs in the tiles repeatedly, 1604 on two occasions, and 1620 once. In the north wall is the name of the artist, probably a Moor: *Me fecit Garrido 1606.* The tiles along the stairway which mounts to the choir are unusual in that they contain pictures, naturally enough scenes of the life of St. Dominic.

The striking feature of the second cloister is the appearance of trefoil arches, even though often rebuilt. That they were so designed in the second half of the sixteenth century is doubtful. At any event they existed in the time of Meléndez (1681), for they can easily be distinguished in the engraving in his book. This testimony suggests that the trefoil cloisters of Santo Domingo were erected in the early seventeenth century. If that be true, they were the earliest of a type which became very popular in Lima.

The cloisters of the novitiate, first built under Domingo de Valderrama (1586–1590)[13] now form part of the Colegio de Santo Tomás. With one side of the structure entirely demolished and the rest drastically modified, the only features of interest are a few trefoil arches in the second story. A handsome arrangement is the composition of repeated arches over the stairway and the wooden dome, also *mudéjar* in flavor, due to the strips which suggest a melon vault (Fig. 120).

Another attachment to the monastery of Santo Domingo is the chapel of the Vera Cruz, a small church of single nave with seven bays of barrel vaults and a dome over the crossing. The style of its Doric pilasters and cornice belongs to the seventeenth century, but it has been restored on many occasions, the last time in 1942–1944. A document recently discovered by Harth-terré establishes the severe and classical portal as the work of the architect, Diego Guillén, in 1613.[14]

[1] Lizárraga, *Descripción de las Indias* (Buenos Aires, 1916), pp. 92–104; List of the provincials with their dates in *Corona centenaria* (Lima, 1921), pp. 164–166.

[2] Angulo, Domingo, "La iglesia de Santo Domingo," *Revista del Archivo Nacional del Perú*, XII (1939), 221–228.

[3] Meléndez, Juan, *Tesoros verdaderos de las Indias . . . orden de predicadores* (Rome, 1681), I, 53–59.

[4] Cobo, Bernabé, *op. cit.*, pp. 237–239.

[5] Angulo, Domingo, *op. cit.*, p. 222.

[6] *Ibid.*

[7] Angulo, Domingo, "La torre de Santo Domingo," *Arquitecto peruano*, March, 1938.

[8] Harth-terré, Emilio, "Una capilla muy galana," *El Comercio* (Lima), June 9, 1948.

[9] *Idem.*, "¿Dibujó realmente el virrey Amat?" *Cultura peruana*, vol. I (1941), no. 1. Juan de la Roca's activity on the church of the Buena Muerte is documented. See p. 272.

[10] Angulo, Domingo, "El primitivo estilo de Santo Domingo de Lima," *Revista del Archivo Nacional del Perú*, II (1921), 527–530; Flores Araoz, José, "La iglesia de Santo Domingo," *Cultura peruana*, vol. III (1943), no. 13.

[11] Gento Sanz, Padre Benjamín, *San Francisco de Lima*, pp. 160–163.

[12] *Rasgos conmemorativos de la inauguración del templo de Santo Domingo, octubre de 1901* (Lima, 1901), pp. 15–22.

[13] Lizárraga, *op. cit.*, p. 102.

[14] Harth-terré, *Artífices*, p. 89.

LIMA: CATALOGUE OF SECONDARY
MONUMENTS

Descalzas de San José

The church is in ruinous condition subsequent to the earthquake of 1940. It preserves a mediocre side portal of the late seventeenth century, and perhaps the floor plan of the original foundation of 1602.

Cobo, *op. cit.*, p. 265; Vargas Ugarte, "Notas," pp. 166, 173, 180.

Descalzos Franciscanos

This branch of the Franciscans came in 1596. The church, consecrated in 1749 according to the inscription on the portrait of Monseñor Joseph Cayetano Paravicino, is notable only for its picturesque location. The single-storied cloisters with square piers belong to the same type as those of Arequipa and the nunneries of Lima. An inner chapel dedicated to Nuestra Señora de los Angeles has a good portal of the late seventeenth century. The monastery possesses a magnificent collection of paintings, the finest in Lima.

Cobo, *op. cit.*, p. 250; Angulo, Domingo, "El barrio de San Lázaro," *Monografías históricas*, II, 120–122.

Desemparados

Founded in 1629 and demolished in 1937 to provide a garden behind the Palacio del Gobierno. It maintained some of the style of the church erected in 1669–1678 until torn down,

although it had suffered badly in the remodeling of 1894–1897.

Torre Revello and Noël, *Arquitectura virreinal*, pp. 145–46; Angulo, Diego, *Planos*, vol. I, pl. 26; Mugaburu, *Diario*, I, 174; II, 16–17; Vargas Ugarte, *Los jesuitas del Perú*, pp. 176–180.

Espíritu Santo

This hospital for sailors which was established in 1573 received its final rebuilding under the viceroy Amat in 1765. In recent years the church had disappeared, but the first story of the patio with its fine trefoil arches formed part of the School of Engineering. The building as a whole was much remodeled. In 1945 it was abandoned in preparation for its demolition to make way for the new basilica of Santa Rosa.

Cobo, *op. cit.*, p. 297; *Memorias de los virreyes* (Madrid, 1859), IV, 464–465; Eguiguren, L. A., *Diccionario histórico cronológico de San Marcos* (Lima, 1940), I, 975–977.

Magdalena la Vieja

This church stood well outside of Lima in the colonial period. It is a modest single-naved edifice in eighteenth-century style, whose wooden barrel vault has often been rebuilt. The neocolonial façade dates from 1931. Although architecturally insignificant, it has a magnificent array of seven gilded retables and pulpit, all of the eighteenth century, and second only in importance to those of Jesús María.

Mercedarias

The present church is neo-Gothic of the years 1927–1930. The principal cloister of single story with square piers and the small domed chapel in the second cloister date from the eighteenth century. The roofs of the cloisters await reconstruction after their collapse in 1940. The convent began as a *beaterio* in 1686 and was elevated to higher status in 1734.

García Sanz, Pedro, *Apuntes para la his. eccl. de Lima* (Lima, 1876), p. 89.

Nuestra Señora del Belén

In 1924 this church, formerly part of the Mercedarian Recoleta, was destroyed to widen a street. The fine collection of eighteenth-century retables and a pulpit of the seventeenth century were transferred to the new Colegio de los Sagrados Corazones (1937).

Cobo, *op. cit.*, p. 253.

Nuestra Señora de la Buena Muerte

This order of fathers of the Cross came to Lima in 1710. The church of single nave is now nondescript, much rebuilt, and largely modern. The well-known architect, Cristóbal de Vargas, was engaged here in 1749. Two designs for the church by another architect, Juan de la Roca, were submitted in 1771, according to an entry in the *Libro de Gastos, 1739–1775*, p. 707, a discovery made by Alberto Santibáñez Salcedo.

Angulo, Domingo, "El barrio de San Lázaro," *Monografías históricas*, II, 161; Harth-terré, "La iglesia del Corazón de Jesús," *Arquitecto peruano*, January, 1942.

Nuestra Señora de la Cabeza

This extremely impoverished parish church has been frequently rebuilt since its foundation in 1617, the last major reconstruction in 1810. Its adobe and wood fabric is totally wanting in architectural interest.

Angulo, Domingo, "El barrio de San Lázaro," *Monografías históricas*, II, 106, 136–140.

Nuestra Señora del Carmen

The first Carmelite nuns came to Lima in 1619 and this house, unlike the second dedicated to Santa Teresa, still flourishes. The church has been frequently rebuilt and restored, the last time in 1943. In general, the style of the eighteenth century prevails in the portal with its volute capitals, but the towers are of nineteenth-century design. The interior belongs to the typically *limeño* group of the mid-eighteenth century with its bracketed cornice. The entablature block arrangement somewhat resembles that of Santo Tomás and the blind arches of the walls are unusual. This simple barrel-vaulted interior with its lower choir to the right of the sanctuary and its upper choir over the entrance is a very effective nuns' church, even though the furnishings and tile dado are modern. Within the convent the portal of a small rococo chapel is preserved.

Cobo, *op. cit.*, pp. 270–272; Harth-terré, "La ermita de la Asunción," *Arquitecto peruano*, July, 1940.

Nuestra Señora de Cocharcas

The first church was inaugurated in 1685, and later rebuilt on another site nearby in 1777. According to an inscription on his portrait, dated 1804, which hangs in the sacristy, the funds for the later edifice were supplied by Santiago Concha y Errasquín. The donor, a canon, petitioned the king in 1792, that he take under his protection the newly erected church, but the request was rejected. The present interior of Latin-cross plan has no architectural character, and its wooden vaults were being reërected in 1944–1945. The façade and its two towers belong to the eighteenth century, although damaged by a coat of cement, applied in 1930.

Mugaburu, *Diario,* II, 160; Fuentes, Manuel, *Estadística de Lima,* p. 512; Noël and Torre Revello, "Contribución documental," *Congreso internacional de historia de América,* II, 539.

Nuestra Señora de la Concepción

One of the oldest convents of nuns (1573), the church of the Concepción has suffered repeatedly from earthquakes and is now a mediocre structure with vaults of wood. The project to destroy the apse to widen a street will leave it in a still more lamentable condition. The side portal and the tower were completed in 1699 by the architect, Diego Pérez de Guzmán. The present tower, however, is identical in design to those of Nuestra Señora de Cocharcas (1777) and hence must have been rebuilt in the second half of the eighteenth century. The retables include a splendid work dedicated to St. John the Baptist by Martínez Montañés (1607–1612) and the high altar by Llorente (1783). Within the convent the principal cloister adheres to the *limeño* tradition for nunneries, in its single story of arches on square piers.

Cobo, *op. cit.,* pp. 261–263; Vargas Ugarte, "Notas," p. 291; —, "El monasterio de la Concepción," *Mercurio peruano,* XXIV (1942), 619–637; *Documentos para la historia del arte en Andalucía* (Seville, 1930), II, 227–232.

Nuestra Señora de Copacabana

First a small hermitage in 1617, and later made a *beaterio* in 1691, various well-known architects including Fray Pedro Galeano (1628) and Manuel de Escobar (1684–1687) worked on this church. It was badly damaged in 1746 and the interior today is a miserable sight, a Latin-cross plan with wooden barrel vaults and a dome. The façade is dated by an inscription just within the portal: *Miguel Rodríguez me fecit año 1700.* It has, however, suffered by much restoration including a coat of cement in recent years. The upper part of the portal with its round window is clearly modern, but otherwise the early eighteenth-century design is evident.

Angulo, Domingo, "El barrio de San Lázaro," *Monografías históricas,* II, 129–135; Vargas Ugarte, "Notas," pp. 170, 172–173, 289, 295.

Nuestra Señora de la Encarnación

The convent of Augustinian nuns founded in 1554 was the first women's order to be established in Lima. Formerly located on the Plaza de San Martín, it was in ruinous condition when torn down in 1944.

Calancha, *Crónica,* pp. 420–432; Cobo, *op. cit.,* pp. 258–260; Portal, Ismael, *Lima religiosa,* pp. 15–19.

Nuestra Señora de Guadalupe

The church was formerly part of the third Franciscan convent of Lima, set up in 1614. It gave way to the site of the new Palace of Justice in 1930.

Cobo, *op. cit.,* p. 256; *Libros de Cabildos de Lima,* XIII, 510.

APPENDIX

Nuestra Señora de Guia

The *recoleta* of the Augustinians, it was founded in 1618–1622, according to the archives of San Agustín in Lima, and often rebuilt. Until recent years a fragment of a portal, dating about 1760, still existed, but now nothing remains.

Angulo, Domingo, "El barrio de San Lázaro," *Monografías históricas*, II, 141–147.

Nuestra Señora de Montserrat

This little church, a foundation of two Benedictines in 1600, erected at the expense of Alonso González de la Canal, still maintains the style of the seventeenth century within, although the mediocre façade is an excrescence of about one hundred years ago. Its small single nave has five bays, a rather large dome, and a slightly projecting sanctuary. An unusual arrangement is presented in the combination of wooden ceiling over the elevated choir and barrel vaults of typical *limeño* cane and plaster in the rest of the church. The simple molded cornice in particular suggests a seventeenth-century date. Two side altars of the eighteenth century are preserved in part.

Cobo, *op. cit.*, p. 251; Córdoba Salinas, "Teatro de la Santa Iglesia metropolitana . . . Lima" (manuscript dated 1650 in the New York Public Library), folio 64.

Nuestra Señora del Patrocinio

This tiny church is conventual in type with single nave, lower choir at the right of the sanctuary, and raised choir over the entrance. The large dome over the sanctuary and the broad cornice with dentils provide an original and interesting composition. The façade with two towers, although one of the dullest in Lima,

has the virtue of a dated inscription with the name of the donor (not the architect, as has been erroneously stated): *A costa de don Juan Joseph Aspur se acabó esta obra el año 1734.* The *beaterio* with which this church is connected was founded by Francisco Villagómez in 1688, according to the legend upon his portrait which hangs in the entrance to the cloister.

Angulo, Domingo, "El barrio de San Lázaro," *Monografías históricas*, II, 151–155.

Nuestra Señora del Prado

Inaugurated in 1640, the church today is a poor structure of brick and wood whose vault collapsed in 1940. The best architectural feature is the side portal of brick and stucco, a work of the seventeenth century. Whether it belongs to the original church of 1640 or was built later in the same century is problematic. It does not seem to meet the description of any one of the three portals designed by Juan de Aldaña in 1638. The style with its rustication, the oval ornament, and the broken pediments is related to the monastery entrance of San Francisco and the façade of the chapel of the Soledad (1669–1674). The Prado portal is the best of its kind except for those of San Francisco. The cloister, of single story and square piers, seems to have been reërected in the eighteenth century. The gem of the convent is a small chapel in the second cloister, the Capilla de los Dolores, which has a large shell-shaped semidome, so characteristic of Lima in the eighteenth century, and a fine trefoil door.

Santibáñez Salcedo, Alberto, *El monasterio de Nuestra Señora del Prado* (Lima, 1943); Vargas Ugarte, "Notas," pp. 161, 171–174; Mugaburu, *Diario*, I, 3; Calancha, *Crónica*, II (Lima, 1653, edited after Calancha's death by Bernardo de Torres), *Libro* V; Harth-terré, *Artífices*, pp. 103–104.

Nuestra Señora del Rosario
(Abajo el puente)

A small humble chapel of wood and plaster reconstructed in 1896, according to an inscription in the church. A fallacious tradition claims it as the first church in Lima, but the date of foundation is unknown. It is not mentioned by Padre Cobo, writing in 1629.

Angulo, Domingo, "El barrio de San Lázaro," *Monografías históricas,* II, 104–105.

Recoleta Domínica

This church is now modern Gothic and connected with the Universidad Católica and no longer owned by the Dominicans.

Cobo, *op. cit.,* p. 254.

San Andrés

Lima's first hospital, established in 1545, has now become a conventual school called the Hijas de María Inmaculada. The small chapel with interesting dome belongs in part to the eighteenth century, but the buildings are otherwise modern.

Cobo, *op. cit.,* pp. 282–287.

San Francisco de Paula Nuevo

The new church and convent were begun on a different site in 1748 because of the havoc the earthquake had caused two years previously. After one year the work was abandoned and completed only in 1812–1814. It still lacks the apse, and the interior of nave and two aisles is mediocre with its barrel vaults and dome of wood. The façade, too, in retarded eighteenth-century style, lacks distinction.

Angulo, Domingo, "El barrio de San Lázaro," *Monografías históricas,* II, 126–127.

San Francisco de Paula Viejo

The complex history of this church which originated as Nuestra Señora del Socorro in 1615 is related by Domingo Angulo. I discovered an entry in the "Actas Capitulares" of Sucre Cathedral, Bolivia (*Años 1682–1701,* folio 225 reverse) under date of December 5, 1691, which concerns a contribution of money to the church of San Francisco de Paula. Severely damaged in the earthquake of 1940, the church has been demolished.

Angulo, Domingo, "El barrio de San Lázaro," *Monografías históricas,* II, 123–128.

San Ildefonso

The Academia de Bellas Artes occupies the former Augustinian college which was founded by papal bull in 1608 and inaugurated in 1616. The main cloister of single story carrying arches on square piers remains essentially in the condition in which it was rebuilt following the earthquake of 1687.

Torres, Bernardo de, *Crónica, Libro* I, pp. 200–210; *Revista del Archivo Nacional Perú,* XII (1939), 33; Rubio, David, *Los agustinos en el Perú* (Lima, 1912), p. 76.

San Lázaro

This famous hospital for lepers was founded in 1563 and abolished in 1822. The present large church of nave and two aisles, rebuilt by Matías Maestro in the early nineteenth century, is now almost entirely modern and without interest.

Angulo, Domingo, "El barrio de San Lázaro," *Monografías históricas,* II, 109–119; Mendiburu, *op. cit.,* VII, "Matías Maestro."

San Lorenzo

A humble wooden chapel, first erected in 1834.

Angulo, Domingo, "El barrio de San Lázaro," *Monografías históricas,* II, 165–168.

San Marcelo

San Marcelo began its existence as the first church of the Augustinian order in 1551–1574. The architect, Esteban de Amaya, was engaged in building the second church in 1561, and a year later Cristóbal López made the *artesonado* ceiling and the choir. This comparatively modest building was superseded by another in the time of the viceroy Esquilache (1615–1621), which Padre Cobo called the best of the parish churches. Damage in the earthquake of 1687 was severe, however, and it was reconstructed under the direction of a famous sculptor of retables, Diego de Aguirre.

The restoration of 1925–1933 was so drastic that San Marcelo can no longer be regarded as a colonial building. One of the best of Lima's façades (Fig. 116), dating about 1750, was destroyed and replaced by a monstrous neo-colonial affair which is an exaggeratedly lavish and misunderstood copy of San José in the environs of Nazca. The interior, too, has been entirely redecorated, using the same church as a model, and, though unsatisfactory, with less disastrous results than in the façade. The numerous retables, some of them formerly in San Carlos, were painted black in the past century. At present an attempt is being made to redeem that stupid blunder and to regild them as they were in the eighteenth century.

Cobo, *op. cit.*, pp. 202–203; Calancha, *Crónica*, pp. 247–250; Angulo, Domingo, *Revista histórica*, III (1908), 246; *ibid.*, XIII (1939), 31; Harth-terré, "La primera iglesia de San Agustín en Lima," *Arquitecto peruano*, December, 1941; Lohmann Villena, *Revista histórica*, XIV (1941), 346; Vargas Ugarte, "Notas," pp. 152, 156.

San Pedro Nolasco

This church, which was originally part of the Mercedarian College, is now a poor small modern edifice. The documents of the foundation in 1649 have been published by Padre Barriga.

Barriga, Víctor, *El templo de la Merced de Lima*, pp. 169–173.

San Sebastián

This, the first parish church in Lima (1554), is unfortunately in wretched condition today, having lost its vaults in the earthquake of 1940. Its single nave may still retain the ground plan of the church designed by Francisco Becerra in 1585, but the elevation is in large part of the past century. The most important feature is the fine high altar of the mid-eighteenth century. The side altars of the demolished church of Santa Teresa were to be installed here.

García Irigoyen, *Santo Toribio* (Lima, 1906), I, 325–327; Cobo, *op. cit.*, pp. 197–198; Harth-terré, *Artífices*, p. 73.

Santa Ana

The hospital of Santa Ana was founded by royal decree in 1553, and its church received the honor of being declared the second parish of Lima in 1570. The hospital has disappeared, and the church of Latin-cross form with vaults and dome of wood is completely modern and devoid of interest. The attribution of the original church to Francisco Becerra in Harth-terré's recent book is undoubtedly a typographical error, since the document given as reference is the contract for San Sebastián.

Cobo, *op. cit.*, pp. 199–201, 288–291; *Revista del Archivo Nacional Perú*, XII (1939), 165–181; Harth-terré, *Artífices*, pp. 25, 73.

Santa Catalina

Founded in 1621 and repeatedly destroyed by earthquakes, the last time in 1940, it has lost all architectural significance. Only a very poor side portal with caryatids, like those so common in *limeño* retables of the second half of the eighteenth century, can be considered colonial.

Meléndez, *Tesoros*, III, 57–81; Vargas Ugarte, "Notas," pp. 159, 166, 182; Harth-terré, "Fray Cristóbal Caballero," *Mercurio peruano*, XXV (1943), 383–388.

Santa Clara

The nuns came in 1604, but this church like Santa Catalina, has often been ruined, and only the façade in part shows any vestiges of the colonial period. The single-naved interior was restored after the earthquake of 1940.

Cobo, *op. cit.*, pp. 266–267; Mugaburu, *Diario*, I, 7; Vargas Ugarte, "Notas," pp. 292–293.

Santa Liberata

First built in 1716, the church has been much restored and today is closed to the cult.

Angulo, Domingo, "El barrio de San Lázaro," *Monografías históricas*, II, 156–164.

Santa Rosa de las Monjas

This convent of nuns dedicated to Santa Rosa, founded in 1704 on the site of the saint's death, was inaugurated four years later. The church of single nave belongs to the nunnery type like that of El Carmen. It resembles the latter not only in plan but also in the typical eighteenth-century cornice with bracket in the center of each bay. Exceptional are the pilasters which do not continue to the floor level, stopping, on the contrary, halfway down. A fine dado of Sevillian tiles is perhaps the loveliest feature of the church which is well cared for, but drab. A large dome rises above the crossing and the usual barrel vaults prevail throughout the rest of the building.

The façade belongs to a series of typical *limeño* structures with its two small towers and volute capitals topping the pilasters. The portal has a fine shell decoration over the doorway, an arrangement very commonly used for eighteenth-century interiors. Another appearance of the device on an exterior is that in the side portal of the Merced in Lima.

Very little can be said of the sanctuary within the convent which encloses the room in which the saint died, since it is unavailable to the public. Judging by published photographs the building is contemporary with the structure of 1704–1708. The large cloister by exception among the convents of nuns has both upper and lower galleries, the former consisting of trefoil arches and the latter of round arches.

Portal, Ismael, *Lima religiosa* (Lima, 1924), p. 75; Flores Araoz, José, "Monasterio de Rosas de Santa María de Lima," *Lima, precolombina y virreinal*, pp. 373–390; Eguiguren, L. A., *Calles de Lima*, pp. 94–95.

Santa Rosa de los Padres

Church and monastery were founded in 1676 on the site of the saint's home, five years after her canonization. The inauguration took place in 1685, but the work was not complete until 1728. The interior of single nave with three shallow chapels at each side is today mainly of nineteenth-century date. To the first period (1676–1685) belongs the elevated choir with an allover pattern of ornament similar to the vaults of San Francisco. The early-eighteenth-century façade also remains intact. The rose windows of the clerestory reveal the neo-Gothic taste of the past century. The five bays of vaulting have a domical section and a tiny lantern stands over the crossing. The general effect of the interior is cold and uninteresting but not disagreeable. The plain walls with dentil ornament add a touch of the Neoclassic style of the past century.

"Cedulario arzobispal," *Revista del Archivo Nacional del Perú*, VIII (1930), 48–49; Mugaburu, *Diario*, II, 168–169.

Santiago del Cercado

This church of Latin-cross plan with wooden vaults is almost completely modern, although still on the site of the Indian parish of 1571. The façade was rebuilt in the neocolonial style in 1942.

Cobo, *op. cit.*, pp. 126–130; Mendiburu, *op. cit.*, IX, "Portillo"; Angulo, Domingo, "El barrio de San Lázaro," *Monografías históricas*, II, 97; Harth-terré, "La iglesia del Cercado de Lima," *Arquitecto peruano*, May, 1942.

Surco

Parish church of a pueblo in the suburbs of Lima; adobe and brick structure of long single nave with barrel vault of cane and mud. The broad façade is clearly of the late eighteenth century as are the retables, one with columns fantastically bent in curves.

La Trinidad

Founded in 1584, the church today is a dilapidated structure of wood and plaster, one of the poorest in Lima. A relief of the Trinity, dating from the eighteenth century, which is located over the portal, and some mediocre retables of the same period survive.

Cobo, *op. cit.*, p. 264.

Las Trinitarias

This small conventual church, inaugurated in 1722, has been preserved intact, although the retables all belong to the post-colonial period. The two-towered façade and the side portal with its statue of St. Michael fit into the same stylistic group as Santa Rosa de los Padres. The small interior has only four bays in the nave, a tiny sanctuary, and in contrast a large dome over the crossing. Broad bands resting on corbels divide the dome into six sections, and four small windows provide the lighting. As usual a simple molded cornice stands at the springing of barrel vaults with each transverse band resting upon a corbel. Even without documentation the corbels would indicate an eighteenth-century date, and likewise the even more typical *limeño* feature, the large shell tympanum over the side doorway. The lower choir is placed within the convent to the right of the sanctuary, and the upper choir is elevated over the entrance. All in all the church of the Trinitarian nuns, though unpretentious, offers the spectacle, infrequent in Lima, of a structure unmodified by subsequent reconstructions.

Bermúdez, J. M., *Anales de la catedral de Lima*, p. 258; García Sanz, *op. cit.*, p. 80.

Bibliography

BIBLIOGRAPHY

ART

Angulo Iñiguez, Diego, *Planos de monumentos arquitectónicos de América y Filipinas,* Seville, 1933–1939.

—— "Las catedrales mejicanas del siglo XVI," *Boletín de la Real Academia de la Historia,* Madrid, CXIII (1943), 137–181.

—— and Marco Dorta, Enrique, *Historia del arte hispano-americano,* Barcelona, 1945, vol. I.

Angulo, Padre Domingo, "La iglesia de Santo Domingo de Lima," *Revista del Archivo Nacional del Perú,* XII (1939), 221–228.

Antúnez de Mayolo, Santiago, "Iglesia de Jesús María," *Lima, precolombina y virreinal,* Lima, 1938, pp. 181–224.

Barriga, Padre Víctor, *El templo de la Merced, Documentos para la historia del arte,* Arequipa, 1944.

—— Articles in *El Deber,* newspaper of Arequipa. See notes of chapter VIII.

Benavides Rodríguez, Alfredo, *La arquitectura en el virreinato del Perú y en la capitanía general de Chile,* Santiago, 1941.

Buschiazzo, Mario J., *Estudios de arquitectura colonial hispano-americana,* Buenos Aires, 1944.

—— "Cabildos del virreinato del Río de la Plata," *Boletín de la Comisión Nacional de Museos y Monumentos Históricos,* vol. VIII, 1946.

Camón Aznar, *La arquitectura plateresca,* 2 vols., Madrid, 1945.

Cappa, Padre Ricardo, *Estudios críticos acerca de la dominación española en América,* Madrid, 1895, vols. XIII–XIV.

Castro, Martha de, "La arquitectura barroca del virreinato del Perú," *Revista, Universidad de Habana,* vols. XVI–XVIII, 1943–1944.

Cuadros, Manuel E., *Historia y arquitectura de los templos del Cuzco,* Cuzco, 1946. Booklet.

Documentos de arte colonial sudamericano, Buenos Aires, 1943–1948: I, *La villa imperial de Potosí;* II, *Chuquisaca;* III, *Las iglesias de Potosí;* IV, *El arte religioso y suntuario en Chuquisaca.*

Documentos para la historia del arte en Andalucía, Seville, 1927–1946, vols. I–X.

Exposición de cuadros y objetos de arte virreinal, Lima, 1942.

Flores Araoz, José, "La iglesia de Santo Domingo," *Cultura peruana,* vol. III (1943), no. 13.

García, José Uriel, *La ciudad de los Incas; estudios arqueológicos,* Cuzco, 1922.

—— "La arquitectura colonial del Cuzco," *Revista universitaria,* XXV (1936), 111–118.

—— "Imagineros y tallistas del Cuzco colonial," *La Prensa,* Buenos Aires, February 7, 1937.

—— "Los Mollinedo mecenas del Cuzco colonial," *La Prensa,* Buenos Aires, March 20, 1938.

—— "Un notable artista peruano de la época colonial," *La Prensa,* Buenos Aires, April 24, 1938.

García y Bellido, "Estudios del barroco español," *Archivo español de arte y arqueología,* V (1929), 21–86.

Gento Sanz, Padre Benjamín, *San Francisco de Lima,* Lima, 1945.

Guide to the Art of Latin America, edited by Robert C. Smith and Elizabeth Wilder, Washington, 1948.

BIBLIOGRAPHY

Guido, Angel, *Fusión hispano-indígena en la arquitectura colonial*, Buenos Aires, 1925.

———— "El estilo mestizo o criollo en el arte de la colonia," *Congreso internacional de historia de América*, Buenos Aires, 1938, vol. III, pp. 474–494.

———— *Redescubrimiento de América en el arte*, Rosario, 1941.

Handbook of Latin American Studies, vols. I–XII, Cambridge, 1936–1949.

Harth-terré, Emilio, *Biobibliografía*, Lima, 1945.

———— *Artífices en el virreinato del Perú*, Lima, 1945.

———— "Francisco Becerra," *El comercio de la tarde*, Lima, April 26, 1944; *El comercio de la mañana*, Lima, January 1, 1945.

Kubler, George, *Mexican Architecture of the Sixteenth Century*, 2 vols., New Haven, 1948.

Lampérez y Romea, Vicente, *Arquitectura civil española*, 2 vols., Madrid, 1922.

———— *Historia de la arquitectura cristiana española*, 2nd ed., 3 vols., Madrid, 1930.

Lima, precolombina y virreinal, Lima, 1938.

Llaguno y Amírola, *Noticias de los arquitectos y arquitectura de España*, Madrid, 1829.

Lohmann Villena, Guillermo, "Noticias inéditas para ilustrar la historia de las bellas artes en Lima durante los siglos XVI y XVII," *Revista histórica*, XIII (1940), 5–30; XIV (1941), 345–375.

López Martínez, *Retablos y esculturas de traza sevillana*, Seville, 1928.

———— *Desde Martínez Montañés hasta Pedro Roldán*, Seville, 1932.

Marco Dorta, Enrique, "La arquitectura del renacimiento en Tunja," *Revista de Indias*, Madrid, III (1942), 463–513.

———— "Arquitectura colonial, Francisco Becerra," *Archivo español de arte*, XVI (1943), 7–15.

———— and Angulo Iñiguez, Diego, *Historia del arte hispano-americano*, Barcelona, 1945, vol. I.

Mariátegui Oliva, Ricardo, *Una joya de arquitectura peruana de los siglos XVII y XVIII*, Lima, 1942.

———— *Una iglesia-relicario, El Carmen de Trujillo*, Lima, 1945.

———— *Escultura colonial de Trujillo*, Lima, 1946.

———— *San Francisco y la Dolorosa de Cajamarca*, Lima, 1947.

Medina, Pío Max, *Monumentos coloniales de Humanga (Ayacucho)*, Ayacucho, 1942.

Montes, Padre Graciano, *La sacristía del templo de San Agustín de Lima*, Lima, 1944.

Morales Macchiavello, Carlos, "La iglesia de las carmelitas en Trujillo," *Arquitecto peruano*, July, 1941.

———— "Iglesia y convento de San Francisco de Lima," *Arquitecto peruano*, July, August, September, 1941.

Navarro, José Gabriel, "Curiosa ordenación," *Archivo español de arte y arqueología*, IV (1928), 179–182.

———— *La iglesia de la Compañía en Quito*, Madrid, 1930.

———— *Religious Architecture in Quito*, New York, 1945.

Neumeyer, Alfred, "The Indian Contribution to Architectural Decoration in Spanish Colonial America," *Art Bulletin*, XXX (1948), 104–121.

Noël, Martín, *Contribución a la historia de la arquitectura hispano-americana*, Buenos Aires, 1921.

———— *Teoría histórica de la arquitectura virreinal*, Buenos Aires, 1932.

———— *El arte en la América española*, Buenos Aires, 1942.

———— and Torre Revello, *Arquitectura virreinal*, Buenos Aires, 1934.

———— and Torre Revello, "Contribución documental a la historia del arte colonial hispano-americano," *Congreso internacional de historia de América*, Buenos Aires, 1938, III, 535–550.

"Relación . . . la compra del sitio y fábrica de la nueva iglesia de los Huérfanos," *Revista del Archivo Nacional del Perú*, X (1937), 53–76.

Rodríguez Casado and Pérez Embid, *Construcciones del virrey Amat*, Seville, 1949.

Sánchez Cantón, "El convento de San Francisco de Lima," *Revista de Indias*, Madrid, IV (1943), 527–551.

Santibáñez Salcedo, Alberto, "La restauración de la sacristía del templo de San Agustín," *Cultura peruana*, vol. V (1945), no. 22.

Schubert, Otto, *Historia del barroco en España*, Madrid, 1924.

Solá, Miguel, *Historia del arte hispano-americano*, Barcelona, 1935.

Torre Revello. See Noël and Torre Revello.

Toussaint, Manuel, "El arquitecto de la catedral del Cuzco," *Anales del Instituto de Investigaciones Estéticas*, Mexico, 1941, no. 7, pp. 59–63.

———— *Arte mudéjar en América*, Mexico, 1946.

Vargas Ugarte, Padre Rubén, "Notas para un diccionario de artífices coloniales," in *Cuaderno de estudios*, Lima, Universidad Católica, II (1942–1943), 151–200, 286–298.

———— *Ensayo de un diccionario de artífices coloniales de la América meridional*, Buenos Aires, 1947.

———— *Historia del Colegio y Universidad del Cuzco*, Lima, 1948.

Velarde, Héctor, *Arquitectura peruana*, Mexico City, 1946.

Weise, Georg, *Spanische Plastik*, 4 vols., Reutlingen, 1925–1939.

Wethey, Harold E., "Iglesias de Cajamarca," *Cultura peruana*, vol. V (1945), no. 23.

———— "La Merced in Cuzco, Peru," *Journal of the Society of Architectural Historians*, V (1945–1946), 35–38.

———— "Saña, a Dead City of Peru," *Michigan Alumnus Quarterly Review*, LIII (1946), 9–14; the same in Spanish translation: "Saña, la ciudad muerta del Perú," *Cultura peruana*, vol. VII (1947), no. 28.

———— "The Problem of Toribio de Alcaraz," *Gazette des Beaux Arts*, XXXI (1947), 165–174.

———— "Hispanic-Colonial Architecture in Bolivia," *Gazette des Beaux Arts*, 1949.

HISTORICAL SOURCES

"Actas Capitulares," vol. I (1547–1591), vol. II (1590–1630), vol. IV (1667–1712); original documents preserved in the Sala Capitular, Cuzco Cathedral.

Anales del Cuzco, 1600–1750, Lima, 1901. See *Noticias cronológicas del Cuzco*.

Anello Oliva, Padre Juan, *Historia del Perú y varones insignes de la Compañía de Jesús*, Lima, 1895.

Angulo, Padre Domingo, *La orden de Santo Domingo en el Perú*, Lima, 1909.

———— "El barrio de San Lázaro" and "La metropolitana de la ciudad de los reyes" in *Monografías históricas sobre la ciudad de Lima*, 2 vols., Lima, 1935.

———— "El monasterio de Santa Clara de la ciudad del Cuzco," *Revista del Archivo Nacional del Perú*, XI (1938), 55–95, 157–184.

———— "El terremoto del año 1687," *Revista del Archivo Nacional del Perú*, XII (1939), 3–45, 131–164.

Arzay, Sánchez y Vela, "Historia de la villa imperial de Potosí" (1720), manuscript no. 2065, Madrid, Royal Palace Library.

Barriga, Padre Víctor, *Documentos para la historia de Arequipa*, 2 vols., Arequipa, 1939–1940.

———— *Los mercedarios en el Perú en el siglo XVI*, Rome-Arequipa, 3 vols., 1933, 1939, 1942.

———— *Memorias para la historia de Arequipa*, Arequipa, 2 vols., 1941, 1946.

Beltrán y Rózpide, Ricardo, *Colección de las memorias y relaciones de los virreyes del Perú*, Madrid, 1921.

Bermúdez, J. M., *Anales de la catedral de Lima, 1534–1824*, Lima, 1903.

Calancha, Padre Antonio de la, *Crónica moralizada del orden de San Agustín en el Perú*, Barcelona, 1638.

BIBLIOGRAPHY

Cieza de León, Pedro de, *La crónica general del Perú* (1553), Lima, 1924.

Cobo, Padre Bernabé, "Historia de la fundación de Lima" (1629), in *Monografías históricas sobre la ciudad de Lima,* ed. by Domingo Angulo, Lima, 1935, vol. I. First published in Lima in 1881 by M. González de la Rosa.

Colmenares Fernández de Córdoba, Felipe, *El día deseado,* Lima, 1771.

Córdoba Salinas, "Teatro de la Santa Iglesia Metropolitana de . . . Lima," unpublished manuscript dated 1650, New York Public Library.

—— *Crónica de la religiosíssima provincia de los doze apóstoles del Perú de la orden de N. seráfico P. S. Francisco,* Lima, 1651.

Cosio, José Gabriel, *El Cuzco histórico, Guía,* Lima, 1924.

Echave y Assu, *Estrella de Lima,* Antwerp, 1688.

Eguiguren, L. A. (Multatuli), *Las calles de Lima,* Lima, 1945.

Feyjóo, Miguel, *Relación descriptiva de la ciudad y provincia de Trujillo del Perú,* Madrid, 1763.

Fuentes, Manuel, *Estadística general de Lima,* Lima, 1858.

García de la Concepción, *Historia bethlehemítica,* Seville, 1723.

García Irigoyen, Carlos, *Santo Toribio,* 4 vols., Lima, 1906.

—— *Monografía de la diócesis de Trujillo,* 3 vols., Trujillo, 1930–1931.

García Irigoyen, Manuel, *Historia de la catedral de Lima,* Lima, 1898.

García Sanz, Pedro, *Apuntes para la historia eclesiástica de Lima,* Lima, 1876.

Gridilla, Padre Alberto, *Cajamarca y sus monumentos,* Cajamarca, 1939.

Herrera, Monseñor Salvador, *Pomata y su templo monumental,* Arequipa, 1934.

"Historia o narración de las cosas sucedidas en este colegio del Cuzco, cabeza de los Reynes del Perú desde su fundación hasta hoy primero de noviembre día de Todos Sanctos año de 1600," manuscript, Library of Congress, Washington.

Jiménez de la Espada, Marcos, *Relaciones geográficas de Indias,* 4 vols., Madrid, 1881–1897.

La Bolsa, Arequipa, newspaper of 1868.

Leguía y Martínez, Germán, *Historia de Arequipa,* Lima, 1913.

Levillier, Roberto, *Gobernantes del Perú, Cartas y papeles, Siglo XVI,* 14 vols., Madrid, 1921–1926.

Libros de Cabildos de Lima, 15 vols., Lima, 1935–1947.

Lizárraga, Reginaldo de, *Descripción y población de las Indias* (circa 1590–1603), Lima, 1908.

Lorea, Antonio de, *Santa Rosa,* Madrid, 1671.

Martínez Compañón: *Trujillo del Perú a fines del siglo XVIII,* drawings made for Bishop Martínez Compañón, 1779–1791; pub. Madrid, 1936.

Mateos, Padre F., *Historia general de la Compañía de Jesús en la provincia del Perú, Crónica anónima de 1600,* 2 vols., Madrid, 1944.

Means, Philip A., "Biblioteca Andina," *Connecticut Academy of Arts and Sciences, Transaction,* vol. XXIX, 1928.

Meléndez, Fray Juan, *Tesoros verdaderos de las Indias . . . de el orden de predicadores,* Rome, 1681–1682.

Memorias de los virreyes que han gobernado el Perú, 6 vols., Lima, 1859.

Mendiburu, Manuel de, *Diccionario histórico-biográfico del Perú,* 15 vols., Lima, 1931–1938.

Mendoza, Diego de, *Crónica de la provincia de S. Antonio de los Charcas, del orden de N. seráfico P. S. Francisco de las Indias occidentales, reyno del Perú,* Madrid, 1664.

Middendorf, E. W., *Peru,* 3 vols., Berlin, 1893–1895.

Miranda Valcárcel y Peralta, Francisco, "Crónica de esta provincia del Cuzco" (1650–1707), manuscript, Library of the Convent of La Merced, Cuzco.

BIBLIOGRAPHY

Miró Quesada Sosa, Aurelio, *Costa, sierra y montaña*, 2 vols., Lima, 1938, 1940.

Monografías históricas sobre la ciudad de Lima, 2 vols., Lima, 1935.

Montalvo, Francisco Antonio, *El sol del Nuevo Mundo*, Rome, 1683.

Montesinos, Fernando de, *Anales del Perú* (1642), Madrid, 1906.

Mugaburu, José de, *Diario de Lima* (1640–1694), Lima, 1917–1918.

"Noticias cronológicas del Cuzco," manuscript copy, New York Public Library. Contains the complete text published in two parts by Ricardo Palma as: *Noticias cronológicas del Cuzco*, Lima, 1902, and *Anales del Cuzco*, Lima, 1901. See Romero, Carlos, for publication of the text of the years 1595–1600, omitted by Palma.

Odriozola, Manuel de, *Terremotos*, Lima, 1863.

———— *Documentos literarios del Perú*, 10 vols., Lima, 1872–1877.

Olivas Escudero, Fidel, *Apuntes para la historia de Huamanga*, Ayacucho, 1924.

Portal, Ismael, *Lima religiosa*, Lima, 1924.

Ramos, Alonso, and Sans, Rafael, *Historia de Copacabana*, La Paz, 1860.

"Relación de las provincias y conventos que la Orden de N. Señora de la Merced tiene en las Indias occidentales," in "Yglesias de Indias," unpublished Spanish manuscript number 1106, Ayer Collection, Newberry Library, Chicago.

Relaciones de los virreyes y audiencias que han gobernado al Perú, 3 vols., Madrid, 1867–1872.

Romero, Carlos, "Noticias cronológicas de la gran ciudad del Cuzco" (1595–1600), *Revista histórica*, V (1913), 209–224.

Salmerón, Fray Marcos, *Recuerdos históricos*, Valencia, 1646.

Sanjinés, Fernando de M., *Historia del santuario e imagen de Copacabana*, La Paz, 1909.

Santibáñez Salcedo, Alberto, *El monasterio de Nuestra Señora del Prado*, Lima, 1943.

Santos, Fray Juan, *Chronología hospitalaria*, Madrid, 1716.

Schofield, Sophy E., *Libros de Cabildos de Lima, Indices, 1535–1601*, Lima, 1946.

Suardo, Juan Antonio, *Diario de Lima* (1629–1634), Lima, 1917–1918.

Torres, Bernardo de, *Crónica de la provincia peruana de los ermitaños de San Agustín*, Lima, 1657.

Tovar, Manuel, *Apuntes para la historia eclesiástica del Perú*, Lima, 1873.

Travada y Córdoba, "El suelo de Arequipa convertido en cielo" (1752), in Manuel de Odriozola, *Documentos literarios del Perú*, Lima, 1877, vol. X.

Urteaga, Horacio, and C. A. Romero, *Fundación española del Cuzco*, Lima, 1926.

Valdivia, Deán, *Fragmentos para la historia de Arequipa*, Arequipa, 1847.

Vargas Ugarte, Padre Rubén, *Historia del culto de María en Hispano América y de sus imágenes y santuarios más celebrados*, Lima, 1931.

———— *Historia del Perú, Fuentes*, Lima, 1939.

———— *Manuscritos peruanos*, 4 vols., Lima and Buenos Aires, 1935–1945.

———— *Los jesuitas del Perú*, Lima, 1941.

Vázquez, Juan Teodoro, "Crónica continuada de esta provincia del Perú de N. P. S. Agustín," unpublished manuscript, dated 1721, Museo Prado, Lima. Another copy in the Archivo Histórico Nacional, Madrid.

Vázquez de Espinosa, Fray Antonio, *Compendium and Description of the West Indies* (1612–1630), trans. by Charles Upson Clark, Smithsonian Miscellaneous Collection, vol. CII, Washington, 1942.

Villanueva Urteaga, Horacio, "Cajamarca prehispánica y colonial," *Revista universitaria*, Cuzco, XXXIII (1944), 97–155.

———— "Hacia la ciudad de Cajamarca la grande," *Revista universitaria*, XXXVI (1947), 197–244.

Zamácola y Jáurequi, *Apuntes para la historia de Arequipa* (1804), Arequipa, 1888.

———— *Relación . . . el espantoso terremoto, el día 13 de mayo de 1784*, Arequipa, 1889.

BIBLIOGRAPHY

PERIODICALS

Cuadernos de Estudios, Instituto de Investigaciones Históricas, Universidad Católica,
Lima, 1938–

Cultura peruana, Lima, 1941–

*Journal of the Society of Architectural His-
torians,* Urbana, Illinois, vol. V (1945–
1946); Special Issue on Latin American
Architecture.

Mercurio peruano, Lima, 1918–

Revista del Archivo Nacional del Perú, Lima,
1920–

Revista histórica, Lima, 1906–

Revista universitaria, Cuzco, 1912–

ARCHIVES

Cuzco, Archivo Capitular.
——— Archivo de la Merced.
——— Archivos Notariales.
Lima, Archivo Capitular.
——— Archivo Nacional del Perú.
Sucre, Archivo Capitular.
——— Archivo Nacional de Bolivia.

Notes

NOTES

CHAPTER I

THE EVOLUTION OF COLONIAL ART IN PERU

1. Leonard, Irving, "Romances of Chivalry in the Spanish Indies," *University of California Publications in Modern Philology*, Berkeley, XVI (1933), 217–372; *Books of the Brave* (Cambridge, 1949).

2. Lanning, J. T., *Academic Culture in the Spanish Colonies* (New York, 1940); Eguiguren, Luis Antonio, *Diccionario histórico cronológico de la real y pontificia Universidad de San Marcos* (Lima, 1940), I, 2.

3. Mecham, John L., *Church and State in Latin America* (Chapel Hill, 1934); Haring, Clarence H., *The Spanish Empire in America* (New York, 1947).

4. Angulo, Diego, *Planos de monumentos arquitectónicos de América y Filipinas* (Seville, 1933–1939).

5. Sanjinés, Fernando de M., *Historia del santuario e imagen de Copacabana* (La Paz, 1909), pp. 114–116.

6. Vargas Ugarte, Padre Rubén, *Los jesuitas del Perú* (Lima, 1941); Mateos, Padre F., *Historia general de la Compañía de Jesús en la provincia del Perú* (Madrid, 1944).

7. See Angulo, Diego, and Marco Dorta, Enrique, *Historia del arte hispano-americano* (Barcelona, 1945), vol. I; Kubler, George, *Mexican Architecture of the Sixteenth Century* (New Haven, 1948).

8. Braden, George S., *Religious Aspects of the Conquest of Mexico* (Durham, 1930).

9. Vargas Ugarte, *Ensayo de un diccionario de artífices coloniales* (Buenos Aires, 1947); "Notas para un diccionario de artífices coloniales," *Cuaderno de estudios*, Lima, Universidad Católica, II (1942–1943), 151–200, 286–298; Harth-terré, Emilio, *Artífices en el virreinato del Perú* (Lima, 1945); Barriga, Padre Víctor, "Documentos para la historia del arte en Arequipa" (unpublished); articles in *El Deber*, newspaper of Arequipa; García, José Uriel, *La ciudad de los Incas* (Cuzco, 1922); "La arquitectura colonial del Cuzco," *Revista universitaria*, XXV (1936), 111–118.

10. Harth-terré, *op. cit.*, pp. 13–24; Schofield, Sophy, *Libros de Cabildos de Lima, Indices, Años 1535–1601* (Lima, 1946).

11. Barriga, *Documentos para la historia de Arequipa* (Arequipa, 1939), I, 79–83, 177–180, 211–212; Wethey, H. E., "The Problem of Toribio de Alcaraz," *Gazette des Beaux Arts*, XXXI (1947), 165–174.

12. Vargas Ugarte, *Ensayo de un diccionario*, pp. 62–64, 101–102, 120–122.

13. Harth-terré, *op. cit.*, pp. 191–197.

14. *Ibid.*, pp. 223–231.

15. Zimmern, Natalie H., "Tapestries of Colonial Peru," *Journal of the Brooklyn Museum*, 1943–1944, pp. 27–52.

16. Arzay, Sánchez y Vela, "Historia de la villa imperial de Potosí" (1720), Manuscript No. 2065, Madrid, Royal Palace Library, folio 494.

17. Guido, Angel, "El estilo mestizo o criollo en el arte de la colonia," *Congreso internacional de historia de América* (Buenos Aires, 1938), III, 482.

18. Cappa, Padre Ricardo, *Estudios críticos acerca de la dominación española en América* (Madrid, 1895), XIII, 103.

19. Wethey, "Hispanic-Colonial Architecture in Bolivia." *Gazette des Beaux Arts*, 1949.

20. Calancha, Antonio de la, *Crónica moralizada* (Barcelona, 1638), p. 488.

21. "Historia o narración de las cosas sucedidas en este colegio del Cuzco, cabeza de los Reynes del Perú desde su fundación hasta oy primero de noviembre día de Todos Sanctos año de 1600" (folio 132, manuscript in the Library of Congress, Washington, D. C.): ". . . hizo también por medio del Padre Juan Ruiz famoso arquitecto de nuestra Compañía la portada de los Indios que sale a una Calle Real de cal y canto y la Portada principal de nuestra iglesia que sale a la Plaça principal del Cuzco la qual toda ella e labrada de sillería perfectíssima con mucha cantidad de columnas y pilares grandes y pequeñas con sus basas, chapiteles, Pedestales y cemborios y a los lados sus encaxes y assientos para sanctos de bulto, todo de cantería ricamente labrada y todo con tanto primor y arte que en todo el Piru de barra a barra no ay obra que le iguale." The same description appears in another manuscript: Mateos, *op. cit.*, II, 33.

22. Anello Oliva, Padre Juan, *Historia del Perú y varones insignes de la Compañía de Jesús* (Lima, 1895), pp. 164, 204–205.

23. Cobo, Padre Bernabé, "Historia de la fundación de Lima" (1629), in *Monografías históricas sobre la cuidad de Lima* (Lima, 1935), I, 52–53; Buschiazzo, Mario, *Estudios de arquitectura colonial hispano-americana* (Buenos Aires, 1944), pp. 29–30; Palm, Erwin E., *Anales de la Universidad de Santo Domingo*, IX (1945), 279.

24. Sanjinés, *op. cit.*, pp. 114–116; Wethey, "Hispanic-Colonial Architecture in Bolivia."

25. Gothic vaults survived to a very late date in Bolivia as well as in Peru. San Agustín (*circa* 1585–1620) and Santo Domingo (early seventeenth century) at Sucre have decorative ribbed vaults in the transept, crossing, and sanctuary. In Santo Domingo at Cochabamba (1778) they occur over the arms of the transept. The cathedral of Sucre, rebuilt in 1683–1692, and the chapel of Santo Rojas (1718) have Gothic vaults throughout.

26. Schubert, Otto, *Historia del barroco en España* (Madrid, 1924), p. 116.

27. Wölfflin, Heinrich, *Principles of Art History* (English edition, New York, 1932).

28. Braun, Joseph, *Spaniens alte Jesuitenkirchen* (Freiburg, 1913).

29. Angulo, Diego, "La Capilla del Pocito de Guadalupe," *Arte en América y Filipinas*, 1936, pp. 161–165.

30. Vargas Ugarte, *Ensayo de un diccionario*, pp. 321–322.

31. Buschiazzo, "Cabildos del virreinato del Río de la Plata," *Boletín de la Comisión Nacional de Museos y Monumentos Históricos*, VIII (1946).

32. *Recopilación de las leyes de los reynos de las Indias* (Madrid, 1841), Book IV, título VII; Tizón y Bueno, Ricardo, "El plano de Lima," *Monografías históricas sobre la ciudad de Lima* (Lima, 1935), I, 401–407; Angulo, Domingo, "Fundación y población de la villa de Saña," *Revista del Archivo Nacional del Perú*, I (1920), 280–289; Solá, Miguel, *Historia del arte hispano-americano* (Barcelona, 1935), pp. 13–21; Harth-terré, "La fundación de la ciudad colonial," *La Prensa* (Lima), July 28, 1938; for Mexico see Kubler, *op. cit.*, I, 68–102.

33. See the costumes of Charles IX of France and his queen, Elizabeth of Austria, in Piton, Camille, *Le costume civil en France de XIII au XIX siècle* (Paris, 1910), pp. 152–153.

34. See Velarde, Héctor, *Arquitectura peruana* (Mexico City, 1946), pp. 126–130.

CHAPTER II

THE SIXTEENTH CENTURY: AYACUCHO, LAKE TITICACA

1. Gridilla, Padre Alberto, *Cajamarca y sus monumentos* (Cajamarca, 1939), p. xvii.

2. See the catalogue of the churches of Lima in the present volume (Appendix). For Spanish prototypes see: Angulo, Diego, "Arquitectura mudéjar sevillana," *Boletín de la Sociedad Española de Excursiones*, XL (1932), 165–212, 245–293; Weise, Georg, *Studien zur spanischen Archtektur der Spätgotik* (Reutlingen, 1933).

3. Medina, Pío Max, *Monumentos coloniales de Huamanga (Ayacucho)*, (Ayacucho, 1942), pp. 9–11.

4. *Ibid., passim.*; Córdoba Salinas, *Crónica de la religiosíssima provincia de los doce apóstoles del Perú . . .* (Lima, 1651), p. 545.

5. Harth-terré, "Iglesia de San Francisco de Asís," *Arquitecto peruano*, March, 1941; Marco Dorta, *Historia del arte hispano-americano*, I, 635.

6. Córdoba Salinas, *op. cit.*, pp. 423–432; Montesinos, Fernando de, *Anales del Perú*, pp. 25–27.

7. Gento Sanz, Padre Benjamín, *San Francisco de Lima* (Lima, 1945), p. 305. See pages 103–104, above.

8. Buschiazzo, "Exotic Influences in American Colonial Art," *Journal of the Society of Architectural Historians*, V (1945–1946), 22.

9. Medina, *op. cit.*, p. 51.

10. Meléndez, Fray Juan, *Tesoros verdaderos de las Indias . . . de el orden de predicadores* (Rome, 1681), I, 96, 99, 318, 399.

11. Mateos, *op. cit.*, II, 400.

12. Meléndez, *op. cit.*, I, 365.

13. Mendiburu, Manuel de, *Diccionario histórico-biográfico del Perú* (Lima, 1931–1938), vol. VII, "Montalvo y Peralta"; Vargas Ugarte, *Ensayo de un diccionario*, pp. 17–18, 71; *Revista de archivos y bibliotecas nacionales* (Lima, 1900), V, 77. La Asunción at Yunguyo may preserve its plan of 1590, but it is otherwise largely rebuilt.

14. Angulo and Marco Dorta, *op. cit.*, I, 576–577.

15. *Revista de archivos y bibliotecas nacionales, loc. cit.*; Marco Dorta, *Historia del arte hispano-americano*, I, 638–639; —"Iglesias renacentistas en las riberas del lago Titicaca," *Anuario de Estudios Americanos*, II (1945), 701–715.

CHAPTER III

THE SEVENTEENTH CENTURY: CUZCO

1. Mendoza, Diego de, *Crónica de la provincia de San Antonio de los Charcas* (Madrid, 1664), pp. 133–136. The preface is dated 1656–1663.

2. Zimmerman, Arthur F., *Francisco de Toledo, fifth viceroy of Peru, 1569–1581* (Caldwell, Idaho, 1938), p. 145; Vargas Ugarte, *Ensayo de un diccionario*, pp. 107–108. The document of October 10, 1559, still exists in the "Actas Capitulares," vol. I, folio 99 reverse, Archives of Cuzco Cathedral. The following volumes of the "Actas Capitulares" are preserved in the Sala Capitular: vol. I (1547–1591), in very fragmentary condition, surely of more than one volume originally; vol. II (1590–1630); (vol. III missing); vol. IV

(1667–1712). The laying of the ground stone and other references in 1560 are recorded in *Noticias cronológicas del Cuzco* (Lima, 1902), pp. 192–196. This publication contains part of the important chronicle of that name which was written in Cuzco in 1749. Ricardo Palma brought out the work in two sections, unaware that they are one and the same history of Cuzco. The second part he had printed as *Anales del Cuzco, 1600–1749* (Lima, 1901), but he omitted entirely the years 1595–1600 which were issued by Carlos A. Romero in *Revista histórica*, V (1913), 209–224. The Palma editions are defective and replete with errors throughout, another proof that creative writers are rarely scholars. Romero attributed the work to a canon of Cuzco, Diego de Esquivel y Navia, because his name is written on the cover of the manuscript formerly in the possession of Dr. Fortunato Herrera of Cuzco. The name may, however, indicate ownership rather than authorship of the manuscript. The two best copies of the work were lost in the fire of the Biblioteca Nacional of Lima in 1943. The library of the University of Cuzco and the estate of Dr. Herrera possess manuscripts of the second half of the chronicle. A complete copy in a good hand belongs to the New York Public Library, the gift of the late Philip Ainsworth Means. Villanueva, Horacio, "Los anales del Cuzco y su presunto autor D. Diego de Esquivel y Navia," *Revista del Instituto Americano de Arte*, Cuzco, IV (1945), 61–72.

3. "Libro de gastos," *protocolo* X, loose sheets dated 1583, Archivo Capitular, Sucre Cathedral; Wethey, "Hispanic-Colonial Architecture in Bolivia."

4. "Actas Capitulares," vol. I, folios 114 and reverse. In an entry of September 22, 1562, Juan Correa petitioned that his salary as *maestro mayor*, then six months in arrears, be paid in full or he would resign. This documentary reference was generously supplied by Monseñor Juan Antonio Casanova. Vargas Ugarte, "Notas," p. 158; —, *Ensayo de un diccionario*, p. 65.

5. Urteaga, Horacio H., and Romero, Carlos A., *Fundación española del Cuzco* (Lima, 1926), pp. 98–114.

6. *Noticias cronológicas del Cuzco*, p. 220.

7. Lizárraga, Reginaldo de, *Descripción y población de las Indias* (Lima, 1908), pp. 80–81; written in the last decade of the sixteenth century. In 1589 the canon, Esteban Villalón, agreed to pay for the construction of one of the chapels in which he was to be interred. This information was supplied by Monseñor Juan Antonio Casanova who will publish the document in his forthcoming history of the canons of Cuzco.

8. Documents in Marco Dorta, "Arquitectura colonial, Francisco Becerra," *Archivo español de arte*, XVI (1943), 7–15; Llaguno y Amírola, *Noticias de los arquitectos y arquitectura de España* (Madrid, 1829), III, 56–58.

9. On Tunja Cathedral see Marco Dorta, *Historia del arte hispano-americano*, I, 557–558; Marco Dorta, "La arquitectura del renacimiento en Tunja," *Revista de Indias*, III (1942), 470–475. The original documents on Bartolomé Carrión's engagement as architect of Cuzco Cathedral are found in "Actas Capitulares," vol. II, folios 119–121. The text was partly transcribed by Vargas Ugarte, "Notas," p. 159; —, *Ensayo de un diccionario*, pp. 64–65.

10. Harth-terré, "Francisco Becerra"; *El comercio de la tarde* (Lima), April 26, 1944; and *El comercio de la mañana*, Jan. 1, 1945; —, *Artífices en el virreinato del Perú*, pp. 80–82.

11. *Anales del Cuzco*, p. 30.

12. Documents discovered by Fray Gento Sanz, *San Francisco de Lima* (Lima, 1945), pp. 351–360; the import of the documents was first published by Harth-terré, *El comercio de la mañana* (Lima), Jan. 1, 1945. Two other architects who had worked on the cathedral, *circa* 1610–1615, Juan de Pontones and Francisco de la Cueva, are also mentioned; Vargas Ugarte, *Ensayo de un diccionario*, pp. 184–188.

13. Harth-terré, *Artífices*, p. 82.

14. *Anales del Cuzco*, p. 76.

15. Montesinos, in *Anales del Perú*, II, 47

(completed in 1642), states that, although Cuzco Cathedral was begun in 1573, it was only half finished or less; *Anales del Cuzco,* pp. 86, 89, 92.

16. Vargas Ugarte, "Notas," pp. 161–164.

17. *Anales del Cuzco,* pp. 102, 123–125, 131, 142. The cathedral was not consecrated until 1668.

18. Vargas Ugarte, "Notas," pp. 163–164.

19. Matto de Turner, Clorinda, *Tradiciones cuzqueñas* (Arequipa, 1884), I, 100. Her source was the *Anales del Cuzco.* Nearly all writers of guidebooks on Cuzco have followed suit. Francisco Guzmán in "La catedral del Cuzco," *Revista del Instituto Arqueológico del Cuzco,* III (1938), 71, makes the same error. Benavides Rodríguez attempted to identify Diego Arias, priest of Pissac and Urubamba, and later canon of Huamanga and Cuzco, with a painter of images in Seville, Spain, a land which it is unlikely he ever saw: Benavides Rodríguez, Alfredo, *La arquitectura en el virreinato del Perú y en la capitanía general de Chile* (Santiago de Chile, 1941), p. 54; López Martínez, Celestino, *Arquitectos, escultores y pintores, vecinos de Sevilla* (Seville, 1928), p. 19.

20. Diego Arias became *obrero mayor* by provision of the viceroy on February 29, 1648. This fact is stated in the manuscript copy of the "Noticias cronológicas del Cuzco," folio 280 reverse (New York Public Library). It does not appear in Ricardo Palma's printed version, which is notable for numerous abridgments and omissions. Vargas Ugarte in *Ensayo de un diccionario,* p. 126, mistakenly says that Arias became *maestro mayor* on February 29, 1641.

21. Miguel Gutiérrez Sencio is called *maestro mayor* of the cathedral in a document of 1625 referring to the purchase of a slave. The document is in the Archivos notariales, Cuzco, Ante Luis Diez de Morales, *escribano.* This information was kindly supplied by Dr. José Uriel García. Gutiérrez Sencio is mentioned, as in charge of the cathedral, in the report of the viceroy, the Marqués de Guadalcázar, dated December 14, 1628: *Relaciones de los virreyes y audiencias que han gobernado al Perú* (Madrid, 1871), II, 47; Gento Sanz, *op. cit.,* pp. 351–360; Vargas Ugarte, *Ensayo de un diccionario,* pp. 182–183.

22. "Recibí del señor licenciado Diego Arias de la Cerda cura beneficiado de Urubamba y obrero mayor de la catedral doscientos pesos de oro reales por el salario que me tocó de tres meses que se cumplen a fin de marzo de 1649 y por verdad lo forme a mi nombre en el Cuzco en veynte y cuatro días del dicho mes y año. Miguel Gutiérrres Cencio" (*Legajo 94,* Archivo de la catedral del Cuzco). The archives of Cuzco Cathedral are in a state of complete disorder, unbound documents wrapped in paper and string being unarranged even as to century or subject matter.

23. *Anales del Cuzco,* p. 110.

24. Angulo, Diego, *Planos de monumentos,* pl. 25.

25. Vázquez de Espinosa, Antonio, *Compendium and Description of the West Indies* (1612–1630), trans. by Charles Upson Clark (Washington, Smithsonian Miscellaneous Collection, vol. CII, 1942), pp. 390, 430.

26. For an important study of the Mexican churches see Angulo, Diego, "Las catedrales mejicanas del siglo XVI," *Bol. Real Acad. de la His.,* Madrid, CXIII (1943), 137–181; —, *Historia del arte hispano-americano,* I, 429–457. I agree with Manuel Toussaint that Francisco Becerra drew the plans of Cuzco Cathedral, but cannot concur in the arguments offered by Toussaint to support the contention. Toussaint's insistence on the similarity between Puebla and Cuzco is not convincing. Indeed, the differences between the plans and elevations of the two churches are very great. Toussaint, Manuel, "El arquitecto de la catedral del Cuzco," *Anales del Instituto de Invest. Estéticas* (Mexico, 1941), no. 7, pp. 59–63.

27. Wethey, "The Early Works of Bartolomé Ordóñez and Diego de Siloe," *Art Bulletin,* XXV (1943), 344.

28. The dimensions of Cuzco Cathedral are approximately as follows: length within church 81.20 meters; breadth of the three naves 28.65 meters; breadth of aisles 5.95 meters; breadth of central nave 9.82 meters; average depth of chapels 6.63 meters; average size of piers 2.53 meters by 2.95 meters at base; average height of church 20 meters; *capilla mayor* raised 1.81½ meters. Dimensions of Cuzco façade are: total breadth 46.25 meters; central portal 14.25 meters; side portals 6.80 meters each; towers 9.30 meters wide each.

29. Lampérez y Romea, *Arquitectura cristiana española* (2nd ed., Madrid, 1930); Angulo and Marco Dorta, *Historia del arte hispanoamericano*, I; Palm, "Rodrigo de Liendo, arquitecto en la Española," *Publicaciones de la Universidad de Santo Domingo*, XXVIII, 1944; —"Documentos y testimonios relativos al arquitecto, Rodrigo Gil de Rozillo, llamado Rodrigo de Liendo," *Anales de la Universidad de Santo Domingo*, X (1946), 281–335; Waterman, T. T., "Gothic Architecture in Santo Domingo," *Bulletin of the Pan-American Union*, LXXVII (1943), 312–325.

30. Wölfflin, *op. cit.*

31. Dated 1606–1680; upper part finished 1728. *Archivo español de arte*, XIV (1941), 545.

32. *Anales del Cuzco*, p. 110; see notes 21–22. J. U. García attributed the façade of Cuzco Cathedral to a man called Francisco Domínguez de Chávez y Arellano who, he said, signed a contract with Diego Arias de la Cerda in 1649. Dr. García also gave the church of the Compañía to the same architect by contract of March 22, 1652. See *La ciudad de los Incas, postscriptum,* and "La arquitectura colonial del Cuzco," pp. 114–115. Dr. García very kindly informed me in a letter of August 9, 1947, that he no longer attributes the two façades to Domínguez de Chávez y Arellano. The following is a quotation from his letter: "Los documentos que poseo sobre el arquitecto Domínguez de Chávez se refieren a contratos con el deán Arias de la Cerda, para obras complementarias en la catedral y con los Jesuitas para la facción de la capilla de San Ignacio, lateral a la Compañía. No tengo la evidencia de que haya tomado a su cargo la confección de la fachadas de ambos edificios, al menos hasta este momento."

33. Mendoza, *op. cit.*, pp. 133–138. The preface is dated in Cuzco in 1657. Mendoza's signature appears five times as witness in 1649 to the profession of young monks in Cuzco. No Franciscan monks were professed in the fateful year of 1650: "Libro de Profesiones," 6–25, folios 102–104, Archives of San Francisco, Cuzco.

34. It was turned over to the Colegio de Educandas in 1848. Gamarra Hernández, Aurelio M., *Datos históricos de los colegios del Perú* (Lima, 1919), pp. 175, 178.

35. Santos, Fray Juan, *Chronología hospitalaria* (Madrid, 1716), p. 367. The church measures 41.40 meters by 5.75 meters. The pulpit and the paintings of the life of St. Andrew (dated 1667–1668) were brought to this church from the chapel of San Andrés, destroyed about 1930. It is difficult to date the patios of San Juan de Dios on style alone. The square Doric columns of the first and second patios have their counterpart in the court of the former hospital of the Almudena, now the local prison, a structure of the second half of the seventeenth century; photograph in Larco Herrera, *Cuzco histórico* (Lima, 1934), p. 205. Yet as late as 1723, the same type of column is used in the cloister of the novitiate in the Recoleta.

36. The length of the nave, not including the choir at the west which is closed off, is 40 meters. The width of the nave is 8.89 meters; the depth of the portals at the side 3.10 meters, and the thickness of the walls about 1.72 meters. The interior of the church has been painted in ugly fashion to imitate marble.

37. The same capital appears in the upper gallery of the large cloister of Santo Domingo, in the cloister of the Recoleta, and in the patios of numerous houses of the seventeenth century,

for instance, the house of the Condes de Peralta in Calle Santa Teresa, and in the cloister of San Bernardo (Municipalidad). A local variant of this capital which is large in proportion and has very big volutes is found profusely in Cuzco: the Casa del Almirante, the house of Garcilasso de la Vega, the arches of the Plaza Mayor and Plazuela de la Merced, the ruined cloister of San Agustín (ruined in 1650 and again later in the century, according to Diego de Mendoza) and many houses in the city.

38. *Anales del Cuzco,* p. 48.

39. García, "La arquitectura colonial del Cuzco," p. 115; also Harth-terré, *Mercurio peruano,* XXIII (1941), 254.

40. For the history of the convent see Angulo, Domingo, "El monasterio de Sta. Clara de la ciudad del Cuzco," *Revista del Archivo Nacional del Perú,* XI (1938), 55–95, 157–184; Mendoza, *op. cit.,* pp. 68–70, 247–248; Marco Dorta, *Historia del arte hispano-americano,* I, 657.

41. Vargas Ugarte, *Manuscritos peruanos* II, 175; Montesinos, *op. cit.,* II, 174–175; Mendoza, *op. cit.,* p. 134. The nave of Santa Catalina consists of four bays and sanctuary measuring 39.55 meters in length, not including the choir at the west which is separated from the nave by a screen. It is exceptionally large, consisting of three bays. The breadth of the church is 10.25 meters. Santa Teresa is smaller with a complete length of 37.20 meters and a breadth of 9 meters.

42. *Anales del Cuzco,* p. 115; Vargas Ugarte, *Manuscritos peruanos,* II, 117.

43. *Anales del Cuzco,* pp. 154, 159; Noël and Torre Revello, "Contribución documental a la historia del arte colonial," *Congreso internacional de historia de América,* Buenos Aires, 1938, III, 536.

44. The original foundation of San Francisco took place in 1534. The convent moved to a second site in 1538 and to the present in 1549. All of the data regarding the church and convent are found in Mendoza, *op. cit.,* pp. 41–43.

45. Length of church including *capilla mayor* 54.65 meters; total breadth 27.14 meters; breadth of nave 9.58 meters and *capilla mayor* 9 meters; *capilla mayor* raised 1.10 meters; piers 1.95 meters square; breadth of right aisle 7.5 meters; left aisle 6.86 meters; measurements vary greatly throughout the church.

46. The combination of barrel vaults in the nave with ribbed late-Gothic vaults over the apse is common in Mexico, especially in Augustinian churches of the sixteenth century. Angulo, Diego, *Historia del arte hispano-americano,* I, 172, 278. In Bolivia the use of decorative ribbed vaults over the apse is persistent in the early seventeenth century. They are combined with groined vaults in the nave in San Agustín and Santo Domingo at Sucre. In San Agustín and Santo Domingo at La Paz, on the other hand, barrel vaults cover the nave and Gothic vaults the sanctuary.

47. Angulo and Marco Dorta, *op. cit.,* I, 673; Camón Aznar, *La arquitectura plateresca* (Madrid, 1945), figs. 20, 45.

48. *Anales del Cuzco,* p. 177.

49. Padre Figueroa of San Francisco informed me that the cloister of Santa Clara (finished 1622), which is in strictest *clausura* and hence not visible, is in Doric style and similar to the second cloister of San Francisco. Other Doric cloisters of the period in Cuzco were: the second cloister of the Merced (1634), apparently of pier construction; the cloister of the Compañía with the two-over-one arrangement (after 1650); the cloister of the Recoleta (founded 1599), with the same scheme. In Quito, Ecuador, the Doric order was employed in the mid-sixteenth-century cloisters of San Francisco and San Agustín. The two-over-one composition occurs in the cloister of La Merced (1646–1648). Navarro, José Gabriel, *Religious Architecture in Quito* (New York, 1945), pp. 7, 12, 20.

50. Mendoza, *op. cit.,* p. 55.

51. The second cloister of Santo Domingo, built in a single story in rusticated stone, looks

like a late-seventeenth-century structure, although built in 1816–1820. Within recent years a second story in crude plaster has been added to three sides without regard for appearances. "Libro Capsae," folio 163, Archives of Santo Domingo. This document was kindly supplied by Padre Morales.

52. Plan of the monastery in Buschiazzo, *Estudios de arquitectura colonial hispano-americana*, p. 103. The dimensions of Santo Domingo are: length 54.60 meters; breadth 22.36 meters; breadth of apse 9.02 meters; breadth of aisles 4.40 meters; piers 2.14 × 1.36 meters.

53. Meléndez, *op cit.*, I, 607; Cappa, *op. cit.*, XIV, 42.

54. Buschiazzo, "El templo y convento de Santo Domingo del Cuzco," *Revista de arquitectura*, Buenos Aires, XXII (1936).

55. The document containing the date of the tower is contained in *Legajo* VIII, folio 261, in the archives of Santo Domingo. This information was generously supplied by Padre Morales.

56. Harth-terré, *Artífices en el virreinato*, p. 85; photograph in Angulo and Marco Dorta, *op. cit.*, I, 559.

57. Miranda Valcárcel y Peralta, Francisco, "Crónica de esta provincia del Cuzco, 1650–1707" (manuscript in the Merced library, Cuzco), folios 18–19; see Wethey, "La Merced in Cuzco, Peru," *Journal of Architectural Historians*, V (1945–1946), 35–38.

58. Miranda, *op. cit.*, folios 15–16: "La maravilla de su hermosura de tanto arte y perfección que viéndola el señor Conde de Lemos, Virrey del Perú, cuando entró en aquella ciudad viendo la arquitectura y suntuosa fábrica de aquella maravillosa casa, dixo podía servir de palacio al rey, nuestro señor, más poderosa soberana reyna para su culto y albergue de sus hijos, previno con divina providencia tan anchuroso y magnífico palacio que a poco costo se depuso, de la cochera, templo de la caballería, refectorio, con sobra de oficinas y alas, puerta, claustro alto y bajo, tan aseadas y tan abun-

dantes celdas que sus techumbres perfiladas de oro . . ."

59. García, J. U., in "La arquitectura colonial del Cuzco," p. 117, says that the cloister of the Merced is the work of Francisco Domínguez de Chávez y Arellano, Juan Samanés, Martín de Torres, Juan Toledano, and Juan de Olmos. The latter was a goldsmith who made the monstrance of the Merced in 1720, long after the cloister was finished. Juan Samanés was a painter of the seventeenth century; Martín de Torres was a sculptor who built the high altar (destroyed) of the Merced in 1631. The other two were presumably architects, but the fact is that neither documentary nor stylistic evidence exists relative to the architect of the cloister.

60. Donatello's Annunciation in Santa Croce, Florence, and Desiderio's tomb of Carlo Marsuppini in the same church.

61. Miranda, *op. cit.*, folio 80.

62. *Ibid.*

63. *Ibid.*, folio 90.

64. *Legajo* VII, *registro* 173, 23 pages. The same architect appears elsewhere in the Merced documents. He signed a petition for wheat (!) due him on March 6, 1637 (*Legajo* IV, *registro* 80, folio 80) and he is mentioned as expert for the monastery in the contract awarded to Martín de Torres for the high altar on February 6, 1631 (*Legajo* IV, *registro* 81). He was architect of Cuzco Cathedral from 1617 to 1649, holding the position of *maestro mayor* most of that time. See notes 21 and 22 above.

65. García, J. U., "La arquitectura colonial del Cuzco," p. 117

66. Note 66 will be found at the top of page 297.

67. Less fortunate was the silver treasure of the Merced, especially several sets of Baroque candelabra, which were sold for silver! The proceeds were used for restorations and for covering the brown stone with a coat of gray paint.

68. García, J. U., "La arquitectura colonial del Cuzco," p. 116; Cosio, J. G., *El Cuzco histórico, Guía* (Lima, 1924), p. 25, attrib-

66.

Measurements compared:	La Merced	San Francisco	Santo Domingo
Length	52.60 meters	54.65 meters	54.60 meters
Total breadth	23.84 meters	27.14 meters	22.36 meters
Breadth of nave	10.80 meters	9.58 meters	9.55 meters
Breadth of aisle	5.25 meters	7.5–6.86 meters	4.40 meters
Breadth of sanctuary	13.55 meters	9.00 meters	9.02 meters

Measurements are taken within the walls of the church.

uted the architecture of the Merced to Antonio Blanco. This is an error. Fray Blanco was famed for his oratory in the mid-seventeenth century. Miranda Valcárcel y Peralta, *op. cit.*, folio 3 reverse.

69. Miranda Valcárcel y Peralta, *op. cit.*, folios 83–84. The refectory, rebuilt in 1699–1702, seems to be the chief exception (folio 86).

70. A passageway through the side into the narthex was closed in the eighteenth century, thus explaining the two pilasters and entablature which are meaningless today.

71. Bishop Mollinedo's escutcheon on San Cristóbal dates it between 1673–1699. The tower of Santa Clara, which is stylistically like the others, surely was erected in the second half of the seventeenth century and is not part of the construction finished in 1622. The tower stands against the church but is structurally free of it. Moreover, there is no suggestion of this tower in the famous view of Cuzco painted after the earthquake in 1650 (Fig. 21). The tower in the picture does not occupy this same position and is of different type.

72. The cornice and a single half column appear in the right tower of San Sebastián (1664) which must be anterior to the Merced tower.

73. "Historia o narración de las cosas sucecidas en este colegio del Cuzco, cabeza de los Reynos del Perú desde su fundación hasta oy primero de noviembre dia de Todos Sanctos, Año de 1600" (Library of Congress, Manuscript Division, Washington), folios 13–14. Additions to the chronicle in different hands continue spasmodically up to the year 1653. Mention is made of two cloisters in the first half of the seventeenth century, one of which consisted of two stories in brick. A third and small cloister, not now extant, was reërected after the earthquake of 1650. Two short extracts from the manuscript are published by Padre Vargas Ugarte in *Los jesuitas del Perú*, pp. 182–184. Vargas Ugarte in *Historia del Perú, Fuentes*, p. 252, ascribes the manuscript to Padre Antonio de Vega. This friar's name appears at the bottom of the first page, but without any indication that he was one of the several chroniclers of the manuscript. (Vargas issued the whole text after my book was in press: *Historia del Colegio y Universidad del Cuzco*, Lima, 1948). The Washington manuscript is certainly related to the *Crónica anónima de 1600*, recently published. The description of the portal of the Jesuit church at Cuzco is the same, word for word: Mateos, *op. cit.*, II, 33; Vargas Ugarte, *Manuscritos peruanos*, IV, 199–200.

74. *Anales del Cuzco*, p. 110.

75. Historia o narración, pp. 219–223; Vargas Ugarte, *Ensayo de diccionario*, pp. 174–177.

76. Vargas Ugarte, "Notas," pp. 169–170; —, *Los jesuitas del Perú*, pp. 182–185; —, *Ensayo de un diccionario*, pp. 174–177. See note 32. Vargas, *Historia del Colegio*, pp. 181–186.

77. *Anales del Cuzco*, pp. 110, 142.

78. Braun, Joseph, *Spaniens alte Jesuitenkirchen* (Freiburg, 1913).

79.

Measurements compared:	La Compañía	San Pedro	El Belén
Length	61.85 meters	56.14 meters	49.40 meters
Breadth of nave	11.44 meters	10.50 meters	9.66 meters
Depth of chapels	2.65 meters	3.00 meters	———

Measurements are taken within the walls of the church.

80. Tamayo, Alberto, *Las iglesias barrocas madrileñas* (Madrid, 1946), pp. 13, 97, 105, 123, 163.

81. Urteaga and Romero, *op. cit.*, p. XCIV. The hospital has been completely destroyed, and the site is now occupied by an orphan asylum.

82. *Anales del Cuzco*, p. 171.

83. Angulo, Diego, *Planos de monumentos, Estudios II*, pp. 94–95, 660–663, pl. 27. The church is also mentioned in Mollinedo's letters as under construction in 1693 and 1696: Noël and Torre Revello, "Contribución documental," 537–538.

84. *Anales del Cuzco*, p. 169; García, J. U., *Ciudad de los Incas, postscriptum.*

85. For comparative dimensions see note 79.

86. Urteaga and Romero, *Fundación española del Cuzco*, p. XCIV.

87. Noël and Torre Revello, "Contribución documental," p. 538.

88. For comparative dimensions see note 79.

89. Urteaga and Romero, *op. cit.*, p. XCIV.

90. Noël and Torre Revello, "Contribución documental," p. 538.

91. Cuadros, Manuel E., *Historia y arquitectura de los templos del Cuzco* (Cuzco, 1946), p. 84.

92. No name of architect is included. Martín de Aragón is mentioned as the priest, not architect, contrary to Vargas Ugarte's interpretation. See Vargas Ugarte, "Notas," p. 294.

93. Noël and Torre Revello, "Contribución documental," p. 536.

94. *Anales del Cuzco*, pp. 257, 287.

95. *Ibid.*, p. 168.

96. *Ibid.*, pp. 276–283; Vargas Ugarte, "Notas," pp. 191, 295; —, *Ensayo de un diccionario*, pp. 204–211.

97. San Antonio, the chapel of the seminary, was rebuilt in the time of Bishop Mollinedo (1678), whose shield appears on its stone doorway. The single-naved church is chiefly notable for its paintings. The portal of the seminary nearby is similar to that of San Antonio and it bears the shield of Bishop Sarricolea y Olea (1736–1740) (Noël and Torre Revello, "Contribución documental, p. 536).

The Jesuit Colegio de San Bernardo (now Municipalidad), founded in 1619 and rebuilt after the earthquake of 1650, has a small chapel and a fine cloister with typical *cuzqueño* volute capitals, here modified by a stilt block with *mudéjar* rolls at the sides (*Anales del Cuzco*, pp. 38, 106).

The Almudena was rebuilt by the Mollinedos who turned it over to the Bethlehemite Fathers in 1698. The church is a long low structure now abandoned and in disrepair, distinguished only by a large dome embellished outside with tiles. The hospital now serves as the local prison, and still preserves a late-seventeenth-century portal of mediocre quality. *Anales del Cuzco*, pp. 169, 195; García de la Concepción, *Historia bethlehemítica*, Seville, 1723, pp. 53–61; Vargas Ugarte, *Manuscritos peruanos*, II, 120–121.

Santa Ana, a mud church with isolated tower and lacking in architectural interest is said to have been rebuilt under Mollinedo.

San Agustín, rebuilt after 1650, was demolished in 1835, but the arches of the cloister still stand, a monument of no importance.

Capilla de San Andrés was demolished in 1930

and its portal of the mid-eighteenth century serves as the façade of a motion-picture theater. A series of paintings, the pulpit, and a small altar were transferred to the Colegio de Educandas and the high altar to a chapel in San Pedro. The chapel of San Andrés was attached to the hospital of the Recogidas, founded in 1629, completed in 1649, and rebuilt after 1650 (*Anales del Cuzco*, pp. 63, 98. Mendoza, *Crónica*, p. 25).

San Blas, an adobe church with pitched wooden roof, has a long single nave, clearly of sixteenth-century type, though much rebuilt.

San Cristóbal, another adobe church with sloping roof of cane, is now in ruinous condition. Its fine stone tower of the late seventeenth century bears Mollinedo's shield.

Beaterio de las Nazarenas, of interest only because the walls of the building are partly Incaic and the portal has a curiously archaic colonial escutcheon flanked by serpents. The society was established by royal decree in 1683 (Noël and Torre Revello, "Contribución documental," p. 541).

La Recoleta has a fine cloister of the seventeenth century with six arches to a side in the lower gallery and double that number in the upper gallery. It was probably rebuilt after the earthquake on the plan of the original foundation of 1599 (Mendoza, *Crónica*, p. 55). The cloister of the novitiate of five square Doric columns, with a second gallery of seven Doric

arches on one side only was built in 1723, according to an inscription there on the portrait of Bishop Arregui. The church is small and without interest, and the tower is a modest provincial version of the Cuzco type, having in this case one-arched openings on each face. According to an inscription on a picture in the refectory, the convent was originally completed in 1601 (García, J. U., *La ciudad de los Incas*, p. 202).

Santiago, founded in 1572, is a poor mud church without interest (Urteaga and Romero, *op. cit.*, p. XCIV; *Noticias cronológicas del Cuzco*, p. 219).

98. Noël and Torre Revello, "Contribución documental," pp. 536–538.

99. Urteaga and Romero, *op. cit.*, p. XCIV.

100. Angulo and Marco Dorta, *op. cit.*, I, 653–655.

101. Noël and Torre Revello, "Contribución documental," p. 537.

102. Mendoza, *Crónica*, pp. 58–59.

103. Noël and Torre Revello, "Contribución documental," p. 537.

104. *Ibid.*; *Anales del Cuzco*, p. 200.

105. Mollinedo's portrait is found in the church of San Sebastián and in the sacristy of San Pedro; and as donor of a Madonna in El Belén, and in the Madonna of the Almudena of the cathedral; and as witness to the death of St. Peter Nolascus in the series of pictures in the cloister of La Merced.

CHAPTER IV

LIMA; PISCO, NAZCA, ICA

1. Vargas Ugarte, *Ensayo de un diccionario;* —, "Notas," pp. 151–200, 286–298; —, *Los jesuitas del Perú;* Lohmann Villena, Guillermo, "Noticias inéditas," *Revista histórica*, XIII (1940), 5; XIV (1941), 345.

2. Harth-terré, *Artífices en el virreinato del Perú* (Lima, 1945).

3. Cobo, Padre Bernabé, "Historia de la fundación de Lima," *Monografías históricas sobre la ciudad de Lima*, I, edited by Domingo Angulo (Lima, 1935). The work was first published in Lima in 1881 by M. González de la Rosa.

4. Angulo, Diego, "Arquitectura mudéjar sevillana," *Boletín de la Sociadad Española de Excursiones*, XL (1932), 165–212, 245–293.

5. Schubert, *op. cit.*, p. 180; Romero de Torres, Enrique, *Provincia de Cádiz* (Madrid, 1934), Figs. 354, 364.

6. Schubert, *op. cit.*, p. 245.

7. *Ibid.*, pp. 140, 293, 400, 405–433.

8. Fernández, Justino, "Santa Brígida de México," *Congreso internacional de historia de América* (Buenos Aires, 1938), III, 438–454; Angulo, Diego, *Planos de monumentos*, pl. 174.

9. Rodríguez Casado, and Pérez Embid, *Construcciones del virrey Amat* (Seville, 1949); —, *Memoria de gobierno del virrey Amat* (Seville, 1947), pp. lxiii–lxxi.

10. Calancha, *op. cit.*, p. 250.

11. Harth-terré, *Artífices*, p. 89.

12. Gento Sanz, *op. cit.*, pp. 141, 171–172; Mugaburu, José de, *Diario de Lima* (1640–1694; Lima, 1917–1918), II, 27; Sánchez Cantón, "El convento de San Francisco de Lima," *Revista de Indias*, IV (1943), 527–551.

13. Harth-terré, "Entalladores del siglo XVII," *Boletín del Instituto de Investigaciones Históricas*, Buenos Aires, XXVII (1943), 153; —, *Artífices*, p. 131; Vargas Ugarte, *Ensayo de un diccionario*, pp. 119, 230.

14. Barriga, *El templo de la Merced*, pp. 11–12, 413–416.

15. Photograph in Montes, Padre Graciano, *La sacristía del templo de San Agustín de Lima* (Lima, 1944).

16. Monasterio, Fray Jacinto, *Recuerdo de la inauguración del templo de San Agustín de Lima* (Lima, 1908), p. 38.

17. Angulo, Diego, *Planos de monumentos*, pl. 209.

18. Vargas Ugarte, "Notas," p. 291.

19. Barriga, *El templo de la Merced*, pp. 252, 272.

20. Meléndez, *Tesoros verdaderos de las Indias*, I.

21. Gento Sanz, *op. cit.*, p. 305.

22. Navarro, *Religious Architecture in Quito*, p. 12; "Curiosa ordenación," *Archivo esp. de arte y arqueología*, IV (1928), 179–182; Angulo and Marco Dorta, *op. cit.*, I, 606; Calancha, *op. cit.*, p. 250.

23. Sánchez Cantón, *op. cit.*, pp. 531–537.

24. Harth-terré, *Artífices*, pp. 165–171; Sancho Corbacho, Antonio, *La cerámica andaluza* (Seville, 1947).

25. Vargas Ugarte, *Los jesuitas del Perú*, p. 186. The work of the Jesuit architect, Diego de la Maza, seems to have been connected with the church which antedated the earthquake. Vargas Ugarte, "Notas," p. 177. Plan and sections published by Harth-terré, in *Arquitecto peruano*, September, 1940.

26. He died in 1725. See Mendiburu, *op. cit.*, XI, 296–297.

27. Schmidt, Max, *Kunst und Kultur von Peru* (Berlin, 1929), *passim*; Kelemen, Pál, *Mediaeval American Art* (New York, 1943), *passim*.

28. Documents in Archivo Nacional del Perú, Lima: "Nazca," *Legajo XVII, cuaderno 442*. The Jesuits of Cuzco had purchased the hacienda of San José de Nazca in 1620; *ibid.*, *Legajo III, cuaderno 81*. A Basque architect, Gaspar Urrunga, was in charge of construction in 1762–1767; see Harth-terré, "Los artífices vascos en el Perú virreinal," *El Comercio* (Lima), September 1, 1948.

29. Vargas Ugarte, *Los jesuitas del Perú*, pp. 23–24; Barriga, *El templo de la Merced*, pp. 280–285.

30. Vargas Ugarte, "Notas," pp. 169, 196, 288; Vélez Picasso, *La villa de Valverde del valle de Ica* (Ica, 1931); Vargas Ugarte, *Ensayo de un diccionario*, p. 157.

CHAPTER V

CENTRAL PERU: AYACUCHO, HUANCAVELICA

1. Medina, Pío Max, *Monumentos coloniales de Huamanga (Ayacucho)* (Ayacucho, 1942); Olivas Escudero, Fidel, *Apuntes para la historia de Huamanga* (Ayacucho, 1924).

2. Medina, *op. cit.*, p. 52; *Annuae litterae societatis Jesu, Anni 1605* (Duaci, 1618), pp. 385–393; Harth-terré, "La casa de los diamantes en Ayacucho," *El Comercio* (Lima), April 21, 1948.

3. Harth-terré, *loc. cit.*

4. Medina, *op. cit.*, pp. 4–7.

5. Medina, *op. cit.*, pp. 17–18; Meléndez, *Tesoros*, I, 609; II, 72.

6. Medina, *op. cit.*, pp. 26–29.

7. Harth-terré, "Iglesia de San Francisco de Asís, Huamanga (Ayacucho)," *Arquitecto peruano*, March, 1941.

8. Vargas Ugarte, "Notas," p. 177; —, *Ensayo de un diccionario*, p. 203. Padre Vargas also states that the work was directed by Diego Gallegos: *ibid.*, pp. 309–310.

9. Gento Sanz, *San Francisco de Lima*, p. 305.

10. Medina, *op. cit.*, contains all documentary information cited here.

11. Meléndez, *Tesoros*, I, 618–619; II, 80.

12. Vargas Ugarte, *Ensayo de un diccionario*, p. 177.

13. Santos, *Chronología hospitalaria*, p. 380.

14. Lascano González, *Monumentos religiosos de Córdoba colonial* (Buenos Aires, 1941); *Documentos de arte argentino*, 25 vols. (Buenos Aires, 1939–1947); Harth-terré, "Arquitectura popular peruana," *Revista Tres* (Lima, 1941); Buschiazzo, "Arquitectura religiosa popular en la Argentina," *Boletín de la Comisión Nacional de Museos y Monumentos Históricos*, Buenos Aires, IV (1942).

15. Photograph in Noël, Martín, *El arte en la América española* (Buenos Aires, 1942), p. 59.

16. Harth-terré, "La arquitectura popular en Valle del Río Mántaro," *Arquitecto peruano*, December, 1940.

17. Vargas Ugarte, "Notas," p. 173; —, *Ensayo de un diccionario*, pp. 189–190; —, *Historia del culto de María*, pp. 477–488; Olivas Escudero, *Apuntes para la historia de Huamanga*, pp. 471–490.

18. Montesinos, *Anales del Perú*, II, 138 ff.

CHAPTER VI

NORTHERN PERU: TRUJILLO, GUADALUPE, SAÑA, CHICLAYO

1. García Irigoyen, Carlos, *Monografía de la diócesis de Trujillo* (Trujillo, 1930–1931), II, 155–160. Many photographs of Trujillian monuments are reproduced in a special issue of *Cultura peruana*, vol. II (1942), nos. 9–10.

2. Pérez, Pedro N., *Los obispos de la orden de la Merced en América* (Santiago de Chile, 1927), p. 128; Barriga, *El templo de la Merced de Lima*, pp. 166–167, 177; Vargas Ugarte, *Ensayo de un diccionario*, pp. 131–132.

3. García Irigoyen, *op. cit.*, III, 119–125.

4. Torre Revello and Noël, "Contribución documental," pp. 542–544; Vargas Ugarte, *Ensayo de un diccionario*, pp. 338–339.

5. Harth-terré, "Catedral de Trujillo," *Arquitecto peruano*, February, 1941. Harth-

terré gives no source for his statement that Cristóbal de Vargas undertook the restorations of Trujillo Cathedral in 1768–1771; Vargas Ugarte, *Ensayo de un diccionario*, pp. 352–353.

6. García Irigoyen, *op. cit.*, I, 167, 283–284; III, 152–158.

7. *Trujillo del Perú a fines del siglo XVIII* (drawings made for Bishop Martínez Compañón, 1779–1791; pub. Madrid, 1936), pl. VI.

8. Córdoba Salinas, *op. cit.*, p. 541; Feyjóo, Miguel, *Relación descriptiva de la ciudad y provincia de Trujillo del Perú* (Madrid, 1763), pp. 67–70; Calancha, *op. cit.*, p. 488; Polo, José Toribio, in *Documentos literarios del Perú*, X (1877), 327–378.

9. Cieza de León, *La crónica general del Perú* (Lima, 1924), p. 338.

10. Calancha, *op. cit.*, pp. 488–498. The Augustinian church today is occupied by Franciscans, and San Francisco by the Carmelites.

11. Meléndez, *op. cit.*, I, 610; III, 774. At what time Padre Bara was prior at Trujillo is not stated. He died in Chuquisaca in 1675.

12. Feyjóo, *op. cit.*, pp. 67–73.

13. Wethey, "Hispanic Colonial Architecture in Bolivia."

14. Feyjóo, *op. cit.*, pp. 70, 142; Morales Macchiavello, Carlos, "La iglesia de las carmelitas en Trujillo," *Arquitecto peruano*, July, 1941; Mariátegui Oliva, *Una iglesia-relicario, El Carmen de Trujillo* (Lima, 1945).

15. García Irigoyen, *op. cit.*, I, 246–247.

16. Santa Ana was one of the earliest churches founded in Trujillo, being mentioned in 1551 and 1555 (García Irigoyen, *op. cit.*, I, 60, 99). The reference to the transfer of the church to the suburb of Mampuesta in 1759 can only mean a temporary transfer of cult after the great earthquake of that year, for Santa Ana today occupies its original site. Noël and Revello Torre, "Contribución documental," p. 544.

17. García Irigoyen, *op. cit.*, I, 238.

18. Angulo, Diego, *Planos de monumentos*, pl. 289, *Estudio*, pp. 616–618.

19. García Irigoyen, *op. cit.*, I, 242.

20. Padre Graciano Montes, provincial of the Augustinians of Peru, informed me that the original act of foundation of 1564 is preserved in the Archivo de la Curia in Trujillo. According to Calancha, the Augustinians took possession of the sanctuary in 1563: Calancha, *op. cit.*, pp. 563, 566. Marco Dorta's attempt to date the church of Guadalupe in the sixteenth century, notwithstanding Calancha's contemporary testimony, is not convincing: *Historia del arte hispano-americano*, I, 623–627, 632.

21. Vargas Ugarte, *Ensayo de un diccionario*, pp. 226–227.

22. Angulo, Domingo, "Fundación y población de la villa de Saña," *Revista del Arch. Nac. Perú*, I (1920), 280–289; Bachmann, Carlos, *Departamento de Lambayeque* (Lima, 1921), pp. 294–310; Lizárraga, *Descripción y población de las Indias*, p. 18; Vázquez de Espinosa, *Compendium and Description of the West Indies*, pp. 393–395; Alcedo y Herrera, *Piraterías y agresiones de los ingleses* (Madrid, 1883), p. 164; Wethey, "Saña, a Dead City of Peru," *Michigan Alumnus Quarterly Review*, LIII (1946), 9–14; — , "Saña, la ciudad muerta del Perú," *Cultura peruana*, VII (1947), no. 28; García Irigoyen, *Santo Toribio* (Lima, 1906), II, 278–285.

23. Santos, *Chronología hospitalaria*, p. 369.

24. García Irigoyen, *loc. cit.*

25. "Relación de las provincias y conventos que la Orden de N. Sra. de la Merced tiene en las Indias Occidentales," section IV, paragraph 13, in "Yglesias de Indias," Spanish manuscript no. 1106, Ayer Collection, Newberry Library, Chicago; Salmerón, Marcos, *Recuerdos históricos* (Valencia, 1646), p. 291. It is possible that Salmerón used the Newberry manuscript, inasmuch as he never visited the Indies and his brief reference to Saña is similar.

26. Vargas Ugarte, *Ensayo de un diccionario*, pp. 226–227.

27. Calancha, *Crónica*, pp. 566, 851–852.

28. Camón, José, "La intervención de Ro-

drigo Gil de Ontañón en el manuscrito de Simón García," *Archivo esp. de arte*, XIV (1941), 300–305.

29. For photograph see: Angulo and Marco Dorta, *op. cit.*, I, 622 and *passim*.

30. Vargas Ugarte, *Ensayo de un diccionario*, pp. 74–75.

31. Vázquez de Espinosa, *op. cit.*, p. 396.

32. Menéndez Rúa, Angel, *Boceto histórico de la yglesia de Lambayeque* (Lambayeque, 1935), pp. 48–50; Bachmann, Carlos, *op. cit.*, p. 318; Arróspide de la Flor, César, "La iglesia de San Pedro de Lambayeque," *Mercurio peruano*, XXVII (1945), 3–10.

CHAPTER VII

NORTHERN PERU: CAJAMARCA

1. The substance of this section was published in an article, "Iglesias de Cajamarca," in *Cultura peruana*, vol. V (1945), no. 23.

2. García Irigoyen, *Monografía de la diócesis de Trujillo*, I, 203; Gridilla, Padre Alberto, *Cajamarca y sus monumentos* (Cajamarca, 1939), pp. xxviii, 10, 16, 39; Mariátegui Oliva, Ricardo, *San Francisco y la Dolorosa de Cajamarca* (Lima, 1947), p. 18.

3. Gridilla, *op. cit.*, pp. 38–39; *Revista histórica*, Lima, I (1906), 474–475; García Irigoyen, *op. cit.*, pp. 116, 207.

4. Pereyra, Emiliano, *Cajamarca, región turística* (Cajamarca, 1943), p. 15.

5. García Irigoyen, *op. cit.*, I, 212; Vargas Ugarte, *Ensayo de un diccionario*, pp. 143–147. *Matriz*: word used in the Spanish and Portuguese colonies for the first-ranking parish church in a city or village.

6. The date of consecration is found on the portrait of Bishop Luna Vitoria which hangs in the right transept of the cathedral: . . . *consagró esta santa iglesia mayor de Caxamarca la grande, día 27 de octubre, año de 1762 que agradecida le dedica en reverendo obsequio esta digna memoria.*

7. Vargas Ugarte, *Ensayo de un diccionario*, pp. 232–251. Apparently nothing was accomplished in 1690 when an attempt to rebuild San Antonio was made. The architect in charge was Juan Manuel Cristóbal de Vera. Gridilla, *op. cit.*, pp. 40–42; García Irigoyen,

op. cit., I, 203–204; Villanueva Urteaga, Horacio, "Hacia la ciudad de Cajamarca la grande," *Revista universitaria*, Cuzco, XXXVI (1947), 213–214, 227–229; Mariátegui Oliva, *op. cit.*, *passim*.

8. García de la Concepción, Fray Joseph, *Historia bethlehemítica* (Sevilla, 1723), *Libro* II, p. 126.

9. Angulo, Diego, *Planos de monumentos arquitectónicos*, pp. 619–620. The monks were finally forced to give up the church in 1815. Gridilla, *op. cit.*, p. 58.

10. The floor plan was first published by Alva Manfredi in *Arquitecto peruano*, July, 1943.

11. *El Hogar, Número extraordinario* (Cajamarca, 1920), p. 41.

12. García de la Concepción, *op. cit.*, *Libro* II, p. 126; Villanueva, Horacio, *op. cit.*, pp. 219–220; Vargas Ugarte, *Ensayo de un diccionario*, pp. 326–327, is mistaken in giving the date of the façade as 1746.

13. Málaga Santolalla, Firmín, *Departamento de Cajamarca* (Lima, 1906), p. 52.

14. Vargas Ugarte, *Ensayo de un diccionario*, p. 236.

15. Lampérez y Romea, Vicente, *Arquitectura civil española* (Madrid, 1922), I, 345.

16. Angulo and Marco Dorta, *Historia del arte hispano-americano*, vol. I, fig. 461.

17. *Se empeçó esta obra el 17 de O del año de 1763 i se acabó el 17 de O de 1767 siendo*

prefecto . . . *Fray Juan de Belén* . . . The interior was rebuilt in 1774. Villanueva, Horacio, *op. cit.,* p. 223; Vargas Ugarte, *Ensayo de un diccionario,* pp. 293–294.

18. Villanueva Urteaga, Horacio, "Cajamarca prehispánica y colonial," *Revista universitaria,* Cuzco, XXXIII (1944), 150; Pita, Vicente, "Colegio Nacional de San Ramón,"

in *Datos históricos de los colegios del Perú* (Lima, 1919), pp. 117–146.

19. Gridilla, *op. cit.,* p. 69.

20. Guerrero, Justiniano, *Cajamarca al vuelo* (Cajamarca, 1936), pp. 15–16.

21. *Iglesias de México* (Mexico, 1927), III, 187.

22. *Ibid.,* VI, 136.

CHAPTER VIII

SOUTHERN PERU: THE MESTIZO STYLE — AREQUIPA

1. The earlier government buildings erected by the architect, Francisco Vélez, after the earthquake of 1784 were lost in the catastrophe of 1868. Plans and documents in the Archivo de Indias are published by Noël and Torre Revello, *Arquitectura virreinal* (Buenos Aires, 1934), pls. XVII–XVIII; also Angulo, Diego, *Planos de monumentos,* pl. 205.

2. Wethey, "The Problem of Toribio de Alcaraz," pp. 165–174.

3. Harth-terré, *Artífices,* pp. 27–28.

4. Documents published by Padre Víctor Barriga in the newspaper, *El Deber* (Arequipa), August 2–11, 1944, and December 28–29, 1944. Vargas Ugarte, *Ensayo de un diccionario,* pp. 161, 214–218; —, "Notas," II, 178; Harth-terré, *Artífices,* pp. 8, 98. The high altar was the work of Antonio de Torres and Joseph Flores in 1733 (*El Deber,* December 1, 1944). A description of the old cathedral is to be found in Travada y Córdoba, Ventura, "El suelo de Arequipa convertido en cielo" (1752), in Odriozola, *Documentos literarios del Perú* (Lima, 1877), X, 101–107.

5. Vargas Ugarte, *Ensayo de un diccionario,* pp. 58–59, 132; —, *Los jesuitas del Perú,* p. 11; Valdivia, Deán, *Fragmentos para la historia de Arequipa* (Arequipa, 1847), pp. 81–82; Harth-terré, *Mercurio peruano,* XXIV (1942), 57; Mateos, *Historia general de la Compañía de Jesús en la provincia del Perú,* II, 187–194.

6. *Missale Romanum* (Ratisbon, 1925), pp. 238–239. The words complete are inscribed on the portal of a house, Calle Santa Catalina 101, in Arequipa.

7. Modern inscriptions under the choir which are copies of the concealed inscriptions in the presbytery say the church was built in 1657 and consecrated in 1740. Padre Víctor Barriga informed me that the unpublished documents give the plan to Juan de Aldana. Harth-terré, *Artífices,* p. 8, also mentions Juan de Aldana as architect of La Merced. His date, 1654, is a typographical error. Valdivia, *op. cit.,* pp. 77–78, says that La Merced was completed by 1661. He dates the large chapel at the right in 1757.

8. *La Bolsa* (Arequipa), August 27, 1868.

9. Padre Barriga informed me that the neo-Renaissance tower was built in 1896, and that its truncated appearance is due to the dismounting of its tottering spire in 1923.

10. *La Bolsa* (Arequipa), August 19, 1868; Zamácola y Jáuregui, Juan Domingo, *Relación . . . el espantoso terremoto el día 13 de mayo de 1784* (Arequipa, 1889), p. 7.

11. It reads, *A mayor gloria de Dios y de la santísima Virgen año de 1873.*

12. This information taken from the notarial archives of Arequipa was generously supplied by Padre Barriga. Vargas Ugarte, *Ensayo de un diccionario,* pp. 122–124; —, "Notas," p. 161.

13. Polar, Jorge, *Arequipa* (2nd ed., Arequipa, 1922), p. 171.

14. The inscription on the vault under the choir, *Año de 1677*, is carved with numerals and letters in reverse. A cartoon must have been applied to the wall backwards!

15. Mendoza, *Crónica*, p. 49; Barriga, "El convento de San Francisco de Arequipa y el fundador, Juan de San Juan," *El Deber*, Dec. 2, 1937.

16. Harth-terré, *Artífices*, p. 27; Vargas Ugarte, *Ensayo de un diccionario*, pp. 58–59.

17. The piers of the nave are 2.71 meters thick, and, in addition, there are deep piers 1.77 meters wide between the bays of the aisles.

18. Valdivia, *op. cit.*, p. 80.

19. Antúnez de Mayolo, Santiago, in *Lima, precolumbina y virreinal*, pp. 202–218; Castro, Martha de, "La arquitectura barroca del virreinato del Perú," *Revista, Universidad de Habana*, XVI–XVIII (1943–1944), Neumeyer, "The Indian Contribution to Architectural Decoration in Spanish Colonial America," *Art Bulletin*, XXX (1948), 117.

20. La Recoleta has two such cloisters. The monastery was founded in 1642 and completed in 1648. A church dedicated to San Jenaro, protector against earthquakes, had been located there since 1600. The present edifice is a huge neo-Gothic affair of 1935. Valdivia, *op. cit.*, pp. 83–84; Echevarría, Francisco J. de, "Memoria" (1804), manuscript in possession of Barriga, pp. 61–63; Barriga, "Para la historia del templo de la Recoleta de Arequipa," *El Deber* (Arequipa), October 30, 1937.

21. Barriga, "El cabildo de Arequipa y la fundación del monasterio de Nuestra Señora de Gracia 1568," *El Deber* (Arequipa), June 21, 1937; Zamácola y Jáuregui, *Apuntes para la historia de Arequipa* (1804; pub. Arequipa, 1888), pp. 35, 52; Valdivia, *op. cit.*, pp. 87–91.

22. *La Bolsa* (Arequipa), August 27, 1868.

23. Travada y Córdoba, "El suelo de Arequipa convertido en cielo," pp. 243–244.

24. *Ibid.*, pp. 267–294.

25. The Augustinian house was founded in 1574. Andrés de Espinoza, the architect from Lima who went to Arequipa to build the cathedral in 1621, also received the contract for San Agustín the same year. He was associated in the project with another architect, Francisco Flores. Barriga, "Contrato para construir el templo de S. Agustín," *El Deber* (Arequipa), November 8, 1944. A basilican church existed in the eighteenth century, but it collapsed in 1868. The present structure is a very poor thing covered by a tin roof. The façade, sacristy, and cloisters still exist. Travada y Córdoba, *op. cit.*, p. 220.

26. Barriga, *Memorias para la historia de Arequipa* (Arequipa, 1941), I, 227. The church originally founded in 1582 was reconstructed in present form in 1678. It is a single-naved structure with barrel vault and enormous curving buttresses. It was much remade in the nineteenth century, and an academic neo-colonial façade was added within recent years. Travada y Córdoba, *op. cit.*, pp. 214–215; Valdivia, *op. cit.*, pp. 74–75. Another single-naved church in Arequipa is San Juan de Dios, in lamentable condition with a corrugated iron roof. Originally the hospital of San Juan Bautista, it was transferred to the order of San Juan de Dios in 1648, and reconstructed after the earthquake of 1784. It has one side portal with a few bits of ornament, and is the least important colonial church in the city. Valdivia, *op. cit.*, p. 82; Zamácola y Jáuregui, *Relación*, p. 9; Travada y Córdoba, *op. cit.*, pp. 230–232.

27. Vargas Ugarte, "Notas," p. 192. The architect, Antonio Pérez del Cuadro, was engaged to draw the plans of the church in 1719. It was consecrated in 1730, at which time the façade was probably finished. Pérez del Cuadro said in 1719 that he was en route to Chuquisaca to build the cathedral. His statement cannot be accepted literally, for the cathedral was rebuilt in 1683–1692. He was probably to erect the large chapel of Santo Rojas, attached to the cathedral, founded in 1718 by a donation of Bishop Morcillo Rubió de Auñón. "Actas

Capitulares, 1713–1732," *Libro* A, folios 127–134, Sucre Cathedral; Taborga, Miguel Santos, *Un capítulo de la historia del colonaje* (Sucre, 1905), pp. 44–45.

28. The vault of the passageway leading to the priest's house near the church has an inscription cut in the stone, *F. A. 1739 Garicochea*. The name may be that of the mason or the priest. Harth-Terré has recently interpreted the name Garaycochea as that of priest and architect of the church; see "Los artífices vascos en el Perú virreinal," *El Comercio* (Lima), September 1, 1948. An inscription in the left aisle of the church states that the priest's house was built in 1803.

29. Barriga, *Memorias*, I, 273–274; Vargas Ugarte, *Ensayo de un diccionario*, p. 290. The inscription *Año 1783 JZJ* is cut into the vault of the left aisle. The other inscription, found on the side wall, follows: *Capilla de Animas fabricada con su campo santo, órgano y ornatos a costa de don Domingo Zamácola y Jáuregui cura de esta parroquia, año de 1802.*

30. A series of paintings of the miracles of the Virgin, located beneath the choir, have the signature of the painter, Jacinto Carvajal, and the date 1780. In the sacristy of the church is a fine small bell with the date 1582.

31. Valdivia, *op. cit.*, pp. 75–76; Barriga, *Memorias*, I, 131, 203, 247, 273.

32. Miranda Valcárcel y Peralta, "Crónica de esta provincia del Cuzco," folio 96.

33. Barriga, *Memorias*, I, 155–156. The tower now has the date 1896 upon it.

CHAPTER IX

SOUTHERN PERU: THE MESTIZO STYLE — LAKE TITICACA, PUNO

1. Harth-terré, "La obra de la Compañía de Jesús en la arquitectura virreinal peruana," *Mercurio peruano*, XXV (1942), 57–58.

2. Neumeyer, "The Indian Contribution to Architectural Decoration in Spanish Colonial America," *Art Bulletin*, XXX (1948), 106.

3. *Iglesias de Potosí, Documentos de arte colonial sudamericano* (Buenos Aires, 1945); Vignale, Pedro Juan, "El maestro anónimo de la portada de San Lorenzo de Potosí," *Arquitecto peruano*, January, 1946; —, *La casa real de moneda de Potosí* (Buenos Aires, 1944); Marco Dorta, "Andean Baroque Decoration," *Journal of the Society of Architectural Historians*, V (1945–1946), 33–34; Guido, Angel, *Fusión hispano-indígena en la arquitectura colonial* (Buenos Aires, 1925); Wethey, "Hispanic-Colonial Architecture in Bolivia."

4. Neumeyer, *op. cit.*, pp. 104–121.

5. Arzay Sánchez y Vela, "Historia de la villa imperial de Potosí" (1720), Manuscript No. 2065, Madrid, Royal Palace Library, folio 495. I am indebted to Dr. Lewis Hanke for his generosity in allowing me to read the photostatic copies of the manuscript in his possession.

6. Arróspide de la Flor, César, "La catedral de Puno," *Mercurio peruano*, XXII (1940), 90–93; Harth-terré, "Tesoros de arquitectura virreinal en Puno," *Mercurio peruano*, XXIII (1941) 627.

7. Toussaint, Manuel, "Arte mudéjar en América," in *Kollasuyo* (La Paz), November, 1939, pp. 3–9; —, *Arte mudéjar en América* (Mexico, 1946).

8. Meléndez, *Tesoros*, I, 318, 447, 619–620.

9. Harth-terré, "Tesoros de arquitectura," p. 629.

10. The inscription on the arch of the atrium has given rise to controversy because

of several puzzling abbreviations. The first part reads: *Siendo cura el S. D. D. Gregorio Stiago de la Concha hizo este arco . . .* The next words, which are extremely problematic, have been freely interpreted by Salvador Herrera and Mariátegui Oliva as follows: *el maestro pica-pedrero Nazario N. S.* The last line is obvious: *Salvador Soto año de 1763.* Harth-terré has made Salvador Soto the builder of the arch. The other two writers point out that the latter was probably the donor, since his name as donor appears over the second chapel to the right within the church. This latter theory seems convincing enough, but the reading of the confused part of the inscription as *el maestro picapedrero Nazario N. S.* is at best hypothetical. See Herrera, Salvador, *Pomata y su templo monumental* (Arequipa, 1934), p. 94; Mariátegui Oliva, *Una joya de arquitectura peruana de los siglos XVII y XVIII* (Lima, 1942), pp. 24, 29; Harth-terré, "Tesoros de arquitectura," p. 629.

11. The same type of pseudoclassical urns are also found in Peruvian textiles of the period. The long palmette so common everywhere, but especially in Santiago at Pomata and San Francisco at La Paz, was used in *keros* of the late Incaic or early colonial period. Kelemen, Pál, *Mediaeval American Art* (New York, 1943), vol. II, pl. 192; Yacovleff, E., and Herrera, F. L., "El mundo vegetal de los antiguos peru-

anos," *Revista del Museo Nacional*, Lima, IV (1935), 51.

12. Neumeyer, *op. cit.*, pp. 120–121.

13. Harth-terré, "La obra de la Compañía de Jesús," p. 62.

14. Noël and Torre Revello, "Contribución documental," pp. 536–537.

15. *Ibid.*, pp. 538, 541. The priest, Juan de la Borda, who was at Ayaviri as early as 1677, was the patron of the new church.

16. *Ibid.*, pp. 536, 538.

17. *Ibid.*, p. 538.

18. Harth-terré, "Tesoros de arquitectura," p. 619.

19. *Ibid.*, p. 622; Harth-terré reads the date as 1711.

20. Buschiazzo, *Estudios en arquitectura colonial hispano-americano*, p. 28.

21. Mendiburu, *op. cit.*, X, 55.

22. Mermaids also occur at Asillo, Cuzco, Huamán, Lampa, Oropesa, and Nuestra Señora de Montserrat (see Index). They are found, likewise, in the minor arts: silverware; colonial textile, Museum of the American Indian, New York; rugs in the church of San Pedro Mártir, Juli, and the Brooklyn Museum; an inlaid box in the Brooklyn Museum. Zimmern, Mrs. Natalie, "A Colonial Pile Carpet from Arequipa," *Bulletin*, Brooklyn Museum, IX (1948), 11–15; —, "A Peruvian Bargueño," *Gazette des Beaux Arts*, XXI (1947), 114.

CHAPTER X

CHOIR STALLS

1. "Cuentas por cargo y del Padre Francisco de Mendia de lo procedido de las mandas que en esta ciudad y obispado se hizieron para la obra del coro de esta santa iglesia catedral," document dated 1592, *Protocolo X*; in the Archivo Capitular preserved in the Sala Capitular, Sucre Cathedral.

"Gastos y pagos que a hecho Lorenzo Ro-

dríguez Navarro," *Legajo XI*, further payment to Christóval Hidalgo in 1599 for work on the choir stalls and for the doors of the sacristy.

"Cuentas de Andrés Martínez de Guilléstegui," payments to Christóval Hidalgo for work on the choir stalls in 1595 (folios 26–27), in 1596 (folios 29 reverse, 35), in 1597 (folios 38, 41 reverse, 42) and other payments to Hidalgo for the frame of a crucifix and for the frame of the altar of Our Lady (folio 28), and for the *cielo del altar mayor* (folio 29 reverse). Christóval Hidalgo appears later, paid for the scaffold of the high altar in 1607 and for sundry work in 1614. "Cuentas de Pedro López, 1607–1610," folio 190 reverse; "Cuentas de Padre Juan Patiño de Oro, 1616–1621."

The account books of Sucre Cathedral, located in the Sala Capitular, are uncatalogued and in complete disorder, scattered throughout packages of miscellaneous papers dating from different centuries. Some are loose sheets and fragments. In a few instances pages are numbered. The earliest papers have the date 1582. I am most grateful to Señor Gunnar Mendoza, director of the Archivo Nacional at Sucre, and to the canons of Sucre Cathedral, who authorized my research in the archives.

2. Angulo and Marco Dorta, *op. cit.*, I, 549.

3. Lizárraga, *op. cit.*, pp. 30–34; Cobo, *op. cit.*, p. 238.

4. See Weise, Georg, *Spanische Plastik* (Reutlingen, 1925–1939), the stalls of Santa María Redonda, Logroño (vol. II, pls. 174–175); Toledo Cathedral (vol. III, pls. 170–175, pls. 410–413); Avila Cathedral (vol. III, pls. 432–435).

5. *Ibid.*, vol. III, pls. 31, 34, 36, 97.

6. Vargas Ugarte, *Manuscritos peruanos*, II, 145; —, "Notas," pp. 180–181; —, *Ensayo de un diccionario*, pp. 211–214.

7. Harth-Terré, *Artífices en el virreinato*, p. 120. The pulpit, which he was also to have carved under Noguera's direction, was delayed until 1664 when it was reassigned to Diego Agnes, after Noguera's death. The pulpit disappeared with the earthquake of 1746 (*ibid.*, p. 126).

8. *Ibid.*, p. 123; Vargas Ugarte, *Ensayo de un diccionario*, pp. 222–223, 227–228; *Documentos para la historia del arte en Andalucía*, Seville, II (1928), 84–85, 291–296; V (1933),

11–12; Ceán Bermúdez, *Diccionario histórico* (Madrid, 1800), III, 292.

9. Noël, *Teoría histórica*, p. 87; García Irigoyen, *Historia de la catedral de Lima*, pp. 71 ff.

10. Vargas Ugarte, "Notas," p. 195.

11. Weise, *Spanische Plastik*, vol. III, pls. 438–439; *Catálogo monumental de la provincia de Palencia* (Palencia, 1930), vol. I, p. 69, pl. 112; Ricci, Corrado, *Baroque Architecture and Sculpture in Italy* (London, 1912), pp. 76–77; Berliner, Rudolph, *Ornamentale Vorlage-Blätter* (Leipzig, 1926), pl. 33. I am indebted for the second and third references to Mrs. Beatrice Gilman Proske of the Hispanic Society of America. Ganz, Paul, and Seeger, Theodor, *Das Chorgestuhl in der Schweiz* (Frauenfeld, 1946), pl. 61.

12. Choir stalls of La Merced, Lima (1628), of San Francisco, Lima, and the façade of San Francisco, Lima (1674); the choir stalls of San Francisco and of the cathedral at Cuzco; the choir stalls of Trujillo Cathedral; various retables and pulpits in Trujillo; the façade of Santa Lucía at Ferreñafe (1690).

13. Choir stalls of La Merced, Lima, of San Francisco and the cathedral in Cuzco, of Trujillo Cathedral.

14. Choir stalls of La Merced, San Agustín, and San Francisco in Lima, of San Francisco and the cathedral in Cuzco, of Trujillo Cathedral.

15. Choir stalls of La Merced and San Francisco in Lima, and of San Francisco in Cuzco.

16. Weise, *op. cit.*, vol. III, pls. 370–391.

17. García, José Uriel, "Imagineros y tallistas del Cuzco colonial," *La Prensa* (Buenos Aires), Feb. 7, 1937.

18. Mendoza, *Crónica*, p. 44.

19. *Ibid.*, p. 135. In a *Relación* of January 1, 1650, the choir stalls of San Francisco are lauded as the finest in the realm. Cappa, *Estudios*, XIII, 67–68.

20. Barriga, *El templo de la Merced de Lima*, p. 120.

21. Vargas Ugarte, "Notas," pp. 163–164;

Torre Revello and Noël, "Contribución documental," p. 536.

22. The other apostles to the right as one stands with one's back to the high altar are Saints John the Evangelist, Andrew, and Simon; on the left are Saints James, Bartholomew, and Matthias. St. Michael stands in the left corner and the Guardian Angel in the corresponding place at the right.

23. The forty-three full-length saints average one meter in height. To the left as one stands with one's back to the high altar are Saints Roch, Charles Borromeo, Medon, Clement, Philip, Anthony Abbot, Denis, Jerome, Augustine, Stephen, Luke, John the Evangelist, Joseph, James Minor, Thaddaeus, and Philip. On the right are Saints Matthew, Thomas, Joachim, Matthew, Mark, Sebastian, Lawrence, Gregory, Ambrose, Antolin, Blas, Anvari (?), Yg (?), Gregory, Paulin, Isidorus. Over the door on the left side which leads into the choir is a figure of the Madonna of the Immaculate Conception and over the opposite door St. Anne.

The lower stalls number twenty-four and are placed lengthwise only, being omitted across the rear wall.

24. *Anales del Cuzco*, p. 167; Vargas Ugarte, "Notas," pp. 161–164; Benavides Rodríguez, *op. cit.*, p. 57. See Chapter III, note 32, above.

25. See Chapters XI and XII.

26. The choir stalls of Santa Clara at Cuzco and of the cathedral at Sucre in Bolivia, both previously discussed, have no figure sculpture. A set of choir seats in Nuestra Señora del Prado at Lima have the same distinction. The backs of some of them have openwork, and the *mudéjar* pointed arch is an interesting and unusual feature. See Santibáñez Salcedo, Alberto, *El monasterio de Nuestra Señora del Prado* (Lima, 1943), pp. 22, 37.

27. *Choir Stalls from the Monastery of San Francisco, Lima, Peru*, "Hispanic Notes and Monographs" (New York, 1928).

28. Sánchez Cantón, *op. cit.*, p. 551; Gento Sanz, *op. cit.*, pp. 140, 190–191. The Hispanic Society has attributed the stalls to Pedro Montes in 1622 on the basis of a letter written them by a former prior of the monastery. I wish to express my thanks to Mrs. Beatrice Gilman Proske and the Hispanic Society for supplying a copy of the following letter:

"El infrascrito, Guardián del Convento de San Francisco de Jesús de Lima, certifica: que estos seis asientos fueron sacados del coro de nuestra iglesia para colocar en su lugar un nuevo órgano. Fueron construidos el año 1622 por el hermano lego fr. Pedro Montes. Las imágenes que están grabadas en los respaldares son de San Luis Obispo de Tolosa, San Jácome de la Marca y San Daniel mártir.

"Y en testimonio de lo cual, expido el presente certificado en Lima, a 2 de agosto de 1911.

[Signed] Fr. Teófilo Belmont"

If the information contained in this letter was taken from documents in the Franciscan archives, they no longer exist. They would refer to a series of stalls of earlier date than those at present preserved. See Burr, Grace H., *Hispanic Furniture* (New York, 1941), pp. 102–103, 207. Mrs. Burr mistakenly associates Padre Cobo's reference to the cathedral stalls with those of San Francisco.

29. The elephant has been known in Europe since antiquity. He was long regarded as a symbol of Christian morality. Heckscher, W. S., "Bernini's Elephant and Obelisk," *Art Bulletin*, XXIX (1947), 170–172; Bond, Francis, *Wood Carvings in English Churches*, I, *Misericords* (London, 1910), pp. 27–31.

30. Miranda Valcárcel y Peralta, *op. cit.*

31. Romero de Torres, *Provincia de Cádiz*, p. 334, fig. 208.

32. Three more reliefs of full-length saints are dismantled and in storage in the monastery at Cuzco. The figures in the upper stalls are identifiable by gold-lettered inscriptions. On the left with one's back to the altar they are: Venerable Fathers Juan Vallejo, Antonio Bautista Santiago Sales, Juan Sorosa, Pedro de Busta-

mante, Diego de Narbona, Bernardo de Corboría, Juan Gil Alberto, Alonso de Sevilla, Guillermo de San Leonardo, Pedro Uraca, Pedro de San Germano, Pedro Amerio Qarto Genera, Antonio de San Erdo; on the rear wall: San Serapio Escoto, San Pedro Armen, San Pedro Nolasco, San Pedro Apóstol, the Trinity over the prior's stall, San Pablo Apóstol, Jaime de Aragón Fundador, San Ramón Nonato, San Pedro Pasqual; along the right wall: Santa María de Socoro, Proto-martyr Raimundo de Blanes, Venerable Fathers Guillermo Sagiamo, Sancho de Aragón, Pedro de Dionisio, Diego de Soto, Gerónimo de Prado, Gonzalo Dias, Vicente Salalito, Pedro Oscavir, Juan Falconi, Miguel el Carmelo, Juan Serco. The statue of the Madonna, seated in a chair, occupies the place behind the prior's stall, in a position similar to that of the Madonna in the choir of the Merced at Lima. The decorative hoods upon the entablature are in

several instances modern restorations, very accurately reproduced.

33. Calancha, *op. cit.*, p. 248; Quintero, Pelayo, "Sillas de coro españolas," *Boletín de la Sociedad Española de Excursiones,* XVI (1908), 19.

34. Monasterio, Fray Jacinto, *Recuerdo de la inauguración del templo de San Agustín,* (Lima, 1908), pp. 12, 23–25; Vázquez, Fray Juan Teodoro, "Crónica continuada de esta provincia del Perú de N. P. S. Agustín," (manuscript dated 1721 in Museo Prado, Lima), vol. II, pp. 12 reverse, 337 reverse.

35. Eguiguren, L. A., *Las calles de Lima* (Lima, 1945), p. 154.

36. It was impossible to see the seated statue of St. Augustine above the prior's chair. Hence I am uncertain whether or not it belongs to the sculpture of 1721–1725. The lower stalls are twenty-eight in number.

CHAPTER XI

PULPITS

1. "Libro de Profesiones, 1606–1664," folios 77–80, manuscript No. 6–25, in the archives of San Francisco, Cuzco. The inscription on the lectern reads, *Se hizo año de 1628 siendo guardián El P. F. Pedro Gómez, Lector Jubilado.* Diego de Mendoza, *op. cit.,* p. 45, mentions the pulpit in 1664 and attributes the workmanship to Pedro Gómez. Vargas Ugarte, "Notas," p. 172, also makes the guardian an artist. The inscription as he quotes it is erroneous. Vargas Ugarte, *Ensayo de un diccionario,* p. 178.

2. Cappa, *op. cit.,* XIII, 67–68.

3. The inscription appears on the lower part of the pulpit and is inlaid in ivory. It reads: *Siendo abadesa doña Catalina de Orue Su administrador Fray Benito Hernández. Año 1637.*

4. Document in Archivos notariales, Cuzco, dated February 28, 1656, before the notary

Lorenzo de Mesa. For this document I am indebted to Monseñor Juan Antonio Casanova.

5. Original document on the Mercedarian altar in the Mercedarian Archives at Cuzco: *Legajo* 4, *registro* 81, February 6, 1631; Vargas Ugarte, *Ensayo de un diccionario,* pp. 270–271. The two others which have disappeared are the retable of the Immaculate Conception in Cuzco Cathedral (1646) and a retable in San Agustín (1639); García, J. U., "Imagineros y tallistas del Cuzco colonial," *La Prensa* (Buenos Aires), February 7, 1937; also Dr. García's notes on the notarial archives at Cuzco which he generously allowed me to examine.

6. See Chapter XII, note 18, below, for further data on Martín de Torres.

7. The paintings from the chapel of San Andrés, also now located in the Colegio de Educandas, are dated by inscription 1667–1668. A legend in the first picture states that

the hospital founded by Andrés Pérez de Castro in 1649 was destroyed in the great earthquake the following year and had to be rebuilt.

8. García, J. U., *loc. cit.*

9. The pulpit in Santa Catalina has a statuette of St. Michael on top of the canopy and St. Dominic beneath it. Four Dominicans, including St. Dominic and St. Peter Martyr, occupy the niches. On the pulpit of La Merced the four Fathers of the Latin Church stand within the niches, while St. Peter Nolascus is carved in relief upon the large panel behind the speaker's place. St. Michael finishes the composition at the top.

10. Dr. García generously showed me extracts from the document which he copied in the notarial archives in Cuzco. He mentions the contract in *La Prensa* (Buenos Aires), February 7, 1937. See Chapter XII, note 21, below for further details.

11. The pulpit of Santa Teresa is not mentioned in Bishop Mollinedo's letter dated 1678, although he does speak of the retable. It may be that the pulpit had not been completed. Noël and Torre Revello, "Contribución documental," p. 536.

12. *Loc. cit.*

13. Angulo, Diego, *Planos de monumentos, Estudios,* pp. 94–95.

14. *Anales del Cuzco,* p. 169. Vargas Ugarte, *Ensayo de un diccionario,* p. 272. See Chapter XII, note 18, below.

15. García de la Concepción, *Historia bethlehemítica,* Libro III, p. 60.

16. García, José Uriel, "Un notable artista peruano de la época colonial," *La Prensa* (Buenos Aires), April 24, 1938.

17. Vargas Ugarte, *Manuscritos peruanos,* II, 120–121.

18. *Anales del Cuzco,* p. 167; Vargas Ugarte, "Notas," pp. 161–164.

19. Noël and Torre Revello, "Contribución documental," p. 538.

20. García, José Uriel, "Los Mollinedo mecenas del Cuzco colonial," in *La Prensa*

(Buenos Aires), March 20, 1938; —, *La Prensa,* April 24, 1938.

21. The gilded pulpit of Santo Domingo is rather dryly cut with a rectangle and cruciform panel in each of the polygonal sides. St. Dominic and St. Thomas Aquinas are the two saints of the canopy and wall panel respectively. The pulpit of San Francisco belongs to the period of refurbishing of the church (*circa* 1712). It has been badly recut and thus ruined in recent times. In its present condition one cannot be sure whether it bore any iconographic relationship to the pulpits of Santa Clara in Trujillo and San Francisco de Paula in Ayacucho. A charming *Purísima* escaped by virtue of her high location at the top. The pulpit of Santa Ana is a small rustic work, yet well gilded. That of San Juan de Dios, of good quality, falls into the usual type of the Ayacucho school. Even in a remote village like Andahuaylas, a fine gilded pulpit, in a general way belonging to this group, embellishes the church.

22. Lohmann Villena, "Noticias inéditas," *Revista histórica,* XIV, 352.

23. Morales Macchiavello, "La iglesia de las carmelitas en Trujillo," *Arquitecto peruano,* July, 1941. Merely for the sake of record, mention should be made of the other pulpits of Trujillo. The one in the church of El Belén, of the first quarter of the eighteenth century, is the usual type with spiral colonnettes, and is now painted white. It has the four Fathers of the Latin Church upon the tribune, the lower part of which has been scraped bare of its ornament, leaving only the nude bust caryatids. The pulpit in Santiago at Huamán is of similar type, but has lost its statuettes. Only the canopy in Trujillo Cathedral is colonial, the tribune being modern (1911). The pulpit of La Merced is so badly ruined as to lack any interest. The last three are reproduced in Mariátegui Oliva, *Escultura colonial de Trujillo* (Lima, 1946), pp. 37, 39.

24. The present chapter is not a complete catalogue of Peruvian pulpits, although it is

hoped that no work of importance has been overlooked. A rustic product of "popular art" like the pulpit of El Belén in Cajamarca, now partly painted white, is charming in its naïve handling of traditional elements. Flat wood carving without any genuine sense of design, when compared with the best of the period, characterizes numerous provincial objects such as the pulpit at Huarás. In San Agustín at Lima a relief of the Madonna giving her girdle to St. Augustine and St. Monica and eight statuettes are fragments of a colonial pulpit.

25. Santa Clara, Ayacucho; Santa Clara, San Francisco, and Santa Catalina in Cuzco; Santa Rosa de las Monjas, Lima; San Francisco, Arequipa.

26. La Merced, La Almudena, and Los Educandos at Cuzco; Lampa; Cajamarca Cathedral; San Francisco de Paula, Ayacucho; Santa Clara, Trujillo.

27. San Blas, San Pedro, and the cathedral in Cuzco; the parish church at Checacupe.

28. Cajamarca Cathedral; San Francisco de Paula, Ayacucho; Santa Clara, Trujillo; parish church, Lampa. Also in the church of El Belén, Trujillo.

29. Ayacucho Cathedral; La Compañía, Pisco.

30. Santa Clara, Trujillo; La Compañía in Arequipa, Cuzco, and Pisco.

31. The cathedral of Cajamarca, dedicated to St. Catherine of Alexandria; the seminary of St. Anthony Abbot, Cuzco.

32. La Merced and Santa Catalina, Cuzco, both by the same artist.

33. The parish church, Checacupe; San Pedro, the cathedral, La Almudena, El Belén, and San Sebastián at Cuzco. The niche statues upon the tribune are lost in the last two churches.

34. San Blas, La Merced, San Pedro, at Cuzco; Santo Domingo, San Francisco, Santa Clara, Ayacucho; St. Joseph on the panel in Jesús María, Lima.

CHAPTER XII

RETABLES; FIGURE SCULPTURE

1. Durán y Sanpere, *Los retablos de piedra*, 2 vols. (Barcelona, 1932, 1934); Zarco del Valle, *Documentos de la catedral de Toledo* (Madrid, 1914), pp. 30–58; Gestoso y Pérez, *Sevilla monumental* (Seville, 1889–1892); Weise, *Spanische Plastik*; Wethey, *Gil de Siloe and His School* (Cambridge, 1936).

2. Toussaint, "Proceso y denuncias contra Simón Pereyns en la inquisición de Méjico," *Suplemento al No. 2 de Anales del Instituto de Investigaciones Estéticas* (Mexico, 1938), p. xviii.

3. Photograph of the Huaro retable: Marco Dorta and Angulo, *Historia del arte hispanoamericano*, vol. I, fig. 790.

4. The second story does not belong to this altar. A side altar of wood in two stories carved with eight apostles in relief, located in La Merced at Sucre (Bolivia), is a provincial Renaissance piece, probably of the late sixteenth century. A small single-storied altar of the same period stands in a chapel at the left in San Lázaro, Sucre.

5. *Revista de archivos y bibliotecas nacionales* (Lima, 1900), V, 77.

6. Byne, Arthur, and Stapley, Mildred, *Spanish Architecture of the Sixteenth Century* (New York, 1917), p. 9.

7. The inscription on the predella reads: *Esta capilla y retablo hizo el Padre Fray Juan Vizcaino siendo prior 1618 . . . Pintólo Dionisio Sebastián Acosta Inca . . .* Its original location as the high altar is recorded in Sanjinés, *Historia del santuario e imagen de Copacabana*, p. 113.

8. *Legajo XI, Archivo Capitular, Sucre*

Cathedral. Attached to the contract of 1604 and the drawing are other papers, including Pastorelo's request of 1607 for more money to cover work on the retable in excess of that originally specified. The retable was evaluated by Miguel de Aguirre, sculptor, and 1,680 pesos were added to the original price of 8,000 pesos.

9. Roque Balduque's retable taken to Panama in 1560 by the bishop-elect of La Plata (Sucre), Fernando Cuesta, who died en route to his new post. Angulo, Fray Domingo, "Los obispos de la Plata en el siglo XVI," *Revista del Archivo Nac. del Perú*, X (1937), 15. Numerous sculptures by Martínez Montañés were sent to America. López Martínez, *Retablos y esculturas de traza sevillana* (Seville, 1928), pp. 36–37, 55–56, 59, 79–80; *Documentos para la historia del arte en Andalucía*, II, 48–58, 227–232; Angulo, Diego, "Dos Menas en Méjico," *Archivo español de arte y arqueología*, XI (1935), 138–152; —, "Martínez Montañés y su escuela en Honduras y Guatemala," *Archivo español de arte*, 1947, pp. 285–291.

10. Lohmann Villena, *op. cit.*, XIII, 14–16; Vargas Ugarte, "Notas," pp. 176–177; Harth-terré *Artífices*; Harth-terré, "Imafronte de la catedral de Lima," *Arquitecto peruano*, June, 1941; Vargas Ugarte, *Ensayo de un diccionario*, pp. 199–200.

11. For documents see: Lohmann Villena, *op. cit.*; Harth-terré, "Entalladores del siglo XVII," in *Artífices*, pp. 115–132; Vargas Ugarte, *Ensayo de un diccionario*.

12. García, José Uriel, "Imagineros y tallistas del Cuzco colonial," *La Prensa* (Buenos Aires), February 7, 1937; Vargas Ugarte, *Ensayo de un diccionario*, pp. 270–272; see Chapter XI, notes 4–5; also below in Chapter XII, note 18.

13. The inscription on the lower left reads: *Acabóse este retablo en 20 de Marzo de 1651, siendo prior y vicario provincial el muy rev. padre maestro Fray Santiago Deosi [?]*.

14. García, J. U., "Imagineros y tallistas del Cuzco colonial."

15. They are used only in the second story flanking the niches. The center of the retable, as in other instances, has been slightly modernized. The subjects of the paintings are as follows: the Madonna of the Rosary at the top, a canvas of St. Joseph at the left, St. John the Baptist at the right; in the second story, the Meeting of St. Francis and St. Dominic (?) at the left, and St. Catherine of Alexandria in prayer at the right. The smaller spaces had images of the four Fathers of the Latin Church. St. Jerome is now replaced by the Madonna. Two characteristic colonial angels, dressed as knights, appear upon the predella.

16. The rectangular frame about the kneeling Christ is modern, and the whole altar is badly damaged.

The altar of St. Joseph in Santa Clara at Ayacucho belongs in part to the period *circa* 1660, but it seems to have been refurbished in the eighteenth century, and also subjected to modern tampering by local carpenters.

The altar of the Infant Christ in the right transept of San Antonio at Cajamarca likewise should be mentioned here as a work of approximately the same date. It has been painted white in part, and the three colonial statues as well as the modern Christ Child do not belong here.

17. Medina, *op. cit.*, p. 5.

18. Monseñor Juan Antonio Casanova generously supplied me with the complete documentation of this altar. The references to Juan Tomás are contained in "Libro de gastos que se hicieron en 13 de junio de 1677 en adelante," folios 87 and following. Eleven payments to him were made in the years 1678–1679. Only one specifically mentions the retable, and that is a payment for gilding it. Little doubt can be entertained that all of the entries were related to the same retable. See also: García, José U., "Un notable artista peruano de la época colonial," *La Prensa* (Buenos Aires), April 24, 1938. Padre Vargas Ugarte's attribution of the retable partly to Martín de Torres (*Ensayo de un diccionario*, pp. 272–273) is mistaken, for

NOTES

Monseñor Casanova quotes payments to a carpenter, named Cristóbal de Torres. For the letter of Bishop Mollinedo in the year 1678, see: Noël and Torre Revello, "Contribución documental," p. 536.

19. The high altar of Santiago de Compostela (1659); the high altar of the Compañía at Granada (*circa* 1660); the retable of St. Paul, Seville Cathedral (1658); the retable of the Hospital de la Caridad, Seville (1670); the high altar of Montederramo (1666) in the province of Orense. García y Bellido, A., "Estudios del barroco español," *Archivo esp. de arte*, V (1929), 44–54; ill. XX (1947), 81, 93. By 1650 it appears on the choir stalls at Muri and Neu St. Johann in Switzerland. Ganz and Seeger, *Das Chorgestühl in der Schweiz*, pls. 78, 84; Hernández Díaz, José, "Papeletas para la historia del retablo en Sevilla durante la segunda mitad del siglo XVII," *Boletín de Bellas Artes*, Sevilla, II (1935), 5–7.

20. Angulo, Diego, "Dos Menas en Méjico," p. 140, Fig. 3. I am indebted to Miss Elizabeth Wilder for information about the spiral column in Mexico which became common there in the eighth and ninth decades of the seventeenth century, just as was the case in Peru.

21. García, J. U., "Imagineros y tallistas"; Dr. García did not include all details of the contract in this article. He allowed me to consult his notes on it. The contract in the Archivos notariales (folio 88) is dated 1675. "Diego Martínez de Oviedo maestro mayor de arquitectura . . . se obliga hacer el retablo mayor y el púlpito de Santa Teresa. El altar será igual al altar mayor de la Merced y el púlpito igual al púlpito de la Compañía o San Agustín o Nuestra Señora de la Merced. El altar debe tener cuatro nichos para colocar los santos . . ." Mollinedo speaks of the retable as though it were finished in 1676 in his letter of 1678. Noël and Torre Revello, "Contribución documental," p. 536.

22. Vargas Ugarte, *Ensayo de un diccionario*, pp. 200–202. The altar was completed by an assistant, Diego de Aller. Possibly Martínez de Oviedo had died or was busy with other work.

23. Ramos, Alonso and Sans, Rafael, *Historia de Copacabana*, p. 146; Sanjinés, *Historia del santuario e imagen de Copacabana*, pp. 114–115.

24. Noël and Torre Revello, "Contribución documental," p. 538.

25. García, J. U., "Imagineros y tallistas," *La Prensa*, February 7, 1937.

26. Lohmann Villena, *op. cit.*, XIII, 5–30; XIV, 345–375; Vargas Ugarte, "Notas"; Harth-terré, *Artífices*; Vargas Ugarte, *Ensayo de un diccionario*.

27. Harth-terré, *Artífices*; —, "Decubrimiento de un artífice virreinal, Pedro de Noguera," *Arquitecto peruano*, July, 1946; Vargas Ugarte, *Ensayo de un diccionario*, pp. 221–223.

28. Harth-terré, *Artífices*, pp. 173–184; Vargas Ugarte, *Ensayo de un diccionario*, pp. 211–213, 227–228, 262–263.

29. Lohmann Villena, *op. cit.*, XIII, 16; Montes, Padre Graciano, *La sacristía del templo de San Agustín de Lima* (Lima, 1944); Santibáñez Salcedo, Alberto, "Un valioso documento del S. XVII," *Cultura peruana*, vol. V (1945), no. 22.

30. Harth-terré, *Artífices*, p. 129.

31. Documents on Aguirre in Lohmann Villena, *op. cit.*, XIII, 10; XIV, 347–348; Harth-terré, *Artífices*, pp. 128–132; Vargas Ugarte, *Ensayo de un diccionario*, pp. 117–119; Vázquez, Padre Juan Teodoro, "Crónica continuada" (manuscript, dated 1721, in the Museo Prado, Lima), vol. I, *Libro III*, p. 157.

32. Vargas Ugarte, *Ensayo de un diccionario*, pp. 119, 230; Harth-terré, *Artífices*, p. 131.

33. Vargas Ugarte, Padre Rubén, letters written to me from Lima, dated Jan. 11, 1948, and Feb. 2, 1948. The original documents are preserved in the Jesuit archives in Rome and in Toledo.

34. Photographs: Pillement and Daniloff, *La sculpture baroque espagnole* (Paris, 1945), pls. 50–51.

35. Navarro, José Gabriel, *La iglesia de la Compañía en Quito* (Madrid, 1930), pp. 65 ff.

36. Lohmann Villena, *op. cit.*, XIV, 350–354; Vargas Ugarte, *Ensayo de un diccionario*, pp. 140–141. The high altar of Jesús María was not gilded until 1744, the gilder being C. Arias. Antúnez de Mayolo in *Lima precolombina y virreinal*, pp. 196, 221. The retable is well preserved except for the ugly paint recently applied to the figures of the Holy Family. The platform on which they stand and the doors of the tabernacle are modern.

37. Antúnez de Mayolo, *op. cit.*, pp. 194, 196.

38. Barriga, "Los altares de San José en Santa Teresa y de San Francisco Xavier en La Compañía," *El Deber* (Arequipa), Dec. 15, 1944.

39. Barriga, *El Deber,* Dec. 1, 1944; Vargas Ugarte, *Ensayo de un diccionario*, p. 351. The date, 1729, is given by Vargas Ugarte.

40. Lohmann Villena, *op. cit.*, XIV, 361, 368. The effigy was carved by Baltasar Meléndez.

41. Paris, 1738. See Gurlitt, C., *Das Ornament des Rococo,* 1894; Berliner, Rudolph, *Ornamentale Vorlage—Blätter* (Leipzig, 1926), pl. 396.

42. For this cult see: Vargas Ugarte, *Historia del culto de María en Hispano-América* (Lima, 1931), p. 15.

43. Mariátegui Oliva, *Escultura colonial de Trujillo* (Lima, 1946), pp. 50, 70–71.

44. The retable of the Via Dolorosa in San Pedro at Lima is a puzzle, because the atlas figures are combined in a salomonic retable which otherwise would be dated about 1710. Perhaps it is a case of a reactionary artist of 1765.

45. *Lima, precolombina y virreinal*, pp. 135–136.

46. Picón Salas, Mariano, *De la conquista a la independencia* (Mexico City, 1944), p. 120. Moreno Villa, José, *La escultura colonial mexicana* (Mexico City, 1942), pl. 124. I also wish to express my thanks to Mr. and Mrs. Pál Kelemen for their generosity in showing me their photographs of Salamanca.

47. Vargas Ugarte, "Notas," p. 190; —, "El monasterio de la Concepción," *Mercurio peruano*, XXIV (1942), 628; —, *Ensayo de un diccionario*, p. 321.

48. Colmenares Fernández de Córdoba, *El día deseado* (Lima, 1771), pp. 29–56. A very poor work is the high altar of El Corazón de Jesús, representative of the new stylistic trend (1765). The artist was a certain Joseph Manuel Palomares. *Revista del Archivo Nacional del Perú,* X (1937), 71.

49. Medina, *Monumentos coloniales de Huamanga (Ayacucho)*, p. 65.

50. *Ibid.*, p. 29. The inscription upon the large painting of the Immaculate Conception in the sacristy says that the high altar, sacristy, and this painting were finished in 1712.

51. *Ibid.*, p. 14. Dr. Medina interprets the date as 1717, but the S-curve of the last number can only be read as eight in this instance.

52. The altar of St. Rose was contracted of Pedro Gutiérrez and Juan Gómez in 1787. Unfortunately I did not study or photograph this work. Vargas Ugarte, "Notas," p. 189; —, *Ensayo de un diccionario*, p. 312.

53. The cult of the Christ of Burgos is very widespread in Peru. The Augustinians in Lima were among the first to promote it. See Calancha, *Crónica*, pp. 258–296.

54. Mariátegui Oliva's suggestion that they were taken from separate retables is difficult to accept, if for no other reason than that both retables in Trujillo Cathedral have the same composition. He is, however, correct in noting the numerous reconstructed altars in Trujillo (*Escultura colonial de Trujillo*, p. 63).

55. Weise, *Spanische Plastik,* 4 vols., *passim.*

56. "Retablo mayor, Arenys de Mar, obra de Pau Costa," in *Anales y boletín de los museos de arte de Barcelona,* vol. II (1944), no. 4, pp. 7–30.

57. Darby, Delphine Fitz, *Francisco Ribalta and His School* (Cambridge, 1938), fig. 17.

58. Photographs in Mariátegui Oliva, *Escultura colonial*, pl. IX.

59. Noël and Torre Revello, "Contribución documental," p. 543.

60. *Ibid.*, p. 544.

61. *In Anno Domini de 1759 finitum hoc opus. Me Fecit Fernandus Collao.*

62. Mariátegui Oliva, *Escultura colonial*, p. 68.

63. *El illmo. sr. dr. Fran. Xavier de Luna Victoria digno obispo de esta diócesis reedificó esta iglesia y construyó a sus expensas este retablo que doró el Mrō Manuel García i se acabó oi 5 de setiembre de 1774.*

64. The existence of three fine bronze baptismal fonts in Trujillo and the vicinity should be recorded. A large round shallow basin is supported by a central vertical column in two of them. The font in San Francisco at Trujillo is decorated with a few vertical acanthus leaves widely spaced. The inscription forms a border of Latin letters on the exterior of the basin, and reads thus: *Ex pecunia del bachiller Juan Sánchez de Arroyo rector de esta santa iglesia catedral Francisco de Rivas faciebat Anno 1670.* The inscription implies that the font originally stood in the baptismal chapel of Trujillo Cathedral. The author was a member of a family of workers in bronze. He assisted his brother, Antonio, on the famous fountain in the Plaza Mayor at Lima. See Harth-terré, *Artífices*, p. 187.

Another, at Ferreñafe, has the date and name of donor but lacks the signature of the artist. It is a small basin without pedestal and the loveliest of the lot. A small row of cherubs' heads alternates with a geometrized leaf. The narrow inscription follows: *Siendo cura i vicario Ferriñafe el bachiller don Bernabé de Alcozer año de 1684.*

The third, in the church at Mansiche, more closely resembles the bronze in Trujillo although the author's name here is given as Pedro de Espinossa and in Trujillo he was Francisco de Rivas. The legend is read with some difficulty in this way: *Soy del pueblo de San Pedro de Túcume i me hisieron el año de 1689, siendo cura el bachiller López Collado-Pedro de Espinossa fecit.* It is interesting that the font was made for the village of Túcume some miles

away. The transfer to Mansiche may well have taken place in recent years.

65. Harth-terré, "Tesoros de arte virreinal en Puno," *Mercurio peruano*, XXIII (1941), 629.

66. For the technical procedure which the Spanish call *estofado* see: Pacheco, Francisco, *Arte de la pintura* (1649); ed. of Madrid, (1866), II, 44.

67. An ecclesiastic (†1702) in the Sagrario; Diego Morcillo Rubió de Auñón (†1730); Joseph Damián de Zevallos (†1743) in the cathedral.

68. Gallagher de Parks, Mercedes, "La escultura costumbrista y popular en piedra de Huamanga," *Actas y trabajos científicos del XXVII Congreso Internacional de Americanistas* (1939), Lima, II (1942), 3–15.

69. Crucifixes in the parish church at Ica, Ayacucho Cathedral, and Santa Domingo, Cuzco.

70. Iglesia del Prado of Lima; San Juan, Juli.

71. The churches at Juli and the Andean region. The Spanish-speaking peoples call these works *arte popular.*

72. Vargas Ugarte, *Historia del culto de María*, pp. 548–551.

73. Statues in Lima erroneously attributed to him are: Crucifix in the choir of Santo Domingo; Crucifix and Calvary, Iglesia del Prado; Santa Apolonia in the cathedral. The latter is a Neoclassic work of the nineteenth century.

74. Padre Barriga has suggested that this crucifix is the one described by Padre Cobo and that it was placed in a chapel founded in 1542. The sculpture, however, should be dated about sixty years later. Barriga, *El templo de la Merced de Lima*, pp. 15, 21.

75. Hazañas y la Rua, Joaquín, *Vázquez de Leca* (Seville, 1918), p. 237.

76. Cobo, *op. cit.*, p. 236. Diego Angulo suggested several years ago that the crucifix mentioned by Martínez Montañés in 1603 might be identified with the one to which Padre Cobo referred. Professor Angulo did not know, how-

ever, that the statue still existed. Angulo, Diego, "Dos Menas en Mejico," p. 150. The crucifix shipped by Martínez Montañés to Lima in 1640 would have been too late in style to be identical with the work under discussion. See Vargas Ugarte, *Ensayo de un diccionario*, p. 87.

77. Pacheco, Francisco, *op. cit.*, II, 319–351.

78. Murillo's "Holy Family": Mayer, A. L., *Klassiker der Kunst* (Stuttgart, 1913), p. 5. There is a colonial painting in the cloister of San Francisco at Cuzco of which many variants exist.

79. Lohmann Villena, *op. cit.*, XIII, 21–22.

80. Echave y Assu, *Estrella de Lima* (Antwerp, 1688), p. 98; Angulo, Domingo, *Monografías sobre . . . Lima* (Lima, 1935), II, 43.

81. Photograph: *Lima, precolombina y virreinal*, p. 120.

82. See pp. 201–202, above; *Anales del Cuzco*, p. 169.

Index

INDEX

Principal page references are in italic type

INDEX

INDEX

INDEX

INDEX

INDEX

INDEX

Illustrations

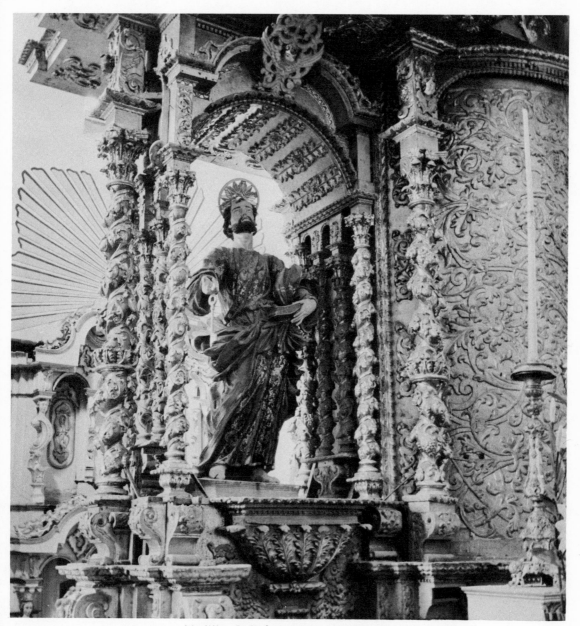

Trujillo, Cathedral, High Altar, Detail

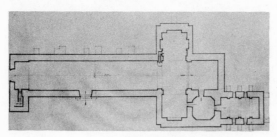

1 Juli, San Juan, Plan (1590)

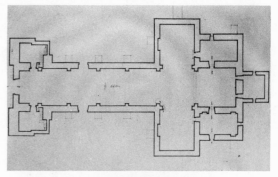

3 Puno, Cathedral, Plan

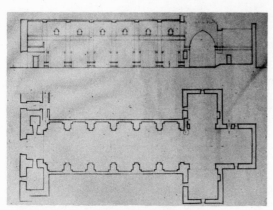

2 Juli, San Pedro Mártir, Plan

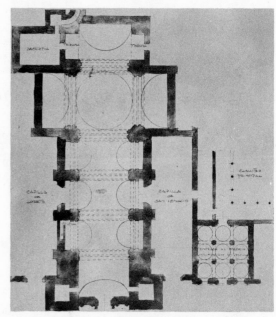

4 Cuzco, La Compañía, Plan (1651)

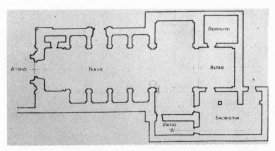

6 Pisco, La Compañía, Plan

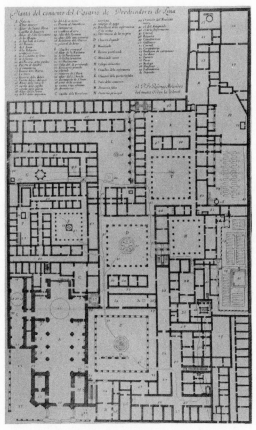

5 Lima, Dominican Monastery, Plan
(after Meléndez, 1681)

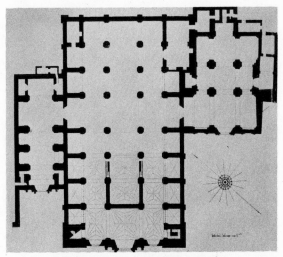

7 Cuzco, Cathedral, Plan

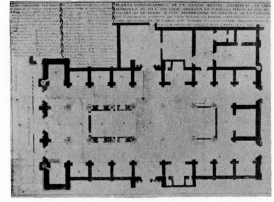

8 Lima, Cathedral, Plan (Drawing of 1755)

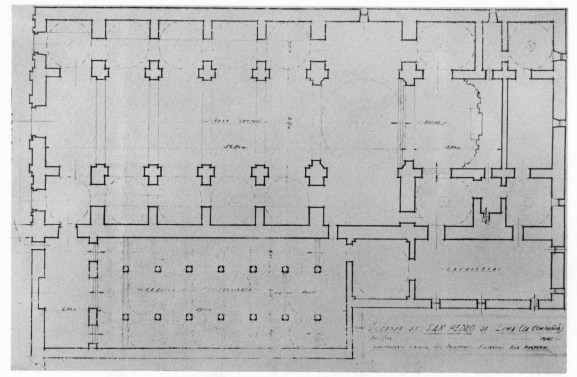

9 Lima, San Pedro (La Compañía), Plan (1624)

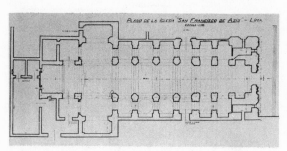

10 Lima, San Francisco, Plan (1657)

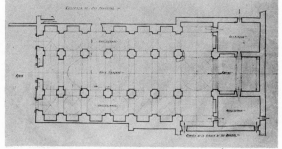

11 Cajamarca, San Antonio, Plan (1682)

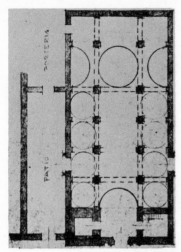

12 Cuzco, La Merced, Plan

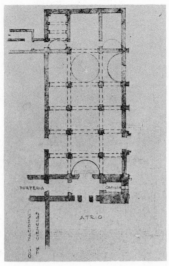

13 Cuzco, San Francisco, Plan

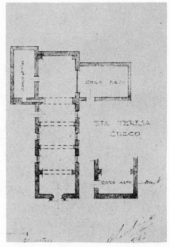

14 Cuzco, Santa Teresa, Plan

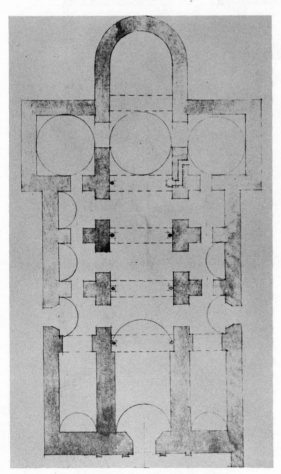

15 Arequipa, San Francisco, Plan

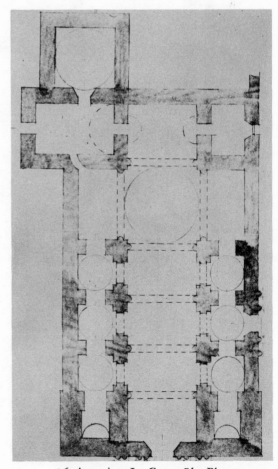

16 Arequipa, La Compañía, Plan

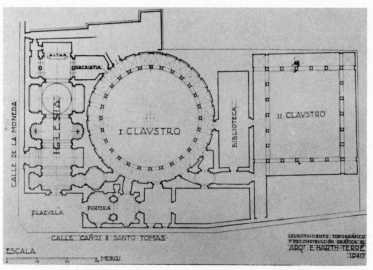

17 Lima, Colegio de Santo Tomás, Plan

18 Lima, El Corazón de Jesús, Plan (1758–1766)

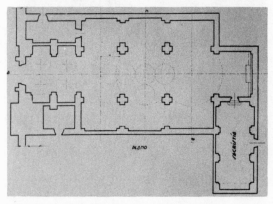

19 Ayacucho, San Francisco, Plan (1712–1723)

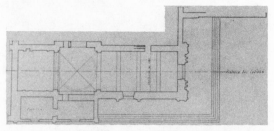

20 Trujillo, Santa Teresa, Plan

21 Cuzco, El Triunfo, Painting: Cuzco in 1650

23 Cuzco, Casa del Almirante, Exterior

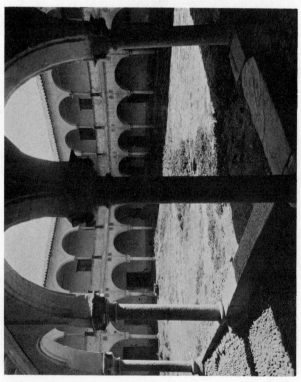

22 Cuzco, Casa del Almirante, Patio

25 Lima, Torre Tagle Palace, Corridor

24 Lima, Torre Tagle Palace, Exterior

26 Lima, Torre Tagle Palace, Patio

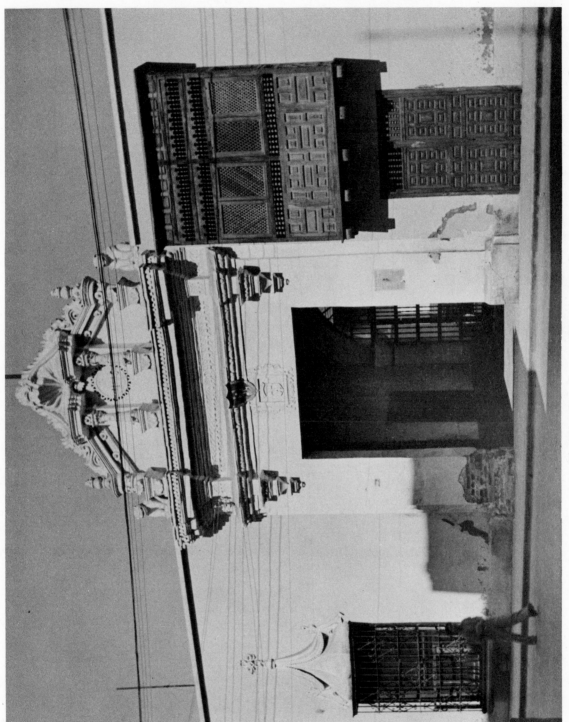

27 Trujillo, Casa Ganoza Chopitea, Façade

30 Cajamarca, Colonial House, Portal

29 Trujillo, Casa de los Herrera, Exterior

28 Lambayeque, Colonial House, Patio

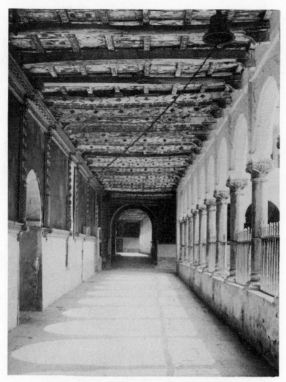

31 Cuzco, San Francisco, Cloister

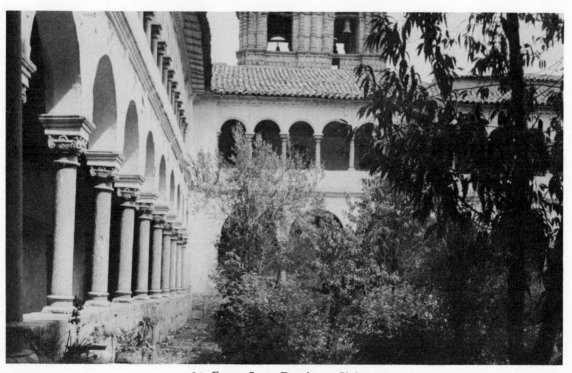

32 Cuzco, Santo Domingo, Cloister

34 Cuzco, San Francisco, Cloister, Detail of Upper Gallery

33 Cuzco, San Francisco, Cloister, Capital of Lower Gallery

36 Ayacucho, La Merced, Façade

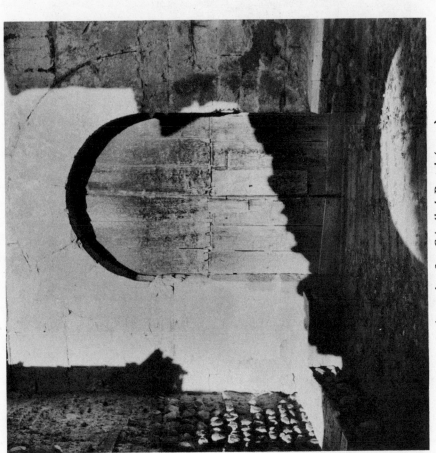

35 Ayacucho, San Cristóbal, Portal (1540)

38 Ayacucho, La Merced, Lateral Portal, Detail

37 Ayacucho, La Merced, Interior

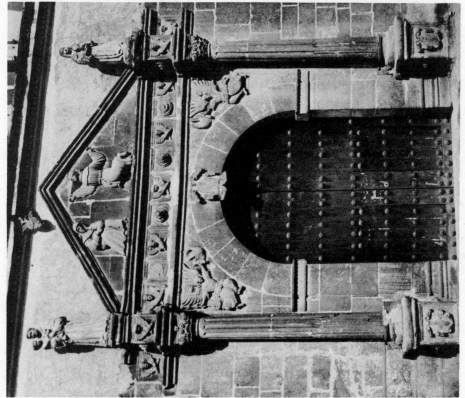

40 Ayacucho, San Francisco, Façade, Detail

39 Ayacucho, San Francisco, Façade

41 Ayacucho, Jesuit Chapel, Portal (*circa* 1570)

42 Ayacucho, Santa Clara,
Orue Escutcheon (1568)

44 Juli, San Pedro Mártir, Crossing (*circa* 1565)

43 Ayacucho, Santa Clara, Portal (1568)

45 Paucarcolla, La Inmaculada, Portal (*circa* 1563)

46 Chucuito, La Asunción, Lateral Portal

47 Juli, San Juan, Front Portal

48 Juli, La Asunción, Lateral Portal

49 Chucuito, La Asunción, Exterior

50 Chucuito, La Asunción, Interior

52 Ilave, San Miguel, Portal of Chapel

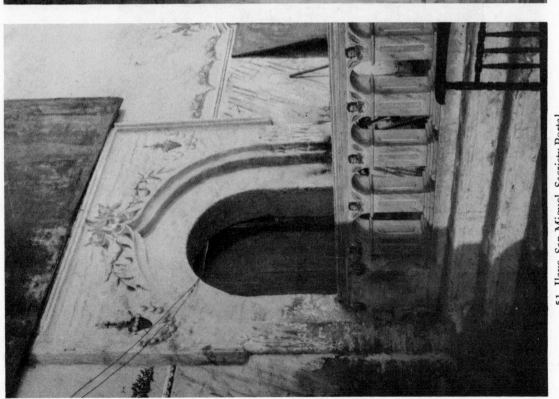

51 Ilave, San Miguel, Sacristy Portal

54 Ilave, San Miguel, Nave

53 Ilave, San Miguel, Lateral Portal

56 Cuzco, La Merced, Front Portal

55 Cuzco, Santo Domingo, Lateral Portal

58 Cuzco, San Juan de Dios, Lateral Portal

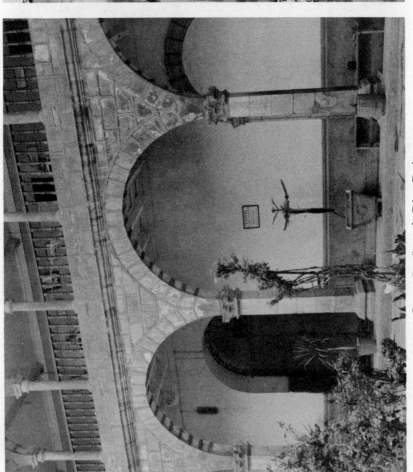

57 Cuzco, San Juan de Dios, Patio

59 Cuzco, Santa Clara, Interior

60 Cuzco, Santa Teresa, Interior

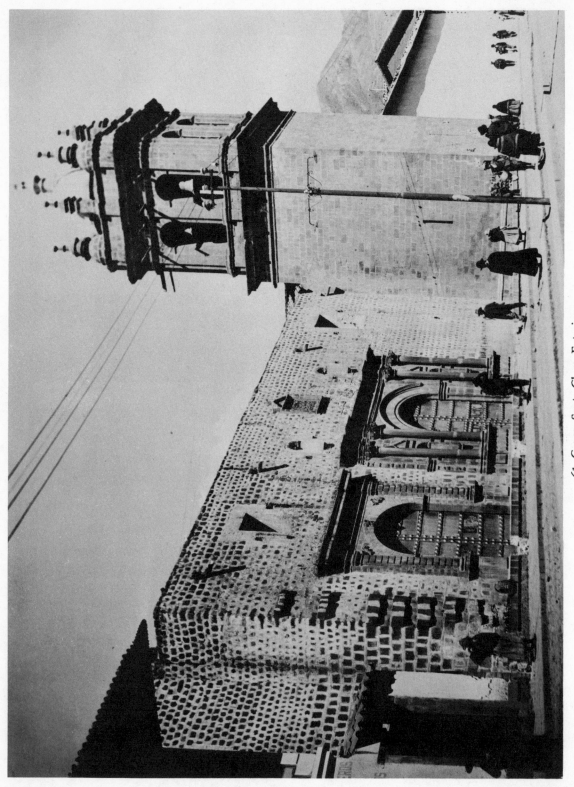

61 Cuzco, Santa Clara, Exterior

62 Cuzco, Cathedral, Exterior

64 Cuzco, La Compañía, Main Portal

63 Cuzco, Cathedral, Main Portal

65 Cuzco, Cathedral, Interior

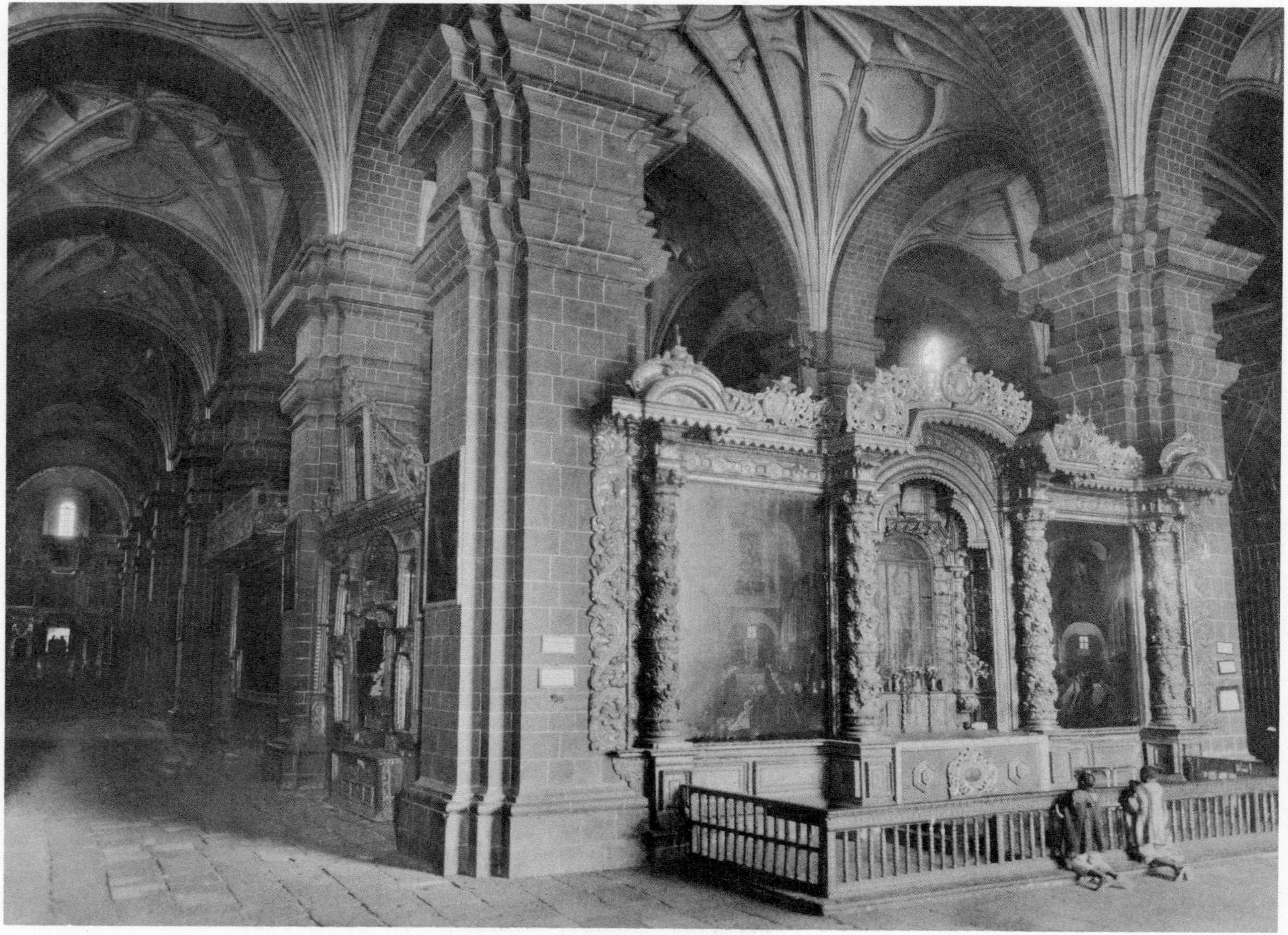

66 Cuzco, Cathedral, Interior

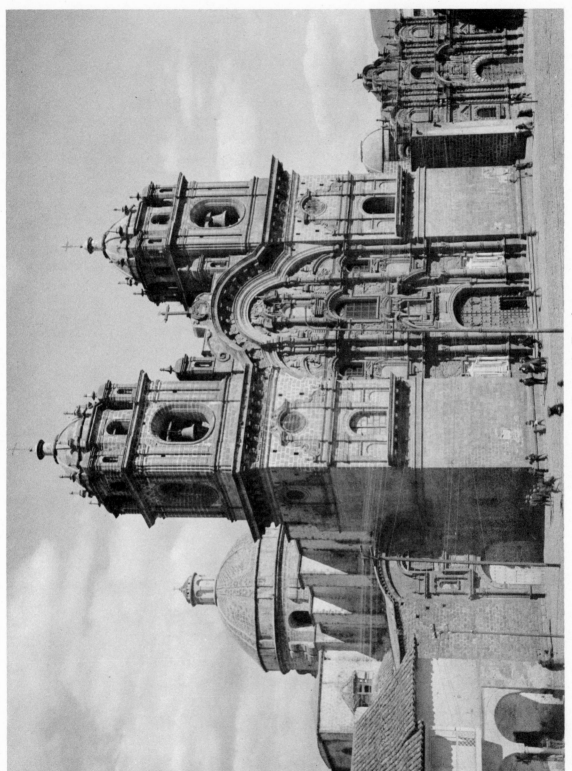

67 Cuzco, La Compañía, Exterior

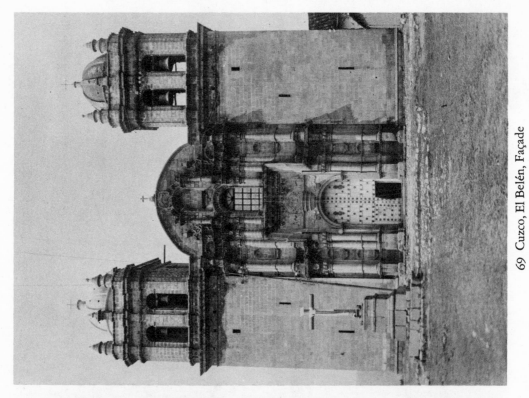

69 Cuzco, El Belén, Façade

68 Cuzco, San Pedro, Façade

71 Cuzco, San Sebastián, Façade, Detail

70 Cuzco, San Sebastián, Façade

73 Cuzco, San Pedro, Interior

72 Cuzco, La Compañía, Interior

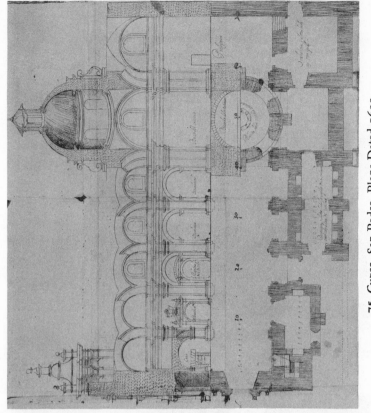

75 Cuzco, San Pedro, Plans Dated 1699

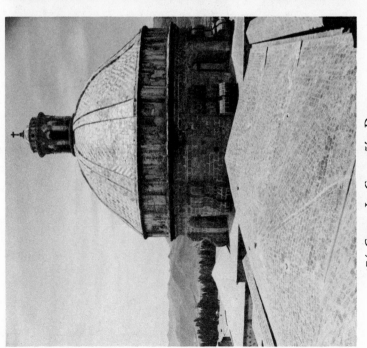

74 Cuzco, La Compañía, Dome

76 Cuzco, San Francisco, Interior

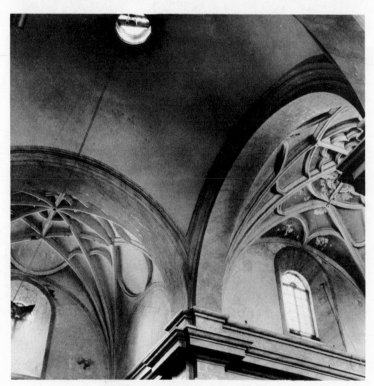

77 Cuzco, San Francisco, Vaults

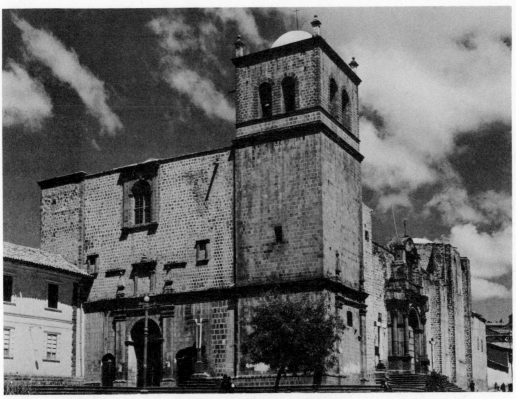

78 Cuzco, San Francisco, Exterior

79 Cuzco, Santo Domingo, Exterior

81 Cuzco, La Merced, Detail of Tower

80 Cuzco, La Merced, Exterior

82 Cuzco, La Merced, Nave

83 Cuzco, La Merced, Stairway of Cloister

84 Cuzco, La Merced, Main Cloister

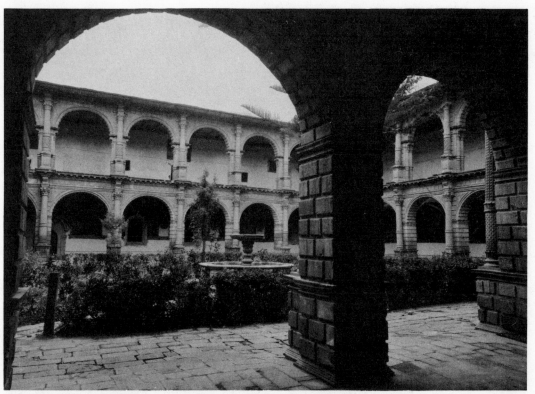

85 Cuzco, La Merced, Main Cloister

86 Cuzco, La Merced, Second Cloister

87 Cuzco, La Compañía, Cloister

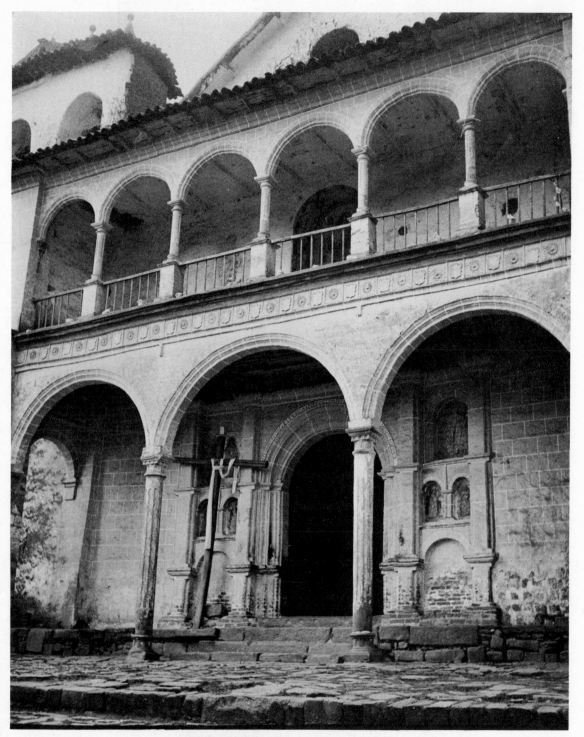

88 San Jerónimo, Parish Church, Façade

89 San Jerónimo, Parish Church, Interior

90 Checacupe, Chapel, Exterior

CHAPTER IV

91 Lima, Cathedral, Interior

92 Lima, San Francisco, Nave

93 Lima, La Merced, Nave

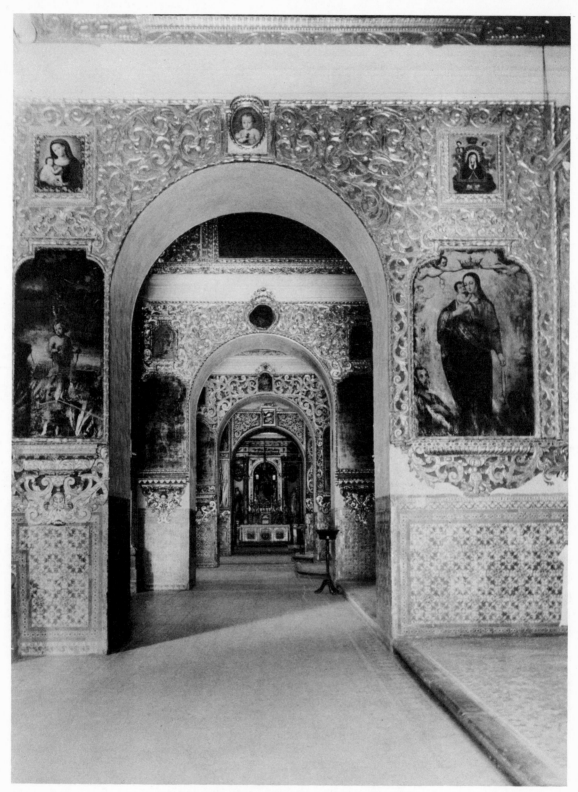

94 Lima, San Pedro (La Compañía), Right Aisle

96 Lima, El Corazón de Jesús, Baptismal
Chapel

95 Lima, El Corazón de Jesús, Interior

97 Lima, Santo Cristo de los Milagros, Interior

98 Lima, Santo Cristo de los Milagros, Wooden Grille

99 Lima, San Pedro (La Compañía), Sacristy

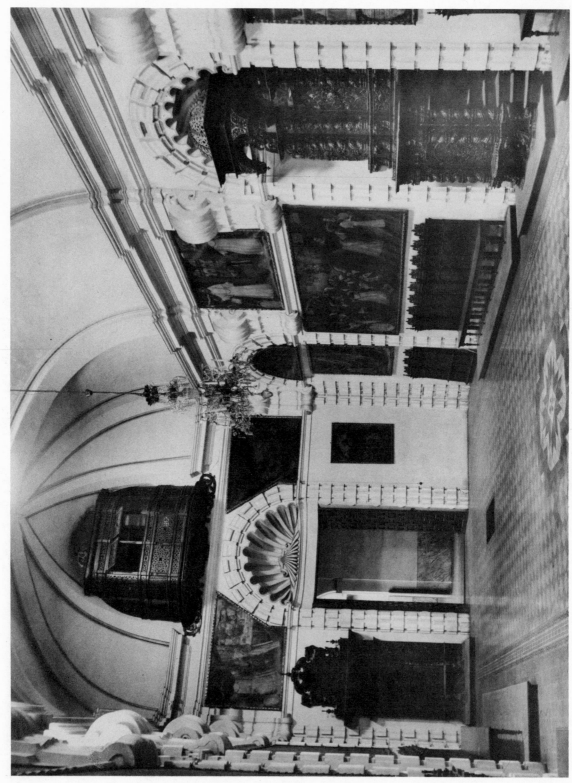

100 Lima, Santo Domingo, Chapter House

102 Lima, Santo Domingo, Exterior (after Meléndez, 1681)

101 Lima, San Francisco, Chapter House

103 Lima, Cathedral, Façade

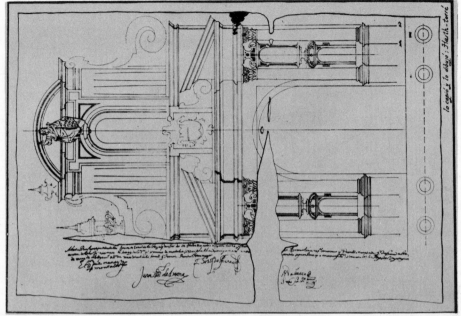

105 Lima, Cathedral, Main Portal, Design of 1626
(after Harth-terré)

104 Lima, Cathedral, Main Portal

107 Lima, San Francisco, Detail of Main Portal

106 Lima, San Francisco, Lateral Portal (1674)

109 Lima, San Francisco, Main Portal

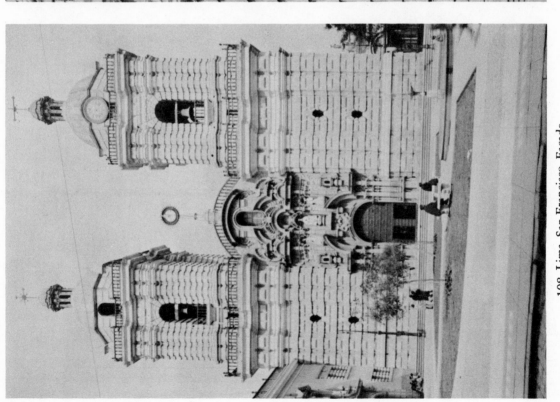

108 Lima, San Francisco, Façade

111 Lima, San Agustín, Façade (1720)

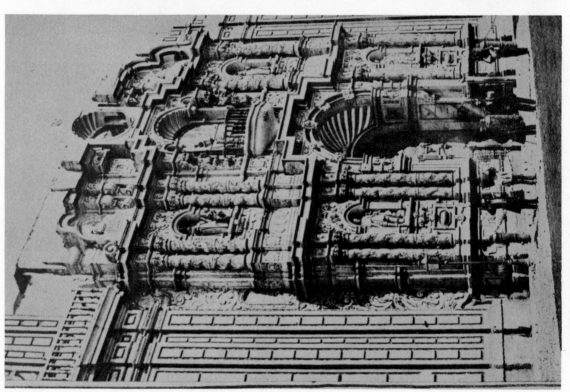

110 Lima, La Merced, Façade (Photograph *circa* 1890)

113 Lima, Cathedral, Rear Entrance (1732)

112 Lima, La Concepción, Lateral Façade

114 Lima, San Carlos, Exterior

115 Lima, Santa Teresa, Façade

116 Lima, San Marcelo, Façade (Old photograph)

117 Pisco, La Compañía, Exterior

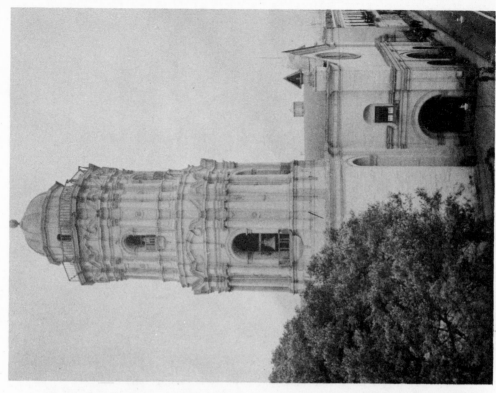

119 Lima, Santo Domingo, Tower (before 1940)

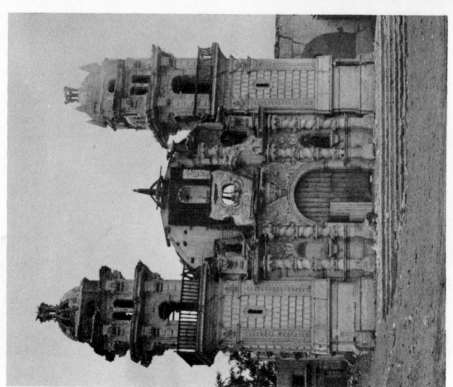

118 Nazca, San José, Façade

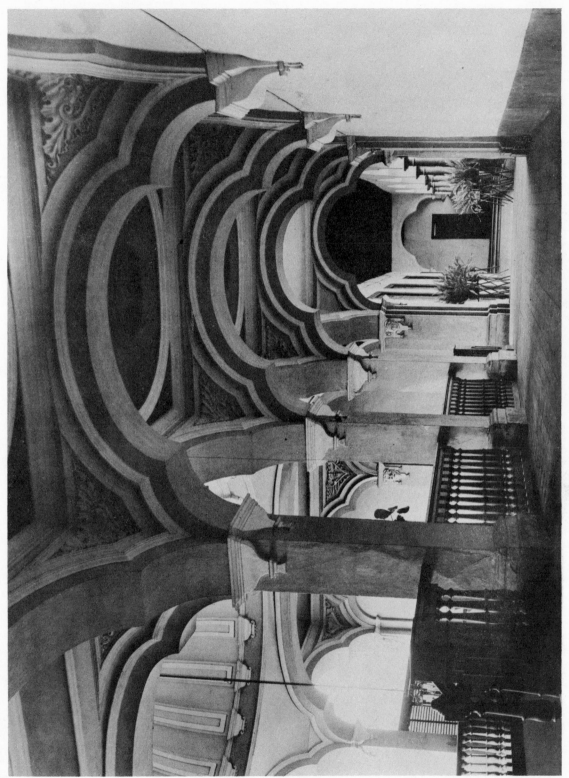

120 Lima, Dominican Novitiate, Upper Cloister

121 Lima, Santa Teresa, Cloister

122 Lima, Santa Teresa, Cloister

123 Lima, La Merced, Cloister

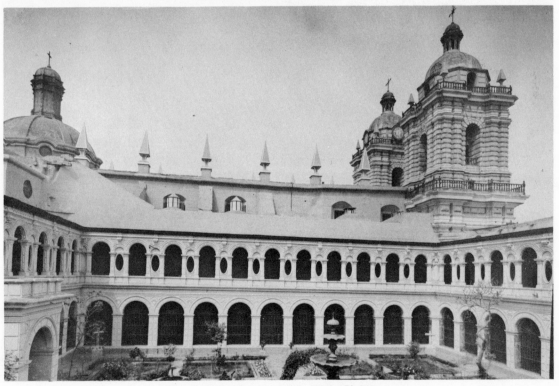

124 Lima, San Francisco, Main Cloister

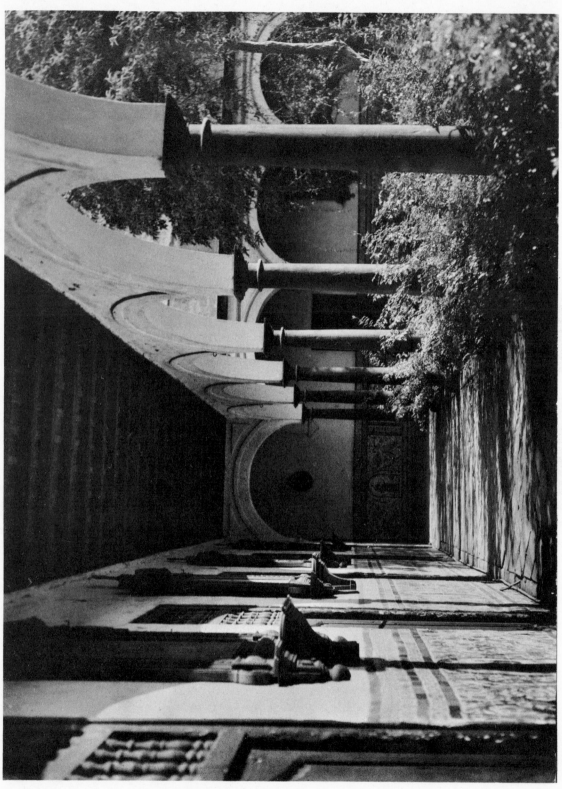

125 Lima, San Francisco, Casa de Ejercicios

127 Lima, Santo Domingo, Tile Revetment (1606)

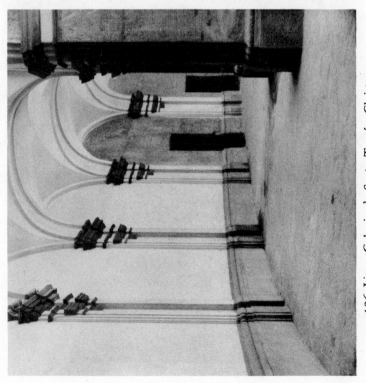

126 Lima, Colegio de Santo Tomás, Cloister

128 Nazca, San José, Façade

130 Nazca, San José, Lateral Portal

129 Nazca, San José, Tower

132 Nazca, San Xavier, Tower

131 Nazca, San Xavier, Exterior

134 Nazca, San Xavier, Interior, Detail

133 Nazca, San Xavier, Façade, Detail

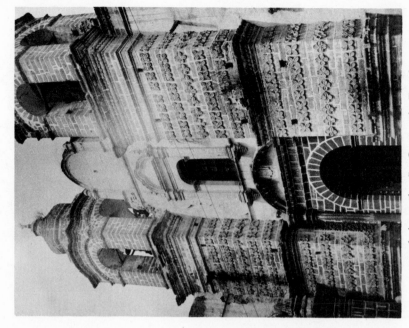

136 Ayacucho, La Compañía, Façade

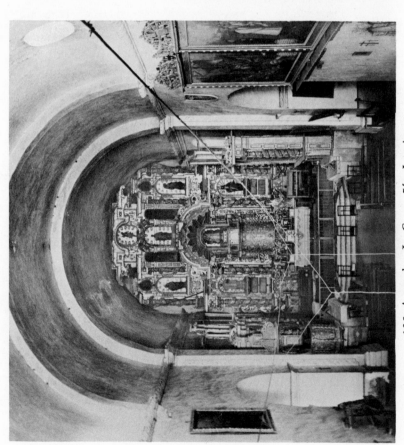

135 Ayacucho, La Compañía, Interior

137 Ayacucho, La Compañía, Left Side

138 Ayacucho, Cathedral, Exterior, Side View

139 Ayacucho, Cathedral, Façade

140 Ayacucho, Santo Domingo, Façade

142 Ayacucho, Santo Domingo, Monastery Portal

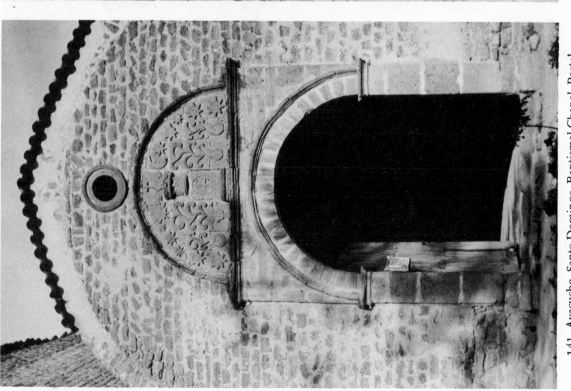

141 Ayacucho, Santo Domingo, Baptismal Chapel, Portal

144 Ayacucho, San Francisco de Paula, Interior

143 Ayacucho, Cathedral, Nave

146 Ayacucho, San Francisco de Paula, Façade

145 Ayacucho, Santa Teresa, Façade

147 Ayacucho, San Francisco, Interior

148 Ayacucho, Santa Ana, Exterior

151 Huancavelica, San Sebastián, Portal

150 Huancavelica, San Francisco, Main Portal

149 Ayacucho, Santa Clara, Tower

153 Huancavelica, Santo Domingo, Façade

152 Huancavelica, Matriz, Façade

154 Huancavelica, Town Hall, Exterior

155 Cocharcas, Nuestra Señora, Façade

156 Mamara, Parish Church, Exterior

157 Mamara, Parish Church, Lateral Portal

CHAPTER VI

158 Trujillo, Cathedral, Façade

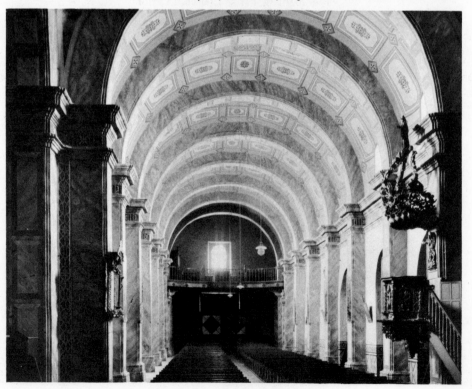

159 Trujillo, San Agustín, Nave

160 Trujillo, Cathedral, Nave

161 Trujillo, Santo Domingo, Nave

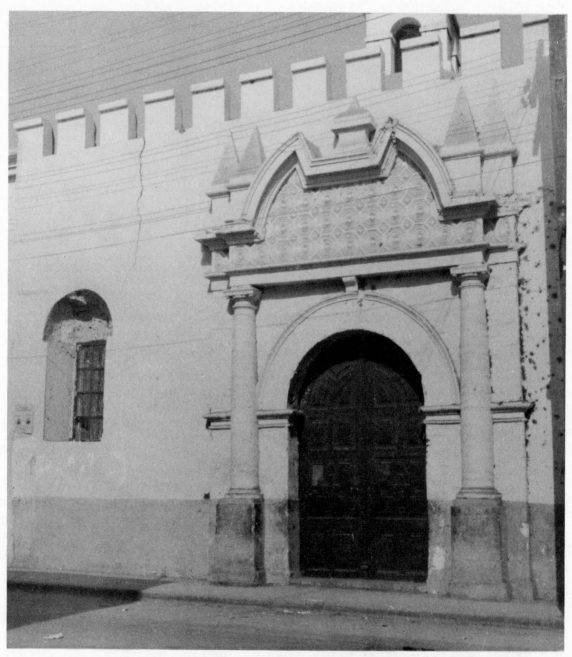

162 Trujillo, San Agustín, Monastery Portal

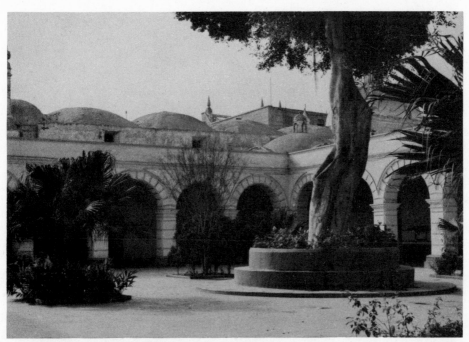

163 Trujillo, La Merced, Cloister

164 Trujillo, La Merced, Pendentive

165 Huamán, Santiago, Façade

166 Saña, Matriz

167 Saña, San Agustín, Exterior

168 Saña, San Agustín, Nave

169 Saña, San Agustín, Vault of Aisle

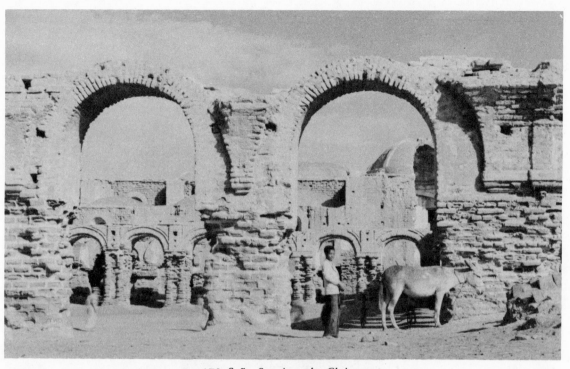

170 Saña, San Agustín, Cloister

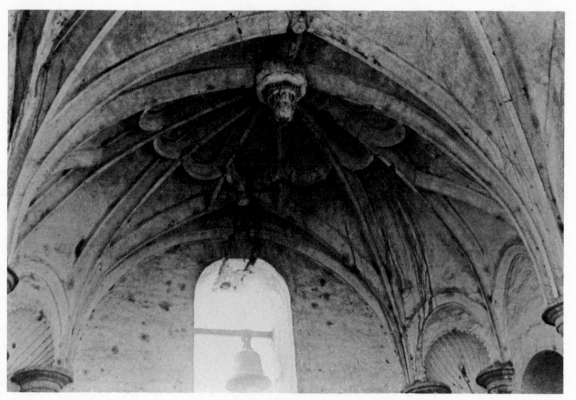

171 Guadalupe, Nuestra Señora, Vault

173 Chiclayo, Santa María, Cloister

172 Chiclayo, Santa María, Exterior

175 Ferreñafe, Santa Lucía, Façade, Detail

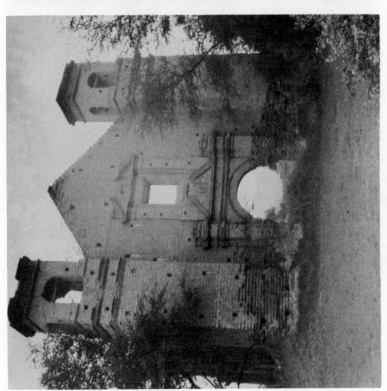

174 Saña, La Merced, Façade

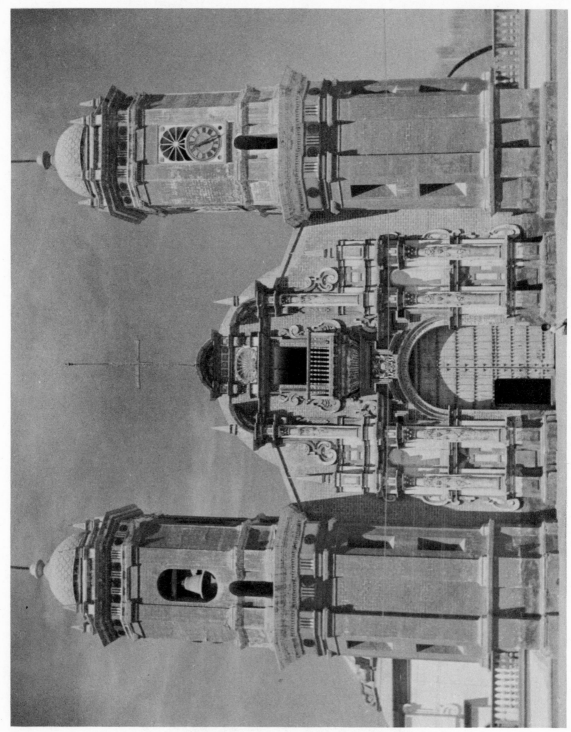

176 Ferreñafe, Santa Lucía, Façade

CHAPTER VII

177 Cajamarca, Cathedral, Façade

179 Cajamarca, Cathedral, Façade, Detail

178 Cajamarca, Cathedral, Lateral Portal (1686)

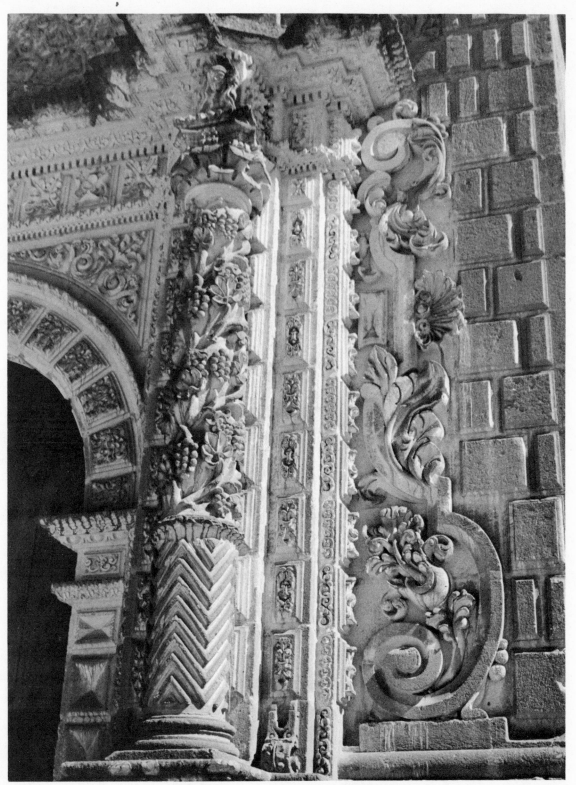

180 Cajamarca, Cathedral, Façade, Detail

181 Cajamarca, Cathedral, Nave

182 Cajamarca, San Antonio, Façade

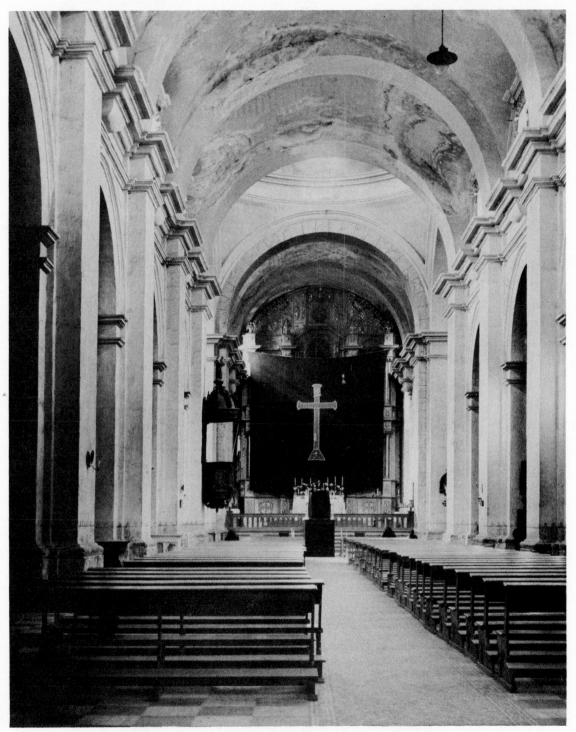

183 Cajamarca, San Antonio, Nave

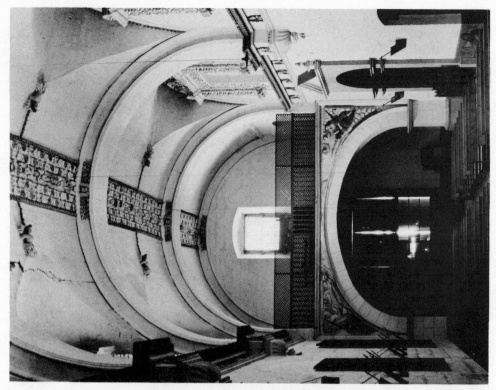

185 Cajamarca, Capilla de la Dolorosa, Interior

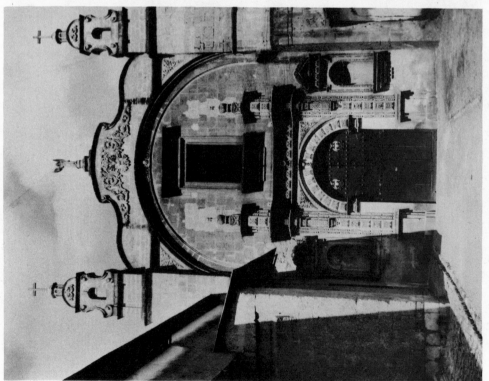

184 Cajamarca, Capilla de la Dolorosa, Façade

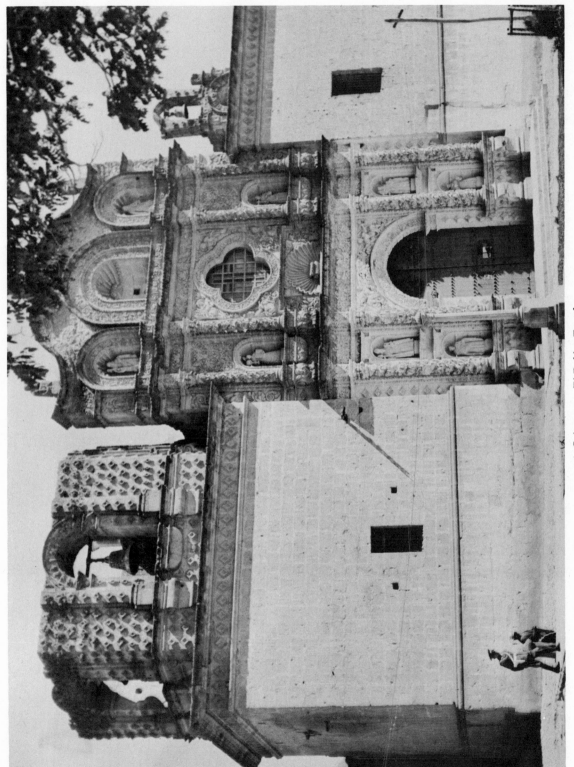

186 Cajamarca, El Belén, Façade

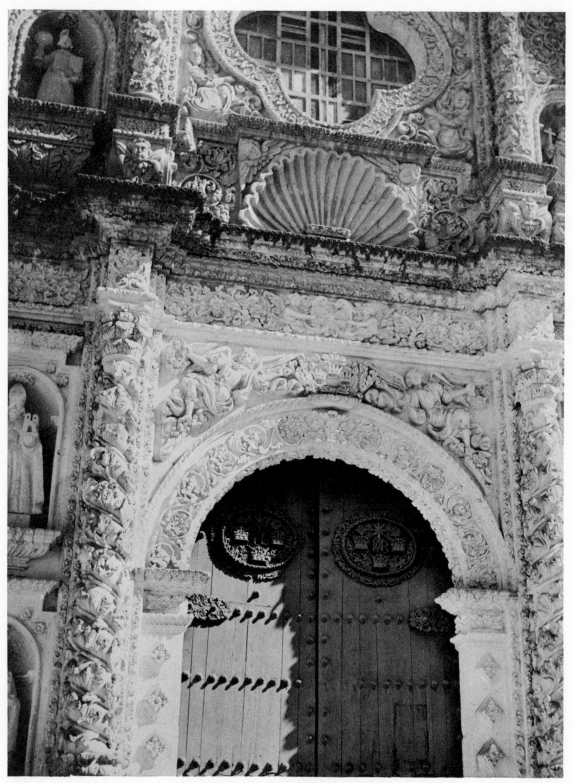

187 Cajamarca, El Belén, Façade, Detail

189 Cajamarca, El Belén, Dome

188 Cajamarca, El Belén, Nave

190 Cajamarca, La Recoleta, Façade

192 Arequipa, La Compañía, Façade, Detail

191 Cajamarca, La Recoleta, First Cloister

193 Arequipa, La Compañía, Façade (1698)

194 Arequipa, La Compañía, Lateral Portal (1654)

195 Arequipa, La Compañía, Nave

196 Arequipa, La Compañía, Cloister

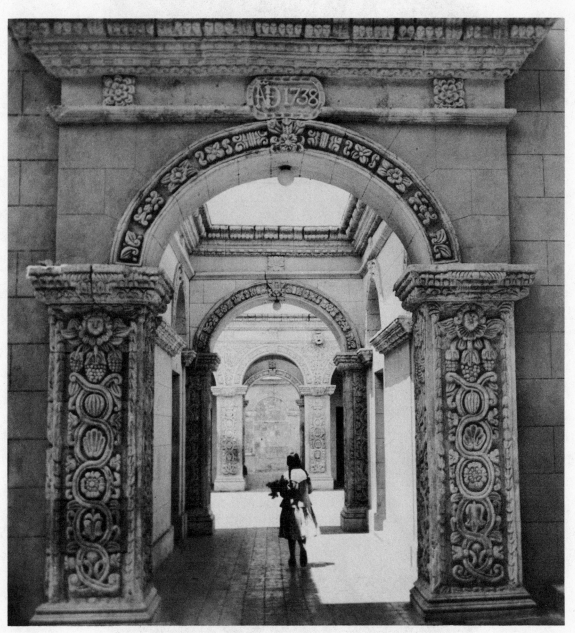

197 Arequipa, La Compañía, Cloister Entrance (1738)

199 Arequipa, San Francisco, Cupola of Aisle

198 Arequipa, Santo Domingo, Cloister

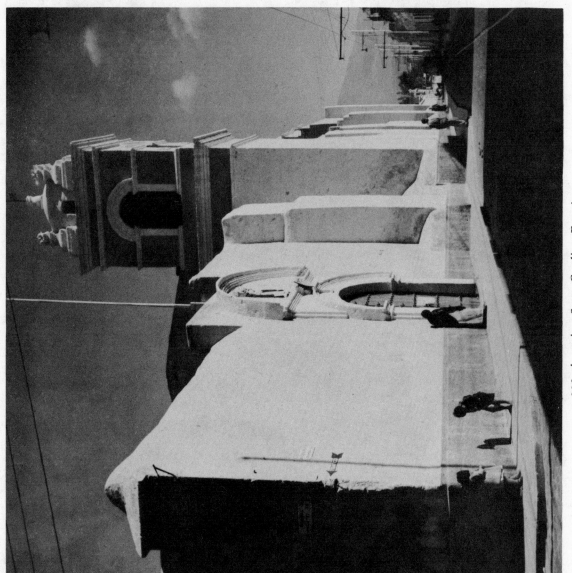

200 Arequipa, Santa Catalina, Exterior

202 Paucarpata, Parish Church, Lateral Portal

201 Arequipa, Santo Domingo, Lateral Portal

204 Yanahuara, San Juan Bautista, Façade (1750)

203 Arequipa, Casa del Moral, Portal

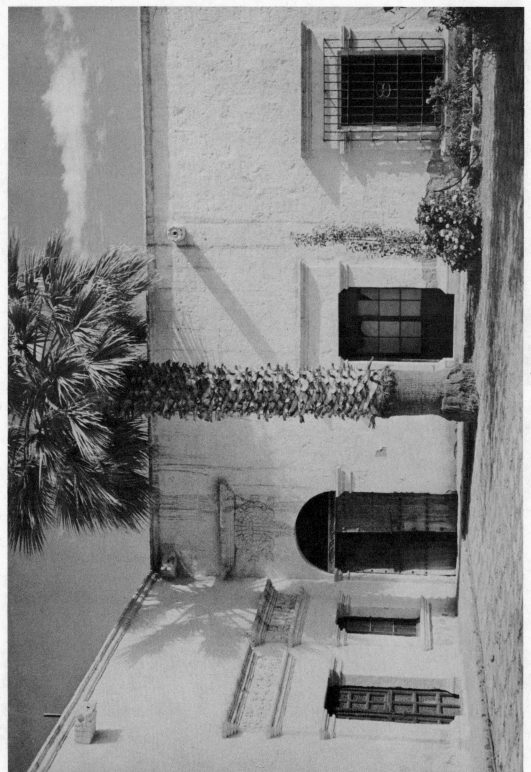

205 Arequipa, Casa del Moral, Patio

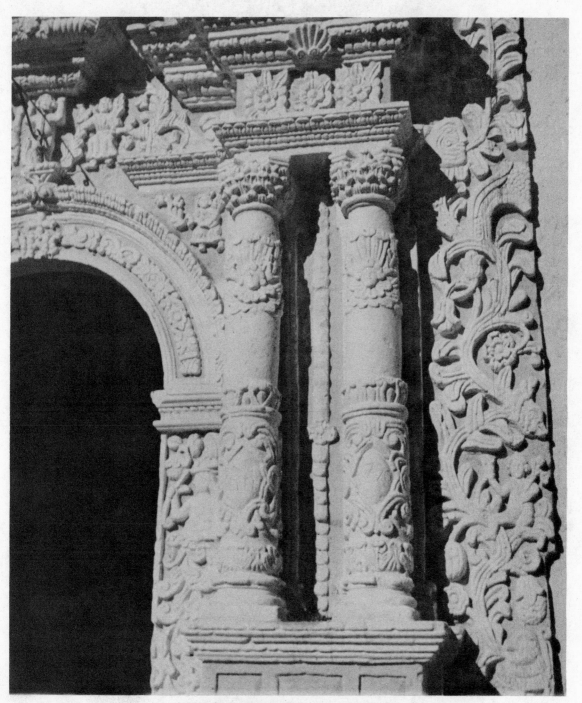

206 Yanahuara, San Juan Bautista, Façade, Detail

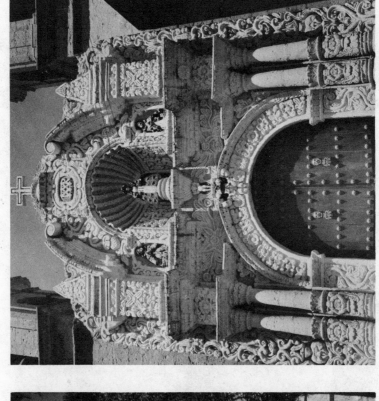

208 Caima, San Miguel, Façade, Detail

207 Caima, San Miguel, Façade

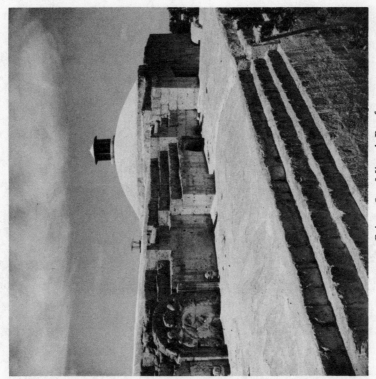

210 Caima, San Miguel, Roof

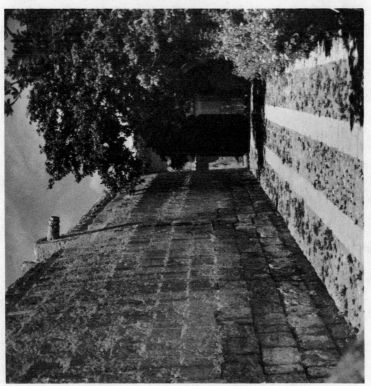

209 Caima, San Miguel, Exterior

212 Caima, San Miguel, Aisle

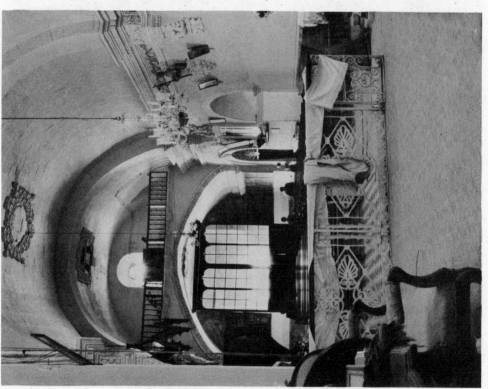

211 Caima, San Miguel, Nave

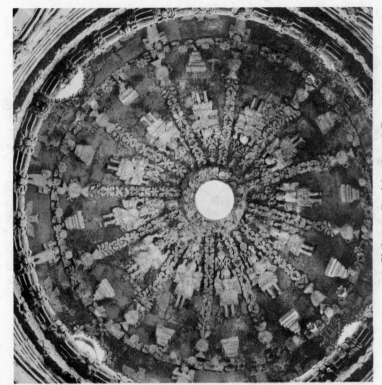

214 Chihuata, Espíritu Santo, Dome

213 Arequipa, San Agustín, Sacristy, Dome

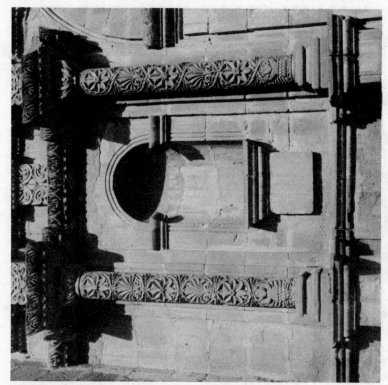

216 Pomata, Santiago, Façade, Detail

215 Pomata, Santiago, Exterior

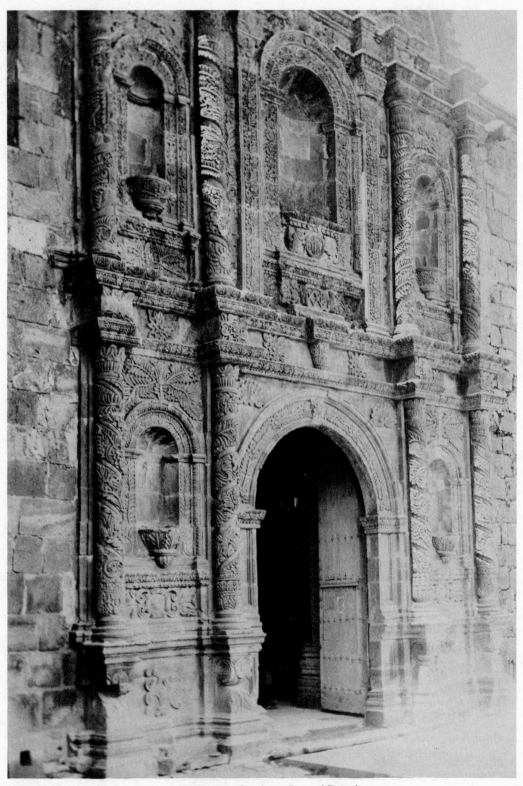

217 Pomata, Santiago, Lateral Portal

219 Juli, San Juan, Lateral Portal, Detail

218 Pomata, Santiago, Lateral Portal, Detail

220 Pomata, Santiago, Nave

221 Pomata, Santiago, Dome

223 Archidona (Spain), Santo Domingo, Dome

222 Olmedo (Spain), La Mejorada, Dome (after Lampérez)

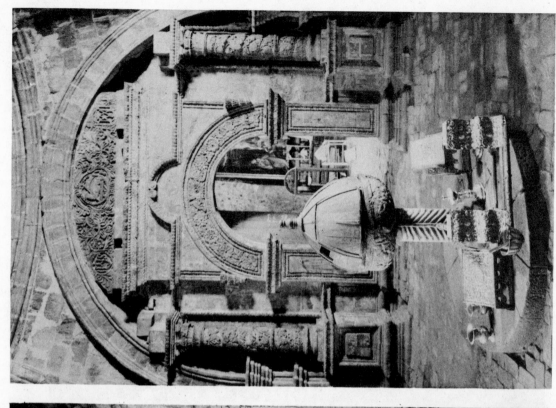

225 Juli, San Juan, Baptistry

224 Pomata, Santiago, Sanctuary

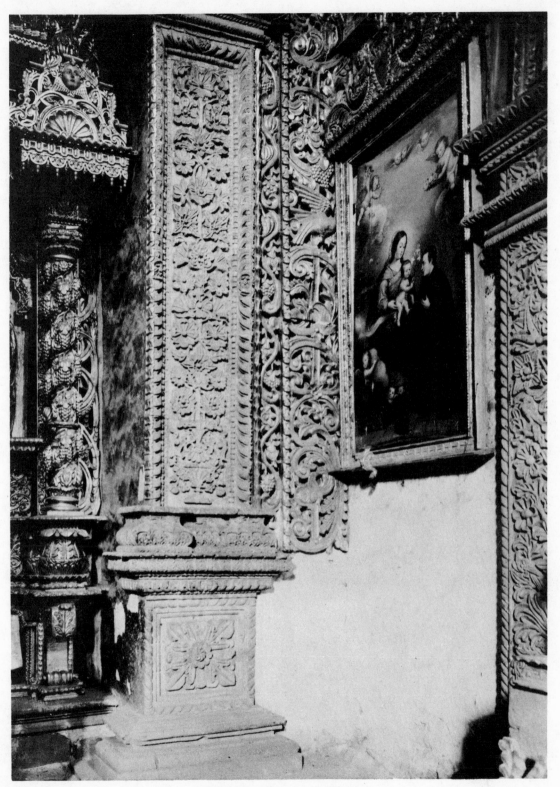

226 Juli, San Juan, Right Transept

228 Juli, Santa Cruz, Right Transept

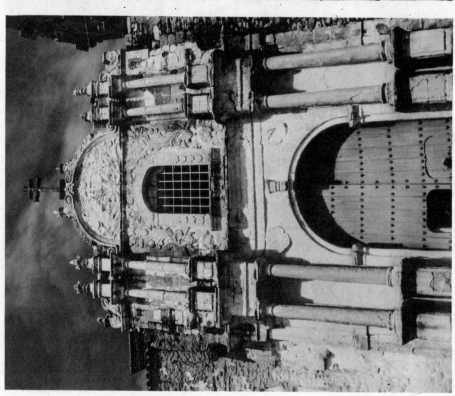

227 Juli, San Pedro Mártir, Façade

230 Sucre, Araña Collection, Colonial Desk

229 Juli, Santa Cruz, Choir Piers, Detail

232 Juli, Santa Cruz, Sanctuary

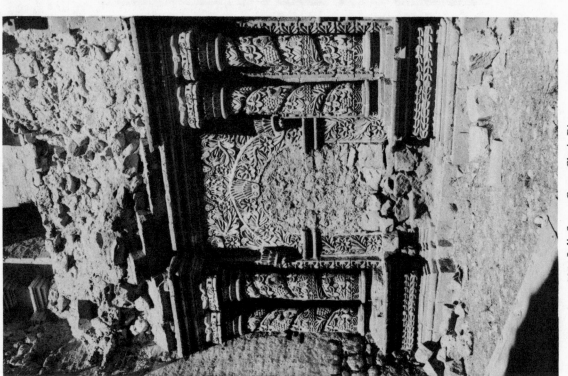

231 Juli, Santa Cruz, Choir Piers

233 Juli, La Asunción, Tower

235 Pomata, San Miguel, Choir Piers

234 Juli, La Asunción, Atrium Gate

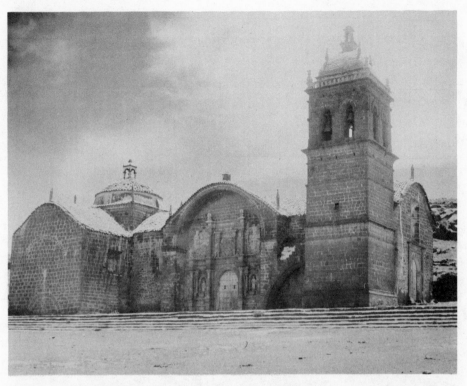

236 Zepita, San Pedro, Exterior

237 Zepita, San Pedro, Lateral Portal

238 Zepita, San Pedro, Lateral Portal, Detail

239 Lampa, Parish Church, Exterior

240 Ayaviri, Parish Church, Lateral View

242 Ayaviri, Parish Church, Façade

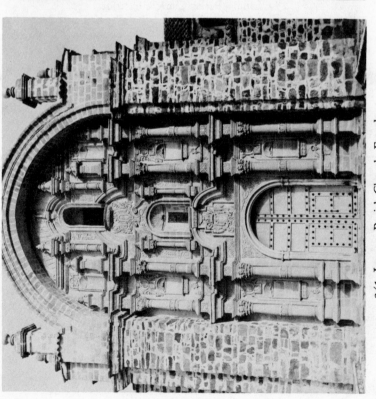

241 Lampa, Parish Church, Façade

244 Asillo, Parish Church, Façade

243 Lampa, Parish Church, Choir Piers

245 Lampa, Parish Church, Nave

246 Ayaviri, Parish Church, Nave

247 Juliaca, Santa Catalina, Exterior

248 Juliaca, Santa Catalina, Nave

250 Puno, Cathedral, Façade (1757)

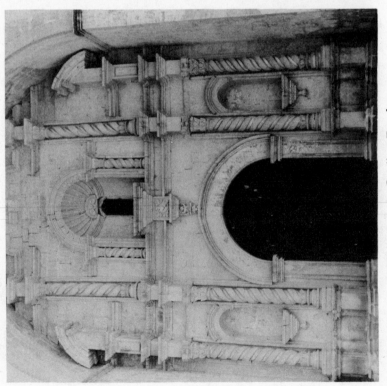

249 Juliaca, Santa Catalina, Façade

251 Puno, Cathedral, Façade

253 Puno, Cathedral, Lateral Portal (1755)

252 Puno, Cathedral, Façade, Detail

255 Sucre, Cathedral, Choir Stalls (1592–1599)

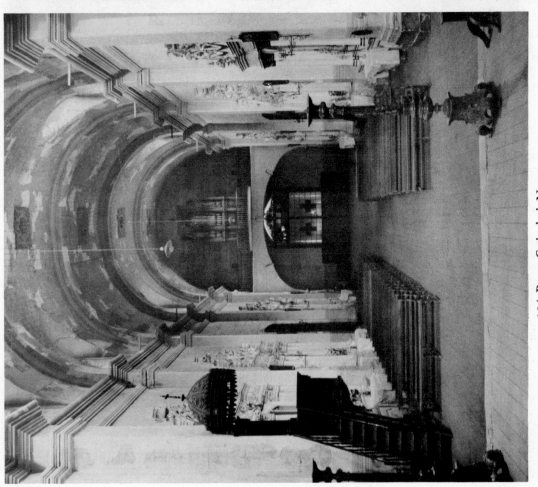

254 Puno, Cathedral, Nave

256 Lima, Santo Domingo, Choir Stalls

257 Lima, Cathedral, Choir Stalls

259 Cuzco, San Francisco, Choir Stalls

258 Lima, Cathedral, Choir Stalls

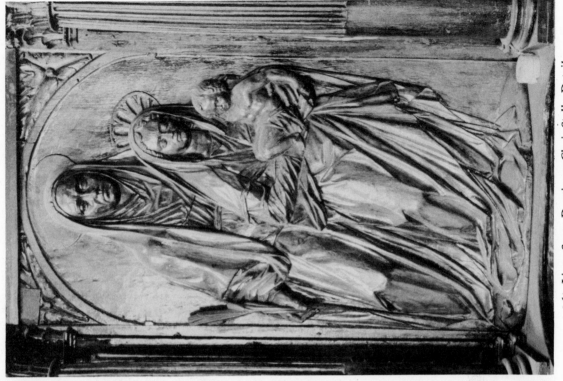

261 Lima, Santo Domingo, Choir Stalls, Detail

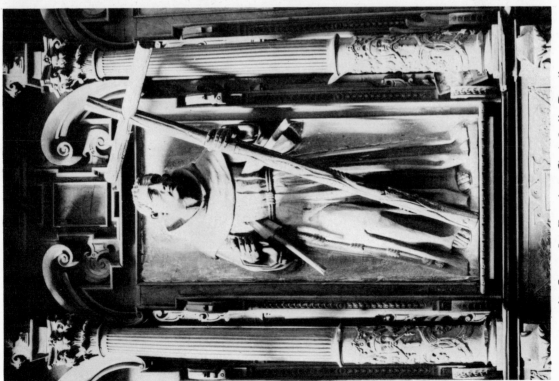

260 Cuzco, San Francisco, Choir Stalls, Detail

262 Cuzco, Cathedral, Choir Stalls

264 Lima, La Merced, Choir Stalls

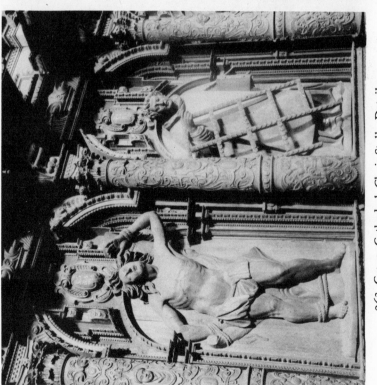

263 Cuzco, Cathedral, Choir Stalls, Detail

265 Trujillo, Cathedral, Bishop's Throne

267 Lima, San Francisco, Choir Stalls, Detail

266 Trujillo, Cathedral, Choir Stalls

268 Lima, San Francisco, Choir Stalls

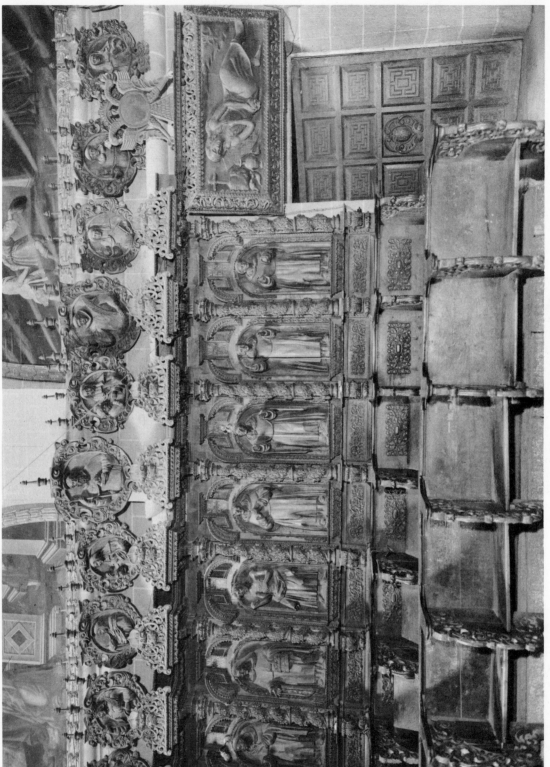

269 Cuzco, La Merced, Choir Stalls

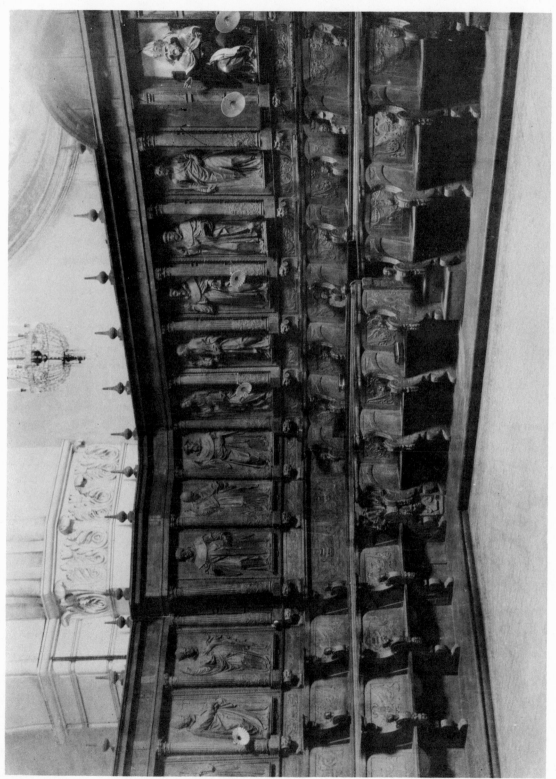

270 Lima, San Agustín, Choir Stalls

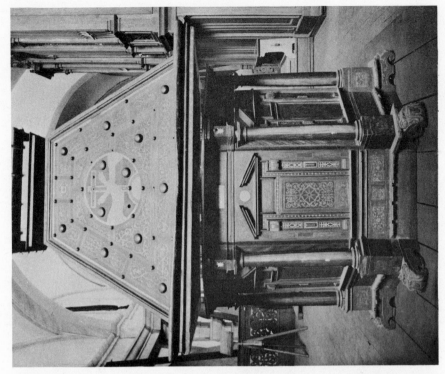

272 Cuzco, San Francisco, Lectern (1628)

271 Lima, San Agustín, Choir Stalls, Detail

274 Ayacucho, Santa Clara, Pulpit (1637)

273 Cuzco, San Francisco, Pulpit

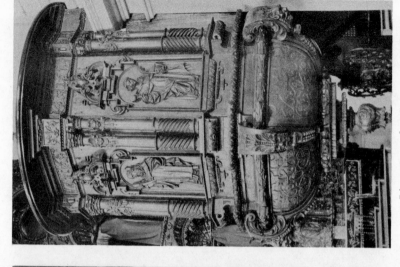

277 Lima, Sagrados Corazones, Pulpit

276 Arequipa, San Francisco, Pulpit

275 Cuzco, Cathedral, Ambo (1656)

279 Cuzco, La Merced, Pulpit

278 Cuzco, Santa Catalina, Pulpit

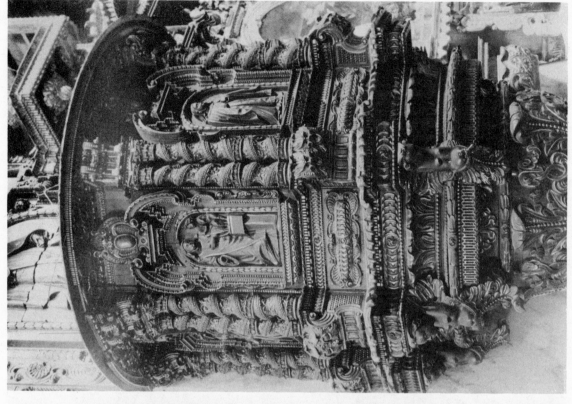

281 Cuzco, Santa Teresa, Pulpit (1675)

280 Cuzco, La Compañía, Pulpit

283 Cuzco, Cathedral, Pulpit, Detail

282 Cuzco, Cathedral, Pulpit

286 Cuzco, La Almudena, Pulpit

285 Cuzco, San Pedro, Pulpit

284 Cuzco, Santo Domingo, Pulpit

287 Cuzco, San Blas, Pulpit

288 Cuzco, San Blas, Pulpit, Detail

290 Cuzco, El Belén, Pulpit

289 Checacupe, Parish Church, Pulpit

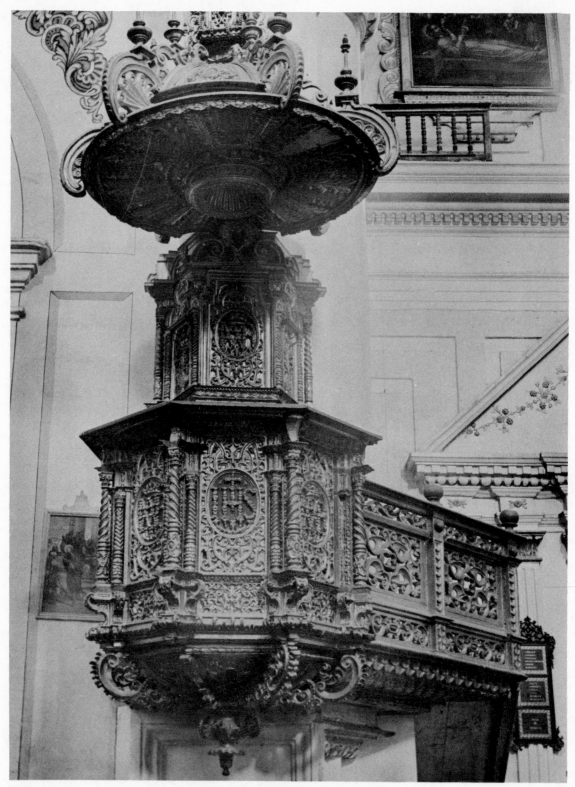

291 Arequipa, La Compañía, Pulpit

294 Pisco, La Compañía, Pulpit

293 Ayacucho, Cathedral, Pulpit

292 Lima, Jesús María, Pulpit

296 Ayacucho, San Francisco de Paula, Pulpit

295 Ayacucho, La Compañía, Pulpit

299 Trujillo, Santo Domingo, Pulpit

298 Trujillo, San Francisco, Pulpit, Detail

297 Trujillo, San Francisco, Pulpit

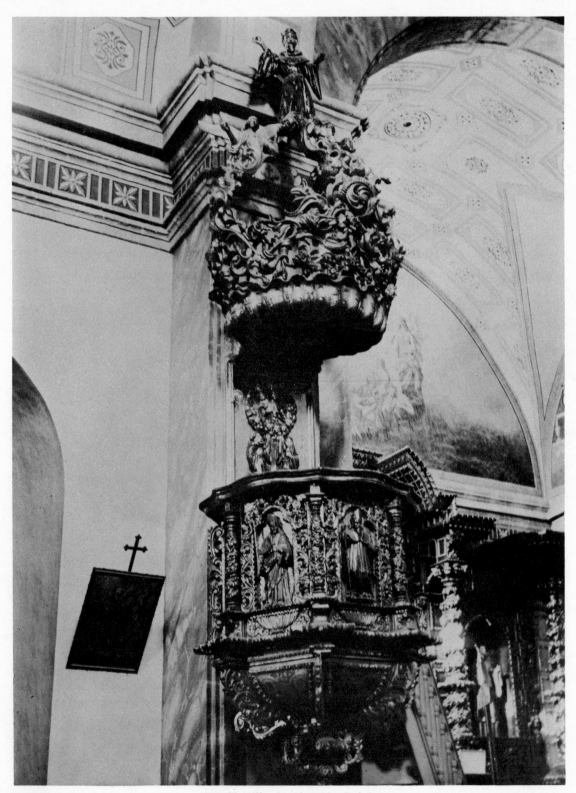

300 Trujillo, San Agustín, Pulpit

302 Trujillo, Santa Teresa, Pulpit

301 Trujillo, Santa Clara, Pulpit

305 Cuzco, Santo Domingo, Cloister Retable

306 San Jerónimo, Parish Church, Altar (1609)

307 Cuzco, San Blas, Altar of Nuestra Señora del Buen Suceso

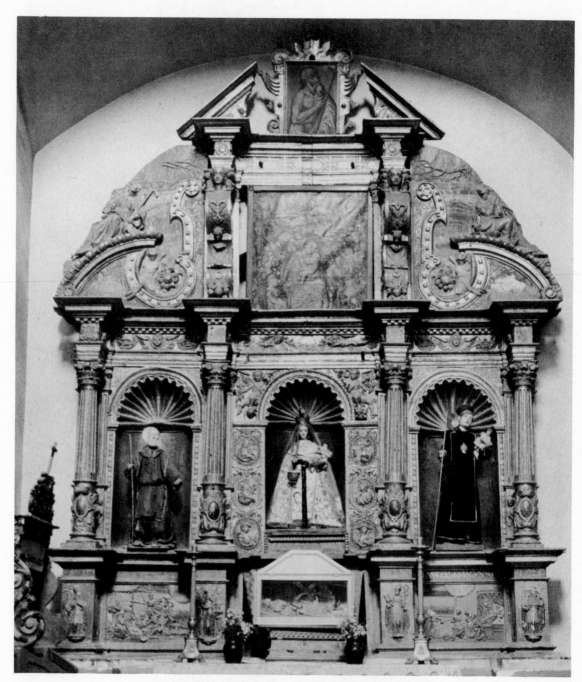

308 Copacabana, Nuestra Señora, Altar (1618)

309 Lima, Cathedral, Apostles (1608)

310 Cuzco, Cathedral, Retable of the Trinity (1655)

312 Cuzco, La Merced, Retable of the Soledad, Detail

311 Cuzco, La Merced, Retable of the Soledad (1660)

314 Cuzco, San Blas, High Altar

313 Cuzco, Santa Catalina, High Altar

316 Ayacucho, La Compañía, Altar

315 Juli, La Asunción, High Altar, Detail

317 Cuzco, Santa Teresa, High Altar (1675), Detail

318 Cuzco, La Compañía, High Altar, Detail

319 Cuzco, La Compañía, High Altar, Detail

320 Copacabana, Nuestra Señora, High Altar

321 Cuzco, San Pedro, High Altar (1720)

323 Cuzco, Santa Catalina, Lateral Altar

322 Cuzco, San Francisco, Sacristy Altar

324 Lima, Cathedral, Altar of the Immaculate Conception

326 Lima, San Pedro, Altar of St. Ignatius

325 Lima, San Pedro, Altar of St. Francis Xavier

327 Lima, Jesús María, High Altar

328 Lima, Jesús María, Altar of Crucifixion

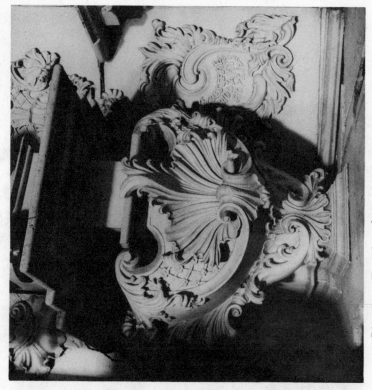

330 Lima, San Francisco de Paula Nuevo, Lateral Altar, Detail

329 Lima, San Francisco de Paula Nuevo, Lateral Altar (1764)

332 Lima, San Carlos, High Altar

331 Trujillo, Santa Teresa, Lateral Altar

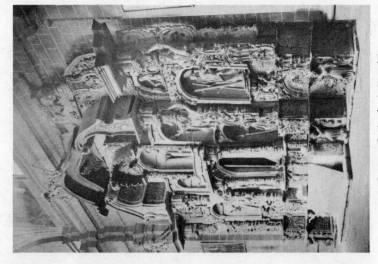

334 Cuzco, Cathedral, Retable

333 Lima, San Agustín, Sacristy

336 Lima, San Sebastián, High Altar

335 Lima, La Concepción, High Altar (1783)

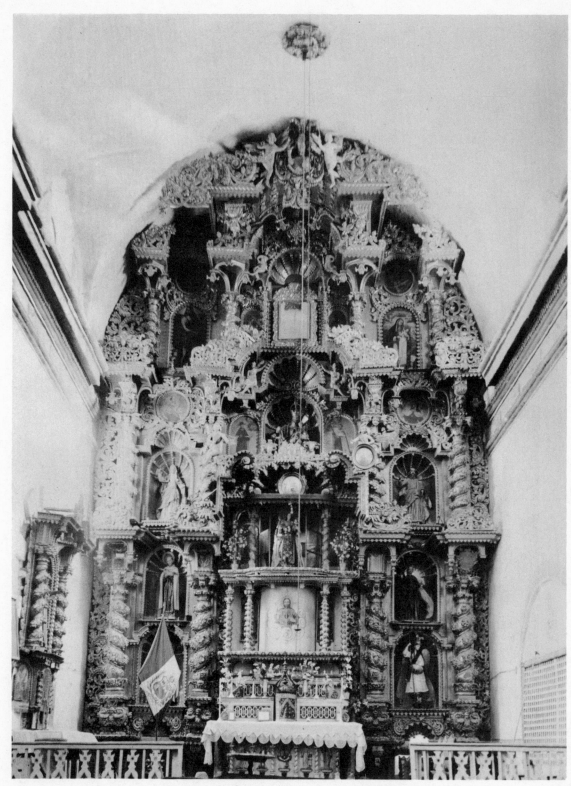

337 Ayacucho, Santa Teresa, High Altar (1703)

338 Ayacucho, Cathedral, Altar of the Immaculate Conception (1764)

340 Trujillo, San Francisco, High Altar, Detail

339 Trujillo, San Francisco, Lateral Altar, Detail

342 Trujillo, San Francisco, Transept Altar

341 Trujillo, Santo Domingo, High Altar, Detail

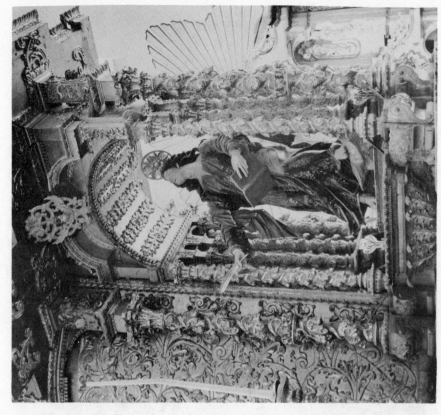

344 Trujillo, Cathedral, High Altar, Detail

343 Trujillo, Cathedral, High Altar

345 Trujillo, Santo Domingo, Altar of the Rosary

347 Trujillo, Santa Teresa, High Altar (1759)

346 Trujillo, Santa Clara, Altar of the Crucifixion

349 Trujillo, Santa Teresa, High Altar, Detail

348 Trujillo, San Agustín, High Altar, Detail

350 Trujillo, San Lorenzo, High Altar (1774)

351 Trujillo, San Lorenzo, High Altar, Detail

353 Pomata, Santiago, High Altar

352 Cajamarca, Cathedral, High Altar

354 Cajamarca, Cathedral, High Altar, Detail

355 Pomata, Santiago, High Altar, Detail

356 Juli, San Juan, High Altar, Detail

358 Cuzco, San Francisco, St. Francis

357 Ayacucho, San Francisco de Paula, St. Anne

359 Cuzco, La Compañía, Lateral Altar

360 Lima, La Merced, Crucifix by Martínez Montañés

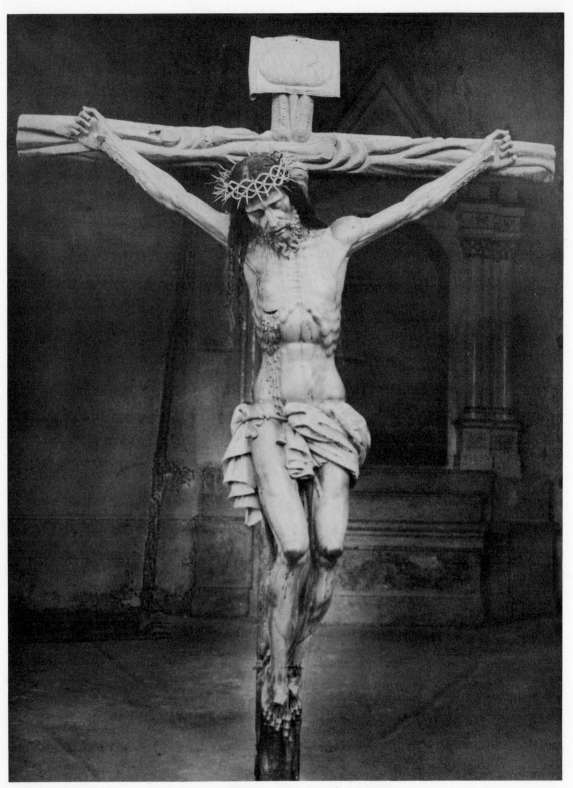

361 Mollepata, Parish Church, Crucifix

362 Lima, Cathedral, Holy Family

364 Cuzco, La Almudena, Madonna (1686) by Juan Tomás

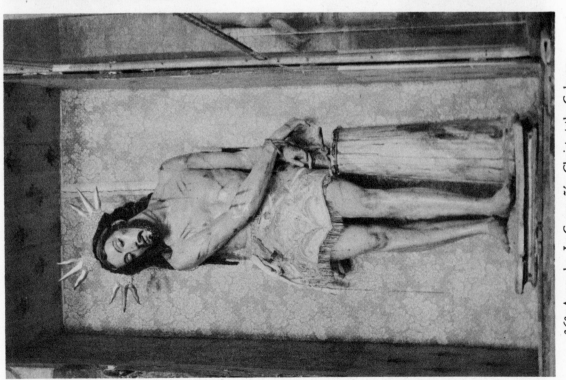

363 Ayacucho, La Compañía, Christ at the Column

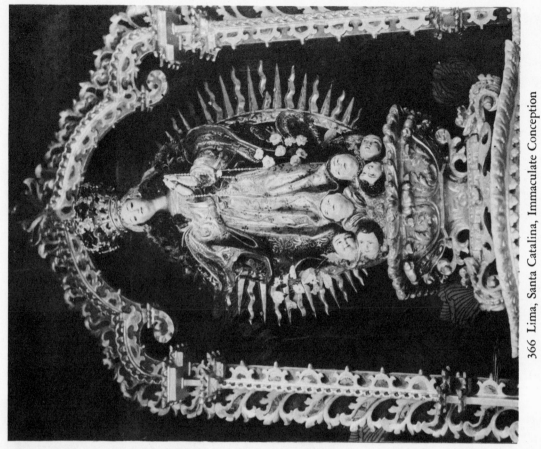

366 Lima, Santa Catalina, Immaculate Conception

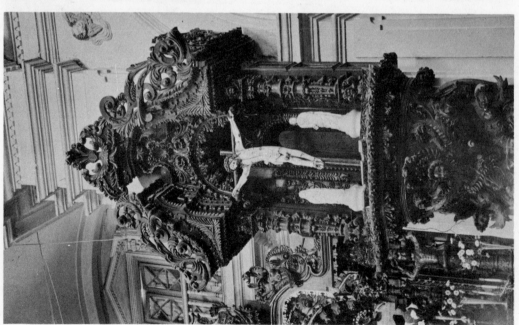

365 Ica, Parish Church, Ivory Crucifixion

Map of the
VICEROYALTY OF PERU

0   100   200

Miles

------- *Boundaries of modern Peru*